Family Mediation

Third Edition

Family Mediation

Third Edition

Lisa Parkinson

Neil Robinson, Editorial Consultant

 **Family Law**

Published by Family Law
A publishing imprint of Jordan Publishing Limited
21 St Thomas Street
Bristol BS1 6JS

British Library Cataloguing-in-Publication Data

A catalogue record for this book is available from the British Library.

ISBN 978 1 78473 025 3

Typeset by Letterpart Limited, Caterham on the Hill, Surrey CR3 5XL

Printed in Great Britain by Hobbs the Printers Limited, Totton, Hampshire SO40 3WX

DEDICATION

This book is dedicated to mediators everywhere

ACKNOWLEDGMENTS

First and foremost, I should like to express my warmest thanks to Neil Robinson, Editorial Consultant, for his tremendous encouragement and support with this new edition. Neil's professional knowledge and expertise, both as a lawyer and as a mediator, are illuminated by his creative imagination and by an eagerness we both share to test and expand the boundaries of mediation thinking and practice. I should also like to express my special thanks to Angela Lake-Carroll for her contributions to Chapter 8, to Philippa Johnson for her help with legal aid statistics and Jane Wilson for information regarding domestic abuse. Paul Gadd helped most generously to transform some sketched diagrams into print-worthy versions. Julian Roskams, my editor, has been very helpful and I should like to thank him too.

I am grateful to Paul Kemp of Worcester Family Mediation Practice for permission to include his screening documents (Appendices C and D) and to the Family Mediation Council for permission (given for the previous edition) to include the FMC Code of Practice for Family Mediators (Appendix B), likewise the Family Mediators Association for permission to include the co-mediation file record (Appendix G) and the Family Mediation Centre, Staffordshire for their additional ground-rules for court-referred mediation (Appendix E). I should also like to thank individual mediators who have kindly provided mediation examples from their practice, including Terry Bastyan, Mabel Edge, Jacqueline Gregory, Jane Staff, Nicola Tiernan, Sabine Walsh and of course, Neil Robinson and the Family Mediation Centre, Staffordshire. All identifying details have been removed from these case examples and the names changed.

I also wish to express my thanks to friends and colleagues in other European countries for responding so readily to requests for 'updated snapshots' of developments in their jurisdictions, especially to Sabine Walsh for her updates on Germany and Ireland and for her helpful comments on Chapter 14 on mediation training, also Pia Deleuran in Denmark, Marianne Souquet in France, Vaula Haavisto in Finland, Paola Farinacci in Italy, Manuela Pliżga-Jonarska in Poland, Professor Juan Carlos Vezzulla in Portugal, Professor Tsisana Shamlikashvili in Russia, Anne Hall Dick and Janie Law in Scotland, Professor Leticia Villaluenga in Spain and Bernt Wahlsten in Sweden. Beyond Europe, I should like to express thanks to Dr Jenn McIntosh and Professor Lawrie Moloney in Australia, Jim Melamed at mediate.com, Cilgia Caratsch and Stephan Auerbach at International Social Service (ISS) in Geneva and Dr Mohamed Keshavjee, formerly with the Aga Khan Foundation. Verena

Schlubach of ISS Berlin kindly provided the ecogram for cross-border family mediation in Chapter 15. Special thanks to Adam Curle and his publishers for quotations from his poems, to Jenn McIntosh for 'Rachel's Poem', John Wiley International for permission to include Christopher Moore's diagram in Chapter 11 and Pan Books for the extract from 'The Prophet' by Kahlil Gibran. Also to Family Law for some material from articles previously published *in Child and Family Law Quarterly*, *Family Law* and *International Family Law*.

My husband, Tim, has given constant support over many years and his computing skills have saved me on many occasions. I am happy that he appreciates our many mediator friends as much as I do.

Although so much is owed to other people, all omissions, errors and other failings in this book are entirely my own responsibility.

Lisa Parkinson
November 2014

FOREWORD TO THE SECOND EDITION

The first edition of this book was published in 1997. By then family mediation in Britain had for nearly twenty years been developing a limited public identity; and throughout that period Lisa Parkinson had been a central figure (arguably even the central figure) in its development.

The depth of the author's experience of family mediation even by then; the level of her intellectual energy; her way with words; her breadth of vision; but above all her skill in communicating with different sorts of people (and in communicating how to communicate): all these qualities were likely to make the book an immediate success. But few could have forecast the level of its success. Reviewers wrote that it fizzed with good ideas; was packed with nuggets, all gold; brimmed with sheer quality; and was the most fitting text for any aspiring mediator. In the light of its necessary relationship with the family law and procedure of England and Wales it is in a way astonishing that the book was nevertheless chosen for translation into Russian, Portuguese, Italian, Spanish and Slovenian.

But it was in part its nexus with our family law and procedure at that time which has rendered the first edition – still in print – seriously out of date. It had been published a year after the enactment of the Family Law Act 1996 and in the expectation that all of it would soon be brought into force. Both expressly and by necessary implication a greatly increased role for mediation was written across much of the Act. In the book Lisa Parkinson addressed it all at length but, with typical prescience, questioned whether the new path to divorce there laid would prove too long and tortuous. In the event, of course, neither Part I nor Part II was brought into force at all.

There was, however, one Part of the Act – Part III – which did come into force; which has survived in a replaced form; and which was to have important consequences for the role of family mediation. Section 29 required most applicants for public funding for proposed applications to the court in private family law matters first to have attended an assessment for suitability for mediation; and public funding was made available for a mediator to conduct the assessment. If, as quite often occurred, mediation then followed, further public funding was made available for it. But, even when it did not follow, the process of assessment brought the possibility of mediation to the attention of one if not both of the parties and, in that it was a mainstream procedure, it came over time to raise the profile of mediation with the general public.

Now, however, we have two dramatic developments; and the result is that the timing of this second edition could not be more apt.

The first is the threatened removal of public funding for almost all applications to the court in private family law. Most mediators, certainly including Lisa Parkinson, are as concerned as are we family lawyers about the effect of its threatened removal on the ability of the family courts to work efficiently and to deliver justice. The proposal however is that in principle public funding of mediation should remain. Although the terms under which the funding for it is to continue will require the closest scrutiny lest they erode its provision through the back door, a situation in which family mediation were to be funded but family litigation were not to be funded would of course transform the landscape in favour of mediation.

The second is the Practice Direction about to be issued by the President which will substantially extend the ambit of the procedure introduced by section 29 of the Act of 1996. Instead of being a prerequisite to the grant of public funding for the making of an application, evidence of attendance at an assessment for mediation will be expected to be filed upon issue of most private law applications, whether the applicant is acting in person or is represented by solicitors privately funded or (in the rare remaining situations) publicly funded. Absent such evidence, the court will at the first appointment consider whether to use its power under rule 3.3(1) of the new Family Procedure Rules 2010, which will come into force on 6 April 2011, to adjourn the proceedings in order to enable the parties to obtain advice about alternative dispute resolution.

For long mediators have been forecasting a breakthrough for family mediation. Today, at least, the forecast is solidly based. The subtitle introduced into this second edition is 'Appropriate Dispute Resolution in a new family justice system'. Yes, the system will be new in various respects. And, yes, mediation will no longer be outside it nor even running in parallel with the system. It will indeed be *in* the system. So, irrespective of whether we are already family mediators or whether (as I do one day) we aspire to be family mediators, all of us who work in the system need a comprehensive understanding of family mediation, the practice of which is far more complex and multi-faceted than the uninformed observer might assume. We will need a *vademecum*. It will be Lisa Parkinson's book.

Nicholas Wilson
Lord Justice of Appeal
President of the Family Mediators Association
31 January 2011

FOREWORD TO THE THIRD EDITION

Lord Wilson's 2011 comments on the second edition were, as always, remarkably prescient. The 'Blue Skies' we anticipated for family mediation have proved to be, for many mediators, turning from grey to black. The unintended consequences of the savage cuts to legal aid are still working through the system; the impressive energy with which Simon Hughes, Minister for Justice, has tried to promote mediation and services for unrepresented or ill-advised litigants has not yet produced either the coherence or the resources which the system so sadly lacks. We may be, as the President of the Family Division has said, 'on the cusp of history', and it would be ungrateful in the extreme not to acknowledge the value of new legislation and regulation in attempting to promote a more holistic, co-operative vision of family justice. Nevertheless, the execution of this vision has been partial and especially challenging for the family mediator, and a third edition of Lisa's book is essential to revisit the context in which we now work and to start to explore how we might respond to these challenges.

This third edition is bigger and better. It reflects the deep conversations Lisa continues to promote across the mediation world, and the lateral thoughts with which she so often illuminates those dialogues. It reflects the changes in legal context, in assessment practice, in standards reform and in funding; it encompasses the most current thinking and research into dispute resolution. It meets the needs of novice and experienced practitioner alike as well as providing an overview for the academic and the interested observer. We are told that the Family Justice System in England and Wales has been 'redefined' by the changes of April 2014; the question for 'family peace-builders' is whether mediation has also been 'redefined' and, if so, for better or worse. The revisions in this edition start to address those questions and suggest some provisional answers.

As a trainer, mediator and consultant, I am unapologetic about my advocacy for this book, which is used as the core textbook on Family Mediators Association foundation courses and recommended by so many other organisations and individuals. This is because it embodies the core skill of the mediator, which is to turn fundamental principles and frameworks into a creative, humane and innovative space with the potential to transform relationships. It is the 'Bible' that family mediators carry with them, not because it provides easy answers, but because it promotes fresh thinking.

Professor Neil Robinson
Editorial Consultant
November 2014

PREFACE

The Children and Families Act 2014 is focusing more attention on the role of family mediation in the family justice system. Family mediators have been given greater responsibility to encourage consideration of non-court dispute resolution processes before application is made to the family court, and to assess the suitability of mediation in particular circumstances. In explaining non-court dispute resolution and in managing the mediation process appropriately, family mediators need to combine awareness, empathy and a high level of knowledge and skills. The nature and scope of the mediation process and requirements for practice have come under sharper scrutiny. Following the recommendations of the Family Justice Review, the McEldowney Report and the Scoping Study led by Dr Stan Lester, the Family Mediation Council has issued revised standards and requirements that cover many aspects of family mediators' training, supervision, accreditation and professional development.[1] Writing about the development of family mediation in the context of these evolving systems is like painting a Forth Bridge that keeps getting longer, or as Angela Lake-Carroll remarked, 'painting the Forth Bridge while an earthquake is going on underneath!'

This edition is more than an update of the previous one, because this is a time of major change in the whole family justice system and in the provision and regulation of family mediation. Despite the major setbacks resulting from LASPO,[2] there are fresh challenges and opportunities. Recent research findings, in particular the Mapping Paths to Family Justice study,[3] show the need for greater flexibility in designing dispute resolution processes and approaches that cater for different needs. A standardised model of family mediation cannot possibly meet the diverse needs of couples and family members from different cultural backgrounds who come to mediation at different stages of separation or divorce or other family crisis, in widely varying circumstances. If the mediation process is not tailored to their circumstances and needs, it is likely to break down, if it starts at all. Mediators need to make careful assessments of mediation's suitability,[4] manage different levels of conflict and provide facilities and skills for different constellations of family members. Recent experience shows that while adhering to the basic principles of mediation, a range of

---

[1] See Chapter 14.
[2] Legal Aid, Sentencing and Punishment of Offenders Act 2012.
[3] Barlow, Hunter, Smithson and Ewing *Mapping Paths to Family Justice – Briefing Paper and Report on Key Findings* (Universities of Exeter and Kent, June 2014), chs 1 and 13.
[4] See Chapter 3.

approaches can be developed for different stages and levels of conflict, not only in private family law disputes but also in other areas, including some public law child cases and hybrid family/civil cases.[5]

Mediation tends to be seen as a problem-solving process, but family problems are complex and solutions rarely simple. Mediators learn from hard-won experience and from other sources of insight. Non-scientists like me can see parallels between mediation and chaos theory and the relatively new science of complexity theory which distinguishes between simple and complex systems. The family justice system is putting greater emphasis on private ordering, with clear expectations that most separating and divorcing couples will resolve issues themselves, with the help of mediators where needed. However, as shown in the chapter on family mediation research, there can be risks and disadvantages in private ordering, as well as significant benefits when it is suitable and practised well.[6] With the trend away from court-dispensed justice towards participative decision-making and collaborative practice, we may find, like the pianist and conductor, Daniel Barenboim, co-creator of the West–Eastern Divan orchestra, that 'the inclusion of all parties in a dialogue ... is not a guarantee for perfect harmony, but it creates the conditions necessary for co-operation'.[7] Barenboim also reminds us that 'spontaneous realisation' is possible only with 'all the repetitions and the familiarity resulting from intense study'.[8] Mediation practice can be enhanced by better understanding of different systems of thinking – intuitive and analytical, fast and slow[9] – and even by comparing the structure of mediation with musical structures. Communication needs language that is imaginative, as well as clear.[10] Poetry and visual arts help us to see with fresh vision, while even limited scientific knowledge can help us to make new connections in useful and practical ways.[11]

Mediation experience over several decades shows that a great deal remains to be explored and considered. There is greater recognition of the need to listen to children and young people in helping parents to make arrangements that take account of their children's needs, feelings and ideas, without putting pressure on the child.[12] Exchanges with colleagues in other countries enrich our own developing practice. I have been very fortunate in having opportunities to take part in conferences and training workshops in many countries, from the French West Indies to Canada and the United States, South Africa, Russia and Kazakhstan and European countries. Irrespective of culture and language, mediators all over the world find that they have the same spirit and share intuitive understanding. A global network of mediators is needed to develop international family mediation in relocation disputes and child abduction cases,

---

[5]   See Chapter 4.
[6]   See Chapter 13.
[7]   Barenboim *Everything is Connected – The Power of Music* (Weidenfeld and Nicolson, 2008), p 59, ch 4.
[8]   Ibid, p 58.
[9]   See Chapter 14.
[10] See Chapter 6.
[11] See Chapter 2.
[12] See Chapters 7 and 8.

using mediators specially qualified in this field. The Hague Conference *Guide to Good Practice on Mediation in the context of the 1980 Child Abduction Convention* was published in 2012, while International Social Service has recently published a guide to international family mediation for parents and professionals.[13]

This new edition is designed primarily for family mediators in England and Wales, whether they are highly experienced practitioners or those embarking on training. I hope it will also be of interest to members of other professions who work with families within or outside the family justice system, as well as to family mediators in other jurisdictions. At a time of bitter struggles and conflicts in many parts of the world, we need negotiators, peace-makers and young people who are trained in conflict resolution, not in waging war. May this book, in however small a way, stimulate reflection and discussion, offer some fresh thinking and encourage the co-operative search for conflict resolution that all mediators endeavour to support.

Lisa Parkinson

Bristol
November 2014

---

[13] See Chapter 15.

CONTENTS

CHAPTER 1

MEDIATION AND THE MANAGEMENT OF CONFLICT

'All of us share this world but for a brief moment in time. The question is whether we spend that time focused on what pushes us apart, or whether we commit ourselves to a sustained effort to find common ground, to focus on the future we seek for our children and to respect the dignity of all human beings.'[1]

CONTENTS

1.1   MANAGING CONFLICT

Aggression arouses anger and causes fear, and reactions to aggression are often of a fight or flight nature. Physical aggression can threaten the survival of an individual or group and may destroy their environment. Lorenz,[2] a biologist who studied the function of aggression in animals, describes behaviours which different species of vertebrates have developed to deal with aggression. There are instinctive, biological reactions among animals, including humans. Many

---

[1]   Barack Obama, speech, 4 June 2009.
[2]   Lorenz *On Aggression* (University Paperbacks, 1968).

animals avoid conflict by surrendering to the individual or group they perceive as the stronger. Human history is dominated by warfare and conquest, but human beings have also developed ways of resolving conflict through peaceful negotiation. All too often, we fail to use them. Reactions to conflict in so-called developed societies are often primitive, with appalling consequences for helpless victims. Some wars, like those in the Middle East, can appear unending, despite the rising death toll among the adult population and the suffering and death of enormous numbers of children.

Conflict is a universal part of life: life without conflict would be static. 'Conflict is everywhere, not only between human beings, but throughout nature, from quantum mechanical particles to dark energy'.[3] Conflict itself is neither positive nor negative: it is a natural force that is necessary for growth and change. What matters is how it is managed. If conflict is managed well, it need not destroy individuals, relationships and communities. The energy that is generated in conflict needs to be used constructively, instead of destructively. 'Resolving conflict is rarely about who is right. It is about acknowledgement and appreciation of differences.'[4] To resolve conflict, purposeful communication is needed and this purposeful communication can lead to changes in perceptions and attitudes. When conflicts are resolved in a participative and integrative way, instead of through contest, relationships can be sustained and strengthened. Dialogue between disputants in an atmosphere of increased openness, listening and co-operation may then radiate out to other members of their family or community. From Buddhist teaching we can learn that:[5]

> 'most of our time is spent in analysing differences. Now concentrate on similarities, on what is common between ... antagonistic opposites. ... Look for the higher thirds above all opposites ... look for this relationship, and you will be kinder to each of the pairs.'

Mediation offers a means of managing and resolving conflict. A neutral third party, the mediator, holds a centred position between disputants and from this balanced position assists them to channel and combine their energies in working out solutions, instead of fighting, surrendering or accepting an unsatisfactory compromise. The Council of Europe's Recommendation in 2003[6] defined family mediation as 'a life-building and life-management process between family members in the presence of an independent and impartial third party known as the mediator.... The primary aim of mediation is not to reduce congestion of the courts but to repair a breakdown in communication between the parties with the help of a professional trained in mediation.'

---

[3]   Cloke *Mediation and Meditation – the Deeper Middle Way* (mediate.com Weekly No 266, March 2009).

[4]   Crum *The Magic of Conflict* (Touchstone, 1987), p 49.

[5]   Humphreys *Zen Buddhism* (Unwin Paperbacks, 1984), p 158.

[6]   Council of Europe *Family mediation and gender equality* (Recommendation 1639, 2003), para 5.

1.2 MEDIATION – ROOTS AND GROWTH

Mediation is often seen as a recent development, but it has a long history in many different civilisations and cultures. As early as the fifth century BC, Confucius urged people to use mediation instead of going to court, warning them that litigation was liable to leave disputants embittered and unable to co-operate. Confucius recommended that, instead of going to court, they should meet with a neutral peace-maker to assist them to reach agreement. Anthropologists have described traditions in African and native Indian tribes to call a moot or meeting where respected senior tribesmen settle disputes between individuals, families or villages.[7] A Cheyenne Indian chief had a duty to act as peace-maker to settle quarrels in the camp. Muslim countries are torn by religious conflicts between Sunni and Shia communities and attacks on Christian minorities, yet the peaceful resolution of conflict is deeply embedded in Islamic religious traditions and rituals.[8] In many countries from Canada to Kazakhstan, Ismaili Muslim communities have set up Conciliation Boards to encourage resolution of disputes with the help of trained mediators. These services are increasingly used by non-Ismailis. There are many early examples of mediation in Europe and North America. In early industrial societies, the Quakers used mediation as their preferred means of settling marital and commercial disputes. The first Boards of Conciliation were set up in the 1860s to help resolve disputes in certain industries. There is also a long tradition of mediation in Jewish communities. The American Jewish community in New York set up the Jewish Conciliation Board in 1920 to encourage consensual settlement of disputes.

Informal kinds of mediation are used every day, while mediation using professionally qualified or specially trained mediators has been institutionalised in many fields – family justice, employment, civil and commercial disputes and the criminal justice system, particularly victim-offender reparation schemes. Community mediation is used to settle disputes between neighbours over boundaries, noise or shared facilities and in housing disputes between landlords and tenants. At an international level, mediators are brought in to help settle disputes between different countries and communities. Mediators helped to achieve a negotiated agreement between Israel and the Palestinians in January 1997 on the withdrawal of Israeli forces from the West Bank city of Hebron. Dialogue between Israeli and Arab leaders, assisted by international mediators, needs to be sustained with the utmost energy and determination. In August 2014, the truce achieved by Egyptian mediators between the Israeli government and the Palestinian Sunni Islamic organisation, Hamas, showed that peace-*making* needs to be resourced as much as armed peace-*keeping*. Nelson Mandela was an outstanding mediator who used his mediation skills in July 2000 to resolve the dispute in South Africa over the cause of AIDS, urging scientists and politicians to work together in the struggle against a disease that was devastating Africa. The Nobel Peace Prize for 2008 was awarded to Martti

---

7   Roberts *Order and Dispute – An Introduction to Legal Anthropology* (Penguin Books, 1979).
8   Keshavjee *Islam, Sharia and Alternative Dispute Resolution* (I.B. Tauris, 2013).

Ahtisaari, former President of Finland. The Norwegian Nobel Committee praised Mr Ahtisaari's achievements in resolving international conflicts:

> 'He is one of the most forward-looking of peace-makers. The world needs more (people) like him. We wanted to focus on successful peace-makers because this world needs peace-makers.'

In some countries, mediation is the normal way of settling disputes. Modern China, with over a billion people, has nearly a million mediators. Mediation is available nearly everywhere and disputes in the family, the community and the workplace are normally referred to mediation. Chinese and Japanese mediators have authority. They are expected to uphold moral values and may reproach one party's wrongdoing and praise the other for acting correctly. Disputants are urged to resolve their differences in a responsible and peaceable manner for the good of the family and society as a whole. This paternalistic approach is accepted in China and Japan where the emphasis on moral precepts and persuasion seems to work well, whereas in other countries mediation generally aims to help participants reach their own decisions and agreements. In every sphere of life, nationally and internationally, mediation offers a means of facilitating communication and seeking the resolution of conflict. Although there are situations in which mediation is neither possible nor suitable, it should be considered as the first step in exploring ways to settle disputes and improve co-operation.

1.3   ADR AND NON-COURT DISPUTE RESOLUTION

Mediation and other dispute resolution processes, including solicitor negotiation, arbitration and collaborative law, have traditionally been grouped together under the collective acronym, ADR, meaning Alternative Dispute Resolution, because these processes offer an alternative to litigation. In many countries, however, dispute resolution processes are increasingly encouraged or even required as the first resort, with the court providing the necessary alternative forum. The Family Justice Review recommended that 'alternative dispute resolution' should be rebranded as 'Dispute Resolution Services',[9] while the amended Family Procedure Rules use the term 'non-court dispute resolution', defined as 'methods of resolving a dispute, including mediation, other than through the normal court process'.[10] The previous edition of this book suggested that ADR could stand for *Appropriate* Dispute Resolution, since the dispute resolution process needs to be appropriate for the parties in their particular circumstances. In some cases, non-court dispute resolution may be used in conjunction with settlement-focused court proceedings, while in other cases the court provides the only possible or appropriate forum.[11]

---

[9]   *Family Justice Review Final Report* (November 2011), para 4.82.
[10]   FPR 2010 2.3 (as amended).
[11]   For further discussion of 'appropriate' and 'autonomous' dispute resolution, see **10.2**.

1.4 DISPUTE RESOLUTION FOR FAMILIES

The nationally representative Omnibus survey in England and Wales[12] found that 44% of respondents had heard of mediation, 32% had heard of solicitor negotiation and 14% had heard of collaborative law. 45% indicated they had heard of none of these. As many as 47% of couples who separated or divorced between 1996 and 2011 did so without taking legal advice. Only 1% went to mediation in this period.[13] Couples who split up without legal advice or mediation do not necessarily agree matters between themselves. In some situations, the parent who leaves the family home, voluntarily or under duress, loses contact with the children and may abandon efforts to see them. Property and financial matters may be dealt with without either partner knowing their legal rights or understanding the longer term consequences. In August 2014 the government announced an expansion to its ongoing campaign to increase public awareness of family mediation and to promote take-up of publicly funded mediation.[14] Work is also in progress to improve the provision and quality of family mediation services, assisted by the findings of a comparative study of client usage, experience and outcomes of non-court dispute resolution processes. Researchers at the Universities of Exeter and Kent studied three processes: solicitor negotiation, collaborative law and mediation.[15] Their findings are referred to in Chapter 13.

1.4.1 Solicitor negotiation

When a relationship breaks down, communication often breaks down as well. Partners who are unable to negotiate with each other may turn to solicitors for advice and support and rely on their legal advisers to settle matters for them. Family lawyers who are members of Resolution follow a Code of Practice that encourages settlement through negotiation as far as possible. Now that legal aid is no longer available for most family matters,[16] some solicitors' firms offer fixed rates and 'packages' to make legal help more affordable. However, individuals on low incomes or welfare benefits may find even fixed rates out of reach, unless they can raise a loan or have family support. More couples are likely to turn to online services. If they cannot settle matters on their own or if solicitor negotiation does not lead to settlement, one party may take a dispute to court, either with legal representation if they can pay privately or as a litigant in person. A small minority, around 10%, of separating and divorcing couples, litigate on family matters. These cases are likely to involve intractable disputes entailing risks of high emotional and financial costs and harmful consequences

---

[12] Omnibus survey 2012, cited in Barlow, Hunter, Smithson and Ewing *Mapping Paths to Family Justice – Briefing Paper and Report on Key Findings* (Universities of Exeter and Kent, June 2014), p 4.

[13] Ibid, p 6.

[14] DfE and MoJ *A Brighter Future for Family Justice* (August 2014).

[15] Barlow, Hunter, Smithson and Ewing *Mapping Paths to Family Justice – Briefing Paper and Report on Key Findings* (Universities of Exeter and Kent, June 2014).

[16] Legal Aid, Sentencing and Punishment of Offenders Act 2012 (LASPO).

for children.[17] As the diagram below illustrates, separated couples who use solicitors to negotiate on their behalf can avoid communicating directly with each other. When settlements are negotiated via lawyers, their clients may remain unable or unwilling to communicate directly. But arrangements for children are likely to depend on good communication between parents and the children of separated parents need parents who can talk and co-operate with each other.

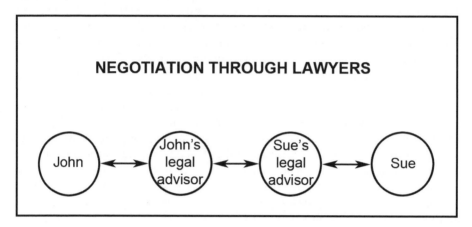

1.4.2   Collaborative law

In collaborative law, each client instructs a specially trained collaborative lawyer. The two collaborative lawyers and their clients work together co-operatively in order to resolve matters without going to court. The aim is to reach settlement in four-way meetings in which the collaborative lawyers provide legal advice and guidance to their clients and encourage them to negotiate with each other. If no settlement is reached, new lawyers in different firms have to be instructed for court proceedings. Legal aid is not available for collaborative law and the process may be expensive, but it has a good success record on resolving financial and property issues, including complex and high asset cases. If there are issues concerning children, a family consultant or mediator may be brought in.

1.4.3   Arbitration

In some cases, the parties to a dispute may decide to go to arbitration instead of going to court. They may ask an independent expert or panel to make or recommend a decision. The arbitrator's decision is usually binding, but may be advisory. The hearing is held in private and the parties may decide on aspects of its form, such as whether or how to record the proceedings. The parties usually have legal representatives at the arbitration hearing.

---

[17]   See Chapter 7 below.

1.4.4   Mediation

The word 'mediation' is in everyday use, but in relation to family matters it is
still liable to be misunderstood as an attempt at reconciliation or even confused
with 'meditation'. In the 1980s, mediation became a fashionable portmanteau
word carrying various bundles of meanings and values. Some policy-makers
and professionals thought it should be directed at 'marriage saving', while
others thought it should be a means of protecting children from the
consequences of an acrimonious divorce. Mediators themselves were likely to
see the main aim as 'empowering' separating and divorcing couples to reach
agreements without going to court. 'That's a great deal to make one word
mean', Alice said in a thoughtful tone. 'When I make a word do a lot of work
like that,' said Humpty Dumpty, 'I always pay it extra'.[18] Members of different
professions and mediation organisations in many countries, not only in the UK,
have shown unfortunate tendencies to compete like divorcing parents to win
'custody, care and control' of the mediation 'child'. With the growth of
mediation nationally and internationally, it is increasingly necessary to agree a
universal definition, to develop harmonised standards of training and practice
and reduce areas of potential misunderstanding.

The word 'mediation', derived from the Latin 'medius, medium', meaning 'in
the middle', is used with only minor variations of spelling and pronunciation in
many European languages – English, French, German, Italian, Spanish and
Portuguese. In Europe, the term *family mediation* is used in preference to
divorce mediation, the term commonly used in the United States, because
family mediation helps *families* – children and parents – and secondly, because
large numbers of couples live together without marrying. Unmarried couples do
not need 'divorce mediation'. The emphasis on *family* is particularly important
because children's needs should be given priority and because disputes in family
situations such as adoption, care of the elderly and inheritance are not confined
to separation and divorce. Family mediation is used primarily by separating and
divorcing couples to settle arrangements for children and/or financial and
property matters. It may also be used to help settle other kinds of family
matters. Grandparents seeking contact with grandchildren in family conflict or
following the death of a parent may come to mediation, also same-sex couples
and members of different generations. Mediation assists family members to
manage or resolve conflict and work out agreed arrangements. The Family
Mediation Council,[19] the representative body for qualified family mediators in
England and Wales, defines family mediation as:

> 'a process in which those involved in family breakdown, whether or not they are a
> couple or other family members, appoint an impartial third person to assist them
> to communicate better with one another and reach their own agreed and informed
> decisions concerning some, or all, of the issues relating to separation, divorce,
> children, finance or property by negotiation'.[20]

---

[18]   Carroll *Through the Looking Glass* (first published 1872, Penguin Books, 1948), p 117.
[19]   www.familymediationcouncil.org.uk.
[20]   Family Mediation Council Code of Practice 2010, 1.2.

1.5 EARLY DEVELOPMENTS IN FAMILY MEDIATION – ENGLAND AND WALES

The surge in the divorce rate in the last quarter of the twentieth century highlighted the need to encourage early settlement between divorcing couples in dispute over their children or other matters and avoid, or at least reduce, the emotional, social and economic costs of litigation. The Finer Report[21] is often seen as a catalyst for the development of family mediation in England and Wales. The Finer Committee called for a unified family court to replace the dual jurisdiction of the divorce county courts and magistrates' courts. The Committee also recommended that conciliation should be used to help separating and divorcing couples negotiate with each other and reach agreements, as far as possible, with the assistance of an impartial third party, the conciliator. The Finer Committee defined conciliation as:

> 'assisting the parties to deal with the consequences of the established breakdown of their marriage, whether resulting in a divorce or a separation, by reaching agreements or giving consents or reducing the area of conflict upon custody, support, access to and education of the children, financial provision, the disposition of the matrimonial home, lawyers' fees and every other matter arising from the breakdown which calls for a decision on future arrangements'.[22]

The Finer Committee distinguished 'reconciliation' – 'the action of re-uniting persons who are estranged' – from 'conciliation' – 'the process of engendering common sense, reasonableness and agreement in dealing with the consequences of estrangement'.[23]

The first family mediation service in the UK – and possibly in Europe – started in Bristol in 1978 in response to the Finer Committee's recommendations.[24] Bristol Family Conciliation Service (the term 'conciliation' was used in the Finer sense) was set up by a small group of family lawyers and social workers who anticipated that it might take some time to set up a single Family Court (it took forty years – see Chapter 3). The Bristol scheme differed from the Finer concept of court-based conciliation in providing independent, out-of-court mediation at an early stage, usually prior to court proceedings. Mediation at the pre-court stage facilitates early settlement of disputes and acts as a filter for disputes capable of being settled by the parties themselves. The aim is not just to reach agreement on limited issues. An important aim is to facilitate communication between family members, especially between parents during the stressful transitions of separation and divorce. In disputes over children, the mediator facilitates a dialogue that helps parents to reach joint decisions that take account of their children's needs and feelings. The first family mediators were qualified social workers and marriage counsellors who mediated on issues concerning children – custody and access, as the issues were then termed.

---

[21] Finer Committee *Report of the Committee on One-Parent Families* (1974), HMSO Cm.5629.
[22] Ibid, para 4.288.
[23] Ibid, para 4.305.
[24] Parkinson *Bristol Family Conciliation Service*, unpublished paper (1978); Parkinson and Westcott Bristol Family Conciliation Service *Law Society's Gazette* (21 May 1980).

During the 1980s, out of court family mediation services were set up in many regions of England and Wales and in Scotland, mainly as independent projects supported by charitable grants or run under the wing of the Divorce Court Welfare Service, then part of the Probation Service. The first national meeting of representatives of local services held in January 1981 led to the National Family Conciliation Council (NFCC),[25] now National Family Mediation (NFM). Many local mediation services had support from local lawyers and judges, but there was also opposition from lawyers who feared mediators would take work away from them. Mediators explained that they were not a substitute for lawyers and that they encouraged clients to seek legal advice. At a meeting with local solicitors in 1980, the co-ordinator of the Bristol scheme mentioned that mediators were referring more clients to solicitors for legal advice than solicitors were referring to mediation. This resulted in greater confidence in the mediation service and more solicitor referrals to mediation.

Mediation experience soon showed that mediation was needed on all issues, including finance and property, since disputes concerning children are frequently linked to disputes over the family home and maintenance. These interrelated issues cannot be mediated effectively in isolation from each other. Mediation on all issues calls for legal knowledge and expertise, as well as knowledge and expertise from other disciplines. Interdisciplinary co-mediation, teaming a mediator from a family law background with a mediator from a social work, counselling or family therapy background, was developed from 1985 onwards in a pilot project in London, Solicitors in Mediation.[26] Henry Brown[27] and John Cornwell, founder of the Solicitors Family Law Association (now Resolution), were both members of Solicitors in Mediation. A two-year grant from the Nuffield Foundation supported the development of a training programme in interdisciplinary co-mediation. Demand for this training and positive feedback from Solicitors in Mediation clients led to the founding in 1988 of a national association, the Family Mediators Association,[28] to develop training and practice in interdisciplinary co-mediation. Initially, the Law Society permitted solicitors to act as mediators only as a separate form of professional practice, outside their legal practice. Subsequently, both the Law Society and the General Council of the Bar modified their professional practice rules to enable solicitors and barristers to act as mediators within their legal practice in accordance with their code of practice for mediation.[29] In 1995, a joint move was made by NFM, FMA and Family Mediation Scotland to set up the UK College of Family Mediators,[30] to establish policy and standards for the training and accreditation of family mediators and to provide a unified voice in representations to central government.

---

[25] Parkinson *Conciliation in Separation and Divorce – Finding Common Ground* (Croom Helm, 1986); Fisher (ed) *Family Conciliation within the UK* (Family Law, 1990).

[26] Parkinson *Co-mediation with a lawyer mediator* (48 Family Law, 1989).

[27] Brown and Marriott *ADR Principles and Practice* (Sweet & Maxwell, 1st edn 1993, 3rd edn 2011).

[28] www.thefma.org.uk.

[29] Law Society Family Mediation Code of Practice 1997.

[30] UK College of Family Mediators *Code of Practice and Standards for Mediators and Approved Bodies* (1995).

1.6 FAMILY LAW ACT 1996

Family mediation gained support from senior members of the judiciary and from evaluations of comprehensive (all issues) mediation[31] and by the mid 90s the government was finally persuaded that mediation constituted 'a happy concatenation of economy and humanity,'[32] (note, economy came before humanity). Although Parts I and II of the Family Law Act 1996, dealing with divorce law reform, were abandoned, Part III, which was implemented, gave statutory recognition to family mediation and provided public funding through the legal aid system. Section 13 (Resolution of Disputes) made provision for referral to mediation as follows:

> '(1) After the court has received a statement, it may give a direction, requiring each party to attend a meeting arranged in accordance with the direction for the purpose—
> (a) of enabling an explanation to be given of the facilities available to the parties for mediation in relation to disputes between them; and
> (b) of providing an opportunity for each party to agree to take advantage of those facilities.'

Section 29 dealt with mediation and civil legal aid:

> 'a person shall not be granted representation for the purpose of proceedings relating to family matters, unless he has attended a meeting with a mediator—
> (a) to determine—
>   (i)   whether mediation appears to be suitable to the dispute and the parties and all the circumstances, and
>   (ii) in particular, whether mediation could take place without either party being influenced by fear of violence or other harm, and
> (b) if mediation does appear suitable, to help the person applying for representation to decide whether instead to apply for mediation.'

Referrals to mediation increased when solicitors became obliged to refer clients seeking legal aid for family proceedings (with some exemptions) to an authorised family mediator for information about mediation and assessment of eligibility for legally aided mediation. The Legal Aid Board, now the Legal Aid Agency (LAA) set criteria and requirements for LAA-contracted mediation services and mediators providing publicly funded information and assessment meetings and mediation.[33] Cases involving domestic violence were initially exempt from the requirement to consider mediation before legal aid could be obtained. These exemptions were later reduced when authorised family mediators were required to screen for domestic abuse and child protection issues in assessing suitability for mediation.[34]

---

[31] Walker, McCarthy and Timms *Mediation: the Making and Remaking of Co-operative Relationships* Relate Centre for Family Studies (University of Newcastle 1994); see also Chapter 13 below.
[32] Parkinson 'A Happy Concatenation?' in Westcott (ed) *Family Mediation – Past, Present and Future* (Family Law, 2004), pp 33–46.
[33] See Chapter 14 below.
[34] See **1.10** and Chapter 3 below.

1.7 FAMILY JUSTICE REVIEW 2011

In 2010, the Ministry of Justice, together with the Department for Education and the Welsh Assembly Government, set up a Review 'to examine the effectiveness of the family justice system and the outcomes it delivers, and to make recommendations for reform.'[35] Recognising that 'long and complicated legal processes are emotionally and financially draining for parents and distressing for children', the aim of the Review was to produce a system 'which allows families to reach easy, simple and efficient agreements which are in the best interests of the children, whilst protecting children and vulnerable adults from risks of harm. Family mediation and similar support should be used as far as possible to support individuals themselves to reach agreements about arrangements, rather than having an arrangement imposed by the courts'.[36]

In his evidence to the House of Commons Justice Committee on 26 October 2010, the Lord Chief Justice, Lord Judge, said that in ordinary private law cases he did not believe that the adversarial system improved parents' relationship with each other as mother and father of their children. Lord Judge expressed his 'most serious reservations about whether the adversarial system is in any way to the advantage of the child'.[37] The views of the Lord Chief Justice were conveyed to the Family Justice Review on behalf of the judiciary. Writing in the *Government Gazette*,[38] Jonathan Djanogly MP, then Parliamentary Under Secretary of State at the Ministry of Justice, drew attention to the overloaded court system and called for greater use of out of court dispute resolution:

> 'At a time when we must spend with the utmost care and when services are already straining to keep up with increased demand, how will we bring about change? First we must ask some fundamental questions about the way we, as a society, use our civil justice system and the role each of us plays in taking responsibility to resolve our own problems where possible. This is where other dispute resolution options other than court have an important, possibly revolutionary role to play.'

The Final Report of the Family Justice Review (Norgrove Report) recommended fundamental reform of the family justice system.[39] However, just two months after publishing its Response[40] endorsing most of the Review's recommendations, the Government took controversial and ill-timed action under the Legal Aid, Sentencing and Punishment of Offenders Act 2012 (LASPO) to withdraw legal aid for nearly all family matters, thus cutting off the main source of referrals to mediators. It was not made clear that legal aid continued to be available for assessment meetings and mediation. Referrals to mediation dropped by 50–80%[41] and some mediation services, including

---

[35]   Family Justice Review, Terms of Reference 2010.
[36]   Ibid.
[37]   Reported at [2010] Fam Law 1252.
[38]   Djanogly 'Going into mediation instead of going to court' (2009) *Government Gazette* 2010.
[39]   Ministry of Justice *Family Justice Review Final Report* (London, November 2011).
[40]   Ministry of Justice and Ministry of Education *The Government Response to the Family Justice Review – A system with children and families at its heart* (April 2012, Cm 8273).
[41]   *Mediation in Divorce* (April 2014) Newsletter.

long-established services in Bristol and Manchester, closed as a result of loss of work and mounting debts. Although a Pre-Application Protocol issued by the President of the Family Division of the High Court in April 2011 had created an 'expectation' that applicants paying privately, as well as those seeking legal aid, should attend a 'Mediation Information and Assessment Meeting' (MIAM) before applying to the court, many applicants took no notice of this expectation and many courts ignored it as well. LASPO resulted in an initial surge of litigants in person and a near catastrophic decline in mediation – the exact reverse of the government's objectives. However, as mentioned at **1.4** above, there is now a sustained campaign to improve this situation and new measures are being introduced to increase public awareness and facilitate access to mediation.[42]

1.8   CHILDREN AND FAMILIES ACT 2014

Forty years after the Finer Report, the Children and Families Act 2014 created the long-awaited single Family Court. The accompanying Child Arrangements Programme (CAP) and Family Procedure Rules give effect to its provisions in private family law, with renewed emphasis on the value of 'private ordering': 'The CAP is designed to assist families to reach safe agreements where possible out of the court setting ... [since] it is well recognised that negotiated agreements between adults enhance long-term co-operation and are better for the children concerned'. Since 22 April 2014 and subject to exemptions, attendance is required at a 'Mediation Information and Assessment Meeting' (MIAM) with an authorised family mediator before a court application is made in private law children and financial remedy cases. As mediators provide information on dispute resolution processes and not only on mediation, the acronym MIAM is misleading. The Mapping Paths study referred to above[43] suggested that MIAMs should be renamed DRIAMs (Dispute Resolution Information and Assessment Meeting). More simply, they could be AIMs (Assessment and Information Meetings).

The Family Procedure Rules recognise that 'there may be over-riding factors which mean the court does not consider attendance at a MIAM is suitable in any particular case'.[44] FPR Rule 3.8(1)/(2) sets out the circumstances in which a requirement to attend a MIAM does not apply.

'In summary, the main exemptions are:
- domestic violence/child protection;
- bankruptcy;
- the unavailability of an authorised mediator within a specified geographic area or timescale;

---

[42]   DfE and MoJ *A Brighter Future for Family Justice* (August 2014).
[43]   Barlow, Hunter, Smithson and Ewing *Mapping Paths to Family Justice – Briefing Paper and Report on Key Findings* (Universities of Exeter and Kent, June 2014).
[44]   *Family Mediation in England and Wales – A Guide for Judges, Magistrates and Legal Advisors* (Family Justice Council and Family Mediation Council, 2014). See Appendix A.

- a MIAM has already been attended in the four months prior to making the application.

The full definition of these exemptions can be found at paragraphs 20–27 of PD3A.'[45]

The information and assessment meeting has two main purposes: first to provide information on non-court dispute resolution (and other sources of help), and secondly, to assess the suitability of mediation in the particular circumstances. The aim is to assist those in dispute on family matters to make an informed choice of process or way forward. Each party must be seen individually, because a careful assessment of suitability cannot be made with both parties present. There may be a history and/or risk of domestic abuse, child protection concerns and significant emotional or power imbalances. Although both partners involved in separation or divorce should have an equal right to information and despite representations from mediation organisations to government ministers, the requirement to attend an information and assessment meeting applies only to the applicant and not to the respondent. The Family Procedure Rules make it clear that the respondent is expected to attend a meeting with a mediator prior to a court hearing and that the judge can direct attendance, but, unlike the applicant, the respondent is not required to attend at the pre-court stage. Filing a court application is likely to exacerbate the dispute. Mediation awareness training is being provided to judges to increase their understanding of mediation and further efforts are being made to raise public awareness and understanding of mediation through online information, posters and a video sponsored by the Ministry of Justice. Solicitors were formerly the main source of referrals to mediation but with access to legal advice sharply curtailed, the media and especially the internet are now the main sources of public information. Services that survived LASPO are experiencing a gradual increase in the take-up of mediation, but referral rates are unlikely ever to regain pre-LASPO levels.

Scotland has not followed England and Wales in requiring consideration of mediation prior to court proceedings. Family mediation in Scotland is provided by Relationships Scotland and CALM (Comprehensive Accredited Lawyer Mediators recognised by the Law Society of Scotland). Legal aid is available on a case by case basis and the confidentiality of mediation provided by members of these two organisations has the formal approval of the Lord President of the Court of Session. The Scottish Civil Courts Review, known as the Gill Review (September 2009) recommended a free mediation service for lower value claims to encourage out-of-court settlements, but did not propose measures to encourage greater or pre-court use of family mediation.

---

[45]　Ibid.

1.9   MEDIATION AND THE COURT

Comparisons between mediation and court proceedings tend to portray mediation as 'good' and court proceedings as 'bad', but such simple comparisons misrepresent both systems. Mediation is not always suitable and where it is used, it does not always lead to agreement. Some disputes need a court decision. But before embarking on the court route, people need to understand the options for dispute resolution so that they can make an informed choice of process. Family mediation encourages co-operation and supportive relationships between separated parents and children and helps family members to settle issues by agreement, if possible. This process is not suitable or 'successful' in all circumstances, just as court proceedings are not invariably adversarial. Judges may be moving away from the adversarial system to a more inquisitorial system. Adversarial litigation is at the opposite end of the spectrum from participative, settlement-seeking mediation. There is scope for various combinations of settlement-seeking processes along this continuum.

Adversarial litigation	Mediation
The parties are regarded as adversaries	Seeks mutual interests and common ground
Issues defined by lawyers in legal terms	Participants discuss issues in their own terms
Lawyers speak on behalf of their clients	Participants talk and listen to each other
Polarises, drives parties further apart	Narrows differences and helps to build bridges
Formal legal rules govern the court process	Informal, private and flexible
Usually takes a long time, involves delay	Agreements can be reached quickly
Parties rely on their legal advisers	Participants reach their own decisions
Focus on past grievances and wrongs	Focus on present and future arrangements
Conflict and stress may be prolonged	Aims to reduce conflict and stress
Possible options may not be explored	Explores all available options
High costs for disputants and the state	Legal costs may be avoided or greatly reduced

Adversarial litigation	Mediation
Orders imposed by judicial authority	Participative decision-making with agreement
Imposed decisions are less likely to last	Consensual decisions are more likely to last

Litigation tends to focus on past wrongs and grievances, whereas mediation focuses mainly on the present and future, generally without exploring past history, although connections between the past and the present may need to be understood.[46] The Family Procedure Rules[47] contain 'the court's duty and powers to encourage and facilitate the use of non-court dispute resolution'. These duties and powers are considerably strengthened from previous versions:

- The court must consider, at every stage in proceedings, whether non-court dispute resolution is appropriate.

- In considering whether non-court dispute resolution is appropriate in proceedings which were commenced by a relevant family application, the court must take into account:
  (a) whether a MIAM took place;
  (b) whether a valid MIAM exemption was claimed or mediator's exemption was confirmed; and
  (c) whether the parties attempted mediation or another form of non-court dispute resolution and the outcome of that process.
  If the court considers that non-court dispute resolution is appropriate, it may direct that the proceedings, or a hearing in the proceedings, be adjourned for such specified period as it considers appropriate:
  (a) to enable the parties to obtain information and advice about non-court dispute resolution; and
  (b) where the parties agree, to enable non-court dispute resolution to take place.

- The court may give directions under this rule on an application or of its own initiative.

- Where the court directs an adjournment under this rule, it will give directions about the timing and method by which the parties must tell the court if any of the issues in the proceedings have been resolved.

This rule accords with Article 13 of the European Directive on Mediation[48] that 'it should be possible under national law for the courts to set time limits for a mediation process. Moreover, the courts should be able to draw the parties' attention to the possibility of mediation whenever this is appropriate.'

---

[46] See **2.3** and **2.8** below.
[47] Family Procedure Rules 2010 (as amended in April 2014 and supported by the Child Arrangements Programme and allied Practice Directions).
[48] European Parliament *Directive on Certain Aspects of Mediation in Civil and Commercial Matters* (2008/52/EC, 21 May 2008).

Despite a clear statement of the principles of mediation in the Guide to Family Mediation for Judges, Magistrates and Legal Advisors,[49] some judges may see mediators as providing a service to the court, rather than recognising mediation as an independent and confidential non-court service for separated couples and other family members. Returns and experience from a number of courts using a duty mediator at court on family first hearing days found that expecting mediators to attend court pro bono, without any guarantee of referrals, was not sustainable in the longer term. Despite positive results, In-Court Mediation Schemes such as the Milton Keynes scheme are therefore no longer viable.[50] Courts, including Bristol Family Court, are increasingly shifting to a telephone rota system in which judges and court staff refer parties to an information and assessment meeting with an authorised mediator at one of the services in their area. It is preferable for these meetings to take place out of court, rather than at court, to avoid mediation being perceived as part of the court system and imbued with the court's authority. Court referral to an accredited mediator should not be confused with court-directed conciliation in which disputes over children are referred to Cafcass, the Children and Family Court Advisory and Support Service. The suggestion that 'the Cafcass officer and the mediator are part of the same team'[51] fails to recognise that in-court conciliation and out-of-court mediation are intrinsically different processes that need to be delivered separately. Conciliation takes place under the court's jurisdiction and Cafcass officers are officers of the court. Mediation is an independent process: mediators are not officers of the court. Mediation is confidential and the content of mediation is not normally reportable to the court.[52] Both processes aim to facilitate settlement and increase co-operation, especially in cases concerning children, but there are significant differences between them. The following table may help to distinguish out-of-court mediation from in-court conciliation.

Family mediation	Conciliation
Mainly pre-court, individuals can self-refer or be referred by lawyers and other agencies	Courts may direct parties to take part in conciliation to resolve contested issues over children

---

[49] *Family Mediation in England and Wales – A Guide for Judges, Magistrates and Legal Advisors* (Family Justice Council and Family Mediation Council, 2014). See Appendix A.

[50] Banham-Hall 'Children Act First Appointment Scheme' [2008] Fam Law 1054–5.

[51] Doughty and Murch 'Judicial independence and the restructuring of family courts and their support services' [2012] 24(3) *Child and Family Law Quarterly* 346.

[52] See **1.10.2** below.

Family mediation	Conciliation
Attendance at a mediation information meeting is required in some countries prior to a court application or hearing, but mediation itself is normally voluntary with a mediator who does not hold statutory duties to the court	Conciliation is imbued with the court's authority. Parties in dispute over children may be directed by a judge to take part in conciliation with a court social worker or expert
Private and independent, usually out of court	May take place in the context of a court appointment
Publicly funded in some countries for qualifying individuals. Private clients are charged fees.	State-funded
May cover any or all issues – children, property, finance and other family matters	Children issues only
Qualified mediators in private practice are regulated by their professional association	Judges and family court social workers are officers of the court, accountable within the justice system
Non-directive: participants are encouraged to explore options and consider their children's needs in reaching agreements	Welfare of child is paramount. Conciliators may give directive advice on children's best interests
Confidential, 'without prejudice and privileged', unless a child or adult is at risk of harm or if the court requires disclosure	Conciliation by family court social workers is not privileged. The outcome is recorded
Often consists of a series of meetings spaced over several weeks or months, flexible	Usually a single meeting, 1 hour on average. Tends to produce standardised agreements
Level of conflict varies	Mainly high conflict disputes over children
Aims to facilitate child-parent and co-parenting relationships in the longer term	Unlikely to change attitudes or relationships[53]

53 Trinder et al *Making contact happen or making contact work? The process and outcomes of in-court conciliation* DCA Research Series 3/06 (2006).

Family mediation	Conciliation
Mediated agreements reached by participants themselves are more likely to last	Conciliated settlements more liable to break down: some parents renegotiate arrangements

Many mediations take place at an early stage, generally before application to the court, but even at Court of Appeal level, it may not be too late to consider mediation. In one case, the presiding judge observed that 'this case supports our conviction that there is no case, however conflicted, which is not open to successful mediation, even if mediation has not been attempted or has failed during the trial process'.[54] Mediation in entrenched disputes is difficult, but should be considered nonetheless. Litigation fatigue may have set in, motivating disputants to settle. Mediation provides opportunities to speak and be heard in ways that the courts do not offer. An intractable dispute on children issues may turn out to be rooted in other family issues that need to be understood. Making connections in mediation between feelings and issues is not therapy, but making connections can have therapeutic effects. Cross-disciplinary knowledge and skills are needed to resolve disputes that span children, finance and other issues. There is scope for further liaison between the courts, Cafcass and mediation services on referral to mediation and in developing the mediation process for complex and entrenched disputes.

Where mediation is offered following a referral from the court in the context of court proceedings, it is essential to explain the key principles of mediation very carefully to each party and make sure they are understood. As Neil Robinson has observed (personal communication), the shift from an arena that is widely perceived as adversarial to a forum for co-operative resolution is hard for many people to understand and accept, yet it offers a real opportunity for those entrenched in court 'warfare' to change direction in a way that could be transformative for them. Mediators who receive referrals from the court may find it necessary to explain the principles of mediation to both parties in more depth and to propose ground rules for the mediation process, as suggested by Neil Robinson in Appendix F.

1.10   CORE PRINCIPLES OF FAMILY MEDIATION

The core principles of family mediation and requirements for the training and practice of family mediators in England and Wales have been established by the Family Mediation Council (FMC), the governing body comprising representatives of six Member Organisations: the College of Mediators, the Family Mediators Association (FMA), National Family Mediation (NFM, formerly the National Family Conciliation Council), Resolution (formerly the Solicitors Family Law Association), the ADR Group and the Law Society. The Law Society does not provide mediation training, but it represents solicitors

---

[54]   Thorpe LJ *Al-Khatib v Masry* [2005] 1 FLR 381, CA.

and manages the Law Society's Family Mediation Panel for solicitor mediators, providing a route to recognition and accreditation as a family mediator.

The FMC Code of Practice defines the aims of mediation as follows:[55]

'2.1 Mediation aims to assist participants to reach the decisions they consider appropriate to their own particular circumstances.

2.2 Mediation also aims to assist participants to communicate with one another now and in the future and to reduce the scope or intensity of dispute and conflict within the family.

2.3 Where a marriage or relationship has irretrievably broken down, mediation has regard to the principles that the marriage or relationship should be brought to an end in a way that a) minimises distress to the participants and to any children; b) promotes as good a relationship between the participants and any children as is possible; c) removes or diminishes any risk of abuse to any of the participants or children from the other participants; and d) avoids any unnecessary cost to participants.'

The FMC Code of Practice is designed to establish the integrity of the mediation process within the boundaries of ethical principles, location, time and confidentiality:

- Neutral ground – meetings take place on neutral territory, not on territory belonging to, or associated with, one of the participants.

- Time boundaries – mediation is normally short-term. Time boundaries help participants to focus on issues and concentrate on their priorities. The use of time in each session needs to be planned and organised well.

- Safeguards – principles and ground-rules are needed to provide security for participants and their children. The confidentiality of the mediation process is explained further below.

The Guide to Family Mediation in England and Wales for Judges, Magistrates and Legal Advisors[56] explains the four core principles governing family mediation.[57]

- Mediation is voluntary.
- Mediation is confidential, except where there is risk of harm to a child or vulnerable adult or where the court requires disclosure.
- Mediators are impartial: they facilitate negotiation towards settlement and have no vested interest in the outcome.
- Decision making rests with participants in mediation.

These four principles are fundamental to the practice of family mediators in England & Wales. They are set out in the FMC Code of Practice followed by

---

[55] FMC Code of Practice 2010, see Appendix B.
[56] *Family Mediation in England and Wales – A Guide for Judges, Magistrates and Legal Advisors* (Family Justice Council and Family Mediation Council, 2014). See Appendix A.
[57] Ibid, p 3.

Member Organisations and are explained both verbally and in writing to those considering and taking part in mediation.[58]

all parties

1.11   VOLUNTARY PARTICIPATION

A requirement to receive information and consider mediation is not in itself mandatory mediation, because participation in mediation itself is voluntary.[59] Mediators ascertain both parties' willingness to take part and explain that they can withdraw at any stage. The mediator may also terminate the process if it is no longer suitable and/or no further progress can be made. Concerns have been raised as to whether a requirement to consider mediation prior to court application contravenes Article 6 of the European Convention for the Protection of Human Rights and Fundamental Freedoms 1950 – the right to access to justice. It may be argued that individuals also have the right to information and that, before embarking on court proceedings, they should be informed of opportunities to reach a settlement out of court. The requirement to attend an information and assessment meeting should not delay court proceedings, since it can usually be arranged quickly.

The FMC Code of Practice states that 'participation in mediation is voluntary at all times and participants and the mediator are always free to withdraw. Where mediators consider that a participant is unable or unwilling to take part in the process freely and fully, they must raise the issue and possibly suspend or terminate the mediation.'[60] The European Directive on Mediation 2008 likewise defines mediation as a voluntary process 'in the sense that the parties are themselves in charge of the process and may ... terminate it at any time'.[61]

1.12   CONFIDENTIALITY AND LEGAL PRIVILEGE

The confidentiality of mediation requires clear understanding by all concerned – participants, mediators, judges, professional advisers – first, that there are different elements or aspects of confidentiality and secondly, that each of these elements can be applied independently and differently from the others.

1.12.1   Confidentiality provided by the mediator, within defined limits

The FMC Code of Practice 2010 states at 5.5 that:

> '5.5.1 Subject to paragraphs 5.5.3, 5.5.4 and 5.5.5 below mediators must not disclose any information about, or obtained in the course of, a mediation to

---

[58]   FMC Code of Practice, see Appendix B.
[59]   See however **3.11** below on refusal to consider mediation.
[60]   FMC Code of Practice 2010, 5.2.
[61]   European Parliament *Directive on Certain Aspects of Mediation in Civil and Commercial Matters* 2008/52/EC 21 May 2008.

anyone, including a court welfare officer or a court, without the express consent of each participant, an order of the court or where the law imposes an overriding obligation of disclosure on mediators.

5.5.2 Mediators must not discuss the mediation or correspond with any participant's legal advisor without the express consent of each participant. Nothing must be said or written to the legal advisor of one party regarding the content of the discussions in mediation which is not also said or written to the legal advisor(s) of the other.

5.5.3 Where it appears necessary so that a specific allegation that a child has suffered significant harm may be properly investigated or where mediators suspect that a child is suffering or is likely to suffer significant harm, mediators must ensure that the relevant Social Services department is notified.

5.5.4 Mediators may notify the appropriate agency if they consider that other public policy considerations prevail, such as an adult suffering or likely to suffer significant harm.

5.5.5 Where mediators suspect that they may be required to make disclosure to the appropriate government authority under the Proceeds of Crime Act 2002 and/or relevant money laundering regulations, they must stop the mediation immediately without informing the clients of the reason.'

1.12.2 Legally privileged and 'without prejudice' negotiations in mediation

Mediation is confidential in the sense that its content cannot be disclosed to the court by one party or their legal representative except with the other party's consent or if required by the court (see **1.12.3** below). This confidentiality is protected by the privilege covering 'without prejudice' negotiations. The 'without prejudice' rule permits parties to actual or potential court proceedings to withhold evidence of settlement negotiations from disclosure to the court in any subsequent proceedings. This immunity from disclosure is based on the public policy principle that parties should be encouraged to settle disputes out of court, without fear that their attempt could disadvantage them in subsequent court proceedings. The 'without prejudice' privilege belongs to the parties jointly and may be waived by them jointly. English courts have long supported the existence of a legal privilege attaching to statements and communications where parties enter into negotiation with the aim of achieving reconciliation.[62] *Re D*[63] extended the privilege to cover mediation on children matters, on the grounds that it is likewise based on a public interest principle. This privilege has been extended further to cover mediation on other issues. The legal privilege attaching to mediation is derived from case-law and a series of legal rulings has established that it is subject to three limitations:[64]

---

[62] See, for example, *McTaggart v McTaggart* [1948] 2 All ER 754; *Pais v Pais* [1970] 3 All ER 491.

[63] *Re D (Minors) (Conciliation: Privilege))* [1993] 1 FLR 932.

[64] *Cross on Evidence* (Butterworths, 6th edn, 1985).

(1)   The privilege belongs to the parties jointly, not to the mediator or the process. The privilege can therefore be waived with the consent of both parties.

(2)   The privilege does not cover statements that are not sufficiently relevant to the dispute that is the subject of negotiation.

(3)   A binding agreement that results from privileged negotiations is not in itself privileged. (For this reason, the confidential mediation summary (Memorandum of Understanding) should record 'proposals subject to legal advice', not 'agreement'.)[65]

The European Directive on Mediation (2008) states:[66]

> 'Given that mediation is intended to take place in a manner which respects confidentiality, Member States shall ensure that, unless the parties agree otherwise, neither mediators nor those involved in the administration of the mediation process shall be compelled to give evidence arising out of or in connection with a mediation process, except:
> (a)   where this is necessary for overriding considerations of public policy of the Member State concerned, in particular when required to ensure the protection of the best interests of children or to prevent harm to the physical or psychological integrity of a person; or
> (b)   where disclosure of the content of the agreement resulting from mediation is necessary in order to implement or enforce that agreement.'

1.12.3   The court's power to override the 'without prejudice' privilege attaching to mediation

Case-law has established that there are 'matters which a court is entitled to investigate and determine by way of exception to the without prejudice rule'.[67] In the case of *Brown v Rice*, the judge found that 'the absence of a written settlement signed by, or on behalf of, each of the parties does not necessarily mean that the parties may never have arrived at a concluded settlement. An acceptance of an offer after the conclusion of the mediation would be regarded as made in the mediation ... It would be an odd result if in any given case the court was prevented from determining the existence of a concluded settlement solely because the alleged settlement arose within the context of a mediation.'[68]

This indicates that in exceptional circumstances the court can require disclosure of all or part of the mediation process because of 'overriding considerations of public policy'. The question of privilege in civil and commercial mediation was addressed further in *Farm Assist v Defra*.[69] The mediator in the case applied to set aside a witness summons by asserting a mediation privilege, but her attempt to assert privilege was rejected by the judge. In his judgment, Ramsay LJ stated

---

[65]   See Chapter 12 below.
[66]   European Directive on Mediation 2008, Art 7.
[67]   *Brown v Rice* [2007] EWHC 625 (Ch), para 25.
[68]   Ibid, at para 25 and 21.
[69]   [2009] EWHC 1102 (TCC).

that there are 'exceptions which permit use or disclosure of privileged communications or information outside the conciliation where, after balancing the various interests, it is in the interests of justice that the communications or information should be used or disclosed'.

It needs to be understood, therefore, that there can be an overriding obligation in law that takes precedence over the 'without prejudice' privilege and that accordingly the judge may require the mediator to disclose the content of mediation discussions and relevant documents. Judges are referring more cases to mediation and it is likely that judges will wish to be informed of the outcome and even also of the content of a mediation. Mediators should be prepared for the confidentiality of mediation to be challenged by the court more often and more robustly. It is extremely important, therefore, that mediators explain confidentiality to clients as carefully as possible and keep on file an Agreement to Mediate that explains this confidentiality and its limits, signed and dated by both parties. Mediators must also head their mediation summaries correctly with the required standard paragraphs[70] so that they can claim the confidentiality of mediation as a 'without prejudice' and privileged process, in accordance with the Guide to Family Mediation quoted below. If mediation participants wish to waive their privilege to facilitate an order being made with consent, their joint consent should be provided in writing, preferably after taking legal advice.

1.12.4 Explaining confidentiality to clients

It is clearly not a simple matter to explain the confidentiality of mediation and its limits to anxious and often already confused individuals at their information and assessment meeting. There are risks of overloading them with too much complex information that they cannot process and of worrying them even more than they are already. However, one of the mediator's tasks at the information and assessment meeting is to explain confidentiality and its limits as clearly and helpfully as possible, in a way that the person concerned can understand. The nature and extent of client confidentiality and the 'without prejudice' privilege are set out in the FMC Code of Practice and contained in the Agreement to Mediate which both parties need to understand fully and sign, in order to confirm their understanding and acceptance before mediation begins. The FMC Code of Practice states at s 5.6:

> '5.6.1 Subject to paragraph 5.6.2 below, all discussions and negotiations in mediation must be conducted on a legally privileged basis. Before the mediation commences the participants must agree in writing that discussions and negotiations in mediation are not to be referred to in any legal proceedings, and that mediators cannot be required to give evidence or produce any notes or records made in the course of the mediation, unless all participants agree to waive the privilege or the law imposes upon mediators an overriding obligation of disclosure upon the mediator.

---

[70] See Chapter 12 below.

5.6.2 Participants must agree that all factual information material to financial issues must be provided on an open basis, so that it can be referred to in legal proceedings.

5.6.3 All information or correspondence provided by either participant should be shared openly and not withheld, except any address or telephone number or as the participants may agree otherwise.

5.6.4 Privilege will not apply in relation to communications indicating that a child or other person is suffering or likely to suffer significant harm, or where other public policy considerations prevail.'

The Guide to Family Mediation in England and Wales for Judges, Magistrates and Legal Advisors states that:[71]

'Any client entering a mediation process is asked to sign an "Agreement to Mediate" which sets out both the scope of, and limitations to, confidentiality. By signing the agreement to mediate, the parties understand that all communications, (except the disclosure of financial information) are made solely for the purpose of attempting to reach a settlement and are made on the basis that the communications are:
(a) confidential;
(b) will not be referred to in evidence in any court proceedings about the same issues;
(c) will not be used in affidavits or statements. However, this promise of confidentiality does not prevent the mediator disclosing information where there is significant risk to the life, health or safety of children, the parties, or anyone else, or in relation to money laundering/other unlawful act/s.'

Mediators may, therefore, feel somewhat reassured that judges are being encouraged to protect the confidentiality of the mediation process and are being given a clear message that mediation needs to remain a safe space where discussions can take place in privacy. Nevertheless, the greater interaction between courts and mediation means that the complexities which are only touched on above will be subject to greater scrutiny in the future.

1.13 IMPARTIALITY OF THE MEDIATOR

Mediators are stated to be impartial and/or neutral, but impartiality is not the same as neutrality. A mediator is impartial in the sense of being non-partisan, non-directive and not having a stake in the outcome of the mediation. Neutrality suggests an absence of values, whereas mediation has value-laden objectives and mediators are not value-free.[72]

The FMC Code of Practice makes it clear that 'mediators must not have any personal interest in the outcome of the mediation, must not mediate in any case in which they have acquired or may acquire relevant information in any private

---

[71] Op cit, p 4.
[72] See FMC Code of Practice and Chapters 7, 13 and 14 below.

or other professional capacity and must not act or continue to act if they or a member of their firm has acted for any of the parties in issues not relating to the mediation'.[73] Even if participants have no objection to a mediator who has advised or acted previously for one or both of them in a different capacity, or who has a colleague who has done so, they may not realise the potential influence in mediation of knowledge and relationships derived through some previous contact. Mediators must decline to mediate if they have prior knowledge or experience of advising or working with either or both parties in another role or capacity.

Neutrality and impartiality in mediation incorporate the concept of 'equidistance', meaning that the mediator gives equal attention to all participants and manages the process in a balanced and even-handed way. 'All information or correspondence provided by either participant should be shared openly and not withheld, except an address or telephone number or as the participants may agree otherwise'.[74] Mediators should be careful not to engage in separate telephone discussions, emails or correspondence with one party, unless the basis for sharing the content of the communication with the other party has already been agreed. Some mediators prefer the term 'multi-partial'. Mediators cannot be neutral in the sense of having no influence, because their professional values and experience and personal conditioning inevitably influence the way they conduct the mediation process. There is a duty to assist parents to understand and respond to their children's needs, but exerting pressure or expressing opinions would be contrary to the principles of mediation. Mediators occupy varying positions along the continuum between passive facilitation and active intervention.[75]

1.14 DECISION-MAKING RESTS WITH THE PARTICIPANTS

The FMC Code of Practice states that: 'Mediators must not seek to impose their preferred outcome on the participants or to influence them to adopt it, whether by attempting to predict the outcome of court proceedings or otherwise. However, if the participants consent, they may inform them that they consider that the resolutions they are considering might fall outside the parameters which a court might approve or order. They may inform participants of possible courses of action, their legal or other implications, and assist them to explore these, but must make it clear that they are not giving advice.'[76]

Mediators assist participants to reach their own, well-informed decisions and arrangements. This principle is sometimes referred to as 'empowerment'. Like neutrality, empowerment has a number of meanings. At one level, there is empowerment through the sharing of information. Mediators explain the need for full financial disclosure and participants undertake in signing the Agreement to Mediate to provide full information and supporting documents. They are

---

[73] Ibid, 5.1.
[74] Ibid, 5.6.3.
[75] See Chapter 10 below on power imbalances in mediation.
[76] FMC Code of Practice 5.3.

encouraged to take legal advice on financial disclosure and whether further enquiry is needed. Mediation should be terminated if a participant declines to provide information or provides information that appears to be deliberately incomplete or inaccurate. At another level, empowerment means autonomy in the sense of freedom to make choices and maintain control over personal decisions and family arrangements.[77] Mediators assist participants to reach their own decisions without advising them or steering them towards a particular outcome, for example by suggesting the kind of order the court might make. The Agreement to Mediate makes it clear that the outcome of mediation is not binding on participants. They are encouraged to take independent legal advice before entering into any agreement that they wish to make legally binding. Mediators should stress the need for great caution and avoid creating expectations of a mediation outcome being enforceable, especially where premature understandings misunderstood as 'agreement' could disadvantage either or both parties.[78]

1.15   FURTHER PRINCIPLES

The four core principles of voluntary participation, confidentiality, impartiality and participant control of outcomes are underpinned by other fundamental principles:

- Suitability and safety.
- Respect for individuals and cultural diversity.
- Child focus.
- Mediator competence.

1.15.1   Suitability and safety

Assessing the suitability of mediation is considered at some length in Chapter 3[79] and also in Chapter 10 on power imbalances. An essential aspect of 'empowerment' is the protection of adults and children from abuse, intimidation or from any form of pressure.[80]

1.15.2   Respect for individuals and cultural diversity

England and Wales has become ethnically much more diverse over the last ten years, with London the most ethnically diverse area. Figures from the recently published Census for England and Wales[81] show that the majority White British population decreased from 91.1% in 2001 to 86% in 2011, while inter-ethnic relationships continue to rise. 9% of those living together as a couple in 2011 were in an inter-ethnic relationship, representing an increase of 7% over the last

---

[77] But see **10.2** on gender imbalances and autonomy in dispute resolution.
[78] See Chapter 12 on mediation outcomes and summaries.
[79] See **3.4–3.6** below.
[80] Ibid and also see Chapter 13 on mediation experience and outcomes.
[81] Office of National Statistics, 2011 Census Analysis, July 2014.

ten years. Many children have a multi-cultural heritage from mixed-race parents with family roots in countries the children may have never seen. Mixed-race adoption is no longer a rarity. For family mediation to be acceptable to multi-cultural and ethnic minority families, mediators need to appreciate and respect cultural diversity and recognise the limitations of a monocultural perspective. In some communities, the interests of the wider family take priority over individual concerns and needs. Family members have strong obligations to each other and it may be normal for children to live with relatives or for a dependent relative to be taken in by other family members. This kind of family system is very cohesive when extended families live in close proximity. But if families migrate, parents can be very isolated. They may live a long way from relatives and separation or divorce may be condemned by their community for religious or moral reasons. Mediators need to be aware of cultural factors and norms that influence willingness and ability to negotiate in mediation. In traditional Asian marriages, the husband is dominant and the wife submissive. Divorce is discouraged, because it brings social stigma and upsets the harmony of the family. Culturally specific mediation literature is needed to identify variables that influence the mediation process. Mediators need sufficient understanding of different cultural and ethnic traditions so that they do not seek, consciously or unconsciously, to apply their own society's norms and values. Even mediators with the same ethnicity as both participants need to appreciate the uniqueness of each family's history, traditions, values and relationships. Cross-cultural mediators should bring the open minds and self-awareness that all mediators need, while mediators who undertake international family mediation in disputes over cross-border relocation or parental child abduction need additional training to develop specialised knowledge and skills.[82]

North American and West European models of mediation need to be adapted to meet the diverse needs of different cultures, communities and legal systems. Partly as a result of increased immigration, many countries have substantial ethnic minority groups and ethnically mixed populations. Members of these communities may shun services provided by a dominant culture that may fail to understand and respect their traditions and values. To be acceptable to other ethnic groups, mediators may need to be members of the same group or at least accepted by demonstrating their flexibility and openness. Cross-cultural mediators need knowledge and understanding of cultural diversity and suppleness in their thinking and practice to adapt to the needs of multi-ethnic families: 'A Western, individualistic, problem-solving model of mediation suitable for a Western context [is] not totally suitable for a communitarian culture to which most of the Ismaili communities belong.'[83] Afro-Caribbean communities have strong societal and family ties. Concepts applicable in Western societies may not have the same importance for them. A core of universal values needs to be based on best mediation practices in the context of

---

[82]   See **4.6**, **6.3** and Chapter 15 below.
[83]   Keshavjee *Islam, Sharia and Alternative Dispute Resolution* (IB Tauris, 2013).

'diversity in unity'.[84] Mediators should demonstrate their openness to different traditions and values and ensure that individuals from every race and culture are treated with equal respect.

1.15.3   Child focus

'On 22 April 2014 the largest family justice reforms for a generation came into effect, firmly putting children at the heart of the system and implementing many of the recommendations suggested by the Family Justice Review.'[85] The Interim Report of the Family Justice Review[86] had observed that:

> 'Every year 500,000 children and adults are involved in the family justice system. They turn to it at times of great stress and conflict. The issues faced by the system are hugely difficult, emotional and important. It deals with the failure of families, of parenting and of relationships. It cannot heal those failures. But it must ensure it promotes the most positive or the least detrimental outcomes possible for all the children and families who need to use it, because the repercussions can have wide-ranging and continuing effects not just for them, but for society more generally.'

The Report went on to observe that:[87]

> 'Parents can agree arrangements for children following separation with minimal involvement from the court – in fact a study has found the great majority (around 90%) do not go to court. For the other 10%, court can become the arena for drawn out intractable disputes over contact and residency of children. Parental conflict damages children. Although courts focus on encouraging parties to reach agreement, parents' perceptions of "having their day in court" and the adversarial system can exacerbate this conflict. Furthermore, we have heard concerns from both parents and others – such as grandparents – that the length of the case means that existing arrangements become entrenched and they lose all chance of meaningful contact with a child. Using the system is complicated and costly, both emotionally and financially. People enter the system because they are either forced to or are unaware of other ways of finding a resolution.'

The Final Report of the Family Justice Review (Norgrove Report) concluded:[88] 'Children's interests are central to the operation of the family justice system. Decisions should take the wishes of children into account and children should know what is happening and why'. For the great majority of parents, whether living together or apart, there is no public scrutiny of the welfare of their children. If parents cannot communicate with each other or cannot agree arrangements for their children, they may need a mediator's help. Mediation should not simply facilitate quick agreement. A series of meetings can offer

---

[84] Fiadjoe *Family mediation in the Caribbean Paper given at the Council of Europe's 7th European Conference on Family Law – International Family Mediation*, Strasbourg, March 2009.

[85] DfE and MoJ *A Brighter Future for Family Justice* (August 2014), p 4.

[86] *Family Justice Review Interim Report* (Executive Summary, November 2011), para 1.

[87] Ibid, paras 101–2.

[88] *Family Justice Review Final Report* (Ministry of Justice, February 2012).

separated parents an extended opportunity to consider and discuss arrangements for their children, including the needs, feelings and reactions of each child, the child's relationship with each parent and the parents' relationship with each other. The need to consider with parents (and/or other family members) the child's needs, feelings and views is addressed in the FMC Code of Practice:

> '5.7.1 At all times mediators must have special regard to the welfare of any children of the family. They should encourage participants to focus on the needs and interests of the children as well as on their own.
>
> 5.7.2 Mediators must encourage participants to consider the children's wishes and feelings. If appropriate they may discuss with them whether and to what extent it is proper to consult the children directly in order to ascertain their wishes and feelings.
>
> 5.7.3 Where mediators and both participants agree that it is appropriate to consult any children directly, the consent of the children must first be obtained. Mediators consulting directly with any children must have been specifically trained to do so and have received specific enhanced clearance from the Criminal Records Bureau. Such mediators must provide appropriate facilities for direct consultation.'

Concern for children's well-being and the right of the child to be consulted does not mean that a mediator acts as advocate for the child or carries responsibility for the welfare of a child. Mediators should not advise parents on what constitutes the best interests of a particular child. They can, however, suggest sources of information and guidance about children's needs in separation and divorce. Parents should be encouraged to consider each child's individual position, needs and feelings in working out arrangements that will work as well as possible for that child. To a varying extent – more so in some countries than in others – family mediators take an educational role to help separated parents become more aware of children's needs in separation and divorce so that their decisions and arrangements incorporate this fuller understanding. Family mediators should be careful not to be prescriptive. In asking questions, rather than giving answers, they encourage parents to consider when and how they will explain to their children about their separation or divorce and listen to their feelings and views on arrangements that affect their lives (see Chapters 7 and 8 below).

1.15.4   Mediator competence

FMC-approved training and accreditation in family mediation open the way to registration in the FMC's national directory of family mediators, subject to meeting continuing requirements for mediation practice, professional practice consultancy and professional development. These and other components of the evolving profession of family mediators are considered in Chapter 14.

1.16   PHASES IN THE EVOLUTION OF FAMILY MEDIATION

Many countries have introduced legislation and procedures empowering the courts to refer cases to mediation. Australia was one of the first states to pass legislation promoting the use of mediation in family disputes.[89] Family members who take part in mediation are experiencing major changes in their lives. Family mediation is likewise evolving through a series of transitions in becoming an established professional discipline. The Australian National Alternative Dispute Resolution Advisory Council identified four phases in the development of mediation and ADR:[90]

- A period of pioneering work.

- Increasing use of ADR and training of mediators.

- Rivalry and power battles among mediation practitioners and organisations.

- Increasing co-ordination and collaboration.

Similar phases in the evolution of family mediation may be traced in many countries. There are tensions and struggles and also positive indications of growing interdisciplinary and international co-operation. Movement through the four phases of development is more cyclical than linear. It is part of the dynamic nature of mediation that it will always be going through periods of change and possibly chaos and turbulence.[91] In England and Wales, LASPO resulted in so much chaos and turbulence in family law that the government realised urgent action was needed. A Mediation Task Force set up in the spring of 2014 under the chairmanship of David Norgrove, who also chaired the Family Justice Review, delivered its report in June 2014.[92] The Task Force recommended a number of measures to improve the take-up of family mediation and make better provision for child-inclusive mediation. Some of these recommendations have been taken forward by the Government.[93] In a joint response from the Department for Education and the Ministry of Justice the Government renewed its commitment to 'make family justice work better for everybody involved.'[94] Under the leadership of Simon Hughes, Minister of State for Justice and Civil Liberties, government officials, academics and mediators are working together to improve the provision and quality of family mediation services. The dynamics of change need determined efforts to drive mediation forwards through joined-up strategies and a confluence of energies.

---

[89]   Family Law Act of Australia 1975.
[90]   NADRAC 2001.
[91]   See Chapter 2 below.
[92]   *Mediation Task Force Report* (Ministry of Justice, June 2014), see also Chapter 3.
[93]   See Chapter 3 below.
[94]   DfE and MoJ *A Brighter Future for Family Justice, Joint Ministerial Foreword* (August 2014), p 3.

CHAPTER 2

FAMILY MEDIATION – THEORETICAL FRAMEWORKS

'Untwisting all the chains that tie
The hidden soul of harmony.'[1]

CONTENTS

2.1   THE FAMILY JUSTICE SYSTEM[2]

'The family justice system is a network of organisations including family courts, the Children and Family Court Advisory and Support Service (CAFCASS), the Child Support Agency, lawyers and also professionals from medicine, social work and therapy.'[3]

This definition of the family justice system accords with an early definition of an organisation as 'the arrangement of personnel for facilitating the accomplishment of some agreed purpose through the allocation of functions and responsibilities'.[4] Dispute resolution practitioners may be seen as having a place in the family justice system, since its objective is to promote the settlement of disputes in the context of potential or actual court proceedings. The Council of the European Union, in issuing its *Directive on Certain Aspects of Mediation in Civil and Commercial Matters,* stated that its aim was 'to promote the

---

[1]   Milton *L'Allegro'* 142.
[2]   The introduction to this chapter is based on a previous article, Parkinson 'The Place of Mediation in the Family Justice System' [2013] CFLQ 200–214.
[3]   www.education.gov.uk/vocabularies/educationtermsandtags/7152 (last accessed 26 April 2013).
[4]   Gaus *The Frontiers of Public Administration* (University of Chicago Press, 1936), p 66.

amicable settlement of disputes by encouraging the use of mediation and by ensuring a balanced relationship between mediation and judicial proceedings'.[5] A relationship implies a connection: it does not follow that all parts of the system are under unified hierarchical control. Angyal, a social scientist, distinguished a relationship from a system:

> 'A relation requires two and only two members (relata) between which the relation is established. A complex relation can always be analysed in pairs of relata, while the system cannot be thus analysed ... A system is made up of a number of constituent parts that can operate independently of each other. In a system, the members are, from the holistic viewpoint, not significantly connected with each other except with reference to the whole.'[6]

Family mediation was perceived well over thirty years ago as having a place in the family justice system. The President of Bristol Law Society wrote to the Lord Chancellor's Department in November 1981 suggesting that the pioneer scheme in Bristol demonstrated that an informal system of conciliation (used in the same sense as 'mediation') 'can work in harmony with a judicial system, the one complementing and supporting the other. In my view, this achievement may well show a direction in which a reform of the whole family law system might proceed'.[7]

The judicial system is part of the wider family justice system depicted in the Interim Report of the Family Justice Review as a series of concentric circles.[8] Children and families are placed at the centre. The surrounding ring contains the courts and the judiciary, Cafcass and expert witnesses, lawyers and local authorities, contact centres and mediators.

The Family Justice Review was so critical of the existing family justice system that it questioned whether it was a system at all. In its Response, the Government stated that 'through our proposed reforms our aim is to create a coherent and effective system which draws on the expertise which all parties bring to it and which delivers effectively for users.'[9] The Government Report, 'A Brighter Future for Family Justice', refers to the establishment of the Family Justice Board in March 2012 as a means of 'brokering culture change across the family justice system and driving through radical form'.[10] Local Family Justice Boards set up across the country are helping to 'build a system centred on children and based on strong partnerships between all the organisations involved.'[11]

---

[5]   European Directive 2008/52/EC of 21 May 2008 on certain aspects of mediation in civil and commercial matters (2008) OJ L 136/3, Art 1.
[6]   Angyal 'A Logic of Systems', in F E Emery (ed) *Systems Thinking* (Penguin Books, 1969), Vol 1, pp 28–29, 32.
[7]   Westcott, unpublished correspondence quoted in Parkinson *Conciliation in Separation and Divorce* (Croom Helm, 1986), p 78.
[8]   *Family Justice Review: Interim Report* (MoJ, 2011), p 45.
[9]   The Government Response to the Family Justice Review (February 2012), p 25.
[10] DfE and MoJ *A Brighter Future for Family Justice* (August 2014), p 15.
[11] Ibid.

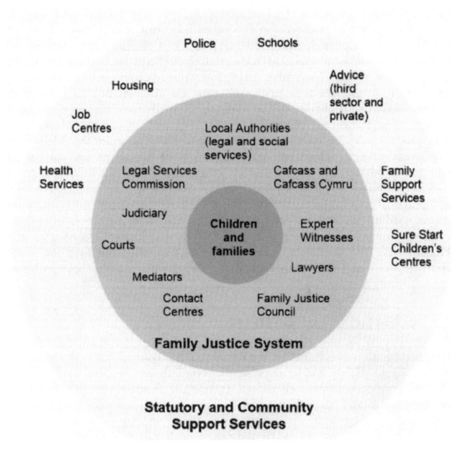

Police   Schools

Housing

Advice
(third
sector and
private)

Job
Centres

Local Authorities
(legal and social
services)

Health
Services

Legal Services
Commission

Cafcass and
Cafcass Cymru

Family
Support
Services

Judiciary

Children
and
families

Expert
Witnesses

Sure Start
Children's
Centres

Courts

Lawyers

Mediators

Contact
Centres

Family Justice
Council

Family Justice System

**Statutory and Community
Support Services**

At central government level, the Ministry of Justice and the Departments for Education, Health, and Work and Pensions are all stakeholders in mediation. While there is evidence of more joined-up thinking between departments, there is still some way to go. In 2013–14 the Ministry of Justice incurred a 'constructive loss' of £56.3 million in a joint venture with a company called (ironically) Shared Services Connected Ltd on an IT system reported by the *Guardian* newspaper as being late, over budget and duplicating a system already developed by the Cabinet Office.[12] This 'constructive loss' has been overshadowed by the £260 million which, according to media reports in August 2014, the Home Office paid to Raytheon, an American arms and electronics manufacturer, to develop an IT system to monitor immigration. In cancelling the contract with Raytheon, the Home Office allegedly incurred liability for a further £224 million, including £50 million for damages. In stark contrast, in the year from July 2013 to June 2014, Legal Aid Agency expenditure on MIAMs and mediation fell from £13,150,000 to £6,738,000 – a reduction of

---

[12]   Ministry of Justice Annual Report and Accounts 2013–14, paras 3.21–3.22, reported by *The Guardian* on 30 June 2014.

virtually 50%.[13] Assessment of eligibility for publicly funded mediation is laborious and has to be correct in every detail, because if any fault is found in the MIAM assessment or in documentary proof of eligibility, payment to the mediator is recouped at audit. MIAMs are free of charge for both parties if one is eligible and from 3 November 2014, for a three-year period and subject to six-monthly review, the first mediation session is also free of charge for both parties where one is eligible.[14] The Mediation Task Force[15] also recommended increased payments to mediators for MIAMs and increased payments to solicitors for advising on and preparing consent orders under the 'Help with Mediation' scheme. These recommendations were not taken up, but on 23 October 2014 the Ministry of Justice announced a new £2 million support package to improve online information for separating couples, increase legal and practical help for litigants in person in the family and civil courts and pilot a safeguarding advisory service run by Cafcass to assist mediators in making risk assessments. Announcing this initiative, the Justice Minister, Simon Hughes, said 'Too many people end up fighting expensive and confrontational court battles and I am determined that more people resolve their problems outside of the courts.'[16]

2.2   VARIATIONS ON A THEME

Family mediation does not exist in a vacuum: it has connections with the family justice system, family and social systems, economic and welfare systems. This chapter considers some well-known theoretical frameworks for mediation before proposing a more holistic or 'ecosystemic' framework. Researchers[17] have found considerable variations among family mediators in the approach and techniques they use. In the United States, mediators tend to have trained in one approach which they may use exclusively, espousing a 'qualitatively distinct approach reflecting fundamental differences of value, principle and philosophy'.[18] Bush and Folger define the aim of transformative mediation as 'changing the parties themselves for the better, as human beings' through helping them to 'recognize and exploit opportunities for moral growth inherently presented by conflict'.[19] In the UK, mediators may not espouse such lofty ideals, seeing mediation more pragmatically as a problem-solving process designed to achieve co-operative settlement.[20] Before considering what is meant by an 'ecosystemic' approach, the following references to three well-known approaches show that each of them has made important contributions to the

---

[13]   https://www.gov.uk/government/uploads/system/uploads/attachment_data/file/358092/legal-aid-statistics-apr-jun-2014.pdf.

[14]   Department for Education and Ministry of Justice *A Brighter Future for Family Justice* (August 2014).

[15]   Mediation Task Force Report (June 2014) Summary of Recommendations.

[16]   Ministry of Justice press release, 23 October 2014.

[17]   Irving and Benjamin 'Research in Family Mediation – an Integrative Review' in Irving and Benjamin (eds) *Family Mediation – Contemporary Issues* (Sage 1995); see also Chapter 13.

[18]   Roberts *An A–Z of Mediation* (2014), p 181.

[19]   Bush and Folger *The Promise of Mediation* (Jossey-Bass 1994), p 12.

[20]   See the FMC and European definitions in Chapter 1.

development of family mediation. These three approaches are known as Structured, Transformative and Narrative Mediation.

2.3   STRUCTURED MEDIATION

The structured or settlement-seeking approach to mediation is based on the system of *principled negotiation* developed in the Harvard Negotiation Project.[21] Fisher and Ury's thinking drew from the pioneering work of Mary Parker Follett[22] in the field of industrial relations. Mary Parker Follett advocated a 'mutual gains' approach to negotiations in place of the traditional system of 'distributive bargaining' that resulted in inflated initial demands and forced concessions. The application of structured, settlement-seeking mediation in resolving disputes in divorce was taken forward by Coogler[23] and Haynes,[24] whose writing and teaching have been major influences in the development of family mediation in many countries. Structured mediation is a staged model with procedures designed to ensure evenly balanced participation through rules and guidelines agreed in advance between the mediator and the participants. The structure provides physical and psychological boundaries that help to contain strong emotions and channel energies towards negotiation and problem-solving. Separate time with each participant may be included during the process, as well as at the outset. The mediator's role is clearly defined and distinguished from other roles.

One of the main features of structured mediation is its focus on interests instead of on positions. A *position* is a statement of one party's preferred outcome. Stating a position usually involves strategic elements such as accusation, overstatement, insisting on one's rights and entitlements and denying that the other party has equal rights. In contrast, an *interest* is an underlying need or goal that needs to be met. Demanding a fixed proportion of capital assets is an example of a position, whereas needing sufficient money to provide adequate housing is an example of an interest. For example, a couple may be arguing over the amount of money each of them is entitled to receive. As parents, they may have a mutual interest in providing stability for their children and avoiding a change of school, if possible.

When mediation is directed towards settlement, the parties are invited first of all to put forward their respective positions. The mediator seeks to identify and understand the interests that underlie these positions and to help the parties recognise that they may have mutual interests and needs, despite being in conflict. Mutual needs are often concrete, such as the need for affordable housing, and there are also psychological needs such as maintaining respect and self-esteem. The mediator helps the parties to look for integrative or 'win-win' solutions which meet as many of these mutual needs as possible. In the

---

[21]   Fisher and Ury *Getting to Yes* (Penguin Books, 1983).
[22]   Follett *Dynamic Administration: The Collected Papers of Mary Parker Follett* Metcalf and Urwick (eds) (Harper, 1942).
[23]   Coogler *Structured Mediation in Divorce Settlement* (Lexington Books, 1978).
[24]   Haynes *Divorce Mediation – A Practical Guide* (Springer Publishing, 1981).

well-known catchphrase, the mediator is 'soft with the people and tough with the problem'. Engaging the parties in a problem-solving approach enables them to work together towards agreement, instead of wasting time and energy in destructive competition. This problem-solving approach relies heavily on negotiation and bargaining techniques. The mediator is likely to use left-brain thinking, characterised as linear, logical, analytical, rational and task-oriented.

Using the techniques of principled negotiation, the mediator aims to:

- separate the people from the problem;
- focus on interests rather than on positions;
- create options for mutual gain;
- reach win/win outcomes instead of win/lose.

Structured mediation consists of a series of stages. Gulliver[25] defined six stages of settlement-seeking as:

1. Searching for an Arena.
2. Defining the Agenda.
3. Exploring the Field.
4. Narrowing Differences.
5. Bargaining.
6. Ritualizing the Outcome.

Fisher and Ury[26] identified four stages in the mediation process consisting of:

1.	Defining the issues	Participants explain their positions
2.	Fact-finding	Gathering and sharing information
3.	Exploring options	Considering needs, concerns and consequences
4.	Reaching agreement	Negotiating a mutually acceptable outcome

These stages of generic mediation may be developed into twelve stages for family mediation.[27]

Haynes defines the final bargaining phase in the settlement-seeking model as one in which 'positions are modified, options traded, and the give-and-take of bargaining occurs'.[28] When the focus is on interests instead of positions, different ways of meeting these interests can be explored and areas of agreement may emerge. The process can work very well where there are mutual interests and motivation to reach agreement on specific issues. For structured mediation to be most effective, participants need to be:

---

[25] Gulliver *Disputes and Negotiations – a cross cultural perspective* (Academic Press, 1979), pp 82–85.

[26] Fisher and Ury *Getting to Yes* (Penguin Books, 1983).

[27] See Chapter 5 below.

[28] Haynes *Alternative Dispute Resolution – the Fundamentals of Divorce Mediation* (Old Bailey Press, 1993), p 4.

- motivated to reach a settlement;
- capable of thinking rationally;
- reasonably clear about the issues they need to settle;
- able to explain and assert their positions;
- able to negotiate;
- able to recognise a fair or acceptable outcome.

Many mediators use structured mediation because the focus is on achieving concrete agreements on specific issues. Lawyer mediators, in particular, are accustomed to playing an active role in working towards settlement. In structured mediation, the mediator can exercise considerable power. If the mediator manages the process in a directive way, there could be risks of disempowering participants instead of empowering them, while attempts to empower a weaker participant could prejudice the mediator's impartiality.[29] There are also risks of mediators steering participants towards a quick settlement, rather than spending time building a mutually satisfactory agreement with both (or all) participants. The aim of structured mediation is to achieve concrete results and practical solutions. These are indeed important goals, whereas improving relationships between participants may not be seen as a necessary or appropriate objective. A mediator using a structured approach may expect strong feelings to be put aside, especially negative feelings about the past. Suppressing emotions or putting them aside may not be possible or helpful during separation and divorce. Structured mediation was not specifically designed for divorce and family disputes. It was designed for civil and commercial mediation and its principles and techniques are extremely useful, but if feelings are not acknowledged and insufficient time is given to family relationships, a settlement may be reached that does not improve communication between separated parents, nor take sufficient account of children's needs.

2.4 TRANSFORMATIVE MEDIATION

> 'The heart of the transformative approach to mediation has been identified as human moral growth in two specific dimensions together: strength of self and relation to other.'[30]

In intense personal and family conflicts, participants may not be capable of negotiating in a calm and rational way. They may be overwhelmed by such strong emotions that they cannot think clearly. Some mediators, especially those from psychotherapeutic backgrounds, found that structured mediation encouraged mediators to take too much control of the process and that they expected too much rationality in resolving disputes. In the *transformative* approach promoted by Bush and Folger,[31] participants are encouraged to take

---

[29] See Chapter 10 below on Power Imbalances in Mediation.
[30] Bush and Folger *The Promise of Mediation* (Jossey-Bass, 1994), p 230.
[31] Ibid.

the lead while the mediator follows, instead of the mediator giving directions that participants follow. Transformative mediation seeks fresh vision through talking and listening. Fresh vision and understanding transform perceptions. Writing on the integration of meditation techniques with mediation, Cloke[32] suggests that:

> 'the deeper, transformational middle way can be accessed through skilful means, which include not only meditation techniques that assist us in becoming more centered, compassionate, and aware of ourselves and others, but mediation techniques that enable us to engage in authentic and committed listening, open hearted communication, empathetic dialogue, creative problem solving, collaborative negotiation, genuine forgiveness and reconciliation.'

The first premise of Bush and Folger's approach is that mediation has the potential to generate transformative effects that are beneficial for the parties and for society. The second premise is that mediation has potential to generate these transformative effects only in so far as the mediator brings a mind-set and methods of practice conducive to the realisation of two key goals – *empowerment* and *recognition*. *Empowerment* encourages self-determination and autonomy, increasing people's capacity to view their situation clearly and to make decisions for themselves. *Recognition* involves participants being able to recognise each other's feelings and perspectives and being more responsive to each other's needs. Empowerment and recognition are intrinsic elements of mediation. Although not unique to the transformative approach, they have much greater emphasis here than in the structured model. Empowerment and recognition help participants to gain mutual understanding so that they can acknowledge each other's needs with more empathy.

Folger and Bush[33] identify ten hallmarks of transformative mediation:

1.   Commitment to empowerment and recognition as the main aim of the process and the main features of the mediator's role.

2.   Leaving responsibility for the outcome with the parties – 'it's their choice'.

3.   Consciously refusing to be judgmental about the parties' views and decisions – 'the parties know best'.

4.   Taking an optimistic view of the parties' competence and motives. Transformative mediators take a positive view of the parties' good faith and decency, whatever the appearances may be. Instead of labelling people as inherently uncaring, weak or manipulative, the mediator sees the parties even in their worst moments as temporarily weakened, defensive or self-absorbed.

5.   Allowing and responding to the expression of emotions – not just allowing the parties a few moments to vent their feelings so that the feelings can be put aside in moving on to the 'real issues'. Transformative mediators

---

[32] Cloke 'Mediation and Meditation – the Deeper Middle Way' *Mediate.com Weekly* No 266, March 2009.

[33] Folger and Bush 'Transformative Mediation and Third-Party Intervention' (1996) 13 *Mediation Quarterly* 4.

encourage the parties to describe their emotions and the events that gave rise to them, in order to promote understanding and shared perspectives.

6.   Allowing for and exploring the parties' uncertainty – their lack of clarity should be seen as positive, rather than negative. If mediators assume that they understand the situation and each party's needs at an early stage of the mediation they may block an important stage of fluidity and ambivalence. Rather than developing a hypothesis which leads in a particular direction, it is preferable for mediators to retain a healthy sense of uncertainty, so that they continue to ask questions instead of drawing conclusions.

7.   Remaining focused in the here and now of the conflict interaction – 'the action is in the room'. Instead of trying to solve problems, the mediator focuses on specific statements as they are made, trying to spot the precise points where the parties are unclear, feel misunderstood or may have misunderstood each other. When mediators spot such points, they slow down the discussion and spend time on clarification, communication and recognition.

8.   Being responsive to the parties' statements about past events – 'discussing the past has value to the present'. Folger and Bush suggest that if the history of the conflict is seen as an evil that must not be dwelt on, important opportunities for empowerment and recognition will be missed. Reviewing the past can reveal choices that were made, options that were available and key turning-points. Reviewing the past can lead to a reassessment of the present.

9.   Viewing an intervention as one point in a larger sequence of conflict interaction. Conflict often goes in cycles, as the parties struggle with doubts and uncertainties. If mediators expect a cycle of moving towards and then away from agreement, they are less likely to panic when progress towards agreement stops or stalls. Transformative mediators may even welcome these cycles as part of the natural ebb and flow of the mediation process.

10. Feeling a sense of success when empowerment and recognition occur, even in small degrees. 'Small steps count'. Mediation is always challenging and often difficult. Allowing ourselves to perceive and enjoy small successes is very important in sustaining our energy and motivation. Instead of defining success solely in terms of the final agreement reached, transformative mediators value each small step that contributes to personal strength and interpersonal understanding and compassion.

Folger and Bush believe that the transformative approach should be preferred over settlement-seeking. However, people come to mediation because they have problems to solve. They are not necessarily seeking 'transformation'. The term 'transformative mediation' may suggest that mediators are miracle workers who transform people or their conflicts in the course of a brief intervention. Even long-term therapy may not produce fundamental change. Folger and Bush do not make it entirely clear whether the aim is to transform people and relationships, or their perceptions of their conflict and each other. A conflict has the potential to be transformed, if it is understood and managed differently, whereas transforming individuals is beyond the mediator's role and a potentially dangerous aim. People do not come to mediation to be transformed and mediators should not impose a process of their own – however creative and visionary – on people who do not want it. If participants want help in reaching a concrete agreement without being expected to change their negative views of each other, they are entitled to receive the kind of help they have asked for. Mediators who feel they have a mission to transform their clients might operate outside the ethical boundaries of mediation. Yet there is evidence that taking part in mediation can be a cathartic experience for some people, leading to changes in their relationship and even in their self-perception. If this catharsis happens without being forced by the mediator, the mediator's role is genuinely transformative. Mediation can have therapeutic effects without being therapy. Folger and Bush's contribution is to emphasise the empathising, visionary and human aspects of mediation, in contrast to the structured approach which can be too cold, logical and limited in dealing with interpersonal relations. It should be recognised, however, that the key elements of acknowledgement and recognition were not introduced into mediation by Bush and Folger: they were used by mediators at least from the 1970s onwards and probably long before that.

2.5   NARRATIVE MEDIATION

> 'The potential to awaken the curiosity of each individual to listen to the narrative of the other and to inspire the courage necessary to hear what one would prefer not to'.[34]

Narrative mediation is based on the idea that mediators and disputants exercise a continuing reciprocal influence on each other throughout their dialogue. Writers with a narrative perspective on mediation[35] conceive it as a story-telling process in which participants are invited to tell their story, with the dual purpose of involving them equally while also helping them towards a shared understanding. Recognising the continuous reciprocal influence that mediators and disputants exercise on each other is seen by Cobb[36] and others as a challenge to the settlement-directed model of mediation in which disputants are guided by the mediator as a series of steps or stages. Stage-by-stage models provide a useful structure for the mediation process, but do not allow for widely differing dynamics or utilise a sufficient range of communication strategies.

---

[34] Barenboim *Everything is Connected – The Power of Music* (Weidenfeld and Nicolson, 2008), p 73.

[35] Burrell, Donahue and Allen 'The impact of disputants' expectations on mediation' (1990) 17 *Human Communication Research* 104–139; Cobb and Rifkin 'Neutrality as a discursive practice' (1991) in Sarat and Silbey (eds) *Studies in law, politics and society* JAI Press, USA.

[36] Cobb 'A Narrative Perspective on Mediation' in Folger, J and Jones, T (eds) *New Directions in Mediation – Communication Research and Perspectives* (Sage Publications, 1994).

Central to the narrative or communication model of mediation is Bateson's[37] concept of 'framing'.[38] Bateson defined a frame as a psychological means of delineating messages. Frames operate by including certain messages and excluding others, just as a picture frame contains the picture to be viewed and excludes subjects outside the frame. Frames also suggest how the message within the frame is to be interpreted. For example, a negative message can be given a positive frame, or vice versa.[39] However, the notion of a frame is static, whereas mediation has taken over the more process-oriented term, *reframing*, to represent an interactive exchange of messages. *Reframing* is widely seen as one of the main tools by which mediators help participants move towards settlement. In much of the literature on mediation, reframing is seen as a unilateral function carried out by the mediator as a planned strategy. In contrast, communication models emphasise the joint influence or 'co-construction of frames'[40] in which participants, disputants and mediators frame and reframe for each other continuously. The influence traditionally attributed to the mediator is fundamentally altered by this perception, with its implications for mediators' shaping or sculpting the mediation process in response to each participant's moves and counter-moves. Bodtker and Jameson[41] offer the metaphor of a kaleidoscope to depict the complexity of interacting frames. Each participant (at least three, if there are two parties and one mediator) brings a frame to the process, like a disk that fits the end of the kaleidoscope. We need a conceptual tool to help us understand the relationship between these three kaleidoscopes during the mutual influence process. What features does the mediator pick out from the disputants' frames as more significant than others, and for what reasons?

Greatbatch and Dingwall[42] investigated mediators' intervention shifts in relation to different responses from the parties – verbal resistance, verbal compliance and silence. Their study illustrates the reciprocal influences of the mediation process. Cobb and Rifkin,[43] in a narrative analysis of mediation sessions, suggest that the sequence of frame bids is important. They report that the party who tells his or her story first has an advantage, because the second party's story is seen as a reaction or challenge to the first story, instead of a story in its own right. The second story becomes a subplot, unless it is skilfully woven into the first story by the mediator. This raises further questions as to whether the mediator invites the parties to decide who is going to speak first, as

---

[37]   Bateson *Steps to an Ecology of Mind* (Chandler, 1972).
[38]   See also **2.7** below and references to Neuro-Linguistic Programming (NLP) and reframing in Chapters 6 and 11.
[39]   See **11.2** below.
[40]   Bodtker and Jameson 'Mediation as mutual influence: re-examining the use of framing and reframing' (1997) 14 *Mediation Quarterly* 3.
[41]   Ibid.
[42]   Greatbatch and Dingwall 'The Interactive Construction of Interventions by Divorce Mediators' in Folger and Jones (eds) *New Directions in Mediation – Communication Research and Perspectives* (Sage, 1994).
[43]   Cobb and Rifkin 'Neutrality as a discursive practice' in Sarat and Silbey (eds) *Studies in law, politics and society* (JAI Press, 1991, USA).

in the Coogler model,[44] or whether the mediator makes the choice as to which party will speak first, having formed a hypothesis about their power relationship or other factors.

Cobb[45] describes conflict stories as 'notoriously rigid, readily re-enacted and recalcitrant to change.' The role of players in each disputant's story are contested and reformulated in the opposing version and the values upheld in one story are denigrated in the other. Haynes[46] describes mediation as opening couples' stories to new interpretations – the kaleidoscope is shaken up. Cobb[47] argues that all three features of a post-structural perspective on narrative – narrative coherence, narrative closure and narrative interdependence – function collectively to challenge traditional views of mediation. Understanding the reciprocal influence of frames and reframing by all participants in mediation provides an analytic frame for understanding interventions. It also leads to the development of new techniques for mediators, whether they are seeking to *transform* disputants' stories or simply encourage greater congruence.

2.6 SYSTEMS THEORY IN ECOSYSTEMIC FAMILY MEDIATION

Mediation is limited and impoverished if mediators fail to integrate elements of different theories and models in an eclectic way, especially when managing complex cases and intractable disputes. Systems theory provides an overarching framework for family mediation. In systems theory, the concepts of first order and second order change provide ways of understanding how social systems change. First order change is change consistent with prevailing values and norms that can be implemented using people's existing knowledge and skills. A change becomes 'second order' when it conflicts with prevailing values and norms or when it is not obvious how it will make things better. Second order change requires consideration of new approaches through 'System 2' thinking which involves reflection, analysis and reappraisal.[48] 'Orderly and creative transformation of social systems ... depends on a capacity for second order learning, which requires a willingness and capacity for challenging assumptions'.[49] Rapoport, a systems theorist, considers that 'the critical issue of peace and the need to convert conflict to co-operation demand incorporation of second order learning in social systems, **and the most effective way to produce social learning is through a participative design process'.**[50]

---

[44] Coogler *Structured Mediation in Divorce Settlement* (Lexington Books, 1978).

[45] Cobb 'A Narrative Perspective on Mediation' in Folger, J and Jones, T (eds) *New Directions in Mediation – Communication Research and Perspectives* (Sage Publications, 1994), p 54.

[46] Haynes *Alternative Dispute Resolution – the Fundamentals of Divorce Mediation* (Old Bailey Press, 1993).

[47] Note 36, at p 61.

[48] Kahneman *Thinking, Fast and Slow* (Allen Lane, 2011), see **14.15** below.

[49] Ramsbotham, Woodhouse and Miall *Contemporary Conflict Resolution* (Polity Press, 2nd edn, 2005), p 46.

[50] Rapoport *The Origins of Violence* (Paragon House, 1989), p 442, emphasis added.

Ecosystemic family mediation addresses the needs of individuals and families as they navigate their way through major changes in relationships and living arrangements.

Connections need to be made between a number of elements:

- Links between the private family system and public systems of family justice and child protection.

- Family systems including children and parents, former partners and new partners, step-parents and members of extended families – not only separating and divorcing couples.

- Connections between different theoretical approaches to mediation and practical learning from experience and research.

- Interdisciplinary partnerships between practitioners from different disciplines.

- The relationship between national family mediation organisations (via the FMC) and central government.

- The role of the mediator in providing a bridge between family members and other professions through hybrid models of mediation.

2.6.1 Links between private family systems and public systems of justice and child protection

Ecosystemic mediation makes connections between private family processes and public systems, including the legal system, employment and economic systems and social support services for families. In a sense, mediators mediate between the private system of family decision-making and public systems of justice and child protection. Mediators work at the interface between these systems, assisting family members to communicate and collaborate more effectively and thus avoid the unnecessary involvement of public systems. When the judicial system needs to be involved – for example, when a court order is needed to give legal force to a divorce settlement or in child welfare mediation,[51] the mediator can facilitate a smooth conjunction, so that the cogs of different wheels can turn without one set of wheels impeding the other. Those who work in the family justice system need to understand the complementary roles and responsibilities of judges, legal advisers, social workers and mediators. Mediators need to understand the boundaries between these roles and the ways in which systems function and interact with each other.

Using an ecosystemic framework, family mediators can select and combine elements from different approaches and practices in designing tailor-made models that fit the needs of participants, rather than expecting them to accept an off-the-peg model that may not be a good 'fit'. A systems perspective helps mediators to take account of legal, economic and social factors that impinge on particular family issues. As Roberts[52] points out: 'an understanding of the

---

[51] See **4.13** and **4.14** below.
[52] Roberts *Mediation in Family Disputes* (Ashgate, 2nd edn, 1997), p 16.

impact of the legal, economic, political, social, gender, cultural, ethnic, family and psychological environment of any dispute between individuals, particularly one involving children, is fundamental to the discussions that occur in mediation'. If negotiations take place in mediation without reference to influences and consequences outside mediation, power imbalances may be accentuated. The changes involved in moving from a two-parent household to two single-parent households – or to family arrangements involving new partners and children from other relationships – require multiple adjustments, for adults and for children. There are many dimensions in which adjustments need to be made – emotional, psychological, legal, economic and social. These dimensions need to be understood and addressed in considering the needs of each partner and their children. A solution that one partner might seek for emotional reasons – such as remaining in the family home – needs to take account of the needs of all concerned, as well as being viable financially. Each family's culture, needs, circumstances and relationships are unique. Arrangements need to be designed by family members, rather than imposed on them, so that they will work in the longer term and not just settle a dispute in the short term.

2.6.2   Family systems

Much of the literature on different approaches to mediation – structured, transformative and narrative – focuses on adult perspectives and adult needs. Children are scarcely mentioned. The words 'child' and 'family' do not feature in the index to 'The Promise of Mediation'.[53] Even where there are child-related issues, children may be regarded as objects of competition or care, rather than as the subject of rights who need a voice in decision-making. Ecosystemic family mediation encourages parents to consider their children's perspectives and needs in maintaining relationships that nurture and support children. Before looking at this approach in more detail, we need to ask: 'Who, these days, counts as family?' The definition of 'family' as a biologically related group consisting primarily of two parents and their children – the traditional nuclear family – is largely obsolete. Many families blend different cultures and traditions within infinite varieties of living patterns and child-rearing arrangements. According to Adoption UK, one in every sixteen adopted children is adopted by two mums or two dads. For many people, 'family' means a pattern of relationships rather than a biological group. Younger children when asked who belongs to their family commonly include neighbours and close friends as part of their family, although even a six-year-old is able to differentiate between 'blood' and 'non-blood' relationships.

> 'In my family I have five parents – my mum and my step-mum, then my dad and my other step-mum, and then my half-sister's dad, and my brothers and sisters and then there's all the pets of course' (Sonya aged 9).[54]

---

[53] Bush and Folger *The Promise of Mediation* (Jossey-Bass, 1994).
[54] Quoted by Neale and Wade *Parent Problems – children's views on life when parents split up* (Young Voice, 2000), p 21.

'My family just **is**. It's different from other people's families but I don't mind, because who says what a family should be like?' (Hope, aged 14).[55]

Enabling children to maintain their attachments to both parents and to others they love – grandparents, aunts, uncles, close friends – may be crucial for their well-being and psychological security. A research study[56] with children aged between eight and fourteen found that from the children's perspectives the key defining characteristics of 'family' were love, care, mutual support and respect. Children shared this concept of 'family' irrespective of differences in their gender, ethnic background and where they lived. Older children were less likely than younger ones to define family in terms of formal relationships and more likely to see the nature or quality of relationships as the defining feature. Tara, a 13 year old, describes a family as:

'a group of people which all care about each other. They can all cry together, laugh together, argue together, and go through all the emotions together. Some live together as well. Families are for helping each other through life.'[57]

Ecosystemic mediation helps family members (couples, families, children and young people, grandparents, step-parents, adult children) to work out arrangements and manage change. Family members are helped to communicate with each other and reach agreed decisions during critical periods of transition and readjustment. Saposnek[58] pointed out that:

'child custody disputes are typically created out of a complex of interactional dynamics ... By viewing custody disputes from a family systems perspective, the mediator is able to understand these contributory elements and utilize interventions to achieve effective resolution ... The children's behaviour may have the effect of further increasing the polarization of each parent's position, because each parent may interpret the children's behaviour as evidence that it is both valid and necessary to assert their own position in order to ensure the well-being of the children.'

If the dispute is viewed in a systemic frame, it may be evident that the reactions and actions of each family member, including children, influence the actions and reactions of other family members in a reciprocal way. Therefore to work solely with the adults involved, without taking account of the needs, feelings and reactions of their children, may be ineffective. Children can block arrangements with which they are profoundly unhappy. Ecosystemic mediation focuses on the family as a whole. Children and other family members are included in this frame, indirectly and directly. The mediator maintains equidistance by helping participants to consider the needs of the family, rather than focusing solely on the dyad of two conflicted parents. Children and young people need opportunities to have a say and be listened to in working out

---

[55] Ibid, p 6.
[56] Morrow 'Children's Perspectives on Families' (1998) *Rowntree Research Findings* 798.
[57] Ibid, p 2.
[58] Saposnek 'Strategies in Child Custody Mediation: A Family Systems Approach' (December 1983) 2 *Mediation Quarterly* 29–30.

arrangements that affect them.[59] In some ethnic groups, children are brought up by members of the extended family, rather than by their parents. Grandmothers and aunts may be the main carers of loosely formed groups of siblings, half-siblings and cousins. Other children live in single-parent households and some of these children may never have experienced life in a two-parent family. Many different carers may come and go – their parent, the parent's new partner or a succession of different partners, childminders and teachers. Mediators should be careful not to assume that the mother is, or should be, the sole or principal carer. Many mothers work full-time and more fathers, step-mothers and step-fathers take an active part in shared childcare. Single-parent households headed by fathers are more common than they used to be. Occasionally, siblings are split between their parents, sometimes for the parents' convenience and sometimes because of children's wishes, or the wishes attributed to them. Siblings who are split between two warring camps may be drawn into the conflict, yet desperately need their parents to present a united front.

Family mediators are presented with complex relationships in dramatically – often traumatically – changing family structures. In practical terms, childcare is often an issue for parents in stable relationships trying to juggle family and work commitments. Many couples who co-parented their children when they lived together continue to co-parent after they separate. Other separated couples do their parenting in parallel, rather than jointly. Parallel parenting needs basic understandings between parents who may have different approaches to discipline and routine and may not communicate readily with each other, except over essentials. Parallel parenting with little communication between the parents may burden children who are used as messengers. A great deal of distress is caused when parents battle over parenting rights and wrongs and the amount of time the children spend with each parent. There may also be conflict over the children's contact with other family members and the involvement of new partners on either side. Step-families have multiple adjustments to make and there can be tensions and disputes between 'old' and 'new' families, especially where a step-family includes 'his' children, 'her' children and 'their' children. When parents and step-parents are able to co-operate with each other, their children feel well supported and are likely to thrive.

2.6.3   Ecograms – understanding family structure and relationships

Family mediators need to understand who is living in each household, whether new partners are seen as part of the family, and if so, by whom. One of the family mediator's first tasks, after welcoming both parents and helping them to understand and engage in mediation, is to draw a 'map', verbally or literally, of the immediate family, as seen by each parent. Questions need to be put to each parent. This may be facilitated by drawing an ecogram on the flip-chart. The ecogram is a modified version of a geneogram, a classic tool in family therapy

---

[59] See Chapter 8 below.

that is used differently in family mediation and for different purposes. Geneograms are by definition diagrams that show family structures, generations and relationships on vertical, generational lines. The term 'ecogram' is used instead of 'geneogram'[60] to depict the 'ecology' of families in transition. When separated parents acquire new partners, the family grows outwards on a horizontal axis, not just downwards. To understand the ecology of the evolving family structure and system, mediators use ecograms to depict the family's *landscape* (using computer terminology here to mean a wider picture) rather than the family in *portrait* format (ie a narrower, linear format).

Another useful feature of the ecogram is to show two horizontal lines connecting the parents, instead of the usual single line. The top line represents the marital or partner relationship that is being disconnected through separation or divorce. The lower line represents the *co-parenting relationship* that usually needs to continue. It is extremely difficult for couples to end their relationship as partners, yet continue to work together as co-parents. The feelings – or threads – of these different relationships often become entangled. Separating them out visually, using a flip-chart, may help parents to see that the threads that they are disconnecting as partners need to be disentangled from the threads that still connect them as parents. If parents continue to raise unresolved marital conflicts, the mediator may need to redirect them, gently but firmly, to the line connecting them as parents, saying, for example: 'You both said you want to work out arrangements for Ian and Jess (see example below), so may we get back to talking about them? Can I ask each of you to tell me a bit more about each of the children'?

The ecogram should show by means of dotted lines (ie permeable boundaries) who lives in each household and who is in contact with whom. It provides a visual focus for parents that may make it easier for them to talk about their children's relationships and contacts with other family members. In the ecogram below, Carol and Hugh have come to mediation to work out arrangements for their children, Ian aged 12 and Jess aged 10. An immediate problem is that Ian is saying he does not want to see his father. Hugh blames Carol for turning Ian against him and for not giving Ian the 'emotional permission' he needs to spend time with his father. Carol accuses Hugh of abandoning her and the children and going off with another woman. She says Ian feels his father has let him down. The ecogram may suggest other possibilities to explore. For example, what does Ian like doing at weekends? How does he feel about spending weekends away from his friends, in the company of two younger girls aged 10 and 5? Would Hugh be able to phone Ian to suggest going to a football match with him (or another activity that would be attractive to Ian)? How might Ian respond to such an invitation? Would Jess feel left out and need a special invitation too? An ecogram helps mediators and parents to look at the sharing of parental responsibilities, the

---

[60]   Bérubé *Workshop at International Family Mediation Trainers Conference* (Edinburgh, April 2002); Parkinson 'A family systems approach to mediation with families in transition' in *Context, the magazine for family therapy and systemic practice* (October 2002).

continuity of child-parent relationships and interactions between 'old' and 'new' family systems, in graphic and helpful ways.

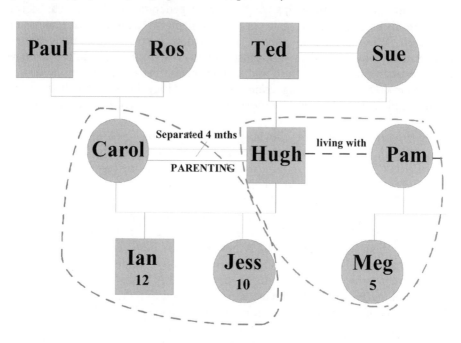

Ecograms are particularly helpful when the family system includes children from previous relationships and new partners, as well as other family members. Some family mediators draw an ecogram on the flip-chart at the start of the mediation, as a means of gathering information from both parents as the picture of their family emerges. This can include information about employment, income and each parent's most urgent issues and priorities. However, it may be inadvisable to include a new partner and other children. Carol and Hugh separated only four months ago and it may be very painful for Carol that Hugh is now living with his new partner, Pam, and with her daughter, Meg. Carol should not be faced with this situation on the flip-chart. If, on the other hand, Carol has a new partner too, it may be helpful to include both new partners and to show, for example, that Meg spends alternate weekends with her father, Robert. The ecogram needs to expand horizontally to cover such situations. Mediators may decide to use all or only part of the ecogram in discussions with parents, or they may draw it later in their case notes as an aid to their own reflection. The ecogram may offer fresh insights on the family's structure and functioning and may also be useful in case discussions with a consultant.

2.7 PRINCIPLES OF ECOSYSTEMIC FAMILY MEDIATION

- Ecosystemic mediation takes an holistic view of families in transition: facilitating communication between family members is of key importance.

- The aim is to help family members to manage change and reach agreed decisions for the future during a critical period of transition and readjustment.

- A separated family is still a family: the needs of family members are interrelated and they may need help to communicate with and listen to each other.

- Participants are helped to work out practical and workable arrangements in relation to parenting of children, housing, financial support and division of assets and beyond these practical arrangements, to value each other's continuing co-operation and support.

- An interdisciplinary approach is needed because mediation takes place within cultural, social and legal contexts. Family mediators need interdisciplinary knowledge and understanding of interrelated contexts.

- Ecosystemic mediation has a relationship with the family justice system while maintaining the independence and confidentiality of the mediation process. Mediation takes place 'in the shadow of the law',[61] helping participants to move out of the shadow of the court in reaching their own agreed decisions.

- Children are individuals with rights of their own, including the right to maintain family relationships that are nurturing and sustaining.

- Children and young people need to understand the changes in their lives. If both parents agree that this would be appropriate, children and young people may be involved directly in mediation, as well as indirectly. Family mediators need further training on the inclusion of children in mediation.

Systems theory offers a means of conceptualising and understanding individual experiences and life events in the context of social and family processes. It offers helpful ways of understanding family structures, relationships and patterns of behaviour. Fragmented or dysfunctional communications between family members may become coherent and can even be seen to have a positive function, if these communications are understood in the context in which they occur. Looking at interactions and patterns of communication helps mediators to move away from linear cause-and-effect explanations that encourage blaming and tunnel vision. When participants in mediation are seen as interconnected and interacting, rather than as detached individuals moving in different directions, the difficulties they bring are easier to understand. This approach is particularly helpful for cross-cultural, cross-border and intergenerational mediation.

The use of systems theory in mediation needs to be clearly distinguished from its use in family therapy, where there are connotations of pathology and treatment. Writers on family mediation have sought to distinguish mediation

---

[61] Mnookin and Kornhauser 'Bargaining in the shadow of the law: the case of divorce' (1979) 88 *Yale Law Journal* 950–997.

from family therapy.[62] A systems perspective in mediation is a conceptual tool, not a form of treatment involving family members. Therapy is a form of treatment, whereas the application of systems theory in industry and other contexts does not have a treatment function.[63] The use of techniques in family mediation that are also used in counselling and family therapy can cause confusion and a blurring of roles. Reframing is often given as an example. Reframing is a communication and conflict management skill which mediators use differently from therapists and for different purposes.[64] Reframing in mediation typically involves re-stating positions or concerns in an accurate and positive way that enables them to be heard and understood. Underlying aims are picked up and made explicit for both parties. Reframing does not mean imposing the mediator's views or values on participants. This would be neither reframing nor mediation. Reframing and circular questioning are invaluable techniques in mediation, where they are used differently from the ways in which a therapist would use them. These techniques are very helpful at a 'micro' level in working with a particular family system. At 'macro' level, an ecosystemic approach makes connections between families, processes and outcomes.

Ecosystemic mediation integrates elements of structured, transformative and narrative mediation in dynamic and flexible ways. It assists family members to reach agreed decisions on matters that have psychological, social, economic and legal implications and consequences. The outcome may be a concrete agreement, as in settlement-seeking mediation. There may be improved communication without a concrete agreement, as in transformative mediation. Connections may be made between the past and the present, as in narrative mediation. Ecosystemic mediation connects different systems and offers cross-disciplinary knowledge and understanding. This broader approach is needed in cross-cultural and cross-border family mediation where different cultural, legal and family systems and their interactions need to be understood. There may be intergenerational issues involving members of extended families. In some cultures and communities, a dispute between a married couple cannot be resolved effectively without taking account of the traditional values, religious beliefs and influences of senior family members, religious leaders and employers. Family members and community leaders may need to be involved in the mediation, directly or indirectly. It is important to clarify who holds power to take decisions and whether third parties need to be involved, directly or indirectly, to ensure that agreements will be acceptable to them. Cross-cultural and international mediators need to be 'multi-partial' and eager to learn about the values and traditions of other cultures.[65]

---

[62] Folberg and Taylor *Mediation* Jossey-Bass (1984); Walker and Robinson 'Conciliation and Family Therapy' in Fisher (ed) *Family Conciliation within the UK* (Family Law, 1990), pp 61–66.

[63] Emery *Systems Thinking: Selected Readings* (Penguin Education, 1969), Vol 1.

[64] See **6.16** below.

[65] See Chapter 15 on international family mediation.

2.8   CONNECTING PAST, PRESENT AND FUTURE

> 'Decision-making is a ... process rooted in the past, carried on in the present, shaping the future ... a deliberate and conscious act of selecting from between at least two alternatives or melding several alternatives into a course of action.'[66]

Some understanding of the past may be necessary to manage the present and consider future possibilities. Mediators need to understand, at least to some extent, the forces that drive powerful emotions and block movement. The past forms part of the present and plays a part in shaping the future. Although mediators do not usually explore the past as many therapists would do, significant events and experiences that have been brushed into the undergrowth of memory may need to be drawn out, because they may be closely connected to the current situation and an obstacle to resolution. Disputes are typically presented in polarised terms, such as whether or how the non-residential parent should see the children. A mother (mothers being more often the main carer) may argue that the children do not want to see their father or that he does not feed them properly or that he does not tell her where he is taking the children. There can be a myriad of objections. The father argues in turn that he has a right to see his children and that they enjoy their time with him and so on. These disputes can run and run. But where do the roots lie? If mediators focus on problem-solving in a tightly structured way, the roots remain buried and feed the conflict. Past-focused questions may be needed[67] to make connections between past experiences, present emotions and future possibilities. Bush and Folger argue that 'steering away from the past and emphasising the future, in order to work towards a concrete settlement, works against exploring parties' perceptions of past conduct in order to surface recognition'.[68] As Paolucci points out, 'decisions are influenced not only by the present situation but also by past decisions. Decisions have a sequential effect: a decision made in the present may be influenced by past decisions and may influence future decisions and actions'.[69]

2.8.1   Mediation example

Philip expressed his despair at the first mediation meeting that his teenage sons, aged 15 and 17, refused to see him and were abusive to him on the telephone when he tried to speak to them. His wife, Sylvia, who had insisted on him leaving the family home, said she was very angry with him and that 'he knew why'. The cause of her anger remained unclear, however. Philip appeared bewildered and at a loss. There were indications that, behind their aggressive façade, the boys were unhappy and felt their father did not care about them. He seemed to know little about them. It emerged that Sylvia and the boys had been extremely close to her own father, who had died the previous year. When her loss and the deep pain in the family were acknowledged in mediation, Sylvia's

---

[66]   Paolucci et al *Family Decision-Making – an Ecosystem Approach* (Wiley, 1977), pp 5 and 54.
[67]   See Chapter 6 below.
[68]   Bush and Folger *The Promise of Mediation* (Jossey-Bass, 1994), p 279.
[69]   Paolucci et al *Family Decision-Making – an Ecosystem Approach* (Wiley, 1977), p 12.

veneer of hostility suddenly cracked and dissolved in a sudden outpouring of grief. Seeing Philip's shocked and compassionate reaction, Sylvia softened and became willing to discuss how he could approach each of the boys with an invitation that would attract each of them. Sylvia suggested that their older son would be pleased if Philip proposed going to a photography exhibition with him (something they had never done before), while the younger one, who was keen on flying, would jump at going to an air-show. Sylvia undertook to encourage the boys to receive and accept their father's invitations. Terms of settlement were reached in two sessions on financial and property matters, but the real breakthrough was in restoring contact and relationships in a family that had been suffering from bereavement and loss. In emotional and practical terms, Sylvia opened a door for Philip to reach his sons. This was not a door that was likely to have been opened through legal proceedings and, had a structured, future-focused approach been used, the significance of the grandfather's death might have been missed entirely.

2.9 TURBULENCE AND CHANGE IN MEDIATING WITH CHANGING FAMILIES

Mediation theory needs to explain the dynamics of the process, irrespective of its outcome. We need a theory to explain how mediation *actually* works, as opposed to how it *should* work. Turbulence and fluid dynamics offer a metaphor and a theory for the process of family mediation, irrespective of outcome. There is a story about the quantum theorist, Werner Heisenberg, on his deathbed. Heisenberg said he would have two questions to put to God: why relativity, and why turbulence. Apparently he added: 'I really think He may have an answer to the first question'.[70] Mediators who see the destructive effects of marital and family conflict may likewise be inclined to ask 'Why conflict?' Conflict in separation and divorce fits the scientific definition of turbulence remarkably well: 'What is turbulence? It is a mess of disorder at all scales, small eddies within large ones. It is unstable. It is highly dissipative, meaning that turbulence drains energy and creates drag'.[71] Conflict in divorce drains energy and creates drag, just as turbulent airflow over the wing of an aeroplane creates drag and destroys lift. Conflict itself is not necessarily destructive. It can produce positive change and growth. But, scientifically speaking, a rough surface uses a lot of energy. Separating couples who are struggling for change or trying to maintain the status quo against the threat of change use a lot of energy. But the energy is often used wastefully and counter-productively – to attack, to threaten or to compete with each other. Mediators need to help couples conserve as much of their energy as possible, so that they achieve forward movement and 'lift'. Instead of draining their reserves of energy, separating couples need to find ways of using it that enable them to pull together in some areas while letting go in others. This is not at all an easy task. As those who work with separating and divorcing couples will know, the movement is typically fluctuating, up and down, backwards as well as

---

[70] Gleick *Chaos – Making a New Science* (Abacus, 1993) at p 121.
[71] Ibid, p 122.

forwards, sometimes purposeful but often chaotic. This reality of irregular rather than smooth movement, with sudden peaks and troughs, is familiar to most mediators.

Turbulence is caused by interactions between forces of stability and forces of instability. In the turbulence that occurs when a couple's relationship breaks down, there is often a struggle as the experience of increasing instability overwhelms efforts to maintain some stability. In this struggle, energy may be used up in generating even more turbulence or it may be directed towards controlling the turbulence. Mediators seek to help couples use their energy constructively instead of destructively, to *manage the dynamics of change*. When turbulence subsides, stability is regained. Another characteristic of turbulence that is highly relevant to mediation is that turbulence produces unpredictable and highly variable results known to scientists as 'surface tension effects'. Surface tension effects are typically small, 'micro' effects (think of snowflakes, all of which are different) that scientists had assumed to be too small to be significant. However, the new ideas of chaos theory caused them to look again at surface tension effects and how they come about. To their surprise, they found that small changes in surface tension effects 'proved infinitely sensitive to the molecular structure of a solidifying substance'.[72] The significance of this finding for mediation is the realisation that even small changes in surface tension effects may influence the development of new family patterns and structures more profoundly than might have been expected. The changing structures of separating families may still be malleable. Relationships may still be ambivalent and flexible, if they have not yet solidified. A crisis in the family, when forces of instability interact most powerfully with forces of stability, creates unique opportunities for change and growth. The timing of the intervention is important: the stage at which mediators become involved affects the level and management of turbulence. Early interventions are usually more influential than later ones, when dysfunctional patterns or structures may be set or stuck and resistant to change.

2.10 CHAOS THEORY

Chaos theory offers some fresh insights for family mediators who wonder why, if they follow the same steps or procedures in working with separating couples, they get such different results. Chaos theory is a science of the global nature of systems. It has brought together thinkers from different fields that had previously been widely separated. The first chaos scientists had an eye for patterns, especially patterns that appeared on different scales at the same time. In the 1970s, scientists in the United States and Europe came increasingly to realise that although physicists had established certain principles to explain the laws of nature, they still had no understanding of the forces that produce disorderly weather patterns, turbulence in water and the oscillations of the heart and the brain. The irregular side of nature, its discontinuous and erratic side remained deeply puzzling. But in the 1970s a few scientists began to seek

---

[72] Ibid, p 311.

links between order and disorder. Edward Lorenz, a scientist at the Massachusetts Institute of Technology found in his study of weather patterns that there were familiar patterns over time, pressure rising and falling, airstreams swinging north or south. But the repetitions were never quite exact. The patterns showed wide and unpredictable variations. From almost the same starting point, two similar weather patterns could grow further and further apart until all resemblances disappeared. What caused these differences? It was assumed that substances such as fluids, that are more easily measurable than the atmosphere, were well understood. However, this was not so.

Gleick[73] took the example of two bits of foam falling over a waterfall and bobbing side by side at the bottom. 'What can you guess about how close they were at the top? Nothing. As far as standard physics was concerned, God might just as well have taken all those water molecules ... and shuffled them personally'. Couples on the brink of divorce may be a long way apart, or they may be quite close to one another. Even if the varying distance between them could be measured, it would not be a reliable predictor of the distance that will exist between them at the end of the mediation process. There are many currents to navigate along the way that may alter each partner's course. Scientists studying unpredictable variations gradually realised that very small differences in input could make a major difference to the final shape of things. In weather systems, Lorenz[74] translated this idea into what is only half-jokingly known as the Butterfly Effect: the notion that a butterfly stirring the air today in Beijing could result in storm systems next month in New York. Had Lorenz stopped with the Butterfly Effect – an image of a tiny, fragile movement having far-reaching but entirely random results, he would not have helped much. But his work showed that a chain of events has critical turning points in which small interventions can be very influential. This new science of chaos theory evolved as 'a science of process rather than state, of becoming rather than being'.[75] Mediation, too, is a science of process rather than state, of becoming rather than being.

---

[73] Ibid, p 8.
[74] Cited in Gleick, see above.
[75] Ibid, p 5.

CHAPTER 3

CONSIDERING MEDIATION AND ASSESSING SUITABILITY

'All roads lay too open, opened too deeply
Every degree of the compass.
Here at the centre of the web, at the crossroads'[1]

CONTENTS

3.1   GATEWAYS TO DISPUTE RESOLUTION

Most people know of the court's existence, but they may have little knowledge of court procedures and as mentioned in Chapter 1, as many as 45% of respondents to the nationally representative Omnibus survey[2] were unaware of ways to resolve family matters through solicitor negotiation, mediation or collaborative law. Efforts are being directed both locally and nationally to increasing awareness and understanding of non-court dispute resolution. The internet is a major source of information. The Government's online service, Sorting Out Separation,[3] provides parents with information concerning separation and ways to resolve or avoid conflict at any stage of separation. The links to mediation are much stronger than in previous versions of the website. As the Mediation Task Force pointed out,[4] there is a plethora of websites for

---

[1]   Ted Hughes *Birthday Letters* (Faber, 1998), p 5.
[2]   Barlow, Hunter, Smithson and Ewing *Mapping Paths to Family Justice – Briefing Paper and Report on Key Findings* (Universities of Exeter and Kent, June 2014), p 4.
[3]   www.sortingoutseparation.org.uk.
[4]   Mediation Task Force Report (June 2014).

separating couples or touching on them, such as Wikiforce[5] and others developed by the CAB or commercial organisations. This morass of information is confusing for separating couples and others in family crisis who are not sure where to turn. Work is ongoing to improve the FMC directory[6] of authorised mediators who have a key role in explaining different paths to settlement and assisting separating couples to make an informed choice of route.

Mediators have been described as gate-keepers,[7] raising 'the crucial question whether mediators can ... become in effect part of the access to justice apparatus'. The same authors suggest that mediators 'exercise considerable power in directing parties down the different paths toward dispute resolution'.[8] This is a misconception of the mediator's role, because mediators do not direct parties down a particular path: they explain different paths and help people to make an informed choice. At the assessment meeting and throughout mediation, the gate to the court remains open. Mediators are gate-openers, not gate-keepers. In separation or divorce, many couples close the gate – or slam the door – between them, too deeply hurt or angry to communicate constructively, if at all. Yet they need answers to questions such as when and how the children will see the parent who has left, whether the family home can be kept for the children's benefit or whether it will have to be put on the market and sold, and how essential outgoings in two separate properties can be afforded. Separated parents with children need to talk to each other, not only to work out answers to these questions, but so that they can go on speaking to each other as their children grow up. The suitability of mediation requires careful assessment: participants need to be willing and 'emotionally ready'[9] to engage in mediation. Gateways to mediation and other forms of dispute resolution need to be open at all stages, including later stages of court proceedings, to facilitate settlement and reduce conflict. Judges, lawyers, social workers and mediators need to understand and appreciate each other's roles and responsibilities and the value of working collaboratively. The family justice system needs to be designed to assist family members to resolve disputes and co-operate better, with clear signposting to different services and access to legal advice. In virtual terms, family mediation should be a circular building with open doors providing easy and direct access. There should be access from the internet and paths that can be travelled in either direction, both to and from lawyers and the family court, and also to and from counselling, therapy and children's services.

The building's circular structure is symbolic, like the round table used for mediation meetings. It should be light and airy with plenty of windows, yet provide privacy and safety for those entering the building. It should be a welcoming place for families, with rooms suitable for different family needs.

---

[5]   www.wikivorce.com.
[6]   www.familymediationcouncil.org.uk.
[7]   Doughty and Murch 'Judicial Independence and the restructuring of family courts and their support services' [2012] CFLQ 333, at p 342.
[8]   Ibid, at p 345.
[9]   See 3.8, 3.9 and 11.8 below.

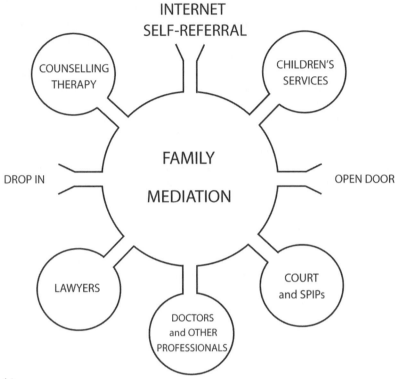

© Lisa Parkinson

The website of Family Mediation Centre Staffordshire[10] shows a family mediation building with rooms for family mediation, counselling, consultation with children and family group meetings. Mediators need to demonstrate to family members, fellow professionals and researchers that they make skilled and careful assessments of suitability. When mediation has been found suitable and both parties are prepared to try it, the stages of the mediation process need to be designed and paced according to the level of conflict and emotional readiness to take part.[11]

3.2 MEDIATION INFORMATION AND ASSESSMENT MEETINGS (MIAMS)

Since 22 April 2014 and subject to certain exemptions,[12] applicants in private law children and financial remedy cases are required to attend a Mediation Information and Assessment Meeting (MIAM) with an authorised family mediator, before making their application to the court. The respondent to the potential court application is expected, but not required, to attend a separate information and assessment meeting. As mentioned in Chapter 1, the purpose

---

[10] www.fmcstaffs.co.uk.
[11] See Chapter 5 below.
[12] See **1.8** above.

of this meeting is for the mediator to explain the processes and potential benefits of non-court dispute resolution and consider with each individual the suitability of mediation or other process in their particular circumstances. As also mentioned above, the acronym, MIAM, is misleading, since the information provided by the mediator covers non-court dispute resolution processes, not only mediation. After attending information and assessment meetings, some couples find they can work things out by themselves and phone in to say they do not need mediation, because they have agreed their arrangements. However, where an application to the court is proceeding, this needs to be made on Form C100 for a child application or on Form A for a financial remedy application. Page 19 of the C100 Form or page 9 of Form A must be completed and signed by an authorised family mediator who ticks the relevant boxes to confirm that:

14a The following MIAM exemption applies:

An authorised family mediator confirms that he or she is satisfied that –
(a)   mediation is not suitable as a means of resolving the dispute because none of the respondents is willing to attend a MIAM; or
(b)   mediation is not suitable as a means of resolving the dispute because all of the respondents failed without good reason to attend a MIAM appointment; or
(c)   mediation is otherwise not suitable as a means of resolving the dispute.

14b The prospective applicant attended a MIAM:

The prospective applicant only attended a MIAM.

The prospective applicant and respondent party(s) also attended the MIAM together.

The prospective applicant and respondent(s) have each attended a separate MIAM.

The prospective respondent party(s) has/have made or is/are making arrangements to attend a separate MIAM.

Mediation or other form of Dispute Resolution is not proceeding because:

The applicant has attended a MIAM alone and
•   the applicant does not wish to start or continue mediation; or
•   the mediator has determined that mediation is unsuitable

Both the applicant and respondent have attended a MIAM (separately or together) and
•   the applicant does not wish to start or continue mediation; or
•   the respondent does not wish to start or continue mediation; or
•   the mediator has determined that mediation is unsuitable

Mediation has started, but has:
•   broken down; or

- concluded with some or all issues unresolved.

As well as exploring the suitability of mediation, authorised mediators assess eligibility for public funding. Those receiving publicly funded mediation are also eligible under the Help with Mediation scheme for a limited amount of legal advice on proposals reached in mediation and the preparation of a consent order.[13] If mediation is suitable and accepted by both parties as their preferred way forward, they need to understand its principles and be clear about the process. Even when the information meeting does not lead to mediation, it is unlikely to have been a waste of time. Individuals who are stressed and confused value being listened to and understood. They may need information about other services. Sometimes the second partner declines the offer initially and accepts later. Many people are confused, distressed or angry, and mediators need to consider the suitability of mediation and dispute resolution with each individual concerned. Screening for any form of domestic abuse or child welfare concerns is discussed below. Mediation is also unlikely to be suitable where there are indications of overwhelming grief, unmanageable anger or mental disorder. The potential for mediation and dispute resolution may be difficult to assess initially. Some conflicts surface only when participants meet for the first time, whereas unpredictable shifts from conflict to co-operation can occur when parents meet and talk about their children. Conflict between separating couples is often channelled into disputes over children or financial matters, and may be associated with one or more of the following:

- The non-mutuality of the decision to separate or divorce.
- A sense of profound betrayal by the other partner.
- Experience of loss and the fear of further loss.
- Blame and recriminations over past events.
- Fear of an unknown future.
- Disillusionment – failed expectations.
- Financial problems.
- Cultural or religious differences.
- Communication problems.
- A need to punish the other partner for inflicting pain.
- Outrage over allegations seen as unfounded and malicious.
- Volatile emotions, lack of self-control.
- Fighting for equality or justice.
- Influence of advisers or other third parties.
- Different views on parenting.
- Disorganised or dysfunctional families.

At information and assessment meetings, the mediator looks for motivation to reach a settlement, willingness to meet with and listen to the other party and capacity to consider the other party's needs, as well as the needs of any children

---

[13] Eligibility can be checked at www.gov.uk/check-legal-aid.

involved. If either party seems to lack this motivation and capacity, displaying only a quest for vindication or determination to defeat the other party, mediation is probably unsuitable, yet there may be risks of emotional harm to children resulting from prolonged warfare between parents and/or other family members. A typology proposed by a family therapist[14] may be applicable to individuals considering mediation. There are three categories consisting of:

- 'Customers' – who know they have a problem and want to achieve change.
- 'Window shoppers' – who are ambivalent, torn between a desire to change and an impulse to stay as they are.
- 'Complainants' – who are not emotionally ready to contemplate change.

This typology is broadly similar to one proposed in a research study on mediator practice at information and assessment meetings (MIAMs).[15] The researchers' categories consisted of:

- 'Engaged' clients, who already have some understanding of mediation and want to move on from the initial meeting to mediation.
- 'Compelled' clients, who are sceptical about mediation, often without knowing much about it, who attend an initial meeting because they are required to do so, or because of financial constraints or emotional pressure.
- 'Unclear' clients, similar to de Shazer's 'window shoppers'.
- 'Strategic' clients, whose underlying aim may be to delay proceedings and maintain the status quo or demonstrate to the court that they hold the higher moral ground, despite having no real intention to settle.

The researchers found that the assessment of suitability varied according to the mediator's views on what mediation is able to achieve, the type of help needed and commercial pressures resulting from the reduction in solicitor referrals.[16] Three key 'types' of mediator were characterised as 'purists', 'realists' or 'optimists'. 'Purist' mediators were most likely to exclude from mediation situations that involved power imbalances and clients whom they judged to be not in an appropriate emotional frame of mind for mediation. 'Realist' mediators were more likely than 'purists' to take on 'marginal' cases. Although seeing these as more challenging, 'realists' recognised the lack of alternative sources of help in the post-LASPO environment. The majority of mediators in the research sample were in the 'realist' category. Collaborative law and solicitor negotiation are seen by many people as unaffordable. For those unable to settle matters on their own, mediation may be the only alternative to going

[14]   De Shazer *Keys to solution in brief therapy* (Norton, 1985) quoted by Cantwell 'Battling Parents: are they getting the right treatment?' [2007] Fam Law 743–748.
[15]   Bloch, McLeod and Tooms *Mediation Information and Assessment Meetings (MIAMs) and mediation in private law disputes – Qualitative research findings* (Ministry of Justice Analytical Series, 2014), pp 18–20.
[16]   Ibid, p 16.

to court as a litigant in person. In marginal cases, rather than offering a 'take it or leave it' standard model, mediators may consider offering co-mediation, shuttle mediation or caucusing.[17]

The third group of mediators in the research sample were termed 'optimists'. Mediators in this group were most likely to take on marginal cases, believing that almost all those willing to try mediation should have the opportunity and feeling confident of their own ability to mediate effectively in most cases. These mediators were more inclined to try to persuade uncertain clients to take part in mediation. The researchers suggested that 'their attitudes may have been influenced by business pressures due to the reduction in solicitor referrals post LASPO'.[18] Mediators need to be optimistic, or they would give up mediating altogether, but they need to be competent realists as well. If they are unable to manage emotional distress and high conflict, there can be risks of participants becoming traumatised in mediation or capitulating under pressure. Skills and techniques to mediate with non-communicating, angry and entrenched couples are considered in later chapters. Many couples come to mediation at an early stage of separation when emotions are running very high. Their positions may be polarised, yet help is needed to contain a crisis that could spiral further out of control. Mediators need to distinguish explosive reactions to recent events, where there may yet be motivation and capacity to reach agreement, from entrenched positions where mediation could be used to prolong conflict, rather than end it.

3.3 MEDIATING IN CRISIS SITUATIONS

The Chinese ideogram for 'crisis' combines two characters, one meaning 'danger' and the other 'opportunity'.

Separation is generally a period of acute crisis for both partners and for the family as a whole. Emotions run high and physical violence may occur for the first time in a way that is out of character for the couple's relationship. In these volatile situations, major decisions should not be hurried or imposed by the

---

[17] See Chapter 4 below.
[18] Bloch, McLeod and Tooms *Mediation Information and Assessment Meetings (MIAMs) and mediation in private law disputes – Qualitative research findings* (Ministry of Justice Analytical Series 2014), p 16.

initiating partner on a shell-shocked one. On the other hand, there may be urgent questions over the non-residential parent's contact with the children and the payment of household bills. Such matters are not helped by delay. At an early stage when everything is in a state of flux, there are usually more options and more scope for change. The highest level of crisis is usually during separation, rather than the legal divorce. Individuals are more ready to accept outside intervention in the early stages of crisis. Help 'purposefully focused at a strategic time is more effective than more extensive help given at a period of less emotional accessibility'.[19] As time goes by, the range of options narrows, positions become entrenched and attitudes harden. If contact with children has broken down or has not even started, the longer the break continues, the harder it becomes to renew contact and rebuild damaged relationships.

A dialogue is needed, but many separating or separated couples find this dialogue very hard to manage on their own. Couples involved in relationship breakdown may be divided into three broad categories: those who are able to talk and work things out, those who argue and fight, and those who cannot talk at all. Couples from all three categories come to mediation and may belong at different times to more than one category. Mediators need to adapt their approach to different levels of conflict and the varying stages each partner may be at in the emotional and psychological divorce. The diagram below illustrates the phases of emotional and psychological separation and divorce, starting with an initial crisis in which one partner leaves the other or announces the intention of doing so. The leaver – shown on the upper trajectory – is more able to cope with a break up that has been pondered over, whereas the unprepared recipient – shown on the lower trajectory – may be inclined, at first, to deny that it is happening. Denial may be followed by intense anger or depression and this phase may be prolonged. If there is not enough help and support, the partner who feels abandoned can slide downwards from depression to despair. David Lodge[20] describes despair as:

> 'a downward spiral movement – like an aeroplane that loses a wing and falls through the air like a leaf, twisting and turning as the pilot struggles helplessly with the controls, the engine note rising to a high-pitched scream, the altimeter needle spinning round and round the dial towards zero.'

When one partner is spiralling downwards and the other partner who can still fly is impatient to move on, the challenge for mediators is how to help them both equally and prevent the gap between them from widening still further.

3.4   ASSESSMENT MEETINGS – A RELIABLE FILTER OR A NET WITH HOLES?

In 2012/13, around 31,000 information and assessment meetings took place where one or both parties were publicly funded, with around half progressing

---

[19]   Rapoport 'The state of crisis – some theoretical considerations' in Parad *Crisis Intervention* (Family Service Association of America, 1965), p 30.

[20]   Lodge *Therapy* (Penguin Books, 1996), p 63.

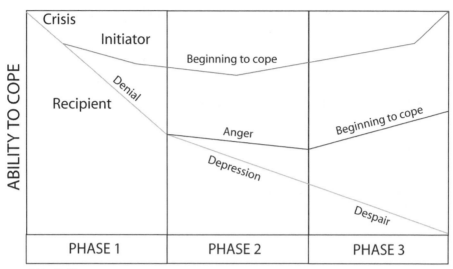

© Lisa Parkinson

to mediation.[21] Mediators need to build rapport with each partner in explaining mediation and exploring its suitability, while potential participants need to gain enough trust and confidence in the process of mediation and in the mediator to decide to give mediation a try.[22] The strongest criticism of assessment meetings is of inadequate screening for domestic abuse. Hester and Radford[23] found around twenty years ago that some mediators considered mediation suitable even when there was a history of domestic abuse. They advocated training for mediators to develop greater awareness of domestic abuse and effective screening for abuse and other risks. Dingwall[24] also expressed concerns that mediators were not screening adequately for domestic abuse and other risks. Although mediators should now be better trained in screening for domestic abuse and assessing suitability, some mediation users who took part in the Mapping Paths to Family Justice study[25] felt that domestic abuse or other concerns had not been checked adequately at the assessment meeting. Contrary to the FMC Code of Practice, some mediators had seen couples together at a joint assessment meeting, while others had allowed their administrator to 'screen' on the phone. These areas of poor practice must be eliminated. Mediators who are authorised to conduct assessment meetings should attend compulsory update training in screening for domestic abuse and other contra-indications for mediation. Individuals must be seen separately,

---

21   Ministry of Justice, 2013, Figure 12.

22   Bloch, McLeod and Tooms *Mediation Information and Assessment Meetings (MIAMs) and mediation in private law disputes – Qualitative research findings* (Ministry of Justice Analytical Series, 2014), p 26.

23   Hester and Radford *Domestic Violence and Child Contact in England and Denmark* (Polity Press, 1996).

24   Dingwall 'Divorce mediation: should we change our mind?' (2010) 32(2) *Journal of Social Welfare & Family Law* 111.

25   Barlow, Hunter, Smithson and Ewing *Mapping Paths to Family Justice – Briefing Paper and Report on Key Findings* (Universities of Exeter and Kent, June 2014).

since effective screening cannot be done in the presence of an abusive or potentially abusive partner or ex-partner.

> 'In all cases, mediators must seek to ensure that participants take part in the mediation willingly and without fear of violence or harm. They must seek to discover through a screening procedure whether or not there is fear of abuse or any other harm and whether or not it is alleged that any participant has been or is likely to be abusive towards another. Where abuse is alleged or suspected mediators must discuss whether a participant wishes to take part in mediation, and information about available support services should be provided.'[26]

> 'All assessments for suitability for mediation must be conducted at meetings on a face-to-face basis ... meetings must include an individual element with each participant to allow mediators to undertake domestic abuse screening.'[27]

Individuals are often apprehensive and confused when they come to an assessment meeting. They may be uncertain whether it is safe to explain their situation and whether the mediator will hold information in confidence. If an address or phone number is provided in confidence, mediators and mediation services must protect confidential addresses and telephone numbers with the utmost care. The mediator needs to build trust by making it clear that information provided at the initial separate meetings is not shared with the other party (or only if it is agreed that certain information may be shared). The suitability of non-court dispute resolution and each party's willingness to take part must be explored with each of them individually. Confidentiality needs to be handled extremely carefully when screening for abuse, child protection issues and potential risks. It is only after screening has been completed and mediation has been found suitable, with both parties' willing consent, that communication between the mediator and both parties can be shared on an even-handed basis. The phrasing of questions to explore fears and risks is very important, with words such as 'abuse' or 'violence' generally avoided, unless the client uses them. For some people, violence means only physical violence, but unremitting verbal and psychological abuse may be even more destructive than physical violence. Initial questions should be low-key, such as *'When you lived together, how were decisions taken? ... What usually happened?'* The screening questions used in Worcester Family Mediation Practice are included in Appendix C, by way of example, and the same practice's sample file screening form is included in Appendix D. The mediator needs to ascertain whether the relationship between the couple involves, or has involved in the past, any degree of abusive or controlling behaviour or other possible contra-indications for mediation. When there are indications of abuse or risk, more specific risk assessment questions need to be asked, as in the Cafcass Mediation Risk Assessment Tool, to ascertain the type and level of risk, whether it is low, medium or high and the corresponding response or action needed.[28] An individual's body language may convey anxiety or fear. The need for a sensitive response to body language is another reason for face-to-face meetings. Assessment by telephone is not

---

[26]   FMC Code of Practice 2010, 5.8.2.
[27]   Ibid, 6.1.
[28]   See **2.1** above, safeguarding advisory pilot scheme announced on 23 October 2014.

normally adequate, although in some circumstances, such as those involving disability or geographical distance, an initial assessment by phone or Skype may enable further steps to be taken safely and appropriately. Where there is any indication of abuse, the mediator needs to ask whether the police were called and/or safeguarding services involved, whether medical treatment was necessary and whether there are, or have been, court injunctions, care orders or personal protection orders. Information should be given about services such as Women's Aid and men's support services. Although no measures guarantee full protection, the circumstances in which restraining orders can be made in the criminal courts offer longer protection to a wider group of people, some of whom might not seek protection through the civil courts. The police have powers to remove a violent partner from the family home, initially for 48 hours, to give the other partner time to obtain advice and support. Individuals who have experienced abuse and/or who fear abuse should not be put under any pressure to take part in mediation, but if they do not trust the mediator and fear retaliation from the (alleged) perpetrator, they may avoid disclosing abuse at an assessment meeting or even throughout the mediation. There are different categories of domestic abuse with varying contra-indications for mediation. Mediators should explore very carefully whether mediation or another process would be suitable and must assess power imbalances that would affect mediation significantly. If mediation is to proceed, the mediator must take steps to manage imbalances, such as establishing ground-rules, structuring the process and identifying needs for legal advice or other form of support. If there are concerns about personal safety, a decision that mediation is not suitable should be taken by the mediator, rather than by one partner. If one partner is blamed for refusing mediation, they may be at risk of repercussions. Mediator should screen for safety and suitability throughout mediation and must suspend or terminate the process if power imbalances cannot be managed adequately, or if there is intimidating or abusive language or behaviour.[29]

Additional sections are needed in the FMC Code of Practice to make it clear that information provided by either party at their MIAM is not shared with the other party prior to both parties accepting and signing the agreement to mediate[30] and secondly, to make it clear that the requirement to share all communications between participants during mediation does not apply to statements indicating that a child or adult is at risk of harm, or where other public policy considerations prevail.

At the assessment meeting, consideration of possible ways forward operates like traffic lights at a cross-roads. Before going ahead, it is essential to slow down and consider whether the lights are red, amber or green and whether they are steady or flashing. If the red light is on or flashing, the path to mediation is unlikely to be suitable. Contra-indications for mediation include:

- Experience and/or fears of domestic abuse, especially where there are continuing risks.

---

[29] See Chapters 4 and 10 below.
[30] See Chapter 5 and Appendix E below.

- Child safety and protection issues.
- Intimidation, threats, overwhelming power imbalances.
- High levels of emotional distress.
- Mental illness.
- Mental disability.
- Substance misuse.
- Evidence of dishonesty and deceit.
- Unwillingness to accept or adhere to the ground-rules for mediation.

Although domestic abuse occurs at all levels of society, perceptions and definitions of violence and abuse often differ. Behaviour that may be condemned in some cultures or communities may be condoned in others. Definitions and value judgements vary among those providing help, as well as among those needing help. Researchers in Bristol found a tendency among professionals to look for circumstances that fitted their personal views and theories, without making careful assessments to check whether factual accounts and subjective experience of abuse supported their assumptions.[31]

3.5   DOMESTIC ABUSE – CATEGORIES AND RISKS

The Legal Aid, Punishment and Sentencing of Offenders Act 2012 (LASPO) defines domestic violence as 'any incident, or pattern of incidents, of controlling, coercive or threatening behaviour, violence or abuse (whether psychological, physical, sexual, financial or emotional) between individuals who are associated with each other'.[32]

Statistics in England and Wales indicate that two women die every week, on average,as a result of domestic violence. Statistics in other countries show similarly high levels. Just over half (54%) of female homicide victims in England and Wales in 2009/10 were killed by their partner, ex-partner or boyfriend. Alcohol abuse is frequently a factor. 45% of UK women have experienced some form of domestic abuse, sexual assault or stalking and for women aged 19 to 44, domestic abuse is the largest cause of death. Women who have recently separated from their partner are at the highest risk (22.3%), compared with other groups. When divorce mediation developed in the United States during the 1980s, there was vehement opposition from women's rights groups and feminists. The strongest objections were to mandatory mediation, where female victims of violence were required to take part in mediation with their male assailant. Critics of mediation objected that physical safety could not be ensured and that risks of further violence would be increased through face-to-face meetings with an abusive partner. Victims of violence were at greatest risk immediately after a mediation meeting, if they left the building at the same time as an angry ex-partner. There has been large-scale debate on

---

[31]   Borkowski, Murch and Walker *Marital Violence* (Tavistock, 1983).
[32]   Legal Aid, Punishment and Sentencing of Offenders Act 2012 (LASPO) Sch 1, Pt 1, para 12.

these issues, involving many different organisations and professions. Legislation was enacted in many states in the USA exempting women who had been victims of violence from mandatory mediation. Women's groups tend to oppose mediation whenever abuse has been experienced, yet some women want mediation because they need an opportunity to talk to their partner or ex-partner in the presence of an impartial, competent and trustworthy third party.[33]

3.5.1 Emotional and psychological abuse, coercive control

A majority of respondents in a research study in Australia on experience of abuse reported that verbal, psychological and emotional abuse occurred daily and was more devastating and long lasting in its negative impact than physical attacks.[34] Emotional abuse includes threats to harm a person or pet or threats to self-harm and blame the partner. Understanding the impact of abusive behaviour on the abused person and on children who witness or overhear it is a key factor in assessment. An abused person may experience fear and humiliation to such an extent that it impairs their ability to assess the risks they continue to face. 'Domestic violence is behaviour that seeks to secure power and control for the abuser and to undermine the safety, security, self-esteem and autonomy of the abused person.'[35]

The level of fear needs to be understood and assessed as part of the screening process. Degrees of fear and risk need careful assessment, since an abused person is liable to underestimate the impact of their experience and risks of continuing and even more severe violence. It is helpful to ask individuals to rate the level of fear they are experiencing on a scale of 1–10. Johnston and Campbell[36] identified five categories of domestic abuse in which mediation may be strongly contra-indicated. Mediators need to recognise and assess different forms and levels of abuse, their impact on abused adults and children and any ongoing risks.

3.5.2 Physical and sexual assaults by the male partner

This kind of abuse is liable to increase in severity over time and such cases are not suitable for mediation. It is the possibility of couples in this category being referred to mediation that causes the greatest concern. If a sufferer of this type of violence is referred to mediation, the greatest care must be taken to help her obtain advice and help, without putting her at further risk. A person who has abused a previous partner is likely to be abusive in a current relationship. Physical violence includes sexual abuse. About a third of women who report

---

[33] Herrnstein 'Women and mediation: a chance to speak and to be heard' (1996) 13(3) *Mediation Quarterly* 229–41.

[34] *Bagshaw Disclosure of Domestic Violence in Family Law Disputes: Issues for Family and Child Mediators* (Conflict Management Research Group, University of South Australia, 2001).

[35] National Family Mediation *Policy on Domestic Violence* (London, 1996).

[36] Johnston and Campbell 'A clinical typology of interparental violence in disputed custody divorces' (1993) 63(2) *American Journal of Orthopsychiatry* 190–199.

violence say that the attacks started when they became pregnant. Reports also indicate that disabled women are liable to experience high levels of emotional abuse and high levels of sexual violence.[37] Nearly a quarter of young teenage girls have reported that they were forced into a sexual relationship. One in two boys and one in three girls in one study said they thought it acceptable to hit a woman or force her to have sex.[38]

3.5.3   Interactive violence used to provoke reactions and gain control

Johnston and Campbell[39] suggest that couples who have an established pattern of provoking each other verbally and exchanging insults often end up having a physical struggle. Either partner may start provoking the other but the overriding response by the man is to assert control by physically dominating and overpowering the woman. The man does not batter her and does not normally use more force than is necessary to obtain her submission.

3.5.4   Abuse by women against men

15% of domestic abuse sufferers are men, but 50% of men who claim to be sufferers of abuse may be perpetrators.[40] Female violence is increasing, however, especially among younger women. Around a fifth of domestic abuse cases involve violence by women against men. A woman who kills a violent partner has usually endured years of violence and abuse from him, but there are also women who explain they felt driven to violence by their partner's passivity or failures. Women typically throw objects or hit their partner, but generally cause less serious injury than men do. Physical attacks by a woman on a male partner are less commonly reported than attacks by men on female partners, because men may have difficulty admitting that they cannot control their partner's abuse. Women who are physically violent are more likely to be arrested than men who are violent.

3.5.5   Abuse between same-sex couples

When there is domestic abuse between a same-sex couple, one partner is usually the perpetrator in a similar pattern of behaviour as those found between heterosexual couples. However, the sufferer in a same-sex relationship is less likely to contact the police than a sufferer in a heterosexual relationship and the sufferer may not realise that threats to 'out' them against their will constitute a form of emotional abuse.

---

[37]   Wilson *Domestic Abuse: Practice and Precedents* (Law Society Publishing, 2010), p 8.

[38]   Burton and Kitzinger with Kelly and Regan *Young People's Attitudes Towards Violence, Sex and Relationships: A Survey and Focus Group Study* (Edinburgh: Zero Tolerance Trust, 1988).

[39]   Johnston and Campbell 'A clinical typology of interparental violence in disputed custody divorces' (1993) 63(2) *American Journal of Orthopsychiatry* 190–199.

[40]   Wilson *Domestic Abuse: Practice and Precedents* (Law Society Publishing, 2010), p 6.

3.5.6 Abuse associated with separation

An incident of physical abuse may occur for the first time during separation in ways that are uncharacteristic of the couple's relationship and previous behaviour towards each other. This kind of abuse typically occurs when an extra-marital affair is discovered or one partner announces the intention of leaving the other. Johnston and Campbell suggest that mediation may be helpful to couples in this category and that they should not be denied the opportunity, if they are willing to mediate. These couples are often loath to admit to an outsider that an argument between them has escalated into physical violence, because they feel humiliated. A mediator who senses this may need to comment that a crisis situation can easily get out of control when stress levels are very high. Especially where a couple indicate that they fear losing control, they need to be asked about any incident/s, the impact on each partner and fears of further incidents.

If there has not been any previous history of abuse and both partners are anxious to work together to regain control, mediation may be suitable, with additional safeguards and conditions as necessary. Arrangements should always be made for separate waiting-areas. If there is high conflict and a risk of confrontation, arrangements should be made for the partners to arrive and leave at different times, to avoid conflict flaring up between them before or after a meeting. In some cases, shuttle mediation may be the only safe and acceptable way to proceed (for examples of screening in and out of mediation, see Chapter 4). Shuttle mediation arranged with each partner on a different day, without either of them knowing the date and time of the other's appointment, may provide a safe forum for discussions that both consider to be necessary and possibly urgent. Experience of mediation and evidence from consumer studies indicate that mediation may be appropriate in situations where one or more incidents of violence or abuse occurred some years ago and where there is no fear of recurrence, or where there has been a single, atypical incident, involving both partners to some extent. A written policy and code of practice should be adhered to, with procedures and safeguards to ensure:

- Initial screening, with full explanation of dispute resolution processes and options, the safeguards available and the ground-rules that would apply if mediation takes place.
- Willingness to participate on an informed and voluntary basis. Mediators must continue to check during mediation that neither partner is participating under pressure and/or in fear.
- Separate waiting-areas, so that neither partner fears waiting in the same area as the other while tension mounts between them.
- It is generally undesirable for both parties in a mediation to arrive and leave the building at the same time. Prior arrangements need to be made for them to arrive and leave separately.
- Mediators need adequate knowledge of levels and forms of domestic abuse and ability to provide information on support services and the protection orders the courts can make.

- Mediators' continuing training in screening and responses to non-verbal signals, so that they can respond and refer appropriately to other forms of help.

- Suitable working conditions and safeguards, including not allowing a mediator to work alone in part of a building at any time. There should be an emergency call system or panic button.

- Where one party alleges abuse by the other, an essential condition for offering or continuing mediation is that the alleged abuser does not deny the basic *facts*. Although views and explanations of causes and reasons are likely to differ, the basic fact that an assault or violent incident took place must be recognised by both parties.

Assessing safety and suitability is particularly complex when the couple is still living together under the same roof and neither is able or willing to leave. If neither considers that there is any form or risk of abuse, but explain that they get caught up in repetitive arguments, they may agree to avoid raising controversial subjects at home and bring them to mediation instead. The mediator may help them to agree a non-verbal signal meaning 'Cut!' or 'Truce!' that either can give and the other will be willing to accept. Both partners need to know the kind of action that could be taken if rules agreed between them are not kept.

3.6   ASSOCIATIONS BETWEEN DOMESTIC ABUSE AND CHILD PROTECTION

Children are liable to have suffered physical abuse themselves in as many as 40–60% of domestic violence cases.[41] 750,000 children annually are reported to have witnessed domestic violence and in 90% of incidents, children were in the same or an adjoining room.[42] Children have described their terror of the violence they could hear taking place: '*I used to hide myself in the smallest part of my bedroom.*'[43] The impact on children of witnessing or experiencing violence and fearing further violence may be devastating and in the longer term, it may have deeply damaging effects. Domestic violence features in the lives of 37% of children who are receiving social work interventions and 60% of those on the child protection register.[44] English law recognises that a child witnessing or hearing domestic abuse is a child protection issue. The meaning of harm to a child was amended in the Adoption and Children Act 2002 to include '*impairment suffered through seeing or hearing the ill treatment of another*'. When there is domestic abuse, questions need to be asked about child abuse and when there is child abuse, questions need to be asked about domestic abuse. Many children remain in contact after separation with an allegedly

---

[41]   Hester, Pearson and Radford 'Family Court Welfare and Voluntary Sector Mediation in Relation to Domestic Violence' (1997) *Rowntree Social Policy Research Findings* No 117.

[42]   *Mills* 'Effects of Domestic Violence on Children' [2008] Fam Law 165–171.

[43]   Cockett and Tripp *The Exeter Family Study: Family Breakdown and its impact on children* (University of Exeter Press, 1994), p 46.

[44]   Children in Need Census 2001.

abusive parent and some continue to live with one. Contact between parents when collecting or returning children may be a flashpoint when further abuse occurs. Screening by mediators for domestic abuse and/or child abuse is not a substitute for child welfare investigations. Mediators may encounter situations of children at risk that have not been reported to a safeguarding agency and which need to be reported.

Example

A young father, 'Sean' explained at his assessment meeting that he was looking after his three children under five years of age, including a six month old baby. His ex-partner, the mother of the children, had left and he did not know where she was living. He thought she was living in a squat about thirty miles away. She had a history of drug-taking. The red light was on, indicating that mediation was unsuitable. Sean wanted to apply for residence of the children. His right arm was in plaster and when the mediator enquired whether he had had an accident and whether his arm was painful, he explained that his ex-partner had arrived without warning and tried to snatch the baby from him. He had resisted, because he did not think the baby would be safe with her and there was a struggle, in the course of which she shut the door on his right arm and broke it. The neighbours heard the row and called the police. Sean said it had taken two policemen to wrestle his partner to the ground. She was arrested and he went to hospital and his arm was put in plaster and then he went back home to look after the children. This incident had occurred two days after a solicitor referred Sean to an information and assessment meeting. The mediator asked if a social worker had visited and Sean said that no-one had come. The police have a legal obligation to inform children's services if they are called to a domestic violence incident and there are concerns for a child's safety. As it is emotionally harmful for a child to see or hear domestic abuse, a referral should be made even when the incident has not placed the child at risk of physical harm.

Sean needed help and the mediator explained the need to call the duty social worker, to which Sean readily consented. The safeguarding service confirmed they had received a call from the police, but they had been given an incorrect address and had been unable to find Sean and the children. Sean provided his address and it was arranged that a social worker would call the same day. As this example shows, even when mediation is unsuitable, an important connection may be made between two systems – in this case, between the mediator providing the assessment and the safeguarding service.

Multi-Agency Risk Assessment Conferences (MARACs) are arranged between local agencies involved in providing services to domestic abuse sufferers. A MARAC is organised regularly to discuss issues relating to the highest risk domestic abuse sufferers in the area. The police chair the meeting and there is an independent MARAC coordinator. In some cases, after allegations have been made, safeguarding checks may find no evidence of harm or risk of harm to a child. The safeguarding agency may then give a green light for mediation to proceed with a child-centred focus, with the aim of reducing the conflict between the parents that gave rise to unfounded allegations. The parents may be asked to give their consent to summaries of mediation meetings and arrangements for their children being shared with the social worker concerned.

3.7   OTHER CONTRA-INDICATIONS WITH POSSIBLE OPPORTUNITIES FOR MEDIATION

Other circumstances needing careful consideration of suitability, where the traffic lights for mediation may be amber or red, include:

- Indications that counselling, therapy or other form of help may be needed.
- Power imbalances that may not be manageable.[45]
- High levels of hostility, conflict and mistrust.[46]
- Allegations or evidence of substance abuse.
- Mental disorder – many individuals experiencing separation have some degree of depression.
- Need for therapeutic help.
- Complex finances where collaborative law may be more appropriate than mediation.
- Language difficulties, illiteracy, deafness.
- Indications that one party wants to use mediation to prolong the status quo, without motivation to settle.

Assessment of the suitability of mediation in these and other complex circumstances should be covered in mediators' training. Special needs should be catered for, such as physical access for the disabled and special assistance for those with speech or hearing difficulties. Some difficulties may be overcome by bringing in specialist help, but this may be hard to access and it brings its own complications. A resource person must be acceptable to all participants and must have good understanding of the mediation process. Mediation where one or both parties are deaf may be possible with the help of a worker for the deaf. There must be prior consultation to ensure that both parties would feel comfortable with the proposed worker. If the worker is already known to one party but not to both, there could be an actual or perceived bias and the other party might not accept the worker as impartial. Mediators and participants need to be able to trust the integrity and professionalism of a specialist worker who joins in the mediation process. If a worker for the deaf signs the mediator's words for one or both parties, the mediator cannot check the accuracy of the translation. The same applies when an interpreter is used to translate to and from another language. Apart from the accuracy of the translation, it can be difficult to convey nuances of language and feeling from one language to

---

[45]   See Chapter 10 on power imbalances.
[46]   See **5.7.2** below and Chapter 11 on mediating with high conflict and 'enmeshed' couples.

another.[47] Mediation should be available and accessible to everyone, in accordance with equal opportunities policy, provided it is suitable and both parties are willing.

3.7.1 Abuse associated with psychotic conditions

Although mediators do not diagnose mental illness, they need to be aware of differences between neurosis and psychosis and between reactive depression and chronic depression. The mediator needs to check for any history or indications of mental illness for either partner. There may be disordered thinking and distortions of reality in psychotic illness that can lead to sudden explosions of violence. There is usually little build-up to these unpredictable attacks. They come out of a clear blue sky and the level of violence may range from moderate to severe. Separation triggers an acute phase of danger. 'Deirdre' came to an initial meeting saying she wanted to take part in mediation. Her account of her situation was at times rambling and incoherent. Careful questioning elicited that she was undergoing psychiatric treatment following a suicide attempt. Mediation would have been unsafe, both for Deirdre and her partner, and they were referred to other professional and support services.

3.8   EMOTIONAL READINESS FOR MEDIATION

The Mapping Paths Study[48] questions whether couples should be encouraged to take part in mediation at an early stage of separation or divorce, when they may be in turmoil and not emotionally ready to take decisions. The decision to separate is rarely a joint decision. Far more often, one partner initiates the separation, sometimes after a period of withdrawing from the relationship. In other situations, the breakdown may be precipitated by a critical event. Some couples accept that they have grown apart and take a mutual decision to separate in a calm and reflective way. But they are not the norm. There is usually an initiator and a recipient. The gulf between their positions and the feelings that accompany them may be so wide that communication breaks down completely and negotiation may be impossible. If one partner discovers that the other has a new relationship, or if a divorce petition arrives without warning, the shock may be extreme. Emotional and psychological adjustment begins earlier for the leaver than for the left partner. A partner who is abandoned is left behind emotionally, as well as physically. Acute feelings of shock, rejection and betrayal often spill over on to children and financial issues. Many individuals come to mediation in a fragile state and are expected to negotiate over arrangements for children and financial matters in a reasonable way, at a time when the ability to think rationally may be temporarily diminished. When decisions are needed on many different issues simultaneously, it is hardly surprising that many people feel overwhelmed. Outrage and

---

[47]   See **6.3** below.
[48]   Barlow, Hunter, Smithson and Ewing *Mapping Paths to Family Justice – Briefing Paper and Report on Key Findings* (Universities of Exeter and Kent, June 2014).

anger can quickly spread from one issue to another. On the other hand, co-operation and agreement in one area help to maintain trust and increase co-operation in other areas.

When mediators explain options for dispute resolution and consider the suitability of mediation, they need to take careful account of each partner's emotional state. Some individuals may not be emotionally ready to negotiate. For them, taking part in mediation could be a very distressing and even traumatic experience, if the suitability of mediation has not been assessed carefully and if the mediator is not sufficiently skilled to manage high conflict or where one partner is paralysed by shock and distress.[49] The divergence between parents' needs and the needs of their children may be widest in the immediate post-separation period. Parents may be too angry and raw to take part in negotiations with each other. They may be unable to absorb information, listen to each other or think rationally. It may be argued, therefore, that mediation should not take place at an early stage of separation. Yet children desperately need reassurance that the parent who has left the home has not abandoned them. Wallerstein and Kelly[50] describe movingly how children wait at the window, yearning for their father (or mother) to appear. Parents need to be encouraged to recognise that their children's needs may differ from their own. Making arrangements for children to keep in touch with the parent who has left may be a first step in mediation, while negotiations over division of assets or the divorce itself may be delayed and can take place at a later stage.

In one case, the wife, 'Julia', explained at her initial meeting that she felt too upset to take part in a face-to-face meeting with her husband, who had recently left her. Julia said there had not been abuse of any kind in their relationship, but she did not feel emotionally strong enough to take part in mediation. On the other hand, she recognised that the children needed to see their father and she herself needed financial security. She could not afford to pay for solicitor negotiation or collaborative law and she was most anxious to avoid court proceedings. The mediator suggested that there could be 'shuttle mediation', at least initially, without the couple meeting directly. Julia said she would feel comfortable enough in a separate room, with her husband in another room and the mediator moving between them. The mediator gave her an earlier arrival time so that Julia would not arrive simultaneously with her husband and she could wait quietly on her own. On the morning of the shuttle mediation, the mediator greeted Julia, who surprised her by saying 'It's OK! I can handle it! I can be in the same room!' The reassurance that her apprehension was understood and the security of separate space if necessary seemed to enable Julia to engage in mediation with more confidence than she had previously thought possible. Julia's husband was co-operative and the mediation proceeded without stressful confrontation.

---

[49]   Barlow, Hunter, Smithson and Ewing *Mapping Paths to Family Justice – Briefing Paper and Report on Key Findings* (Universities of Exeter and Kent, June 2014), p 14.

[50]   Wallerstein and Kelly *Surviving the Break-up – how children and parents cope with divorce* (Grant McIntyre, 1980).

Mediation at an early stage should not be hurried. Intervals between sessions allow time to reflect and opportunities to take advice and prepare for the next meeting. There are, however, understandable concerns about premature decisions being taken under pressure. Skilled mediators should be aware of these risks and able to help couples work out interim or holding arrangements without pressure to take long-term decisions. Independent legal advice is needed alongside mediation to make sure that both partners understand their legal position and possible disadvantages if the status quo should be prolonged. Time management is important in planning an agenda that incorporates both partners' needs. A staged process can give the bereft partner time to catch up and engage in decision-making, instead of remaining on the receiving end. Rigid positions may soften when couples find they can agree 'holding arrangements' without dealing with everything at once. A significant advantage of mediation is that the process can go at the clients' pace (adjusted for each client's individual pace) rather than at a pace forced on them by the legal process or the court. Assessment meetings undertaken sensitively at an early stage of separation enable *pace* to be assessed, as well as *process*.

3.9   GRIEF AND LOSS

Mediators need to be aware of grief reactions and different stages of grieving, when considering whether a partner who is deeply bereft is ready and strong enough to take part in mediation. There is a great deal of literature by psychologists and psychiatrists about attachment, bereavement and loss.[51] Different stages in the grieving process have been described as an initial phase of numbness and shock, then yearning and searching for the lost person, followed by a phase of disorganisation and despair leading, usually, to gradual recovery and reorganisation. People who come to mediation in the initial phase of numbness and shock are unlikely to be in an emotional state to reach decisions or negotiate on financial issues. Comparisons have been made between grieving following death and grieving in separation and divorce. A study of widows and divorced wives[52] showed that both groups experienced similar feelings of loss and grief and had similar difficulties in adjusting to the loss, reconstructing their lives and coping with economic problems. Despite these similarities, grieving in separation and divorce differs significantly from grieving the death of a partner. A partner who leaves the marriage has exercised a choice. The voluntary nature of the decision causes deeper hurt and rejection and more anger than where the loss occurs involuntarily through death. Death involves funerals and 'rites of passage' that help to establish the reality and finality of death, whereas a partner who has been left may refuse to accept the breakdown as a final one. Maintaining contact through the children may prolong and intensify pain, with its constant reminders of the former partner's continuing existence and refusal to return. The Kübler-Ross[53] model of stages

---

[51]   See also **5.3** and **11.12** below.
[52]   Kitson, Lopata, Holmes and Meyering 'Divorcees and widows: similarities and differences' (1980) 50 *American Journal of Orthopsychiatry* 291–301.
[53]   Kübler-Ross *On Death and Dying* (Macmillan, 1969).

of grieving and differences between losing one's partner through separation, rather than through death, are discussed further at 5.3 on attachment and loss.

Mediators need to recognise and understand the emotional stage that each partner seems to have reached, especially in the common situation where they are at different stages. The partner who initiated the separation may have spent a long time thinking about it and preparing for it. The one who is left may be stunned, unable to accept the fact of the separation or to see any justification for it. The wider the gulf between them in seeing that their relationship is over, the harder it is to mediate on the issues that need to be settled. Acknowledging this gap explicitly may help a little. The gulf between the partner wanting separation or divorce and the partner who wants to continue the relationship is a very common problem in mediation. Mediation can be tried, to see whether the partner who has made the break is willing to slow down and allow the other one to 'catch up' emotionally. The second partner may become more able to acknowledge the reality of the breakdown of their relationship. In other words, mediation may be able to bridge the gap between them. Mediation can also be suspended while counselling takes place. The difficulty about this is that there are often urgent issues regarding the children and immediate financial matters. Discussion of these issues is extremely difficult and may not be appropriate, when one partner is very distressed. On the other hand, it may not be possible to put urgent questions on hold, while counselling takes place over a period of months. Mediation may take place concurrently with counselling, but this also has its problems. There has to be enough clarity about the different focus of work in each process. Otherwise, clients can get confused about what they are supposed to be doing with whom. There may be overlap and duplication of effort.

There are situations in which grief and loss are so intense that it is inappropriate to mediate. Mediators need to take account of:

• how recently the separation took place;
• whether there are multiple losses occurring simultaneously;
• the extent to which decisions are being taken unilaterally by one partner;
• the degree of distress shown;
• willingness and capacity to engage in mediation.

3.10 AMBIVALENCE

By the time they come to mediation, many couples say that they have already seen a counsellor or that it is too late for them to go to counselling to resolve the problems in their relationship. Some individuals, however, need supportive counselling alongside mediation. Ambivalence about ending a close relationship is very common. Mixed feelings may be hidden under a defensive shell of anger. Mediation facilitates communication and when blocked feelings are expressed, there can be new perceptions and a major shift in attitudes to separation. Mediators need to be sensitive to signs of ambivalence and able to recognise a need for counselling to help one or both partners reflect on and if necessary accept the ending of their relationship. Counselling may be needed to help an individual or couple explore their relationship in more depth and have support over a longer period.

One partner may be more in need of counselling than the other, but the suggestion of counselling should be put forward for both to consider, if they have not already done so. The mediator should be able to give information about accredited counselling services. Some couples work out a divorce settlement in mediation and then decide not to divorce after all.

Example

Cathy, who was in her 50s, had filed a divorce petition. Her husband, Owen, was 15 years older. There were frequent stormy rows between Cathy and their 18 year old daughter, Tessa, who would then appeal to her father for support. Tessa's two younger brothers were described by both parents as closer to their father, whom they found more patient and less volatile than their mother. Cathy felt isolated and had decided she wanted to move out of the family home and live independently. She was anxious to obtain a 50% share of the profits from Owen's recently sold business, as well as half the difference between his higher pension and her own. Owen did not accept that the marriage needed to end. Tessa had become occupied with college and a new boyfriend and he felt that she and her mother were getting on better. Cathy admitted that she felt ambivalent. Cathy and Owen decided to go to counselling, but the problems continued and they returned to mediation. Acknowledging that she still had some mixed feelings, Cathy pressed on with divorce proceedings. They each took legal advice and in mediation they were able to reach arrangements for a final settlement in divorce. Owen, still trying to persuade Cathy to stay, said at the last meeting that Tessa was away on holiday and when the boys were not around, he and Cathy were enjoying time on their own. Cathy did not disagree and she seemed more relaxed. A year later, the mediators heard that the divorce had not proceeded beyond the 'decree nisi' and the couple were still together.

Although mediators do not provide counselling or therapy, the process of mediation facilitates communication and increases insight and understanding. Some couples discover a new understanding in mediation that enables them to stay together with a stronger relationship than before. If, however, their relationship breaks down again, they may return to mediation feeling clearer about the need to separate or divorce. Parents who remain apart are helped to separate their anger and distress as partners from their mutual concerns for their children, so that they can deal with practical arrangements at a pace they can both manage, working together as co-parents who share love and care for their children. When there are signs of ambivalence, it may be helpful to ask how much change is being looked for, and in what area/s. Some people may be looking for a complete change with a new life, possibly with a new partner.

Others may be looking for a change in their partner's behaviour. Changes in behaviour and perceptions may be achieved through mediation, sometimes with 'transformative' outcomes.

3.11 THE MEDIATION PARADOX

Taking part in mediation may put more pressure on separating couples at a very stressful time. A basic paradox in mediation is to expect more from couples who are splitting up than would normally be expected from those living together in relative harmony. Many individuals are likely to decline mediation because they find these expectations of reasonable negotiation too daunting, or impossible to imagine. In mediation, co-operation is looked for even where one partner may have just walked out of the relationship, possibly without warning. Although the couple may not have spoken to each other since separating, they are invited to sit down together to discuss arrangements for their children and financial and property matters. There are expectations of reasonableness when reason may be swamped by anger and grief. Many people in the middle of relationship breakdown are more inclined to retreat into a corner, yell at their partner or weep, rather than meeting face to face to negotiate. Discussions about future arrangements make the ending of the relationship more real and painful. Agreements may be looked for to finalise a divorce that one partner does not want at all. Holmes and Rahe[54] developed a scale of 43 stressful life events and asked four hundred people to rate the level of stress they associated with each event. Divorce scored the second highest score, next in level of stress to the death of the spouse, although the stress of selling one's home and buying another property is also very high. Redundancy, imprisonment, or a close friend's death were all rated as less stressful than divorce. Mediators need to be aware of the trauma and adjustments faced by separating couples in every area of their lives. The emotional and psychological impact of separation is profound and far-reaching. It is not like an illness from which one suffers and recovers. It is an extremely complex and painful process requiring the restructuring of identity and integration of past experience in a series of transitions. Many people turn to relatives, friends and lawyers for support. The stage at which they seek and accept help and the nature of the help they are given affect their passage through separation, and in some cases, divorce. When individuals come to assessment meetings, they are at a crossroads and need to understand the different paths to settlement or resolution, some of them longer and more costly than others and none with a guaranteed outcome. Mediators explain these different paths and help individuals to decide which of these paths they feel able and ready to take. The mediator's understanding and empathy may enable tentative steps to be taken along the mediation path, with reassurance that the process can be halted at any time if it is not found to be productive or helpful. Even when no form of settlement can be reached,

---

[54] Holmes and Rahe 'The social readjustment rating scale' (1967) 11 *Journal of Psychosomatic Research* 213.

mediation should not be seen as having 'failed' or wasted time, because important information and different points of view may have been shared and considered.

There is however a further paradox in that participation in mediation is voluntary, yet there is the potential penalty of a costs order being made against a party who refuses 'unreasonably' to consider mediation. The Court of Appeal has heard a number of cases in relation to civil mediation. For example, in *Cowl v Plymouth City Council* in 2001 and *Dunnett v Railtrack* in 2002, the Court of Appeal made it clear that parties who unreasonably refused to mediate their disputes would face the risk of a serious cost consequence at the end of the litigation. Lord Justice Dyson decided in *Halsey*[55] that it is wrong to compel unwilling parties to mediate and that such compulsion would be a breach of the right of access to the courts required by the European Convention on Human Rights (ECHR). Lord Dyson added that, even if he were wrong on the ECHR point, he found it difficult to conceive of circumstances in which it would be appropriate to order mediation in the face of objection from one or more parties. Whilst it seems that the courts will not compel parties to mediate against their will, the Court of Appeal expects consideration of mediation to be at the forefront of judges' minds in case management and of the parties' legal advisers in giving advice, with the concomitant risk of serious cost sanctions at the end of a trial where there has been a refusal to mediate. Civil mediation and litigation have very different principles and processes from those that apply in family proceedings. However, in the case of *Mann v Mann*,[56] judgment was given in financial remedy proceedings in which the husband had failed to make payments agreed under the Court of Appeal mediation scheme. The wife issued a statutory demand in respect of the sums owed and her demand was withdrawn on the agreement that the matter was to be resolved by further mediation. Such mediation did not take place, each party blaming the other. Mostyn J reviewed the current law against compulsion and 'robustly encouraged them to engage in mediation' by means of an Ungley Order. This formulation, previously known only in civil cases, requires the parties to consider non-court dispute resolution and raises the possibility of a costs order against a party who unreasonably refuses to consider it. There appears to be a grey area as to what would constitute an unreasonable refusal to consider mediation and who is able to make a finding of 'unreasonableness'. Is this the start of the erosion of the 'voluntary principle' by the courts? If so, is this to be used where litigants behave unreasonably and disproportionately in financial litigation, as in *Mann v Mann*, or could it also be used where judges consider that the best interests of the child have been compromised by the refusal of an intransigent parent to consider non-court dispute resolution? The Family Justice Review[57] recommended that 'judges should retain the power to order parties to attend a MIAM session and Separated Parents Information Programmes and may make a costs order where it is felt that one party has behaved

---

[55] *Halsey v Milton Keynes General NHS Trust* and *Steel v Joy and Halliday* [2004] EWCA Civ 576.
[56] *Mann v Mann* [2014] EWHC 537 (Fam).
[57] Family Justice Review, para 118.

unreasonably'. The Government response is that in child arrangement proceedings, the court can make an Activity Direction and this can include attendance at a MIAM, and secondly, that the court already has the power to make cost orders.[58] Rather than urging anxious or angry people into mediation for fear of incurring a penalty for non-attendance, participation should be encouraged by an assurance of careful and sensitive management by the mediator and by the finding that almost three-quarters of a sample of mediation users said they were satisfied with the mediation process.[59]

---

[58] Department for Education and Ministry of Justice *A Brighter Future for Family Justice* (August 2014), p 34.

[59] Barlow, Hunter, Smithson and Ewing *Mapping Paths to Family Justice – Briefing Paper and Report on Key Findings* (Universities of Exeter and Kent, June 2014), p 10.

CHAPTER 4

DESIGNING MEDIATION MODELS

'Having the structure in mind is only part of the necessary path to a real understanding of the music.'[1]

CONTENTS

4.1 DESIGNING THE MODEL

A standard model of mediation would be inadequate to meet the diverse needs of couples and family members who come to mediation at different stages of the family life-cycle and in widely varying circumstances. If the mediation process is not adapted to their circumstances and needs, it is likely to break down, if it gets off the ground at all. Mediators need to be flexible in responding to different kinds of disputes and able to provide facilities and skills for different constellations of family members. It is possible to maintain the

---

[1]   Daniel Barenboim *Everything is Connected – The Power of Music* (Weidenfeld and Nicolson, 2008), p 58.

basic principles of mediation while designing a range of models that can be adapted for different stages and levels of dispute and varying circumstances. As Brown and Marriott suggest, dispute resolution practitioners 'can devise a permutation of procedures and approaches which fit all the nuances of the parties' needs and circumstances without being constrained by prescribed rules.'[2] In proposing innovative approaches for out of court dispute resolution, Neil Robinson has considered 'creative options for dealing with an ever greater variety of family conflicts ... [through] modifying the model and working in partnership'.[3] He cautions, however, that practitioners may modify the model, but should not 'break the mould'.[4]

Mediation needs to be designed to fit the needs of participants, rather than expecting participants to accept a standard process that may not suit them well. In other words, family mediation should be tailor-made, rather than 'off-the-peg'. There is scope for creative variations. Daniel Barenboim, pianist, conductor and co-founder of the West-Eastern Divan orchestra, describes variations on a musical theme as a '*process of transformation*'.[5] Robinson suggests analogies between mediation and jazz as 'spontaneous invention within a theoretical framework'.[6] However, before becoming too creative, there are questions to consider such as the physical setting for mediation, the use of one mediator or two, and the pros and cons of shuttle mediation and caucusing.

4.2   THE SETTING AND PHYSICAL ARRANGEMENTS

First of all, the setting and physical arrangements need to be considered carefully. Mediation needs to be conducted in a private setting away from the court, with sessions arranged at intervals to suit the needs of participants. Court-referred mediation is usually less flexible. When proceedings are adjourned to allow mediation to take place, the court may set a deadline. Participants need a private forum for meetings, free from disturbance and providing suitable facilities. The ambiance should be pleasant and welcoming. Careful consideration should be given to the suitability of premises, waiting-areas, mediation rooms and facilities. The court is not a suitable location for mediation or even for initial information meetings. In out-of-court mediation, mediators are in charge of their own environment and the atmosphere it conveys. Many prefer to use a round or oval table. Chairs need to be be placed at a comfortable distance from each other in the mediator's line of vision, so that the mediator can keep equal eye contact with participants, without turning from one to the other like an umpire at a tennis match. Participants should not sit opposite each other, because this can encourage confrontation. They need to be able to look at each other and at the mediator, without sitting too close or opposite one another.

---

[2]   Brown and Marriott *ADR Principles and Practice* (Sweet & Maxwell, 1993), p 19.
[3]   Robinson 'Developing Family Mediation' [2008] Fam Law 926.
[4]   Ibid, p 928.
[5]   Barenboim *Everything is Connected – The Power of Music* (Weidenfeld and Nicolson, 2008), p 32.
[6]   Robinson 'Developing Family Mediation' [2008] Fam Law 927.

Sole Mediator

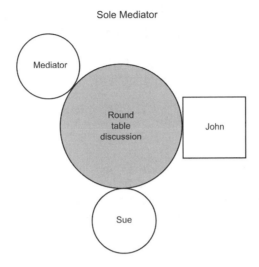

4.3 GENDER ISSUES[7]

With a sole mediator, there is inevitably a gender imbalance in the room, unless the mediator and the couple are all of the same sex. Gender issues tend to run through family mediation like an electric current. Mediators have to be careful not to make assumptions, such as assuming that the children live, or should live, with their mother. Such an assumption would destroy trust in the mediator's impartiality. The children may be living with their father, who may have looked after them while the mother went out to work. Gender issues are closely linked to power imbalances in mediation and mediators need to be aware that among mediation users there is 'a strong and regularly stated perception of gender bias.'[8] Many men who took part in the Mapping Paths to Family Justice study felt that the mediation process, and indeed the whole family justice system, was biased against them. Some mothers, on the other hand, felt that the system was biased towards fathers and a few women who had used a male mediator said they had felt disadvantaged or not well understood.[9] The great majority of mediators are female, but female clients do not necessarily see this as an advantage, fearing that the female mediator will be 'seduced' by their ex-partner or be unable to stand up to a dominant male. Mediators need to gain each partner's confidence that they will not be drawn into taking sides and that they will be strong and skilled enough to manage power imbalances. Impartiality needs to be emphasised with comments such as: 'You know, mediators are used to hearing two sides of things and we don't take sides or make judgements as to who is right or wrong', or 'I think trust usually breaks down, when a relationship breaks down. It is difficult for separated parents to trust each other. We'll look at the kind of reassurances you both need

---

[7]   See also **3.7**, Chapter 10 on Power imbalances and Chapter 13 on research findings on gender issues.

[8]   Barlow et al *Mapping Paths to Family Justice – Briefing Paper and Report on Key Findings* (2014), p 11.

[9]   Ibid.

where the children are concerned'. Same-sex couples may want a mediator of the same gender as themselves, but freedom from bias is more important. All clients need assurances that the mediator is open-minded and will not make value judgements. The Mapping Paths researchers recommend that gender-balanced co-mediation should be more widely available and used more often.

4.4   CO-MEDIATION

The old adage, 'two heads are better than one', is particularly apt in mediation. Provided that co-mediators work well together and enhance each other's strengths, a co-mediating team has greater capacity than a sole mediator to manage difficult conflicts and power imbalances. Some mediation services offer male/female co-mediators, but in general, female mediators predominate. Two female co-mediators would compound the gender imbalance and there is resistance to the idea of co-mediation by two male mediators. If co-mediation is offered with same-sex mediators, participants should be asked whether they would find this acceptable and there should be further enquiry during mediation to ensure they are comfortable with the process. The model of male-female co-mediation offers great advantages in addressing gender issues and power imbalances.

When co-mediators come from different professional disciplines, generally an experienced family lawyer trained in mediation working with a co-mediator who is a qualified social worker or therapist, they combine two sets of knowledge and experience. Co-mediators from family law and human science backgrounds complement each other in very valuable ways. The Family Mediators Association (FMA) has a continuing commitment to this 'uniquely robust and flexible model of Appropriate Dispute Resolution'.[10] Interdisciplinary co-mediation offers a wider range of knowledge and experience than a single mediator can provide. The combination of a mediator from a legal background working with a mediator from a human sciences discipline (counsellor, therapist, social worker, psychologist) is particularly helpful in dealing with inter-related children and financial issues. Knowledge and skills in understanding the emotions of separating couples and family issues needs to be combined with expertise on legal and financial aspects. Co-mediators should not be restricted, however, to their original field of expertise. Mediators' training should blend interdisciplinary knowledge and skills.[11] When co-mediators mediate across the whole range of family issues, moving with confidence in each other's professional territory, the benefits of co-mediating are greatly increased. There are always some kinds of power imbalances and co-mediators can help maintain a balance in the unfolding process of emotional, family, financial and legal divorce. A sole mediator may find it hard

---

[10]   FMA 2011; www.thefma.org.uk.
[11]   See Chapter 14 on mediator training.

to keep all these different dimensions in simultaneous focus. At a practical level, one mediator can focus on gathering financial data while the other mediator focuses on interactions in the room.

Co-mediation may be used for different purposes:

- training – helping an inexperienced mediator to learn from a more experienced mediator;
- to provide gender balance;
- to manage high conflict, entrenched positions and difficult dynamics;
- to provide balanced understanding and response to different perspectives;
- to provide special expertise and knowledge within the mediation;
- to facilitate cross-cultural mediation, using co-mediators from different cultural backgrounds;
- to allocate tasks to each mediator in a way that maximises effectiveness;
- to give scope for more complex strategies;
- to bridge geographical distance, where participants live too far apart to travel to the same location. A mediator in each location may meet with one party and liaise with the other mediator.[12]

4.4.1 Benefits of co-mediation

Family members at different stages of relationship breakdown bring discordant views, conflicting needs and a complex mix of issues – marital, parental, financial and legal. Co-mediators may be more able than a sole mediator to contain conflicting needs and high emotions in mediation. One of the benefits is when co-mediators have complementary knowledge, professional knowledge and personal qualities. They can draw from each other's strengths, contribute different abilities and provide support to each other. A period of co-mediation practice as a stage of practical training is important to broaden perspectives and develop new skills. Interdisciplinary co-mediators can contain strong emotions and complex issues in mediating on inter-related matters that neither a lawyer nor a therapist could manage on their own. 'A legal resolution that ignores the client's psychological needs is as inappropriate as a psychological resolution that conflicts with the client's legal needs'.[13] Co-mediation also provides the safeguard of each mediator being able to check or amplify the other's input.

4.4.1.1 Balance

Co-mediators can provide physical and psychological balance. 'It probably sets you more at ease to have two. Otherwise it is like having someone in charge,

---

12 See also Chapter 15 on international cross-border family mediation.
13 Steinberg 'Towards an Interdisciplinary Commitment' (July 1980) *Journal of Marital and Family Therapy*, p 261.

whereas with two it is not a case of being in charge.'[14] Male-female co-mediators provide gender balance in the room and a model for power balancing. Some research has suggested that male-female mediation teams facilitate fairer and more balanced agreements.[15]

4.4.1.2 *Wider perspectives to understand different points of view*

'It was also useful having two people there because you could perhaps get two slightly different views on something which certainly helped both of us to have an option.'[16]

Many couples have different ethnic backgrounds from each other and/or from the mediator. Cultural diversity needs to be respected in mediation, but culturally-informed practice can be difficult for a sole mediator who is perceived as belonging to the majority culture. Co-mediators bring different personal backgrounds, experience and perspectives that can help them address cross-cultural issues that a sole mediator, with experience confined to a single culture, might miss. When parents in mediation are divided by nationality, religion or culture, co-mediators, each of whom shares the same cultural background as one of the parents, can introduce a dynamic of understanding, recognition and therefore safety in the mediation process, without becoming aligned with one parent against the other.

Example

Sabine Walsh, a mediator and trainer in Ireland and native German speaker, provided this example of a cross-cultural co-mediation with a German-Irish couple and her Irish co-mediator. The German mother spoke English fluently, so language did not present a problem in itself. The dispute between the parents was over their child's education and the relative merits of the German and Irish school systems. The mother wanted the child to go to the German school in Dublin, whereas the father argued in favour of the local gaelscoil (Irish-speaking school). The mother had felt that her point of view was not being heard or understood, because nobody in her community knew anything about the German education system and its ethos. In the co-mediation, Sabine, as the German-speaking mediator, was able to facilitate the mother explaining the values of the German system, while the father felt the process was balanced by the presence of a male Irish co-mediator. The co-mediators, working together effectively as a team, were able to strengthen the parental 'team' so that the parents became able to work together co-operatively instead of competitively, and reach a joint decision for their child.

---

[14] Mediation client quoted by Walker, McCarthy and Timms *Mediation: the Making and Remaking of Co-operative Relationships* (Relate Centre for Family Studies, University of Newcastle, 1994), p 128.

[15] Adler and Barnes 'Mediation and Lawyers – the Pacific Way' (1983) 18 *Hawaii Bar Journal* 37–52.

[16] Walker, McCarthy and Timms *Mediation: the Making and Remaking of Co-operative Relationships* (Relate Centre for Family Studies, University of Newcastle, 1994), p 125.

4.4.1.3 *Dynamics*

A sole mediator may put questions to each party in turn, gathering information from each of them and making sure they have equal opportunities to respond. This question and answer dynamic might be described as linear, whereas co-mediators facilitate round-table discussions – a circular dynamic. Co-mediators encourage discussion and debate, without giving the impression of one person taking control.

4.4.1.4 *Complementary styles and skills*

Co-mediators bring different personal qualities, styles of working and range of skills. Different personalities and styles are appreciated by participants who may see that it is unrealistic to expect one person to have all the qualities and skills they are looking for.

4.4.1.5 *Greater creativity*

Greater creativity is possible in generating options and ideas. Brainstorming is more effective when co-mediators bring complementary experience and ways of thinking – analytical and intuitive.[17] They spark ideas off each other and encourage couples to generate their own ideas.

4.4.1.6 *Fresh vision and learning*

A newly trained mediator learns from co-mediating with a more experienced mediator. Experienced mediators also learn from less experienced ones who bring fresh vision and who may question an approach or challenge an assumption.

4.4.1.7 *Modelling*

Co-mediators can model constructive debates on different points of view. They can openly disagree, provided they discuss differences in a constructive way and avoid contradicting each other in an argument that competes with the couple's argument (see ground-rules for co-mediation, below). When co-mediators discuss differences in a friendly dialogue, they model positive ways of exploring disagreements that help participants to discuss them too, instead of fighting over them.

4.4.1.8 *Maintaining good practice*

The presence of a co-mediator helps to guard against oversights and omissions. A sole mediator's practice cannot be monitored closely, unless a supervisor is present or the sessions are recorded on audiotape or video. A mediator working

---

17 Kahneman *Thinking, Fast and Slow* (Penguin Books, 2012); see also **14.15** below on mediator training.

alone may step outside the role, develop inappropriate ways of working or miss important points, without anyone realising that this is happening. Co-mediators learn from each other and provide informal monitoring of each other's practice. If either has cause for concern or discomfort, this needs to be raised and explored between the two mediators and may need discussion with a peer group or a supervisor.

4.4.1.9 Support for mediators

Co-mediating provides support for mediators, as well as for participants. Mediation is stressful work that demands a high level of concentration. There is a great deal of information to absorb. A sole mediator addresses matters that may be intellectually demanding and emotionally draining. The presence of a co-mediator is both supportive and reassuring. Responsibilities can be shared and tasks divided. Provided the co-mediators work comfortably together as a team, the stresses are lower than when mediating alone.

4.4.2   Disadvantages of co-mediation

4.4.2.1   Cost

The main disadvantage of co-mediation is its higher cost. In cases involving significant assets or financial complexity, privately paying clients may wish to consider the options of collaborative law or mediation. If there are issues concerning children as well as financial matters, collaborative lawyers might call in a family mediator as well, thus involving three professionals rather than two. When there is high conflict and/or disputes on interrelated issues, parents who are both in paid employment may see the benefit of having co-mediators from different professional backgrounds and be willing to pay the higher cost involved. Mediation services should explain the advantages of co-mediation, such as maintaining balance and encompassing all issues, with a special focus on children's well being. If a case has been assessed as unsuitable for sole mediation but suitable for co-mediation, clients may accept the cost in preference to lawyer negotiation, collaborative law or going to court. In publicly funded mediation, the Legal Aid Agency allows an additional disbursement for co-mediation but there must be strong justification recorded in the case file. Otherwise, the additional disbursement may be recouped on audit. The Agency has stated in relation to co-mediation that:[18]

> 'whilst you do not need our prior authority to use Co-mediation, any decision to use Co-mediation will need to be recorded on the file including, where appropriate:
> *   reasons as to the complexity, legal, psychological or otherwise of the case;
> *   a risk assessment for the participants and/or Mediator;
> *   any reasons as to the requirement of specialist and/or expert skills;
> *   any management issues for the Mediation.'

---

[18]   Legal Services Commission *Family Mediation Specification* (December 2009), para 2.23.

It is critical to record the justification adequately, using a pro-forma such as the one devised by the Family Mediators Association.[19]

4.4.2.2   Logistics

Travel costs and time also need to be considered, if co-mediators are based in different locations.

It is more difficult to schedule sessions with co-mediators. If one mediator is unwell or unavoidably delayed, should the other mediator continue alone? Postponing a session may have serious disadvantages for participants and re-scheduling may involve considerable delay.

4.4.2.3   Time

As well as the time needed for co-mediation sessions, time is needed for consultation and planning beforehand and for discussion and feedback afterwards. Written summaries of mediation should be checked by both mediators and signed by them both.

4.4.2.4   Competition or confusion

If both mediators are eager to intervene and/or take matters in different directions, the resulting confusion may endanger the mediation. These problems are more likely to occur if co-mediators have not had similar training and lack experience.

4.4.2.5   Becoming split, taking sides

There are risks of co-mediators being split by a warring couple, consciously or unconsciously. Participants often try to persuade mediators to take sides. If co-mediators do not understand each other well, the couple's conflict could be projected on to them and used to split them. Discussion with co-mediators who are working at cross-purposes would not assist a couple in crisis.

4.4.2.6   Combined pressure

The combination of two assured and knowledgeable mediators may be overpowering for nervous clients. Mediators who constantly affirm each other's statements make it more difficult for participants to disagree with the mediators' joint view. Well-trained mediators should not allow this to happen (and should take care to avoid stycomithia – speaking single lines alternately – a technique used in verse drama)!

---

[19]   See Appendix G below.

4.5 DIFFERENT MODELS OF CO-MEDIATION

- **Co-pilots**: both mediators operate the controls and can take over from each other at any stage of the flight (process). They provide balance and support, especially in managing power imbalances. But there can be duplication in the sharing of controls and tasks. There could also be confusing changes of direction, if one co-pilot cuts across the other.

- **Pilot and Navigator**: the pilot operates the controls so that the craft moves forward, steering through headwinds or strong currents. The navigator studies the map and tracks the course. The navigator may notice particular landmarks or see a new route opening up. The navigator may intervene less often than the pilot and focuses on dynamics, rather than on content. The navigator has more time to observe body language and to think about underlying issues, while the pilot keeps the process in movement. The pilot/navigator roles may alternate, as in the co-pilot model, but the allocation of tasks is planned beforehand and more clearly delineated. For example, if one mediator leads the discussion while the other records key points or figures on the flip-chart, the pilot flies the plane while the navigator records the flight-path.

- **Pilot and Apprentice**: opportunities to observe, learn on the job and gain confidence.

- **Pilot and Controller (Advanced Flying Test!)**. This may be used for supervision or in testing competence. Differences in seniority and experience between co-mediators may need to be explained to participants. It may be possible for the Controller to take a back seat and provide support, allowing the pilot to fly independently, unless there is risk of crashing!

4.6 PRE-REQUISITES FOR EFFECTIVE CO-MEDIATION

- **Trust your co-mediator.** Co-mediators need confidence in each other's integrity and competence and need to be able to trust each other. A partnership built on mutual trust and respect provides a strong anchorage in working with stormy couples.

- **Consider professional and practice issues,** including premises, facilities, model of practice, charging and professional indemnity cover. Co-mediators need to be clear about their joint or separate accountability and the basis on which fees are being charged. They also need to consider 'what if?' questions, such as what one mediator would do, if the other mediator has to cancel at the last minute. Clients may have come a long distance and may need mediation urgently.

- **Training for co-mediation.** Co-mediators should have trained with the same training organisation and should have practised co-mediating in role-play. Co-mediators must use the same standard documents and adhere to their organisation's policy and practice requirements. They must be clear about line management and preferably have the same professional practice consultant. There must be clarity on complaints procedures and responsibilities in dealing with any complaint from a client.

- **Agree roles and tasks.** Co-mediators need to consider how to allocate responsibility for different tasks or parts of the process. The mediators may alternate in taking the lead at different stages. Will both mediators take notes and maintain duplicate sets of records?

- **Agree whether both mediators are equally in charge, or whether one is apprenticed to the other.** One mediator may be more experienced than the other. Mediation often takes place in one mediator's premises and the other mediator may be a guest on the other's territory. It is important for co-mediators to discuss questions of seniority and status and to make sure that both feel at ease. Power imbalances between mediators could have an unfortunate impact in mediation.

- **Give each other openings to join in discussion.** It is not necessary for both mediators to have equal input and unhelpful if they feel a need to compete. A mediator who listens and observes has a very important role that can be explained to the parties as a listening role. However, when one mediator is leading, it is important to provide openings for the other one to come in: 'Is there anything you would like to add?' 'Shall we move on to …?' 'What do you think about …?' Regular consultation avoids the second mediator feeling superfluous or frozen out. Seating arrangements should enable co-mediators to keep eye contact with each other.

- **Understand each other's views and values.** Co-mediators need to understand each other's views and values, especially where they differ. Mediation may involve controversial issues, such as children visiting a transvestite father. Co-mediators need to be able to accommodate each other's view and values and be skilled in reading signals from each other. They need to manage differences in ways that enhance their complementary roles.

- **Mutual support.** Co-mediators do not need to agree on every point but must give support to each other and be ready to rescue each other from a difficulty. When they disagree, they should be careful not to contradict or undermine each other.

- **Speak the same language.** Mediators from different backgrounds need to speak the same language, avoiding jargon from their own professional fields. One mediator sometimes needs to clarify or amplify what the other mediator has just said.

- **Preparation and debriefing.** Co-mediators need to prepare for mediation sessions and debrief afterwards. This means allowing additional time for each session. Planning and debriefing, when thinking is shared and tension offloaded, are both important. Co-mediators need to give each other positive feedback as well as questioning each other, if necessary. Once a good working relationship has been built up, most co-mediators develop an intuitive understanding that enables them to work together creatively.

- **Have a fall-back plan.** Preparation may go out of the window when couples come in with an unexpected turn of events or change of direction.

Co-mediators need to be able to alter course easily, when the situation requires. Familiarity with each other and ability to read signals reduces the need for lengthy discussion.

- **A good sense of humour.** It is difficult to imagine co-mediation working well if co-mediators lack a sense of humour, or if they are unable to use humour sensitively.

- **Consider practical details.** Seating arrangements should facilitate discussion, maximise eye contact and avoid alignments.

- **Professional practice consultancy and cpd.** Case discussions with a consultant and continuing professional development are needed to develop practice and skills.

4.7   STRATEGIES AND SKILLS IN CO-MEDIATION

- **Consulting openly.** eg 'Do you think we should talk about x first, or y?' The process becomes a conversation between four people, instead of one mediator addressing participants in turn.

- **Picking up on non-verbal signals and pre-empting.** If one mediator misses signs of participant's bewilderment, distress, frustration or anger, the co-mediator may notice these signs and respond.

- **Giving information.** It may be difficult for a sole mediator to volunteer information without seeming like an expert, whereas a co-mediator can give a prompt: 'Do you think it would be useful to discuss ...?' Relevant information may be provided impartially, reducing the need for couples to go backwards and forwards between mediation and lawyers.

- **Strategic debates.** Mediators from different backgrounds tend to have different perspectives ad approach questions from different angles. These debates may be used strategically to reduce power imbalances. Provided co-mediators are comfortable in discussing dilemmas and do not undermine each other, they may question or challenge each other in helpful ways. The reduction of tension in the room is often palpable. Participants who feel different needs or views are heard may feel validated and better understood. Constructive disagreements between co-mediators can be used to model positive conflict management and as an impasse strategy.[20] It is important that neither mediator undermines the other or puts the other down. The tone should be reflective and friendly and may involve some humour, if appropriate.

- **Using humour to reduce tension.** Co-mediators often use humour in commenting on their own differences of approach, as a way of lightening the atmosphere. Provided there is sensitivity, mutual respect and trust, a humorous remark between co-mediators may ease the couple's tensions. Timing is important and awareness of the feelings in the room. Humour alters the dynamics and often encourages participants to use humour too.

---

[20]   See Chapter 11 below.

- **Brainstorming.** Co-mediators can generate options that draw on different knowledge and perspectives. They can play hard/soft negotiator and use a range of impasse strategies.

- **Preparing written summaries.** A blend of skills is needed in preparing mediation summaries.[21] Summarising and 'mutualising' skills need to be combined. Consultation on the content and style of the written summary provide learning opportunities for mediators from different professional backgrounds.

4.8 THE SYNERGY OF CO-MEDIATION

Co-mediation should be an essential component of mediation training. It provides on-the-spot learning, builds confidence and allows mediators to see what does or does not work. Newly trained mediators welcome the safety net provided by an experienced mediator and their fresh vision encourages experienced mediators to think differently about the way they work. Although potentially costly in its use of resources, co-mediation enables issues to be tackled more efficiently, because co-mediators can work in tandem more flexibly. The process can be structured in different ways to suit different needs and circumstances. As Neil Robinson suggests,[22] (borrowing from a jazz musician) co-mediation allows 'contrapuntal interplay' in which the mediators 'play different instruments' (for example, bass and alto sax may be a good combination to provide solid process and creative improvisation!). The mobility of co-mediation helps to maintain momentum. Co-mediators who enjoy working together create a lighter atmosphere that helps clients to regain their own strength and creativity. Co-mediation provides synergy – combined energy and ideas – while maintaining equilibrium. Co-mediators need to hold the destructive forces of polarity within a contained emotional, psychological and physical space, while possible changes are explored and negotiated.

A balance needs to be kept between stability – *homeostasis* – and change – *morphogenesis*. There are many pressures in mediation that threaten this balance. The stresses on a single mediator can be very heavy. Co-mediators have greater resources for managing stress, because they can support each other, offload together and stimulate fresh thinking. Together, they offer a well of resources. Clients can draw from this well to replenish their own depleted energy and limited resources. Mediators need to replenish their energies when they feel drained. Co-mediation offers many benefits for participants – for the mediators as much as for the mediated. 'There is now a greater readiness among mediators to explore different ways of working, to adapt accepted processes and models, and to work with other professionals.'[23]

---

[21] See Chapter 12 below.
[22] Personal communication.
[23] Robinson 'Developing Family Mediation' [2008] Fam Law 926.

4.9   SHUTTLE MEDIATION AND CAUCUSING

Although the aim is to encourage direct communication and negotiation, face-to-face meetings may inflame conflict between couples who tend to be confrontational. Shuttle mediation and caucusing, using co-mediators if possible, enable options to be explored more calmly. In shuttle mediation and caucusing, mediators meet with each party separately, instead of with both together.

Shuttle mediation is commonly used in civil and commercial mediation. After an introductory meeting, the parties and their lawyers may be placed in separate rooms while the mediator 'shuttles' between them, conveying clarifications, proposals or counter-proposals. Shuttle mediation is less often used in family mediation because the aim is to facilitate direct communication between family members. Separated parents need to be able to talk directly with each other about their children after mediation ends. If they are seen separately, they do not listen to each other and may be unable to communicate directly either before or after mediation. However, in cases involving domestic violence or other form of abuse, shuttle mediation may be a possible model. In situations where it would be unsafe for ex-partners to meet face-to-face, or where one of them refuses to do so, shuttle mediation may provide a means of negotiating issues such as division of joint assets or responsibility for debts. It may be the only possible option in domestic violence cases involving some degree of continuing risk or fear. Attendance at a joint meeting could be negotiated later, if any further risk or fear has been clearly overcome and both parties are willing to meet face to face. Shuttle mediation is also used in international, cross-border cases where the parties live too far apart for face-to-face meetings.[24]

Caucusing differs from shuttle mediation in combining some short separate discussions during, or apart from, joint meetings. The word *caucus* is derived from an Algonquian Indian word for tribal leader and its original transcription from the Algonquian language – *cawcawwassoughes* – suggests interminable and repetitive discussions! Caucusing can be structured in various ways. If a participant appears extremely emotional, without concerns about domestic violence or abuse, it may be helpful to suggest that the first mediation meeting could include a short discussion with each partner separately, with the expectation that they will be able to manage a joint meeting for the remainder of the session. A brief initial caucus can reduce high levels of tension at the outset and provide reassurance to each participant about the other one's mood and willingness to discuss matters in a contained and constructive way. This builds a stronger bridge for both participants to meet face to face. Alternatively, a mediation meeting may begin with a joint meeting, followed in situations of particular difficulty by a short caucus with each partner on their own and then a continuation of the joint meeting. Participants feel freer to disclose an underlying fear or to put forward a tentative proposal, without the other party

---

[24]   See Chapter 15 below.

being present. The mediator can give one-to-one support and encouragement, but must be careful not to give any impression of forming an alliance.

Caucusing is very useful as a fall-back strategy, rather than as a model of choice. If mediation is on the verge of breaking down, proposing a short caucus can prevent a 'walk-out' and allow recovery time when emotions are running high. Caucusing should be used with care and takes time, but it enables more mediations to be 'held'. Some mediators are opposed to caucusing in principle because it interferes with the transparency of the mediation process and may blur the mediator's role. Other mediators have found that caucusing has not borne out these fears in practice. Confidentiality needs to be clarified carefully with participants before caucusing or shuttle mediation take place.

4.9.1 Confidentiality in shuttle mediation and caucusing

In civil/commercial mediation, the content of separate meetings is confidential and the mediator may carry only authorised information from one party to the other. A civil/commercial mediator may therefore know, on a confidential basis, the terms on which each party would be willing to settle. The mediator uses this knowledge to bargain, negotiate and look for leverage, without revealing either party's position to the other party. Holding information in confidence is also used in 'hybrid' cases such as inheritance disputes whose subject matter straddles family and civil jurisdictions. In family mediation, 'shuttling' between participants in separate meetings is based on the principle that 'all information and correspondence provided by either participant should be shared openly and not withheld'.[25] The mediator establishes a 'no secrets' ground-rule at the outset, to avoid problems of holding information in confidence from one party or disclosing what they believed they had said in confidence. A family mediator cannot continue to mediate while holding confidences such as 'Don't tell Jim that I am going to take the children away.' A family mediator should establish that information provided by either participant in a caucus meeting, or in mediation as a whole, should be shared, except where it involves risk to a child or adult. Holding information in confidence does not appear to compromise the mediator's impartiality in civil/commercial mediation, but it could do so in family mediation, especially on child-related issues. When information gathered in separate meetings is shared with both participants, it does not mean that the mediator repeats every word that was said during a caucus, exactly as it was said. The mediator needs, as always, to use acknowledging, prioritising and reframing skills in giving feedback to both participants together. They should be invited to confirm or clarify the feedback from their own perspectives.

Henry Brown[26] argues that the family mediation principle of all communications being shared openly with both parties is overly restrictive and that the confidentiality of separate meetings should be 'transferrable' from civil/commercial mediation to the mainstream of family mediation. While this

---

25 FMC Code of Practice, 5.6.3
26 Henry Brown *Enhancing the Practice Model* John Cornwell Memorial Lecture, FM Annual Conference, 24 September 2014.

might be envisaged in financial negotiations between separating or divorcing couples, where the mediator might hold each party's 'bottom line' in confidence, when the issues concern children and future family relationships, holding information in confidence could make the mediator's position untenable. If mediators accept confidences relating to children, they could find themselves caught in a sticky web of 'secrets'. Before sanctioning any use of confidential caucuses in family mediation, the FMC Code of Practice and the agreement to mediate would need to be modified and guidelines on good practice, to clarify principles and boundaries, would be essential.

Before offering shuttle mediation or caucusing, it is important to consider possible benefits and disadvantages. How might it affect each participant and the process? Would it help them to feel safer? Might it draw them further apart, while drawing the mediator into a supportive, counselling role? The partner who feels left out when the other one is being seen may become anxious and suspicious about what is being said behind their 'back'. Caucusing may be useful as a crisis strategy, however, when emotions cannot be contained or the discussion becomes so heated that a participant is about to rush from the room. A stormy departure can be anticipated and pre-empted, if possible. Offering a short time with each participant alone may be helpful if the couple can no longer remain in the room together. It also gives distressed participants some recovery time. If there are co-mediators, mediation services may have a policy of caucuses being co-mediated, to safeguard one mediator from being targeted as the vulnerable messenger. Both co-mediators may meet with each participant alternately, but if time is short, one mediator could meet with one party while the co-mediator meets with the other. Feedback from these separate meetings is then shared with both participants jointly, if they are able to continue together. Before caucusing, the ground-rules on impartiality and open communication must be clarified and accepted. There may be gender issues to consider, if a male mediator were to meet with the male partner and the female mediator with the female partner, this could create an impression of gender alliances, even if the arrangement were to be reversed on a later occasion. After caucusing participants are usually calmer and often feel able to come back together. Co-mediators do not need to withdraw and confer privately: they can summarise key points and proposals and encourage participants to add to them. More often, a sole mediator works alone, without the support of a co-mediator. When there is high conflict, a short caucus may enable a 'stuck' mediation to continue with lower conflict and more clearly defined focus. Haynes[27] gives reasons for caucusing similar to those mentioned above, suggesting that it is useful 'when the level of hostility is so high that it prevents rational discussion', or when 'continual ventilation of grievances by one person impedes the progress of the negotiations.' Before caucusing, there should be consideration both of its potential benefits and its disadvantages.

---

[27] Haynes *Alternative Dispute Resolution – the Fundamentals of Divorce Mediation* (Old Bailey Press, 1993), p 38.

4.9.2 Benefits of shuttling and caucusing

- Enables mediation to take place safely in situations involving domestic abuse.
- Helps to manage power imbalances and volatile emotions.
- Can reduce perceptions of gender bias.
- Enables each participant to feel heard more fully.
- Builds trust in the mediator – increases rapport.
- Provides impartial support for participants overwhelmed with distress.
- Avoids or curtails destructive confrontations.
- Calms inflamed situations – gives opportunities to acknowledge, reassure and refocus.
- Helps to pre-empt a walk-out and breakdown of the mediation.
- Screens out blaming, accusations, aggressive body language etc.
- Helps mediators to gain fuller understanding of each party's position and needs.
- Explores underlying fears and feelings, such as a desire for reconciliation, that may be suppressed in joint meetings.
- Allows time for cooling down and reflection.
- Increases mediator control of process (but see disadvantages also).
- Avoids loss of time through interruptions, sidetracking etc.
- Helps to maintain future focus, positive ways forward, promotes agreement.
- Explores scope for compromise, sources of resistance and blocks to settlement.
- Addresses special needs – illness, disability, need for an interpreter.

4.9.3 Disadvantages of shuttling and caucusing

- Risks loss of impartiality; may create perceptions of mediator taking sides.
- Loss of trust in the mediator, suspicions of bias.
- Fears and fantasies of what is being said 'behind one's back' – feelings of abandonment.
- Difficulties of carrying negative messages between parties ('shoot the messenger').
- Additional resources – eg two rooms may be needed.
- Time-consuming.
- Confidentiality issues, if one party does not want information disclosed to the other party.
- Empowers the mediator but may disempower participants.
- Who is seen first? Disadvantages for the second party in responding to first party's position or proposals, without first explaining their position or proposals.

- Mediators may be directive and manipulative – no check by both parties.
- Enables couples to avoid direct communication.
- Enables couples to opt out and let the mediator do the work.
- May prolong mediation to no avail.
- If distressed clients are seen alone, the boundaries of mediation may become blurred with counselling or therapy.
- Selective sharing of information risks distortion and misreporting of positions.
- Inclusion of a third party in a caucus, such as a grandparent or new partner, could cause problems of imbalance and confidentiality. Careful use of shuttle mediation or caucusing can enable high conflict couples to reach pragmatic settlements, even if they do not change their relationship or views of each other. Arrangements for children may involve working out ground rules for ongoing communications between the parents that will be less likely to re-ignite their conflict.

4.10 MEDIATING ONLINE

For young people and parents, texting has become the main means of communication, but texting can bring a fresh set of problems. Text messages and social media can cause further arguments. However, if mediation is to be relevant to modern families, 'we need to meet people where they are and that is online'.[28] Family members have access to a range of communication options that mediators need to understand and utilise. 'There is a fascinating, ever-evolving relationship between online communication and experience and face-to-face communication and experience. Well-utilized, each wonderfully enhances the other ... The online world is an extension of the physical world and offers new capacities that have not previously existed.'[29] Melamed goes on to say (personal communication) that family and divorce mediation is evolving to be a 'choreography of communication' in which mediators and other professionals can help participants to identify valuable online information, as well as making progress toward agreement in their own time. 'Participants are able to take on more active drafting roles in terms of what will work for them and their family, often by "asynchronous", thoughtful and edited comments, rather than impulsive, often destructive real time declarations. A mediator may act as a buffer and diplomat in supporting these communications. Mediators of the future will be wise to focus on utilising communication modalities strategically and on tailoring this use to the particular needs and preferences of individual participants.'

For those with access to the internet, online communications are mostly instant and cheap. Although correspondence by e-mail is not an adequate substitute for meeting face-to-face, it offers a practical way of sending out mediation forms and fast-forwarding negotiations, where both partners are equally comfortable

---

[28]   Melamed 'The Internet and Mediation' (2009) *mediate.com weekly* 298.
[29]   Ibid.

using email and wish to expedite the mediation process. The same rules on confidentiality should apply as in caucusing. Settlement proposals can be clarified through exchanges of emails. If there is a scheduled court hearing and time is short, a draft Memorandum of Understanding can be emailed to participants for them to check, before hard copies are sent for them to take to their legal advisers. Mediators may choose to use tools such as 'track changes' in Microsoft Word, in order to engage participants further in the drafting process.

Mediating online or by telephone is generally less satisfactory than face-to-face meetings, but it is a useful resource and in some circumstances may be the only way to mediate.[30]

4.11 WIDENING THE SCOPE OF FAMILY MEDIATION

Family mediation still takes place mainly with separating/divorcing couples but its scope is widening to embrace family conflicts of many kinds. The legal basis for the dissolution of same-sex relationships is now similar to that for married couples, whereas the unsatisfactory state of the law for separating heterosexual cohabitants gives them a further incentive to use mediation.[31] Another growing area is the arrangement of finances where there may be no dispute but a series of competing interests, such as estate planning or pre-nuptial arrangements for subsequent relationships, particularly where there are children.[32] Interdisciplinary family mediation has capacity for hybrid models that give participants scope for advice, reflection and other steps between meetings. Another area that is ripe for development is the use of mediation in child care cases.

4.12 CHILD WELFARE MEDIATION

A quarter of the 100,000 children who run away from care or home each year are found to be at serious risk of harm. There are 'serious shortcomings in a system that is supposed to protect children in care'.[33] The Family Justice Review[34] made a powerful call to reduce delay in child care proceedings:

> 'Delay really matters and damages children. Delay in proceedings:
> (i) may deny children a chance of a permanent home, particularly through adoption;
> (ii) can have harmful long term effects on a child's development;
> (iii) may expose children to more risk; and
> (iv) causes already damaged children distress and anxiety.'

---

[30] For mediating online in international cases see **15.10** below.
[31] See **9.18** below.
[32] See **9.17** and **9.18** below.
[33] All Party Parliamentary Groups for Looked After Children and Care Leavers and for Runaway and Missing Children, 18 June 2012.
[34] Family Justice Review *Final Report* (February 2012, Ministry of Justice, London), para 56.

When the Family Justice Review reported in 2011, proceedings in child care and supervision cases were taking 55 weeks on average. Since then, reforms in the family justice system have reduced the length of proceedings to an average of 32 weeks.[35] The Family Justice Review suggested that 'mediation also has potential and a pilot on the use of formal mediation approaches in public law proceedings should be established.'[36] In its Response,[37] the Government considered the proposal for a pilot mediation scheme to 'identify areas in which formal mediation is currently used in public law proceedings and work with the Family Mediation Council, HMCTS, the Legal Services Commission, local authorities in England and Wales, Cafcass, CAFCASS Cymru and other organisations with an interest to develop options for undertaking a pilot. Careful consideration will be given to when mediation may be appropriate in these types of cases.'[38] More recently, the Government has stated that mediation in public law proceedings is not being taken forward at the present time, but 'further consideration may be given over the coming months'.[39]

Mr Justice (now, Lord) Ryder,[40] in his Judicial Proposals for the Modernisation of Family Justice, pointed out that 'care cases can be complex and each family is unique and deserving of the court's full attention (para 40). The problem to be solved is essentially placement, which of course includes the potential success of rehabilitation and the feasibility of family and other kinship options and contact. Good practice demands that these options are identified ... at the beginning of the proceedings and this is much more likely to occur where family group conferencing or similar early engagements with families have occurred to identify alternative placements for the child'[41] (para 47). As suggested in Chapter 2, ecosystemic mediation provides a framework for conflict management and dispute settlement between participants themselves and also between private systems of family decision-making and public systems of law and child protection. Mediators work at the interface between these systems, assisting private family systems to function effectively and avoid unnecessary or further involvement of public systems. There are bound to be power imbalances in mediations involving family members and public authorities. These power imbalances need to be taken into account. Mediation on specific issues may be suitable and mediators can use a range of interventions that help to empower families and promote children's well-being.[42]

Previously, cases involving child welfare issues were considered unsuitable for referral to mediation, but new ways of providing mediation in these cases are being developed. Many childcare cases involve the return of a child to his/her

---

[35] Department for Education and Ministry of Justice *A Brighter Future for Family Justice* (August 2014), p 5.

[36] Family Justice Review, para 99.

[37] Government Response to the Family Justice Review (February 2012).

[38] Ibid, Recommendation 95.

[39] Department for Education and Ministry of Justice *A Brighter Future for Family Justice* (August 2014), p 41.

[40] Ryder LJ *Judicial Proposals for the Modernisation of Family Justice* (MoJ, July 2012), para 40.

[41] Ibid, para 47.

[42] Barsky *Conflict Resolution for the Helping Professions* (Wadsworth, 2000).

own parents or to the care of another family member. Rebuilding relationships is a priority. Family Group Conferences are highly successful, with good outcomes reported by family members and social workers. Children's services are overloaded and in some circumstances, an independent mediator may assist the child protection social worker and the family by gaining the trust and co-operation of all concerned, precisely because the mediator has no power to decide or influence the outcome. Mediation at the end of a care order can support the return of a child from foster care or residential care to a parent or family member. Supportive relationships between carers and parents can be encouraged. In one case, a one-year-old child was found to have been injured non-accidentally by his father in circumstances denied by both the young father and the mother. Mediation was used to rebuild fractured relationships between the maternal grandparents, who became the child's guardians and carers, the parents who had since separated from each other, and the paternal grandmother. These family members had previously competed with each other to 'win' the child.

Some childcare cases may need mediation because the social workers involved may not be perceived as impartial by the parents or family. The social worker's efforts to build a co-operative relationship with the family are hampered if the parents see them as agents of social control and resist their intervention. Social work reports may be critical of parents and strenuously opposed by them. It is very difficult for social workers to use their authority to protect the child, while at the same time forming a supportive and co-operative relationship with the child's parents. The primary concern must be the protection and welfare of the child. After the child's safety has been been investigated and assured, referral to mediation can be considered with the parents' understanding and consent to the outcome being reportable to the social worker. When family members are in dispute with each other as well as with the child protection system, a mediator can help parents to focus on the best interests of their children and work out an agreed plan to present to those with authority over their children.

Family members and social workers may need to turn to mediation as an independent process that can facilitate mutually agreed decisions in the best interests of the child. It may not be necessary for social workers to participate directly in the mediation, provided that they support the referral to mediation. The Agreement to Mediate may need to be modified to allow the outcome of the mediation to be reportable to social services and, if necessary, the court. Mediators may also need some background information from social workers in order to carry out mediation with full information and awareness of child protection issues. Some mediation services may therefore ask to see the initial and/or final Social Work statement. Parents or other carers may need to agree that outcomes and arrangements for children are shared with the social worker concerned. It is important to recognise that the role of mediator is not compatible with holding statutory responsibility, such as the duty to prepare reports for the court. Lawyers and social workers involved in childcare cases are not in a position to act as mediators if they have a statutory duty to report to a public authority with decision-making power. Mediation skills needed for child welfare mediation include:

- engaging with some or all of the parties;
- clarifying issues;
- understanding different priorities and points of view;
- facilitating dialogue and negotiations;
- exploring options and objectives;
- drawing up written agreements.

In a case referred to mediation with the support of the social worker, background information was not required. The foster-parents came to mediation with their 18-year-old foster daughter, Cara, who had left their care and moved into her own apartment a few streets away. Cara had a three-year-old daughter, Molly, who continued to live with the foster-parents. Cara had a close and trusting relationship with her foster-parents and there was a ready consensus in mediation between Cara and her foster-parents that Molly's residence should remain with her foster-grandparents and that Cara would visit her every day, whenever she wanted. The social worker supported this agreement.

The Public Law Outline 2014[43] envisages greater use of mediation and other forms of out of court dispute resolution before, during and after care proceedings. Active case management under paragraph 3.20 includes: 'where it is demonstrated to be in the interests of the child, encouraging the parties to use an alternative dispute resolution procedure, if the court considers such a procedure to be appropriate and facilitating the use of such procedure.' Whilst power imbalances are inevitable in mediations involving family members and a public authority and these need to be taken into account, mediation on certain issues may be suitable and accepted. Mediators can use a range of interventions that help to empower families and promote children's well being. A growing area is the use of mediation at the end of care proceedings to support the move of a child in foster care to a family member under Special Guardianship. In this way, supportive relationships between the prospective carers and the parents can be encouraged. There is a risk, however, that mediators could become unwilling participants in the Local Authority relinquishing its responsibilities at too early a stage. In a case referred to the Family Mediation Centre Staffordshire, mediation was used to rebuild fractured relationships between the maternal grandparents who became the child's Special Guardians, the separated parents, and the estranged paternal grandmother, all of whom had taken competing positions concerning the child.

Mediators can work collaboratively with judges, Cafcass and local authority social workers, provided they maintain the integrity and boundaries of the mediation process and pay careful attention to confidentiality. Suitability and

---

[43] Public Law Outline (Ministry of Justice, 2014).

prerequisites for mediation in public law child proceedings, possible models and stages of the process were considered on a two-day course in Stafford, 27–28 November 2012.[44]

4.13   MEDIATING WITH EXTENDED FAMILIES

> 'My family is my brother, step-dad, half-brother, mum and dad and my dad's fiancée. I've got two homes. My dad, brother and I live here and my mum's side live fifteen miles away.'[45]

Most family mediations involve two parties – mainly, separating or separated couples. However, many separated parents have new partners, who, like grandparents, may help to look after the children. The co-operation of family members may be critical if arrangements agreed between parents are to work in practice. If key family members feel excluded from decisions reached in mediation, they may sabotage the agreements. Yet if a new partner or grandparent is involved on one side but not the other, bringing a third party into the mediation would unbalance the process unacceptably. Sometimes both parents are living with new partners. Are foursomes fearsome and to be avoided at all costs? If planned carefully with all concerned, it may be helpful in some circumstances to invite the former couple and their new partners to take part in a four-way mediation meeting. In some circumstances, some form of shuttle mediation or caucusing may be more appropriate. Careful assessment is needed to consider the inclusion of other adult family members (for child-inclusive mediation, see Chapter 8) and their actual or potential influence, both within and outside the mediation. Mediators need to assess possible benefits and risks in involving them directly. Different ways of structuring meetings need to be explored and pre-conditions agreed, before involving other family members and designing the mediation process. Mediation techniques and skills can be used to help family members and professionals who support them to reach agreement on arrangements including care of the elderly, social isolation and homelessness, adoption and post-adoption support, care of the disabled and inheritance disputes.

Co-mediators are likely to be needed for mediation with a large family group. In disputes involving step-parents, mediation can help those involved to understand the options available – such as shared residence, step-parent adoption or other form of agreement – so that they can consider the needs of the child concerned and the objectives and potential consequences of each option. Negotiated agreements provide a better basis for future childcare than a court order, since arrangements are more likely to work where there is agreement and co-operation over what constitutes the best interests of the child. Those with parenting responsibilities should be encouraged to consider appropriate consultation with and explanations to the child.

---

[44]   Parkinson *Child Care Mediation in Public Law Proceedings* (presented at The Family Mediation Centre course in Stafford, 27–28 November 2012, unpublished).

[45]   Sally, aged 12, quoted by Neale and Wade *Parent Problems – children's views on life when parents split up* (Young Voice, 2000), p 7.

Example

This mediation involved the paternal grandparents, George and Mary, their daughter-in-law Sara (mother of Chrissy, aged 3), her new husband, Will, and two co-mediators (male/female). Chrissy's father did not take part in the mediation because he was receiving treatment in a drug addiction centre and a court order barred him from contact with his daughter. When Sara came to a MIAM, she explained that she had been through a very difficult time because of her ex-partner's drug addiction and trouble with the police. She and her new husband, Will, were now eager to establish their own family. Sara was expecting their baby in a few months' time. She would have liked to forget about her ex-partner and his family, but she understood that grandparents have a right to seek contact with their grandchildren and she also felt that Chrissy would need some knowledge of her father's family, as she grew up. At the first mediation meeting, the mediators enquired about Chrissy, her personality, favourite toys and activities and so on. The atmosphere became more relaxed and an interim agreement was reached that Sara would invite George and Mary for coffee at her home, so that Chrissy would begin to know them better. After this visit, George and Mary would take Chrissy to the zoo, as she loved animals. Once Chrissy was at ease and happy to see them, her grandparents would take her out once a month and when she was over four years old, she might stay with them overnight, if she was happy to do so. It was recognised that Chrissy had three sets of grandparents and used different names for each of them. All the family members needed to know Chrissy's names for each grandparent, so that they would know whom she was talking about. The mediators drew a circle on the flip-chart with Chrissy in the centre, with lines showing her relationship to the family members who encircled and supported her and the names she used for each of them. The mediators provided a written summary of the arrangements worked out in mediation. Court proceedings were not needed.

4.14   INTERGENERATIONAL MEDIATION

Consensual decisions on future care are often needed in relation to the care of the elderly. Medical advice may be needed on the elderly person's mental capacity, functioning and ability to represent their own interests in any negotiations. Decisions about the residential care of an elderly relative can cause deep rifts in families. Mediators can help family members to consider the options available, facilitating family discussions and decision-making with professional advice. When elderly parents are unable to manage their own affairs, mediation can assist adult children to negotiate and reach agreement over their parents' care and property and management of their assets.

Example

An estranged elderly couple were being looked after in separate residential care homes. They had been married for only six years. Each of them had a middle-aged daughter from previous marriages that had ended in divorce.

Sadly, their late marriage to each other had broken down as well. The wife, Frances, aged 82, had begun to suffer from dementia and her husband, Arthur, aged 84, was unable to look after her. They had begun to argue a great deal and neither of them wished to be placed in the same residential home. Arthur's daughter from his first marriage, Linda, was aged 58. Frances' daughter from her first marriage, Carla, was aged 53. Arthur and Frances had each appointed their daughters as their legal representatives because they were not capable of reaching decisions or taking part in mediation themselves. The two principal protagonists were therefore Linda and Carla. The family member who made the first approach to seek mediation was Arthur's daughter, Linda. Linda and Carla met separately with the mediator and were able to reach agreement on the sale of their parents' family home and the division of the sale proceeds. The mediated agreement enabled the costs of their parents' residential care to be covered more comfortably and also settled some minor disputes over family possessions.

Intergenerational mediation to resolve issues over the care of elderly family members may include elderly persons who are able and willing to take part in discussions with their adult children. Some intergenerational mediations are undertaken by social workers who have trained as mediators, but if the mediator holds authority and is accountable to a public service, the principles of mediation cannot be fully applied. Social workers employed in a public service may be required to make recommendations and take decisions for which they would accountable to their local authority. Discussions with family members would not be legally privileged and there could be conflicts of interests and responsibilities between the duty towards family members and statutory duties that include the care and protection of individuals and society as a whole. These questions need careful consideration and adaptations to provide new forms of child welfare or intergenerational dispute resolution. Intergenerational dispute resolution may also be helpful in resolving disputes between adolescents and their parents, for example after an adolescent has run away from home.[46]

4.15   MEDIATION IN INHERITANCE DISPUTES

Disputes over the terms of a Will (or in the absence of a Will), for example, between the family and cohabitant of the deceased, or between adult children, can be fuelled by similar feelings to those experienced in separation and divorce – bitterness, grief, rejection, loss, anger and resentment. Mediation gives opportunities to recognise and express these emotions in negotiating over the terms of a disputed Will, whereas these painful feelings risk being further inflamed by court proceedings. Litigation in inheritance disputes also carries high risks of the value of the estate being consumed by legal costs and culminating in the permanent breakdown of relationships between siblings.

---

[46]   See also **8.14** below on child-parent mediation.

A mediator trained both in family and civil/commercial mediation can respond to the intense emotions of inheritance dispute, while also having financial expertise developed in civil mediation. This model needs to be developed to help family members resolve a wide range of financial and property matters, in conjunction with related issues concerning their children.

4.16   MEDIATION IN ADOPTION AND POST-ADOPTION SUPPORT

Mediation can help resolve issues over continuing contact between an adopted child and birth parents. It may not be possible to bring birth and adoptive parents together for face-to-face meetings, because, unlike separated parents, they are strangers who have not previous contact with each other and they may feel too vulnerable and anxious. Shuttle mediation can be used, however, to explore a child's post-adoption contact with birth parents and to work out practical details. As 'open adoption' becomes more common, mediation may be needed to facilitate communication between birth and adoptive parents and between the child and both sets of parents. Agreed arrangements for contact can be recorded in a written agreement that is provided to all concerned, including the child, and approved by the court if necessary. There should be provision for reviewing arrangements and modifying them as circumstances change and the child gets older. This is again an area for 'working in partnership'. Many adoption organisations have excellent practice in relation to post-adoption support.

4.17   MEDIATION INVOLVING PEOPLE WITH DISABILITIES

A more controversial use of mediation is in relation to complaints involving discrimination against people with physical and mental disabilities. Some disability advocacy groups have been alarmed by this development, fearing that hard-won battles for legal rights could be lost if disabled people are not represented adequately. One of the concerns about mediation involving people with certain forms of disability is their ability to communicate and negotiate fully. As Maida[47] has pointed out, there is the problem of ensuring informed participation and secondly, the problem of power balancing. Effective communication in mediation requires adequate mental capacity and techniques that allow everyone to participate fully. Many people question the use of mediation with someone who does not have full mental capacity or only intermittent capacity. Mediators have an obligation to ensure that individuals are able to participate fully and that their interests are adequately represented. There are a number of strategies that may be used to level the playing-field and manage actual or potential power imbalances. Medical advice may be needed in the first instance on the suitability of mediation. If mediation is suitable, the disabled person may need someone to provide additional physical and emotional support in the mediation process. The role of supporters and the

---

[47]   Maida 'Mediating disputes involving people with disabilities', Ch 12 in Kruk (ed) *Mediation and Conflict Resolution in Social Work and the Human Services* (Nelson-Hall, 1997).

extent to which they speak on behalf of the disabled person need careful consideration. Systems theory provides a framework for mediators to understand the tangled web of facts, perceptions, communications and feelings that may need unravelling to help family members reach consensual decisions.

In circumstances where Skype is not available and disability precludes face-to-face meetings, the telephone may be the only means of communication. In one such case (provided by Neil Robinson), the couple, Clarice and Mike, had been married for 30 years. Up to their separation nine months earlier, they lived together in the family home owned in Mike's sole name. Their son John (25) suffered from Asperger's Syndrome and was unable to manage independently. Clarice was physically disabled and the property where she and John were now living had been equipped for her needs. Clarice and Mike were not speaking to one another, although they co-operated in supporting John. They both wanted to use mediation to resolve a number of issues. The common ground between them was their joint concern to protect John's interests. Mediation proceeded by way of:

• Initial telephone discussion with Clarice.

• Initial telephone discussion with Mike.

• A mediation meeting at Clarice's home, with Mike available on the telephone, followed by a meeting with Mike, with Clarice on the telephone. Then a telephone discussion with both on the line and finally, meetings with Mike and Clarice separately to go through the draft Memorandum of Understanding.

4.18 LAWYERS IN MEDIATION

Brown and Marriott[48] devote a chapter of their book to considering the role of lawyers who advise and assist clients in different forms of dispute resolution. Lawyers complain that mediators 'take work away' from them, but mediators are a source of referrals to lawyers. Many individuals come to mediation without having taken legal advice. Mediators encourage them to take legal advice during mediation, as well as at the end. The roles of lawyers and mediators are different and complementary. Although mediation should reduce litigation, questions frequently arise in mediation on which participants need independent legal and financial advice before making proposals for settlement.

In civil/commercial mediation, the parties' lawyers attend with their clients and advise them during the process. This is not general practice in family mediation, but in some cases it may be worthwhile. The logistics are more difficult in family mediation than in civil/commercial mediation that may last a whole day and be concluded on the same day, whereas family mediation normally takes place over several sessions held at intervals of weeks or even months. In some American states it is common for lawyers to attend family mediation sessions, whereas in Britain and other European countries this is uncommon. Lawyers

---

[48] Brown and Marriott *ADR Principles and Practice* (Sweet & Maxwell, 1993).

who take part without understanding the mediation process might try to take
control and inhibit their clients from talking with each other. If lawyers seek to
use mediation as an opportunity for advocacy, the nature of the process would
change fundamentally. In a survey in Florida, well over half the lawyers said
that over the previous twelve months they had attended family mediation
sessions with their clients in 75% of their family law cases. The majority said
their reason for attending was to facilitate agreements being reached. Another
reason given by many of them was the need to protect their client. A lawyer's
presence can give support to an anxious and vulnerable client who might
otherwise refuse to take part in mediation. Some lawyers admitted that they
attended mediation in order to learn about the mediation process and the
mediator's abilities. Once they were satisfied that the mediators were competent
and knowledgeable, they were more comfortable to allow their clients to
participate. The survey showed that after attending mediation sessions, lawyers
found that the benefits of mediation outweighed any potential disadvantages.
One of the advantages of having lawyers present is that there can be a break
during the mediation session in which the parties withdraw with their own
lawyer for a short separate meeting or caucus. When legal advice is given on the
spot, a great deal of delay is avoided. Lawyers can advise their client, if they
perceive that the client is being obstructive, for example by explaining that their
position is unrealistic or unhelpful. Mediators cannot spell things out in this
way. Lawyers can also be very helpful in assisting negotiations and finalising a
settlement.

Before legal advisers are invited to attend a mediation meeting, it is important
that some ground-rules are established with them so that the lawyers
understand and respect the mediation process. The Agreement to Mediate needs
to be adapted for lawyers and they should be asked to sign it so that the
confidentiality of the mediation process is not breached in subsequent litigation.
A number of other aspects also need to be clarified with lawyers. They need to
know whether they are being invited to as passive observers, whether they are
invited to contribute actively and whether there will be opportunities for them
to withdraw with their client at intervals to give further advice. Roles and
structure need to be agreed and it needs to be established that the mediator is
not responsible for paying the costs of lawyers who attend mediation with their
clients.

4.19   HYBRID FAMILY/CIVIL MEDIATION

Some mediators who are cross-trained in family and civil mediation are well
equipped to mediate in hybrid family and civil cases that have potential for
lengthy and costly litigation in different courts. Robinson[49] has given examples
of the use of mediation in such cases. In one case, intergenerational litigation
over interests in a family farm involved both Chancery and family proceedings.
The final hearing in Chancery proceedings was stayed pending mediation
between four parties, two of whom were divorcing spouses involved in ancillary

---

[49]   Robinson [2009] Fam Law 253.

relief proceedings. The ancillary relief proceedings had been stayed pending the outcome of the Chancery proceedings. The total costs to the parties over the four years of these proceedings had already climbed to over £30,000. A merged family/civil mediation was set up and attended by the four parties and their solicitors or Counsel. The mediation lasted one day and culminated with a Memorandum of Understanding produced in respect of the ancillary relief proceedings and a Tomlin Order in the Chancery proceedings. The cost of the mediation to the four parties averaged less than £500 each.

4.20   MEDIATION IN COMPLEX SYSTEMS

A simple system is programmed to be predictable, like a car engine. Simple systems can of course be faulty and behave unpredictably, usually at highly inconvenient moments, but in general, a simple mechanical model is designed to be predictable. Mediation is neither simple nor predictable. It offers a means of resolving disputes in complex family systems and cases that span civil and family jurisdictions, also in care proceedings linked with family proceedings.

At a family mediation conference in Italy in October 2013,[50] Dr Mazzei, a family therapist, talked about the differences between 'complicated' and 'complex' in their Latin and Italian forms. 'Complicato', complicated, enfolded, suggests hidden folds of meaning ('plicato', folded). The meaning is comparable to 'contortus, perplexus, implicato', whereas 'complesso', complex, is more positive in conveying a sense of 'embracing' as well as complexity and therefore relates to the work mediators do to help preserve and rebuild family bonds. Family mediation is complex. In many situations, especially those involving entrenched conflict, it is complicated as well. Expertise and creativity need to be combined in designing mediation models for complex family systems and complicated situations. Mediation 'in complex and entrenched cases is likely to involve working in partnership with other professional colleagues and the court process – a far more evolved multi-disciplinary approach than we have previously embraced.'[51] As Daniel Barenboim says,[52] 'the inclusion of all parties in a dialogue … is not a guarantee for perfect harmony, but it creates the conditions necessary for co-operation'. Barenboim also reminds us that 'spontaneous realisation' is possible only with 'all the repetitions and the familiarity resulting from intense study'.[53]

Complex systems differ from simple systems in having the capacity to create something new – a new order and new structures – through developing different forms of interaction and relationship.. Complexity theory is based on the study of the collective behaviour of complex systems. It is rooted in chaos

---

[50]   Conference of the Italian family mediation association, Società Italiana di Mediazione Familiare (SiMeF), Florence, 4 October 2013.

[51]   Robinson 'Developing Family Mediation' [2008] Fam Law, 927.

[52]   Barenboim *Everything is Connected – The Power of Music* (Weidenfeld and Nicolson, 2008), p 59.

[53]   Ibid, p 58.

theory[54] in which chaos is viewed as extremely complex information, rather than as an absence of order. Complex systems possess the potential for qualitative change while retaining their systemic integrity. Arnon Bentovim, consultant psychiatrist, family therapist and jazz musician, wrote that:

> 'practitioners of jazz and family therapy have to respond to the moment, the atmosphere, the emotional climate, and to be aware of the rhythm, the melodies and counter melodies, variations and familiar cadences. They need to forget technique to create genuine dialogue, to create a transformative musical experience or to transform the lives of the families we work with.'[55]

In a similar way, to create genuine dialogue, mediators need to respond to the moment, the atmosphere and the emotional climate and be aware of 'melodies and counter melodies'. While adhering to the core principles of mediation, mediators need to use empathy and intuition in reconnecting fragmented systems and designing new pathways to help families to manage change.

---

[54] See Chapter 2 above.

[55] Bentovim 'Jazz and family therapy – my journey' (June 2011) *Context, the magazine for family therapy and systemic practice*, p 33.

CHAPTER 5

NAVIGATING THROUGH MEDIATION

'What we call the beginning is often the end
And to make an end is to make a beginning,
The end is where we start from'.[1]

CONTENTS

5.1 DIMENSIONS OF SEPARATION AND DIVORCE

Separation and divorce involve major changes in relationships and living arrangements. This very stressful period calls for simultaneous adjustments in many different dimensions. Bohannan[2] identified six dimensions of adjustment in separation and divorce: emotional, psychological, parental, legal, economic and social. How many of us could manage adjustments in all these areas at once? It may not be possible to work out arrangements for children without addressing interrelated housing and financial issues. In mediation, interrelated issues can be considered in conjunction with each other, whereas the court deals with children and property matters in separate proceedings. Emotional and psychological issues are not the main focus of mediation, but ignoring their impact may increase conflict and distress and block the resolution of disputes.

---

[1]   T S Eliot *Four Quartets 'Little Gidding'* (Faber, 1959), p 58.
[2]   Bohannan *Divorce and After* (Doubleday, New York, 1970).

5.2   TOWARDS A TYPOLOGY OF SEPARATING AND DIVORCING COUPLES

Communication problems are often both a cause and an effect of relationship breakdown. Researchers at the Centre for Marital and Family Studies at the University of Denver, Colorado[3] have suggested that it is not *whether* couples argue that matters, it is *how* they argue. Disagreements are normal and relationships without any conflict would be abnormal. How couples deal with conflict is the critical factor. Each relationship is unique, but some patterns are discernible. It is useful for mediators to recognise patterns, not to place couples in categories or encourage assumptions, but to help design an approach that is likely to be helpful to the couple concerned. Conflict patterns may change over time and one partner may show features of one response, while the other partner shows features of another. Some patterns are deeply engrained and strongly resistant to change. Mediators are not clinicians who make diagnoses as a prelude to treatment, but as suggested in the previous chapter, they need to design the mediation process to meet different sets of needs. The mediator's interventions can reduce surface tensions,[4] even if they do not reach the roots of the problem. Different combinations of knowledge, intuition and skills are needed to mediate between couples who range from the potentially co-operative to intractably opposed. Researchers have proposed various typologies to describe patterns of reaction and interaction between separating and divorcing couples. Kressel and colleagues[5] described four patterns: 'disengaged', 'direct conflict', 'autistic' (non-communicating) and 'enmeshed'. Ahrons[6] distinguishes between 'perfect pals', 'co-operative colleagues', 'dissolved duos', 'angry associates' and 'fiery foes'. The following typology identifies some patterns of communication, conflict and dysfunction drawn from mediation experience:

- Co-operative couples.
- Semi-detached couples.
- Business managers.
- Conflict avoiders.
- Angry fighters.
- Transferred conflict.
- Clinging by one partner.
- Triangulation of third parties.
- Entrenched conflict.

5.2.1   Co-operative couples

Co-operative couples may seek mediation without having a dispute, because they want to reach agreements and maintain their co-operation. If there are

---

[3]   Markman, Stanley and Blumbers *Fighting For Your Marriage* (Prentice Hall, 1996).
[4]   See Chapter 2 above.
[5]   Kressel, Jaffe, Tuchman, Watson, Deutsch 'A Typology of Divorcing Couples' (1980) 19(2) *Family Process* 101–116.
[6]   Ahrons *The Good Divorce* (Bloomsbury, 1994).

financial and property issues, they may need a mediator's help in working out their financial settlement. Co-operative couples are able to move relatively easily through stages of mediation: gathering information, exploring options and working out arrangements. Reality-testing by the mediator is important, however, because financial plans may not have been fully considered and longer term consequences may have not been clearly understood. Mediation with co-operative couples is usually low-key and may be easy going, but mediators need to be ready for a sudden flaring of anger or pain.

A new relationship or partner on either side is liable to upset previous co-operation between parents. Mediators can anticipate difficulties by putting hypothetical questions,[7] such as asking when a parent plans to tell their children about a new relationship and in what way. Parents may decide to return to mediation if a new relationship on either side necessitates a review of their existing arrangements. It may be helpful to mention to co-operative parents that whilst they are clearly helping their children by working together so well, children can be confused by the very amicability they see between their parents. Children may misinterpret friendliness as a sign that their parents are getting back together. Younger children, especially, may find it hard to understand why there is any need for separation or divorce, since their parents seem to get on so well. Co-operative parents may value the opportunity to discuss how they will explain things to the children and consider how they can have a say. Some parents avoid talking to their children about separation or divorce because it is a painful subject and they are not sure how to explain something they do not fully understand themselves.[8]

5.2.2 Semi-detached couples – apart, but not fully detached

Semi-detached couples are often ambivalent about separation or divorce. They may demonstrate this by preferring to leave some things in the air. Mediation may help them to clarify decisions and options and in the process they may be able to express uncertainties, insecurity and mixed feelings. Some couples may need to work out clearer boundaries concerning their separation and contact with each other. A partner who makes frequent visits – 'just passing by and thought I would drop in' – may justify this as keeping in touch with the children. But unplanned visits may be disruptive and can be an excuse for checking up on what is going on in the other parent's home. It may help both partners to work out when and how they will communicate with each other and how far this should be by prior arrangement. When visits are planned, children as well as parents need to be emotionally prepared. If there is ambivalence and some unresolved conflict, there may be a knot of tangled feelings. Many semi-detached couples can talk on their own to some extent, but they may need a mediator's help to tackle difficult questions that they otherwise avoid or shelve. Some admit that, while wanting to be fair and reasonable, they have an urge to hit back at a partner who has caused hurt. Mediators can help them address matters that they shy away from, but need to resolve.

---

7 See Chapter 6 below.
8 See Chapter 8 on talking with children.

Example

Stephen and Rhoda had been to Relate for counselling the year before they came to mediation. When they came to mediation they had been living apart under the same roof for over a year and both of them accepted that their fifteen-year marriage (without children) had broken down irretrievably. They were detached from each other to a considerable extent, but still had emotional, financial and legal ties to unravel. Although fully prepared to split their assets on a 50/50 basis, Stephen did not see why he should share his pension with Rhoda. Rhoda was concerned about her long-term security as she had a much lower income and only a small pension. Stephen felt she could increase her income and her pension. They had both consulted solicitors. Rhoda's solicitor suggested mediation and Stephen agreed to attend. Rhoda was ready to address difficult issues that Stephen was inclined to avoid. In mediation, the issues were addressed systematically, with concerns noted and acknowledged. A careful use of humour proved a helpful way of engaging with them and the discussions became lighter and freer. Three mediation sessions were spent defining issues, gathering and clarifying financial facts and needs and exploring possible options and time-scales for settlement. Stephen and Rhoda were encouraged to take legal advice and their settlement was approved by the court in a consent order.

5.2.3 Business managers

There are some dual-career couples whose relationship seems to have been based on mutual convenience and friendship, without deep feelings on either side. Their relationship may have been short, without strong investment or attachment. These couples are less likely to have children. A career move for one partner may precipitate a decision to separate and the couple may approach separation as though it were a business negotiation. Practicalities may be addressed briskly, without any mention of feelings. Mediators are expected to be highly efficient on technical matters. Any enquiry into emotions may be seen as intrusive and brushed aside. Couples who treat separation or divorce as a piece of business to get through as efficiently as possible are entitled to receive an efficient mediation process. Mediators should, however, have their antennae well tuned to pick up signs of pain and distress that may be well concealed beneath a cool exterior.

Example

Howard and Caitlin had lived together for two years before they married. They owned a large and expensively furnished flat in London. They did not have children. Both of them worked long hours and Howard, who worked for an international telecommunications company, travelled a great deal. He paid the mortgage from his salary and Caitlin paid the housekeeping bills. They had rarely discussed financial matters as they had separate bank accounts and were largely independent financially. Once their various assets and income had been listed in mediation and values agreed, there was agreement to divide everything on a 50/50 basis – until it came to the candlesticks. These were a valuable pair of silver candlesticks that had emotional as well as monetary value. Howard and Caitlin acknowledged that the candlesticks were precious because they had bought them on a special occasion that held memories for both of them. Having previously seemed quite cold and detached towards each other, they then spoke with sadness about the ending of their relationship. Both were close to tears. Had the mediator attended only to questions of financial equality, Howard and Caitlin would have left mediation with a financial settlement, but the sadness they both felt would have remained unspoken.

Business managers may include older couples whose feelings for each other have withered away. Sometimes they have formed new relationships and come to mediation ready to dissolve a marriage that is no more than an empty shell. If financial issues are relatively straightforward and there is no anger or resentment on either side, they may choose mediation as a private and low cost means of 'private ordering'.

5.2.4   Conflict avoiders

In this common pattern, one partner may withdraw from the other, seeking compensation in work, leisure activities or a new relationship – or all of these. Communication may be limited and may have ceased altogether. Some couples continue to live under the same roof, but each partner withdraws into a shell, closing up like a clam and refusing to talk to each other. Their silence may convey hurt, anger and feelings of mutual rejection, sometimes in a passive-aggressive pattern. Yet there may be hidden affection and attachment and a fear of abandonment. Typical reactions are avoidance, retreat, non-communication and fear of confrontation. If one parent leaves the home without any prior discussion, the remaining parent may be unable to tell the children if, when or how they will see the parent who seems to have walked away. This pattern of avoiding conflict and communication may be passed on to the next generation. Emotional and practical issues may be unresolved and new partnerships may be formed, when old ties remain knotted.

Sometimes both partners avoid discussing the breakdown in their relationship. In mediation, one may throw a sudden accusation into the air like a verbal grenade and then retreat behind the barriers. At other times, one of them seeks discussion and is frustrated by the other's clam-like retreat into a closed shell. This shell can remain closed for years. If one partner leaves without having given any clear warning, the abandoned partner may experience profound shock, followed by disbelief, distress, anger or an unmanageable mixture of emotions. The leaver may insist that he or she tried to talk, but felt constantly rebuffed. The gulf of blocked communication may be so wide that it is difficult to conceive of any bridge capable of spanning it. Counselling could help the partners to understand what has happened and why, but they may not be willing to go to counselling. Some couples who avoid talking to each other directly may be able to talk in mediation. Separate initial meetings with each partner are essential in helping the mediator to understand the stage that each partner is at and the strength of suppressed emotion and conflict. The pace of mediation may need to be slow, especially to start with. Mediators need to be attentive to body language, able to pick up unspoken feelings and aware of the dynamics of rejection, counter-rejection and ambivalence. Good listening and communication skills are very important, especially in the phrasing and focusing of questions.

Example

Bill and Glenda sat down at their first mediation meeting without looking at each another. Both were silent. In response to a question from the mediator, Glenda said: 'Well, we've split up. So what do we do now?' Sensing a frozen atmosphere, the mediator asked if it would help to begin by explaining different ways of structuring a separation or divorce to see whether any of these ways would be helpful for them. Both nodded. The mediator explained different ways of structuring a separation or divorce, starting with the least formal way and moving on to reaching a formal and final settlement in divorce. Getting back together was also mentioned, without giving it special emphasis. Headings were put on the flip-chart and questions arising from these headings were used to encourage dialogue between Bill and Glenda. In the course of explanations and discussions they became visibly less strained. By the end of the session, they had identified and discussed a number of specific issues. At the following session, they were helped to explore further questions together, taking one step at a time.

5.2.5   Angry fighters

Mediating between participants who are in open conflict with each other needs a very different approach from mediating with conflict avoiders. Angry couples who fight openly need more rule-setting, quicker interventions by the mediator and careful structuring of sessions.[9] The aim is to channel the energy generated by the couple's anger into resolving issues, instead of prolonging the battle. Couples who fight over the spoils of the marriage may find these dwindling away, the more they fight over how much each should get. Mediators need to shift the focus from individual rights and wrongs to mutual concerns and interests. Disagreements can be reframed as valid concerns, with a range of possible options to consider. When the separation is recent and feelings are raw, anger may be loud and strong. However, couples who were formerly able to co-operate as parents may be able to regain this capacity. They need to express their anger and it has the positive function of asserting values and needs. Although explosive anger risks blowing a mediation apart, its expression in a safe forum can have a cathartic effect (danger and opportunity).[10] If there is motivation to move on, angry couples may respond well to mediation. Some couples show a disconcerting ability to switch suddenly from fury to hilarity. If

---

[9]   See 5.7.3 below.
[10]   See Chapter 3 above on crisis management.

the mediator begins to understand the dynamics of their relationship and the kind of humour that works for them, humour may be as effective as reasoning and common sense.

5.2.6 Transferred conflict

Some couples fight openly on overt issues. Others use disputes over children as a vehicle for conflict that is seething below the surface. Attempts to settle the overt dispute may make little headway if the underlying conflict is not addressed. One parent's time with the children may be blocked because the resident parent is distraught or enraged by the other parent's departure, especially if a new partner is involved. One of the strongest arguments for mediation on all issues is that it enables emotional and practical links between issues to be understood and worked on. Disputes over children may be based on disagreements over parenting values or discipline, but more often, they are fuelled by unresolved marital issues. Some disputes over children embody genuine concerns over child welfare, but they are often a channel for anger about 'the other woman' or 'that bloke you're seeing.' There may be an underlying strategy to secure occupation and sole ownership of the family home. Children can be employed as weapons or used in bargaining tactics. Some parents who come to mediation admit that they have been fighting each other through the children. Realising how much this affects the children may motivate them to stop fighting and work out solutions.

Example

David and Alison were referred to mediation because of disputes over the children's visits to their father. David was living with a new partner called Lynne. Alison was struggling to make ends meet and she deeply resented David and Lynne's higher standard of living. Alison felt David wanted everything his own way, including the children. David reacted by accusing Alison of punishing him through the children and trying to turn them against him. His anger may also have served as a defence against his guilt feelings about leaving Alison for Lynne. It was necessary for David and Alison to express some of their anger, to acknowledge it and accept it as normal and understandable. This acknowledgement was combined with encouragement to start looking at ways forward. Before focusing on arrangements for the children, the mediator enquired about other areas of agreement or disagreement. Asking these questions was important, because it enabled anger on other issues to surface. Alison complained that David was not paying adequate child maintenance. The links between child arrangements and financial issues became clearer. Another issue was Lynne's role in relation to the children when they visited their father. Mediation involved discussion of these interrelated issues, with acknow-ledgement of deeply personal feelings and encouragement to give priority to the children's needs and feelings.

5.2.7   Clinging by one partner[11]

The most prolonged anger in separation and divorce may stem from one partner's continuing intense need for the other. It is not only children who harbour fantasies of reconciliation. When continuing attachment on one side is not reciprocated, the abandoned partner's feelings of grief and anger may make rational discussion impossible. An emotionally desperate partner may embroil the other in prolonged disputes as a way of clinging on and maintaining involvement – rather like a limpet that cannot be prised off a rock that provides security against the incoming tide. The other partner may be more like a sea anemone than a rock. Sea anemones are mobile: they can close their tentacles and withdraw into an impregnable lump. If the 'limpet' refuses to accept the 'sea anemone's' withdrawal, mediation may be impossible. Referral to counselling may be needed, but both partners may refuse it. Legal advice is important when one partner is seeking a divorce that is strongly resisted by the other. If they come to mediation, it is important to recognise with both partners that they are looking in opposite directions. It may be helpful to acknowledge that ending a relationship involves more than the loss of the partner. Expectations of a safe future with financial security may be lost as well. Enforced changes of lifestyle, usually involving a lower standard of living, may intensify bitterness. One partner may accuse the other of failed promises and commitments. Disillusionment fuels anger. Although anger over failed hopes and dreams may be mutual, the partner who is seen as responsible for ending the relationship is expected to carry the blame. Blaming the other enables the 'innocent' partner to take the role of victim and avoid responsibility for any part in the failed relationship.

Mediators do not analyse the causes of breakdown or provide therapy, but they can facilitate a change of attitude through acknowledging and legitimising anger over failed expectations. The great difficulties and in some cases impossibility of mediating where one partner is unable to let go of the other are discussed further in Chapter 11 on deadlocks and impasse strategies. Mediators may help those who are struggling to hold on to a former partner to recognise irreconcilable needs and look at hypothetical outcomes, whether agreement is reached or not. In some cases, it may be possible to work out interim arrangements. 'Holding arrangements' for children and/or financial arrangements help to recognise the reality of separation without looking for final decisions. Some issues may be left open, at least for a time. Although time does not necessarily bring acceptance, intervals between mediation meetings may be helpful. Gradually, the partner who was clinging on may realise that support is still there and that it is possible to contemplate the future.

5.2.8   Triangulation of third parties

Triangulation is a term derived from family therapy which is used to describe third party involvement in interpersonal conflict. In mediation, it may relate to

---

[11]   See also **11.9** below on one partner's inability to let go of the other.

parents using children as pawns or weapons in their battles with each other. Children become 'triangulated' when they side with one parent against the other as a result of manipulation or in conscious or unconscious moves to protect themselves from being torn apart, or sometimes to protect one parent from the other.[12] New partners, step-parents and other family members may also be triangulated.

As Mathis, a family therapist, suggests,[13] mediators are also potential targets for triangulation by clients who seek to manipulate the mediator or the mediation process. The first party to attend an assessment meeting may predict that the other party will be unwilling to attend. Although this pessimism may be well founded, the second party should have an equal opportunity to consider mediation. The first party may be trying to gain moral superiority or help for their sole benefit. Another family therapist using a systemic approach called this the Battle for Initiative and the Battle for Structure.[14] Mediators experience the battle for control when one party seeks to win their support before the other can do so. Separating couples often look for allies, experts or other third parties to enlist on their side. Mediators need to be aware of the risks of triangulation, especially if they mediate alone. Couples in conflict may embark on a series of moves and counter-moves in which increasing numbers of third parties are liable to become involved. These moves are strategic. As the supporting army of relatives, friends and professionals grows on each side, other people's vested interests may escalate and obscure the original dispute. Mediators need to understand the strategic moves that may be made, so that they can respond with impartial yet engaging strategies of their own. Even at an early stage, there may be moves to take control of the mediation process and its outcome. There may be moves by one party to take control of the new territory in which the 'game' is to be played.

The first move might be called 'Seize the Initiative'. One party finds out about mediation before the other one and puts the other at a disadvantage by knowing more about it, claiming the higher moral ground of 'wanting mediation' and stating that they have been offered, or have already attended, a meeting with the mediator. The second party may be highly suspicious that the mediator is then inevitably biased in the first one's favour, unless the mediator's impartiality is made very explicit. The second move may be called: 'Let me explain the problem'. One party may try to influence the mediator and take control of the process by saying 'Let me explain the problem' or 'Here is the correspondence to give you the background'. Mediators need to explain the principles and ground-rules of mediation clearly and adhere to them from the outset. It is easy to underestimate the skills and time involved in engaging both parties in mediation in a carefully balanced way. It is worth taking this time and trouble, because clear information and careful assessment increase the likelihood of mediation taking place. Family mediators hold a centred and

---

12 See **7.15** below.
13 Mathis 'Couples from Hell: Undifferentiated Spouses in Divorce Mediation' (Jossey-Bass, 1998) 16(1) *Mediation Quarterly* 37–49.
14 Whitaker 'Process Techniques of Family Therapy' (1977) 1 *Family Process* 4.

balanced position between couples who are often feeling overwhelmed and confused. Early research in the UK[15] found that individuals who went to mediation often had difficulty explaining the issues they needed to settle. Many of them said they needed to 'sort everything out'. Arrangements for children, property and financial issues are often tied up in a tangled knot of unsettled questions. Teasing out the knotted threads is an essential part of mediation. Mediation can involve turning the knot around and seeing which threads can be loosened first. The knot may begin to unravel if the threads are teased out gently, whereas tugging at them only tightens the knot.

5.2.9   Entrenched conflict[16]

Even in a harmonious relationship, each partner is likely to have a set of experiences and perceptions that does not coincide with the other's perceptions. In separation and divorce, these different perceptions tend to diverge sharply. Each partner may recount and reinterpret the breakdown of their relationship in a narrative designed to bolster their own self-esteem and enlist other people's support and sympathy. Each partner's version of 'the truth' may sound very convincing, until the other side of the story calls it in question. Friends, relatives and professional advisers who hear only one side of the story may be drawn into making biased judgements that escalate the conflict and drive the couple still further apart.

Experience of loss, and the fear of further loss, can trigger a psychological defence mechanism known as 'splitting', in which each partner's perceptions of what was 'bad' in their relationship, or in their own self, is split off from the 'good' part. All the 'bad' part is then projected on to the other partner. This splitting mechanism generates a self-perpetuating pattern of recriminations and counter-accusations in which each partner's self-image and beliefs come under increasing attack from the other.[17] When people become 'enmeshed'[18] in conflict, they may feel a deep emotional need to keep the fight going, despite the pain and suffering it causes. Couples may become addicted to fighting to the extent that they sabotage any chance of agreement in order to prolong their battle. They want war more than they want peace. The potential for settlement may be very low in such cases, but should not be ruled out because movement in mediation is unpredictable. Some couples who have fought for a long time may have reached a stage where they are tired of fighting and are ready to move on. Their anger needs to be acknowledged and possible ways forward can be explored. Where children are involved, the position and feelings of each child need to be discussed. Parents may be encouraged to look forwards, not only backwards, in considering the impact on their children if the battles continue.

---

[15] Walker, McCarthy and Timms *Mediation: the Making and Remaking of Co-operative Relationships* (Relate Centre for Family Studies, University of Newcastle, 1994).

[16] See also **11.8** below.

[17] Johnston and Campbell *Impasses of Divorce – the Dynamics and Resolution of Family Conflict* (Free Press, 1988).

[18] Kressel, Jaffee, Tuchman, Watson, Deutsch 'A Typology of Divorcing Couples' (1980) 19(2) *Family Process* 101–116.

Children who experience prolonged parental conflict risk suffering emotional and psychological harm that may continue to affect them as adults. For the sake of the children as well as the adults involved, mediators should not exclude 'enmeshed' couples from opportunities for mediation. A carefully planned approach, employing a range of mediation skills and strategies, can lead to a breakthrough between some parents that can bring lasting benefits, for them and for their children.[19]

5.3   ATTACHMENT AND LOSS

Mediators need to understand the multiple losses of separation and divorce and the vital importance for each family member of having anchors that hold them and prevent them being swept away.[20] The theory of attachment and loss provides a means of understanding the devastation of loss and the safety of continuing attachment:

> 'The dimensions of meaning and belonging are at the core of the experience of separation and divorce; they form the arc of relatedness to others, the bonds we all need to live. Divorce transforms and shifts these bonds. Each person feels its meaning differently; belonging is an issue for each. Links within the family, and connections to the broader social realm, can only be recreated over a long period of time. The family needs temporary buttressing while new foundations are laid, new beams put in place.'[21]

Mediation helps couples who are experiencing turmoil and loss to find anchors for themselves and their children, offering help at different stages of separation:

- pre-transition help: opportunities to consider and prepare for a transition that will allow continuity in some areas (co-parenting of children) while managing changes in other areas.

- mid-transition help, working out 'holding arrangements', managing crisis.

- post-transition help, to review arrangements and assist with further adjustment.

Understanding the importance of attachment in personal relationships may be a key to understanding what is happening below the surface of the issues brought to mediation. Attachment is clearly very important where children are involved. The non-resident parent fears losing their relationship and contact with their children, especially if they dread being replaced by a step-parent. For children, the sudden loss of a loved parent may be devastating. If they do not receive enough love and 'buttressing' to cope with this loss, their future development and capacity to form relationships may be affected. Family mediators who work with couples and, indirectly or directly, with children, need to understand the importance of attachment and the effects of losing a person to whom one is

---

[19]   See Chapter 11 below.
[20]   See also **3.9** above on grief and loss.
[21]   Hancock 'The dimensions of meaning and belonging in the process of divorce' (1980) 50(1) *American Journal of Orthopsychiatry* 27.

deeply attached. Although Bowlby's ideas on infant-mother attachment were questioned, his later work[22] and other studies[23] are supported by evidence from clinical research. This evidence shows the importance of secure attachments for children's healthy development and suggests that the quality of parenting a person receives in childhood may affect the quality of care he or she later gives as a parent.[24] Those who experienced insecure attachments to their own parents or who lost a parent through death or divorce may have greater difficulty providing the solid base on which their children in turn rely in becoming securely attached to them. Thus a cycle may be formed in which an insecure pattern of attachment may be passed on from one generation to the next. Bowlby[25] suggested that attachment to parents has become even more crucial for children, because other family members are now more distant or occupied than they used to be. Grandparents and other relatives may be working and less available to the children. Attachment to parents gives children a secure base from which to begin exploring the world around them. As they get older, children show progressively less attachment behaviour and more exploring behaviour. Two types of behaviour indicative of insecure attachment in infancy are avoidance behaviour and clinging. Clinging may seem the opposite of avoidance, but it is also evidence of insecure attachment.[26] Clinging children have learnt to use frequent and intense attachment behaviour to keep reassuring themselves of their mother's (or father's) availability.

Clinical studies suggest that both clinging and avoidance behaviour is liable to persist in adolescence and adulthood. Whereas these patterns may have served a useful function in childhood, they can have the opposite effect in adult life. The excessively clinging partner may find that being very possessive of the other partner may result in rejection – the very result that the clinging was intended to prevent. Fear of rejection intensifies the clinging and thus the cycle of clinging/rejection/tighter clinging is repeated. One partner's inability to let go of the other, long after their relationship has effectively ended, is often a feature of a very difficult divorce. In contrast, an independent person who appears not to want close attachments may be left in isolation, because other people interpret the lack of signs of affection as indifference. Over-dependence and careful avoidance of dependence may be learnt responses to insecure attachments in childhood. When these behavioural patterns continue in adult life, they impair a person's ability to cope with further loss and change. Problems in coping with loss and change have been found to be precipitating factors in a number of mental illnesses. For example, losing one's mother before the age of eleven is associated with increased vulnerability to depression following other critical life events.[27] One reason for the particularly traumatic effect of losing a deeply

---

[22]   Bowlby 'Loss: Sadness and Depression' (Hogarth Press 1980) 3 *Attachment and Loss*.
[23]   Ainsworth 'Attachment: Retrospect and Prospect' in Murray Parkes and Stevenson-Hinde (eds) *The Place of Attachment in Human Behaviour* (Tavistock, 1982), pp 3–30.
[24]   Murray Parkes *Bereavement* (Tavistock, 1972).
[25]   Bowlby 'Loss: Sadness and Depression' (Hogarth Press 1980) 3 *Attachment and Loss*.
[26]   Ainsworth 'Attachment: Retrospect and Prospect' in Murray Parkes and Stevenson-Hinde (eds) *The Place of Attachment in Human Behaviour* (Tavistock, 1982). pp 3–30.
[27]   Brown 'Early Loss and Depression' in Murray Parkes and Stevenson-Hinde (eds) *The Place of Attachment in Human Behaviour* (Tavistock. 1982), pp 232–268.

loved partner or parent is that this person is often the very attachment figure to whom the bereaved one would normally turn for support in a time of crisis. A bereaved person often feels that the whole sense or meaning of life has been lost as well: '*My whole world has been turned upside down.*' Those whose early relationships were relatively secure tend, after a period of grieving, to be able to resume normal life and can form new attachments, whereas those who had insecure or permanently broken early relationships are more likely to show pathological reactions to loss. They may find it very difficult to form and maintain lasting attachments that allow both intimacy and space within the relationship.

Essential elements in helping people to cope with loss and avoid pathological or chronic grieving are recognition of the psychological need to grieve and giving reassurance to grieving people that their overwhelming and fluctuating emotions are normal, not abnormal. Acknowledging the normality of these feelings helps parents to cope with their own and their children's reactions, recognising that they may need to give extra reassurance to a child who is anxiously clinging and demanding extra attention, or to comfort a child who seems detached and remote. One of the most widely known theories of grief is the Kübler-Ross[28] model of the stages of grieving that a bereaved person traverses: denial, anger, bargaining, depression and acceptance. The MIAMs researchers referred to this model to demonstrate the varying states of emotional readiness for mediation presented by clients.[29] However, as Emery and Italian colleagues[30] have pointed out, a key difference between loss of the partner through death and loss through separation and divorce is that instead of moving through the stages from denial to acceptance in a linear way, as a bereaved person may do, a separated individual tends to swing between these stages, sometimes uncontrollably. This *cyclical model of grieving* is unpredictable. In the course of a mediation session, both partners may swing between all these stages in rapid and exhausting succession. Some get stuck at one stage, with the needle of their emotional compass pointing only in one direction, while others have outbursts of anger and distress, yet manage to reset their compass to negotiating and accepting before they finish the session.[31]

Mediators need to understand the importance of attachment and loss even though they are not providing counselling or therapy. They need to be aware of and able to acknowledge the pain that may be expressed. Mediators also need to consider whether there is need for individual counselling or therapy. Understanding the harmful effects of loss is helpful in working with parents to prevent unnecessary losses that they do not want to happen. Cycles do not repeat themselves inexorably. Parents may alter their perceptions and

---

[28] Kübler-Ross *On Death and Dying* (Macmillan, 1969).

[29] Bloch, McLeod and Tooms *Mediation Information and Assessment Meetings (MIAMs) and mediation in private law disputes – Qualitative research findings* (Ministry of Justice Analytical Series, 2014), p 23.

[30] Emery, Margola, Gennari and Cigoli 'Emotionally Informed Mediation: processing grief' in Cigoli and Gennari (eds) *Close relationships and community psychology: an international perspective* (FrancoAngeli, 2010).

[31] See Chapter 11 below.

expectations of each other and of themselves. Learnt behaviour and communication patterns may change. It may be possible to manage a painful loss with increased strength and go on to form new and lasting relationships. Mediators need optimism, as well as empathy and understanding, to provide a temporary life-raft for parents who are experiencing loss, to help them support their children and avoid further loss for their children and themselves. Examples of mediating with parents during these difficult and painful transitions are included in later chapters.

5.4   NAVIGATING THROUGH MEDIATION BY APS

As discussed in Chapter 3, each partner's emotional state needs to be taken into account in assessing the suitability of mediation. The assessment meeting is an essential prelude to the mediation process, both in formal terms and in building rapport and trust with each participant and gaining commitment to mediation. Situations involving domestic abuse, high levels of conflict and distress and/or significant power imbalances may be unsuitable for standard mediation using a sole mediator, but other models, such as gender-balanced co-mediation, shuttling and caucusing may be considered in some cases. If there are special needs, one or more mutually acceptable third parties may need to be brought into the process. The mediation model needs to be designed for the participants in their particular circumstances, drawing from the mediator's ability to adapt the process to cater for different kinds and levels of conflict, subject to the resources available.[32]

Instead of navigating by GPS (global positioning system), mediators navigate by APS: Assessment, Planning and Skills. These are the key reference points in navigating from the assessment meeting through to conclusion of the mediation process. While there are consecutive phases or stages to traverse, it is essential to combine assessment, planning and skills in each phase. Skills are needed in initial assessment meetings and throughout the process, while assessment (of needs, issues, concerns and risks) is not a separate task that is concluded before mediation begins. Assessment and re-assessment need to be continuous, because situations and reactions can fluctuate during a mediation and fresh difficulties or risks may arise. Planning begins in initial meetings, when the mediator may offer a model or approach that is designed with and for the participants in their particular circumstances – tailor-made, rather than 'off-the-peg'. Further planning is needed for each successive mediation session. The acronym APS – Assessment, Planning, Skills – may be a useful tag in helping mediators to navigate through an often turbulent process, although lovers of Bach may prefer to think of Bach's Three-Part Invention No 5 in E flat major, BWV 791, in which movement through the three parts is both disciplined and creative.

Structured mediation[33] consists of a series of stages to identify issues, gather information, explore options and work towards reaching agreement, working

---

[32]   See Chapter 4 above.
[33]   See **2.3** above.

at a pace that both participants can manage. Explaining these stages helps to reduce anxieties and unrealistic expectations of getting everything settled in a single session. Whether mediation consists of a one-off meeting or a series of meetings over a period of time, there is a beginning, middle and end. Mediators are responsible for managing beginnings, middles and endings as clearly and constructively as possible.

The six stages of mediation referred to in Chapter 2,[34] commonly used in a structured, problem-solving approach, may be extended to twelve stages in family mediation. After the opening stages, the sequence can be varied according to participants' needs and priorities. The following twelve-stage model, developed independently from Moore's twelve-stage model,[35] shows interesting parallels between the two, although Moore's stages are not designed specifically for family mediation. Family mediators, in particular, should encourage flexible movement, rather than following a prescribed sequence as though it were a set text or musical score. See below.

---

[34] Gulliver, P *Disputes and Negotiations* (Academic Press, 1979).
[35] Moore *The Mediation Process* (Jossey-Bass, 1986), pp 32–33.

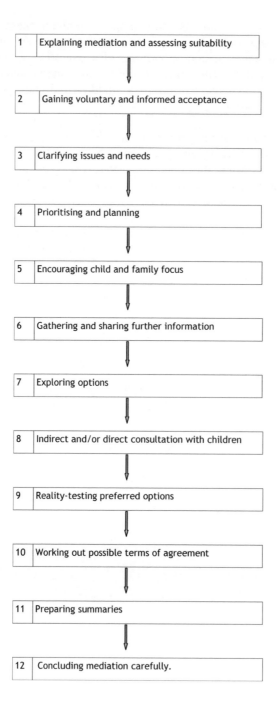

1	Explaining mediation and assessing suitability
2	Gaining voluntary and informed acceptance
3	Clarifying issues and needs
4	Prioritising and planning
5	Encouraging child and family focus
6	Gathering and sharing further information
7	Exploring options
8	Indirect and/or direct consultation with children
9	Reality-testing preferred options
10	Working out possible terms of agreement
11	Preparing summaries
12	Concluding mediation carefully.

5.4.1 Stages 1 and 2: explaining mediation and gaining voluntary and informed acceptance

These opening stages were considered in Chapter 3. The objectives, principles and conditions of mediation are explained at initial information and assessment meetings, when each party's concerns and willingness to accept mediation are explored. Once it has been established that mediation is suitable and that both parties understand its objectives and terms and are willing to take part, they are invited to sign the Agreement to Mediate[36] before mediation can proceed. Signing the Agreement to Mediate has symbolic as well as practical significance in confirming their acceptance of mediation and willingness to work together. The mediator retains a copy of the Agreement signed by them both. This signed copy might be needed if the confidentiality of mediation is questioned at a later stage or if a complaint is raised by a participant which the Agreement to Mediate could show to be unfounded.

5.4.2 Stage 3: clarifying issues and needs

The issues that need to be resolved and each party's main concerns should have been established to some extent at the information and assessment meeting. These issues and concerns need to be revisited and clarified at the first mediation meeting. Circumstances may have changed. Each participant needs to explain matters from their point of view and feel heard, but this does not work well if they have free rein to state opposing positions in an aggressive and challenging manner. If the mediator asks warmly: 'So, Maureen, would you like to explain what brings you to mediation and then I'll ask you the same question, Chris', Maureen may seize the opportunity to explain that Chris has left her to live with Sharon and he isn't giving her any money and she can't pay the rent and the children are so upset they don't want to see him and only last week he said … and then she said … Maureen may need to vent her feelings, but if the mediator lets her rant at Chris, he is likely to become increasingly angry and may walk out. This could be the end of the mediation when it has barely begun. Rather than letting one participant take the floor, an open question may be put to each of them in turn, such as 'Maureen/Chris, what would you like to achieve at this meeting?' or 'What is your main priority at the moment?' Focused questions of this kind help to reframe differences into needs – there may be an immediate practical need or a need for reassurance. Each partner's responses provide information on matters that need to be settled and give indications of urgency or priority. Couples are often so preoccupied by their disagreements that they overlook areas of fundamental agreement. Setting the agenda for mediation begins in preliminary assessment meetings and continues in an ongoing dialogue with both partners together. Listing concrete issues provides the focus for discussions but risks polarising positions if they are presented too starkly. To help participants move from their positions to their needs, it may be helpful to pose questions such as 'What do you need to work

---

[36] See Sample Agreement to Mediate, Appendix E below.

out in mediation?' before, as well as during, the first session, to encourage mindfulness that this is a joint undertaking.

The order in which questions are put to participants needs to alternate, so that neither partner is invariably responding to what the other has just said. Varying the order is important to show the mediator's balanced attention and impartiality and to avoid giving too much space to any participant (including the mediator!). To start with, it may be helpful to put an initial question to the more hesitant or reluctant party, rather than to the one who seems dominant or more confident. In the example above, the mediator notices that Maureen is keen to do most of the talking, while Chris seems sullen and withdrawn. Chris might therefore be asked what he thinks needs to be settled, first of all. Then Maureen may be asked the same. Sometimes it is useful to ask for headings first, with fuller discussion to follow. The way in which questions are phrased by the mediator influence the answers that are given.[37] It is very important, especially in the opening stages, for mediators to ask appropriate questions and to phrase them with care. It may be possible to underline a mutual wish to settle issues by agreement if possible, despite different points of view: 'You both say your main concern is to work out arrangements for your children (and financial arrangements). Your objectives fit very well with the aims of mediation'. Mediators need to acknowledge feelings of anger, stress and insecurity, keeping eye contact with both partners, smiling when appropriate and talking with them both in a calm and friendly way.[38]

5.4.3   Stage 4: prioritising and planning

Very often, both partners raise the same issues but they do not necessarily share the same priorities. A mother living with the children in the family home may be in urgent need of child support, whereas the father's priority may be contact with his children. If there are competing priorities that each parent needs time for in the first meeting, the time to be allotted to each issue can be divided equally, leaving time for summarising, planning the next steps and listing tasks to be undertaken. Alternatively, it may be agreed to discuss certain issues at the first meeting and others at the following meeting, when further information can be made available. Unproductive arguments can be pre-empted by saying 'With regard to child support, I can give you some general information but it would help a lot if each of you could fill in the questionnaire I will give you, to provide details of your income and monthly outgoings, and bring your completed form to the next meeting so that we can see how each of you is managing at the moment – or not managing – and look at possible options.'

It may also be helpful to list issues needing attention on the flip-chart,[39] to show participants that they have been heard and to provide a common focus. There may be areas of agreement that help to put disagreements into a broader

---

[37]   See Chapter 6 below.
[38]   See **5.7.1** below on acknowledgement.
[39]   See Chapter 9 below.

perspective. Urgency or priority need to be recognised. If the flip-chart is used, colours or asterisks can be used to highlight questions and show urgency.

5.4.4 Stage 5: encouraging child and family focus

Many parents want matters concerning their children to take priority over financial or other issues. Arrangements for children may be needed urgently. Working out interim arrangements helps to provide reassurance and increase motivation to continue. Most parents want their children to maintain their relationship with them both. They may disagree, however, over the frequency and length of visits and over the involvement of third parties. Further sessions are likely to be needed to gather and share information concerning each child, to consider each child's feelings and needs and explore possible arrangements. These matters lie at the heart of mediation and are discussed in Chapters 7 and 8.

5.4.5 Stage 6: gathering and sharing further information

Gathering and sharing financial information is an essential prerequisite before proposals for settlement are considered. A financial questionnaire needs to be completed by each participant and copies of their completed forms are then provided to them both. Supporting documents are also needed. The mediator goes through the completed forms and documents systematically with both partners and seeks to fill in gaps, clarify discrepancies and generally help them both to gain a full understanding of their financial situation and needs. Participants may be asked to complete schedules of their current and/or projected average monthly expenditure and to check their borrowing capacity. Methods and skills to gather and share financial information are the subject of Chapter 9.

5.4.6 Stage 7: exploring options

Possible options for settlement and their potential benefits and disadvantages need to be identified. Further information may be requested and participants may need to take legal and/or financial advice before going any further. An interim note of mediation or interim summary may assist them to take advice on possible options and how a settlement might be structured.

5.4.7 Stage 8: indirect and/or direct consultation with children

Children need to understand and co-operate with decisions and arrangements if they are to work well in practice. Parents may need to discuss when and how they are going to explain their arrangements to their children and give them the reassurances they need. They also need to consider whether, and if so in what way, their children should have the opportunity to be consulted directly, either in mediation or in some other way.[40]

5.4.8   Stage 9: reality-testing preferred options

Children's needs, feelings and views need to be taken into account in exploring and reality-testing possible arrangements. Research findings referred to in Chapter 13 show the importance of checking the longer-term implications of a proposed financial settlement to make sure that neither parent is likely to find themselves lacking sufficient means to support themselves and the children.

5.4.9   Stage 10: working out possible terms of agreement

Terms of agreement may be limited to arrangements for children or may cover detailed proposals for a full and final settlement on all issues as a basis for a consent order in divorce proceedings. Mediators need a range of skills to address and overcome blocks to agreement. Power imbalances within or outside the mediation are considered in Chapter 10, while problems of 'stuckness' and entrenched positions are considered in Chapter 11.

5.4.10   Stage 11: preparing written summaries

The confidential and legally privileged mediation summary or Memorandum of Understanding sets out proposals for settlement, whereas financial information is summarised in an 'open' Financial Statement, with supporting documents attached. Participants are invited to confirm the accuracy of both summaries before taking them to legal advisers to formalise arrangements.[41]

5.4.11   Stage 12: concluding mediation

Even where mediation ends without any agreement, it has not necessarily failed because issues have generally been clarified and differences may have been narrowed. Participants should have gained a better understanding of their options and possible ways forward. The issues may be resolved more quickly if the dispute is taken to court.

5.5   LIMITATIONS OF A RIGID STRUCTURE

Although it may be necessary to move systematically from one stage to the next, adhering to a rigid sequence has limitations that may impede progress:

- It may be necessary to go back to a previous stage, for example where there is reluctance or hesitation to move forwards.

---

[40]   See Chapter 8 below.
[41]   See Chapter 12 below.

- Sometimes a couple will benefit from 'fast forwarding', where they both want to run through an outline agreement before considering other possible options.

- Agreement may not be the couple's main goal. There can be other more important goals, such as establishing or re-establishing communication. Kelly[42] found that a substantial proportion of mediation users were pleased with the process although they did not reach agreement, because it brought other benefits.

- Mediators may focus on concrete issues and avoid more difficult emotional or relationship issues which block real progress.

- Mediators may try to drive participants forwards in a direction that neither of them wants.

- Participants may find it hard to explain their needs if the mediator moves briskly from one stage to the next.

- Going part of the way is enough for some couples. They may not be ready to go any further. This does not make it a 'failed mediation'.

Structured and 'transformative' approaches[43] need not be mutually exclusive. Mediators may combine them in a flexible structure in which the sequence of stages and pace of progression can be varied.

5.6   CIRCULAR MOVEMENT IN MEDIATION

Some couples move steadily forwards in mediation towards a mutually satisfactory outcome. Others seem more inclined to remain in the past or even to move backwards. They may be so stuck in their failed relationship that they need to keep going over the hurts and wrongs they have suffered. These couples are much harder to work with and they need more skills from the mediator. If they achieve a few steps forward, a real or imagined threat or accusation may be all it takes to throw them backwards again. Listing their priorities on the flip-chart is helpful, as turning to the flip-chart can be a way of reminding them of their stated objectives ('Do you think this ties in with what you were wanting for the children, Sam?' or 'Would it help if we have another look at the information you have provided, Naomi, before ruling out that option?').

Forward and backward movements in mediation are very common. These movements are not just linear – very often they are circular, following a familiar – in both senses – circular path. Discussions or accusations may go round and round without getting anywhere – the gerbil wheel problem. Mediators try to help participants to get off their particular gerbil wheel, when they are willing to do so. If the mediator puts a question to each participant in turn, they tend to respond to the mediator, without talking to each other. Mediators encourage couples talk to each other – sometimes for the first time after a long period of

---

42   Kelly, 'Mediated and Adversarial Divorce: Respondents' Perceptions of their Processes and Outcomes' (1989) 24 *Mediation Quarterly* 71–88.
43   See Chapter 2 above.

not talking. One way of facilitating their communication is to ask one of them to explain a particular concern to the other, rather than to the mediator: 'Philip, it might help if you could explain to Margaret how you see...' This approach enables discussions to *converge*, instead of *polarising*. In the diagram below, the mediator's linear approach shows communication between the mediator and each partner separately, but not between the couple themselves. In the converging, circular approach, communication moves more freely between the participants and the mediator.

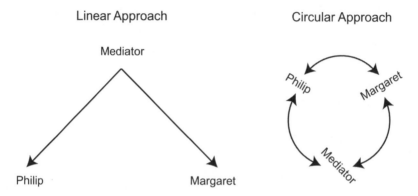

5.7 KEY SKILLS IN THE OPENING STAGES

Although needed throughout the process, there are key skills of critical importance in the opening stages, to help participants engage without pressure or further distress and to enable the mediation to progress constructively. These skills include acknowledging, asking helpful questions, conflict management, reframing and refocusing, time management and, in general, the combination of process, interpersonal and problem-solving skills. The mediator seeks to control tempo and volume, enabling voices to be heard and managing a sequence of movements.

5.7.1 Acknowledging feelings and concerns

What happens when one is angry? Physically, there is an increase in adrenalin, the heart rate quickens and blood pressure rises. Breathing quickens and muscles are tensed. It is hard to listen when one is angry. Participants may need to express anger before they are able to hear each other. Mediators should acknowledge anger explicitly, rather than trying to stifle it: 'I understand that you are both feeling very raw and angry at the moment'. As suggested above, it may help to observe that feeling very angry in these situations is entirely natural and normal. Acknowledging anger and referring to it in a normalising and mutualising way may make it less necessary for couples to show their anger in aggressive statements and loud voices. The mediator needs to calm participants after an angry outburst, to help them to move on, in spite of their anger: 'I know it's very difficult to talk about the house being sold, when it's your home and the children's home too, and you are both feeling so stressed. But can we look at what options there may be and how they would work?'

Acknowledging participants' feelings and concerns is one of the mediator's most important skills. Feelings should be acknowledged with empathy and as far as possible in a mutualising way: 'So you are both feeling very stressed ... concerned'. Strong emotions need to be named. 'I can see that you are both feeling very angry at the moment ... I can see that you are both extremely stressed ... It's very difficult to cope with the children's distress, as well as your own....' It takes a big effort to come to mediation and it may be very difficult to reach joint decisions. Recognising that partners have difficulties communicating with one another or that communication has broken down completely may be stating the obvious, yet it can have a calming effect, because the acknowledgement is accurate, non-judgmental and empathetic. Acknow-ledgements need to be phrased as 'I can see that ...' or 'I am hearing that ...' and not as 'I understand ...', because a mediator who claims to understand may be sharply rebuked, whereas not having heard accurately may be forgiven. The use of different types of question and the phrasing and timing of questions are important skills that are considered in Chapter 6 on communication in mediation.

5.7.2 Conflict management

Managing high levels of conflict and emotion in mediation is very challenging. Hugh McIsaac,[44] writing from his long experience as director of family court services and conciliation in Los Angeles County Superior Court, identified parents who seem to need conflict in order to survive as the most intractable and difficult to work with. Both parents are involved in an 'ongoing emotional morass'[45] and children who become caught in this morass suffer a great deal. Couples who are enmeshed in conflict[46] drain professional resources and may seek to use mediation as another battle-ground. Mathis[47] identified 'emotionally attached, undifferentiated couples' who fight, negotiate and renegotiate endlessly. Sclater and Richards[48] suggest that the roots of entrenched conflict may lie in earlier life experiences of loss, rejection and unfulfilled attachment.

Some couples come to mediation determined to score points over each other. 'We are so patterned in our lives to think of conflict as a contest that life becomes a big scoreboard'.[49] Arguing and blaming test the mediator's ability to

---

[44] McIsaac 'Towards a Classification of Child Custody Disputes: an Application of Family Systems Theory' (1986/7) 14/15 *Mediation Quarterly* 39–50.

[45] Ibid, p 48.

[46] Kressel et al 'Typology of Divorcing Couples' (1980) 19(2) *Family Process* 101–116; see **5.2.9** above and Chapter 11 below on mediating with enmeshed couples.

[47] Mathis 'Couples from Hell: Undifferentiated Spouses in Divorce Mediation' (Jossey-Bass, 1998) 16(1) *Mediation Quarterly* 37–49.

[48] Sclater and Richards 'How Adults Cope with Divorce – Strategies for Survival' [1995] Fam Law 143.

[49] Crum *The Magic of Conflict* (Touchstone 1987), p 37.

maintain control. Ground-rules may be needed to manage discussions and are often accepted with relief. It is the mediator's responsibility to make sure that rules are agreed and adhered to. If rapport is established with each participant in initial meetings, the mediator can intervene more easily when an angry outburst turns into a tirade. The mediator needs to intervene in an empathetic but firm way, so that ground-rules are kept and each participant has a chance to speak, knowing that the mediator will control attacks and interruptions. Point scoring and verbal attacks need to be curtailed (see Chapter 10 on verbal goading and one-upmanship tactics in mediation). Mediators also need to be firm in outlawing offensive or inflammatory language. 'Look, sorry, Barry/Brenda, I'm not going to be able to help you unless we all agree that certain language cannot be used here – is that OK?' Mediation skills and techniques in mediating with enmeshed couples are considered further in Chapter 11.

5.7.3   Ground-rules

Mediators do not always set ground-rules at the outset. It may be helpful to ask participants if they would like to suggest some ground-rules, or for the mediator to propose them, if necessary. Most participants appreciate knowing that there are certain ground-rules and when conflict is high, they are essential. Ground-rules are likely to include:

- Equal opportunities for each participant to explain their views and concerns.
- Participants listening to each other without interrupting, even if they disagree.
- The mediator discourages fault finding and blaming: the focus is on ways of reaching settlement.
- Respect: discussions need to be civilised and differences need to be understood.
- Participants are asked not to interrupt each other, but the mediator may interrupt if necessary, to keep discussions on track. There may be a way of saying this which can raise a smile: 'I know it seems unfair that you are asked not to interrupt each other, but I am allowed to interrupt you! If I do interrupt at all – and I may not need to – it would be to help us keep on track and to use time as well as possible. Time runs away fast, so may we move on to … ?'.
- Focus on the present and future, more than on the past.

Ground-rules are discussed further in Chapter 10 at **10.8** as a means of managing power imbalances.

5.7.4 Reframing and refocusing

Conflict management does not mean suppressing negative outbursts. There may be opportunities to pick up a position and reframe it.[50] 'So, Julie, you disagree strongly about overnight stays but you said you think it's important for the children to go on seeing their father?' 'So, Steve, you are saying you want your share of the house but you appreciate that Julie says she supports your relationship with the children?'

These opportunities need to be grasped quickly, because when anger is open and direct, arguments escalate fast. Mediators need to be quick and confident in their use of conflict management skills, including empathetic but firm control, acknowledging, reframing and refocusing. Pragmatic questions such as 'So, what do you think might help?' can elicit a simple suggestion that has not been put forward before, because the couple were too angry to think about anything else. Future-focused questions may be useful, such as:

> 'How long do you think it will take the two of you to reach some kind of settlement/agree arrangements for your children?'

> 'When your children are older and are asked what this period of their lives was like, what do you think they will say?'

When parents are caught up in blame and recriminations, the ecogram can be used to refocus them on their children's feelings and needs. The use of strategies such as caucusing is discussed further in Chapter 10 on deadlocks and impasses. However, some intractable disputes remain intractable. Cantwell[51] points out that there may be serious child welfare concerns, including risks of long-term emotional harm to children. Intractable disputes may need Cafcass and the court, rather than mediation. There may also be need for referral for therapy or psychiatric assessment.

5.7.5 Time management

> 'The speed of a harmonic progression, just like the speed of a political process, can determine its effectiveness and ultimately the reality it seeks to influence'.[52]

Barenboim suggests that the Oslo peace process in the conflict between Israel and Palestine was doomed to fail because of faulty time management. In his view, the preparation was too hasty and the process itself too slow and frequently interrupted. Mediators need to manage pace and tempo in conducting mediation sessions. In practical terms, they need a clock in their line of vision and they may need to draw attention to the passing of time: 'I see we are already halfway through the time for today's appointment. Do you think we

---

50   See **2.5** and **2.7** above on reframing and **6.16** below.
51   Cantwell 'Battling Parents: are they getting the right treatment?' [2007] Fam Law 743–748.
52   Barenboim *Everything is Connected – The Power of Music* (Weidenfeld and Nicolson, 2008), p 15.

should move on to talking about ... ?' Or 'I'm aware we are running out of time for today's meeting, so shall we use the last quarter of an hour to recap where we have got to and to discuss whether you would like to arrange another meeting?'

Sessions of an hour and a half are commonly used because an hour may be too short and two hours too long and exhausting for most couples. It is important to plan time so that key questions and issues are addressed, and unwise to ask in the last five minutes: 'Is there anything else you wanted to discuss today?' Participants need to know that times of meetings will be kept: extending time should be resisted because time boundaries have symbolic as well as practical importance. There are usually unresolved issues to come back to. The mediator may say: 'Yes, it really is important that you've mentioned that and it does sound as though it needs full discussion, but unfortunately there isn't enough time left today. Shall we start with this issue next time, if you both think it should have priority?' Or 'I realise we haven't had time today to cover everything that is concerning you. If there are things you haven't had time to raise yet, or which occur to you when you get home, could you make a note of them, so that you can raise them next time we meet?' This helps to reduce frustration at the end of a session and encourages participants to reflect between sessions. Many couples come to the second meeting having reflected further: some have met and talked together. The atmosphere in the second session is often strikingly different from the first. The date and time of the following session should be agreed with both participants before they leave. If there is substantial financial information to collect, an interval of a month may be needed. But if the couple is in crisis and the level of conflict is high, it may help to contain the crisis if a meeting is arranged for the following week.

5.8   TASKS IN THE OPENING STAGES OF MEDIATION

Tasks	Example of use	Aims
Creating a forum and positive atmosphere	Friendly welcome	To put people at ease, enable them to engage in dialogue
Explaining, informing	'Shall I explain how I can help you both deal with this question?'	To help people reach informed decisions and avoid being pressurised into agreement
Questioning	Choice of question form, how? what if? etc	To understand the issues better, focus on ways forward
Listening	Mediator's eye contact, facial expression, posture, tone of voice	To show full attention is being given to what is being said
Acknowledging	'I can see that you are finding it hard to ...'	To help people feel heard and understood

Tasks	Example of use	Aims
Clarifying	'Could you say more about ... explain what you mean by ...'	To check understanding and encourage fuller explanation
Managing conflict without suppressing it	'Could you just let Tony finish and then I'll ask ...'	Controlling interruptions, balancing the discussion
Prioritising	'Which is the most important issue for you at the moment?'	To focus on immediate issues, agree the ordering of issues
Balancing	Putting questions to each participant in turn	To manage power imbalances, maintain impartiality
Building trust	'Could you reassure Sally that you will ...'	To restore or maintain sufficient trust that the other party can be relied on
Managing pace	'Should we spend more time on the question you raised about ...?'	To work at a pace both parties can cope with
Summarising	'Shall we recap on the things you are each going to find out before our next meeting?'	To be clear about the next steps and encourage participants to take charge themselves

5.9 COMBINING PROCESS, PERSONAL AND PROBLEM-SOLVING SKILLS

The table below lists skills that mediators need to combine and use selectively, depending on the dynamics and level of conflict. Mediators have different personal styles, as well as different methods of working. Many mediators are efficient problem-solvers who maintain the pace from one stage to the next. They may however lose participants if they do not provide enough warmth and acknowledgement of feelings. Mediators who have strong interpersonal skills may be less comfortable gathering financial information and analysing figures. Effective mediators need to integrate process management, interpersonal and problem-solving skills, varying the blend at critical points to manage 'surface tension effects' and facilitate forward movement.

PROCESS SKILLS	INTERPERSONAL SKILLS	PROBLEM-SOLVING SKILLS
Intake assessment	Engaging with participants	Defining issues
Setting up the first session	Active listening	Questioning and exploring

PROCESS SKILLS	INTERPERSONAL SKILLS	PROBLEM-SOLVING SKILLS
Intake assessment	Engaging with participants	Defining issues
Explaining process and aims	Acknowledging feelings	Prioritising
The Agreement to Mediate	Mutualising concerns	Gathering, giving information
Structuring the process	Managing conflict	Analysing financial information
Maintaining ground-rules	Easing communication	Exploring options
Time management	Focusing on children	Future focus
Referral for professional advice	Managing power imbalances	Brain-storming
Managing pace of negotiations	Reframing	Narrowing gaps and negotiating
Producing written summaries	Reality testing	Anticipating and pre-empting
Concluding process	Ending with care, leaving the door open for re-referral	Seeking proposals for interim/final settlement

The choice of intervention at a particular moment is sometimes compared to using a box of tools: a spirit-level to check for good balance, a finely pointed chisel to probe delicately for further information or a plane to smooth out differences! Mediating involves far more, however, than picking up tools and mediation training is not simply the addition of a skills-sets for dispute resolution to existing qualifications.[53] The following chapter on communication will hopefully demonstrate that professional knowledge, imagination and creativity are needed, as well as craftsmanship.

5.10   MEDIATING STEP BY STEP

Apprehension ...

Fear ...

---

[53]   See Chapter 14 below on becoming a mediator.

Will he be angry? Or cold?
I feel sick.
I'll agree to anything. And get out.

Well, we spoke.
He's not insisting we sell the house.
We agreed what we'll say to Harry and Chloe.
And what we won't say.

We met for coffee first.
We talked summer holidays.
And birthdays.
But not Christmas.
I can't.

The house is sorted now, and his pension.
He'll come to Harry's Sports Day and Chloe's concert.
So much remains unsaid.
But we laughed about the rabbit.
'Parents are forever', they said.

CHAPTER 6

COMMUNICATION SKILLS IN MEDIATION

'And so each venture
Is a new beginning, a raid on the inarticulate
With shabby equipment always deteriorating
In the general mess of imprecision of feeling,
Undisciplined squads of emotion ...'[1]

'I was much further out than you thought
And not waving but drowning.'[2]

CONTENTS

---

[1]   T S Eliot 'East Coker' in *Four Quartets* (Faber, 1959), pp 30–31.
[2]   Stevie Smith *Selected Poems* (Penguin Books, 1978), p 167.

6.1 COMMUNICATION

Family conflict is rooted in differences between the needs, demands and perceptions of individual family members and also between the needs and perceptions of 'old' and 'new' family systems. There may also be conflict between family members and their social environment. A great deal of conflict is exacerbated or caused by lack of communication or by dysfunctional communication. Effective communication is necessary for conflict management and for participative decision-making. Improving communication between family members is therefore of the greatest importance in increasing their mutual understanding of each other. Greater understanding and better communication between family members facilitate informed decisions and arrangements. Decisions and arrangements that are considered and planned jointly are more likely to work harmoniously for the family as a whole.

The essence of mediation is communication. Different means of communication therefore need special attention in mediation. There can be language without communication and communication without language. Our perceptions of other people and the outside world are determined by a number of filters, including experience, beliefs and language. Depending on the meanings that are conveyed and the ways in which they are interpreted, language has great power to arouse feelings and evoke images. Words can confuse or clarify, infuriate or soothe. The words we use have layers of associations – personal, cultural, conscious and unconscious. These associations influence the way we see the world around us and condition our responses to people and events. We convey ideas through language and use it to organise our thoughts and shape them into messages. Dysfunctional communication erodes relationships. It is both a cause and effect of relationship breakdown. Couples who come to mediation have frequently become stuck in dysfunctional patterns of communication. They often cannot sustain a dialogue on their own because their arguments are too heavily freighted with emotions and accusations. Simply observing that they have problems communicating with one other can bring a measure of relief for several reasons. First, the mediator's observation shows understanding and empathy, secondly, both partners generally agree with it and thirdly, it recognises a shared problem without implying responsibility or blame. Exchanges between couples in mediation are often part of a familiar script in their personal drama. Both partners know the script and a cue from one of them triggers the replay of an angry scene in front of the mediator – a new audience whose sympathy each of them hopes to engage. Mediators need to be good listeners as well as good communicators. They need to listen sensitively with what John Haynes called a 'third ear' to pick up unspoken messages. Timely interventions from the mediator can help to shift the script in a different direction. With the mediator's involvement the dialogue becomes a 'trialogue' in which the mediator elicits responses from both participants and organises their communications in more manageable ways.

6.2   ACTIVE LISTENING AND CENTRED POSTURE

Mediators show that they are listening actively through their posture, facial expression and eye contact, as well as through their words. The mediator's posture needs to convey ease and attentiveness, neither leaning forward intrusively nor too relaxed. The Japanese martial art of Aikido, which is concerned with responding to aggression rather than instigating attack, emphasises the importance of a stable and well balanced posture in dealing with conflict and stress. A well-balanced and centred body position enables the mind to move freely. A mediator who is well centred can keep eye contact with both partners, glancing from one to the other to see how each is reacting and noting their posture and body language. Some mediators make non-committal noises of the 'mm' or 'yes, I see' variety. Others prefer to listen quietly. It is essential to show equal attention and empathy and to avoid giving more attention to one participant than another. Daniel Barenboim[3] stresses the importance of *thoughtful listening*: 'Listening is hearing with thought, much in the same way as feeling is emotion with thought.'

6.3   NON-VERBAL COMMUNICATION

Verbal communication may be considered the core of mediation, but non-verbal communication is very significant. In a large study involving forty different cultures, Morris[4] identified twenty common gestures that had a different meaning in each culture. Shaking one's head can mean 'no' in some cultures and 'yes' in others.

Early research on non-verbal communication found that in a presentation before a group of people, 55% of the impact was determined by body language (posture, gestures and eye contact), 38% by tone of voice and only 7% by the content of the presentation.[5] Mediators need to be alert to participants' body language and aware of non-verbal messages that may be passing between them. The mediator's own body language – eye contact, facial expression, gestures, seating position – also conveys messages to participants that the mediator needs to be aware of giving.[6] Hands can be used to emphasise even-handedness and balance, but too much hand movement may be distracting. A warm smile to both participants at an opportune time can help them to feel welcome and more relaxed, whereas a mediator who shows no warmth of expression and only fleeting eye contact is likely to increase the tension in the room. Smiling invites a smile in response. Rapport is created as much through body language and tone of voice as through words.

---

3   Barenboim *Everything is Connected – The Power of Music* (Weidenfeld and Nicolson, 2008), p 37.
4   Morris *Bodytalk: the Meaning of Human Gestures* (Crown Trade Paperbacks, 1995).
5   Mehrabian and Ferris 'Inference of Attitudes from Non-verbal Communication in Two Channels' (1967) 31 *Journal of Counselling Psychology* 248–252.
6   See Chapter 14 below.

Mediators look for eye contact as a sign of listening and responsiveness but need to be aware that in some Asian and black families, eye contact with a person seen as an authority figure may be considered disrespectful. It is also possible that a person who has difficulty with eye contact could be on the autistic spectrum. A father in mediation was described by the mother as seemingly unable to understand or respond to the social and emotional difficulties of their son, who had been diagnosed with Asperger's Syndrome. Theoretically, it was possible that the father was suffering from the same condition as his son. Although mediators are not equipped to make diagnoses, asking the father about responding to other people's feelings might open up another level of understanding and encourage him to be more patient with his son.

Some kinds of body language in mediation need a response from the mediator, whereas others do not need any comment. When a mediator notices someone's hands gripping papers tightly or a foot jigging up and down, it is important to acknowledge that experiencing separation is extremely stressful and that mediation seeks to reduce stress, often by taking one step at a time. Arms folded across the chest, hands clenched, legs tightly crossed – these may be defensive positions indicating vulnerability, fear of attack, or suppressed anger. Participants may keep their eyes down and avoid looking at each other. They often turn away from each other. Mediators can help them to feel safer by seeking mutual reassurances that may not be offered spontaneously. If a participant avoids eye contact, constantly looking down at the floor or out of the window, this is a signal that something needs to be done to make the person feel safer or more involved. It is important to ask a question that re-engages the person who has withdrawn and invites eye contact. A sprawling posture, leaning back in the chair with legs stretched, may indicate feelings of superiority, yet mediators should be cautious in interpreting body language. A participant who closes their eyes may be avoiding confrontation, but the closed eyes may mask hidden fears or suppressed anger. Frowning or fierce looks, a pursed or quivering mouth, a hand kept over the face – these expressions need to be noted and responded to, in some way.

6.4   SILENCE

The use and value of silence in communication vary markedly from one culture to another.[7] In Western cultures, silence tends to be viewed negatively. It may be interpreted as an expression of coldness, disapproval or resentment or alternatively, it may be understood as a sign of tacit or grudging consent. In Asian cultures, silence may be positive and entirely acceptable as a sign of mutual respect and affirmation. Silences often occur in mediation and mediators need to take care in the ways they respond and interpret the silence. Feelings of sadness and understanding may be shared silently between a couple and the mediator should not hasten to fill an emotionally meaningful silence. If the unspoken feelings are sad and reflective, the mediator should allow space

---

[7]   Robinson L *Cross-cultural Child Development for Social Workers* (Palgrave Macmillan, 2007).

for them. If, on the other hand, the silence feels threatening, the suppressed tension needs to be acknowledged and words found to release it, to avoid a damaging explosion during the mediation or afterwards.[8]

6.5 COUPLES WHO ARGUE WITHOUT LISTENING

When couples separate, their arguments are often fast and furious rather than quiet and reflective. Neither may hear what the other is saying, like two humming tops spinning away from each other in a whirl of words. Mediators need to slow them down, providing a structure in which each person can speak and be heard. The whirl of words may be an outlet for energies that the mediator needs to catch and channel more constructively. Many people have difficulty putting feelings into words. It is frequently necessary to seek information and clarify meanings. Words can accumulate layers of meaning that overlay their original significance. Mediators frequently need to seek clarification. When a parent raises a general objection to children having contact with the other parent, it may be helpful to ask for an example: 'To help me understand the difficulties when Dave picks up the children, could you give an example of what happened last time he called to pick them up ....' It is useful to repeat what each partner says, especially when they are upset and angry. 'So you are worried that ... and Dave is worried that ....' Reflecting each participant's position back to them as accurately as possible helps to calm them because it shows they have been heard. These techniques are essential ingredients of mediation. They help to slow the pace of fast-firing arguments. In high conflict situations, the mediator's use of language is particularly important. Strong words need to be used to acknowledge strong feelings, without implying judgements. Unacceptable *behaviour* can be distinguished from the *person* responsible for the behaviour.

6.6 CONFLICTING VERSIONS OF 'THE TRUTH'

Separating couples often become locked in circular arguments about what happened when and who did or said what to whom and who is now giving the 'right' account. Accounts of events are inevitably subjective, clouded by feelings and coloured by values about what is right or wrong, acceptable or unacceptable. Events, experience and perceptions are woven into a kind of tapestry that makes up our picture of the world. An important need in talking with others is to recount experiences in a way that confirms our perceptions and self-image. The very process of recounting experiences alters the way they are relived in the mind and engrained in the memory. With each retelling, the speaker becomes more convinced that the event took place in the way described. When separated couples argue over conflicting versions of the same event, this is more deeply threatening to them than mere differences of recollection. Each partner has an internalised picture that they seek to present to the outside world, but in face-to-face encounters it is confronted and

---

[8] See also **10.4.7** below on the power of silence.

affronted by the other partner's picture. If the confrontation is stark and one picture shatters into fragments, its owner may feel as though their whole self is falling apart. Mediators need to be aware of the extreme vulnerability of people who are struggling to hold on to a fragile sense of identity. Although mediators are not counsellors or therapists, they need to show understanding by acknowledging fears and stress in strong and warm terms. The power of acknowledgement is considerable. It is important, however, not to acknowledge distress in a way that may increase or expose one party's vulnerability to the other.

6.7   ASKING QUESTIONS

Mediators spend a lot of time asking questions. The questions need to be balanced, well focused and sensitively put, neither interrogating people nor asking the kind of questions that a therapist might ask. Researchers[9] have found that good questioning by mediators was associated with positive outcomes, whereas mediations that broke down were associated with inadequate questioning techniques. Asking useful questions is a very important skill in mediation. Asking questions helps mediators to avoid making statements, offering opinions or giving answers. It is important for mediators to continue to ask questions, even when they think they know the answer. The same question should be put to both partners in turn as they are likely to give different answers. The order in which each partner is asked a question should alternate. 'Open' questions invite a free-ranging response, but may risk opening the floodgates. 'Closed' and focused questions help mediators to obtain specific information and contain high conflict. Unlike Aristotle, mediators do not normally begin by asking 'Why?' Enquiring about causes invites blaming and self-justifying answers that can be very upsetting.

Focused questions help to maintain structure and manage conflict. Many people are extremely nervous when they first come to mediation. An open question, such as 'Could you explain your current situation?' invites them to speak freely. However, it can also put them in the dilemma of not knowing where to begin or end. If one partner launches into a long tirade directed against the other partner, the latter may fear not getting a chance to speak and may lose confidence in the mediator. People are very afraid of losing control and of getting hurt. Some also fear inflicting hurt on each other. Many people find it easier and safer to answer focused questions such as 'Where you are living at the moment?' 'Was the decision to separate a joint decision?' (rather than 'Why did you split up?), or 'at what time would you like to pick up the children next Saturday?' In this way, the mediator can gather information and identify issues in a systematic way that couples may find less stressful.

---

[9]   Kressel et al 'Research in Contested Custody Mediations' (1989) 24 *Mediation Quarterly* 55–70.

Kressel and colleagues[10] found that skilled mediators tended to use an identifiable structure in the type of questions they used and the timing of each question. The structure was rather like a pyramid, with broader information-gathering questions gradually tapering to finely tuned questions, as the mediation progressed. The following examples show how questions can be used to structure the mediation process and to focus attention on the present, the future or the past. Many couples have become locked in the past and need future-focused questions to help them to look forwards instead of backwards. Counsellors and therapists generally believe that some understanding of the past is necessary before beginning to help people to deal with the present and future. Mediators tend to focus on the present and the future, without asking when and how the couple's relationship began to unravel. Quite often, couples refer spontaneously to what each of them sees as the cause of the breakdown, but the mediator's role is not to explore it or make value judgements about what went wrong. Questions that help couples to look forward, rather than backward, are more helpful. 'So, what do you think needs to happen? What would work better?' Future-oriented questions help people to put grievances behind them and to look at how they want the future to be. 'Do you think things are likely to be easier in another year or two? If so, what do you think will have changed?' 'If Poppy is asked when she's 15 (or 25) what is was like for her when her parents separated/got divorced, what do you think she is likely to say?' 'What would you like her to say?'[11]

6.7.1 Present-focused questions

It is usually necessary to ask about current arrangements in order to understand the present situation. If parents are already separated: 'How often are you seeing the children at the moment? What is the usual pattern? How does each of you feel it is working?' It is also important to ask about children's relationships with siblings (how do they get on?) and with other family members. Grandparents often provide a haven of security for children when parents are splitting up. Are there other relatives living in the same area? Is there anyone else who is especially important to a child? The ways in which parents reply to these questions, as well as the content of their answers, shows the mediator how they communicate and whether they listen to each other. It is important to discover whether parents see their children as individuals and whether they are able to separate their children's needs from their own. This is particularly difficult where there is only one child. Sometimes a parent's professed concern about the children is part of a hidden agenda, such as maintaining occupation of the family home. Mediators need to use all their observations – verbal and non-verbal – in formulating further questions, whether concerning children or financial matters.

---

[10] Ibid.
[11] For other examples of future-focused questions, see **11.8.3, 11.8.5** and **11.8.10** below.

6.7.2   Past-focused questions

As suggested in Chapter 2,[12] some understanding of the past may be necessary
to manage the present and contemplate the future. The past impacts on the
present. Therefore, the way parenting was managed in the past may be very
relevant to arrangements for the present and future. Although mediators focus
forwards, it may be helpful to ask how children were looked after before their
parents separated and to what extent the parents shared parenting tasks and
responsibilities. Their answers are likely to indicate their willingness and
capacity to co-parent, or may suggest that it is more realistic to think in terms
of parallel parenting or separate roles as primary and secondary carer. Going
further back, it may be illuminating to ask about each parent's experience of
being parented, as a child. Many parents refer to experiencing parental
separation themselves, as a child or adolescent, and may realise that they are
repeating experiences they had as a child, while others say that, having
experienced losing a parent, they want their children to keep their relationships
with both parents and to have a much better experience than they had
themselves, as children. Examples of past-focused questions are:

- When you lived together, did you share looking after the children?
- Did either of you put the children to bed and get up to see to them during
the night?
- When they started school or nursery, who usually took and collected
them?
- (If both parents were working,) who stayed at home when a child was ill?
- Who usually took the children to the doctor or dentist?
- Did you agree about how to discipline the children?
- Did you both go to meetings with teachers and help with homework?
- Who usually bought the children's clothes and birthday presents for their
friends?
- Was religion an important aspect of bringing up your children?
- Were decisions about the children generally discussed and agreed, or were
they mostly taken by one parent alone? Did you argue over these
decisions?
- Did the children get on well with each other, before you separated? Do
they get on well now, most of the time?

Asking these kinds of questions helps to understand previous patterns of
parenting and relationships. It should not be assumed, however, that what
worked well or did not work before the separation should necessarily form the
basis for what will work in future. The purpose is to explore whether shared
parenting was possible previously, so that realistic plans can be made now. It is
useful to ask parents whether they are able to consult with each other about the
children's education, health and religion, distinguishing major areas of parental
responsibility from day-to-day care and the way children's time is shared.

---

[12] See **2.8** above.

Parents' own experience of having two loving parents, or of their parents splitting up when they were young, is often a strong motivator to manage things equally well or better for their own children.

6.8   DIFFERENT TYPES OF QUESTIONS

Type of question	Purpose	Example
Open	Invites a general, free-ranging response	'So what are your main aims in coming to mediation?'
Closed	Restricts the information that can be given in response. Keeps control of the process	'What type of mortgage do you have?'
Non-directed	Allows either participant to answer	'Could you tell me the present arrangements?'
Directed	Addressed to one party, usually to each in turn	'Have you looked at house prices, Anne … John, have you had a look yet …?'
Past-oriented	Gathers information about the past when necessary	'Did you put the sale proceeds from the flat into buying your house?'
Present-oriented	Clarifies current arrangements	'How often are you seeing the children at the moment?'
Future-oriented	Focuses attention forwards	'How would you like this to work in around six months' time ?'

6.8.1   Thinking about the function of questions

Moore[13] lists different types of questions and their functions, including active listening questions, clarification questions, confrontation questions (identifying a discrepancy, to be used with care) and summary questions. It is important to think about the function of the question and whether the same question is to be put to both participants and if so, in which order. Some examples of different types of questions include:

- **Opening questions**: to build rapport and clarify each participant's main concerns and aims: 'Could you say what you would like to achieve through coming to mediation?'

- **Information-seeking questions**: 'How often do you see the children at the moment?' 'You are explaining that this is a savings account which is earmarked for tax purposes. When do you expect to get the next tax demand?'

---

[13]   Moore *The Mediation Process* (Jossey Bass, 1983), pp 91–92.

- **Negotiating questions:** 'What could you do to make it easier ...?' 'What would be workable for you?'

- **Reality-testing questions:** 'What would happen if ...?' 'Who will provide the transport each weekend?'

- **Option development questions:** 'Are there any other possibilities that either of you can see?' 'Have you considered ...?'

- **Questions to clarify priorities and facilitate communication:** 'What is your main priority right now?' 'Could you explain what you want Bill to understand better ...?'

- **Reflective questions:** put slowly and thoughtfully, a reflective question from a mediator may help participants to consider an aspect they had not thought about before. It may open a window to a fresh view: 'I wonder what you would like your children to be able to say when they are grown up and someone asks them what it was like for them when you two split up?' 'If Louisa decides to get married sometime in the future, do you think she would want both of you to come to her wedding, without worrying that there might still be bad feeling between you?' If these are useful questions, one can see in parents' eyes that 'thought bubbles' are forming in their heads. Sometimes they can be a turning point in the mediation.

- **Hypothetical questions:** hypothetical questions help people to imagine a possible scenario, without being committed to it or feeling trapped. These questions can free people from their current situation, helping them to project themselves into the future and view possibilities, like running a film forwards. They can be asked about the changes they are looking for and then asked about the conditions that would make such changes possible to achieve. Suggestions from the mediator may be 'embedded' in a question, provided they are not put forward as recommended solutions. Hypothetical questions are very useful in exploring options and negotiating towards settlement.

- **Circular questions:** circular questions are a means of gathering and clarifying information derived from systems theory. It is a technique used in family therapy that may be used in mediation, but not for diagnosis and treatment. Circular questions explore perceptions, relationships and communications between couples and between family members. It is a mode of enquiry designed to make a person pause and think about another person's feelings and needs. Circular questions focus on communications and interactions *between* participants in mediation and *between* them and their children. They broaden the focus of enquiry beyond linear, two-way communications from each participant to the mediator. Circular questions explore *connectedness*, rather than differences between the parties' own views and positions. They are useful because they disrupt habitual cause-and-effect explanations that encourage blaming. Questions that invite someone to explain how they think *another* person – who may or may not be present – may be thinking or feeling about an issue, instead of asking those questioned to say how they *themselves* feel about it, encourage shifts of perspective which can lead to a different understanding or a fresh view. This technique is particularly useful in helping parents consider their children's needs and feelings. If both parents respond by describing a child's feelings or needs in similar terms, the mediator can mutualise their concerns and move on to exploring options or arrangements. If, however, they disagree, further circular questions can be asked about how a child may be showing different feelings to each parent, at different times. Each parent may be asked what they think their child, or children, would say, if they were asked about their feelings, or what they are most anxious about, at the moment.

Circular questions often invite some kind of comparison, such as a before/after comparison or asking what might make something better – or worse – for children. Parents are asked to put themselves in a child's place and see their children as individuals who have feelings and needs of their own, rather than as extensions of each parent. They are helped to compare their perceptions of their children's feelings and reactions, without either parent being seen as right or wrong. Circular questions help participants to look through someone else's eyes – especially, through their children's eyes – and perhaps see things in a different light.

The following table offers examples of the functions of some different types of questions. It does not set out to provide a complete list of different questions and their functions.

6.9   THE FUNCTION OF DIFFERENT KINDS OF QUESTIONS

Question	Function	Example
Clarifying	Seeks more information, encourages a fuller reply	'Could you say a bit more about...?'
Reality testing	Helps people to explain their proposals in concrete terms	'How would you see this working in practice...?'
Summarising	Punctuates, gives a focus	'So have I understood that the main question for you now is...?'
Strategic	To change direction or side-step an argument	'Is it possible to put this on one side for a moment and look at...?'
Reflective	To encourage thought, to offer another perspective	'I wonder whether it would be useful to talk about...'
Hypothetical	Allows exploration without asking people to commit themselves	'Jane, if you decided to work full time, would you need more help with childcare?'

Question	Function	Example
Circular	Helps understand perceptions and relationships in families	'If Billy were here and you asked him what his main concern is at the moment, what would Billy say?'

6.10 FILTERING OUT NEGATIVES

Couples often talk at cross-purposes – sometimes very cross-purposes – and often denigrate each other. 'Trevor is useless', 'Judy can't be trusted.' As Fisher and Ury[14] emphasise, it is important to separate the people from the problem. Mediators need to show respect and empathy, using positive language as far as possible. Asking one partner to give a recent example to explain a particular difficulty seeks specific information about the problem, instead of a global judgement of the person. A specific incident can illustrate the problem in concrete terms. The other partner can then fill in further details ('but what I actually meant was...'). Explanations often change perceptions of a particular incident and may begin to question the image of the other person.

When couples are in conflict, it is helpful to use positive language in talking about 'your plans (or arrangements) for the future' instead of repeating words like 'dispute' and 'disagree'. A verbal message can defuse or heighten conflict. Separating parents are very sensitive to language. For example, it helps to talk about *their concerns for their children*, rather than *disagreements over the children,* and about *child support*, rather than *maintenance.* Mediators should avoid using the term 'absent parent' because it can imply that a parent has chosen to abandon the family. Similarly, the term 'one-parent family' is judgmental and hurtful, because it implies that there is only one parent. Mediators include both parents by saying 'both of you, as parents...', 'the family as a whole', 'to help both of you and the children', 'to make things easier for all of you', to show that they are concerned to help children *and* parents. Family mediation is not confined to helping adults settle adult issues. It may be stating the obvious but nonetheless worthwhile to observe that 'the separation [divorce] ends your relationship [marriage], but you are still parents. The family may be changing but it still exists'. It is helpful for parents to realise that there are many positive aspects of family life and relationships that need to continue after they separate. The questions are about what needs to continue, as well as about what needs to end.

Mediators tend to filter out accusatory words and judgemental labels. For example, if a mother says about the father: 'He doesn't care what the children eat', a mediator would avoid repeating the words 'doesn't care' in asking: 'So is the kind of food the children eat when they are with their father one of the things you would like to discuss here today?' Sometimes mediators risk giving

---

[14]   Fisher and Ury *Getting to Yes – Negotiating Agreement Without Giving In* (Penguin Books, 1983).

offence because they neutralise too much. People can feel unheard or devalued if a mediator rephrases a powerful emotional statement so weakly that it loses its force. Mediators need to use strong words in a non-judgemental way. If a mother says: 'I get mad when he (the father) does whatever his mother tells him to do', she is likely to get more angry if the mediator says: 'So you feel a bit annoyed', because 'annoyed' is not an adequate substitute for 'getting mad'. At the other end of the scale of emotions, the word 'happy' may be used insensitively. In training role-plays, mediators often say: 'So you would be happy with Len having the children every other weekend?' Couples who are separating may experience relief, but they are hardly ever happy. It is more acceptable for the mediator to ask: 'So you are saying that it would be all right with you for the children to go to Len every other weekend?'

6.11   PLAIN LANGUAGE

When people are stressed, their ability to absorb information is limited. Plain language is easier to understand. We all have habitual ways of expressing ourselves and we need to listen to ourselves in order to hear how we sound to other people. People who are angry and distressed are easily confused by long sentences or specialist terminology from law or psychology. The way we talk is influenced by our family background, education, friends and leisure activities, as well as by the work we do. Speech varies according to cultural background and social class. People from different regions or social backgrounds may find it difficult to understand professional language and manner of speech. Mediators should watch out for bemused expressions on people's faces.

Couples in mediation may not be from the same culture as the mediator. English may be their second language or a language they use with difficulty. Using ordinary language helps them to understand and to feel that they are being treated as equals. There is usually no need to use legal terminology. When legal terms are necessary, some explanation or commentary is often very helpful. Mediation, like other disciplines, tends to develop its own specialist vocabulary. Mediators talk about 'caucusing', 'empowering' and 'mutualising'. This kind of jargon can mystify a process that should be transparent. We should be able to explain mediation clearly enough for a child of five to understand what it means.

6.12   LANGUAGE IN CROSS-CULTURAL MEDIATION

Participants with little English or none at all need a mediator who speaks their own language. However, bilingual or multi-lingual mediators are scarce. More than a quarter of councils in England and Wales have communities in which people speak little or no English. Thirty local authorities have wards where 10% or more of the population cannot speak English or have only minimal English. According to the 2011 census, 138,000 people in England and Wales could not speak any English, while almost 750,000 could not speak it well. Leicester City Council's translation unit caters for 140 languages and provides translation services to other local authorities. There is a great shortage of bilingual or multi-lingual mediators, especially ones speaking a second language well enough to mediate in it. If they are aware of mediation services, ethnic minority communities may see mediation by white Caucasian mediators as not catering for them in any way. Misunderstandings in cross-cultural mediation result not only from misinterpretation of a spoken language but also confusion because gestures and facial expressions mean different things in different cultures.

Mediating in a second language (as a participant or mediator) may involve additional strain and difficulty and can be extremely tiring. There is increased anxiety about understanding everything that is being said. These effects are likely to be magnified in situations of high emotion and conflict.

Additional challenges and needs arise where:

- One or both parents have different first languages from the mediator/s but appear to be sufficiently fluent in the chosen common language for mediation.
- The parents have different first languages and use one language in speaking with each other, but with different levels of fluency and/or understanding.
- The parents use a third language as their common language.
- A co-mediator translates what one parent says in their first language to the other parent and the other mediator, in the mediation.
- An interpreter is needed (see **6.13** below).

These situations may not be suitable for mediation, because of the linguistic skills that are needed and the difficulties of relying on an interpreter or their unavailability. Language conditions thought and perceptions.

Even when we speak a foreign language well, we need to beware 'faux amis' (words that seem to mean the same in both languages but which are actually different, like 'normalement' in French and 'normally' in English, or 'discusiòn' in Spanish, which may mean an argument rather than discussion). The use of an interpreter presents further difficulties if the mediator does not understand communications between the interpreter and the couple and cannot check the accuracy of translation. An interpreter may fail to convey the mediator's exact words or nuances of language and feeling. An interpreter also needs to be briefed in advance on the mediation process, confidentiality and the nature of their role in the process. If available, a co-mediation team in which one mediator, at least, speaks the same language as one or both participants, provides a better model than bringing in an interpreter. An example of a cross-cultural co-mediation with a German-Irish couple may be found in Chapter 4.[15]

---

[15]   See **4.4.1.2** above.

6.13   LANGUAGE, HEARING OR SPEECH DIFFICULTIES

Where one or both partners have hearing problems, a specialist worker with the deaf may be needed. A third party who joins in a mediation to provide a special resource, such as signing for the deaf, must be equally acceptable to both (or all) participants and needs to have a good understanding of the mediation process. There should be prior consultation to ensure that all participants would feel comfortable with the proposed special helper. If the helper is already well known to one partner, the other partner may not accept the helper as impartial and there may be a real or perceived bias. It is essential to address questions of balance and impartiality, the specialist role of the helper and their potential impact on the process and its outcome.

Example

Theo, who was profoundly deaf, was referred to mediation and came to an information and assessment meeting with Jo, his worker for the deaf, provided by Bristol City Council. Jo seemed to have a natural understanding and flair for mediation, with the result that Theo's eye contact with the mediator conveyed positive and congruent responses to her questions and acknowledgements. His ex-partner, Alexia, had less impaired hearing and she was able to lip-read. Alexia said she was keen to work out arrangements for their six-year-old son, Nikos, in mediation. She definitely did not want to go to court and nor did Theo. There had been some misunderstandings between them over Theo's commitment to Nikos and willingness to pay child maintenance. Alexia was content to accept Jo, whom she knew, to sign both for Theo and herself in mediation. There was only one mediation meeting in which Jo showed her ability as a co-mediator. Both parents were motivated to work out a regular schedule for Nikos and co-operate with each other. Nikos himself did not have a hearing problem and both parents said that he helped them to communicate, when they had a difficulty.

6.14   GENDER CONDITIONING IN THE USE OF LANGUAGE

Although gender stereotypes oversimplify differences and may be misleading, linguistic studies suggest that men and women tend to use different modes or styles of speech because of cultural conditioning.[16] When feelings between a couple are running high, it is easy for one partner to misinterpret what the other partner is saying or to be annoyed by the way it is said. Many arguments are based on misunderstandings or different perceptions, rather than on actual disagreements. Men may be more comfortable talking about activities and practicalities and may find it hard to talk about feelings. Women, on the other hand, often discuss relationships and share their feelings more readily with each other. Men who find emotions too intense to deal with may withdraw. The more one partner withdraws, the more agitated the other one is likely to become and frustration can boil over. Mediators may be able to draw off some

---

[16]   Tannen *That's Not What I Meant* (Virago, 1992).

of the steam by commenting on the pattern they have just observed in a way that is empathetic to both partners: 'When it is hard to talk, it makes everything harder for both of you. May I check that I have understood the main concerns for each of you? Sandra, you were saying that ... and Gordon, you were saying that ....' Some couples have got into a habit of talking loudly whenever they disagree. They may have got used to shouting at each other, or there may be a pattern in which one partner turns up the volume and the other one switches off. Mediators see these patterns in action. When one partner seems to be blocking out while the other one is shouting with increasing desperation, the mediator may pick up the message and repeat it in a quiet, unthreatening tone. The blocking partner may be receptive to the mediator's quiet voice. The louder partner, seeing this, may turn down the volume.

6.15   SKILLS IN THE LANGUAGE OF MEDIATION

6.15.1   Encouraging people to speak for themselves

Angry couples sometimes talk about each other in the third person, even when the other one is present in the room. 'The problem with Jemima/Jeremy is that she/he ....' Or they may even refer to each other in a distant and patronising way as 'Mr Smith' or 'Mrs Smith', as though the other person had been married to someone else. Mediators seek to change these unhelpful tendencies by encouraging participants to speak for themselves and explain what they need, using the first person ('What I am looking for ... I would really like it if ....'), instead of telling the other person what he or she ought to do, using the third person.

6.15.2   Acting as referee, keeping the ground-rules

Couples in conflict often try to score points against each other. If one party is taking all the air space, the mediator may need to interrupt, as constructively as possible: 'George, let me stop you there. If I've understood you, you are saying that ... and Celia, you said just before that ...?' The mediator needs to show that both parties are getting equal attention and that neither will be allowed to dominate the discussion. Balancing and rebalancing can be done through maintaining equal eye contact, giving time to each party, proposing and enforcing ground-rules. If one party uses offensive or threatening language, the mediator needs to be firm and confident enough to make it clear that this has to stop, if the mediation is to continue.

6.15.3   Repeating and summarising

Repeating what each person has said, using the words they have used, is important in mediation for several reasons:
*   It shows that you are listening carefully and that you want to understand.

- It gives each person an opportunity to confirm or to correct you, if necessary.
- It slows things down, if the argument is running too fast.
- Although words are repeated, the mediator's tone of voice may change the climate.
- A different tone of voice may enable the other party to hear.
- Repeating can give strong reinforcement to a positive statement or joint concern.
- A short summary helps to take stock and plan the next step.

Mediators may need to rephrase rather than repeat, because repeating a negative statement may suggest that the mediator agrees with it.

6.15.4 The mediator as translator

A separated wife wrote on her referral form before the first mediation meeting: 'Matthew and I need to rebuild our lives. There are bound to be parts we disagree on. We sometimes don't speak the same language and a third party may be able to interpret what one or both of us are saying to each other.' An interpreter seeks to convey the essential meaning of what has been said. Mediators may 'translate' by rephrasing statements or asking further questions to help couples understand each other better. The same message spoken by a third person who is not emotionally involved may be heard differently. As well as repeating statements, the mediator may need to rephrase or reframe them so that the speaker feels understood and the other partner can hear them. The listener may then respond positively, instead of aggressively. When the mediator substitutes different words, it is important to check with the speaker that the meaning or message is being conveyed accurately.

6.16 FRAMING AND REFRAMING

We construct our reality out of a mixture of perceptions, beliefs, interpretations of past experience, hopes and fears for the future. It is not surprising that separating couples present inconsistent and contradictory pictures of the same situation or same incident. Each of them has constructed a 'frame', a kind of filter through which they perceive their world as they see it. These 'frames' are used to define reactions and responses, even when they produce self-defeating results. Neither 'frame' is right or wrong: each has its own validity. But as long as separating couples argue about whose view is right or wrong, they will fail to make progress in working towards agreed solutions. In listening, clarifying and summarising, mediators show that they are interested in and accept these contradictory pictures, without preferring one picture over another or making judgements about them. In the early stages of mediation, each participant often portrays the other in a negative light. Explanations may be given in blaming or accusatory terms. The challenge for mediators is to re-phrase accusatory statements in a way that fits the picture, yet puts another frame around it so that it may be seen from a different perspective. For further discussion of 'frames' and their use in Neuro Linguistic Programming (NLP) and mediation, see Chapter 11.

Offering a different perspective may enable a view to be seen in a different light. Thus, when a mediator re-frames a perspective, this can help to modify attitudes without the mediator being directive or judgemental. Reframing involves rephrasing statements or ideas to offer a different way of understanding them, without substituting a new meaning belonging to the mediator. It can be used to shift the focus from one parent's opinion of the other parent to their joint concerns for their children. Regular reframing keeps the children in the forefront of the parents' attention. It is not uncommon for parents then to repeat the language and expressions the mediator has used. Reframing requires sensitivity and skills. It may involve changes of words and syntax, to help switch the energy flow from negative to positive. Timing is important, with careful attention to the impact on both parties.

6.16.1   How does positive reframing work?

- It puts a word or statement in a different way: a particular facet is turned to catch a different light. The intention is to clarify and ease the communication between the two parties, not to impose the mediator's own personal view. One way to do this is to ask a question instead of making a comment, to check that the speaker's underlying concern or objective has been understood. If this is not so, their correction provides clarification. If, on the other hand, the re-frame is accurate and sensitive, there is an affirmative response, usually in the form of an appreciative nod and eye contact.

- If negative words and phrases are repeated, the repetition gives them added weight and reinforcement. A positive reframe does not blame, accuse or denigrate anyone.

- Positive reframing assumes good motives. People can be given the benefit of the doubt, until they provide further evidence of having only destructive motives. Offering a positive explanation for a negative position helps people feel better. They are often aware of behaving badly. Being offered some form of validation helps restore the self-esteem that is often extremely low during the process of separation and divorce.
  A positive reframe picks up underlying concerns that may be hidden underneath angry or defensive reactions. If the mediator expresses these as mutual concerns, shared by both parents, common ground between them can be opened up and explored.

- A reframe addressed to one party needs to be balanced by a parallel re-frame or acknowledgement to the other. It is very important to balance and mutualise – to identify common ground and common concerns, even when focusing on one party's statements.

- Especially when there is a high level of emotion or tension, reframing in a calm, reflective way lowers the emotional temperature. Active listening becomes easier. Reframing may be used as a step towards other questions that need to be explored.

6.16.2   The pace and timing of reframing

Inexperienced mediators tend to miss cues for reframing and lose valuable opportunities to intervene at a critical moment. If these opportunities are missed repeatedly, conflict may escalate and both parties may lose confidence in the mediator's ability to contain it. On the other hand, a reframe that is slid in too quickly and glibly may not help. It must not come across in a patronising way, nor diminish the importance of the speaker's original statement. Reframing is not a technique used in isolation: it is part of a process in which each intervention by the mediator must be made with care and lead to the next step.

6.17   MESSAGES AND META-MESSAGES

Some couples do not fight openly. They give each other coded messages. Mediators need to develop the skill of 'third ear listening' to pick up and decode these coded messages. A 'meta-message' is an underlying message conveying information about feelings, relationships and attitudes. The underlying message may contradict what is being said overtly. Coded messages or 'meta-messages' may be subtle and more wounding than an outright attack, especially if they undermine the other partner through sarcasm or ridicule. Coded messages may be attempts to draw the mediator into an alliance, sometimes using apparently innocuous words to convey a message that the other party is unreasonable, stupid or ridiculous.

6.18   PUNCTUATION

Mediators need to orchestrate discussions and manage the tempo. It is useful to have a concept of 'punctuation' – underlining, putting a full stop, beginning a new paragraph. Structure can be maintained by marking the end of each step before going on to the next one. The mediator needs to be pro-active – not just reactive – in managing structure and pace.

Punctuation helps to:
- keep participants on track;
- draw a line under a particular discussion;
- emphasise progress and reinforce co-operation;
- mark stages of the process;
- plan the next stage or steps.

Punctuation is usually verbal, but the flip-chart can be used as a visual tool to structure discussions and to help participants draw a temporary line under one issue and move on to the next one.

6.19 IMAGES AND METAPHORS

'When the imagination sleeps, words are emptied of their meaning.'[17]

Arguments are often repetitive. If the mediator uses an appropriate and arresting metaphor, it may help to change the pattern and convey more vividly something may otherwise be missed. A well-chosen metaphor can catch the imagination and stay in the memory, whereas a flow of words may go unheard or be quickly forgotten. However, an inappropriate metaphor might be patronising, insensitive or just ridiculous. It is useful to think of metaphors or images that are likely to have resonance for the couple, picking up an echo of something they have said. The following suggestions include some obvious metaphors that come into the category of overworked clichés. Others may prompt mediators to invent metaphors of their own. An unexpected metaphor may sow the seeds of an idea that takes root gradually.

6.19.1 Territory, middle ground

Mediation is often described as 'finding the middle ground'. Mediation meetings take place on neutral territory and mediators help participants find common ground that is firm and safe to build on. Mediators often talk about establishing some ground on which separated parents feel able to work together, or about building foundations for future co-operation, or about defining the boundaries for difficult discussions or the practical limits of contact or financial arrangements.

6.19.2 Journeys

There are likewise many obvious metaphors about roads and pathways, travelling forwards, choice of route, roads leading in different directions, crossroads, roadblocks and the need for signposts. Different options may be presented pictorially on the flip-chart as different ways forward involving decisions that can be taken at different stages. Some situations seem to have no way out, but identifying all available routes and brainstorming possible options may open up a way forward. Are both partners aiming to reach an ultimate destination or a short-term one?

6.19.3 Bridges

Even burnt bridges may continue to exist in the mind. Mediation is a bridge which participants approach from either side. It can require great effort, and

---

[17] Camus *Resistance, Rebellion and Death* (1960).

some hope for the future, to venture on to the bridge at all. Some people move on to it readily without needing much support, whereas others need encouragement and support before they can venture on to the bridge and trust it enough to take a few steps. In engineering terms, a cantilevered bridge rests on foundations built from each bank. People using the mediation bridge want to know if there is adequate support. The mediator is responsible for seeing that the bridge is adequately constructed, with sound supports both in emotional and practical terms. Those who are reluctant to let go of the past may be helped in mediation to take some steps on this bridge, towards a future that may feel very uncertain. In concrete terms, the bridge may consist of a period of financial support. Metaphorically, mediation discussions are a bridge that spans a gulf between conflicting views and needs. Bridges are needed between parents and children, as well as between the parents themselves. A parent who has lost all contact with a child or adolescent may feel completely rejected and cut off. This parent may need encouragement to go more than halfway across the bridge – writing or phoning regularly, even where there is no response. The child needs to see the parent's commitment to keeping the bridge in place, possibly over a long time, and may eventually feel able to respond. In stuck situations where a child is refusing to see the other parent, it may help to talk about keeping the bridge open and letting the child know that the bridge is still open.

Emma Turner, Managing Director of Family Mediation Centre Staffordshire, uses the metaphor of stepping-stones to encourage doubtful people to come to an information meeting and consider mediation. 'You can take just the first step and see if the next one looks safe enough. If it doesn't, you can always step back again.'

6.19.4 Elastic

Mundane objects can also be used as metaphors. Everyone knows how useful elastic is. It stretches and gives and retains its shape. But if elastic is stretched too hard or for too long, it begins to sag. A child's resilience is like elastic. Some children maintain their resilience and normal development, despite being pulled between conflicting feelings or forces. Others become vulnerable to pressures that are so great or prolonged that they lose their resilience and capacity to adapt. Parents may become more understanding of a child who is struggling to cope with major changes if they think of the child like a piece of elastic that has great resilience, provided it is not stretched too hard or for too long. Elastic is constructed from a number of small threads that are bound together. When several threads give way, there is little elasticity left. In the same way, most parents and children rely on a number of special bonds with other people. If these bonds (with a partner, parent, grandparents, friends) are suddenly cut, the whole structure may collapse. It is then very important to consider how additional supports can be provided, even temporarily, to maintain existing bonds.

The psychiatrist, Michael Rutter[18] emphasised that stress is normal and that a child who learns how to cope with stressful situations can become stronger rather than weaker. Resilience is not achieved by avoiding stress, but by dealing with it in a way that increases self-confidence and competence. This may involve taking responsibility for one's own reactions to a stressful situation, instead of blaming others for causing it. Resilience is influenced by many factors, including temperament, personal strengths, early life experiences, events in later childhood and adolescence, 'buffering factors' such as family support and the ability to form close relationships. None of these alone determines the response to a major life change but, woven together, they can create a fabric that is elastic, rather than brittle.

6.19.5   Jigsaw puzzles

Arrangements for children and related financial and housing matters are like interlocking pieces of a jigsaw puzzle. Jigsaw puzzles are a useful source of metaphors when mediating with separated couples on all issues – children, finance and property. It is important to acknowledge that many people feel overwhelmed in trying to deal with so much at once, especially when they are extremely stressed. Comparing the complexity of their problems to doing a jigsaw puzzle might be insensitive and appear to trivialise the profound seriousness of their situation, if such a comparison were made without sufficient empathy and understanding. However, recognition that different elements of family re-organisation need to fit together, if they are to work in practice, can help to reduce anxiety. The mediator can point out that just as a puzzle cannot be completed until missing pieces are to hand, in the same way it is necessary to collect further financial information and valuations. Independent financial advice may be needed. Participants are helped to prioritise in planning a step-by-step approach in which missing pieces are identified and gradually slotted into the picture. Doing a jigsaw puzzle involves picking up pieces that look as though they might fit together. If they do not fit, they have to be put aside while the search continues for the right piece. This is like exploring options in mediation. 'Working out a settlement has different parts that need to fit together – the children and the home and money. It's a bit like doing a jigsaw. If there are pieces that don't fit, we need to look for other ways.' Some people like to start a jigsaw by doing one corner, while others prefer to do the outside edges before filling in the centre. 'Where would you like to start – by discussing the outline of what you are looking for, or is there one particular area that is a priority for you?'

A seemingly impossible situation may appear more manageable, if it is approached bit by bit. Jigsaw puzzles provide a homely and reassuring metaphor for a step-by-step approach, rather than expecting an immediate global solution.

---

[18]   Rutter 'Resilience in the Face of Adversity' (1985) 147 *British Journal of Psychiatry* 598–611.

6.19.6   Doors and keys

Finding the key to a problem is a common metaphor. Overworked though it is, the image of a key may help people shift into a problem-solving mode. When they are asked what they see as a key to solving the problem, it is surprising how often they come up with a useful suggestion. Could there be more than one key that would fit the lock?

6.19.7   Trees

Mediators who respond to a dispute about property by talking about trees risk rapid dismissal. Metaphors need to be appropriate and used with care. The concept of a sheltered place, protected from the hurly-burly of everyday life, is, however, fundamental in mediation. In the Camp David talks, Jimmy Carter invited President Sadat of Egypt and Prime Minister Begin of Israel to meet with him in a garden, away from the press and the outside world. He described the garden as 'sheltered by a thick growth of stately oak, poplar, ash, locust, hickory and maple trees ... [in] an atmosphere of both isolation and intimacy, conducive to easing tension and encouraging informality'.[19] At Camp David, Jimmy Carter mediated a peace agreement between Egypt and Israel.

6.19.8   Water and rivers

Metaphors about water offer an abundance of images. Water symbolises movement and change. It can flow fast or gently, or it can be still. Still water may stagnate, but sudden change is like a tide that sweeps people along on currents they feel unable to control. Being swept along is a very frightening experience. Mediators can help make the currents more manageable, recognising the fear of being swept along and noticing when, where and how the current flows fastest. Even those who seem in relatively calm waters can hit rocks or rapids. Asking participants if they foresee some rocks further downstream may help them anticipate and steer clear of future difficulties. The image may also help to strengthen their confidence in their joint ability to steer and keep control.

The process of mediation itself can be compared to water. Water can penetrate small crannies and trickle down. A trickle of water seems insignificant, yet it has the power to crack a block of stone.[20] New ideas, proposals and changes often need to be absorbed gradually, rather than being injected by force. Encouraging people to consider and accept changes by degrees, rather than all at once, is a useful approach in facilitating children's adjustment to change, as well as the adjustments that adults need to make. Water reflects light. Reflecting means thinking. Thinking may throw some light on a dark area, whereas the inability to see ahead in darkness causes panic. Although light does not necessarily provide answers to problems, light, like water, can filter through

---

[19]   Carter *Keeping Faith: Memoirs of a President* (Bantam Books, 1982), p 324.
[20]   See also **11.1** below.

narrow chinks. It can illuminate the process of exploring problems. Reflections may be projected – thrown forwards – from one surface or angle to another and be seen in a different light.

Capacity to change is affected by the ambient temperature. Cold or frozen materials are very brittle. They snap under pressure. Water frozen into ice splinters and cracks, whereas boiling water is too hot to touch and evaporates as steam. Mediators need to register temperature, like a thermometer. If the temperature is too hot, it needs to be cooled in a careful and considerate way, before changes are looked at and discussed. When it seems very cold or frozen, mediators need to offer warmth and understanding, acknowledging fears and easing painful discussion. Warmth makes feel people more comfortable. It also increases pliancy and flexibility.

The importance of language, imagery and non-verbal communication in mediation cannot be overestimated. Even small differences in the angling of a question or the tone of a reflection may affect surface tensions. Managing surface tensions can facilitate change at a deeper level. The language/s that mediators use, verbally and non-verbally – choice of words, tone of voice, pace and rhythm, metaphors and images – play a significant part in the process of mediation and may affect its outcome.

6.20   THE KALEIDOSCOPE – DIFFERENT FACETS OF THE MEDIATOR'S ROLE

A kaleidoscope, each time it is shaken, would reveal different components of the mediator's role:

- **The catalyst**: The mediator is a catalyst who initiates dialogue between participants. If their communication has broken down, they may have been unable to talk with each other for a considerable time.

- **The manager**: The mediator manages the mediation process and provides a structure for negotiations. Participants are helped to define their issues, agree an agenda and move from one stage to the next.

- **The referee**: The mediator sets and maintains ground-rules, giving time for each participant to speak, controlling interruptions and aggressive behaviour.

- **The facilitator**: The mediator helps participants to communicate better and to explain their concerns. The anger that is expressed is sometimes a cover for hurt and fear. Mediators also need to be sensitive to feelings that remain unspoken. Humour may be used, when appropriate, to relieve tension.

- **The interpreter:** the mediator helps couples to listen to each other and to look at issues in new ways, often by reframing negative statements as positive objectives and concerns. Mediators look for common interests and shared commitment – particularly to children – that transcend parents' differences.

- **The information-giver:** Mediators help participants collect and consider relevant information. Mediators are also a resource to both parties, explaining relevant legal or other information. Good communication skills are needed to give legal or other information to both parties jointly, in a sensitive, balanced and clear way.

- **The bridge to new family structures:** Mediators provide a bridge to support families – parents and children – in transitions from one kind of family structure to another. Separating parents often need short-term support to help them maintain or rebuild good parental relationships while ending their marital relationship.

- **The reality tester:** Mediators explore possible options, raises questions and checks the viability of proposals. Sometimes one party makes demands or puts a proposal based on wishful thinking or inadequate knowledge. Exploring how proposals would work in practice helps people look at their real situation.

- **The conductor:** A mediator is a conductor in verbal, musical and scientific terms: verbal in the sense that the mediator helps people convey to each other what they need to say; musical in the sense that the mediator orchestrates different voices and blends them from discord into harmony. The noise of warring couples is discordant and clashing. Mediators need to control the sound so that each voice can be heard, keeping a balance between them and orchestrating the tempo during stages or movements in the process. This involves 'punctuating' or closing each phase, to help signal the next movement. Orchestrating the voices can produce a new form of harmony.
  Mediators are also conductors of energy. The energy people bring to mediation is often negative – being angry uses up a lot of energy. Mediators try to switch the flow of energy from negative to positive so that everyone's energy is used constructively.

- **The synthesiser:** Mediators need summarising and drafting skills to blend disparate statements and to summarise mediation outcomes in a way that assists both participants and their legal advisers. Mutually acceptable proposals need to be clearly drafted, to provide a basis for legally binding agreements. If there are no proposals for settlement, the mediation summary needs to clarify outstanding issues and the parties' positions, to assist further negotiations via lawyers or, if necessary, litigation. The language of mediation is important in building a synthesis out of discordant parts.

- **The juggler:** Skilled mediators are rather like jugglers in their ability to catch ideas and toss them so that different surfaces catch the light. The juggler's skills are open and visible, unlike the magic tricks of a conjurer. Although not trying to emulate a juggler's dazzling speed, mediators need balance, dexterity of movement and intellectual suppleness to keep information and ideas circulating freely. Entertaining an idea or throwing a suggestion into the air need not trivialise the difficulties.

The word 'trickster' has negative connotations, but Benjamin[21] compared the mediator's role to that of 'a folkloric trickster' who may 'confront the harsh, jagged reality of conflict' in seeking to turn things on their heads, transforming settled views and perceptions. Mediators may need to question conventional thinking and assumptions, not to lead people away from directions they wish to take, but to encourage innovative ideas and fresh vision when they are unclear or stuck. If mediation is heavy going, like wading through treacle, people are more likely to want to extricate themselves from it. There need to be ways of lifting the spirits – moments when couples who are sad or angry find themselves able to laugh again. If being in mediation gives them a lift, rather than casting them down, they are more likely to retain what was said and reflect on it afterwards.

---

[21]   Benjamin 'The Constructive Use of Deception: Skills, Strategies and Techniques of the Folkloric Trickster Figure and their Application by Mediators' (1995) 13(1) *Mediation Quarterly* 17.

CHAPTER 7

CHILD-FOCUSED MEDIATION

'I think when parents get divorced, they both have special responsibility towards their children', Lulu aged 8.[1]

'Families have to care for each other or it doesn't work', Rosie, aged 9.[2]

'I always think, no matter what I feel or how hurt I am, that he is the children's father and this is going to be it for the rest of their lives and so we have to get on.'[3]

CONTENTS

7.1 CHILDREN AND PARENTAL SEPARATION

It is estimated that around one quarter of the 12 million children in the UK are likely to experience parental separation before reaching the age of 16. In 2012

---

[1]   Krementz *How It Feels When Parents Divorce* (Gollancz, 1985), p 17.
[2]   Neale and Wade *Parent Problems! – children's views on life when parents split up* (Young Voice, 2000), p 16.
[3]   Mother quoted by Trinder, Beek and Connolly, J 'Making contact: How parents and children negotiate and experience contact after divorce' (2002) *Joseph Rowntree Foundation Findings* 092.

there were 118,140 divorces in England and Wales (an increase of 0.5% over the number in 2011)[4] and almost half (48%) of these divorcing couples had one or more children under the age of 16. According to reports in the media, around 100,000 children under 16 in this country experienced their parents' divorce in 2013. If children of unmarried parents are counted as well, the number of children experiencing parental separation annually is likely to total over 200,000. In 2006, the NSPCC sent a survey to children and young people whose parents had separated and who had been involved in court proceedings over where they should live and with whom they should have contact.[5] The NSPCC received replies from 93 girls and 48 boys aged between 11 and 18. Nearly all of them (95%) said they were satisfied, or mostly satisfied, with where they were living. Arrangements for seeing other family members were OK for nearly two-thirds of them and 'mostly OK' for a further quarter. One in seven living with one parent did not see as much of the other parent as they would have liked, and one in three did not see as much of their grandparents as they would have liked.[6] Separation or divorce often involved moving house and changing school. A quarter of the children had moved to a new area and a new school.

If children receive enough support and reassurance, the majority are able to adjust to parental separation and resume a normal pattern of development.[7] Studies[8] have shown that when separated parents co-operate in continued joint parenting, children's adjustment is greatly eased. Parental separation is a process rather than an event, beginning before one parent leaves the home and continuing long afterwards. Children feel the impact of separation throughout their childhood and into adulthood. Their experiences and reactions vary greatly. The quality of the child's relationship with each parent and the parents' relationship with each other are major influences in the child's adjustment.[9] A review of over two hundred research studies found that although the absence of a parent-figure is not the most influential factor in a child's development, key factors in the child's adjustment are continuing positive contact with the non-resident parent and good communication between parents, and also

---

4   Divorces in England and Wales 2012, Office for National Statistics, 6 February 2014.
5   Timms, Bailey and Thorburn *Your Shout Too!: a survey of the views of children and young people involved in court proceedings when their parents divorce or separate* (NSPCC Policy and Practice Series, 2007).
6   Ibid, *Young People's version*, p 2.
7   Rodgers and Prior *Divorce and separation: the outcomes for children* (Joseph Rowntree Foundation, 1998); Dunn and Deater-Deckard 'Children's Views of their Changing Families' (2001) *Joseph Rowntree Research Findings* 931.
8   See for example Wallerstein and Kelly *Surviving the Break-up – how children and parents cope with divorce* (Grant McIntyre 1980); Johnston and Campbell *Impasses of Divorce – the Dynamics and Resolution of Family Conflict* (Free Press, 1988); Hetherington and Clingempel 'Coping with Marital Transitions – A Family Systems Perspective' (1992) 227 *Society for Research in Child Development* 57.
9   Hawthorne, Jessop, Pryor and Richards 'Supporting children through family change' (2003) *Joseph Rowntree Foundation Findings* 323; Fortin, Scanlan and Hunt 'Taking a longer view of contact: the perspectives of young adults who experienced parental separation in their youth' [2013] Fam Law 104.

between the child and both parents.[10] Close attachments buttress a child's ability to cope with change. However, it cannot be assumed that all children are alike in needing or wanting the same things. Smart and Neale[11] found that boys in some families were happy with arrangements that did not suit their sisters, while some older siblings were unhappy with arrangements that worked well for younger siblings. During and following parental separation, a minority of children do not fare well. Some develop difficulties that continue to affect them as adults. Factors associated with poor outcomes for children are high levels of parental distress, financial hardship and multiple changes of family structure. In one study,[12] children who had experienced separation and divorce were found to be more at risk than children in 'intact' families of having health problems (especially psychosomatic disorders), needing extra help at school, lacking friends and suffering from low self-esteem. A significant factor was the amount of physical and emotional upheaval the children experienced. Those who had experienced three or more different family structures were likely to describe themselves as 'often unhappy' or 'miserable'. Many separating parents are aware of their reduced ability to communicate with each other and care for their children when they are under extreme stress.

In Australia, McIntosh et al[13] identified three categories of separated parents according to their patterns of co-operation or conflict (see **7.8** below). An earlier study of thirty families two years after separation found likewise that they tended to fall into three groups: co-operative co-parent families, conflicted two-parent families and absent-father (or mother) families.[14] Family mediators in Stafford[15] have also suggested that parents coming to mediation fall into three categories: Type A – basically co-operative, for whom referral to mediation provides a co-operative form of working that is immediately attractive; Type B – initially antagonistic, but able to see the benefits of agreement on children's needs or shared financial objectives and showing potential for a more amicable relationship; Type C – locked in hostility, but able to understand the pragmatic benefits of mediation for achieving cost-effective solutions and capable of attaining limited objectives through mediation.

---

[10] Rodgers and Prior *Divorce and separation: the outcomes for children* (Joseph Rowntree Foundation, 1998).
[11] Smart and Neale 'It's My Life Too – Children's Perspectives on Post-Divorce Parenting' [2000] Fam Law 163–169.
[12] See note 11 above.
[13] McIntosh et al *Post-separation parenting arrangements and developmental outcomes for infants and children* (Family Court of Australia, Attorney-General's Department, 2010); Trinder 'Shared Residence: A Review of Recent Research Evidence' [2010] Fam Law 1192–1197.
[14] Lund 'Research on divorce and children' [1984] 14 Fam Law 198–201.
[15] Robinson and Brisby 'ADR Professional' [2001] Fam Law 59–64.

7.2 PROTECTING CHILDREN FROM HARM

'The protection of children from risk of physical and emotional abuse must always take precedence in any "best interests" consideration.'[16]

It is essential that mediators explore carefully at assessment meetings whether there are, or have been at any time, concerns about a child's safety and welfare. If so, it is necessary to enquire whether these concerns have been reported and if so, when, by whom and to whom, and whether a safeguarding service is currently involved. When there are indications at an assessment meeting that a child is or may be at risk of harm, the mediator must contact the local safeguarding service immediately.[17] New statutory guidance on safeguarding children came into effect on 15 April 2013,[18] replacing the previous framework for assessing children in need and their families. Researchers in Australia found that a significant minority of children – as many as 25% – in shared care arrangements following parental separation had a family history entailing abuse or where one parent raised concerns about the child's safety and exposure to dysfunctional behaviour.[19] Some of the concerns that parents express do not indicate any risk of harm but indicate a need for medical, therapeutic or other help. Mediators should be aware of child welfare law and the application of the welfare principle in law and they should be able to provide parents with information about helping agencies and resources.[20] The following chapter (Chapter 8) considers the importance of listening to children themselves and taking account of what they say.

Concerns may arise in the course of a mediation and mediators must not hesitate to contact the local safeguarding agency. Mediation can be suspended while a check is made. Some allegations of child abuse turn out to be unfounded, arising from a parent's mistrust and anger and sometimes a malicious intention to cause trouble for the other parent. When safeguarding social workers find no evidence to support the allegations, they may recommend that mediation should continue and some parents may be able to rebuild trust and co-operation through mediation. In a case referred to mediation following prolonged dispute and litigation in which each parent had made allegations of child abuse against the other, investigation failed to find any evidence to support the allegations. The parents, who were unmarried, accepted mediation and with the mediator's help they were able to reach an outcome in which they withdrew their accusations against each other. They acknowledged that their accusations had been made in anger and through fear of losing their daughters, aged 8 and 10. Assisted by Mabel Edge, a mediator

---

[16] Bryant *An Australian perspective on the Family Justice Review* – paper delivered by the Chief Justice of the Family Court of Australia at the International Family Law Lecture, (London 2012) 24.

[17] *FMC Code of Practice for Family Mediation* 5.5.3.

[18] *Working Together to Safeguard Children: A Guide to inter-agency working to safeguard and promote the welfare of children* (HM Government/DfE, March 2013).

[19] Kaspiew et al *Evaluation of the 2006 family law reforms* (Australian Institute of Family Studies, 2009).

[20] See **7.12** below, *Getting It Right for Children*.

with extensive professional experience in the field of child protection, these parents regained their ability to communicate and co-operate with each other. Having agreed to waive their privilege covering the confidentiality of the mediation, they took the mediation summary of arrangements for their children to the court review hearing and the court approved their arrangements.

7.3 SEPARATED PARENTS INFORMATION PROGRAMMES (SPIPS)

In response to a widely felt need for information and advice, Separated Parents Information Programmes (SPIPs) have been welcomed by separated parents struggling to make arrangements for their children. Under a section of the Children and Adoption Act 2006 brought into effect on 8 December 2008, family courts may embody a direction or condition in a contact order that the parents should attend a Separated Parents Information Programme, to help them co-operate as 'parents apart'. In New Zealand, attendance at a Parenting Information Programme is a mandatory requirement prior to court proceedings over children. Parents have reported that attending a SPIP changed their behaviour and/or that of their ex-partner in important ways, including listening more to their children and jointly attempting to avoid conflict and confrontation in front of them.[21]

The Mediation Task Force recommended a review of the relationship between SPIPs and mediation to promote inter-agency partnership, with parents as the central focus. There is currently a major disconnect between SPIPs and mediation that needs to be rectified. Until recently, access to SPIPs was available only after proceedings had been started. Although this has now changed, the cost of attending a SPIP as well as paying for mediation may be out of reach for many parents, unless they are in receipt of a 'passporting' welfare benefit. Yet the combination of a Separated Parents Information Programme with referral to an information and assessment meeting with a mediator could assist conflicted parents to access the help they need to resolve disputes and co-operate better over their children. The Government has stated that it will undertake further work to look at how MIAMs and SPIPs can be used together more effectively, away from court.[22]

7.4 PARENTAL CONFLICT AND CHILDREN'S ADJUSTMENT

Prolonged parental conflict seems to be a consistent predictor of psychological difficulties for children. Continuing high conflict between parents shows significant associations with children's behaviour problems, somatic and psychosomatic symptoms, underachievement at school and low self-esteem.[23] Conflict is a normal part of family life. What matters is how parents deal with

---

[21]   Dancey 'Contact Activities: Parenting Information Programmes' [2010] Fam Law 1101–1105.
[22]   Department for Education and Ministry of Justice *A Brighter Future for Family Justice* (August 2014), p 39.
[23]   Emery *The Truth about Children and Divorce* (Viking, 2004); Johnston and Roseby *In the*

it. American researchers[24] found that a child whose father was verbally aggressive towards the mother showed more behavioural problems and had lower self-esteem. Mothers who were verbally aggressive towards the father tended to have poorer relationships with their children. These children were often solitary and played alone. When parents were able to co-operate, the children showed better psychological adjustment and lower levels of aggression. Conflict generally diminishes within a few years of separation, but when parents remain in high conflict, the child's life 'often continues to be lived in the middle of a war zone'.[25]

Adults often underestimate children's capacity to understand feelings and relationships. Parents who think a child is too young to understand what is happening may be seeking to protect themselves, rather than the child. Although children's reactions to separation do not necessarily correspond to their chronological age, professionals who work with parents need knowledge of child and adolescent development. It is equally important to seek to understand the individual personality of each child and the family's culture, history and circumstances. When children are struggling and not getting enough support, they often show their distress in behaviour, rather than words. The way they show their feelings may cause further difficulties, because the parents tend to interpret the behaviour differently and give different meanings to it. Each parent then blames the other for causing the problems. The following summary lists reactions among children in a study of 60 families in California who were going through divorce.[26] There were 131 children in the study group and the follow-up continued over a five-year period. The group was not representative of divorcing families generally and the findings should not be generalised to all children experiencing parental divorce. However, where parents continue to be very distressed and/or caught up in prolonged disputes, their children are more likely to show negative reactions. These are the parents and children most likely to need professional help. Contrary to widely held views, boys are not more adversely affected than girls and the age at which children experience separation is less significant than the quality of their experience.[27]

Name of the Child: a developmental approach to understanding and helping children of conflicted and violent divorce (Free Press, 1997).

[24] Camara and Resnick 'Marital and parental sub-systems in mother-custody, father-custody and two-parent households: effects on children's social development' in J Vincent (ed) (Greenwich, 1987) 4 *Advances in family assessment, intervention and research* 165–196.

[25] Trinder 'Conciliation, the Private Law Programme and Children's Well-being' [2008] Fam Law 341.

[26] Wallerstein and Kelly *Surviving the Break-up – how children and parents cope with divorce* (Grant McIntyre, 1980).

[27] Rodgers and Prior *Divorce and separation: the outcomes for children* (Joseph Rowntree Foundation, 1998).

7.5 COMMON REACTIONS AT DIFFERENT AGES

7.5.1 Pre-school children: 2–5 years

- Confusion, anxiety and fear: young children may be very confused about the changes in their family life, if parents are unable to explain the changes to children of this age.

- Strong reconciliation fantasies: children cling to hopes that their parents will get back together again. They may make up fantasies to comfort themselves.

- Increased aggression: the children's anger often stems from their feelings of loss and rejection. Their sense of loss when one parent disappears from their lives, often unaccountably, may lead to aggressive behaviour towards siblings, parents and in school. The remaining parent may be so preoccupied that the child receives less attention from this parent as well, increasing their sense of loss and rejection.

- Guilt feelings: young children may imagine that they are to blame for their parents not getting on together. They may assume that their own naughtiness was the reason for a parent leaving them.

- Regression: children may demonstrate their anxiety and insecurity by lapses in toilet training, reverting to bed-wetting, showing increased clinging behaviour.

- Increased fears – of the dark, for example – or developing feeding problems. Parents who are already strained may find these behaviour problems very hard to understand and tolerate.

7.5.2 Primary school age: 5–7 years

- Pervasive sadness and grieving: this may be related to the level of turmoil in the home, but many children feel intensely sad even when the parent they live with is not sad.

- Yearning for an absent parent: similar to grieving for a dead parent, but with greater feelings of rejection.

- Feelings of abandonment and fear: there are often fears of being forgotten and of losing the remaining parent as well.

- Anger: children often direct their anger at the parent they hold responsible for the breakdown.

- Conflicts of loyalty: a child who feels pulled between parents often does not know how to be loyal to both of them.

- Worry about parents' ability to cope: the more the child experiences a parent's problems in coping with separation, the more the child fears that the parent is no longer going to be able to care for them.

- Reconciliation fantasies.

7.5.3 Middle school: 8–12 years

- Children at this stage are more aware of the causes and consequences of separation and more likely to take sides in parental conflicts.
- May have profound feelings of loss, rejection, helplessness and loneliness.
- May feel shame, moral indignation and outrage at their parents' behavior.
- May show extreme anger, temper tantrums, demanding behaviour, or fears, phobias and denial.
- Increased psychosomatic complaints: headaches, stomach aches, sleep disorders.
- Making judgements: identifying one parent as the good parent and the other parent as the bad parent; rejecting the 'bad parent'.
- Forming an alliance with one parent – not necessarily with the one to whom they feel closest.
- Reduced self-esteem: the child may have difficulty concentrating at school and under-perform at school.
- Acting out: some children, especially boys, are more likely to act out their distress and may become involved in delinquent behaviour.

7.5.4 Adolescents: 13–18 years

- Loss of childhood: older children may be burdened by increased responsibilities for younger siblings and by the need to support overburdened and distressed parents.
- Pressure to make choices – some parents expect older children to make their own decisions about visiting the other parent or which parent they want to live with.
- Conflict between wanting to see an absent parent and wanting to keep up with peer group activities.
- Worry about money: resentful that they may receive less than their friends, pressure on parents to compensate for the divorce by giving them more materially.
- Heightened awareness and embarrassment about their parents' sexual behaviour and parents' involvement with new partners.
- Jealousy of a parent's new partner.
- Fears about forming long-term relationships and putting trust in people.
- Depression: withdrawal, refusal to communicate.
- Delinquency: stealing, drug-taking.

7.5.5 Young adults: 18 upwards

Young adults are often left out of discussions on the grounds that they are independent and less affected by their parents' break-up than younger children may be. Both these assumptions may be wrong. Students in higher education need a home to come back to and may be dependent on financial support from parents. Equally importantly, many grown-up children worry a great deal about their parents and some are very involved emotionally in their parents' troubles. Some parents depend heavily on older children – as well as on younger ones – for emotional support and practical help. Parenting roles are sometimes reversed. A child may consciously accept responsibility for looking after a parent who is unwell or unable to function properly. Taking care of an emotionally dependent parent is a great burden for a child or young person and it can be very difficult for sensitive and conscientious children to free themselves from this burden and get on with their own lives.

7.6   CHILDREN'S ADJUSTMENT TO PARENTAL SEPARATION

Children have complex psychological tasks in adjusting to their parents' separation and divorce.

Wallerstein[28] defined these tasks as:

- Recognising the breakdown in their parents' relationship.
- Disengaging from their parents' conflict and distress and resuming their own activities.
- Coping with loss.
- Resolving feelings of anger and self-blame.
- Accepting the permanence of their parents' separation or divorce.
- Achieving realistic hope regarding trustworthy relationships.

Children need to:

- Understand what is happening, with appropriate explanations according to their age and understanding and reassurance that they will continue to be loved and cared for.
- Keep attachments and relationships with both parents and with other important people in their lives. Wider kin networks, especially grandparents, can play an important part in supporting children and grandchildren around the time of separation.
- Feel reassured that they are in no way responsible for the break-up.
- Have emotional permission from each parent to go on loving the other parent.
- Have regular and reliable contact with the parent who leaves home, including overnight stays and holidays, unless there are contra-indications involving harm or continuing distress to the child.
- Remain in familiar surroundings, if possible. Although a move may be inevitable and sometimes welcomed, most children are attached to their

---

[28]   Wallerstein 'Children of Divorce – the psychological tasks of the child' (1983) 53 (2) *American Journal of Orthopsychiatry* 230–243.

home as well as to their parents. The disruption of moving home and changing schools adds to their confusion and stress and compounds the loss they experience.

- Maintain their daily routine as far as possible – at school and at home. When their familiar world is changing, children benefit from extra attention and nurturing, especially at bedtime.

- Be supported financially so that they do not experience a sudden drop in living standards.

- Have parents who can make thoughtful decisions and arrangements without involving the children too much or using the children for emotional support.

- Know that each parent is able to cope, despite living apart.

- Have parents who have time to play and have fun with them.

7.7   THE 'NO ORDER' PRINCIPLE AND LEGAL LABELS

There is now wider recognition that arrangements agreed by parents themselves are likely to work better than an order imposed on them by the court. The family courts expect separated parents to agree arrangements for their children, with the help of mediation where needed.[29] The effect of the 'no order' principle in the Children Act 1989 is that the court will make a child-related order only where there is continuing dispute and/or where there are concerns about a child's welfare, or where it is considered necessary and in the best interests of the child for the court to make an order, rather than no order at all. This policy of non-intervention by the courts is in harmony with the aim of mediation to help parents reach joint decisions and arrangements for their children. However, some parents look for legally binding child arrangements that cannot be cancelled suddenly by one parent on a whim, without apparent justification. The guidance on child arrangements in the CAP and the revised Parenting Plan issued by Cafcass in March 2014[30] seem to challenge the 'no order' principle and since 22 April 2014 it appears there may now be possibilities of the court making consent orders on child arrangements. It remains to be seen whether the no order principle will be modified and if so, in what way and with what effect.[31]

Over a decade ago, researchers at the Centre for Research on the Child and Family at the University of East Anglia[32] found that the 'no order' principle of the Children Act was working well. However, with the cuts in legal aid under LASPO, recently published figures show a sharp drop in the number of private family law cases. There are concerns that more children may be losing contact with their non-resident parent and that desperate parents might take the law

---

[29]   Midland Region Family Judges and Magistrates *What the Family Courts expect from Parents* (Judiciary of England and Wales, 2011), see Appendix H.

[30]   See **7.12** below and **12.8** on consent orders for child arrangements.

[31]   See **12.9** below.

[32]   Trinder, Beek and Connolly, 'Making contact: How parents and children negotiate and experience contact after divorce' (2002) *Joseph Rowntree Foundation Findings* 092.

into their own hands and abduct their child. Cafcass statistics show 2,928 new private law cases in July 2014 – a 36% fall on the same month last year. Previously, it was estimated that 1 in 10 children of non-resident parents were subject to arrangements ordered by the court.[33] It is not clear whether the marked decrease in private family law cases since October 2013 is due solely to the lack of legal aid, but it is clearly not due to a greater take-up of mediation. Although referrals to information and assessment meetings show signs of a gradual increase following the Children and Families Act 2014, the number of publicly funded mediations is unlikely ever to return to pre-LASPO levels. There is no evidence of a major re-channelling of cases away from the courts and into mediation.

Another contributory factor in the drop in contested proceedings in private child law could be the change in legal labels for child arrangements, since these legal labels have been found divisive in themselves. Parents can no longer fight for 'custody' or 'joint custody' of their children, since the Children Act 1989 (England and Wales) and the Children (Scotland) Act (1995) abolished this term, with its negative implications of possession, and introduced a range of new terms including 'residence', defining where the child lives (either sole residence or shared residence, where the child moves between two homes), and 'parental responsibility', emphasising that parents have joint and shared responsibilities towards their children, rather than rights over them. Separation and divorce do not end joint parental responsibility, unless in exceptional circumstances this responsibility is removed by the court from one or both parents. The evidence suggested, however, that instead of fighting over 'custody', some parents were still fighting over 'residence', 'shared residence' and 'contact', rather than over the actual substance of care. The Norgrove report[34] therefore recommended the introduction of the neutral term, 'child arrangements order', to replace contact and residence orders and to cover all issues related to a child's upbringing. This recommendation was enacted in the Children and Families Act 2014 and in the accompanying Child Arrangements Programme (CAP). It is too soon to measure its effect.

7.8 SHARED PARENTING AFTER SEPARATION

'A clear principle in case law is that it is in a child's best interests to have a continued, meaningful relationship with both parents following separation where this is safe.'[35]

The Norgrove Report cited above made a strong recommendation against legislation that would embody a presumption in favour of shared parenting after separation, on the grounds that such a presumption could create perceptions of separated parents having the right to substantially shared or

---

[33] Office for National Statistics *Non-resident parental contact* (Omnibus Survey Report 2008, No 38).

[34] Family Justice Review Final Report, 2011, para 4.15.

[35] Ibid, para 4.14.

equal time with the child. The Final Report stated that international and other evidence on 'shared parenting' showed that:

> 'people place different interpretations on this term, and that it is interpreted in practice by counting hours spent with each parent, disregarding the quality of the time. The thorough and detailed evidence from Australia showed the damaging consequences for many children.'[36]

A consortium of children's charities led by Coram Children's Legal Centre campaigned successfully for the term 'parental involvement' to be used in place of 'shared parenting'. The Children and Families Act 2014 added the following to s 1 of the Children Act 1989:

> 'A court ... is ... to presume, unless the contrary is shown, that the involvement of [each] parent in the life of the child concerned will further the child's welfare provided s/he can be involved in the child's life in a way that does not put the child at risk of suffering harm ... [i.e.] ... unless there is evidence that involvement of that parent in the child's life would put the child at risk of suffering harm whatever the form of the involvement.'

A further late addition states that the 'involvement' of a parent may be direct or indirect and does not imply any particular division of a child's time. It remains to be seen whether this change in the law will produce any real change of attitude or whether parents will continue to litigate over the issue or nature of a parent's involvement. Mediators are frequently dealing with cases where one parent is preventing the other parent from seeing a child, or where parents disagree over the division of the child's time. Follow-up studies suggest that equal or substantially shared parenting after separation can work well for some children but not for others, especially if there is continuing conflict between parents and if the child's time is divided between parents in a rigid way.[37] An Australian study by McIntosh et al[38] collected data on children's satisfaction with arrangements. The researchers found that children in early adolescence were less satisfied with shared care than their mothers or fathers. Children in shared care were less satisfied than children in all other kinds of arrangements and were most likely to want to change the arrangements. Children in rigid arrangements were most likely to be dissatisfied. McIntosh et al concluded that 'equal or substantial sharing of time may in some circumstances be an arrangement better suited to parents than to children'.[39] A more recent longitudinal British study[40] of children's experiences of post-separation arrangements contains important messages for parents, family lawyers, mediators and all those working in the family justice system. The researchers

---

[36] Ibid, para 4.23.

[37] *Caring for Children after Parental Separation*, Department of Social Policy and Intervention, University of Oxford, Family Policy Briefing 7, May 2011.

[38] McIntosh, Smyth, Kelaher, Wells and Long *Post-separation parenting arrangements and developmental outcomes for infants and children* (Family Court of Australia, Attorney-General's Department, 2010).

[39] Ibid at p 78.

[40] Fortin, Scanlan and Hunt 'Taking a longer view of contact: the perspectives of young adults who experienced parental separation in their youth' [2013] Fam Law 104.

undertook a survey of nearly 400 young adults to explore their experiences during and following their parents' separation and identify the main factors that affected the quality of their experience. A key message for parents and for family law professionals is that each child needs to be considered and understood as an individual, with needs that vary according to the child's age and stage of development, the quality of the parents' relationship and their communication with each other and other factors including the strength of the child's attachment to each parent. Overall, the research indicates that 'different children will be satisfied with different amounts of contact and that the quantity of contact is less important than the quality of the child's experience'.[41] This message underlines the importance of the detailed, child-focused attention that parents are encouraged to give in mediation to each of their children.

Individual children, family culture, parents' circumstances and family relationships all vary a great deal. In some communities, children are brought up by the extended family rather than by their parents. Some children grow up in a single-parent household and hardly know their other biological parent, if at all. Other children grow up with same-sex parents living in a civil partnership or married under the Marriage (Same Sex Couples) Act 2013. Many children are looked after by relatives or childminders. Although mothers still tend to carry the major share of household and childcare tasks, fathers play a much more active role in childcare than they used to do. Single-parent households headed by fathers are more common than formerly and many fathers play a full part in caring for their children, whereas others may have less involvement, often for work reasons. A separated father who has not previously been fully involved in childcare needs to be able to look after a young child on his own. Each parent needs to trust the other's parenting abilities. Mediators help parents to work out arrangements tailored to the child's needs and each parent's availability to care for the child. Separated parents need to consider their continuing joint involvement and how they will share the care of their children in practice. Having two homes can work well for children, provided there is co-operation and good communication between the parents. But there can be practical difficulties and confusion. 'The only drawback is that we forget things we want – like toys and music stuff. It takes a lot of doing, getting it from the other house.' 'It didn't work for me having two bases because you've got like two bedrooms and two of everything and I was getting mixed up who I was' (Caroline, aged 17).[42] Parents are helped to consider in mediation how they will exchange information concerning the child, perhaps using a notebook that travels to and fro with the child. When parents live some distance apart, children may spend longer periods away from their familiar environment and friends. The child's age, views, out of school activities and emotional resilience need to be considered carefully if the child is to manage frequent moves between two different homes and environments. Children who are shuttled to and fro frequently may be unable to maintain their activities and friendships.

---

[41] Quoted in Parkinson 'Taking a Longer View of Contact: messages that adults need to hear' [2013] Fam Law 294.

[42] Fred aged 10 and Caroline aged 17, quoted by Neale and Wade (Young Voice, 2000) 12–13.

These become increasingly important as they get older. Some parents want their child's time to be divided equally between them and some children want this too, but parents need to listen to their children and be aware that their needs and views are likely to change as the child gets older.

The Australian study by McIntosh et al[43] found that different groups of parents established different types of shared care that were associated with different longer-term outcomes. The three groups identified were:

- Co-operative parents, who were more likely to have higher income and education levels. These parents had good parent-parent and father-child relationships at mediation intake and sustained positive relationships over the four years of the study.

- A rigid 'shared care' group with fixed arrangements that lacked flexibility. This group started and continued with higher levels of conflict, higher rates of litigation and lower levels of fathers' regard for mothers' parenting.

- A 'formerly-shared care' group, where shared care was tried following mediation but broke down and reverted to primary mother care. This group also had high rates of pre- and post-mediation litigation and high levels of acrimony.

Children have a keen sense of fairness and those who try to be fair to both parents may sacrifice their own needs in trying to remain loyal to both parents. They may therefore accept arrangements that keep both parents happy at the expense of the child. Arrangements that work well at one stage may need to be varied as the child gets older. Some children want to spend more time with one parent at a particular stage of their development, but may fear hurting the other parent by saying so. Circular questions are particularly helpful in asking parents to put themselves in the child's place, without the mediator expressing opinions or giving advice. Parents often assume that their children's needs and feelings coincide with their own, but this is not necessarily so. Some children who move frequently from one parent to the other manage the transitions very well, whereas others experience anxiety or depression or have significantly higher hyperactivity scores.

Steinman[44] found that some form of shared parenting arrangements can work well for children if:

- there is good co-operation and communication between parents and clarity about who is responsible for which tasks;

- both parents are willing to be flexible, within a clear structure;

- travelling time is not too long and tiring for the child;

- the child is free from worries about being fair to both parents;

---

[43] McIntosh, Smyth, Kelaher, Wells and Long *Post-separation parenting arrangements and developmental outcomes for infants and children* (Family Court of Australia, Attorney-General's Department, 2010).

[44] Steinman 'The Experience of Children in a Joint Custody Arrangement' (1981) 51 *American Journal of Orthopsychiatry* 403–414.

- practicalities are sorted out: having duplicates of some things in each home avoids the child having to carry everything to and fro all the time;
- the child's friendships and activities are respected – this becomes increasingly important as the child gets older;
- parents listen to their child and are able to hear when the arrangements need adjusting.

Smart[45] identified three factors that distinguish successful from unsuccessful shared parenting arrangements:

(1) whether children's needs are prioritised, or whether the arrangement is based on the needs and wishes of the parents;

(2) whether the arrangements are flexible rather than rigid;

(3) whether the children feel equally 'at home' with both parents.

For many parents, shared parenting of children is impracticable because of their work, the lack or cost of large enough accommodation and the time and cost of transport between two households. However, even where children spend only a small proportion of their time with the non-resident parent, the three factors identified by Smart are still very important for their continuing well being.

7.9 MAINTAINING CHILDREN'S ATTACHMENTS AND RELATIONSHIPS

Wallerstein and Kelly[46] found that 'the relationship between visiting father and child is at its most malleable immediately after the father has moved out of the household and as the visiting pattern emerges. The foundations of the new visiting relationship are laid down during the immediate post-separation period. The visiting parent and child also have a second chance at this critical juncture to break out of past unhappy relations and establish a new bond.' The parent who leaves often fears losing the children and without the resident parent's co-operation – usually, the mother – the father may be confined to a minor role or possibly deprived of any role at all. Maintaining children's relationships with the non-resident parent requires sustained effort by both parents. Some parents find this extremely hard. In one mediation, a father expressed his bitter feelings towards the mother for abandoning her children, as he saw it. The mother explained that she had taken the extremely difficult decision to leave the home because the marriage had become deeply unhappy and she felt the strained atmosphere in the home was affecting their three children. As the father was not willing to leave, she decided to leave herself and move into rented accommodation in the same area. In the first stage of mediation, the parents agreed a schedule for the children to visit their mother on a regular basis. This schedule became more relaxed and flexible after settlement was reached on financial and property matters.

---

[45] Smart 'Equal shares: rights for fathers or recognition for children?' (2004) *Critical Social Policy* 484.

[46] Wallerstein and Kelly (1980), p 131.

The following account of mediation concerning contact with a small child comes from a family mediator in Staffordshire:[47]

'A referral was made to mediation by the court to assist the parents with their arrangements for their son, Bobby (not his real name), aged eighteen months. On the day of the mediation meeting there was snow, ice and sub-zero temperatures. However, amidst reports of airports closing down and four hundred stationary lorries on the M25, both parents and the mediator managed to get to the meeting. It had been agreed that Mum would drop Bobby off at his nursery beforehand and Dad would collect him later. Because of the weather, after dropping Bobby off at nursery, Mum had gone to buy him his first pair of Wellington boots. She brought the boots with her to the meeting so that Dad would have them when he collected Bobby later from nursery. So that she would not forget about the boots, Mum took them out of her bag and placed them on the table. And this is where they remained, in the middle of the mediation table, throughout the whole session. These were not any old Wellington boots. They were tiny (baby size 5) wellies in shiny plastic camouflage greens and browns with sparkly soles. So there, in the middle of the table, was a reminder of what was important:

• Talking about a tiny vulnerable child whose feet were so small as to fit into these little boots.
• The army camouflage imitated toughness, but with these little boots any semblance of toughness was deceptive. Their small wearer needed care and protection.
• The boots were made of flimsy plastic and not substantial. Dad was going to add thick woolly socks.
• The boots would fit Bobby now and keep his feet dry, but he would soon grow out of them. His parents would need to think about his changing needs, as he grew up.

Neither of the parents nor the mediator attempted to move the boots from their prominent position in the middle of the table. The mediation had a successful outcome.'

7.10 OVERNIGHT STAYS FOR YOUNG CHILDREN

From an early age, a child is able to form attachments with more than one person and these additional attachments benefit the child.[48] Cohen and Campos[49] found that most infants aged ten months showed attachment to both parents. This finding was based on observations of each infant's reactions to the presence of their mother, father and two strangers, in varying combinations. The incidence of exclusive mother attachment was consistently low, occurring in about 10% of infants. Lamb[50] found that even at seven months, the age when focused attachments first emerge, the infants in the study wanted to be

[47] Jane Staff, *Salmons Mediation* (December 2010).
[48] Schaffer *Making Decisions about Children – Psychological Questions and Answers* (Blackwell, 1990).
[49] Cohen and Campos 'Father, mother and stranger as elicitors of attachment behaviour in infants' (1974) 10 *Developmental Psychology* 146–54.
[50] Lamb 'Father-infant and mother-infant interaction in the first year of life' (1977) 48 *Child Development* 167–81.

held by or reached out to either parent. Children with multiple attachments have greater emotional resources to draw from. Understanding the importance of attachment in child development is essential in appreciating the psychological consequences of disrupting attachment, especially if this occurs without the child's comprehension. The child's age, stage of development and attachments need careful consideration so that arrangements are made to meet the child's needs, rather than the parents' needs.

Professionals, as well as parents, may have conflicting views about overnight stays for babies and young children. Leach's recent book[51] came under attack from separated fathers for cautioning against overnight stays for children under four years old. Some studies suggest that repeated and prolonged absence from the primary caregiver may be uniquely stressful for an infant or child under four years old. The human brain, about 30% formed at birth, expands threefold during the first three years and much of its growth during this time is *experience dependent,* meaning that the brain's development is affected by the nature and quality of care the infant receives. As Schore and McIntosh[52] explain:

> 'Attachment in the first year of life, when the brain circuits for attachment are still setting up, is different from attachment in the third or fourth year of life, when the system is going, so to speak. That is, to stress a developmental system while it is organizing in the first year will have a much more negative impact in response to the same stressor than if you did it when the child was four.'

Prolonged stress is harmful for children under four years old because the immature nervous systems of babies and infants are unstable and highly reactive. 'Stress in infancy is particularly hazardous, because prolonged stress in the early months of life produces high levels of cortisol that can affect the development of other neurotransmitter systems whose pathways are still being established, making it more difficult for the individual to regulate himself in later life.'[53]

It is unfortunate if questions concerning the care of young children become gender wars or, as McIntosh calls them, 'Baby Wars'.[54] In her keynote address to the inaugural conference of the AFCC Australian Chapter, McIntosh set two conditions which must be met before considering arrangements including overnight stays:

(1)   The young child is safe with, and can be comforted by, both parents.

(2)   The young child is protected from harmful levels of stress.

---

51   Leach *Family Breakdown* (2014).
52   Schore and McIntosh 'Family Law and the neuroscience of attachment' Part 1 (2011) *Family Court Review* 49.
53   Gerhardt *Why love matters – how affection shapes a baby's brain* (Routledge, 2004), p 65.
54   McIntosh *Beyond the Baby Wars – toward an integrated approach to the post-separation care of very young children,* keynote address to the inaugural conference of the AFCC Australian Chapter, August 2014.

When both these conditions are met, parents can be helped to work out arrangements that support and develop the child's attachments to both parents and which ease the child's transfers from one parent to the other. The key question is not whether babies form attachments to their father as well as their mother, or whether they need continuing relationships with both parents, but about the degree of stress and disruption of routine a young child could experience in overnight stays with an unfamiliar, or less familiar, carer in an unfamiliar environment. An infant who is handed from one loving parent to the other in an atmosphere of mutual trust and taken to another home not far away, where the child settles down easily, has an entirely different experience from an infant who is removed from the primary carer in a hostile atmosphere and taken to an unknown place. In either case, the child does not know how long he or she will be away from the main carer. Child-focused mediation helps parents to consider optimal arrangements from the child's point of view, so that stress and anxiety for the child can be avoided or minimised as far as possible. Parents who want to know more about child development and how to help children adjust to separation can be referred to useful sources of information and guidance. Many parents can be helped in mediation by detailed discussion of the child's current stage of development and routine. Although it may be assumed that children under five, or even under ten, would not take part in child-inclusive mediation, there are possible ways of including them with their parents that can be considered and explored.[55]

7.11   MOVING FROM CONFLICT TO CO-OPERATION

Many parents have so many problems to deal with when they separate that it is not easy for them to consider what their children may be experiencing. One of the benefits of mediation reported by parents is that they were helped to focus on their children as individuals and to consider their children's feelings and needs, as well as their own. Parents generally want to put their children first and welcome encouragement to do so. Children need time to adjust to major changes and there are practical difficulties for parents with irregular working hours and inadequate accommodation for overnight stays. Mothers (and fathers) often want to be reassured about sleeping arrangements and bedtime routines. A father who has never put a young child to bed needs to know the child's routine, while parents of older children may need to help them with their school work. There are some parents who use disputes over children as a vehicle for unresolved feelings over the ending of their own relationship. Even then, many parents are able to agree about their children's basic needs, despite disagreements over shared care or visiting arrangements. When parents recognise fundamental areas of agreement, their differences can be addressed in a more positive way. Most parents agree that children need:

- to be loved;
- to be taken care of, physically and emotionally;

---

[55]   See Chapter 8 and **11.5** below.

- to be reassured that their parents will look after them, although they no longer live together;

- to be able to enjoy good relationships with both parents, without experiencing conflicts of loyalty;

- to maintain relationships with other family members and key people in their lives;

- to have as much stability as possible;

- to have parents who can take decisions and provide safe boundaries, even if the rules in each parent's home are not the same;

- to have parents who are actively involved and show interest;

- to have opportunities to pursue their own activities and develop new interests;

- to develop as individuals, without being burdened by worries about their parents.

7.12 HELPING PARENTS TO WORK OUT CHILD ARRANGEMENTS IN MEDIATION

Family mediation provides a forum in which parents can discuss their children's needs in constructive ways and work out arrangements in broad terms or in detail. Family mediators assist parents by:

- emphasising positives;

- helping parents to focus on each child individually;

- increasing co-operation and reducing conflict over children;

- encouraging parents to accept each other's continuing role in the children's lives;

- helping them to consider areas of parental responsibility and how these will be shared or entrusted to one parent;

- helping parents to work out arrangements that free children from conflicts of loyalty or pressure;

- helping parents to work out how they will support the children financially;

- considering with parents how they will talk with their children and explain arrangements to them;

- helping parents to be more aware of what their children may be experiencing;

- considering with parents whether, and if so, in what way, children and young people should be consulted or included in the mediation process, so that their views and feelings can be taken into account without giving them responsibility for decisions.

Separated parents need to agree the extent to which day-to-day parenting will be shared between them or carried out mainly by one parent, with back-up from the other parent and often from other family members. Many parents make their own child arrangements without using lawyers or mediators.[56] Those who disagree or whose communication has broken down may come to mediation to work out child arrangements generally, or to agree certain aspects, including:

- time with each parent, overnight stays, school holidays, hand-overs and transport;
- who else will be present during visits, introduction of new partners and their children;
- health care in general and care during illness;
- education – choice of school, school subjects, homework, school meetings and events;
- religious upbringing;
- holidays, festivals and birthdays – presents, parties, outings;
- sport and leisure activities, music lessons, dance classes – paying costs and ferrying children;
- communication – sharing information, when and how to review or change arrangements;
- relationships and visits with other family members;
- discipline – rules and boundaries, respecting the other parent's rules, agreeing whether anyone else has any responsibility for disciplining the child;
- responsibility for the child's security and development – sex education, teaching about drugs;
- emergencies – contacting the other parent.

A useful tool is Cafcass's updated version of the Parenting Plan,[57] a guide for separated parents in making decisions concerning their children and working out practical arrangements. The updated Parenting Plan is available as a pdf download and also in interactive online and Word versions that can be filled in by one parent or by both together. The Parenting Plan recognises that it can be hard for parents to work out arrangements for their children when emotions are running high. It provides information about children's needs when parents split up and includes online modules to help parents modify their communication style, listen more and stay calm when involved in a dispute. There is a step-by-step guide on negotiating constructively to reduce conflict over children and avoid emotional harm to the child. The safety of the child is a predominant theme: completion of the Plan is not suitable where there are risk issues. The revised Parenting Plan is incorporated in Getting it Right for Children, a skills development programme produced by One Plus One[58] and hosted by the Parent Connection.[59] Separated parents have not always

---

[56] Barlow, Hunter, Smithson and Ewing *Mapping Paths to Family Justice – Briefing Paper and Report on Key Findings* (Universities of Exeter and Kent, June 2014), p 6.

[57] www.cafcass.gov.uk/grown-ups/parenting-plan.aspx.

[58] www.oneplusone.org.uk.

[59] See also **12.10** below on formalising agreements on child arrangements.

considered or been able to discuss all the aspects of bringing up children and taking care of them. Mediators may suggest that they use the parenting plan to work through these considerations and practical details, making it clear that the parenting plan may be shown to the court, whereas the mediation summary of child arrangements is confidential and privileged.

In mediation, separated parents can talk with each other directly in a supportive forum that may not be available to them elsewhere. Mediators can encourage and prompt their discussions with questions such as 'Have you thought about?' or 'What happens when …?' It may be particularly helpful to 'reality-check' the details of hand-overs. For example, when one parent collects the child or brings the child back from a visit, will the child be handed over at the door or walk alone to or from the car? Will the parents speak to each other when picking up or returning children? Can they avoid discussing anything in front of them that might lead to an argument? Parents need to agree how they will manage hand-overs to give their children emotional support and avoid angry scenes. In a mediation where communication between the parents had broken down completely, the mother complained that the father was collecting their four-year old daughter, Emily, without speaking or greeting her or giving her a hug. The mother said Emily was becoming more and more resistant to leaving her. The father said that Emily stopped crying and was fine once she was in his car, but he agreed that although he and the mother were not on good terms, Emily needed a 'warm carpet' to help her move from one parent to the other. He undertook to greet her and give her a hug and both parents said they would try to lighten the atmosphere for Emily.

In another example, the mother was willing for Grace, aged three, to go out with her father every Saturday, but only if the handover took place in a public place, because at the time of the parents' separation there had been a single incident involving some physical violence. The police had been called and the father arrested, but released without charge. The fight had arisen in an argument over ownership of a car. This issue was resolved in mediation, but the mother was not willing for the father to come to her home in case there was another argument. They had tried handing Grace over to each other in the street and were distressed that Grace went silently from one parent to the other with tears rolling down her cheeks. The parents decided in mediation that they would make the hand-over easier for Grace by meeting together in a café, where they would have a drink or snack and one parent would then leave Grace gently with the other parent. Arrangements for Grace's birthday and holidays were also worked out in mediation. Both parents reported subsequently that Grace was finding it much easier to move between them.

7.12.1 Step-by-step agreements

Parents with a high level of conflict over children may find it easier to work out step-by-step arrangements than to commit to a long-term plan. Interim arrangements may be accepted on the basis that the parents will review them in mediation and discuss modifications as necessary. Particularly for infants and young children, step-by-step arrangements can work well, as parents can gradually extend the period the child spends away from the primary carer in a way that supports the child's psychological and physical development and resilience. Mediators need to be aware, however, that interim arrangements may become established and that some parents may seek to use delaying tactics to their own advantage.

7.12.2   Asking parents for a 'portrait' of each child

Parents tend to bring conflicting versions of events in order to justify their own point of view. A helpful way to start is to ask them to describe each of their children. Parents are proud of their children and like talking about them. Describing each child's personality and interests, with each parent filling in some details, helps to focus on each child as an individual so that they can talk and listen to each other without feeling under attack. This also serves a number of other purposes:

- Sharing information about the children. Often the parent who is involved in the day-to-day care of the children knows more than the other. Asking this parent to start giving the picture can be a means of updating the parent who knows less.

- Seeing how far the parents agree or disagree about the child's personality, temperament and attachments. Often, there is a large measure of agreement even between parents who are in dispute over parenting arrangements. Areas of agreement can be emphasised and used for the next stage of work. Some parents are very surprised to find how far they are in agreement.

- Easing communication in a positive way, encouraging parents to talk about interests they share that are not upsetting or controversial.

- Establishing ground-rules, making it clear that the mediator will ask each parent and allow time for each of them to respond and be heard, without interrupting each other.

- When conflict is high, mediators can ask focused questions that provide a clear and firm structure.

Gathering information about children includes asking about:
- the child's personality and temperament;
- the child's stage of development – physical, emotional, intellectual;
- how the child is getting on at school – school work and friends;
- how the child gets on with siblings;
- the child's health;
- the child's interests and activities;
- any special needs or difficulties;
- how do the parents know when the child is happy?
- how do they know when the child is upset? How do they respond?

Many parents who come to mediation want to give priority to their children and are motivated to co-operate. Even if they disagree, the atmosphere usually lightens as they describe each child. They often smile and look at each other more readily. It is then easier to move on to questions about current and future arrangements. In one case, parents who had not been speaking to each other and who were in high conflict over their sons, relaxed visibly as they talked about each boy's personality and activities. They then became able to work out time-sharing arrangements.

7.13   METHODS AND SKILLS IN MEDIATING ABOUT CHILDREN

These are some examples of methods and skills that have been referred to in earlier chapters.

7.13.1   Questioning skills, including past-, present- and future-oriented questions and circular questions[60]

Mediators often use future-focused or hypothetical questions for parents to think about before the next meeting. 'If the children are going to live with you (mother) or with you (father), how much time do you think they should spend with the other parent? The children may have one main home or move between two homes, but what part does each of you want to have in their upbringing and general development – what do you see as your strengths and contribution as a parent? In what ways would you see the other parent having a role in the children's upbringing? What support would you look for from the other parent? Are there major questions – such as health, education, religion – on which you would agree to consult each other when necessary? What kind of information about the children would you expect to share with each other?'

Parents may be asked to imagine their child in, say, five years' time, and the questions the child might ask then. A mother who thinks that a child under three will not miss her father may be asked to imagine the child at twelve or fifteen, asking why her father did not love her enough to keep in touch.

7.13.2   Normalising

'many children show signs of ...', 'children often ...'

When parents blame each other for a child's reactions, the mediator may be able to comment that this is normal or a commonly experienced problem. Toddlers who have tantrums and uncommunicative teenagers are found in a great many intact families. Parents tend to blame each other. Instead of looking for cause and effect, the mediator may find that each parent needs more help and support from the other parent. Parents often respond to a request for help

---

[60]   See Chapter 6 above.

and support, once they realise that they are not being blamed for causing the problem. It is important to acknowledge parents' efforts and the support they need, without suggesting that they are failing to meet their children's needs. Criticism, whether overt or implied, increases defensiveness and resistance. When parents constantly blame and find fault with each other, the child's reactions may be reinforced and the parents may turn to experts, having lost confidence in their ability to help their children. One of the difficulties is that children's behaviour may be ambiguous and capable of being interpreted in different ways. Conflict increases when parents interpret the child's reactions differently. To help them realise that they could both be right and that there could be other possible explanations, mediators need to understand how children may hide their feelings or act them out.

- Acknowledging and mutualising – 'you both care a great deal about the children.' Anger and concerns can be acknowledged while keeping the focus on the present and future: 'So you are both concerned to work out arrangements for … (names of the children) that would help them manage these changes as well as possible?'

- Reframing blaming statements, eg 'so you are both looking for reliable arrangements?'

- Prioritising – 'what do you think is most important for the children right now?'

- Information – 'the courts prefer parents to reach their own agreements.' 'Have you come across these books for children?' It is not the mediator's role to lecture parents on their children's best interests. Many parents are, however, in need of information and guidance on how to help their children adjust to their separation. There are helpful books, DVDs and websites for parents and books for children that parents can read with young children or give to an older child. Mediators should have a selection of books and other materials to show parents who are interested and copies of a resource list to give to them.

7.13.3   Using the flip-chart, drawing an ecogram

The flip-chart is very useful for highlighting key questions, providing a common focus and prioritising. Listing parents' issues and options helps to show which areas of parental responsibility are agreed and which areas are not agreed. It may be helpful to draw a calendar on the flip-chart showing a five-week (or any other) period, with each day divided between am and pm. Parents may be invited to explain their current arrangements and the arrangements they are each looking for. Marking these on the flip-chart, possibly with different colours, helps to highlight how much time the children are spending with, or could spend with, each parent. The contrast between two Saturdays a month with their father, compared with around twenty-eight days with their mother, shows more clearly on the flip-chart than in discussion.

7.13.4 Timing and structure in mediating about children

'Shall we decide the order in which we are going to discuss these questions?' Mediators need to focus on the main issues and keep an eye on the clock. Discussions about children can take a long time and mediation is not therapy. Questions and comments need to be focused and the pace of discussion needs to be managed. If the priority is next weekend, it is important to allow time to deal with this, rather than embarking on a wide-ranging discussion which leaves no time to sort out next weekend's arrangements. Sensitivity and skills are needed in deciding how many questions to ask about the children, and at what stage. Questions about what each parent has said – or allegedly said – to the children are often highly sensitive and may be a subject to come back to at another meeting, after they have worked out interim arrangements. 'Have the two of you explained things with the children together, or do you talk to them separately?' Or 'Have you told the children that you are coming to mediation?' Generally, children seem to welcome being told that their parents are meeting together to work out arrangements. Many children are able to understand the idea of mediation and even young children can understand the need for a person who does not take sides.

7.14 CHILDREN'S ROLES IN PARENTAL CONFLICT

Sometimes children are passive bystanders who watch from the sidelines. But if parents continue to fight, the children may be drawn in. A child may become caught in an emotional triangle in which the parents' unresolved conflicts are channelled through the 'triangulated child.' Children may react in ways that seem attention seeking or manipulative, but their reactions may be a way of showing their needs and the pressures they are under. Children try to protect parents, as well as themselves and in some circumstances, their behaviour is the only means they can find of showing needs they cannot express in words.

7.14.1 Roles that a child may take on to try to resolve conflict between parents

	Child's role	Role of mediator
1	Messenger, go-between	Helps parents talk with each other directly, instead of communicating via the children
2	Reconciler (tries to bring parents together)	Helps parents agree what needs to be explained; helps parents discuss how to reassure the child
3	Peace-maker (tells each parent what s/he wants to hear)	Helps parents resolve conflicts

	Child's role	Role of mediator
4	Ally enlisted by one parent to give support	Helps parents reach agreements and resolve conflicts to free the child
5	Decision-taker	Helps parents take responsibility for difficult decisions
6	Scapegoat (tests out, fears being abandoned by both parents)	Helps parents give reassurance and agree necessary limits, define rules etc.
7	Confidante	Helps parents consider how to avoid burdening the child
8	Substitute partner (replacing spouse who has left)	Helps parents feel more secure so that they depend less on the child
9	Substitute parent or carer (looking after a parent or younger siblings)	Helps parents feel more secure so that they depend less on the child. Help parent/s understand the child's needs
10	Judge (encouraged to blame a parent)	Discusses with parents how they can help children understand, without condemning either parent
11	Fugitive (truancy, delinquency)	Discusses risks and concerns with parents. Seeks greater parental involvement
12	Mourner for lost family. Shows grief that parents are repressing	Helps parents recognise and share sadness as well as anger

It is normal for children of all ages to dream that their parents will get back together. The desire to reunite separated parents is often intense and of long duration. Children may develop physical symptoms associated with emotional stress. They may also fantasise that both parents will come together again to care for a child who is ill.

Example

Sarah, aged six, complained of feeling unwell whenever she was due to visit her father.

Mother's interpretation: the visits are distressing Sarah – especially as her ex-husband has a new partner. It would be better for Sarah to reduce the visits or to stop them altogether for a while.

Father's interpretation: his ex-wife is turning Sarah against him because she is jealous of his new girlfriend. If his ex-wife is blocking his relationship with his daughter, it would be better for Sarah to come and live with him. His girlfriend has children of her own and she is an excellent mother.

Possible outcomes if the dispute is not resolved:
- Sarah may lose her relationship with her father.
- The family doctor, teachers, child psychologist and solicitors may all become involved.
- A social work report may be called for.
- If a court order is made, arrangements may not work in practice if Sarah continues to resist.
- The dispute may escalate further.

Mediation may help the parents to:
- Focus on Sarah: how do they describe her? Do they have other children? If Sarah is an only child, the pressures on her may be particularly intense.
- Clarify the present situation and the main questions.
- Consider how Sarah can keep her relationship with both parents.
- Consider how to give Sarah as much support and reassurance as possible. What are the options and practical possibilities? Might Sarah need some time alone with her father? What about the length of time and frequency of visits? If the parents argue when they meet, could Sarah move between them without the parents meeting, at least for a time? Could grandparents help?
- Explore what is troubling Sarah: could it be that she loves both her parents and does not understand why they cannot stay together? Maybe she hopes her father will come and help her mother look after her, so that they can all go on living together? Maybe Sarah is trying to protect one or both parents by preventing them from seeing each other?
- An interim or step-by-step agreement may pave the way for gradually increased visits so that Sarah does not have to cope with too much change too quickly. This may help to reassure Sarah's mother of the need for stability, while reassuring her father that her time with him can increase by degrees.
- Does Sarah need to be reassured that her mother supports her relationship with her father? And that she need not worry about her mother being alone while she is away? Can her mother give her these reassurances?
- Helping Sarah be clear about dates and times. Suggesting that her mother marks the dates on a calendar may be helpful.
- Consider what has been said to Sarah so far? What may she need to hear from both parents? How can she be helped to understand and come to terms with their separation?
- Are there any other changes that would make things easier? Can Sarah's father also phone her?

- Particularly when there is reluctance to agree a fixed schedule, it may help to suggest a further mediation meeting some weeks later, to review how the arrangements are working and whether changes are needed.

Mediators should be careful not to reject a parent's interpretation of a child's behaviour or to claim to know better than the parents. Ideas may be seen as possibilities, rather than as a solution. Parents may take a new idea on board and need time to think about it. If it opens up a fresh perspective, it may help them work together in a problem-solving way, rather than in a confrontational way.

Example

Jake, aged 13, was caught stealing DVDs from a local shop.

Mother's interpretation: Jake is in need of more discipline and control. He is rude, sullen and goes out all the time. She cannot cope with him – she has tried and she has had enough. She cannot make him go to school. At this rate he will end up a criminal. It's time his father took responsibility for him. He can go and live at his father's.

Father's interpretation: Jake is getting out of control. His mother never did handle him very well. Maybe she is right about Jake needing to live with him instead of with his mother – but it's no good expecting him to be at home when Jake comes out of school. The lad will have to do as he is told and stay out of trouble. Otherwise, he'll end up in care. He'd better be aware that this is what will happen if he carries on stealing.

Possible outcomes if Jake does not get the help he needs:
- Further arguments between the parents about whose fault it is that Jake is getting into trouble.
- Neither parent helps Jake to feel loved and wanted.
- Jake re-offends.
- Social workers become involved.
- Jake is taken into care.

Mediation could help the parents to:
- Focus on Jake: What was he like as a small boy? And now? Do his parents think he is unhappy? Angry? Worried? Do they have other children?
- Discuss Jake's needs. What are the present arrangements for Jake? Can they co-operate in meeting his needs? If he lives with his mother, can she rely on his father backing her up over questions of 'boundaries' (staying out late) and discipline?
- Settle other related issues, including financial issues. Might these be affecting Jake? Does he get pocket money?

- Consider whether Jake is angry with both parents. Maybe he imagines they don't care what happens to him? Maybe he is hoping that if he is in trouble, they will get together somehow and sort it out?

- Can the parents to talk with Jake together? Jake needs to be consulted in his own right – how can this be done? If, having considered other possible options, both parents think that offering Jake the opportunity to meet with the mediator on his own would be their preferred plan, would they be willing to put this suggestion to him?[61]

7.15 CHILDREN'S PROTECTIVE STRATEGIES

Children become very anxious when they realise that one parent is unable to cope or that it is not safe for their parents to meet. They may engage in protective strategies to keep everyone safe and protect one or both parents from hurting each other. 'Everything is all right as long as I don't let Mum and Dad speak to each other.'[62] Some children seek to protect their parents and themselves by refusing to see the other parent – even when, deep down, they want to do so. Many children try to help their parents by telling each parent what that parent needs to hear.

Example

Daniel, aged nine, did not want to hurt either parent by choosing one and rejecting the other. He told each of them what he thought they needed to hear from him. He told his father he would like to live with him. He assured his mother he wanted to stay with her. Daniel was unsure if his mother could manage without him. He knew she depended on him.

Mother's interpretation: Of course Daniel wants to live with her. She has always looked after him and they are very close. His father is putting words in Daniel's mouth and pressurising him. This is irresponsible and wrong.

Father's interpretation: Daniel is a boy and it is understandable that he has reached an age where he wants to live with his father. Unfortunately his mother cannot see this. She is over-protective. Daniel should be allowed to decide and then it will be clear where he wants to be.

Possible outcome if the parents cannot agree: If their dispute continues following an application to the court, the court may consider that either parent could provide good care for Daniel and encourage some form of shared parenting. Court proceedings could heighten conflict between the parents and result in Daniel feeling pulled between them more than ever.

Mediation could help these parents to:

---

[61] See Chapter 8 below.
[62] Six-year-old child quoted by Cockett and Tripp, *The Exeter Study* (1994), p 43.

- Focus on Daniel and his needs, through use of present-focused, past-focused and future-focused questions. When Daniel was a baby, did both parents share in looking after him? How did this work? Did they contribute to looking after him in similar or different ways? Did they each value the other parent's support? Or did they wish the other parent had done more? How could both of them be involved now?

- Think about their particular qualities as parents (as mother/father, with their different personalities, interests and abilities) and what each of them can give to or share with Daniel in complementary ways.

- Identify and consider options for shared parenting and how these would work in practice.

- Consider immediate issues in the context of longer-term needs.

- Consider whether and how Daniel can be helped to express his feelings and needs, without being caught up in conflicts of loyalty. According to each parent, how mature do they think he is for his age? Should he be offered an opportunity to meet with a child counsellor or mediator qualified in child consultation, to talk about his feelings and concerns and how he thinks things could work better?[63]

Even parents who are angry with each other usually say that what matters most is their child's well-being. Mediators need to acknowledge how hard it is to continue as parents while ending a close relationship, supporting parents in disentangling the pain and anger of ending their own relationship from their effort to maintain child-parent and parent-parent relationships. Many parents welcome the offer of guide-lines on parenting after separation that both of them will endeavour to follow. As well as drawing attention to the Cafcass parenting plan, mediators may find it useful to give parents who are in continuing dispute over their children a copy of the Midland Region Judges and Magistrates guidelines, 'What the Family Courts expect from Parents'[64] and discuss it with them.

7.16   EXPLAINING TO CHILDREN

Separated parents may be able to agree with each other, but need help to agree how to explain their decisions and arrangements to their children. A parent's inability or unwillingness to explain a painful situation to a child may combine with children's tendencies to suppress their feelings. A collusive wall of silence may be built around the parent who has left. The longer this wall remains, the harder it becomes to dismantle it. It is understandable that many parents feel unable to talk about the separation with their children. They are already overwhelmed by their own pain and worry. When children are asked what would have helped them, they nearly always say that they needed more information, explanation and reassurance from their parents than they actually

63   See Chapter 8 below.
64   Midland Region Family Judges and Magistrates *What the Family Courts expect from Parents* (Judiciary of England and Wales, 2011), Appendix H.

received. Family mediators can help parents to discuss the difficult questions of what should be explained to the children, by whom and at what stage. Many parents who come to mediation have reassured the children that the separation is not their fault, but they may not have been able to tell the children whether they will go on living in the same home or how much time they will spend with each parent. When parents blame each other for the separation or divorce, children are liable to be given conflicting accounts. Mediators help parents to work out agreed explanations, appropriate to the age of the child, that they can give separately or together without contradicting or denigrating each other to the children.

7.16.1   Reassurances that parents need to give their children

- Both parents love their children very much and will always love them.

- They are still a family and their parents will continue to take care of them.

- They will go on living in the same home (or, if a move may be necessary, they will be told about it and involved in new arrangements).

- They will continue to spend time with the parent they no longer live with. (Children need to know where this parent is/will be living).

- The separation is not their fault: they are in no way to blame for the separation.

- Both parents are sorry about the separation.

- They decided to separate because they were making each other unhappy (or some variation that fits the parents' situation. Telling children that their parents are splitting up because they no longer love each other can make young children fear that their parents might stop loving them too).

- They will tell the children about any new arrangements that affect them.

- They are working out new arrangements for the family with a mediator, explaining to the children what this means. Even young children can understand the idea of mediation very well (sometimes better than adults do).

- The children's views and feelings are important and they will be listened to. Their parents will work out decisions that take the children's views into account, as far as possible.

- The parents understand that these changes may be very upsetting and that the children may feel angry or sad or both; these feelings are natural and understandable and they can talk about them.

- If something worries them at any time, they need to tell one or both parents about it, so that they can help.

- Even if the parents divorce, there is no divorce between children and their parents.

Most parents prefer to talk with their children in their own home but may be unsure how to go about it. Mediators can help them plan the timing and content of a joint discussion with children and agree what should *not* be discussed with the children. Parents need to be aware that children can react in very different ways. Some cry and show distress, whereas others may appear unconcerned, barely listening and then asking 'What are we having for tea?' Even if children appear not to be listening, they are usually taking in what is said. They may need to hear it more than once, especially the reassurances, in order to absorb them fully. Mediators can help parents anticipate how a particular child might react ('what if …?'), by asking how they would respond to an angry outburst directed at one parent in particular. Parents who are well prepared are more able to cope with their own feelings and back each other up in front of the children. Sometimes parents are at a loss to know what they can say to a child to help the child understand. One way to help them is for the mediator to place an empty chair and ask them to imagine that the child is sitting there and expecting some explanation from them. Although this may sound artificial, it can be very powerful. Parents may talk to their imaginary child with great emotion and intensity. What matters is not so much what the parents want to say as what children need to hear and who is listening to them. Opportunities for children to have a say in parents' arrangements for them are the focus of the next chapter.

7.16.2   Rachel's Poem[65]

My Mum and my Dad are inside who I am.
They are part of me wherever I go.
When they divorced, they hated each other.
And that was like they hated me.
And when they hurt each other they hurt me.
When Mum did not want me to see Dad, she wasn't seeing me.
When Dad didn't want me to love Mum, he wasn't loving me.
Now that's stopped and they get on OK.
So I can be who I am, with my Mum and Dad inside me.

---

[65]   Reprinted with permission of Jenn McIntosh *Because it's for the Kids. Building a Secure Parenting Base after Separation* (2006).

CHAPTER 8

CHILD-INCLUSIVE MEDIATION

I couldn't get my ideas heard; mum wouldn't let me go to court.' 12-year-old girl[1]

'I've not come across anyone I can speak to – I don't always want to share things with my mum.' 13-year-old boy[2]

CONTENTS

8.1   HEARING THE VOICE OF THE CHILD[3]

'Through most of the calls, there was a picture of children ... lacking or being refused information or feeling unable to talk with their parents or ask them questions for fear of upsetting them further.'[4]

---

[1]   Office of the Children's Commissioner *Don't Just Listen. Act* (Consultation Response to the Family Justice Review, July 2011), p 22.
[2]   Ibid.
[3]   My special thanks to Angela Lake-Carroll, family mediator and trainer, for her helpful comments on this chapter.
[4]   ChildLine, 1998, p 23.

'We needed to know what was going on, what was happening, how things would work out ... We needed help from outside, but there just didn't seem to be the right person to turn to. No one seemed to be there to help us, especially us, the children. Mum and Dad had the lawyers, but we had no one.'[5]

'The court and parties should be conscious of the need to ensure that children are involved, as appropriate in the context of their age and level of understanding, in the decision-making process'.[6] When parents make arrangements for their children following separation, many children and young people want to be listened to and have their views and feelings taken into account.[7] Very often, however, they are left in the dark when their parents separate. They may not be told what is happening and rarely feel that their views have been taken into account. A quarter of children whose parents had separated said that no one had talked to them about the separation when it happened. Only 5% said they had been given full explanations and a chance to ask questions.[8] It was left to the mother in over 70% of families to tell the children about the separation. Some mothers told them only that their father had left, without any explanation.[9] One girl said about her mother 'She didn't understand how I felt. She was too busy being angry.'[10] A boy remarked: 'You're the first person who's ever bothered to ask me how I felt'.[11] Morrow[12] found that most children wanted to have a say in matters affecting them. Even young children could understand and talk about the notion of being listened to. Some want to be heard and involved in decision-making, whereas others want to be consulted without having any responsibility for decisions. Many teenagers insist they should be included in decision-making that will have a profound impact on their lives. One 15 year-old girl pointed out: 'We are people too and shouldn't be treated like low-lifes just because we are younger. I think kids deserve the same kind of respect that we are expected to give so-called adults'.[13]

Rutter[14] has pointed out that 'it matters greatly how people deal with adversities and life stressors – perhaps not so much in the particular coping strategy employed but in the fact that they do **act** and not simply react ... The promotion of resilience does not lie in an avoidance of stress, but rather in encountering stress at a time and in a way that allows self-confidence and social

---

5   Lyon, Surrey and Timms *Effective Support Services for children and young people when parental relationships break down – a child-centred approach* (University of Liverpool, 1998), p 5.
6   Child Arrangements Programme (CAP), President of the Family Division, 2014.
7   Smart and Neale 'It's My Life Too – Children's Perspectives on Post-Divorce Parenting' [2000] Fam Law 163–169; Fortin, Scanlan and Hunt 'Taking a longer view of contact: the perspectives of young adults who experienced parental separation in their youth' [2013] Fam Law 104.
8   Dunn and Deater-Deckard 'Children's Views of their Changing Families' (2001) *Joseph Rowntree Research Findings* 931.
9   Cockett and Tripp *The Exeter Family Study: Family Breakdown and its impact on children* (University of Exeter Press, 1994).
10   Mitchell *Children in the Middle* (Tavistock, 1985), p 94.
11   Ibid, p 81.
12   Morrow 'Children's Perspectives on Families' (1998) *Rowntree Research Findings* 798.
13   Quoted by O'Quigley *Listening to Children's Views* (Joseph Rowntree Foundation, 2000), p 30.
14   Rutter M 'Resilience in the Face of Adversity' (1985) 147 *British Journal of Psychiatry* 608.

competence to increase through mastery and appropriate responsibility'. Nicola Watson[15] has described how teachers, instead of taking control of arguments between primary school children, can use them as opportunities for emotional and social learning with potentially transformative benefits for the children. Studies by Rutter and others[16] show that resilience is a dynamic process, rather than an inherited trait, thus underlining the importance of talking with children and young people, explaining to them, discussing and consulting with them and listening to what they say. There can be misguided attempts to protect children by excluding them, instead of enabling them to participate in family decision-making in ways that increase their self-confidence and self-esteem. Giving children 'appropriate responsibility' does not mean asking them to make choices or judgements: appropriate responsibility comes through appropriate involvement. Many children understand this better than adults do. 'I think there should be some kind of agreement between the children and the parents as to what should happen. I think the people who are involved should get to decide, not by themselves, but by helping each other to reach some kind of agreement as to what would be best' Jake, aged 11.[17]

The importance of hearing children and young people involved in family proceedings has been emphasised in the House of Lords by Baroness Hale of Richmond:

> 'There is a growing understanding of the importance of listening to the children involved in children's cases. It is the child, more than anyone else, who will have to live with what the court decides. Those who do listen to children understand that they often have a view that is quite distinct from that of the person looking after them. They are quite capable of being moral actors in their own right. Just as the adults may have to do what the court decides whether they like it or not, so may the child. But that is no more reason for failing to hear what the child has to say than it is for refusing to hear the parents' views.'[18]

The recent investigation of child abuse in Rotherham is uncovering the extent to which children's statements and complaints were dismissed by the adults who were responsible for protecting them. In an early study of justice and child welfare in divorce, Murch[19] criticised the preventive approach that was then taken to the protection of children's welfare in separation and divorce, pointing out that there was no evidence of its effectiveness. Murch suggested that paradoxically, a participant approach 'might well prove the correct way to be efficiently preventative'.[20] A participative approach to the consideration of children's needs and well-being includes parents and/or other carers and also, in

---

15 Watson 'Looking for Trouble' (2014) vol.4.2 Every Child Journal 44–52 www.teachingtimes. com.

16 Schaefer et al 'The health-related functions of social support' (1981) 4(4) *Journal of Behavioral Medicine* 381–406; Fortin, Scanlan and Hunt 'Taking a longer view of contact: the perspectives of young adults who experienced parental separation in their youth' [2013] Fam Law 104.

17 Neale and Wade *Parent Problems! Children's views on life when parents split up* (Young Voice, 2000), p 32.

18 *Re D (A Child) (Abduction: Rights of Custody)* [2006] UKHL 51 [2007] 1 AC 619.

19 Murch *Justice and Welfare in Divorce* (Sweet and Maxwell, 1980).

20 Ibid, p 206.

appropriate ways and conditions, children and young people themselves. The NSPCC study referred to in the previous chapter[21] found that three-quarters of the children involved in family court proceedings over child arrangements felt they had been able to have a say. However, only half of them thought it had made any difference. Therefore, it is not just a question of whether children and young people have any say in arrangements, but who actually listens and takes account of their views and feelings in a way that is helpful to the child.

8.2   THE CHILD AS SUBJECT OF LEGAL RIGHTS

Until the middle of the nineteenth century, children were treated as small adults who were put to work at an early age, without considering their needs as children. By degrees, child welfare campaigns and public concern led to laws being passed to protect children from exploitation and to provide them with education. However, it was not until the later part of the twentieth century that children were recognised as having rights, as well as needs for care and protection. Article 12(1) of the United Nations Convention on the Rights of the Child 1989, adopted by the UK in 1991, states that in any matter or procedure affecting the child, the views of the child should be given due weight, in accordance with their age and maturity. Those capable of forming opinions should be assured of 'the right to express their views freely' and should be given opportunities to express their views 'either directly or through a representative or an appropriate body' (Article 12(2)). The Brussels II Revised Regulation of 27 November 2003 concerning recognition and enforcement of judgments in matrimonial matters and matters of parental responsibility, likewise upholds the right of the child to be heard in accordance with the child's age and maturity on matters relating to parental responsibility over the child (Article 4).

In public child law proceedings, where a child is in care or where adoption is considered, the court or local authority should as far as practicable ascertain the wishes and feelings of the child having regard to the child's age and understanding.[22] Under the Children Act 1989, the court is required in any proceedings concerning a child to have regard to 'the ascertainable wishes and feelings of the child concerned (considered in the light of his age and understanding)'.[23] In public law proceedings, the child automatically becomes a party to the proceedings and in private law proceedings the child can become a party and be legally represented. The Children (Scotland) Act 1995 requires all those with parental responsibility to have regard, so far as practicable, to the views of the child concerned. A child aged twelve or over is assumed in Scotland to be of sufficient age and maturity to form a view. A study of public and private law child proceedings commissioned by the Ministry of Justice to inform family justice developments[24] found that 10% of divorces involved

---

[21]   Timms, Bailey and Thorburn *Your Shout Too!: a survey of the views of children and young people involved in court proceedings when their parents divorce or separate* (NSPCC Policy and Practice Series, 2007).

[22]   Children Act 1975, ss 3 and 59.

[23]   Children Act 1989 s 1(3).

[24]   Cassidy and Davey (2011) *Ministry of Justice Research Summary* 5/11.

child-related proceedings and these were likely to be high conflict cases. The sample consisted of 602 children involved in 393 private law cases. 58% involved Cafcass reports, 37% expert reports and 53% involved allegations of domestic abuse or concerns about abduction or harm to children. The father was the applicant in 77% of these applications and the mother in 20%. 53% of cases involved one to four court hearings, 31% involved five to nine hearings and 16% involved ten or more hearings. The average length of case was 46 weeks. Cases that resulted in a final order lasted on average 51 weeks – almost a year in the child's life. If there are no interim arrangements, it may be very difficult to re-establish the child-parent relationship after a long break, especially if parents are unable to communicate positively where the child is concerned. Litigation can last for six or even eight years in some cases and the loss of the child-parent relationship may be irreparable.[25] Some parents who were referred to mediation only at a very late stage in proceedings suggested that much earlier referral to shuttle mediation or child-inclusive mediation could have helped them to work out arrangements before their children lost touch with the non-resident parent.

The NSPCC study[26] found that half the children involved in court proceedings had found their Cafcass worker helpful or very helpful. However, a quarter thought their Cafcass worker had not helped them at all. Some children felt they had been talked down to or patronised or that the Cafcass worker had not listened to them. 'I didn't like talking to people who I don't know and who don't know me.'[27] Hunt found that 60% of children seen by a Cafcass worker were seen for half an hour or less.[28] The Final Report of the Family Justice Review emphasised that 'children's interests are central to the operation of the family justice system. Decisions should take the wishes of children into account'.[29] 'Children and young people should be given age-appropriate information to explain what is happening and should be supported and enabled to make their views known. Older children should be offered 'a menu of options, to lay out the ways in which they could – if they wish – do this'.[30] The Family Justice Young People's Board is working on a National Charter for Child-Inclusive Family Justice and the Mediation Task Force drew further attention to 'the urgent need to review the culture that tends to exclude children and young people and to address the misperceptions about the purpose of hearing children's voices.'[31] . In his speech to the Family Justice Young People's Board 'Voice of the Child' Conference on 24 July 2014,[32] Simon Hughes,

---

25 See Chapter 11 on impasses between a parent and a child.
26 Timms, Bailey and Thorburn *Your Shout Too!: a survey of the views of children and young people involved in court proceedings when their parents divorce or separate* (NSPCC Policy and Practice Series, 2007).
27 Ibid, p 4, quotation from a child.
28 Hunt *Parental Perspectives on the Family Justice System in England and Wales: a review of research* (Report for the Family Justice Council, December 2009).
29 Family Justice Review, Final Report 2011, Executive Summary, para 8.
30 Ibid, para 9.
31 Mediation Task Force Report, June 2014, para 86.
32 Rt Hon. Simon Hughes MP, Speech at the Family Justice Young People's Board 'Voice of the Child' Conference, 22 July 2014.

Minister of State for Justice and Civil Liberties, announced his intended policy
for all children of ten and over involved in family proceedings to have the
opportunity for access to the judge, in person or in an appropriate way, and to
have opportunities for consultation in mediation. 'Children and young people
of ten and over will therefore be given the chance to make known their views in
person or if preferred in another way.' Simon Hughes stated his intention 'to
start immediately a dialogue with the family mediation profession about how
we can make sure that the voice of the child and young person becomes a
central part of the process of family mediation.'

8.3   THE CHILD'S ACCESS TO THE JUDGE

Following these recommendations, the Government has made the commitment
that 'all children from the age of ten involved in family court hearings in
England and Wales will have access to judges to make their views known. The
Family Justice Young People's Board has produced tools for Cafcass Officers to
collect the views of children and young people which are now provided
alongside Cafcass reports to the judge'.[33] Some children ask to see the judge
who is responsible for deciding their future, but many children feel scared.
There is a fine balance between involving children and inviting their input on
arrangements that affect them, while also protecting them from pressure and
from risks of being blamed for the court's decision, or feeling disillusioned that
their views made no difference to the outcome.

Judges who see a child in chambers are encouraged[34] 'to enable children to feel
more involved and connected with proceedings in which important decisions
are made in their lives.' A former President of the Family Division gave strong
reasons in favour of the judge seeing a child who is at the centre of a dispute.[35]
Some judges may feel, however, that they lack the necessary training and
expertise to meet with children and are also troubled by the dilemma of
explaining a judicial decision to parents without betraying a confidence from a
child. Judges may therefore be reluctant to see the child, 'preferring that the
voice of the child in private law proceedings is heard either through a Cafcass
report or through a r 9.5 guardian. However, circumstances do arise where it is
not just appropriate but actually necessary for the judge to hear the voice of a
child before making his decision.'[36] There are risks, nonetheless, of children
being coached by each parent on what they should say to the judge and if the
judge is obliged to tell the parents what their child has said, this can have
repercussions for the child. In Australia, 'interviews by other professionals have
long since replaced judicial interviews as the normal means of ascertaining the

---

[33]   DfE and MoJ *A Brighter Future for Family Justice* (August 2014), p 36.
[34]   *Guidelines for Judges Meeting Children who are subject to Family Proceedings*, produced by
       the Family Justice Council and approved by the President of the Family Division [2010] Fam
       Law 654.
[35]   Potter [2008] IFL 140.
[36]   Bellamy, Platt and Crichton 'Talking to Children: the Judicial Perspective' [2010] Fam Law
       647.

views of children'.[37] The Australian researchers suggest that the focus should be, not only on how children are heard in legal proceedings, but on how they can be better heard in families to help them resolve their conflicts without going to court.

8.4 CHILD-INCLUSIVE MEDIATION

The Council of Europe's Recommendation 2003[38] stated that where children are concerned, the child 'should also be heard in the mediation process because he or she is recognised as having rights. Children should be allowed their say if a solution is to be found that is genuinely in their best interests.' A number of studies[39] have shown, however, that children and young people are rarely included in mediation. The Mapping Paths to Family Justice study[40] found that child-inclusive mediation was used infrequently and had rarely taken place in their sample of mediation users. Parents and mediators may have similar misgivings, fearing pressure being put on the child and the risk of repercussions for the child. Child-inclusive mediation, also known as Direct Child Consultation (DCC), offers opportunities for children and young people to be listened to, feel respected and contribute to the process of working out arrangements. Mediators should explore these opportunities with parents first of all and encourage them to consider the potential benefits and any concerns they may have in relation to their child being able to meet with a specially trained professional, alongside or within the mediation process, whether individually and/or with their siblings and possibly also with the family together. Seeking a child's views and feelings may imply that the aim is to seek views and feelings *from* the child. Communication needs to be two-way, not one-way, because children need explanations and reassurance, especially when communication between a child and a parent has broken down. The views and wishes that a child expresses – or be unable to express – depend to a large extent on the child's perceptions. These perceptions may change as the child gains more understanding. A child's rejection of a parent may be a reaction to feeling rejected by that parent. A child needs to understand the reasons for a parent not being in touch for some time. In some cases the child needs an apology from a parent, as well as an explanation of the reasons, before being willing to resume the relationship or, in some cases, to build a relationship from scratch. Consulting children should mean having conversations with them, not plying them with questions and extracting answers for the benefit of adults who 'need to know'. The main value of such conversations is to unblock channels of communication so that children and parents can listen to each other and talk together with more understanding. The mediator's role can be a catalyst in

---

[37] Parkinson and Cashmore 'Judicial Conversations with children in parenting disputes: the views of Australian judges' (2007) 21 International Journal of Law, Policy and the Family 160.

[38] Council of Europe Recommendation *Family mediation and gender equality* (No 1639, 2003, para 6).

[39] Hayes 'Family Mediators in the UK' [2002] Fam Law 760; Murch *The Voice of the Child in Private Law Proceedings* [2005] IFL 8.

[40] Barlow et al *Mapping Paths to Family Justice – Briefing Paper and Report on Key Findings* (Universities of Exeter and Kent, June 2014).

facilitating better child-parent communication. It should not be in any way directive or controlling. Sensitive interventions by mediators can help parents to work out practical arrangements and consider how to help their children adjust, while also enabling children and young people to feel that their views matter too and that their parents are taking them into account. Mediators may draw on their understanding of attachment and systems theory, crisis and chaos theory, family interactions and communications. All these are relevant to mediating with parents, children and young people and other family members. Mediators who take part in helpful and supportive conversations with a child or young person can reassure the child that their feelings about what is happening in their family are normal and understandable, without the child feeling interrogated or put under pressure. Both parents need to give their consent to their child's direct involvement and if one parent declines, the mediator cannot take it further. Parents may have concerns about the emotional impact on their children, while mediators may fear that seeing children directly may undermine and 'disempower' parents, instead of 'empowering' them. It also needs to be borne in mind that a large proportion of disputes between parents over arrangements for their children concern very young children who are too young to be consulted directly. 20% of the children in private law cases in a study conducted for the Ministry of Justice[41] were under two years old and a further 18% were under four years old. Three quarters of the children (76%) in contested family proceedings were under ten years old. The emotional maturity of a child is not congruent with their chronological age and when children are not only of an age but mature enough and willing to be involved directly, calls to Childline indicate that they are 'perfectly able to enter into discussions about the future, so long as they are not being asked to choose in an atmosphere of acute conflict where they feel caught in the middle ... These calls are a very persuasive argument in favour of a mediation service which includes children ... an outside person to help everybody talk ... could be of considerable help to children, as well as to parents, in managing the feelings that threaten to overwhelm them.'[42]

Studies of child-inclusive mediation in Australia, Canada and New Zealand[43] suggest significant benefits for children and their parents, provided there is careful planning with both parents and agreement as to the objectives, conditions and manner of including the child. Mediators need to make sure that pre-conditions for involving the child can be met and parents need to understand and agree the conditions, timing and nature of any direct child involvement.[44] Pre-requisites include the suitability of child-inclusive mediation in the circumstances, clarity about the role of the family mediator or other professional who will meet with the child, the principles and limits of confidentiality (a) for parents and (b) for the child, before, during and following a meeting with the child, and the need to seek the child's informed

[41] Cassidy and Davey (2011) *Ministry of Justice Research Summary* 5/11, p 8.
[42] Childline *Unhappy Parents, Unhappy Children* (1998), p 25.
[43] Mediation Task Force Report, June 2014, Appendix 1.
[44] Parkinson 'Child-Inclusive Family Mediation' [2006] Fam Law 483–488.

consent. Mediators should follow guidelines covering these pre-requisites[45] and parents must give written agreement to the terms of the child's involvement. Mediation in Divorce (MID), based in Twickenham, provides a range of services for adults and children – child-centred and child-inclusive mediation, adult and child counselling and the Family Bridges Project.[46] MID routinely invites young people to come in for a conversation about family changes and arrangements.

> 'Previously, it was always possible to involve children directly in mediation, but in practice it rarely used to happen. We were cautious about undermining the authority of parents in mediation and we tended to think that the best people to talk to children were usually their parents. Several factors caused us to review our policy, including the emphasis given in the European Convention of Human Rights to children's rights to have their views heard, and more importantly, the research findings resulting from interviews with children whose parents had separated/divorced. Offering children a more direct voice in the mediation process is not so much a change of policy, more a change of emphasis. We present the idea to parents in a more positive way, and at an earlier stage. We don't consider children's participation as an exceptional option, but rather as something we actively encourage because we see that most children appreciate the opportunity to be heard directly.'[47]

When mediators are positive about the benefits of including children, they are more likely to be able to reassure anxious parents. An early study in Scotland[48] found that children were involved in only 36 out of 186 cases (19% of cases). The main reason was that the children were too young (average age 3.5 years), while half the parents (42 out of 84 cases) did not think it necessary, saying they were able to talk with their children at home. Other reasons given by parents were that the issues did not involve the children (14 cases) or one parent was not in favour (nine cases). In considering with parents, first of all, whether their child could be included in some way, it is essential to discuss the benefits and possible disadvantages, primarily from the child's point of view.[49]

8.5 POSSIBLE DISADVANTAGES OF INCLUDING CHILDREN IN MEDIATION

- Involving children increases their distress and confusion.

- Children will be upset if they become more aware of parental conflict.

- Children do not share legal responsibility with their parents. Their parents hold responsibility for them and children should not be drawn into parental disputes.

---

[45] See **8.7** below.
[46] www.midmediation.org.uk.
[47] Pendlebury 'Divorce and separation: listening to children and young people in mediation' [2008] Fam Law 1255.
[48] Garwood *Children in Conciliation* (Scottish Association of Family Conciliation Services, 1989).
[49] See also Cantwell 'The Emotional Safeguarding of Children in Private Law' [2010] Fam Law 84–90.

- Children should not be used as judges or arbitrators in parental negotiations.

- Power imbalances between parents and children lie outside the boundaries of mediation.

- Empowering children risks 'disempowering' one or both parents.

- Parents' decision-making authority is undermined if the child or the mediator is seen as the expert.

- The mediator's role may be confused with the role of counsellor or child advocate.

- Involving children may create expectations that things will be made better for them.

- Children may feel under pressure to express their views and feelings.

- Children may fear being asked to make a choice.

- Children may not be reliable judges of their own long-term interests.

- The mediator may become triangulated between parents and child.

- The mediator could be left holding secrets or confidences from a child that the child does not want shared with parents: this would be an untenable position for the mediator.

- The child's conflicts of loyalty may be heightened.

- Parents may be unable to manage their distress in front of the children.

- Parents may brief the child on what to say and put pressure on the child.

- Parents who are unable to co-operate do not necessarily gain this ability through hearing what their child says: they may refuse to take the child's views and wishes on board.

- Feedback to parents afterwards may result in them being angry with the child or interrogating the child.

- Young children who see their parents talking in a friendly way may think their parents are going to get back together again – feeding hopes of reconciliation.

8.6 POTENTIAL BENEFITS OF INCLUDING CHILDREN IN MEDIATION

- Research comparing child-focused mediation with child-inclusive mediation indicates that child-inclusive mediation offers significant additional benefits in terms of positive relationships and agreements being maintained, with positive feedback from children.[50]

- Children need explanations and reassurance that their parents may have been unable to give them.

- Children adjust more easily if there is better communication and they understand their parents' decisions more clearly.

---

[50] Mediation Task Force Report, June 2014, Appendix 1.

- Involving children shows them that their wishes, views and feelings matter and that they are being treated with respect.

- Listening to children is a way of showing care.

- Involving children in mediation helps both parents to listen to their children.

- Parents may choose to explain their decisions and arrangements to their children in a family meeting (some parents need the mediator's support to do this).

- Dispelling misunderstandings: for example, that a child does not want to see a parent when the child actually wants to do so.

- Enabling children to ask questions, comment and contribute their ideas.

- Enabling children to express a worry or concern, such as where the family's pets will live.

- Easing communication and reducing tensions in parent-child relationships.

- Giving children an opportunity to see the mediator alone and talk about their feelings and concerns, without being anxious about how the parents will hear them.

- Helping children to work out the messages they may want to give to their parents (or other people involved) and to feel able to give these messages.

- Enabling a child to receive a message from a parent who cannot give it directly, for some reason.

- With the child's agreement, giving feedback to parents to help them understand the child's concerns and feelings, so that these can be taken into account in the parents' decisions.

Positive reasons for including children need to be weighed against potential risks and problems. When both parents agree that their child should be included in order to help the child, there are different options and considerations to work through. The flip-chart is a helpful tool in considering each option. Some parents would like to include the children in a family meeting with the mediator present, to help them explain things to the children with the mediator's help. Other parents, depending on the age of the child and the particular circumstances, may ask if a child counsellor or a mediator could see a child alone. Adolescents, in particular, may wish to talk with a person who knows both parents but who is not emotionally involved in the situation. Some adolescents need a space to talk through their feelings and decisions, especially when they are old enough to take decisions themselves. Occasionally there are direct requests from children who ask to meet the mediator, because they are aware that the mediator already knows their family situation, whereas a counsellor would not have this knowledge and is not in contact with both parents. Many schools now have peer mediation programmes and some children may know more about mediation than their parents do and see it as a normal and constructive way to sort out disagreements. Children are also anxious not to be singled out as needing counselling, as though they had something wrong with them. Even young children are able to understand that mediation is not the same as counselling or therapy and that the mediator is not a social worker or decision-maker. Some services use a specially trained counsellor, others may use a second mediator to meet with children on their own. Should siblings be seen together or separately? Will feedback be given to the parents afterwards? There are many questions to consider and it is helpful to have a checklist to work through, although obviously not in a rigid or bureaucratic way.

8.7 PRE-REQUISITES FOR DIRECT CHILD CONSULTATION AND CHILD-INCLUSIVE MEDIATION

Three FMC member organisations (FMA, NFM and Resolution) provide training in child-inclusive mediation and all three training programmes adhere to the Standard and Guidelines issued by the former UK College of Family Mediators, recently adopted by the FMC.[51] These guidelines have not been reviewed since 2002. The Mediation Task Force called for a review of mediators' training, registration and supervision in child-inclusive mediation and for guidelines to be updated. A checklist of pre-requisites should cover the following considerations and may need further extension:

- Suitable rooms and facilities for meetings with children and young people.

- Before meeting with children, the mediator must be trained in child consultation/child-inclusive mediation and be registered by the FMC as qualified in this area. They must have a Professional Practice Consultant with this additional training.

- The mediator must have the necessary clearance by the Disclosure and Barring Service.

- A co-mediator or colleague should be available for safeguarding purposes.

- Assessment has not found any evidence or concerns about child welfare and safeguarding issues (mediators must follow policy and procedures on safeguarding of children).

- The mediator should enquire whether any professional is, or has been involved, on matters concerning the child (if so, mediation itself may not be suitable).

- Good understanding is needed of the family's situation, culture and current issues.

- The mediator should seek to get to know the child through the parents first of all – the child's personality, stage of development, activities, relationships, etc. – before exploring options for involving the child directly.

- The mediator should ask parents what each of them has explained to the child so far.

- Careful consideration is needed as to whether the child is of sufficient age and maturity to be consulted directly, or otherwise involved in some way.

---

[51] UK College of Family Mediators *Children, Young People and Family Mediation – Policy and Practice Guidelines* (2002).

- Exploration with parents of possible options for child-inclusive mediation, potential benefits and potential disadvantages or risks.

- The setting, objectives and role of the child counsellor or mediator need to be clarified and agreed with both parents.

- Explaining the extent of confidentiality: (a) for the parents, and (b) for the child and exploring with parents how this might best be explained to their child in a way the child will understand.

- Parents' willingness to receive feedback, including a negative message from a child, and ability to accept that a child may not want any message or feedback to be given.

- Considering with parents the next steps they would or could take in the absence of any message or feedback from their child.

- Parents' agreement on the stage and timing of child-inclusive mediation.

- Parents' written acceptance of the mediator's charges, or confirmation of public funding.

- Discussion and agreement on the structure of the meeting – for example, children and both parents initially for introductions, then children seen alone? Siblings together or separately? Can children choose? What is likely to help the child feel most at ease? What contingencies need to be considered/agreed in the event of the child becoming upset or changing their mind about being willing to talk with the mediator?

- Date for a subsequent mediation meeting, when agreed feedback may be given.

- Parental agreement if another adult is to accompany the child to the meeting – if so, who this would be and what role they would have.

- Agreement as to whether one or both parents will explain to the child/ren what is being proposed and the opportunity to 'rehearse' this explanation.

- Agreement as to whether and how the mediator will also write to or contact the child with an invitation.

- Agreement as to whether the child may be offered a follow-up meeting, if the child wishes to come again.

- Parents sign their consent to child consultation/child-inclusive mediation.

- The child accepts the invitation and is willing to meet with the mediator.

- Parents give permission for the mediator to offer the child a drink (water/juice?), biscuits/fruit?

8.8 CONFIDENTIALITY

It is very important for mediators and parents to consider the boundaries of the mediator's discussions with a child or young person. Confidentiality cannot be absolute and is conditional on a number of factors and considerations. Safeguarding procedures must be followed where a child is said or believed to be at risk of harm. The mediator's duties in these circumstances must be made clear in advance to all concerned, including the child and must be explained in an age appropriate way. Parents must give written consent and it also needs to be clear whether, if the child requests it, a message or other feedback may be given to parents following the meeting with the child. As a child may not want any message to be given, the parents need to accept that they might not receive any feedback. This does not mean that meeting with the child was a waste of time. The child may find it helpful to talk with someone who has no stake in the conflict and may feel more confident, after talking things through, to say to their parents what they need to say, without using the mediator as intermediary. Younger children may wish to send a message which they ask the counsellor or mediator to give to their parents. For all these reasons and circumstances, it is therefore critical that the mediator and parents assess carefully and thoroughly together whether and if the parents are able to understand, accept and agree to the terms for any direct consultation/discussions with their child or children and explore how they will each and both manage the preparation for and any outcome from the mediator's discussion with the child or children (including the possible outcome that their child may choose not to share any part of the discussion with them, or that messages from the child may not be what they expect or hope to hear).

The confidentiality in law of a child's views and wishes expressed in mediation, in terms of being non-disclosable to the court, is not yet sufficiently clear. This means that other factors in relation to the confidentiality of discussions between mediator and child are important to bear in mind. For example, if there are subsequent proceedings, parents – or the Judge – may believe that it is important to know what the child has said in any private discussion with a mediator and may argue or consider that there is an over-riding obligation in law that would allow for any confidentiality of those discussions to be lifted. In the case of *Re J (A Child: Disclosure)*[52] the Court of Appeal was faced with a hard choice between respecting a child's confidentiality on the one hand, or providing justice to a parent, on the other. The Court observed that the stakes were high on both sides of the equation and came to the conclusion that the balance of rights came down in favour of disclosure of information concerning the child. Mediators are likely to worry that, despite the privilege covering the mediation process and the confidentiality afforded to discussions within mediation, in exceptional circumstances the mediator could be called on to testify in court.[53] Experience drawn from the limited practice of child-inclusive mediation in England and Wales has not found that seeing a child alone has left a mediator burdened with confidences from children that they do not want anyone else to know. Children often want to give their messages to their parents themselves, at home or with the mediator's help. These are likely to be positive messages about how the child has been trying to help the parents, or about the kind of help the child would like from a parent. If a child asks the mediator to explain something to their parents on the child's behalf, the child's message should be written down and checked back with the child. If the message is negative and would be hurtful to a parent, the child may be helped (and in fact may wish to be helped) to think of a less hurtful way of expressing it.

---

[52] [2012] EWCA Civ 1204.

[53] Ramsay LJ, *Farm Assist v Defra* [2009] EWHC 1102 (TCC), see **1.10.2** above.

8.9 THE APPROACH TO THE CHILD

Parents need to explain to children why they would like them to take part in mediation, to allay their anxieties and encourage a positive response. With both parents' consent, it is usually helpful for the mediator to send a personal invitation to the child as well, because this shows the child or young person that they are being treated with respect as an individual in their own right. It also upholds the core principle of voluntary participation. Children need to understand what is being offered and to be reassured that they can accept or decline the invitation, as they wish. They need to know that they will not be asked difficult questions. If they wish to talk, they will be listened to, but they are not being asked to make choices, or take responsibility for decisions. Parents need to agree that they will not brief the child beforehand, nor question the child afterwards about anything the child may or may not have said. Children need reassurance that they can speak freely, without fearing that they will get into trouble or hurt their parents in some way. Parents need to accept that the purpose of involving the child is to help the child feel respected and listened to, with the opportunity to express their feelings, view and wishes, and perhaps to gain more understanding of their situation, or more ability to come to terms with it and know that none of it is their fault. The purpose is not to use the child as judge or arbitrator. Great care must be taken at all stages – before, during and afterwards – to avoid causing further distress to children.

Children are usually anxious about talking to an outsider and may fear saying something that will upset one or both parents. They are usually very protective of both parents, or they may side with one parent against the other parent. They may also fear adding to their parents' worries. Children may worry about things that their parents can deal with, once the parents understand what these worries are ('Where will our dog live?'). Mediators can help children explain their worries to their parents and this can free children from some of their anxieties. Mediators also need to be aware that children may not be able to put their fears into words – and have the humility to recognise that they cannot alleviate a child's pain. There are family situations in which a great deal of loss has already occurred and where a child feels deeply estranged from one parent. There are also situations in which a child needs a parent to apologise for saying or doing something that has hurt the child. If the parent concerned is able to say to the child that he/she is genuinely sorry (sometimes there has been a misunderstanding between a parent and a child), considerable healing may take place.

Involving children in mediation can help them to feel clearer and more confident about what they want to say to their parents, as well as what they need to hear from their parents. There are occasions, however, when the child wants help to explain something to their parents. This needs to be planned first with the child and then with the parents. There can be considerable relief if parents understand that sending messages to each other via the child is distressing the child. Even a limited agreement on a small step may be valuable in helping parents and children to talk and listen to each other. In talking with children, it is important not to see it as a one-way process of seeking their views and feelings. It is equally important to give explanations that are appropriate to their age and to convey reassuring messages, especially when communication between a child and a parent has broken down. The feelings and views children may express – or be unable to express – depend on the child's perceptions. These perceptions are liable to change as they gain a better understanding of their parents' positions and feelings. A child's rejection of a parent is often a reaction to feeling rejected by that parent. The main benefit of involving children directly is to re-open channels of communication between the child and both parents, so that they can listen and hear each other with more empathy and understanding.

Example

After three years of court proceedings, a shared residence order broke down immediately because the twelve-year-old boy did not consider that the order met his recorded wishes and feelings. He flatly refused to see his mother at all, who took this to be yet more evidence of manipulation by his father. The mother's solicitor referred the matter to mediation (Family Mediation Centre Staffordshire) rather than seeking enforcement of the order. The parents refused to meet together, and even in shuttled sessions refused to consider any co-operation, the father stating he was following his son's wishes and the mother re-asserting her belief in his manipulation and bullying by the father. In a separate session, the boy told the mediator that he wished to see his mother, but on a more limited basis than as set out in the court order. He had withdrawn from contact because he was angry that the court had not listened to him. Whilst not expressing any judgement, the mediator found no evidence of current manipulation. In the two following sessions, the mediator invited the active participation of the parents' solicitors, who:

• supported their clients in these highly emotive and distressing circumstances;

• with the parents' agreement, met with the mediator to plan process and consider permutations;

• gave independent advice about the difficult question of returning the matter to court or re-involving experts;

• supported interim arrangements so that the boy's relationship with his mother could be rebuilt; and

• worked with the mediator and the parents to draw up a binding agreement that would supersede the court order, so as to avoid the necessity of return to court.

8.10   STUDIES OF CHILD-INCLUSIVE MEDIATION

The use of a Children's Resource Worker in Devon Family Mediation Agency found the following benefits:[54]

- Offering this service encouraged parents to consider whether it would help their children.

- The focus on the child's position and feelings.

- Children valued the opportunity and left the meeting looking happier and more relaxed.

- The mediator acts as facilitator and helps everyone feel comfortable before and after the meeting.

A study in Scotland[55] found that, despite their initial uncertainty, almost all the children who met with the mediator spoke very positively about their experience. Benefits experienced by the children included:

- Feeling 'relieved', 'much easier', less anxious about being pulled between parents.

- Better communication between children and parents.

- Better contact arrangements, feeling happier about contact visits.

- More understanding of their situation ('we like going to dad's now that we understand more' said an eight year old girl, speaking for herself and her sister).

- Having the opportunity to express their own feelings. One teenager said she had not spoken to anyone before about what she was feeling, and she now felt that she and her parents understood each other better.

- Realising they were not alone in having these feelings.

- Asking the mediator's help to convey a message to their parents or to make requests, such as making phone calls to an absent parent.

- Borrowing books to help them understand what was happening.

- Being able to keep out of issues between parents that did not concern them.

Nearly all the children interviewed (24 out of 28) felt they had definitely benefited from seeing the mediator. The other four said everything was all right for them anyway, so it had not made much difference. The findings suggested that:

- There can be considerable benefits for children in being involved in mediation.

- Parents and children agree about the benefits.

- Children would come more readily if they understood the purpose better.

---

[54] Personal communication quoted in Parkinson 'Child-Inclusive Family Mediation' [2006] Fam Law 485.

[55] Garwood *Children in Conciliation* (Scottish Association of Family Conciliation Services, 1989).

- Confidentiality should be clear: there should be a code of practice on involving children in mediation.

- Parents should be willing to accept feedback, if the child wants them to have it.

- Mediators should have additional training before involving children in mediation, to equip them with the necessary understanding and skills.

- Experience and skills in working with children should be shared more.

- More children could be helped in this way, if mediators are clear about the benefits for children and more confident in discussing these benefits with parents.

McIntosh and colleagues[56] have reported on experience in Australia where parents are offered opportunities for their child to meet with a trained child counsellor. If the parents and child accept, and the child consents to feedback being given, the child counsellor joins in a subsequent mediation session to give feedback to the parents and the mediator. The use of a child counsellor alongside the mediation process was found to have many positive benefits for children and their parents. Child-focused mediation, in which children did not take part directly, was compared with child-inclusive mediation in which children met with a child counsellor. In both groups in the year following mediation, the researchers found lasting reductions in levels of conflict and improved management of disputes, as reported by the parents and the children. The child-inclusive group showed more significant improvements in parental and child-parent relationships, particularly between fathers and children, and more noticeable benefits in children's developmental recovery from high-conflict separation. Child-inclusive mediation 'offered children a safe, specialist avenue for their views and needs to be considered and indeed to impact significantly upon the way in which their parents were able to resolve their parenting disputes.'[57]

Research and the experience of practitioners in Britain[58] and Australia[59] suggest that children are more competent to take part in family decision-making than adults generally believe. It is important to take time and trouble to listen to what children tell us and to understand how they feel. The challenges of consulting with children and young people concerning changes in their family life are considerable for all concerned. Adults need sensitivity and awareness, non-judgemental attitudes and a good sense of humour. With these qualities and good professional training, mediators are likely to find conversations with children illuminating and life-enhancing, despite the sadness and anger felt by many children when they lose the security of living with both parents in an intact family. Children understand far more than adults generally imagine.

---

[56] McIntosh, Smyth, Wells and Long 'Child-Focused and Child-Inclusive Divorce Mediation' (2008) 46 (1) *Family Courts Review* (Association of Family and Conciliation Courts).

[57] Ibid, p 22.

[58] Smart and Neale 'It's My Life Too – Children's Perspectives on Post-Divorce Parenting' [2000] Fam Law 163–169.

[59] McIntosh 'Child-Inclusive Mediation' (2000) 18(1) *Mediation Quarterly* 55.

Insights and practical suggestions from children can often help parents to resolve problems in ways that will make life easier for the family as a whole. Two brothers commented with regard to their parents: 'We knew they could not do it without our help.'

Example

In a mediation undertaken at Gilbert Stephens Family Mediation Service in Exeter, an 11-year-old boy had chosen to remain with his father in the family home because, as he explained, he and his dad were both keen on football, while his 13-year-old sister had decided to leave the home with her mother. The parents were locked in intractable conflict, each of them convinced that they knew best. The parents agreed that their children should be involved in the decision-making process, recognising that no arrangement would work if the children were not prepared to go along with it. The mediator met with the brother and sister together. Although the 13-year-old girl was initially unresponsive, both children became interested when the mediator sketched possible plans on the flip-chart. The children then wanted to contribute their own ideas. With their consent, the children's suggestions were put forward at the next mediation meeting. Their ideas had not occurred to the parents, who had been caught up in fighting each other. Both parents agreed with the arrangements proposed by the children and a further application to the court was withdrawn.

Example

ANNA (AGED ELEVEN) AND JAMES (AGED SEVEN)

Carl and Tricia both felt it would help their children – Anna, aged eleven and James, aged seven – to talk with the mediator without their parents being present. Anna was showing reluctance to visit her father and neither parent wanted to force her. They thought she might talk more easily to someone outside the family. All the pre-conditions for involving Anna and James were discussed and agreed. Tricia would invite them to come and explain the arrangements to them. Anna and James accepted the invitation. It was agreed with the parents that, after initial introductions, Anna and James would be seen together, while Carl and Tricia waited in the reception area. Carl and Tricia would then rejoin the meeting. If the children wanted to share anything with them, the mediator would help them do so, but they would not be pressed to say anything, if they did not want to. The parents said they would listen to what the children wanted to say, without getting angry or upset with them. They accepted that (subject to the usual limits on confidentiality regarding child protection) Anna and James should decide whether they wanted anything shared with their parents afterwards. Tricia and Carl thought this freedom would help the children to feel less worried about hurting either of them and that giving them an opportunity to talk, without pressure, would be helpful for them.

The following extracts recalled more or less verbatim may help illustrate the content and style of the discussion with Anna and James. Both children talked readily and showed great insight and sensitivity to their parents' difficulties. They also made suggestions, increasingly with a strong sense of humour:

Mediator: James, do you have any friends at school whose parents don't live together?

James: Yes, I do – I have a friend called Gary and his parents … (etc).

Mediator: How do you think Gary is getting on – is it OK for him?

James: Well, Gary says the thing to do is to tell your parents jokes, to stop them arguing. I tried that … I tried to tell my Mum and Dad a joke about a monkey but they didn't listen. They went on arguing. Anyway I hadn't finished making up the joke.

Mediator: You really are trying hard to help your parents. I think they'd like to know the way you are trying to help them. Could you tell them about it?

James: Yes, I will ….

Mediator: Anna, you said just now that it was just small things you don't like about going to your Dad's at weekends and that you didn't think they were worth bothering about. But sometimes small things can hurt a lot.

James: Yes, that's right. Sometimes I have a scratch that really hurts and other times when I fall off my bike I've got a real gash I hadn't noticed ….

Anna: What I don't like is when Dad picks me up from school he is talking all the time on his mobile and I've told him I don't like it and my friends tease me about it. But he still does it ….

Mediator: So you'd like your father to listen and take more notice of what you say?

Anna: Yes, he doesn't listen properly ….

Mediator: What kind of things do you like doing when you go to your Dad?

Anna: Well, I quite like playing on his computer but the thing is, when I tell him I've got stuck, he just comes and takes over.

Mediator: You mean, you'd like him to show you what to do to get unstuck?

Anna: Yes, he just does it all himself.

Mediator: I think he would show you, if he understands you'd like him to show you.

James: Yes, and I want him to show me too.

Carl and Tricia looked extremely apprehensive when they joined the meeting. They listened very attentively to what the children explained to them with great liveliness and spontaneity. Their eyes filled with tears when James told them he had tried to tell them jokes to stop them arguing. But they also smiled. The atmosphere relaxed and lightened, as both parents understood that they had not 'failed' as parents and that the children were not judging or blaming them. The meeting helped them realise, however, the great importance of listening carefully to their children. Things that the parents had not noticed, or which they had dismissed as unimportant, were extremely important from the children's perspective. Anna's withdrawal, which had troubled them both, turned out to be her way of showing resentment that when she did tell them something, they usually forgot about it. Tricia and Carl might not have realised the significance of these apparently small things in talking with the children at home, because they were looking for 'something bigger', through the other end of the telescope. The children might also have felt inhibited in talking with the mediator in the presence of both parents. Feedback from the children and the parents after the meeting was extremely positive: 'We can talk more easily now.'

Example

TOM (AGED 15)

Tom's mother, Jenny, was leaving her second husband, Wilf, to live with a new partner, Harry. Jenny wanted Tom to come to live with her and Harry, while Wilf thought Tom should stay with him, as he had helped to bring Tom up since he was small and Tom had no contact with his natural father. Both parents were concerned that Tom was staying out late in the evenings, not bothering with his school work and becoming increasingly aggressive and uncommunicative. They could not get a response from him about where he wanted to live and were worried that if the situation continued, he might get involved in drugs and petty crime. They were not sure if he would come to see the mediator but thought it was worth a try.

Tom came. Initially silent, he listened to the positive message from his mother that Jenny had asked the mediator to give him. Jenny's anger and frustration – and possibly guilt feelings – had led to a barrier between her and Tom. Their discussions invariably turned into arguments. Tom began to talk with the mediator, whom he accepted as impartial and not making judgements. He explained that he was angry with everyone in his family and very upset. At the end of the discussion, he told the mediator that he felt he could handle talking with his mother, provided she was willing to try too. He thought it would help if the mediator would also explain to his mother and stepfather how he was feeling, so that they would understand better when he talked to them. He particularly asked the mediator's help in conveying a request to his mother not to keep pressing him to live with her and Harry. He needed more time and he did not want to have to choose between his parents.

His mother was receptive to the feedback from the mediator, which the mediator had checked through with Tom. Jenny and Tom then found they could talk more easily on their own, without arguing as they had done before. Tom also said he would be willing to go out for a walk with his stepfather, which he had previously refused to do. The trouble had been that his stepfather always asked him too early in the morning. Mornings were not Tom's best time.

8.11   APTITUDE, KNOWLEDGE AND SKILLS FOR CHILD-INCLUSIVE MEDIATION

However experienced they may be in other professional fields, family mediators need personal aptitude, knowledge and skills for child-inclusive mediation and family mediators in England and Wales are required to have additional training recognised by the Family Mediation Council and to be registered by the FMC as qualified in this area. Their professional practice consultant must also have this additional qualification. Skills should include:

- Helping parents to understand children's needs in separation and divorce, their reactions to separation, conflict and loss and the rights of the child.

- Engaging both parents in considering whether the child should be included in mediation and if so, when and in what way – exploring suitability, options and objectives.

- Discussing a child's conflict of loyalties – some children may be unable to say what they want or feel. Discouraging parents from coaching their child on what they should say.

- Seeking both parents' written consent to child consultation and the child's confidentiality (unless safeguarding needed).

- Agreeing the approach to the child and the form of invitation from the mediator to the child that will help the child to understand that this is an invitation, not a demand to come.

- Engaging with children, putting them at ease – explaining who you are, what your role is and how you are seeking to help. Explaining reasons for the meeting and the nature and extent of confidentiality in a way that is appropriate to the child's age and level of understanding.

- Listening to children, 'third ear' listening – imaginative understanding to enter into children's anxieties and frustrations, fantasies and wish for magic solutions.

- Communicating clearly – use of language – not talking down to children.

- Acknowledging and normalising a child's feelings. Helping them to understand that some things cannot be changed, however much they want them to change.

- Using humour appropriately and sensitively (beware patronising jokes).

- Using images, anecdotes, books and other materials for children and parents.

- Giving a message from a parent to a child (where a parent is unable or not yet able to communicate directly with the child) and reassurances from parents.

- Tuning in to what is important from the child's perspective.

- Helping children to feel more confident in talking with their parents.

- Giving agreed feedback from children to parents and helping parents to take the feedback on board.

- Offering a follow-up meeting to the child, where this is needed and agreed.

- Knowledge of the type and nature of resources available to children, young people and their parents through local face to face services and/or telephone helplines and online services. The Government report, 'A Brighter Future for Family Justice', has an accompanying Young Person's Guide 'to what's happened since the Family Justice Review looked into things'.[60]

While there has been considerable investment in online information services for separated parents, there has not been comparable investment in online services for children of separated parents. The new charity, Kids in the Middle,[61] is raising funds to help plug this hole in provision by means of a special online service in which children and young people trained as peer mentors offer help to other children and young people who are going through parental separation and divorce.

8.12   CHILD-PARENT MEDIATION

Conflict between adolescents and their parents is a normal part of growing up. Many parents have strained relationships with a withdrawn or rebellious teenager. A separated parent may feel inclined to give up unrewarding efforts, rather than press for contact. It is a tragedy, however, for parent and child if parents give up too readily. Some adolescents need recovery time. If they have lost trust, they may need to be reassured of the absent parent's ongoing love and commitment to them. Wallerstein and Kelly suggest that 'the visiting parent and child also have a second chance at this critical juncture to break out of past unhappy relations and establish a new bond.'[62] Researchers have found that children who are resistant to seeing or staying with their non-resident parent generally have strong reasons for their opposition.[63] Catherine, aged 20, referred to her disappointing visits to her father: 'He sometimes made you feel

---

[60]   DfE and MoJ A Brighter Future – *Young Person's Guide* (August 2014).
[61]   www.kidsinthemiddle.org.uk.
[62]   Wallerstein and Kelly *Surviving the Break-Up* (Grant McIntyre, 1980), p 131.
[63]   Fortin, Scanlan and Hunt 'Taking a longer view of contact: the perspectives of young adults who experienced parental separation in their youth' [2013] Fam Law 104.

that you weren't that important and it didn't matter if you weren't there. He's not warm or emotional, not someone I can talk to about **me**'.[64]

Generally, quarrels between adolescents and their parents are part of the child's growing up process and do not threaten the core of the parent-child relationship. But in others, arguments may escalate into a painful, exhausting and increasingly desperate battle in which anger, depression and self-doubt erode the love and affection that children sorely need. Some children and teenagers run away from home following a bitter argument with a parent or step-parent or run away from local authority care. In 2012 there were 65,520 children in local authority care in England and Wales. A quarter of the 100,000 children who run away from care or home each year are at serious risk of harm. There are 'serious shortcomings in a system that is supposed to protect children in care'.[65] Research by the Children's Society[66] shows that running away is often preceded by conflict with parents or carers, family breakdown or poor relationships, experiences of abuse or neglect, or problems at school. The need to focus on children's experiences in child protection processes was highlighted in the Munro review: 'treating children and young people as people, not objects, requires spending time with them to ascertain their views, helping them understand what is happening to them and taking their wishes and opinions into account in making decisions about them.'[67]

In certain circumstances and subject to pre-conditions being met,[68] mediation may be possible to explore whether a child who has run away from care or from home might be able to return to the care of their parents or other family members under conditions acceptable to the child and the parent/s (or other carers), as well as those with statutory responsibilities for their care. If there are child protection issues, the mediation process needs to be adapted to take account of them.[69] Children need to know that their needs and feelings will be listened to and that solutions can be worked out through involving all concerned in carefully managed discussions. Social workers, schools and colleges need to be able to give children, young people and parents' information about family mediation and details of websites.[70]

---

[64]   Neale and Wade *Parent Problems! Children's views on life when parents split up* (Young Voice, 2000), p 15.
[65]   All Party Parliamentary Groups for Looked After Children and Care Leavers and for Runaway and Missing Children, 18 June 2012.
[66]   Children's Society *Here to Listen?* (London, 2013).
[67]   Munro *The Munro Review of Child Protection – a child-centred system* (DfE, 2011).
[68]   Parkinson *Child Care Mediation in Public Law Proceedings* (paper presented at Stafford, 27–28 November 2012, unpublished).
[69]   See **4.14** above.
[70]   Such as www.oneplusone.org.uk.

8.13 MEDIATION INVOLVING CHILDREN, PARENTS AND TEACHERS

Disputes between children and teachers escalate when irate parents become involved. Children need encouragement to discuss learning or discipline problems and they may need to be directly involved in working out a contract with parents and their school that all concerned can accept. There are of course major power imbalances between children, parents and education authorities. Mediation will not always be appropriate or possible, but it should be considered at an early stage before problems accumulate and positions harden. Family mediators with expertise and experience in working with children and young people, as well as with adults, could offer mediation to schools – for children, parents and teachers – through a new sector of the family mediators' register.

8.14 GROUPS FOR CHILDREN OF SEPARATED PARENTS

Discussion groups for children of separated parents that cater for children of different ages are not easy to find. In the 1980s, some teams of divorce court welfare officers used to organise discussion groups for children based on American models. In France and Quebec there are 'Groupes de Paroles' for children and in Italy, 'Gruppi di Parola'. These groups, led by family mediators, consist of four sessions, each lasting two hours. The children share their experiences and realise that they are not alone. They are helped to express their feelings and to develop ideas for 'coping strategies' through talking, drawing pictures and writing individual or group letters to their parents, explaining what they would like the parents to understand better. These letters are very moving and can have a powerful effect on parents. The children read out their group letter to the parents together, without their parents knowing which message comes from which child, and the parents are helped to write a group letter in response, which they read out to the children. A research study in Milan studied videotapes (made with the written consent of parents and children) of twenty groups involving 113 children aged from 6–12. The researchers found that these groups offered a private place where children could 'give voice' to their experiences of parental separation and divorce, share ideas on how to cope better and help their parents, as well as each other.[71]

8.15 TRAINING CHILDREN AS PEER MEDIATORS AND PEER MENTORS

Children are intrigued by conflict. They watch how adults react and may get satisfaction from acting out aggressive and violent scenes. Children understand more about the nature of relationships at an earlier age than many adults realise. They can learn to manage their own anger and non-violent ways of dealing with conflict. Instead of arguing with parents, teachers, siblings or

---

[71] Marzotto (ed) *Gruppi di parola per figli di genitori separati* (Vita e Pensiero, 2010).

classmates, children can learn about mediation and be trained in mediation skills.[72] Drama groups in schools may be used to explore ways of expressing and managing conflict. One method of teaching children conflict management skills has been developed from drama exercises with adults created by the Brazilian theatre director, Augusto Boal.[73] Boal was nominated for the Nobel Peace Prize in 2008 and in 2009, shortly before his death, UNESCO awarded him the title of World Theatre Ambassador. In drama groups for children, children as young as seven can take part in role-plays led by a skilled trainer and/or mediator. A quarrel or fight may be acted out. It is then acted out a second time and this time any child in the group can shout 'stop' at any point and take over one of the roles, showing how the conflict could be managed differently. Constructive ways of managing conflict are discussed and tried out. Following this training, class teachers have reported that relationships between children are greatly improved and disagreements sorted out more easily. There has been a steady growth in the use of peer support, buddy groups, anti-bullying strategies and mediation.[74] These schemes have high rates of success. In Scotland also, many schools have peer mediation programmes. Services affiliated to the Scottish Mediation Network provide training on mediation in schools.

The charity, Kids in the Middle, mentioned at **8.11** above, is training young people as peer mentors for others experiencing parental separation and divorce who may wish to confide their feelings safely to someone of a similar age who is likely to understand how they feel and who can provide support and suggestions. The website www.kidsinthemiddle.org.uk has videos made by young people for young people.

8.16   CHILDREN'S EXPERIENCES OF CHILD-INCLUSIVE MEDIATION

Child-inclusive mediation may strike parents, children and mediators as daunting. Mediators should take heart from this report of a mediator's first consultation with a child, provided by Jacqueline Gregory and quoted with her consent:

> 'My first child consultation on Friday was truly amazing and left me with goose bumps all over at the power of the children's voices. The transformation of the way the parents behaved compared to the previous week was astonishing – once they saw their children's handwriting with messages for them on the flip-chart they became totally child focussed and stopped bickering. Wow! The children were so sweet and I felt privileged that they felt safe to open their hearts to me as they did. They came out with some cracking lines as well – the little 7 year old girl was not sure at first if she wanted her parents to have feedback, then she said "I have never kept secrets from my Mummy and Daddy before so I am not about to start". The

---

[72]   See **8.1** above, Watson 'Looking for Trouble' (2014) 4.2 *Every Child Journal* www.teachingtimes.com.

[73]   Boal *Games for Actors and Non-Actors* (Routledge, 1992).

[74]   See www.peersupportworks.co.uk.

parents e-mailed to thank me and said they both felt it had really helped their children. They said that their communications were much improved and the benefits to the children were clear.'

A child who took part in a study of child-inclusive mediation in Australia said:[75]

'It helped to have someone listen to what I said, for it to be confidential, but also she would pass on to my parents what I wanted them to know. I was allowed to speak and say what I want. I could speak about problems. Afterwards I felt really good, like much better.'

8.16.1 On Children

Your children are not your children.
They are the sons and daughters of Life's longing for itself.
They come through you, but not from you,
And though they are with you yet they belong not to you.
You may give them your love but not your thoughts,
For they have their own thoughts.
You may house their bodies but not their souls,
For their souls dwell in the house of tomorrow,
which you cannot visit, not even in your dreams.
You may strive to be like them, but seek not to make them like you.
For life goes not backward nor tarries with yesterday.

Kahlil Gibran 'The Prophet' (1926)

---

[75] McIntosh, Wells, Smyth and Long 2008 46(1) 'Child-Focused and Child-Inclusive Divorce Mediation: Comparative Outcomes' *Family Court Review, Association of Family and Conciliation Courts*.

CHAPTER 9

MEDIATING ON MONEY MATTERS

'The world is too much with us: late and soon,
Getting and spending, we lay waste our powers'[1]

'The sadness of lives and the comfort of things'[2]

CONTENTS

9.1   RELATIONSHIP BREAKDOWN AND POVERTY

Financial worries and debts contribute to the breakdown of relationships that may be already under strain. Many families face unemployment, cuts in welfare benefits and rising fuel bills and many couples have large debts. Far from solving their financial problems, separation and divorce make things worse, since two households cost more than one and the separation itself involves further costs. Two-income couples may not earn enough to support two households. A parent who leaves the family home may be unable to rent a small apartment, while a parent who remains in the family home may be unable to

---

[1]   William Wordsworth Sonnet.
[2]   Miller *The Comfort of Things* (Polity Press, 2008).

pay the costs of keeping it. The future may be bleak for them both. Separated
parents who have no other accommodation may move in with their own
parents, renewing an unwanted dependency and losing privacy. The
non-resident parent needs enough room for the children to stay overnight: this
may not be possible. Children in separated families tend to grow up in
households with lower incomes, poorer housing and greater financial hardship
than intact families, especially those headed by lone mothers.[3] Child poverty is
associated with lower educational achievement.

With the loss of legal aid for family law matters, mediators need to tackle
challenges previously handled mainly by solicitors, to help couples struggling in
poverty to make the best possible use of scarce resources by working
co-operatively.

9.2   THE SIGNIFICANCE OF MONEY AND PROPERTY

Having enough money brings security and peace of mind. Money is also a
source of power and means of control.[4] When a couple decide to live together
and buy a property, their investment is far more than a purely financial one. It
is also an investment in their relationship and future happiness, in building a
home for bringing up their children and furnishing and decorating it to their
mutual satisfaction. If, later on, the couple's relationship breaks down, the
occupation or sale of the family home is likely to be a highly emotive issue for
them both. Asking for a valuation of the property in mediation can cause great
distress, if it suggests that the home will inevitably be sold. The idea of
becoming homeless may instil a paralysing fear. Home provides security –
having a roof over your head – and privacy, a refuge to retreat to from the
hurly-burly of life, where you are free to live as you wish, without unwanted
intruders. Living in your own home also means having social status and being
part of a community, with neighbours, friends and maybe relatives nearby or
within reach. In emotional terms, the home contains memories of the past, the
challenges of daily life and dreams for the future. Memories include the hard
work put into maintaining and improving the property. If there are children, it
is the children's home too. Parents have memories of their children being born
and growing up and the joys and trials of each stage. But the home may have
unhappy associations, as well as pleasant ones. There may have been cracks in
the couple's relationship long before the actual break-up. If the atmosphere in
the home has become very strained, with parents not speaking to each other or
constantly arguing, or if there has been domestic violence and/or relentless
psychological abuse, the home is no longer a refuge. It may be a prison where
abuse continues unchecked and unheard. In mediation, it is very important,
therefore, to understand not only the legal ownership and financial value of
property, but also the meanings it holds for both partners, in emotional and
symbolic terms.

---

[3]   Rodgers and Prior *Divorce and separation: the outcomes for children* (Joseph Rowntree
      Foundation, 1998).
[4]   See Chapter 10 on Power Imbalances.

9.3 INTER-RELATED ISSUES – CHILDREN AND FINANCIAL MATTERS

Discussions about children often need to be combined with discussions about financial issues, because they may be closely linked. If parents do not own their home and have no income apart from welfare benefits, day to day child arrangements may be the only issue. More often, arrangements for children are entangled with other questions, such as whether the family home will be retained or sold and where the non-residential parent will live. Mortgage payments on the family home, the cost of renting alternative accommodation, loans, debts and the payment of maintenance are relevant factors to be taken into account in working out whether the family home can be retained or whether it has to be sold. Some fathers question why they should pay child maintenance, if the mother is refusing to let them have contact with the children. Some mothers argue that the father has no right to see the children if he is not supporting them. The changing status of child support/maintenance has not put an end to this kind of retaliatory behaviour. Many parents accept that supporting children financially and providing a home for them are essential components of parental responsibility, inseparable from their day-to-day care, yet the law deals with financial and property issues separately from proceedings over children. The connections between these issues in emotional and practical terms are not addressed in the legal system, although arguments and worries about money often ignite conflict over children. It may be impossible to agree arrangements for children until it is clear where they will be living and how they will be supported. Mediation on all issues provides a forum in which these interrelated issues can be addressed in conjunction with each other, instead of being artificially fragmented.

9.4 LACK OF A STATUTORY FORMULA FOR FINANCIAL SETTLEMENTS

In some countries, standard principles make it easier to settle financial issues because a statutory formula determines the level of child support to be paid. In Norway, each partner keeps what he or she brought into the marriage and they divide equally what they have acquired during the marriage.[5] Norway has guidelines for determining the level of spousal maintenance or child support, based on gross income. Mediators without legal qualifications need to be aware of s 25(2) of the Matrimonial Causes Act 1973 which contains the criteria for the making of financial remedy orders. A continuing criticism is that these criteria leave too much scope for uncertainty. Although formulae exist for the calculation of child maintenance, these are now primarily to assist informed 'private ordering' rather than being imposed as a mandatory requirement.[6] Current government policy is to encourage 'family based arrangements', ie privately-reached agreements between parents. There is a child maintenance

---

[5] Tjersland 'Mediation in Norway' (1995) 12(4) *Mediation Quarterly* 339–351.
[6] Section 16 and Sch 4 of the Child Maintenance and Other Payments Act 2008.

calculator website[7] which shows how much the Child Maintenance Service would require the non-resident parent to pay, but a formula does not necessarily resolve matters. The court and welfare systems do not provide swift or sure outcomes. Mediation provides parents with opportunities to find their own solutions. They know their children's needs better than anyone else and in the same way, they are likely to be best placed to make informed decisions about their financial resources and needs. Mediation encourages them to use their own judgement in finding a workable solution, instead of asking a judge to decide on their behalf. Case-law on the division of (in most cases, exceptional) assets and income on divorce may be equally bewildering for lawyers and clients in attempting to predict the likely outcome of an application on financial matters. Mediators should explain the parameters to participants, without advising on the likely outcome if they take their dispute to court. Questions can be identified for each partner to take to financial and/or legal advisers.[8] In this way, participants are helped to make an informed evaluation of the options available to them and encouraged to use their own yardsticks and creativity in working out what they think is fair.

In some countries, such as Germany, there are fixed principles and mechanisms for pension splitting on divorce. However, in England and Wales pensions are considered within the general discretion provided by s 25 of the MCA 1973 and the Court's powers under the Welfare Reform and Pensions Act 1999. There are no formulae, and attempts to impose general principles have been frowned upon by the Courts. Within mediation, as in litigation, the choice is between 'offsetting' against other assets, or by pension sharing ('splitting') or pension attachment ('ear-marking'). Over the ten years of availability of the pension sharing option, it has not been as popular as might have been expected, but nevertheless around 11% of all financial orders now include a pension sharing provision.[9] It should be borne in mind that:

- pension sharing is only available by way of order on divorce;
- pension sharing or attachment will have significant administrative costs;
- consideration of pensions, including in mediation, is a highly technical matter and requires expert assistance.

This does not mean that mediators should fight shy of dealing with pensions; indeed they must deal with them and must equip themselves to do so. Mediators need to be able to explain available pension options in broad terms, to help participants understand the possible advantages and disadvantages of each option. Mediators therefore need enough knowledge to understand different kinds of pension schemes and to enquire about additional voluntary contributions and benefits payable on death in service or when retirement age is reached. However, there are questions relating to pensions on which expert advice is needed and participants must be encouraged to take this advice. The value of the mediator's knowledge of pensions may therefore be to acknowledge

---

[7] http://www.cmoptions.org/en/calculator/.

[8] See **11.10** below.

[9] Salter 'A Decade of Pension Sharing' [2010] Fam Law 1294–1298.

the importance of what s/he does not know. Expert advice may be made available within mediation much as an Independent Financial Adviser (IFA) is used within Collaborative Law. Mediation summaries need to record the extent to which pension options were considered in mediation and that the participants were encouraged to seek independent legal and financial advice.

9.5 MEDIATING WITH UNMARRIED COUPLES

Opportunities for mediation created by the discretionary and sometimes unclear application of divorce law rules and precedents are even greater in financial disputes arising from the separation of unmarried couples. In contrast to considerations of fairness in divorce-related financial proceedings, fairness is *not* the guiding principle in litigation between former cohabitants. Cohabitants who are unable to resolve their respective interests in a home legally owned by only one of them, although contributed to by them both, face lengthy and costly litigation in the civil jurisdiction under the Trusts of Land and Appointment of Trustees Act 1996. If dependent children are involved and Schedule 1 to the Children Act 1989 is also invoked, matters become even more complex. It is estimated that one sixth of couples living together in England and Wales are unmarried, a proportion predicted to rise to one in four by 2031. 25% of children are born to unmarried parents. Cohabitants who believe that they have legal rights as 'common law' spouses are shocked to find on separation that this is not the case. This is an area of law in urgent need of reform. The President of the Family Division said in February 2011:[10]

> 'I am in favour of cohabitees having rights because of the injustices of the present system. Women cohabitees, in particular, are severely disadvantaged by being unable to claim maintenance and having their property rights determined by the conventional laws of trusts.'

The President's views strengthen the case for legislative reform in this area, a reform for which Resolution has long been pressing. In the future, the courts would then have the same discretion to award maintenance payments, a lump sum or a share of the property. The Justice Minister, Simon Hughes, has said that reform of this area of law is one of his two remaining priorities. Meanwhile, as current law fails to provide the remedies they need, many more unmarried couples may choose to come to mediation to reach financial settlements that they both regard as fair in their particular circumstances (see example of mediation with an unmarried couple below). Mediators need to be familiar with the principles set out in *Stack v Dowden*[11] and *Kernott and Jones*.[12] A useful summary of the current law is provided by Mostyn J in a 2014 case.[13] With up-to-date knowledge of the law, mediators with cross-disciplinary training and experience can provide a forum where needs, resources and 'fairness' can be balanced and where the history of contributions can be

---

[10] (2011) *The Times*, 3 February.
[11] [2007] UKHL 17, [2007] 2 AC 432, HL.
[12] [2010] EWCA Civ 578, [2010] 2 FLR 1631.
[13] *Bhura v Bhura* [2014] EWHC 727 (Fam) [38].

explored as part of a collaborative information-sharing exercise rather than in destructive and adversarial ways.[14] This is an area that is developing, both in mediation and in collaborative law. Same-sex couples not in an existing legal marriage or civil partnership are able to marry under the Marriage (Same Sex Couples) Act 2014. The first such marriages took place in March 2014.

9.6   MEDIATION COMPARED WITH DISPUTE RESOLUTION IN DIVORCE FINANCIAL RELIEF LITIGATION

It is often argued that, particularly once proceedings have started, Judge-led Dispute Resolution offered by the First Directions Appointment (FDA) and Financial Dispute Resolution (FDR) appointments is likely to be more effective than mediation. This is a claim which is strengthened by the changes to Rules and forms in April 2014 that are intended to increase the 'inquisitorial' and case management roles of the District Judge, particularly when dealing with 'Litigants in Person.'[15] The Court may be the only or most appropriate forum for the few truly entrenched cases that are pursued up to a contested final hearing, but clients who have experienced the pressures of in-court negotiations may have different views. Negotiation 'at the Court door' led by Counsel may produce a forced settlement without genuine agreement. It is possible to demonstrate that mediation provides a sound basis for comprehensive financial disclosure that may be more effective than interlocutory Court orders – before even beginning to consider the comparative costs! Essentially, those who engage in mediation or collaborative law invest in a co-operative exercise to share information and explore options, whereas Court-led Dispute Resolution remains grafted on to an adversarial process. There are of course cases where the authority of a Judge is required to guide progress and direct co-operation. In these cases, ways may be devised to combine the strengths of court proceedings and mediation in a settlement-seeking process, rather than in an adversarial one.

Mediation services may offer flexible models of intervention sometimes called 'Informal FDR', meshing the Court's authority with participation in mediation.

9.7   FINANCIAL DISCLOSURE IN MEDIATION

Mediators explain at the initial information and assessment meeting that if there are financial issues, full financial information with supporting documents will be needed in order to work towards a settlement in mediation. A provisional settlement reached in mediation can form the basis for a consent order providing a full and final settlement in divorce. Mediators generally use financial questionnaires similar to those used by family lawyers and the courts (Form E). Participants need to understand that financial information provided in mediation is 'open' (ie can be disclosed to the court), unlike discussions

---

[14]   See Robinson [2009] Fam Law 253.
[15]   For an initial critique of this approach see HHJ John Mitchell 'Inquisitorial family justice' [2014] Fam Law 1180.

which are confidential and privileged. Information gathered in mediation is shared and considered with both partners together. If they work out terms for settlement, the mediator produces an 'open' Financial Summary that they are encouraged to take to lawyers for advice. If no settlement is reached or if the court needs to see the information on which a consent order is sought, it can be made available to the court since there would be wasteful duplication in collecting the same information again. It is important for participants to understand that if the level of disclosure is not satisfactory and does not meet Form E requirements, legal advisers and the court, will be less likely to approve the proposed settlement. Judges have discretion to refuse a settlement if they are not satisfied that it falls within the MCA 1973 'band of reasonableness'. Mediators need to be able to provide neutral legal information in a comprehensible way, explaining s 25 of the MCA 1973 and the 'band of reasonableness' so that participants are clear what the Judge will look for, if they seek a consent order. Giving information in mediation is particularly useful, as clients may have received a different level or quality of information from their lawyers, or none at all. The lack of a standard formula in the MCA 1973 means that mediation clients have the advantage of being able to come to their own decisions (ie be empowered) whilst being aware of the MCA 1973 requirements. The same level of legal information in mediation is needed for ToLATA and Schedule 1 applications. In terms of obtaining financial disclosure, reluctant clients co-operate more readily if they understand the benefits of reaching agreement and the criteria that need to be satisfied.

The first step, generally, is to help couples plan how they will gather information about their financial circumstances as a basis for exploring their financial needs and options. Just as shared knowledge of children's needs informs the debate about how to meet those needs, so couples cannot negotiate usefully on financial matters until they know the value of their assets and extent of their liabilities. Some individuals come to their first mediation meeting with spreadsheets already prepared. Others, when asked, have no idea what assets they have or what the other partner earns. Helping both partners equally to determine the value of their assets and the level of their incomes and liabilities is more important in the first instance than explaining s 25 criteria. Different ways of obtaining professional valuations may need to be considered. The cost of obtaining expert valuations can be more than the asset is worth. Participants may wish to consider instructing a Single Joint Expert (SJE) who has not previously acted for either of them individually. If either partner has a solicitor, their lawyers should be involved in the selection of the SJE. There may need to be correspondence on this issue with possible approval of a joint letter of instruction drafted by the mediator on a 'without prejudice basis' until agreement has been reached as to whom is to be instructed.

In helping couples to gather and share financial information, mediators need to combine process management, interpersonal and problem-solving skills. Filling in a lengthy form is very daunting for some people. The mediator needs to watch for signs of anxiety or resistance and make sure that both partners are willing to fill in their form and feel able to manage it. Some people are anxious that they cannot fill it in because they do not have the information. The mediator should reassure them by explaining that the other participant may be able to provide the information:

> 'Don't worry if you don't know the current mortgage balance. Brenda says that she has the mortgage statement and she will bring it. Put down all you can and we will go through both forms next time and see if the information from both of you gives a complete picture.'

The mediator should make it clear that each participant should fill in their own form, even if they know little about the family's finances. Sometimes one partner offers to fill in the other's form, but normally this should be discouraged even if it is a genuinely helpful offer and not an attempt to take control. If each partner fills in their own form the mediator can see how much information is available to each of them and how far they agree about figures and valuations. Some couples, especially those who are still living together, may get into arguments if they discuss on their own the figures they are putting down on their forms. It may be sensible to discourage them from comparing notes and discussing figures on their own and preferable to suggest going through their forms and looking at differences in mediation, when the mediator is there to help them. Couples generally see the sense of avoiding arguments that would be premature, at this stage. On the other hand, there is no need to discourage co-operative couples from discussing financial matters together. The amount of time that people need to complete their questionnaires and obtain supporting documents needs to be discussed with them. If their circumstances are straightforward, three weeks may suffice, but it can take much longer to obtain pension statements. It may be possible to start working on income and outgoings while information on pensions is being obtained, if participants have collected other necessary information.

As always, mediators need to avoid being over-prescriptive. Although they must keep an eye on the adequacy and comprehensiveness of disclosure from the Court's point of view, the detailed completion of a financial questionnaire is beyond the competence of many clients and is not always necessary. Some services adopt a default form that is much simpler than the 'Mediation Form E'.

Anxious or confused people need reassurance and step-by-step guidance. Mediators can explain how to obtain the surrender value of a policy and discuss with them how they will organise getting valuations. Some couples come to mediation wanting a settlement that they have already worked out together in broad terms. Others do not know where to begin. The pace of mediation needs to be adjusted for couples at varying stages of separation and for partners who are generally at a different stage from each other in adjusting to the separation or divorce. Often, one of them is much more knowledgeable about financial matters than the other, creating a power imbalance that needs to be managed.[16] It is important to encourage participants to find Independent

---

[16] See Chapter 10 below.

Financial Advisers (IFAs) specifically trained in divorce and pensions, because not all IFAs have the necessary knowledge and skills.

The mediator needs to discuss the supporting documents that will be needed in the mediation and plan who will provide them. Co-operation is sought by asking, for example, 'It would be useful if we could have ...' or 'Do you think you could help us by getting hold of ...?' The documents each partner is asked to produce should be listed and recapped at the end of the session. The quantity of supporting documents varies according to the financial circumstances. Mediators need to consider the amount of documentation that participants will need to inform their discussion, and that legal advisers will need in order to advise. The key is proportionality. The level of trust, or mistrust, between partners also needs to be taken into account in considering how much verification will be needed to satisfy both of them. Gathering and considering full financial information in mediation and collaborative law can take considerable time, but it should still be much quicker than correspondence between lawyers, because the information is clarified with both partners together. A timescale should be agreed for the completion of forms and obtaining valuations and documents, as the following mediation meeting would need to be rescheduled if the information is not available.

Where pensions are concerned, unless the fund is very limited, a professional pension report is essential. The clients should consult their lawyers, as their lawyers need to approve the pension report provider and the letter of instruction that is prepared prior to the clients commissioning the report. There may need to be consideration as to which fund should be split and how that is to be achieved with the necessary court order: such considerations can make a significant difference. Some pensions are underfunded and some CTVs (Cash Transfer Value) do not reflect the real value of that pension. Service pensions are particularly complex. With the clients' solicitors' approval, a pension report can be commissioned during the mediation process and a copy of the report may be attached to the confidential mediation summary (not to the Open Financial Statement, as the report may contain recommendations that are not agreed). The same applies if clients have business interests and a forensic valuation of a company is required. In these circumstances, the approval and involvement of the lawyers in the commissioning of the report is equally essential and the report can be annexed to the confidential mediation summary. Another possibility for difficult valuation work is the use of dual experts working together in a cost-effective way.[17]

---

[17] Adam-Cairns 'Why Instruct a Single Joint Expert Valuer?' [2010] Fam Law 656–657.

9.8   PROCESS AND PROBLEM-SOLVING SKILLS[18]

9.8.1   Using the flip-chart to display information and consider options

The flip-chart provides an efficient method of displaying figures gathered from financial forms and documents, before exploring options systematically. Some mediators enter the figures on a spreadsheet on their laptop, but the laptop screen faces the mediator and it may be too small for participants to read the figures easily. A flip-chart overview can be updated as the mediation progresses, when formal valuations are provided and agreed. The summary of finances on the flip-chart can then be transcribed in the 'open' financial summary provided at the end of the mediation. Clients interviewed in the Mapping Paths to Family Justice study[19] commented favourably on the use of flip-charts to show their financial position and options for property division.

There are, however, potential pitfalls and disadvantages in using the flip-chart, as well as advantages. Realisable and 'not yet' realisable assets, such as pension funds, should not be totalled together as this would give a misleading picture of capital available to fund property purchase.

9.8.1.1   *Disadvantages of using a flip-chart*

- A mediator standing at the flip-chart can seem like a lecturer talking down to participants. Many flip-charts are adjustable and can be set at seating level, so that the mediator does not jump up and down like a jack-in-a-box.

- When the mediator writes on the flip-chart, eye contact and dialogue with participants are easily lost if the mediator's back is turned.

- Participants may fear that what is written is 'tablets of stone' that cannot be changed. They may be alarmed to see the value of the family home written up, fearing this means that their home is going to be sold.

- Listing assets that one participant regards as their own personal possession – such as a savings account or jewellery – can cause intense anger and distress if it gives the impression that a treasured possession is to be disposed of or shared with the ex-partner. Mediators need to reassure participants that what is written up for consideration does *not* imply any assumptions or decisions concerning division.

- Flip-chart pages used in mediation are confidential and need to be stored safely.

- Participants may be offended if facts and figures are written in an untidy scrawl. Professional presentation of flip-chart information is very important. Figures need to be neat and legible and lines need to be straight!

---

[18]   See Chapter 5 above.
[19]   Barlow, Hunter, Smithson and Ewing *Mapping Paths to Family Justice – Report on Key Findings* (June 2014).

9.8.1.2 *Advantages of using a flip-chart*

- Financial information is collated and displayed in a clear and systematic way.

- A visual overview enables both participants to consider the information together.

- Participants and mediators look at the same figures at the same time.

- The mediator keeps eye contact and notices changes in facial expression, whereas if participants keep heads lowered to look through forms, it is more difficult to see emotional reactions.

- Errors or differences in values can be identified quickly.

- When there are differences about estimated values, these can be shown as a range, avoiding unhelpful arguments. For example, one partner may exclaim:

    'That's a ridiculous figure. It's worth far more than that.'

The mediator can clarify each partner's valuations (how recent, by whom):

    'So you both think your property is worth between x and y? Shall we use x and y as the range for now and then come back to how you agree an actual figure?'

- Symbols can be used to record queries or issues needing further attention – question marks, asterisks, arrows.

- Different colours can distinguish assets held in sole names from those held in joint names.

- A visual display can be very powerful, showing realities that participants need to grasp.

- A flip-chart is preferable to a whiteboard, because information generally needs to be referred to and updated at the next meeting. It is a working document that encourages movement and focused thinking. Several flip-chart pages may need to be displayed alongside each other, so that capital assets and incomes/outgoings can be considered in conjunction with each other. Some flip-charts have 'wings' that can be extended.

- Flip-chart figures can be copied onto a spreadsheet or printed summary sent to participants to help them consider options and take professional advice.

Flip-chart skills hardly figure in mediation literature, but they are very important. As a visual aid, the flip-chart can be used creatively as well as efficiently to gather and share information and explore options. When considering the information displayed on the flip-chart, one partner may propose spontaneously that a particular asset should remain in, or be transferred to, the other partner's name. Provisional proposals can be marked on the flip-chart in a different colour or shown in some way. It is very important, however, for the mediator not to remain standing at the flip-chart while options are discussed, for in so doing the mediator becomes separated from the problem-solving circle and risks adopting the role of teacher or expert.

9.8.2   Structuring and planning

High levels of conflict may be manageable if a plan is agreed for addressing and working on issues. Priorities need to be identified. The agenda for each meeting needs to be reviewed at the start, as circumstances may change between meetings. At the end of each meeting, the agenda for the next meeting may be agreed, so that participants can make enquiries, take advice and consider possible options. Time for reflection between mediation sessions may be very beneficial.

9.8.3   Setting manageable tasks

A task that is easily manageable for one person may be overwhelming for another. Some people have all the financial information at their fingertips, whereas for another, it may be the first time that they phone a bank or building society. Proposing manageable tasks that need to be undertaken before the next session helps to build confidence, as well as gathering information. 'Homework' tasks should be recapped at the end of the meeting and both parties should have a written note to refer to. Some people need the mediator's help to understand the questions that need to be asked, before they can begin to look for answers.

9.8.4   Considering expenditure and needs

When there are issues involving a need for spousal maintenance and/or child support, the mediator needs to discuss how each participant will provide details of current monthly expenditure and budgets of estimated future expenditure. Some people do not know how they spend their money, only that they spend it. The mediator helps them to plan how they will record their current expenditure, as a basis for working out future needs. Detailed monthly budgets help to work out future housing needs and child support payments. A monthly budget form lists all items of expenditure – housing costs, insurance, gas, electricity and other essential utilities. Expenditure on food, housekeeping, clothing, health, cars, travel to work etc needs to be itemised. There should be a special section on costs connected with the children – shoes and clothing, education, school trips, pocket money and presents. The mediator may need to explain that while some expenditure can be put in a separate category for the children, child maintenance payments by the non-residential parent should include an element of housing and general costs to help maintain a home for them.

'Monthly' needs to be defined as a calendar month – not as four weeks. Mediators need to be sensitive to the embarrassment felt by a person who is unable to work out monthly figures and who needs some help to do so.

Discussion of monthly incomes and expenditure can be productive if there are clear objectives and if discussions are managed carefully by the mediator. If they are managed well, predictable arguments can often be pre-empted and avoided. Mediators also need to ask whether participants are claiming the welfare benefits to which they may be entitled. Many single parents do not claim the benefits to which they are entitled, because they do not know about them.

Arguments flare up quickly if the mediator is passive and allows each parent to attack the other's expenditure: 'Do you really spend that much on clothes every month?' 'Are you telling me you can afford to have all those meals out? Lucky you!' Arguments about 'needs' can take a long time without getting anywhere. Expenditure generally exceeds income and shortfalls need to be highlighted in red on the flip-chart. Both parents may be asked to think of possible ways of reducing their own expenditure and/or increasing their income and to come back next time with revised figures. If one parent's monthly budget is for that parent alone, whereas the other budget is for the other parent and the children, this needs to be shown clearly on the flip-chart. It is helpful to total the figures and combine the totals under the headings of 'Family Income' and 'Family Outgoings'. A parent bringing up children on a low income may be unable to cut a tight budget any further. There is understandable anger and resentment if further cutbacks are expected. The mediator's sensitive use of language is therefore very important. Parents may accept the notion of a 'survival budget', as a means of working out immediate and essential needs, while also considering their needs for the longer-term. Prioritising essential outgoings is more useful than a laborious examination of what each party spends or claims to spend on every item, including holidays and leisure activities.

Parents quite often come up with their own ideas and may respond to suggestions. Some parents decide to open a bank account for the children to which they will each contribute an agreed amount per month in proportion to their income. This account will be used by either of them to purchase clothes or other items for the children. The purpose of this account needs to be agreed and the level of expenditure that would require joint consent. These kinds of arrangements can work well for dual-career parents who are committed to sharing their parenting responsibilities.

9.8.5 Debts and liabilities

Parents are sometimes so worried about debts that they are reluctant to admit how much money they owe, but it is clearly necessary to obtain a complete picture of their financial position and potential risks. If arrears are accumulating, mediators can help couples to prioritise and encourage them to take reliable advice on debt management, such as negotiating an arrangement with their lenders. If mortgage payments are overdue, there may be ways of avoiding the repossession of the family home. If lenders have difficulty making contact with the borrower and the borrower makes no effort to explain their difficulty, the lender is more likely to start repossession proceedings. A person who is in debt may need to write a letter or arrange an appointment with the bank or other lender, explaining their problems and asking for a break or reduction in their repayments until their financial affairs are in order again.

Clients are often able also to arrange a freeze on credit card interest payments and may be able to negotiate manageable reduced payments of outstanding debts. Again, communication with lenders is the key. Other 'money management' suggestions for those on very tight budgets may include using a price comparisons website for changes to utility, phone and insurance costs. Advice agencies such as the CAB may help with checking ongoing reliance on credit cards rather than switching to debit card usage where credit card expenditure continues to mount.

9.8.6   Filling in gaps

There are often omissions and errors that are not deliberate. Mediators need to look out for errors, accepting that it is easy to make a mistake, but watching for any sign of dishonesty and bad faith. Mediators need knowledge and experience to analyse financial information and spot the gaps or inconsistencies. Although participants generally accept the need for disclosure, there are some who see mediation as an easy option and who hope to pull the wool over the mediator's eyes, as well as over their partner's eyes. Deceiving an experienced mediator and their former partner at the same time may, however, turn out to be harder than expected. Some individuals may hope to conceal some of their savings. Mediators need to watch for any sign that a person is being less than frank, such as a life-style not explained by the income declared. A probing question from the mediator may be picked up by the other party: 'But, Archie, I distinctly remember your mentioning that account we had in Switzerland'. The mediator needs to be alive to power imbalances in relation to each participant's understanding of financial information and the management of their income and assets. Where one partner is better informed or astute than the other, as is often the case, mediators need to use power-balancing techniques in addition to other mediation skills.

9.8.7   Anticipating and pre-empting

It is not easy for mediators or for participants to think ahead to the next stage when they are in the middle of managing the present stage. However, mediators need to foresee difficulties and help participants to anticipate and avoid them by putting 'what if?' questions: 'You mentioned earlier, David, that you have a big tax bill to pay soon. If this demand comes in, would it help to discuss …?' Or : 'I know this sounds rather pessimistic, but what would you do if …?'

Clients who are determined to stay in the family/former matrimonial home, despite their inability to meet the outgoings, may be inclined to switch to an interest-only mortgage. Before taking out an interest-only mortgage or converting an existing repayment mortgage to interest only, they should be strongly encouraged to consult an IFA, so that they understand that they will have to plan for a sale at the end of the mortgage term, unless they have some other potential repayment vehicle in place. Where it is necessary to agree a reduced budget, mediators can help participants to explore options for changes in the future, such as working more hours when a child moves to secondary school and finding out what this would produce in terms of increased income. Those contemplating a further training course would need to know what income they could expect after the qualification is achieved. Sometimes an IFA can assist with cashflow forecasting that alleviates fears preventing settlement and gives clients a window on future changes that allow for planning and more control of their finances.

9.8.8   Option development

Mediation itself is an option and exploring options is one of the main elements of the mediation process. After gathering and understanding all the information, the next stage is to identify and explore possible options, looking at what would be possible and examining advantages or disadvantages from the point of view of each participant and the children. Broad options may be divided into sub-options. Future housing needs are usually a dominant concern and the starting-point for identifying possible options. Housing options can be listed under broad headings. A preferred option or options can then be examined in more detail in terms of capital needs, income needs, priorities for the children – such as staying at the same school – and priorities for the parents – such as the area they would prefer to live in. Exploring housing needs provides a framework for considering both parties' monthly income and expenditure. After working through income, expenditure and future budgets, housing plans may need to be looked at again and scaled down. Some options may be rejected, but it is better not to cross them out. A previously rejected option may need re-examining. Mediators should not dismiss what may seem an unrealistic idea, as it may turn out to be workable. If participants seem be stuck, the mediator can suggest other possible options, even putting forward an apparently outlandish idea to encourage brainstorming, wider perspectives and fresh thinking. Exploration of options can be shown graphically on the flip-chart and considered more freely and positively in mediation than in the court setting.

9.8.9   Achieving finality

It is important to clarify whether a full and final settlement is looked for and to distinguish a final settlement on financial matters from arrangements for children that need to be kept under review. Arrangements for children change as they get older or because family circumstances change, whereas once a consent order has been made in divorce, a former partner cannot ask for a bigger share. It is very important for mediators to explain the difference between realisable assets and unrealisable ones such as pensions, so that participants understand why these forms of assets should be treated differently. These differences should be shown clearly on the flip-chart.

9.8.10   Summary of process and problem-solving skills

- Explain process and objectives.
- Identify issues and time-scales – interim, long-term or both?
- Discuss completion of financial questionnaires, valuations, CTVs, supporting documents.
- Plan and prioritise, consider degree of urgency.
- Maintain balance in gathering/giving information.
- Display information on flip-chart for focus and clarity.
- Analyse figures, identify gaps and discrepancies.
- Set tasks – enquire about borrowing capacity, cost of alternative accommodation.
- Current income and anticipated changes, adjustments in tax credits, benefit entitlements.
- Income needed to fund borrowing, loan payments, essential outgoings.
- Identify need for professional advice – legal and financial, pensions.
- Identify and explore options.
- Discuss factors to take into account – children, earning capacity, health etc.
- Reality-testing – viability and effects of each option.
- Spousal maintenance?
- Child maintenance – information about the formula, budgets for children, additional contributions, sport and leisure activities, birthday and Christmas presents.
- Recap on any proposals and outstanding issues.
- Identify range in which settlement may be reached – convert figures into percentages and vice versa, use BATNA and WATNA questions.[20]
- Consider alternative routes to final settlement, if necessary.
- Produce accurate interim/final financial summaries.

9.9   COMBINING PROCESS, PROBLEM-SOLVING AND PERSONAL SKILLS

It is fashionable today to deride consumerism and preoccupation with material possessions, 'but the paradox is that as more and more of our lives are mediated by screens and keyboards, and the virtual world of word and image dominates, the enchantment of things intensifies.'[21] A loved object may have precious associations with special events or past generations, providing a link in the construction and continuity of identity. Possessions may be heavily charged with emotional value. Furniture, pictures and jewellery may have an emotional value that bears little relation to their financial worth and participants may

---

[20]   See **11.11** below.
[21]   Bunting 'Our history told in just 100 objects' (2011) *Guardian Weekly*, 7 January, p 24.

become distressed if assets and possessions are valued solely in monetary terms. In one case, a carpet bought by the couple on their honeymoon was wanted desperately by both of them, because it was a symbol of their investment in each other and hope for happiness. If there are children, couples may agree that a treasured possession will be held by one of them in trust for a child. If there is more than one child, it is obviously helpful if there is more than one possession in this special category. Emotional attachments to possessions need to be understood and acknowledged whenever questions of valuing them are raised.[22] A question put hypothetically, in a sensitive way, is less disturbing than a closed, factual question. Mediators need to facilitate the recognition and empowerment that are central elements in transformative and family-focused mediation. A mediator using a settlement-seeking approach may concentrate on figures without giving enough attention to strong feelings that, for one or both participants, may turn the figures into a blur.

Combining the 'hard' discipline of process and problem-solving skills with the 'soft' empathy of interpersonal skills presents many challenges for mediators. Logical 'left-brain' thinking needs to be combined with intuitive 'right-brain' thinking and imagination. Power imbalances need to be addressed and managed and there may be high levels of emotion. Managing this high level of mental processing and interpersonal skills may be easier for co-mediators than for a sole mediator.[23] Interpersonal skills that need to be used throughout the process and not overlooked when gathering and totalling figures include:

- Acknowledge feelings – anger, fear, confusion – and concerns.
- Motivate participants to undertake manageable tasks.
- Mutualise concerns (for security) and needs as far as possible.
- Give clear and verifiable information in a balanced way.
- Crisis management.
- Prioritise and plan.
- Manage conflict in gathering and sharing financial information.
- Facilitate communication, awareness of non-verbal communication.
- Build trust and seek reassurances.
- Manage power imbalances – recognising money as a source of power and means of control.
- Manage time well.
- Understand emotional value of property and assets.
- Encourage constructive negotiation.
- Encourage co-operation in considering children's needs in relation to financial means.
- Use impasse strategies.
- Maintain notes and records.

---

[22] See mediation example in **12.1** below.
[23] See Chapter 4 above.

9.10   CAN MEDIATION DEAL WITH COMPLEX FINANCES?

Mediating on complex financial issues and high-value assets requires mediators
to have the necessary levels of expertise and experience. With suitably qualified
mediators, mediation offers a means of reducing or avoiding lengthy and costly
correspondence between legal advisers and extremely expensive litigation. It
may also be less expensive than collaborative law. The question of valuing
assets has been touched on earlier. In mediating with a couple who owned six
properties in sole or joint names, valuations were particularly difficult because
two of the properties were overseas and one was half-built. The couple
discussed in mediation how realistic valuations could be obtained and agreed.
The wife recognised that the half-built property was not worth as much as their
original investment and that it would be sensible to agree a value pragmatically,
based on a single valuation, without incurring even more expense.
Collaborative dispute resolution in which mediation is combined with
independent legal and financial advice provided to participants outside – or
inside – the mediation process and drawn on by them in mediation meetings,
can be harnessed in a problem-solving approach, instead of an adversarial one.
In complex and straightforward cases, the motivation of participants is the key
factor. Mediators offer space, time, positive energy – and knowledge and skills
– to help people find keys that can turn a set of locks in their own particular
gateway to conflict resolution. As in dealing with complex emotions and
interconnected systems, mediators need to offer a variety of models – in this
case, mediation, collaborative law, multi-disciplinary approaches and even
family arbitration – that are designed to meet the needs of complex financial
problems.

9.11   PRE- AND POST-NUPTIAL AGREEMENTS

The Supreme Court ruled in *Radmacher v Granatino*[24] that:

> 'the court should give effect to a nuptial agreement that is freely entered into by
> each party with a full appreciation of its implications, unless in the circumstances
> prevailing it would not be fair to hold the parties to their agreement.'

Nevertheless, the parties cannot by agreement oust the jurisdiction of the Court
and in financial relief proceedings the Court is not obliged to give effect to
nuptial agreements. The Court must, however, give appropriate weight to such
agreements. Robinson suggests that mediators should approach pre- and
post-nuptial negotiations with caution, 'but there is then no reason why the
same forensic information gathering could not take place as, for example, when
considering the history of contributions in a cohabitation case'.[25] Negotiations
in mediation involving a pre- or post-nuptial agreement should involve lawyers
directly, offering ways in which legal advisers and mediators work jointly with
a settlement-seeking focus, yet keeping their different roles distinct and clear.

---

[24]   [2010] UKSC 42.
[25]   Robinson 'A Mediator's Guide to Pre and Post Marriage Agreements' [2011] Fam Law 529.

Cases involving pre-nuptial agreements often involve high and complex assets and these cases are likely to lie beyond the expertise of the average family mediator. However, 'the crux of the matter is a proper exploration of process options. Just as in other complex cases which come to mediation assessment, it will be the relative cost-effectiveness and expertise that will decide. Collaborative law would seem an ideal place to create a pre-nuptial agreement. Nevertheless, mediation may well be a perfectly appropriate alternative where funds for costs are limited and the expertise of the mediator is known.'[26]

9.12   CIVIL PARTNERSHIP DISPUTES

Since 1989, when Denmark became the first country to recognize civil partnerships, the legal recognition of same-sex relationships has been accepted in many countries. Half the Member States of the EU have now introduced legislation on the recognition of same-sex relationships. A civil partnership is a legal marriage between a gay or lesbian couple, giving them responsibilities and rights comparable to those of heterosexual married couples. The Civil Partnership Act 2004 came into force on 5 December 2005 in England and Wales. Civil partners have the same property rights as heterosexual married couples and acquire joint parental responsibility for the children of one partner. To dissolve a civil partnership, the couple must have been in a civil partnership for at least a year and a petition must be filed on the same basis as a divorce petition, citing similar 'facts', together with a Statement of Arrangements for any child residing with the couple.

If their relationship breaks down, more civil partners and same-sex couples may come to mediation if they are better informed of its availability and reassured that family mediators offer the same help and empathy to same-sex couples as they do to any couple. A lesbian couple referred themselves to mediation because they wanted to resolve property matters privately through mediation, without going to court. The dynamics of 'the leaver' and the 'left' and their turmoil of anger, grief and continuing attachment were no different from those of male/female partners. In this particular case, the couple had two dogs that they loved like children. Working out shared care and contact arrangements for their dogs was more urgent and important for them than settling financial matters. Mediation provides a forum to negotiate and settle inter-related issues that a court would not consider, as well as issues that could lead to prolonged litigation and high costs.

9.13   MEDIATION IN INHERITANCE DISPUTES

Disputes arise quite frequently over the terms of a will (or in the absence of a will) between family members and the cohabitant of the deceased, or between adult children. These disputes are often fuelled by similar feelings to those experienced in separation and divorce – bitterness, grief, rejection, loss, anger

---

[26]   Ibid, 530.

and resentment. Mediation gives opportunities to recognise and express these emotions in negotiating over the terms of a disputed will, whereas these painful feelings risk being further inflamed by court proceedings. Litigation in inheritance disputes also carries high risks of the value of the estate being consumed by legal costs and culminating in the permanent breakdown of relationships between siblings.

Henry Brown has written (personal communication):

> 'It is certainly a common experience that inheritance disputes may disguise other emotional issues between the parties. An underlying and unstated issue may for example be "Who did daddy – or mummy – love best?" In addition to these emotional aspects, mediating inheritance disputes may be very practical, for example relating to claims for provision and redistribution under the Inheritance (Provision for Families and Dependants) Act 1975, where the process may involve discussion and businesslike negotiation between the parties, or organising the allocation and management of inherited assets and beneficial interests.'

Cross-trained family and civil/commercial mediators may offer a model of mediation in inheritance disputes that is sensitive and responsive to the intense emotions between estranged family members, while also providing the lawyer-assisted financial negotiation characteristic of civil mediation.

9.14 CHOOSING THE APPROPRIATE DISPUTE RESOLUTION PROCESS FOR FINANCIAL DISPUTES

Mediation offers one way to resolve disputes on financial and property matters. Lawyers may consider that collaborative law offers a 'better' process, possibly involving a family mediator to assist with child-related issues. These different forms of dispute resolution should not be seen as competing with one other: each of them has strengths and limitations. Mediation, especially interdisciplinary co-mediation, and various 'hybrid' models that fall outside the scope of this book, can help family members to resolve an increasingly wide range of financial and property matters in conjunction with related issues concerning children and other family matters.

9.15 MEDIATION EXAMPLES

9.15.1 Mediating with Matt and Rachel

Mediating with Matt and Rachel combined elements of structured, transformative and narrative approaches in an ecosystemic framework. They did not have children together. Matt had been married previously and he had a son from his first marriage. Matt and Rachel explained that they were coming to mediation because they were divorcing and needed to reach a settlement on the division of property and other assets. Following separate information and assessment meetings, they came to their first mediation meeting. They behaved very politely towards each other, with no visible anger or raised voices. Feelings were kept under tight control. In a typology of separated couples they would belong to the 'suppressed conflict' or 'non-communicating' group. Both Matt and Rachel seemed to feel hurt and rejected by each other, but they could not say so. They needed reassurance that mediation was not marital counselling and that the mediator would not enquire about the breakdown of their relationship. However, some elements from the past seemed to have a direct bearing on the present. Matt's son lived with his mother and he needed to be provided for. Some pieces of narrative helped to clarify how past relationships were affecting present ones.

Matt and Rachel needed a structured mediation process to identify issues and agree an agenda. Their shared aim was to reach a fair and balanced financial settlement, as quickly and inexpensively as possible. After gathering and sharing financial information and supporting documents, they were invited to explain their priorities and needs, to consider possible options and the implications of each option. This structure offered emotional security in analysing their financial assets without fear of attack or blame. Logical reasoning was important. On the surface, the negotiations were about the share of financial assets that each of them would receive. However, when underlying feelings were acknowledged in a mutualising way, Matt and Rachel began to express their positive feelings towards each other and to explain their emotional needs, as well as financial ones. Each of them then found words to express appreciation of the contribution the other had made to their relationship and recognise that not all the positives were lost. Instead of being drawn apart through acrimonious legal proceedings, Matt and Rachel remained friends. They said that if they had come to mediation a few years earlier, they might not have separated at all. Although they felt it was too late to get back together, mediation helped them to preserve links of mutual respect and affection, good communication and a shared sense of humour. They laughed in mediation in a way that they would never have laughed in court.

This mediation combined different theoretical models and methods. Using the structured settlement-seeking model, the flip-chart was used to analyse financial information. Technical skills were needed to compute figures, explain possible claims and explore a range of settlement options, converting figures into percentages and vice versa. Family mediators need to be efficient information-processors, but equally importantly, they need to acknowledge strong feelings and manage intense emotions. Matt and Rachel wanted a concrete settlement and they achieved it. The mediation process was not therapy, but it had therapeutic effects in facilitating communication, transforming perceptions and enhancing their post-divorce relationship.

9.15.2   Mediating with Joanna and Richard

A married couple in their thirties, Richard and Joanna, came to mediation to settle issues arising from their separation. Richard, an accountant, had left the family home three months previously. He was renting a one-bedroom flat.

Joanna was a teacher, teaching two mornings per week. Their children, Adam and Lucy, aged seven and five, were living with her in the three-bedroom family home, a property owned in joint names with a mortgage. Richard wanted to sell the family home and buy a property of his own where the children could come to stay. Joanna objected strongly to the sale of the family home and argued that this would upset the children even more. Assets and liabilities were listed and estimated values considered. Incomes and pensions were noted and discussed. The next step was to explore available housing options and test the viability of each option. The options were listed on the flip-chart, showing the advantages and disadvantages that Richard and Joanna identified from their own points of view and for the children.

	Option 1 Sell the family home		Option 2 Joanna and children to remain in the family home	
	Advantages	Disadvantages	Advantages	Disadvantages
Richard	Would be able to buy own home	None	None	Unable to buy a home of his own
Joanna	None – wants to stay where she is	Would have to move to a smaller property, away from friends	Many	Financial cost of maintaining the family home
Adam & Lucy	Would be able to stay overnight with their father	Loss of the home they know. Change of school? Further away from grandparents?	Many	May be unable to stay overnight with their father in small rented flat

Further questions included:
- If the family home is kept, could the mortgage be transferred to Joanna's sole name?
- Could Joanna afford the mortgage payments?
- The monthly income that Joanna would need to remain in the family home, with child support payments from Richard.
- Whether Joanna could increase her working hours.
- If the home were sold, the asking price and costs of sale.
- Price ranges of suitable new properties and how a purchase could be funded.
- How other assets, including pensions, would be taken into account.
- Responsibility for debts.

- If the family home remained in joint ownership, when, at the latest, would this end and in what way?

Richard thought the obvious solution was for Joanna to return to full-time work so that she could afford a bigger mortgage. Joanna felt the children had suffered a great deal of upset and said she was not willing to work full-time until Lucy was older. Joanna also said she did not want to make a direct claim on Richard's inheritance from his father, which he had invested. Richard responded by proposing that Joanna should keep a savings account into which she had been paying her earnings, as Richard earned enough to support the family. These assets were provisionally allocated as proposed on the flip-chart as a worksheet visible to all participants. Richard and Joanna decided to split a joint savings account on a 25/75% basis in Joanna's favour. This proposal was added.

At the beginning of the third meeting, the mediator recapped areas of provisional agreement. Joanna and Richard both wanted a full and final settlement in divorce and were in agreement that the children should continue to live with Joanna and spend alternate weekends and part of their holidays with Richard. Richard said he would continue to pay the mortgage for at least the next six months and make child maintenance payments to Joanna. Options were worked on intensively in two further meetings, with Richard and Joanna each taking legal advice from their lawyers. Their joint preference, finally, was for Richard to register a charge on the family home, payable to him on the earliest of the usual 'trigger' events. Joanna took on more teaching hours and as her income increased, she became able to pay more of the outgoings on the family home. Richard could then afford to rent a bigger flat where the children could stay with him. In the longer term, Joanna envisaged being able to buy Richard out of his share of the home long before Lucy reached the age of 18. Joanna and Richard had come to mediation as embattled antagonists. They gradually became joint problem-solvers who, in pooling their ideas and using their resources and energies for the benefit of the family as a whole, found that they could reach their own solutions and keep their legal costs to a minimum.

9.15.3 Mediating with Gemma and Martin

Gemma, aged 29 was unemployed and dependent on welfare benefits and child benefit. Martin aged 31, was a transport manager earning just on £2,000 net per month. They had recently separated after an 11-year marriage. No third parties were involved. Gemma and Martin had two children, Rose aged 11 and Samantha aged 9. Both the children were said to be in good health and doing well at school. Gemma and the children were living in the family home and Martin had moved into rented accommodation. Gemma's solicitor was preparing a divorce petition. Martin had also taken legal advice. Both parents understood that they would continue to share parental responsibility for their children, who would be based with Gemma and see their father often. Their arrangements for the children were agreed before they came to mediation. The children were staying Friday and Saturday nights with their father on alternate weekends and would also spend part of their school holidays with him. If either parent wanted to change their arrangements for a particular weekend, they agreed to give each other as much notice as possible and to schedule a regular meeting to review how the arrangements were working for the children and to discuss any minor problem at an early stage. Martin was paying the mortgage and an agreed monthly amount for the children.

Valuations of the family home and the mortgage balance were obtained and after allowing for costs of sale at 3%, the notional net proceeds of sale were worked out. Martin was willing for Gemma and the girls to remain living in the family home until the earliest of the usual 'trigger' events:

- Gemma remarrying or cohabiting for more than six months;
- Samantha reaching the age of 18;
- Gemma's death.

On this basis, Martin was willing take a charge on the property registered in his name equivalent to a percentage of its gross value. His name would remain on the mortgage and Gemma would use her best endeavours to have his name removed from the mortgage as soon as she was able to do so. Gemma and Martin had three joint bank accounts, with an overdraft on one of them. Martin was paying into this account and as soon the overdraft was cleared, it would be closed and the other two split equally and closed. They had cars of roughly comparable value. Martin was willing for Gemma to keep the contents of the family home, apart from some items in the garage that he was arranging to collect.

9.15.4   Mediating with Edward and Vera

There are many couples who are caring parents and committed to maintaining their co-operation. Other couples come to mediation after years of wrangling and with no goodwill towards each other at all. Edward and Vera were in their early seventies and drawing their pensions. They were living separately under the same roof and barely speaking to each other. Their marriage had broken down eight years previously but they could not agree financial matters and the divorce proceedings had stalled. Edward had refused an earlier offer of a mediation information and assessment meeting. Six months later, he decided to accept it. He had not taken legal advice because he did not want to incur legal costs and was afraid the allegations in Vera's 'unreasonable behaviour' petition would prejudice his position on financial matters. Once this misapprehension was cleared up through the mediation information meeting and an initial half hour with a solicitor, Edward was ready to negotiate a settlement with Vera. Communications between them in two mediation meetings were civilised, although not amicable. As neither could afford to buy the other out, they decided, having taken further legal advice, to sell the matrimonial home and split the proceeds equally on the basis that Edward would pay spousal maintenance to Vera to equalise their pensions. There was a history to the breakdown of their marriage that caused great bitterness between them and resulted in rifts in the extended family as well. Vera and Edward agreed, however, that they did not want to go over the past and that they needed to get on with the rest of their lives. Once they had worked out a way to do so, hostility between them began to ease. In the final mediation session, Vera reported that she had mislaid her house keys and car keys and that Edward had helped her to find them. Previously, as they both acknowledged, this incident would have caused an argument over who was to blame.

To protect ourselves from the cold winds of poverty, it is natural to try to pile up a reassuring stack of material assets and possessions. But the straw of material goods can scatter and blow away. What really matters is 'the growing germ, the very source of life'.

> *'And so from day to day and birth to birth*
> *We must go on, but sometimes sensing*
> *That beyond the straw there must be grain,*
> *The growing germ, the very source of life.'*

> *Adam Curle, 'Straw'.*[27]

---

[27] Curle *Recognition of Reality: Reflections and Prose Poems* (Hawthorn Press, 1987), p 100.

CHAPTER 10

MANAGING POWER IMBALANCES IN MEDIATION

'The balance of power'[1]

'All power is a trust, we are all accountable for its exercise'[2]

CONTENTS

10.1   DIFFERENT FRAMES FOR VIEWING POWER

The word 'power' has mainly negative associations associated with coercion and control. When it involves domination of other people or the seizure of territory, there is an 'abuse of power'. However, power can also be seen in a positive frame in terms of 'capacity, competence and responsibility'. Power that is exercised in consensual and democratic ways can serve collective or mutual needs. With adequate safeguards, it can be exercised beneficially, whereas without safeguards or consensus, power can be used to dominate, manipulate or abuse other people. Power imbalances are often found in relationships that work well: couples rarely have equal power in all areas of their relationship. Different capacities and resources may be used in complementary ways for the benefit of the whole family. Inequalities need not cause resentment and competition, if different strengths are valued. When one partner or parent has greater resources, strengths or responsibilities in some areas, these can be used to mutual benefit. One of the mediator's main functions is to help participants

---

[1]   Sir Robert Walpole, Prime Minister, Speech to Parliament, 13 February 1741.
[2]   Benjamin Disraeli.

identify their resources as well as their needs, so that they can consider how
these resources can be used most effectively for the family's maximum benefit.

10.2 POWER AND GENDER

Power imbalances in family mediation are closely linked to gender. Domestic
violence is an extreme manifestation of the abuse of power through
gender-linked domination, more often by the male partner.[3] Such cases are
either excluded from mediation altogether or possibly offered a safe model such
as shuttle mediation, without any face-to-face contact between the couple.
Differences between the economic position of each parent and in their parental
roles and responsibilities also create significant power imbalances, especially
where one parent has stayed at home or worked part-time while looking after
the children, while the other has built up a successful career. On average, men
earn substantially more than women and have larger pension funds. The male
partner may be more knowledgeable on financial matters, although sometimes
the female partner earns more and manages the family's finances. Mediators
need to be alert to an individual aiming to bulldoze an unsuspecting partner
into a quick financial settlement or to a parent dictating the conditions on
which the other parent is permitted to see the children. Power imbalances in
mediation may be compounded not only by lack of information on financial
assets but by not knowing what questions to ask. If one partner controls the
finances and withholds information, the other cannot assess what would
constitute a reasonable settlement. Disparities of income tend to widen in
divorce, with many single-parent households falling into poverty. Women tend
to have poorer career prospects than men, even if they are equally qualified. In
some cultures, women are taught to be subservient to men. It may be very
difficult for a woman to put her case strongly in mediation if this is contrary to
her upbringing, religion and culture. An Asian wife brought up in a traditional
Asian culture would consider it wrong to assert herself.[4] Although women are
often disadvantaged economically, most divorce petitioners are women. On the
other hand, a man faced with losing his partner, the family home and daily
contact with his children is likely to feel the loser on all counts.

Objections have long been raised to mediation on the grounds that private
ordering leads to unjust outcomes.[5] Genn warned that mediation 'does not
contribute to substantive justice because [it] requires the parties to relinquish
ideas of legal rights during mediation and focus, instead, on problem-solving ...
The outcome of mediation, therefore, is not about *just* settlement, it is *just
about settlement*.'[6] This judgement on mediation may itself be unjust. It may

---

[3] See **3.4–3.6** above.

[4] See 'cross-cultural mediation' in Chapter 3 above.

[5] Hart *Gentle jeopardy: the further endangerment of battered women and children in custody
    mediation* (1990) 7, 4 *Mediation Quarterly* 317–330; Grillo T 'The mediation alternative:
    process dangers for women' (1991) 100(6) *Yale Law Journal* 1545–1610.

[6] Genn 'What is civil justice for? Reform, ADR and Access to Justice' (2012) 24(1) *Yale Journal
    of Law and the Humanities* 15. See also Genn *Judging Civil Justice* (Cambridge University
    Press, 2009).

not have been based on an evaluation of family mediation and is in any event open to challenge. How is justice defined in child-related matters? The Children Act 1989 established that parents have responsibilities towards children, rather than rights over them. Arrangements that take account of children's needs and feelings and which work well in practice do not necessarily represent 'justice' in terms of equality between parents. Children are individuals, not possessions, and research findings both in Australia and the UK show that equally or substantially shared parenting after separation may not be conducive to the welfare of the child.[7] Family mediators have a special concern for children as well as adults: they seek to help parents to consider their children's needs and co-operate better in the longer term. Even on financial matters and division of property, the court does not apply a set formula to determine just outcomes and the courts do not invariably deliver a gold standard of justice. Out of court dispute resolution does indeed give rise to some worrying reports of financial arrangements that disadvantage one party (more often, the primary carer). Examples of unsustainable arrangements resulting from mediation and also from collaborative law are given in the Mapping Paths study.[8] But unbalanced outcomes do not seem to be the norm. Well-trained and experienced mediators assist participants to reach informed, balanced and sustainable outcomes, with legal advisers checking proposals for financial settlement before applying for a consent order.

Critics argue that if mediators fail to address power imbalances and ignore legal rights, mediation:

- fails to compensate women for their inherently disadvantaged position in a male-dominated society in which women have lower status, lower incomes and less bargaining power;

- disadvantages women further, by removing the protections of formality and due process;

- fails to deal with inequalities of power during mediation, because a mediator, acting impartially, cannot protect a vulnerable woman from a forceful, financially more astute and controlling partner;

- is biased towards shared parenting after separation in ways that benefit fathers more than mothers and which disadvantages the mother financially;

- takes advantage of women's greater compliance, anxiety for co-operation and distaste for hard bargaining;

- fails to recognise that violence takes many forms and that it is often concealed by both partners.

More recently, Diduck[9] has warned that private ordering is a form of justice 'that has come to mean nothing more than facilitating the exercise of choice

---

[7] See **7.8** above.

[8] Barlow et al *Mapping Paths study*, (2014), p 24.

[9] Diduck 'Justice by ADR in private family matters: is it fair and is it possible?' [2014] Fam Law 616–619.

regardless of outcome'.[10] She suggests that the 'A' in ADR should stand for Autonomous, since private ordering enables parties to reach their own agreements, on their own. But are they truly autonomous? There is no genuine autonomy if one partner gives way under pressure from the other or if dispute resolution practitioners steer both parties to a quick settlement.[11] There may be pressure from third parties outside the mediation room. Abel warned that informal institutions 'claim to render parties more autonomous when they actually engage in more subtle manipulation'.[12] While some critics object that mediators exercise too much control over the process and its outcome, others complain that they do not exercise enough. In Mnookin and Kornhauser's well-known phrase, separating and divorcing couples do not negotiate in a vacuum: they 'bargain in the shadow of the law ... The outcome that the law would impose, should no agreement be reached, gives each parent certain bargaining chips'.[13] These bargaining chips are the legal principles and precedents that guide the court's decision, taking each party's needs and circumstances into account. Imbalances are increased if an inexperienced or inept mediator lacks necessary knowledge and fails to see or manage tactics that the more astute partner may have been coached to use.

Mediation is intended to empower people, but there can be risks of it doing the reverse. If participants reach ill-informed agreements without knowing their rights and claims in law, there are risks of unfair or unsustainable outcomes. To provide the checks and balances necessary for equitable settlements, participants need independent legal advice before, during and following mediation, to understand their legal position fully and the implications of settlement proposals. The stance taken by each party's legal adviser in giving proper attention to a proposed settlement is a further important factor. When both legal advisers are collaborative lawyers and/or have trained as mediators, they are likely to give their clients legal advice that balances and complements mediation, without undermining it. However, since the drastic cuts in legal aid and more stringent requirements to qualify for public funding for mediation, many people can neither qualify for public funding nor pay privately for legal advice. Consequently, there are greater risks of mediated agreements being reached without independent legal advice. Publicly funded participants can obtain only a limited amount of legal advice and assistance under the Help with Mediation scheme.

Mediators need a high level of knowledge and skills to help participants consider how to divide assets and allocate income to meet needs, while also planning how to share parenting responsibilities and child care. Power imbalances need to be addressed through reality-testing, focusing on children's needs and maintaining the ground-rules of the mediation process. Although mediators do not give advice, they provide general information on the law and

---

[10] Ibid, p 617.
[11] See also **13.6**.
[12] Abel, *The Politics of Informal Justice* (Academic Press, 1982) vol 1, p 9.
[13] Mnookin and Kornhauser 'Bargaining in the shadow of the law: the case of divorce' (1979) 88 *Yale Law Journal* 950–997.

should identify questions on which legal advice is needed to test the fairness of a proposed settlement.[14] They should assist participants to 'reality-test' their proposals and consider how arrangements will work in practice, both in the shorter and longer term. Mediators can also inform participants that 'the resolution they are considering might fall outside the parameters which the court might approve or order'.[15] The assumption that men are more powerful than women is not always confirmed in mediation. It is more helpful to think in terms of personality traits than gender stereotypes. Traits of gentleness and caring that may be thought of as typically female are also shown by men. Gilligan[16] suggests that those who function in a 'female mode' – whether biologically male or female – are willing to negotiate because they value co-operation highly. Individuals with more forceful, aggressive personalities – whether men or women – tend to value co-operation less highly. In mediation, they may be ready to exploit their partner's greater willingness to settle. Although there are some worrying reports of unfair and unbalanced outcomes, research studies have not found evidence of women being systematically disadvantaged in mediation.[17] Women tend to report more benefits than men do. There is no simple dichotomy based on gender alone. Although one partner may appear more powerful than the other, it often emerges in mediation that each has significant power or influence in certain areas. It is important for mediators not to assess too quickly who has more power and where the power lies. Provided there is careful screening for violence, abuse and power imbalances so that situations unsuitable for mediation are screened out, women report more benefits than men. Research findings underline the importance of mediators' training and experience in enabling them to recognise and manage different power imbalances, including their own use of authority and power.[18]

Power is a fluid, rather than a solid, entity. It can be observed shifting and fluctuating during a mediation session and often from one session to the next. Fluctuating power is often seen in mediation, because power relationships tend to change during marriage breakdown and divorce. Although some patterns remain the same, one partner's decision to leave the other may alter the previous balance of power, sometimes dramatically. Other factors may come into play for the first time. It was suggested in the previous edition of this book that the A in ADR could stand for 'Appropriate', on the basis that the process of dispute resolution, whether it takes place out of court or at court, needs to be appropriate for the parties and for the particular case. In some cases, the court is the appropriate forum. Appropriate Dispute Resolution is a more inclusive term than either 'Alternative' or 'Autonomous'. Appropriate dispute resolution can take place out of court and at court, using combinations of processes that should incorporate legal advice. It may include direct consultation with a child or young person, recognising the rights of the child and enabling the child to

---

[14] See **11.8** below.

[15] Family Mediation Council 2010 Code of Practice, 5.3.

[16] Gilligan *In a Different Voice: psychological theory and women's development* (Harvard University Press, 1982).

[17] See Chapter 13 below.

[18] Kelly 'Power Imbalance in Divorce and Interpersonal Mediation: assessment and intervention' (1995) 13(2) *Mediation Quarterly* Vol 85–98.

contribute ideas, feelings and wishes on child arrangements. Research findings on mediation practice and client experiences of mediation in relation to gender issues, power imbalances and dispute resolution outcomes are considered further in Chapter 13.

10.3   COUPLES WHO SHARE THE DRIVING

The essence of a good partnership is that it functions well. In many relationships that work well, it suits both partners for each of them to be in the driving-seat at different times. One may look after the children full-time, while the other goes out to work. Other couples choose to share both kinds of driving – childcare and careers – more or less equally, changing drivers when convenient. Either parent may take over from the other by arrangement, following a general direction that is agreed between them. The wheels go on turning, whichever partner is driving, because they are both competent and trust each other. However, when partners disagree as to who should drive or about the direction they ought to take, both may struggle to grab the wheel from the other. They may then find themselves stuck and unable to move in any direction at all.

The diagram below illustrates different kinds of capacity, resource or power that are frequently encountered in mediation. The diagram is itself constructed in the form of a wheel, each segment representing an area in which one partner may have more power or strength than the other. One partner may be more powerful in having greater social prestige and influence, higher earnings and better career prospects. In relation to children, however, it is the parent who has day-to-day contact and close emotional bonds with the children who is in the stronger position, compared with a parent who is distant from the children, geographically or emotionally, or both. The partners' internal and external resources usually differ. The outer segments of the wheel represent external resources that may not be equally available to both partners, such as support from family and friends, work opportunities and access to legal advice. The segments are clearly inter-related and need to be looked at as a whole. However, when there is conflict, attention is drawn to the particular area or areas in which dispute is evident. Power imbalances in these areas are like spokes protruding through the rim of the wheel, upsetting its balance and impeding its movement. The diagram suggests some of the 'spokes' which impede balanced negotiations and make forward movement difficult.

Differences may become accentuated and protrude like jagged spokes in a broken wheel. A partner who feels abandoned, without any part in ending the relationship, generally feels powerless. On the other hand, family and friends may rally round to give support to the abandoned partner and ostracise the 'leaver'. It may then be the parent who leaves who is rejected, even, on occasion, by their own family.

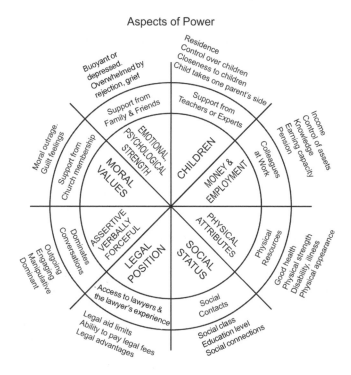

Aspects of Power

10.4 POWER IMBALANCES IN FAMILY MEDIATION

There are many different kinds of power imbalance that affect the dynamics in mediation. These include:

- all forms of physical, psychological and emotional abuse;[19]
- power to end the marriage or relationship;
- power to resist or block change;
- emotional strength and resilience;
- children's residence, established pattern of child care;
- children's emotional loyalty to one parent, alliance with a parent;
- knowledge, control of financial assets, higher income, earning power;
- personality, confidence and assertiveness;
- physique, health and strength, physical appearance;
- verbal skills, use of language;
- intelligence, education or intellectual power;
- gender;[20]
- sexual power, seductiveness;
- ability to manipulate others, especially children;

---

[19] See Chapter 3 above.
[20] See **10.2** above and **13.8** below.

- age;
- moral power – values and religion, support from religious leaders;
- social status, social influence;
- having a new partner;
- family support;
- support from friends and colleagues;
- access to legal services, eligibility for public funding.

Some comments about power imbalances and their impact in mediation may be helpful, before considering some techniques that mediators may use to manage them.

10.4.1   Power to end the marriage or relationship

The decision to end the marriage or relationship is not usually a mutual decision. A unilateral decision to end the marriage, taken by one partner without the other's acquiescence, is associated with anger, bitterness and lengthy disputes. Mediators see many couples whose decision to separate or divorce is not a mutual one. The partner who initiates the break-up starts a train of change that the other partner may resist. Although initiators also suffer loss and grief, they are stronger because they have commenced the process of adjustment earlier, often after considerable time thinking through their decisions and future intentions. It is difficult for mediators to maintain a balance in giving equal support to both partners who are facing in opposite directions and reacting in entirely different ways. Difficulties in bridging these divisions are referred to in Chapters 3 and 11.[21]

10.4.2   Knowledge

Knowledge is a major source of power. Lack of financial information or unfamiliarity with financial documents and business accounts are major disadvantages in financial negotiations. Although there are traditional marriages in which the wife has stayed at home and left financial matters to her husband, there are also many marriages in which the wife manages the family finances. Sharing knowledge reduces feelings of powerlessness. One of the mediator's main tasks is to identify and piece together the information that needs to be shared. Participants are helped to gather and share full information. The mediator also helps them gain information which both may be lacking. Both partners may be encouraged to seek legal advice before the next mediation meeting, so if possible, that they can discuss matters on an equally informed basis.[22]

A useful technique is to put words into the mouth of one party's lawyer: 'I'm sure Julie's lawyer will want to know about this loan. Is there a limit on how

---

[21]   See **3.9** above and **11.9** below.
[22]   See Chapter 9 above.

much you can borrow?' Mediators need enough financial knowledge to ask probing questions and request supporting documents. They also need to be careful not to engage in a dialogue with one participant that leaves the other one feeling excluded or confused. Discussions need to involve both participants equally, without cross-questioning either or patronising one who is less informed. One parent may have more financial knowledge, while the other parent may know more about their children's stage of development and activities. Mediators encourage parents to share knowledge of their children and their finances. One parent's day-to-day experience of looking after the children needs to be shared with a parent who sees them occasionally, or very little.

10.4.3 Power to resist or block a settlement

An apparently powerless and passive partner may exercise power through blocking and resisting. Delaying tactics postpone decisions and settlements. It is naïve to imagine that both parties who accept referral to mediation are necessarily seeking a settlement. Their motives vary. One party's apparent acquiescence with the referral may disguise a profound determination to resist agreeing to anything at all. Accepting mediation may be a delaying tactic in itself. Mediators need to watch out for delaying tactics and recognise the advantages for one party in prolonging the status quo. Both the duration and the pace of mediation need to be kept under review.

A parent who tries to block the children's continuing relationship with their other parent, or who resists a financial settlement, may be using these issues to punish their ex-partner for leaving them. If this unresolved conflict is not addressed, disputes over children and finance may be prolonged. Mediation may be accepted by a resistant partner, not to reach agreement but to prolong the conflict and emotional involvement. Mediators need to be careful not to be drawn into one party's delaying tactics, believing that mediation is facilitating settlement but actually assisting one party to avoid it. The disadvantages of a prolonged status quo need to be considered when one party asks for more time, despite little or no sign of movement to settle.

10.4.4 Emotional pressure and manipulation

Sometimes one partner seeks to manipulate the other one by playing on fears or guilt feelings. An over-generous offer prompted by guilt feelings may be regretted later on, when there has been more time for thought or advice and the consequences are clearer. Mediators should acknowledge offers and concessions but they should also ask 'what if?' questions, applying the brakes to reduce the risks of premature or ill-considered agreements. Both parties need to be in possession of all the relevant information and have time to consider their positions carefully, before an agreement is reached. Showing extreme distress can also be a way of putting pressure on the partner who has left the relationship. The grief of the 'left' partner may be overwhelming and entirely genuine, but it can also be used to manipulate the other partner. It may be impossible – and inappropriate – to continue a mediation session when one partner continues to weep. Tearfulness in mediation is common and may be a much needed release of feelings that brings some relief. Sometimes both partners are upset and both cry. But one partner's persistent weeping makes it impossible to discuss any issues. If mediation is abandoned or postponed, possibly to allow for counselling or psychotherapy, this can have the effect of stopping the other partner from moving in any direction. Ending or shelving mediation so that a distraught partner can seek help may be necessary, but it can shackle the other one indefinitely. When there is great distress, it is still worth asking both partners what could help them in some way, given the existing situation, and whether easing stress on a relatively small area or issue could alleviate some distress.

10.4.5   Verbal dominance and assertiveness

Sometimes one partner tries to take control in mediation by talking at length and preventing the other one from speaking. The quieter party may be less articulate, more anxious or generally less able to put their needs and feelings into words. Another kind of one-upmanship is talking to the mediator over the partner's head, using technical terms to the mediator that the other partner does not comprehend. The mediator needs to recognise the power game that is being played and make sure the other partner is involved in the discussion. Being articulate does not correlate with intelligence and education. Highly intelligent people may be unable to discuss emotional issues: they may be traumatised and overwhelmed by stress.

One partner's domineering behaviour and the other's submissiveness may be a long-established pattern. One partner may also suffer an acute loss of self-esteem, having discovered that a relationship of love and trust has fallen apart. Mediators need to combine personal warmth and sensitivity with sufficient firmness in holding back one partner while encouraging the other one to come forward. This is part of the art of mediating. The disadvantages of low morale and feelings of inferiority may be only temporary. Mediation can help restore self-esteem, by giving careful and balanced attention to both partners. Changes in dress and posture are often noticeable from one mediation session to the next and these may be signs of a gradual recovery of self-esteem. If, however, despite the mediator's efforts, a participant shows no sense of self-worth and no ability to express a need or point of view, mediation is inappropriate and should be carefully terminated. The personal support of a legal adviser is likely to be needed in these situations and probably therapeutic help as well.

Example

At the start of the mediation, Alan appeared to speak for himself and his wife, Zena, explaining what they needed to settle in a quiet and unemotional way. Zena answered questions blankly, with little eye contact. When the mediators sought to draw more from her, she responded with a mixture of passivity and resentment: 'Alan knows about that. There's no point asking me.' Alan was keen to put forward terms of settlement that were purportedly agreed between them. Zena seemed inclined to accept whatever was allotted to her, but her manner was dissatisfied and bitter. When asked about her own needs and priorities, she again took a position of helplessness, saying Alan had always decided everything. There was a sudden change when the mediator said to her: 'Zena, this is your opportunity to decide the kind of life you want for yourself from now on.' Zena's demeanour changed. She stared at the mediator intensely, as though the question had penetrated her inner consciousness and she was absorbing it. From then on, she engaged in mediation and negotiated actively. Alan seemed relieved. He gave the impression that he had only taken the lead previously because Zena's refusal to participate had left him no other option.

10.4.6 Suicide risks and death threats

The experience of losing a partner through death or divorce is known to be a precipitating factor in suicide. Any risk of suicide must be taken very seriously and referral for medical or other help may be needed urgently. On the other hand, suicide and death threats are sometimes used as a form of emotional blackmail that puts enormous pressure on a partner not to leave, or to return home. Mediators should not underestimate the risks of suicide and homicide, including extreme risks to children. The need for professional help may be discussed in mediation if both partners are able to do so, but the mediator may need to seek permission to provide further information to either or both participants, following the session. This permission is normally given readily. A departure from the usual rules of balanced engagement can be made to provide further information without taking on an advisory or therapeutic role. Concerns should be discussed without delay with a consultant or supervisor and normal rules of confidentiality must be breached in a life-threatening situation and/or where children are at risk of harm.

10.4.7 The power of silence

Silences in mediation can be very powerful, in positive or negative ways.[23] They may be a space in which strong positive feelings need to be shared between the couple, without words. Mediators should respect these silences and be careful not to intervene too quickly. At other times, a refusal to answer may be a sign of assumed superiority, intended to frustrate or intimidate. Quite often, it is the decibel level and tone of voice that one partner uses which intimidates the other. The louder the harangue, the more apprehensive or stubborn the silence. The mediator needs to intervene in an angry silence, putting a question to the silent partner in a quiet voice that is not emotionally charged. The silent partner usually responds to a thoughtful and considerate question from the mediator.

---

[23] See **6.4** above on silence and cultural differences.

10.4.8   Physical and emotional closeness to children

Many fathers have higher earnings, better pensions and more control of financial assets, while mothers who are the primary carers of the children are strongly placed to 'know' what the children want or need. Fathers who work long hours or whose work takes them away from home inevitably have less contact and involvement with their children. They may have had little opportunity to build a close relationship, particularly with a baby or infant who is not ready for overnight stays. Many parents fear losing their children, when they separate. In mediation, the mother may show that she is more supportive of the children's relationship with their father than he had imagined. But in some situations, there are deep fears of the children being taken away, even to another country. Mediators must be alert to fears and risks of child abduction.[24] If one parent reassures the other, directly and sincerely, that the children will never be removed because of the pain and harm this would cause for the children, the emotional relief may be very considerable. Positions on other issues may then shift. Separation may provide fresh opportunities for a non-resident parent to build relationships with the children. Parents can manage short absences from the children more easily if they trust each other's commitment and co-operation as a parent. Mediation at an early stage reduces risks of children being used as pawns or weapons in parental battles. Once children become caught up in power battles and alliances, the conflict may be very hard to resolve.[25]

10.4.9   Cultural factors, moral power, religion

When a couple's cultural or ethnic background differs from the mediator's, there may be religious or social traditions affecting the relative strength of their positions. Mediators need to show their interest in these traditions and ask questions that encourage the couple to explain their values to each other, as well as to the mediator. This is very important, especially when moral values and religious precepts are a dominant influence. For example, for mediation with Muslim couples, it may be necessary to involve family members and/or community or religious leaders.[26]

Where one or both partners speak English as a second language, the mediator needs to clarify and summarise frequently, checking assumptions and whether nuances of language are understood. Actually, this is not very different from mediating between couples whose first language is English. Their inability to comprehend each other is sometimes so great that they might just as well be speaking two different languages. Where English is a second language or where there is some form of language disadvantage or disability, mediation may not be appropriate. If there is willingness to try mediation, detailed attention needs to be given to checking both partners' understanding of what is being said, clarifying meanings and giving information as clearly as possible. Although the

---

[24]   See Chapter 15 above.

[25]   See Chapters 7 and 8 above.

[26]   Keshavjee Islam *Sharia and Alternative Dispute Resolution* (IB Tauris, 2013).

mediator can assist comprehension through rephrasing, there may be need for a co-mediator or interpreter with language or signing skills. A specialist third party, such as a translator for the deaf, needs to be acceptable to all participants and should have a short preliminary meeting with the mediator to be clear about their role in the mediation process and to counter-sign the Agreement to Mediate.[27]

In a mediation with a middle-aged English father and a young Thai mother concerning their three-year-old daughter, the Thai mother confirmed that despite her limited English she could understand well, provided the mediator spoke slowly and used clear language. The parents both wanted to use mediation rather than going to court. They worked out a shared care arrangement (the mother was working and the father unemployed) and after some practical problems had been sorted out, they became able to work together in caring for their daughter.

10.4.10 New partners, relatives, friends and third parties

New partners are likely to wield considerable influence. The stance they take varies a great deal, ranging from hostility towards the new partner's ex-partner to a helpful and conciliatory approach and even taking on the role of mediator. When a new relationship is formed after separation, the ex-partner may accept the new partner more easily, but not necessarily so. The new partner may be thrown into the discussion like a hand grenade – 'your boyfriend is not coming anywhere near my children ...' When arguments rage over who is dictating what to whom, the mediator needs to intervene. There are questions to be asked, such as 'do the children already know Sophie?' It is particularly difficult when Sophie was formerly the mother's best friend or next-door neighbour. On the other hand, 'Sophie' or 'George' may be a complete stranger to the children and the other parent, who may need reassurance about the children's gradual introduction to the newcomer and when and how he or she will be introduced to them. If a new partner is peripheral as far as the children are concerned, the mediator may need to focus both parents' attention on what their children are currently feeling and needing from them, as parents. The battle between the parents may be more 'marital' than parental. Rather than keeping the spotlight on the emotive issue of a new partner – who may be peripheral, as far as the children are concerned – mediators need to focus both parents' attention on what their children are experiencing. What would help the children? Focusing on the children's needs may help parents to work out arrangements they can both accept, possibly on a step-by-step basis. Sometimes there is new partner on both sides and adjustments may be difficult.

Research studies have shown widely differing reactions from children, especially in the early stages.[28] Many children form good relationships with stepfathers as well as keeping a good relationship with their father. It may be important to draw parents' attention to the findings from research that,

---

[27] See **6.12–6.13** above.
[28] Ferri and Smith *Parenting in the 1990s* (Family Policy Studies Centre, 1996).

generally speaking, children do not regard a step-parent as a replacement or substitute for their mother or father. Dunne and Deater-Deckard[29] found that although a large proportion of children did not feel emotionally close to a resident step-parent, 91% of children thought a step-parent should be a parent or a friend or both. Only 9% of children thought a step-parent should not be accepted as a parent or as a friend. Families, especially grandparents, give crucial support following separation, and their opinions and attitudes may carry great weight. The American researcher, Judith Wallerstein, compared the circle of relatives, friends and advisers who line up behind the divorcing couple to the chorus in a Greek tragedy.[30] The surrounding chorus laments the breakdown and gives much-needed support. But stoking the flames of conflict may serve other people's emotional needs. If there is a larger or more forceful family clan on one side, one parent can deploy more emotional and practical support than the other.

10.5   EMPOWERING PARTICIPANTS IN MEDIATION

In mediation, each participant frequently perceives the other as controlling. A frequent cross-accusation is that the other is 'controlling' or 'has all the control,' typically where one partner is seen as controlling the children while the other is seen as intimidating and bullying. These perceptions are very powerful in themselves. The more each partner fears losing something they greatly need or value, the more they ascribe power to the other and take up defensive positions. An aggressive or threatening stance may be a cover for feelings of powerlessness and fear. The reality, which the mediator may uncover, is that both feel 'out of control' and begin to feel 'empowered' only when they feel heard and begin to act in concert. Mediators seek to 'empower' participants through helping them to consider relevant information, possible options and the needs of those involved. When participants have comparable resources in emotional, financial and other terms, they can negotiate with each other on a level playing field. In the real world, however, their resources are rarely equal. The negotiating table is often tipped in one partner's favour. Sometimes one holds all the cards and the other has none. More often, each partner has some cards that the other one wants. One parent may hold the financial cards while the other parent holds cards relating to the children. Stalemate may result if neither parent is prepared to share their cards and reach a fair deal.

Mediators do not have power to shuffle the pack and deal out the cards more fairly. Yet mediation claims to provide fair and balanced outcomes. If mediators are impartial and do not accept responsibility for ensuring the fairness of the outcome, how are the interests of the more vulnerable party protected in mediation? Could a weaker partner be put under pressure to give way, in the interest of getting an agreement?[31] Assisting participants to recognise that their

---

[29]   Dunn and Deater-Deckard 'Children's Views of their Changing Families' (2001) *Joseph Rowntree Research Findings* 931.
[30]   Wallerstein and Blakeslee *Second Chances – Men, Women and Children a Decade After Divorce* (Bantam Press, 1989).
[31]   See **13.8** below on satisfaction with outcomes.

different areas of power and control can be negotiated over, 'balanced' and shared differently is an important mediator skill.

10.6 HOW INTERVENTIONIST SHOULD MEDIATORS BE?

There is an inherent tension between impartiality and empowerment, both of which are key principles in mediators' code of ethics. Remaining strictly impartial at all times would limit interventions by the mediator to assist individual participants at particular moments. Pro-active mediators are likely to:

- acknowledge emotions and respond to the dynamics in the room;
- intervene more frequently to manage open conflict;
- apply ground rules to prevent one partner taking control of the mediation;
- raise questions that neither partner has raised;
- help participants recognise that a certain manner of speaking or acting may be counter-productive or hurtful;
- consider caucusing;
- offer suggestions, without proposing them as solutions.

Pro-active mediators have been found more effective than passive facilitators,[32] provided the mediator does not lose participants' trust. Agility and empathy are very important in responding to individual needs, while maintaining balance in the process as a whole.

10.7 MANAGING POWER IMBALANCES IN MEDIATION

Mediators' training should develop awareness of power imbalances and skills in managing imbalances at each stage:

- Initial meetings – considering and assessing with each person individually whether mediation would be a suitable and acceptable way forward.
- Terminating mediation, if despite initial assessments the situation turns out to be unsuitable for mediation. Mediators need to watch for any signs of intimidation by one partner and submissiveness from the other, terminating mediation if the imbalance is extreme and not responsive to mediation.
- Mediators should show respect and look for respect and civility between participants. They should take active steps to control abusive language or threatening behaviour.
- Mediation involves equal participation. If a participant constantly interrupts the other and tries to dominate, the mediator should not allow this to continue.

---

[32] Ibid at **13.10** below.

- The mediator has an active role in creating space for both to speak and be heard. A partner who may have felt oppressed or depressed may be able to speak for the first time, feeling safe to speak in the mediator's presence.

- The mediator should control the documents that are brought into mediation, explaining that the only documents that can be accepted in mediation are those that both participants and the mediator agree to be relevant.

- Sharing information. Obtaining information and sharing it openly are fundamental elements of mediation that can greatly reduce knowledge imbalance.

- Identifying and understanding needs, both present and future needs. The process of identifying and exploring each party's needs and the needs of the children must be done thoroughly and systematically. This helps to balance negotiating positions.

- Information provided by the mediator may affect the parties' expectations and positions. Mediators should not shy away from giving information that both parties need to have. The information should be factual, given in a neutral way and able to be double-checked. For example, information about what the court would consider a joint asset may stop one party claiming that this asset does not come into the reckoning.

- Legal advice. A basic principle of mediation is that both parties should seek independent legal advice before committing themselves to an agreement that may be legally binding. Independent advice provides checks and balances and participants should be strongly encouraged to take legal and financial advice as far as possible.

- All available options need to be explored – not just one party's solution. Mediators may prevent one party forcing 'the obvious answer' on the other by ensuring that other possible options are identified and considered fully.

- Impartiality is not immobility. The small moves mediators make in the course of a mediation session should maintain rapport with both parties and an overall balance.

- Awareness of those who may be exercising power outside the mediation. Children, new partners, grandparents may be very powerful. Mediators help parents consider who has or who should share in decision-making power and whose co-operation is needed, if their decisions are to work in practice.

- Written summaries of mediation. Summaries should explain proposals for settlement and the extent to which all options have been considered. Attention should be drawn to points on which legal advice is needed.

- Quality control of mediation. National standards for the training of mediators, accreditation and monitoring of practice help to provide safeguards for mediation clients and for mediators.

- Mediators need to learn from client feedback and research studies in order to improve their practice and develop their skills.[33]

10.8   SETTING AND MAINTAINING GROUND RULES IN MEDIATION

'We've already got an agreement and we just want you to write it up for us. Can you do that now so that we can both sign it?'

Some people want a quick agreement without providing any information. Mediators need to explain as clearly and diplomatically as possible that providing the necessary information is an essential part of reaching a full and final settlement. Participants can decide the forum in which they provide information, but not whether to provide it. If the court forum is used, the court will require information. Many participants prefer to provide information in mediation, rather than in court. A reluctance to provide information may be acknowledged as a concern to maintain privacy (reframing the refusal to co-operate as concern about privacy). However, mediators should beware allowing mediation to continue without obtaining supporting documents. A wily participant may promise to provide documents but avoid doing so. In such cases, a deadline should be set and if it is still not met, the mediation should be terminated. If there is genuine difficulty rather than unwillingness, for example in obtaining pension information, both participants may decide to extend the time-scale for mediation. It should not be extended indefinitely, however, where one partner appears to be playing for time to gain an advantage or maintain the status quo.

Most participants accept and respect ground-rules,[34] but when the emotional temperature is high, ground-rules may need to be reinforced to control interruptions and disrespectful language. Participants need to be asked to speak for themselves and not for each other. The mediator's ability to remain calm and empathetic, even when responding firmly, helps to reassure individuals who fear loss of control. Sometimes, particularly where court proceedings have been suspended while mediation takes place, it may be important also to work out ground-rules that separated parents will apply between themselves, outside the mediation room.

10.9   THE MEDIATOR'S USE OF POWER

The more mediation becomes institutionalised, the greater power mediators may acquire and be expected to use. Mediators carry authority in having knowledge, experience and familiarity with the problems of separation and divorce. They often have professional qualifications and are likely to impress

---

[33]   See **13.6–13.7** below on recommendations for improving mediator practice.
[34]   See also **5.7.3** above on setting ground-rules.

their clients as confident and articulate people. They may also have strong personalities. Diffident people may find mediators with all these qualities decidedly intimidating.

Mediators may be seen as taking on some of the court's authority if they provide mediation on court premises or even in taking referrals from the court. Some judges may expect the mediator to be directive in settling the dispute, but mediators must resist this pressure, since they seek to empower others. The four core principles of family mediation are voluntary participation, confidentiality, impartiality and empowering participants to reach their own decisions.[35]

> 'It is the preservation of these principles which has enabled mediation to provide a highly effective Out of Court Resolution process. The advantage to this is that, where mediation succeeds, there is far less likelihood of a return to the court process.'[36]

Notably, this comment is not replicated in the 2014 version[37] of the Guide to Mediation for Judges, Magistrates and Legal Advisors, which points out that 'mediation differs fundamentally from Cafcass and CAFCASS Cymru dispute resolution services. These are court based services which can be quite directive in nature and which does not require the consent of the participants; it is court directed and the outcomes of Cafcass and CAFCASS Cymru dispute resolution can be shared with the court. Mediation on the other hand is facilitative and consensual and confidential.'

In adhering to the core principles of mediation, mediators need to resist pressure from participants, fellow professionals and, on some occasions, their own inclinations to intervene in a directive way. Mediators are sometimes perceived as having a 'child-saving' agenda that leads them to prioritise what they believe to be in the best interests of the child over parents' views and needs. In listening to parents and exploring what would promote a child's well being, mediators do not hold responsibility to protect the welfare of the child. They must refer child protection concerns to the appropriate agency for investigation. In mediation, children's well being and the well being of each parent are closely interconnected. The children quoted in Chapter 8 believe that they can help their parents to reach agreements through parents and children listening and talking with each other. The mediator's role is to support this process, helping parents to recognise that children have their own feelings and views. Although these do not always coincide with parents' opinions, children's views need to be taken into account. Mediators can turn a multi-faceted subject around so that different facets catch the light, without directing how the subject should be viewed. Participants are encouraged to look at it from different angles, with increased reflection, in both senses of the word.

---

[35] See **1.10** above.

[36] *Independent Mediation – Information for Judges, Magistrates and Legal Advisers* (FJC and FMC, 2011).

[37] *Family Mediation in England and Wales: A Guide for judges, magistrates and legal advisors* (FJC and FMC, 2014), see Appendix A.

Some participants press the mediator to judge who is right or wrong, but mediators must resist any pressure to make judgements or express opinions. They need to be aware of their values and conditioning so that their attitudes are not determined by their culture, experience and assumptions. Faced with wavering or tediously argumentative clients, mediators would not be human if they did not sometimes feel sorely tempted to tell them what to do. Participants may expect the mediator to express an opinion, perceiving the mediator as an expert who is expected to know the answers. Some mediators step outside their role in expressing opinions, making judgements and exerting influence. A directive mediator controls the process vertically from a superior position, exerting influence explicitly or implicitly from the apex of the mediation triangle to participants on the base line, as shown in Figure 1.

Figure 1

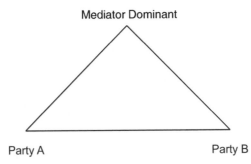

A passive mediator, on the other hand, may not intervene sufficiently to prevent one partner from dominating the other one and the mediator as well. The dominant partner may then exercise control from the apex of the triangle, while the mediator gives ineffectual support to the other on the base-line, as shown in Figure 2.

Figure 2

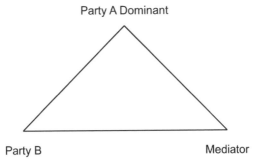

There are also possibilities of a mediator becoming aligned with one partner, consciously or unconsciously. One partner may make an apparently reasonable proposal for settlement and the mediator may be anxious to secure an agreement. The triangle could then turn upside down, with the mediator and the stronger party aligned along the top and the weaker one left alone at the bottom, as shown in Figure 3.

Figure 3

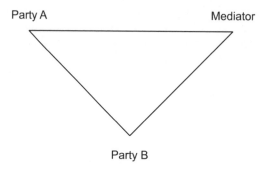

Party A   Mediator

Party B

Shattuck undertook a study of mandatory mediation on child-related issues in the United States, exploring differences between mediators who intervened too much, those who intervened too little and those who kept the balance about right.[38] The study group included recently separated parents who had problems communicating with each other; parents with particularly difficult issues and parents with a long history of conflict and entrenched attitudes. Each group contained parents who looked to the mediator for personal support, sympathy and opinions in their favour. These parents wanted the mediator to exercise authority and were loath to take any responsibility for finding solutions themselves. Shattuck found that that when mediators used five elements of their role in appropriate and balanced proportions, many high-conflict parents managed to reach agreements concerning their children. Mediators who used one or more elements to excess, exerting too much authority and control, tended to steer parents towards the mediator's favoured outcome. These forced agreements were unlikely to last. In contrast, when mediators did not intervene enough and failed to maintain adequate control over the process, parents continued to battle and no agreements were reached. Trinder et al made similar findings in studies of in-court conciliation by Cafcass.[39]

The table below, adapted from Shattuck, is relevant to mediating on all issues, as well as in child-focused mediation.

---

[38] Shattuck 'Mandatory Mediation' in Folberg and Milne (eds) *Divorce Mediation – Theory and Practice* (Guilford Press, 1988).

[39] Trinder, Connolly, Kellett, Notley and Swift 'Making contact happen or making contact work? The process and outcomes of in-court conciliation.' (2006) *DCA Research Series* 3/06; Trinder and Kellett *The Longer Term Outcomes of In-Court Conciliation* (Ministry of Justice 2007); Trinder 'Conciliation, the Private Law Programme and Children's Well-being' [2008] Fam Law 338–342. See also **13.2** below.

Five elements of family mediation

	Element	Purpose	Results of over-use	Results of under-use
1.	Use of rules and procedures to draw people into mediation	To encourage settlement of disputes	Mediation used inappropriately. Parties put under pressure	Mediation easily bypassed, parties turn to the court
2.	Conflict management	To define issues, reduce conflict, set boundaries	Parties not given enough time to explain concerns	Parties get bogged down in repetitive arguments
3.	Focus on children	To help parents consider their children's needs and position	Parents may feel their own concerns and needs have not been heard	Parents may make decisions which suit them, without considering their children
4.	Giving information about children	To help parents understand how to help their children adjust	Parents may be lectured and may feel guilty and disempowered	Parents deny impact of their separation on the children
5.	Seeking agreement	To help parties reach mutually acceptable arrangements	Mediator too directive, imposes solutions	Parties continue their power battles

10.10 MAINTAINING FLEXIBLE BALANCE IN MEDIATION

Mediating is like standing at the tipping-point of a see-saw. If the mediator stands passively at the centre, the see-saw may remain tipped one way or the other, in the same position it was in at the start. If, on the other hand, the mediator shifts weight towards the participant at the lower end of the see-saw, the see-saw may become more level, but the mediator's perceived or actual impartiality may be lost. Skilled mediators manage to make small moves in either direction in managing power imbalances in the room. Whether working singly or in pairs, they may make frequent small shifts of position. Temporary shifts from a midway position include actively seeking and sharing information, enabling a less articulate party to speak and encouraging one who seems overwhelmed. As mediation continues, the see-saw that was initially tipped one way may gradually settle in a more level position. The levelling out depends on each participant and on the circumstances, as well as on the skills of the mediator or co-mediators. Even when the see-saw seems very unbalanced, effective mediators can help participants explore where the balance could or should lie. Different positions may be considered and tried out, before any position is firmed up. In financial terms, different sets of figures may be run through on the flip-chart, to see what they would produce for each partner, before there is any notion of settlement. A male-female co-mediating team can help managing gender issues and power imbalances.[40] Male-female co-mediators provide a visible balance that reassures participants. There are also increased opportunities of bringing in different perspectives and managing power imbalances strategically. Many mediators believe that co-mediation is the most effective model, because there are always some kinds of power imbalance. It is highly desirable for mediators to have experience of co-mediating during their practical training so that they can learn from other mediators and recognise when a co-mediator is needed.[41]

The discussion in this chapter has been mainly about power imbalances that are potentially manageable in mediation. It must be recognised, however, that there are forms and degrees of power imbalance in which mediation would be unsuitable. Circumstances unsuitable for mediation, such as those involving serious degrees of intimidation, violence or abuse, mental incapacity or psychotic illness, should normally have been screened out at the initial assessment stage, but some forms of abuse or mental illness may only become apparent during mediation. Problems or issues impeding settlement may surface during mediation. Mediators need to demonstrate a combination of empathy and firmness in managing power imbalances in mediation or deciding to terminate it. A pendulum swinging through arcs of emotion has difficulty settling in the middle.

Preoccupation with balance may seem a modern concern. However, an ancient instrument known as 'the balance' was used in early societies as a practical tool and as a symbol. *Al-Mizan*, the Arabic word for balance, was applied to the 'spirit level' used by surveyors and builders and also, symbolically, to the search for 'justice and harmony' in human endeavours. The balance became the focus of a branch of science in the medieval Islamic world, the science of weights. Dozens of treatises on the theory, construction and use of the balance dealt not only with weighing scales with equal arms, but also with the steelyard which had 'unequal arms and a sliding counter-weight' (such as mediators sometimes need!). A major text on the science of weights, completed in the year 1121, viewed the balance as an artefact placed in a larger moral framework – perhaps an early example of ecosystemic thinking?

---

[40] See Chapter 4 above.
[41] See Chapter 14 below on training as a mediator.

'The most important lesson
but one that's seldom adequately learned
is that, like sub-atomic particles,
everything with life exists
within a field of force
in which all affect and are affected
by each one of the others;
and that we, the individuals,
and all other individuals like
a blade of grass, whale or bacterium,
are not self-existent, but the products
of this unceasing reciprocity.'

Adam Curle, 'The First Lesson'[42]

---

[42]   Curle *Recognition of Reality – Reflections and Prose Poems* (Hawthorn Press, 1987), p 1.

CHAPTER 11

DEALING WITH DEADLOCKS

'Progress in knowledge is not a tower to heaven built of bricks from the bottom up, but a product of impasse and breakthrough, yielding a bizarre and circuitous structure that ultimately rises nonetheless.'[1]

CONTENTS

11.1   CONFLICT CYCLES AND TRAPS

The concept of a struggle between two opposing forces, the force of Love, which attracts, and the force of Discord, which separates, dates back to Aristotle and even earlier to Empedocles in the 5th century BC. Empedocles was a philosopher and scientist who posited the idea of twin forces of love and discord interacting with each other in a cycle of construction, destruction and reconstruction. The struggle between these two opposing forces is often seen in mediation, where discord often defeats love, but love sometimes reasserts itself. Ending a couple relationship is very difficult and painful. Conflict may be an inevitable part of the emotional and psychological transitions of separation and divorce. Although the adversarial system is often accused of causing and prolonging conflict, conflict in marriage breakdown is not generated solely by the adversarial system. Deep-rooted conflict is not resolved by denying its

---

[1]   Stephen Jay Gould *Eight Little Piggies* (Jonathan Cape, 1994), p 146.

existence or by suppressing it, nor by stigmatising it as pathological. Separated couples need to find ways of integrating their disillusionment and negative emotions with positive feelings, good memories and self-esteem, as they traverse the difficult path from 'breaking up' as a couple to achieving a new identity as separate, whole and autonomous selves.

Mediators need some understanding of the psychological processes that drive or resist change. A bewildering mixture of contradictory emotions is experienced in the reconstruction of families and selves. Some couples find it very hard to let go of their differences and move on. These couples are hard to work with. If they take a small step forwards, a negative comment from one of them is enough to throw them both back into the vortex of accusing and blaming. The vortex spirals downwards and threatens to suck the mediator down as well. Mediators need to resist the 'downward gravitational tug of antagonisms'[2] and encourage movement, upwards and forwards. Systems theory helps us to think about family circles and family processes whose function is to maintain existing systems and resist change. The circle – or dance – which some couples display in mediation may be part of a long-established pattern. Mediators who intervene for a brief period may not understand the family's patterns and dynamics. Should we try to change a revolving cycle without understanding its function? Change that has not been thought through can be dangerous for the couple and also for the mediator. Mediation offers opportunities for families to end negative cycles of communication or behaviour, without forcing unwanted change on them. It can open up safer paths of communication and allow new patterns to develop. Not all conflicts are negotiable and some should not be negotiated. Mnookin[3] identifies two opposing sets of 'traps' surrounding decisions whether to negotiate or not. He suggests that negative 'traps', particularly demonisation of opponents and the need for control, have the effect of fuelling anger and discouraging people from negotiating when they probably should. Positive 'traps', involving religious beliefs and moral values, self-denial and the need for peace at any cost, may encourage people to negotiate when perhaps they shouldn't.

11.2   DIFFERENT TYPES OF CONFLICTS

Some kinds of conflict are much harder to resolve than others. In his *Sphere of Conflict – Causes and Inteventions*,[4] Moore portrays a wheel of different types of conflict and recommends interventions for mediators to use in managing each kind of conflict. Moore differentiates conflicts of interest or values from structural and relationship conflicts and from data conflicts. The following diagram from Moore's book, *The Mediation Process*, is reproduced by kind permission of his publishers. Data conflicts that stem from lack of information,

2   Cloke 'Mediation and Meditation – the Deeper Middle Way' *Mediate.com Weekly*, No 266 (March 2009).
3   Mnookin *Bargaining with the Devil – When to Negotiate, When to Fight* (Simon & Schuster, 2010).
4   Moore *The Mediation Process – Practical Strategies for Resolving Conflict* (1986) Copyright Jossey-Bass Ltd., Christopher W. Moore and Wiley Global Permission, p 27.

misinformation or misunderstandings, or from different interpretations of factual information are generally easier to resolve than other kinds of conflicts.

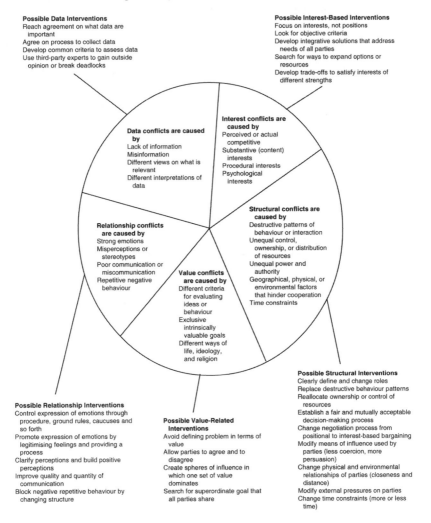

Possible Data Interventions
Reach agreement on what data are important
Agree on process to collect data
Develop common criteria to assess data
Use third-party experts to gain outside opinion or break deadlocks

Possible Interest-Based Interventions
Focus on interests, not positions
Look for objective criteria
Develop integrative solutions that address needs of all parties
Search for ways to expand options or resources
Develop trade-offs to satisfy interests of different strengths

Data conflicts are caused by
Lack of information
Misinformation
Different views on what is relevant
Different interpretations of data

Interest conflicts are caused by
Perceived or actual competitive
Substantive (content) interests
Procedural interests
Psychological interests

Relationship conflicts are caused by
Strong emotions
Misperceptions or stereotypes
Poor communication or miscommunication
Repetitive negative behaviour

Structural conflicts are caused by
Destructive patterns of behaviour or interaction
Unequal control, ownership, or distribution of resources
Unequal power and authority
Geographical, physical, or environmental factors that hinder cooperation
Time constraints

Value conflicts are caused by
Different criteria for evaluating ideas or behaviour
Exclusive intrinsically valuable goals
Different ways of life, ideology, and religion

Possible Relationship Interventions
Control expression of emotions through procedure, ground rules, caucuses and so forth
Promote expression of emotions by legitimising feelings and providing a process
Clarify perceptions and build positive perceptions
Improve quality and quantity of communication
Block negative repetitive behaviour by changing structure

Possible Value-Related Interventions
Avoid defining problem in terms of value
Allow parties to agree and to disagree
Create spheres of influence in which one set of value dominates
Search for superordinate goal that all parties share

Possible Structural Interventions
Clearly define and change roles
Replace destructive behaviour patterns
Reallocate ownership or control of resources
Establish a fair and mutually acceptable decision-making process
Change negotiation process from positional to interest-based bargaining
Modify means of influence used by parties (less coercion, more persuasion)
Change physical and environmental relationships of parties (closeness and distance)
Modify external pressures on parties
Change time constraints (more or less time)

11.2.1 Lack of information or different interpretations of information

Lack of information is a very common problem in mediation. Couples cannot negotiate safely, if at all, if one or both partners do not know about assets held in sole or joint names, pension funds, debts or levels of income. Mediators help participants to gather and share relevant information and also provide them with information they need, without angling the information towards either participant. A couple who disagree about the value of an asset may need guidance on how to obtain a joint valuation. A parent who has lost touch with a child needs information from the other parent about the child's development, routine and activities. Mediators' tasks and skills in helping couples to obtain financial information and make full financial disclosure were referred to in

Chapter 9.[5] The mediator's expertise is needed to explain in general terms what kind of information the court would be likely to consider in relation to a particular dispute, such as allegations of (mis)behaviour by one party, and what the court would be unlikely to consider. To avoid straying from information-giving into advising, mediators should always encourage participants to check the information provided by the mediator with an independent adviser, even where the mediator is an experienced family lawyer.

11.2.2   Misunderstandings

Incorrect information, assumptions or misunderstandings can give rise to unrealistic expectations. If participants seem to be relying on information or advice that may be incorrect, the mediator should encourage them to check further. If, however, the information is said to come from a legal adviser, this is more delicate as mediators should take care not to destroy a client's trust in their legal adviser. Clients may have misunderstood the advice or heard only what they wanted to hear. Mediators can suggest questions for them to take to their lawyers, possibly providing a written note as an aide-mémoire and encouraging them to ask for a written response.[6] If a client seems to have misunderstood or is possibly misinformed, the mediator should consider whether a second opinion is a possible option, but should be careful not to advise clients to change their lawyer or to use one particular lawyer. If a mediator is asked to recommend a solicitor, a list should be given of solicitors in the area who are known to subscribe to Resolution's Code of Practice and The Law Society's Family Law Protocol.

Misunderstandings also occur at a more fundamental level, to the extent that some couples seem almost to speak different languages.[7] Even a word or phrase may be used in one sense by one partner and understood in a different sense by the other. A husband's reference to his wife as 'a very successful artist' clearly annoyed his wife. When the husband was asked to clarify what he meant by 'successful', he explained that she was a highly skilled artist. Whether or not this was his original meaning, his wife was mollified. Mediators need quicksilver awareness to note facial reactions of bewilderment or annoyance so that they can intervene rapidly to seek clarification or offer a reframe that facilitates better understanding.

> 'We had the experience but missed the meaning.
> And approach to the meaning restores the experience
> In a different form.'[8]

---

[5]   See **9.7.1** above.
[6]   See **11.8** below.
[7]   See Chapter 6 above.
[8]   TS Eliot *The Dry Salvages*.

11.3 CONFLICTING VALUES

Disputes may stem from values and principles founded in different moral values, religious beliefs, ideologies and cultural norms. The dispute referred to in Chapter 4[9] between an Irish father and German mother centred on the values they each attributed to different educational systems. Even within the same culture, husbands and wives may have very different notions as to what would constitute a fair outcome, both with regard to the division of assets and also in relation to children. Sometimes a commentary from the mediator about different ways of looking at fairness may be helpful:

> 'There is a question of principle here. You have ideas of fairness that are based on different ways of looking at it, so naturally you don't agree. There are different ways of defining what's fair. There is fairness based on what you each feel you need, or are entitled to, and on this, you differ. There is the court's approach in which the court takes relevant considerations into account and seeks to strike a fair balance. But even when the judge decides what is fair, an order may be made which neither party feels is fair. I can explain the factors the court takes into account, if you would like me to. But it may be useful, first of all, to look at your incomes and outgoings and see how big the gap is between what is coming in and what each of you needs to live on?'

The Mapping Paths to Family Justice study[10] found that husbands predominantly sought a 50% share of capital assets on a 'clean break' basis, whereas wives were mainly concerned to meet their needs, usually (though not always) due to their status as the children's primary carer. Some agreements reached in mediation were based on formal equality, while in one collaborative law case, the wife accepted a settlement which met her immediate needs but constituted less than 50% of the assets. The predominant norm held by fathers in children's matters was also based on equality – their equal right to shared parenting, whereas mothers' main concerns were child welfare and maintaining the status quo as primary carer. One father explained after mediation:

> 'I'm still trying to get 50:50 access to my children. I get 45:55 ... In this equal rights world ... it is difficult ... I did do really well but, you know, it'd be nice to have an equal share.'[11]

Helping parents to shift from parental rights to parental responsibilities, considering their children's needs rather than their own ideas of fairness, is the focus of many mediations (see Chapters 7 and 8). The Mapping Paths study identified the need for mediators and collaborative lawyers to intervene more strongly and consistently in focusing on children's welfare. When a non-resident parent is pressing to have a child on a 50:50 shared care basis, mediators need to focus on the child's needs – current routine, schooling, distance between two homes, continuation of out-of-school activities and time with friends. Parents

---

[9]   See **4.4 1.2** above.
[10] Barlow, Hunter, Smithson and Ewing *Mapping Paths to Family Justice – Briefing Paper and Report on Key Findings* (June 2014).
[11] Ibid, p 22.

282 *Family Mediation*

need to consider time-sharing arrangements from the child's point of view and be willing to listen to their children. For children, the quality of their relationship with their parents matters more than quantity of time.[12] Parents may work out arrangements that although not equating to 50:50 shared care, may be accepted by them both as giving priority to their children's needs and feelings. Whilst children and young people should not be used to arbitrate on what would be 'fair' from their perspectives, careful consideration should be given to opportunities for them to express their views and feelings and feel heard (see Chapter 8).

11.4 RELATIONSHIP CONFLICTS

11.4.1 Mistrust

When a close relationship breaks down, trust usually breaks down as well. When considering the suitability of mediation, it is not realistic to look for complete trust. What needs to be considered is the nature and extent of mistrust. 'Trust is like a glass vessel. If it breaks once and the pieces are big enough you can put it back together. But if you take those bits and break them again, then eventually they will get so small that you will be left with lots of tiny shards.'[13] Discovery of a partner's long-term infidelity, possibly with a person previously considered a good friend, may shatter trust irreparably. Some couples have lost all trust in each other as partners but are still able to trust each other as parents. Others do not trust each other as parents, either. Giving detailed attention to specific anxieties can overcome some barriers, for example if an undertaking is given which can be put to the test and found reliable. An agreement for the primary carer to speak to the child on the phone at certain times when the child is with the other parent can be a means of reassurance that the child is settled and having a good time. Even a young child may also need reassurance that the parent they have left at home is not miserable on their own. Children worry about their parents, as well as parents worrying about their children.

Mediators need to be alert for any expression of mistrust and quick to acknowledge it. If it is ignored, the mistrust is likely to grow. It is important to acknowledge how hard it is to trust a former partner after the relationship has broken down. If one partner accuses the other of being unreliable or dishonest, the mediator can acknowledge mistrust without losing impartiality. One way of doing this is to reframe the mistrust as the need to be fully satisfied, convinced or reassured.[14] One partner's doubts about the other's honesty on financial matters do not automatically mean that that the other partner is seeking to deceive or withhold information. In explaining and going through the stages of

---

[12] See Chapter 8.
[13] 'David' quoted in Fehily *Split – True Stories of Relationship Breakdown in Ireland* (Y Books, Dublin, 2011), p 67.
[14] See Chapter 6 above on reframing.

mediation, mediators should stress the need for full information and supporting documents before options for settlement are considered.

> 'So, Wendy, to feel completely clear [about the value of these shares] ... reassured that [this payment has been made], you would like to see a document showing ... Jim, do you think you could satisfy Wendy by bringing [this document] to our next meeting?'

One partner may have previously resisted providing financial information. Angry demands or correspondence between lawyers tend to increase resistance, whereas mediators may lower resistance by putting the request in a different way:

> 'Jim, Wendy says she would like to be clearer about ... It would be really helpful if you could bring ... to our next meeting. Would that be possible?'

Asking for supporting documents is a means of clarifying and verifying information without intrusive questioning: 'Could you bring ...? It would be useful to have ...' If there is still resistance, it can be pointed out that in court proceedings there is not a choice between providing financial information or not providing it. The choice is the forum in which it will be provided – in mediation or in court (or both). Mediators assist participants to provide full, concrete and verifiable information. They explain the documents the court would need, the questions that legal advisers may ask and supporting documents that will be needed.

If the couple mistrust each other *as parents*, mediators need to enquire into their fears and suspicions. Is there an implied allegation of child abuse, or is it a concern about giving children fizzy drinks and crisps instead of a proper meal? How the mediator responds depends on the allegation or degree of mistrust. If there is risk of harm to a child, the mediator must refer to the Agreement to Mediate, explaining that confidentiality is not absolute, and that the mediator must if necessary contact the local safeguarding agency.[15] In contrast, less serious concerns over suitable food or bedtime routines can be discussed in mediation.

11.4.2 Bad faith

There is an important distinction between building trust and recognising deliberate deceit. It would be naïve to believe that all those who come to mediation are honest and trustworthy. Those who hope to avoid examination of their financial disclosure in court may seek to deceive the mediator, as well as their partner.[16] A mediator who spots double accounting or what might be an intentional omission can ask 'innocent' questions ('Could you help me to understand ...?'), without pinning the person to the wall. However, where one

---

[15] See Chapter 3 and Appendix B.
[16] See **9.7.6** above.

partner – and/or the mediator – remain convinced that assets are being concealed, the mediation has to be terminated.

11.4.3 Power struggles, conflicts of interest

Conflicts associated with power imbalances, gender issues, unmet needs and different interests were the focus of the previous chapter.

11.4.4 Implacable hostility

Couples who seem determined to defeat the mediator, as well as each other, may belong to the category described as implacably hostile or 'enmeshed'.[17] There may even be an unconscious collusion between them that prevents any professional intervention being 'successful'. If settlement is reached and the arguments stop, what would take their place? A do-nothing option may need to be considered. What would be better, worse or the most likely outcome, and for whom, if no agreement can be reached?[18] When mediation is deadlocked, it may be useful to consider, not what would be gained from a settlement but what would be lost from it, and by whom? Some people dread the void of emptiness more than a continuing battle. When there is a battle, there is the prospect of winning and the triumph of inflicting defeat, whereas settlement could mean loneliness and depression. Some couples have a deep emotional need to fight and become addicted to the fight itself. They are sometimes referred to as 'hostility junkies'. They seem to get high on the adrenalin of fighting and develop a greater investment in keeping the conflict going than in ending it. They know exactly which button to press to raise the temperature and renew the battle. Mediators are increasingly mediating with entrenched couples referred by the Court as a last resort, where battles look set to continue for years to come.

11.5 TESTING COMMITMENT TO MEDIATION

Mediators need to watch for lack of commitment to mediation indicated by:

- lack of punctuality or failure to attend a meeting;
- body language conveying lack of engagement;
- delaying tactics or, alternatively, pressure to get an agreement as quickly as possible;
- delay or reluctance in providing financial information and supporting documents;
- evasive answers to questions from the mediator or the partner;
- figures which do not add up: income not tallying with expenditure;
- sabotaging or failing to keep to arrangements or interim agreements;

---

[17] See Chapter 3 above.
[18] See **11.7** above.

- offering plausible excuses in order to continue negotiations, despite not keeping undertakings;

- posturing and playing for time, with no real evidence of motivation;

- evidence of ulterior motives, eg to maintain the status quo on children or financial issues;

- if paying for private mediation, forgetting to bring a chequebook or credit card.

Mediators can test commitment to mediation by:

- Demonstrating their own commitment to absolute transparency and balance throughout the process.

- Making sure that ground-rules are clear and accepted.

- Being firm in relation to mediation procedures. If apologies are accepted for failure to provide information, being clear whether there is a deadline for providing it.

- Considering terminating the mediation if, having offered a further opportunity, there is continuing lack of commitment.

11.6   LOCATING THE BLOCK

Co-operation is a two-way street. A deadlock may seem a dead-end, with no way forward. This may occur in the first mediation meeting or at any stage during the process. Some participants seem to prefer fighting to agreement. Johnston and Campbell[19] identified three different levels in their typology of 'impasses': external, interpersonal and 'intrapersonal.' The word 'block' is used here instead of 'impasse', because 'impasse' implies that there is no way forward, whereas there may be different ways of getting round, over or under a block or shifting it in some way. Mediation is a process in which possibilities of circumventing barriers and blocks or even dissolving them altogether can be explored and tried out. A rock may be unyielding, yet water can penetrate stone and carve a channel through a rocky chasm. Mediation is short-term and opportunities for change may be resisted, as well as limited. There can be transformative moments for participants and for mediators when perceptions and attitudes suddenly change. These moments compensate for the more frequent frustrations of grinding away and apparently not getting anywhere. Immediate outcomes are not a reliable indication, however, of the potential for longer-term change. The diagram below, derived from Johnston and Campbell's typology of external, interpersonal and 'intrapersonal' blocks, shows that different levels may be connected.

It is useful to have a conceptual map to work out where the main block may be located. Although the aim is to work as openly as possible, mediators do not share all their thinking with participants. In planning for each session, the mediator should think about the objectives and structure of the session,

---

[19]   Johnston and Campbell *Impasses of Divorce – the Dynamics and Resolution of Family Conflict* (Free Press, 1988).

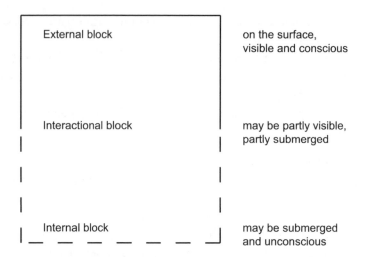

External block	on the surface, visible and conscious
Interactional block	may be partly visible, partly submerged
Internal block	may be submerged and unconscious

possible ways forward and whether other forms of help are needed. If there seems to be a deep internal block, one participant or both may need counselling, psychotherapy or family therapy to reach the roots of the conflict, rather than working to no avail on the surface of the dispute. Systemic treatment may be needed, rather than repeated application of ineffective solutions. Sometimes other family members – children, new partners, grandparents – are closely involved in the conflict and may fuel the flames with their own needs. Family members can have a stake in keeping the conflict going. A feud between two families, like the Capulets and Montagues, can prevent a couple from reaching agreements they actually want to reach. A child may become actively caught up in the conflict. When children feel so much hurt or anger that they reject a parent completely, an agreement between the parents may not resolve the child's feelings.[20] Arrangements for children may also depend on the co-operation of new partners and/or grandparents, whereas in some situations the parental coalition may need to be strengthened to withstand interference and control by others. Would it help or hinder to involve new partners? Some new partners take on a very helpful role as mediators between the ex-partners, whereas involving other third parties directly in mediation would be destructive and harmful.

11.6.1   Level 1: external blocks

These are difficulties beyond the control of the participants, such as accrued debts or inability to sell their home. Recognising these problems does not solve them, but mediation can help couples to look for possible sources of help and support, instead of blaming each other. A breakdown in a relationship may be associated with one partner's change of employment or loss of work. It may not be possible to shift an external block through mediation, but considering how to deal with it may encourage more effective management.

---

[20]   See **11.7** below and also **8.12** above.

11.6.2   Level 2: interpersonal blocks

Interpersonal block lie between the participants themselves. As described above, these blocks frequently involve communication problems, conflicting values and an emotional investment in continuing the struggle.

11.6.3   Level 3: internal blocks

Blocks which are external to the couple or which lie between them are generally apparent, whereas an internal block within an individual may be less evident and even unrecognised by the person concerned. Blocks in thinking or perception may be unconscious, especially if they stem from childhood experience. A deeply buried block is not likely to be unblocked in mediation. However, as different levels of blocks are interconnected, renewed co-operation at surface level[21] can reduce fears and ease resistance at a deeper level. Before looking at skills and techniques to mediate in entrenched conflicts, attention needs to be given to another 'location' of deadlock: one that exists, or which is alleged to exist, between a child and one parent (or occasionally, between the child and both parents).

11.7   CHILD-PARENT REJECTION

Children who are very affected by parental conflict may become aligned with one parent and alienated from the other. When this happens, the rejected parent may give up and walk away, or may embark on litigation to claim his rights as a parent (more often, his rights), in a struggle to defeat the parent who is accused of brainwashing the child. The family dynamics in these cases are complex and usually dysfunctional. If lawyers are enlisted to take up each parent's claims, the dispute may escalate into a conflict that engulfs the family, the court and other systems. Johnston and Roseby[22] provide a thoughtful analysis of the multiple contributory factors in these cases. As they point out, high-conflict parents may be ambivalent or sceptical about the importance of the child's relationship with the other parent. Instead of reassuring and encouraging the child, they may increase the child's anxieties by revealing their own anxieties and fears. Much fuller consideration is needed than is possible here of the syndrome (a term that is itself controversial) of parental alienation. The following examples illustrate some different degrees of alienation between children and parents that may be addressed – and possibly overcome – in mediation.

---

[21]   See Chapter 2 'surface tension effects'.
[22]   Johnston and Roseby *In the Name of the Child* (The Free Press, 1997).

Example

<small>TOTAL REJECTION</small>

Trevor and Sheila were referred to mediation by the High Court after six years of litigation and no previous mediation. Trevor claimed he had requested mediation three years earlier and that Sheila, on legal advice, had turned it down. Although Trevor no longer had legal representation, three firms of solicitors were involved. The elder daughter, Nicola, now 15 years old, was separately represented, while the younger daughter, Susie, aged 13, had a solicitor and guardian. The girls had not seen their father for over six years and were reportedly bitterly resentful of his persistent attempts to see them. Trevor believed Sheila had told the girls that he had abused them when they were little. These allegations had been investigated at the time and no evidence had been found. Sheila considered that the girls were now old enough to speak for themselves and insisted that their views and wishes should be respected. Both girls made it clear via their legal representatives that they wished to have nothing to do with their father and wanted to be free to get on with their own lives. After years of fruitless court proceedings, Trevor's application for direct or indirect contact was finally rejected. The barrier between the girls and their father remained insuperable. Trevor continued to believe that mediation at an early stage could have made a difference. Sheila engaged willingly in shuttle mediation following the High Court referral and there were indications that she might have accepted it at an earlier stage when the girls' relationship with their father was frayed, but still had some threads intact.

Example

<small>A CHILD'S FEAR</small>

Dave and Stacie had a tempestuous break-up three months before coming to mediation. There had been a couple of incidents in which they had screamed and lashed out at each other, but each of them confirmed separately that there was no previous history of abuse of any kind. Their three-year-old daughter, Mel (Melissa) had witnessed the incidents and been terrified by them. Consequently, she screamed if she saw Dave approaching and clung to Stacie. Dave and Stacie had worked through their crisis and wanted to agree the terms of their separation, including Mel's time with her father, but Mel's desperate clinging prevented it. Neither parent wanted to force her, fearing this would cause more harm. A plan was worked out in mediation that Stacie would explain to Mel that she was going to take her to a place where there were toys for her to play with and a person called … (the mediator), who would make sure everything was all right. Her daddy would look in to say 'hello' and he would play with her for a short time, if this would be OK. Stacie would be there all the time. Mel said this would be all right. This first meeting went very well and Mel was not upset at all. She said 'Bye, Daddy', when he left. On the next occasion, Stacie explained to Mel in advance that she would need to pop out for a few minutes to go to the post office, which would be boring for Mel, so she could stay to play with daddy and Stacie would be back in a few minutes. Mel accepted this as well. Gradually she regained trust that her parents could meet together safely and that she did not need to protect either of them or herself.

One of the barriers to overcoming child-parent alienation is that child consultation and child-inclusive mediation take longer and involve higher costs. Parents' availability to attend meetings may also be limited. In Dave and Stacie's case, the cost of four carefully planned 'child-inclusive' meetings was covered (at a low rate) by Stacie's public funding and by Dave's private contributions. Court costs would have been far higher (legal aid was available at the time). Supervised contact at a contact centre would not have led to a sustainable relationship between Mel and her father, because she needed to experience her parents meeting together in a safe and amicable way.

Example

INTRODUCING A LONG-ABSENT FATHER TO THE CHILD

When Andrew and Soraya came to mediation, Andrew had not seen his six-year-old daughter, Tahiri, since she was three months old because he had been in prison following convictions for drug offences and burglary. In prison he had undergone extensive rehabilitation and his progress was being monitored by his probation officer and a social worker at the addiction unit. He and Soraya explained movingly that they had met on two occasions before coming to mediation and Andrew had made a profound apology to Soraya for all he had put her through. Each of them now had a new partner. Andrew and his partner were expecting a baby. Andrew said he longed to see Tahiri and that he now felt worthy to be her father. Soraya feared a relapse and was reluctant to disturb Tahiri's untroubled life in any way. Tahiri was aware that she had a natural father who had gone a long way away. Soraya accepted that Tahiri should get to know her father at some stage but felt the time had not yet come. After reassurance at the assessment meeting that she would not be put under pressure, Soraya was willing to come to mediation and acknowledged that she felt ambivalent.

The first mediation meeting focused on an agreement for Soraya to talk with Andrew's probation officer, social worker and a third person, to obtain their assessments of Andrew's rehabilitation. Tahiri was close to her stepfather and showed no interest in her natural father. At the second mediation meeting, Soraya recounted that she had been playing 'mummies and daddies' with Tahiri and an opportunity arose for her to show Tahiri a photograph of her as a small baby in Andrew's arms. Tahiri asked: 'Does he look like that now?' and Soraya answered: 'He looks a bit older now'. She and Andrew both laughed about this. Arrangements were made for Andrew to write to Tahiri and send her small presents. At the third meeting, three months later, Soraya said that Tahiri had been very pleased with Andrew's presents and she had sent him a thank you card. Andrew said his side of the family was pressing him to seek regular direct contact with Tahiri through a court order, whereas Soraya said her side of the family was urging her not to put Tahiri at risk. Soraya and Andrew recognised the pressures that each of them was under and the anxieties they both felt about the next steps. Rather than asking Soraya how soon she thought Tahiri could meet her father for the first time, the mediators asked both parents for their suggestions as to where a possible meeting could take place. Soraya thought it would be easiest for Tahiri if Andrew would come to their home, where Tahiri would be happy to show him her favourite things. With encouragement from the mediators (which the parents barely needed), Soraya and Andrew decided that both grandmothers would be invited as well (with careful briefing!) to a small tea-party that would be arranged at Soraya's home during half-term. They assured each other that their new partners were fully supportive of Andrew's introduction to Tahiri. Soraya did not live with her new partner and she said he would readily accept not being present at the tea-party. Both parents emphasised that, on their own, they could not have worked out and agreed a plan for Tahiri to be introduced very gradually to her father. Andrew said he felt overjoyed, while Soraya said she felt completely reassured about their ability to co-operate for Tahiri's benefit and that it felt as though a great weight had been lifted off her shoulders.

11.8 MEDIATING IN ENTRENCHED CONFLICTS

11.8.1 Structure

Providing structure in the early stages of mediation was considered in Chapter 5. For any form of conflict resolution, it is important to provide a safe space and allocate appropriate time. Ground-rules need to be explained and agreed.[23] The mediator needs to be calm, focused and self-aware – not always easy! Confidence is needed to structure and manage discussions in highly emotional situations. Otherwise, unproductive circular arguments increase anger and frustration. Mediators need to provide a structure, possibly with time boundaries for each issue or sub-issue. If participants accept these time boundaries, they need to understand that at the end of each time-span, they will have to leave the issue and move on to the next one, whether any progress has been made or not. This helps them to realise that they cannot spend the whole session arguing over the same issue. This is useful in itself. The higher the conflict, the more necessary it is for mediators to ensure that all issues and options are listed systematically – using the flip-chart – and examined. The pros and cons of each option can be marked on the flip-chart. Often this shows that further information is needed before a particular option can be considered properly. If participants are encouraged to seek this information and bring information and ideas to the next session, they are encouraged to shift from confrontation to problem-solving and mutual recognition. Encouragement to consider and reality-test all the options conveys optimism that a solution may exist somewhere. This positive belief helps to counteract the depression and may change the direction of the spiral so that it begins to lead upwards, instead of downwards. Structure helps to contain and manage strong emotions: it does

---

[23] See **5.10** and **10.8** above.

not mean that emotions are ignored or put aside. The structure needs to be flexible and designed to take account of the complexity of the issues and different levels of conflict.[24]

11.8.2   Pacing

Some couples come to mediation with unrealistic hopes of a solution being produced by the mediator. But even the most experienced mediator has no magic wand to wave. Participants' own willingness and motivation to settle are critical factors. Inevitably, there are situations in which mediation is inappropriate. When little movement seems possible, mediators need to consider the use of time more carefully – the use of time in mediation and the length of time between sessions. Allowing ideas to take root gradually, instead of pushing a seedling into the ground and jumping on it, helps delicate plants to grow. Interim arrangements are sometimes like seedlings that need to be allowed some light and air. Time is needed to give these small plants a chance to grow. At a further meeting a few weeks later their 'cultivators' can consider whether the seedling they planted jointly needs to be trimmed back or whether it should be given more space. Many parents are afraid of committing themselves to new arrangements. They may be reassured to realise that it is possible to work out interim arrangements before reaching final decisions.

11.8.3   Asking questions

Mediators can ask reality-testing, hypothetical and reflective questions[25] without interrogating. Rambling or irrelevant answers can be cut short by bringing people back to a focused question that has just been posed and a reflective question for participants to think about before the next meeting. Useful questions might be 'What would make it possible for you to …?' or 'What do you think the situation between you will be like in two (or five) years' time? Do you think things will be just the same? If the situation might be better by then, what might have changed? Could these changes begin any sooner?' A future-focused question could be: 'If … (child) is asked in five years' time (or ten years, or any period) what it was like when you split up/got divorced, what do you think he/she will say? What would you like her/him to be able to say? Could you give any reassurance now that you are trying to make things better?'

Questions may be put forward for further reflection or interim arrangements worked out in the very short term. It may be important to ask how direct communications will be managed. Are parents willing to telephone each other, if anything should occur to prevent either of them keeping an arrangement? If one parent complains of the other's unpunctuality, how many minutes are they prepared to wait beyond the agreed time? What could cause delay? What would they do if an arrangement breaks down? Would they be willing to come to a further mediation session?

---

24   See Chapter 4 above and **11.13** below.
25   See Chapter 6 above.

Powerful questions need to be asked carefully at a suitable stage: 'What do you fear most?' 'What is the worst thing that could happen to you now?' If both participants name their worst fears, they may find they have the same overwhelming fear. Mutual reassurance may be possible when they understand each other's worst fears and realise that they share them.

11.8.4   Getting to the nub of the problem

It is natural to try to resolve disputes by getting to the nub of the problem. De Bono[26] points out, however, that this may be unhelpful. If the conflict is stoked by a fire of anger, both parties are quick to throw more fuel on the flames from opposite sides. Encouraging them to extinguish the fire may only make the flames burn more fiercely, because this would involve conceding closely guarded territory. Focusing on the flames may increase the heat. A highly contentious issue can be put on the back burner, but remember to come back to it. How significant is this issue? Does it have to be dealt with now? If it is not urgent, or if it is minor in terms of the overall situation, it may be possible to note it and move on. It may be more helpful to work on areas that are not so hotly guarded. Often, there are significant areas where participants are already in full or partial agreement. Mutual concerns – over children, in particular – can be given priority and the disputed issue sometimes fades away and lose its importance. Alternatively, after progress has been made on some matters, discussion of disputed areas may be possible in an easier atmosphere.

On the other hand, it may be necessary to let participants focus on the fundamental differences that set them at odds. This is a key area where approaches and experience drawn therapeutic disciplines can be valuable (see the discussion of models, theories and interventions at Chapter Two above). Mediators often describe the nub of the process as assisting movement from 'positions' to 'interests'. This movement can be looked for and encouraged at the outset by asking participants what they really want to *achieve*. It is a key mediation skill to identify when to assist the search for underlying meaning and when to let it lie.

11.8.5   Dividing problems into smaller parts

When the situation as a whole seems an impossible jumble, like a pile of mismatched bricks, time and energy are needed to take the pile of bricks apart and sort them out in some kind of order. With the mediator's help, participants may decide to put some bricks aside while they concentrate on fitting just a few interlocking bricks together. Spreading them out makes it easier to see which ones may fit. It also helps participants to identify the keystones that provide a firm foundation for a new edifice, such as the continuing co-operation needed to support a new structure of post-divorce parenting. 'Chunking' is a term from information technology that means breaking things into smaller pieces. 'Chunking' (or 'stepping down' in NLP) moves from the general to the specific.

---

[26]   De Bono *Conflicts – A Better Way to Resolve Them* (Penguin, 1991).

'Chunking' or 'stepping down' moves the focus from an overwhelmingly large issue to one aspect of it that can be worked on. The flip-chart is a very useful tool for dividing big problems into smaller parts and for seeing how one part relates to the whole.

Inevitably, there are situations where nothing fits, because participants are too far apart. Mediators are bound to feel tempted sometimes to knock heads together, tell people what they ought to do – or just give up. Instead of succumbing to the depression that may weigh down the participants, mediators need to maintain their psychic energy and ability to ask useful questions about immediate next steps. The map that was drawn earlier – verbally or on the flip-chart – may need to be looked at again and fresh stock taken of the choice of route – back to lawyers and the court, or staying in mediation? All options should be identified and re-assessed. If participants are willing to continue in mediation a little longer – even for the remainder of the session – it may be worth identifying the block to settlement and asking what would happen if the block no longer existed.

> 'I can't agree to Luke staying for the weekend, because he doesn't want to go.'

> 'What would happen if Luke said to you one day that he would like to spend a weekend with his father?'

Or:

> 'If you can imagine him changing his mind (even though you think this is very unlikely), would you see this as a good thing, or would you still have concerns about it?'

11.8.6 Confronting and challenging

Mediation practice varies in challenging participants who may be procrastinating, withholding information or possibly giving false information. A direct challenge is a high-risk strategy. There are risks if mediators seek to assert authority, since one of their main strengths is not having authority. Too direct a challenge may jeopardise the mediator's impartiality. Alternative strategies to a direct challenge include:

- Being puzzled.
  If there is a discrepancy, the mediator may say in a puzzled, rather than inquisitorial tone:

  > 'I'm sorry, I don't quite understand how what you just said ties in with the figures on page x of your financial form. Could you help me understand how …?'

- Identifying contradictions between words and behaviour.
  Where there is a contradiction between words and behaviour, it may be necessary to point it out, but there needs to be good rapport to help the

participant recognise the contradiction without feeling alienated. A gentler way may be suggesting that it is often very difficult to do something, when it comes to the point. Acknowledgement and empathy make it easier for participants to admit difficulty and recognise ambivalent feelings. If a parent misses an agreed visit, he or she needs to be asked how they can show that arrangements made in mediation will be adhered to and how a parenting plan can be given more force. If one partner undertakes to provide a financial document and fails to do so, the reasons need to be sought and if another chance is given, there should be a deadline.

11.8.7   Reversing roles

Sometimes it is useful to ask partners to take each other's position, even swapping chairs for the purpose of the exercise. Alex could be asked to imagine himself in Katie's place and say what he thinks her main concerns are and what might be acceptable to her. Then Katie could be asked to imagine herself in Alex's place. Looking at a situation through the other's eyes can sometimes change the way they each see it.

11.8.8   Setting tasks

Where there are doubts about commitment and lack of motivation to find a solution, it may help to identify tasks that participants agree to undertake before the next session. This can be a useful test of motivation. Letting each other down is more difficult when they know the mediator will be monitoring whether the tasks have been carried out. Each parent may be asked to suggest something they could do personally which might help.

11.8.9   Co-mediating

Raging tirades can have a galvanising function for individuals who are otherwise close to despair. But these couples are liable to annihilate each other. The virulence of their onslaughts may paralyse the mediator, who may feel like a rabbit caught in the glare of oncoming headlights. Couples who are addicted to fighting usually have a well-rehearsed pattern of argument. They may get perverse satisfaction in acting their script. They like having an audience and the mediator is another audience, even if the actors have to pay. They may combine forces to keep the fight going. The mediator's usual techniques of setting rules, agreeing structure, exploring options are unlikely to have an effect because this is what the couple expect. It is worth trying to make them forget their script, by doing something unexpected. Co-mediation is needed with entrenched couples and it may be helpful to have an impromptu debate between co-mediators in front of the couple. This is particularly useful if co-mediators take up different positions and engage in a genuine debate, with one mediator saying, for example, to the other:

'Jim, I don't think I see this in the same way as you do. I am not clear why Roy (husband) needs to be satisfied that Barbara (wife) is choosing suitable housing for herself. It seems to be that this is a matter for Barbara to decide for herself?'

Jim may reply:

'Well, I think Roy is saying he's worried whether Barbara can afford to buy and maintain another property.'

A debate between co-mediators can rehearse the couple's arguments and change the dynamics in the room. It can model a way of disagreeing amicably. The couple can then be invited to comment. Even if their positions have not changed, their manner of putting them forward may be softened by the atmosphere of the co-mediators' debate.

11.8.10 Unexpected interventions

When couples are arguing endlessly, it can be useful to enquire – while making it clear that this would be a 'worst case scenario' – what would happen in an emergency, such as one parent becoming seriously ill. This kind of question can have a very sobering effect. The need to draw up fresh Wills may need to be considered in any case and parents need to be encouraged to think about what matters most. One couple who had broken off all communication with each other met at their child's bedside in hospital, following her operation for appendicitis. The parents said they looked at each other across her hospital bed and realised they needed to get along with each other, for her sake.

Sometimes, arguments reach such a pitch that the mediator cannot be heard. In this situation, if the usual interventions have no effect, it may be necessary to stand up and say you are sorry you cannot help. Standing up is likely to stop the couple in mid-flow and this momentary lull can be used to focus on a limited, short-term objective. Surprise people! Instead of responding in the way they expect, do the opposite! Some mediators ask questions that take people by surprise. These need to be used with care – and with empathy.

Examples:

'Maybe it is safer for you both not to try to agree anything at the moment. Would it be better to leave things as they are?'

(With a smile):

'Would you rather discuss this on your own? It wouldn't cost you as much!'

'If Jodi (daughter) is asked by her friends whether the two of you are getting things sorted out now, what do you think she will say? ... What would you like her to be able to say?'

The conscious use of surprise in mediation is worth thinking about and cultivating. Brian Cantwell[27] has written extensively about the dynamics and dysfunctions of entrenched couples, the risks of mediators intervening inappropriately or inadequately and potential therapeutic interventions, using a systemic approach.

11.8.11   Anticipating a walk-out

When one participant is on the verge of walking out, their body language usually gives clues before they get up to leave. If the mediator notices signs of fidgeting, staring out of the window or mounting anger or distress, a walk-out may be prevented by the mediator saying something like:

> 'Karen, you are looking very upset (fed up). People often feel so desperate at times that they just want to give up and get out of here. Is that how you are feeling at the moment? ... Do you think you could manage just another five/ten minutes? If you could, maybe we can concentrate on immediate steps to make things slightly easier for you both?'

It may be possible to pre-empt a walk-out by offering a short caucus,[28] but if a person leaves the mediation room, the mediator needs to consider whether to let them go – sometimes they come back again – or whether the person is acutely distressed and the mediator should try to catch them before they leave the building. Careful attention to body language and eye contact helps to recognise signs of distress or frustration before a person gets up to go. An additional room should always be available where the person can recover or wait safely.

11.8.12   Brainstorming

Mediators should refrain from taking responsibility for resolving a deadlock and encourage the participants to come up with their own ideas. 'Can we spend the next five minutes thinking of any ways forward that could help?' Mediators can add further suggestions and options, provided these are not presented as the solution. All the ideas and options should be written on the flip-chart. Symbols and colours can be used to help participants select and prioritise. They may be encouraged to copy the list on the flip-chart and think about the options at home. At the next meeting the flip-chart can be looked at again. A suggestion that seems 'off the wall' may cause laughter. Feeling more relaxed may unfreeze thinking that has become firmly set. A divorcing couple who could see no solution to their housing problems were invited to brain-storm. After some minutes, one of them came up with an original idea that took the other's breath away, because it was ingenious and practical. This breakthrough would probably not have happened without encouragement to brainstorm and

---

[27]   See Cantwell 'CAFCASS: In-court Conciliation and Out-of-court Mediation' [2006] Fam Law 389–392 and 'Battling Parents: are they getting the right treatment?' [2007] Fam Law 743–748.
[28]   See Chapter 4 above.

the emotional intensity of the meeting. Building rapport with participants and focusing their energy can produce unexpectedly positive results.

11.8.13   Summarising and time keeping

Mediators need to summarise and reframe frequently so that participants feel equally heard and understood. Options should be listed for further reflection. Sometimes a couple come back later to an option they had previously ruled out. If an interim agreement is possible – for example on child arrangements in the short term – legal advice may not be needed on the details. A written note or interim summary should be provided quickly. Time limits need to be emphasised. If participants seem to be wasting time, the mediator may look at the clock and point out how much time remains. The last part of each session is needed to recap, prioritise and discuss next steps. If there is to be a further meeting, allow time to agree the date and time of the meeting.

11.9   NLP TECHNIQUES AND MEDIATION

Successful negotiations often take place without third party intervention. Mediation can facilitate negotiations between participants who are disposed to negotiate, but it is more often needed where face-to-face negotiation is problematic. Many of the concepts and techniques used in mediation have parallels in neuro-linguistic programming (NLP), without being direct borrowings. NLP teaches patterns, techniques and skills for effective communication, personal development and accelerated learning. These techniques and skills were developed in the early 1970s in collaboration between an American professor of linguistics and a doctoral student of psychology. Their work was strongly influenced by Gregory Bateson.[29] The 'neuro' part of NLP recognises the fundamental reality that all our behaviour stems from neurological processes of sight, hearing, smell, taste, touch and feeling. We experience the world through our senses. We make 'sense' of the information we receive and react to it. NLP is concerned with how we organise our subjective experience and how we edit and filter the outside world through our senses.

Map-making provides an analogy for people's different constructions of reality. People construct maps of their reality as they see it, their representation of the world they live in, which they use to guide their route and condition their responses. Inevitably, these maps are selective. They show certain features and landmarks, but there may be crucial gaps. In mediation, each participant's map depends on the selective filters they use to interpret what they see, the landmarks they pick out and the pathways they want to follow. The filters they use may leave out crucial information and awareness of aspects they may have missed, like a blind spot. Mediators help participants to look at their 'maps' at the same time, comparing what appears on each of them and spotting features that appear on one, but not the other, or which may be missing altogether.

---

[29]   See **2.4** and **6.21** above.

Something that appears on one map may be missing on the other map, such as pieces of financial information or reactions a child is showing. In putting the two maps alongside each other, mediators can highlight key features or critical gaps and help participants to create a new 'overlay' that offers them other ways of looking at things, without imposing different views. Mediators' systematic use of questions (corresponding to the Meta Model in NLP) helps to gather additional and more precise information and to gain a fuller understanding shared between all participants. The Meta Model is a series of questions designed to fill gaps in communication, to clarify generalisations, unravel confusions and explore possibilities. Used with sensitivity and rapport, selective questions can elucidate meanings and give choices, without asking blame-inducing 'Why?' questions. Mediators need to be aware that they use maps too. Asking questions that seem irrelevant to participants and outside the 'mediation frame' may create 'Meta Mayhem, Meta Muddle and Meta Misery'![30]

11.10   BATNAS, WATNAS AND MLATNAS

The Mapping Paths study found, both in collaborative law and in mediation, that where a 50:50 split of assets was agreed, generally on a 'clean break' basis, the equal division of moderate assets was likely to leave the children and their primary carer insufficiently provided for.[31] In one collaborative law case, the wife who had been a stay-at-home mother agreed to a 50:50 split of assets with maintenance that was inadequate for her support needs. The researchers advocated more rigorous reality-testing of proposed agreements. Fisher and Ury[32] developed the concept of the BATNA – the Best Alternative to a Negotiated Agreement – and its opposite, the WATNA – the Worst Alternative to a Negotiated Agreement. These may be used as benchmarks against which a proposed agreement may be tested. Mediators may also ask participants to predict what they see as the Most Likely Alternative to a Negotiated Agreement (MLATNA). BATNAs, WATNAs and MLATNAs are extremely useful tools when a mediation is stuck on competing notions of fairness and on the point of breaking down without agreement being reached. The mediator may say:

> 'This is a very difficult situation and you may need the court to decide it for you. But before you ask a judge to decide, there are some important questions to consider. Would it help to make a list of these questions?'

Questions to consider, which can be written down for participants to put to their legal advisers, include:

- If a judge decides, what is the best outcome I would get? (BATNA, Best Alternative to a Negotiated Agreement).

---

[30]   O'Connor and Seymour *Introducing NLP – Neuro-Linguistic Programming* (Thorsons, 1995), p 108.

[31]   Barlow, Hunter, Smithson and Ewing *Mapping Paths to Family Justice – Briefing Paper and Report on Key Findings* (June 2014), p 24.

[32]   Fisher R and Ury W *Getting to Yes – Negotiating Agreement Without Giving In* (Penguin Books, 1983).

- What is the worst outcome I could get? (WATNA, Worst Alternative to a Negotiated Agreement).
- What is the range between 'best' and 'worst' outcomes, in terms of percentages?
- How long might it take to get a final court order?
- What might the total costs be, if the issues are strongly fought by 'the other side'?
- Do judges vary in the view they take and the decisions they make?
- What do you think, realistically, I am most likely to get? (MLATNA, Most Likely Alternative to a Negotiated Agreement). Could you guarantee that I will get this? (Obviously, not.)
- Can I be certain of the final court outcome?
- Could there be other consequences of going to court that I need to think about?

The mediator helps participants to identify these and other relevant questions and can provide a written note of them or encourage participants to write them down. If they take legal advice, their lawyers are likely to advise outcomes within a certain range. If they wish, the clients can discuss their legal advice at a subsequent mediation meeting and consider a basis for settlement within the range they have each been given, without any pressure from the mediator. It is useful to convert percentages into figures and vice versa. The difference in percentages may be relatively small when converted into figures, but however big the gap, it is important to quantify it. In some cases, the difference may be less than the costs that would be incurred through litigation. The time needed to obtain a final court decision may also motivate the couple to accept a negotiated settlement.

Even when they are close to agreement, participants should be encouraged to put BATNA, WATNA and MLATNA questions to their lawyers, to check that their proposed settlement will meet longer as well as short term needs, and that it falls within the range of outcomes that the court would be likely to endorse. Clients should be forewarned that some lawyers' reactions to a proposed settlement might be: 'Oh, you'd do better if you went to court'. Instead of abandoning their negotiations, clients should be encouraged to ask BATNA, WATNA and MLATNA questions. Lawyers cannot guarantee the 'better deal' their client would get in court and the costs need to be taken into account. Clients should ask their lawyers to put their advice in writing. Encouraging clients to take these questions to their lawyers does not mean that lawyers give poor advice. On the contrary, clients are encouraged to seek legal advice as guidance towards well-informed and well-considered decisions. There are risks of premature and/or unbalanced agreements being reached in mediation. Participants may be anxious to reach a settlement without realising the risks. One party may pressurise the other and there are risks for them both, if they do not understand the full consequences of their decisions, especially if an inexperienced mediator does not perceive the pitfalls. Suggesting questions to take to their lawyers is not a sign of failure on the mediator's part, but rather a way of assisting the lawyers to 'invest in' the process of settlement. If BATNA, WATNA and MLATNA questions are used, a couple who had been stuck on 'what's fair' may return to mediation with renewed willingness to settle. Questions for lawyers should be defined and their advice given on a 'without prejudice' basis, so that their responses can be considered within the confidentiality and legal privilege of the mediation process.

11.11 SUMMARY OF TECHNIQUES

• Co-mediate if possible, preferably gender-balanced and interdisciplinary co-mediation.

• Acknowledge participants' feelings – frustration, anger, disappointment – in a balanced way. Acknowledge difficulties and efforts in coming to mediation. Be positive, patient and encouraging.

• Maintain ground-rules. Interrupt pleasantly but firmly to maintain control of discussions.

• Apply ground-rules firmly, explaining that mediation can continue only if they are kept.

• Ask participants whether they were able to trust each other, before they separated?

• Anticipate and pre-empt. A quick agreement may break down if problems are not foreseen and plans made to avoid or pre-empt them.

• If there is time, suggest a break – a cup of coffee? Loosening up physically and shifting physical positions can help.

• Occasionally think of telling a short anecdote. An anecdote can be effective if it is well chosen and non-judgemental.

• Don't see a deadlock negatively. It may be better than a bad solution.

• Use humour – sensitively and if appropriate.

• Show genuine concern to help improve situations and seek feedback on progress or outcomes.

• If a mediator feels exasperated or alienated by one participant, this may be an indication of becoming more aligned with the other one. Examine these reactions and discuss them with a consultant. Are negative reactions linked with the mediator's difficulty with a certain kind of personality?

• A mediation that ends without agreement should not be seen as having failed, because some understanding may have been achieved, and the mediator has not failed personally. Some couples re-refer themselves to mediation after a period of time, saying they now feel ready to reach a settlement.

11.12   INABILITY TO LET GO

The dimensions of loss and intensity of grief experienced before, during and following separation have been referred to in earlier chapters.[33] Some individuals cling to their grief and to their former partner, despite all the evidence that the separation is permanent. This desperate clinging may be shown in various ways:

- inability to contemplate the future or to discuss ways of settling issues;
- inability to express any needs apart from the need for the partner's return;
- great distress, continuous weeping during mediation;
- repeated assertions that the other partner will soon 'come to his (or her) senses' and return home;
- strong moral judgements, especially if the other partner has a new relationship;
- denial of the breakdown coupled with refusal to acknowledge having contributed in any way to the other partner's decision to leave;
- blocking and delaying tactics, refusal to fill in forms etc;
- lack of co-operation over the children, possibly as a means of punishing the other parent or putting pressure on him/her to return home; emotional threats or blackmail, such as suicide threats;
- attempts to manipulate others, including children and mediators, into seeing the abandoned partner as the innocent victim.

Mediation cannot resolve the profound loss and grief of separation and divorce. The grieving process may take years and may be unending. Mediators are not therapists, but they need to be aware of people's pain. Understanding can be conveyed non-verbally in attentiveness and eye contact, as well as in verbal acknowledgement, without taking sides or making judgements:

> 'It's frightening when one isn't sure what is happening next week, let alone next month.'

> 'I can see that you are extremely upset/worried.'

People seem appreciative of these comments. There must be eye contact with both partners and the words need to be said with real warmth and sincerity. When one partner becomes very distressed, the other partner may also be distressed, but may show it less. It is important not to acknowledge the distress of one partner in a way that suggests the other one is not distressed. It is preferable to include both of them in acknowledgements of distress. The partner who assumes that he or she is suffering far more than the other one can be stunned to realise the suffering of the other. These moments are very powerful and must not be hurried. Acknowledgement through illustrating positions on the 'loss cycle', perhaps by use of a pre-prepared sheet or the flip chart, can mutualise loss and grief in powerful ways. Mundane practical details

---

[33]   See **3.9** above.

may seem trivial, but it is essential to have a box of tissues, to avoid having to go out to look for one. When people break down in tears, as they quite often do, it is important to ask, after a few moments, whether they want to continue the meeting or whether they would prefer to stop. Often they say they want to continue. Someone who is crying may need reassurance that it is normal to be upset in these situations. Offering water, tea or coffee to both partners and/or a short break may also be helpful.

11.12.1   Short-term focus

When the level of distress is very high, a short-term focus on how to manage the next week or month is more helpful than looking for long-term or final solutions. Dividing a future that seems like an endless desert into 'chunks' of weeks or months helps people to cope with one chunk at a time.

11.12.2   Enabling a grieving person to express anger

Those who are overwhelmed by grief often find it difficult to express anger. It may help to acknowledge that it is normal to feel angry, as well as sad. Anger needs to be expressed, but kept under enough sufficient control. Anger is an energising force that can protect against depression and despair. Referring to anger in an accepting, normalising way can help a partner who is expressing anger, or one who is suppressing anger. Naming and accepting anger may reduce the need to show it in behaviour. However, allowing the safe expression of anger in mediation does not mean allowing verbal (or physical) abuse.

11.12.3   Making connections between anger and grief

The rejected partner usually experiences and shows the most acute grief, whereas the initiator of the separation commonly experiences grief also but may have greater difficulty in showing it. It is safer for the initiator to express anger than grief, because grief might be interpreted as regret and a change of mind. If one partner expresses all the grief and the other expresses all the anger, they may each remain stuck in these emotions until both can share in the grief and the anger. When one or both partners are locked in anger and unable to express grief, it may help to speak of the sadness that often underlies anger, saying how hard it can be to show sadness when one is extremely angry. The timing of such a comment is important, as well as its sensitivity. One partner, sometimes both, may cry. When anger turns into sadness, the pain may be acute but may be mitigated by awareness that it is shared. Some exceptionally bitter divorces involve the death of a child. If the parents have been unable to grieve their child's death together, their unresolved grief can turn into bitter anger against each other. These situations are deeply tragic and indicate a need for counselling or therapy.

Even where counselling or psychotherapy is sought, there are often practical issues that still need to be settled. Settlement can be helped by the realisation that anger is often linked with grief. The distinction between the roles of mediator and that of therapist is that the mediator is not exploring grief and anger in depth and offering therapeutic help. The mediator acknowledges feelings and helps to make connections. The aim is to ease communication, rather than working with individuals on emotional problems.

11.12.4   Valuing dreams and aspirations

When there is a tendency to idealise the other partner and the marriage that has been lost, it may be possible to recognise the deep disappointment of recognising that there were expectations that may not have been fulfilled. People need to value their dreams and aspirations, yet also acknowledge that a dream is over:

> 'It must be a profound disappointment for both of you that the relationship you invested so much in hasn't worked out in the way you hoped. People often feel that they have failed. But there hasn't necessarily been a failure. It may be a question of different needs and expectations not matching up any more, despite real efforts.'

11.12.5   Using metaphors and analogies

The use of metaphors in mediation and analogies was mentioned in chapter 6. Sometimes it helps to say something on these lines: 'Maybe you both feel you are in the middle of a black tunnel, with no light showing at the end of it' (observe both participants and see if there is a non-verbal or verbal response). 'This is probably the hardest stage of all, right now. But it is surprising how often people find after a year or so that their situation has changed in ways they had not expected to happen. It's impossible to know how things will change or maybe to believe that they can change. But over time things do change. They can get better.'

Optimistic comments may be received with scepticism, but they can bring a smile. Empathy must be shown equally to both partners, keeping eye contact with both and showing warmth to both. Metaphors need to be chosen with care and attuned to clients' language and feelings.

11.12.6   Referral to counselling or psychotherapy

When grief is particularly acute and prolonged, especially when the grief may be linked to earlier unresolved loss, therapeutic help may be needed. Many people seek help from their doctor for symptoms associated with the distress of separation. Although some doctors write out a prescription for medication, many recognise the value of therapy and some employ a counsellor in their practice. Experienced mediators may be able to manage situations of high conflict and difficulty, but however skilled and experienced the mediator, there must be discretion to terminate a mediation which is inappropriate or unworkable, making suggestions of other sources of help. Referrals to counselling must be made with care, however. A recommendation to go elsewhere could be interpreted as a Pontius Pilate kind of gesture, increasing the sense of rejection felt by a person already abandoned by their partner.

Deciding when and how to suggest counselling or therapy needs to be sensitive. A suggestion that counselling might be helpful should be made to both partners equally, without appearing to suggest that one needs counselling, whereas the other does not. Counselling to repair the marriage is only one form of counselling. Counselling to cope with relationship breakdown, or divorce counselling, may help both the initiator and the non-initiator of the separation to understand what has happened between them so that they can move forward with less pain or self-blame. People often want to know what help others have found useful in similar situations. Information about local services may encourage individuals to seek help, without feeling stigmatised. A list of counselling agencies and private therapists can be given to those who want it or posted to them afterwards. Some situations are not suitable for mediation because there are problems of individual psychopathology, a history of mental illness, alcoholism or drug abuse. Mediators cannot and should not be expected to mediate in such cases.

Some couples' intense anger masks a fear of showing grief. If one says 'I wish you were dead', the wish may be mutual and yet they may realise they depend on keeping the anger going, as they might not survive without it. This realisation can be cathartic. But it may be necessary for these couples, as well as the mediator, to recognise that they have come to mediation without actually wanting to agree anything. When this is the case, mediators should not struggle on indefinitely. They must be able to decide when 'enough is enough' and terminate a mediation where no progress can be made or where ant progress is immediately sabotaged by one or both participants, in an almost triumphant way. Legal advisers can spell things out to battling clients in a way the mediator is unable to do. Referring clients back to their legal advisers is not a sign of failure on the mediator's part. Paradoxically, it can result in them returning to mediation with greater readiness to negotiate.

11.13   BLOCKS WITHIN THE MEDIATOR

Mediators need to accept that getting stuck is not confined to participants. It may be the mediator who feels stuck. Sometimes there is a failure to grasp an important point or difficulty relating to one of the participants. Feelings of irritation or frustration – or plain dislike – may impede the mediator's ability to hold a balance and think creatively. Mediators need to tune into their own feelings and examine their own subjective reactions in order to understand what is happening in the room. It is possible to become triangulated into the couple's conflict. Participants' comments or reactions may resonate with the mediator's personal history, consciously or unconsciously, or their attitudes or values may seem so alien that the mediator is unable to engage with them. Whenever there are difficulties like this, the mediator should seek to discuss them with their professional practice consultant, before concluding that no progress can be made. Reflecting with a consultant or supervisor may lead to a different perspective and generate new ideas.

11.14   SOME CONFLICTS REMAIN ENTRENCHED

> *'I deserve it*
> *because I have it.*
>
> *You have not got it*
> *therefore you do not deserve it.*
>
> *You do not deserve it*
> *because you have not got it*
>
> *You have not got it*
> *because you do not deserve it ... etc.'*[34]

Some couples remain entrenched despite sustained efforts to resolve their conflict. In one case referred to mediation by the court, the unmarried parents had been in dispute over contact throughout the life of their five-year-old daughter, Maya. They appeared to make some headway in the first co-mediated meeting. Arrangements for the next six weeks, including Christmas, were written up in an interim mediation summary. However, the father insisted on overnight contact and the mother adamantly refused this. The parents had never lived together in an established partnership and the father had seen very little of Maya when she was a baby. His name was on her birth certificate and he had obtained a court order for regular contact every Saturday. The mother claimed that the father had breached the contact order by keeping Maya for three days without consent. There were other difficulties that contributed to the deadlock:

- The parents lived sixty kilometres apart.
- The father did not drive and he needed members of his family to provide transport.
- His mother and other members of his family supported him against the mother.
- He worked in a retail store with a variable schedule. He usually worked at weekends and had two days off during the week, but in spite of requesting his schedule as far in advance as possible, he generally received it about a week ahead. The mother argued that she could not be expected to change her arrangements at short notice and also that Maya was too tired at the end of her school day to go out with her father for a couple of hours.

The mother cancelled the second mediation meeting at short notice and asked for it to be rearranged. The father had booked a day's leave for the meeting and he was incensed. At the end of the rearranged second meeting, the deadlock

---

[34]   RD Laing *Knots*.

between the parents showed no sign of shifting. What could be learnt from this 'failed mediation'? Maya was five years old and both parents described her as bright and articulate for her age. An experienced child counsellor might have met with Maya with the agreement of all concerned and through therapeutic play might have elicited messages that she wanted her parents to hear. Children's paintings and messages can have a powerful effect on warring parents, helping them to reach agreements that are not the child's responsibility, but which are informed by better understanding of their child's needs and feelings.

11.15   KNOT THEORY AND MEDIATION

Knot theory – the study of surfaces and interconnections – is a branch of science. Without attempting to understand the mind-boggling mathematics involved, mediators may find parallels between getting stuck in mediation and the invariance of knots – that is, knots which cannot be untied. Knot theory studies linkages and interconnections. In a similar way, mediators disentangle communications between family members whose relationships have changed or which are in the process of changing. Mediation helps people to gain information, better understanding, time to think and fresh perspectives. Although the problems may be insoluble, the tangle of crossed lines may loosen if the benefits of agreement and co-operation become clearer.

Neil Robinson has suggested (personal communication) that another way to approach the challenge of deadlocks and impasses in mediation is to build a new structure, using experience from other fields such as civil mediation. Such models are beyond the scope of this book. 'The key will often lie in the balance of creativity and boundary, of improvisation and form. The Family Mediation Centre Staffordshire uses training events to develop new structures to address these challenges. In so doing, they are like musicians who improvise and create new dialogues over a ground – a set pattern of notes or harmonic progression – with examples ranging from Henry Purcell's 'Dido's Lament' to Tord Gustavson's 'The Ground'. Managing change, like managing a crisis,[35] needs courage, because it involves danger as well as opportunities. 25 centuries ago, Empedocles sought to reconcile changing phenomena with the concept of underlying unchanging existence. Those who resist the profound and life-threatening changes of disassociating from a broken relationship need support so that they can hold on to their own identity and find there is still firm ground beneath their feet:

> 'We shrink from change, yet is there anything that can come into being
> without it?'[36]

---

[35] See **3.3** above.
[36] Marcus Aurelius *Meditations Book Seven*, 18.

CHAPTER 12

SKILLS IN ENDING MEDIATION

'However the battle is ended
Though proudly the victor comes,
With flaunting flags and nagging neighs
And echoing rolls of drums;
Still truth proclaims this motto
In letters of living light,
No question is ever settled
Until it is settled right.'[1]

'Begin at the beginning', the King said gravely, 'and go on till you come to
the end: then stop.'[2]

CONTENTS

12.1 SKILLS IN ENDING MEDIATION

When a mediation ends very positively, with a proposed settlement on all the issues and conflict resolved, there should be no victor, 'flaunting flags' or 'nagging neighs'. In the somewhat hackneyed phrase, the outcome of mediation should be 'win/win', not 'win/lose'. Some mediations end at an early stage or partway through, because one or both participants are unwilling to participate further and/or because the mediator finds it unsuitable for mediation to

---

[1] Ella Wheeler Wilcox *Settle the Question Right* (Poems of Pleasure, 1900).
[2] Lewis Carroll *Alice in Wonderland*, p 107.

continue, whether because of child protection concerns, domestic abuse, non-disclosure, unmanageable power imbalances or because attempts to settle the dispute have been exhausted. Obstacles to agreement were considered in the previous chapter. Some obstacles are insuperable, but even an 'unsuccessful' mediation (which may nonetheless have produced some benefits) should be brought to a considered end as calmly and pleasantly as possible, without either or both participants experiencing further loss or disadvantage. The mediator's careful management of high conflict situations and attention to body language, as well as verbal reactions, should as far as possible avoid abrupt and traumatic endings in which one participant leaves the room in distress or where a furious altercation has to be terminated by the mediator. Each stage of mediation, including the final stages, needs the mediator's continuing combination of interpersonal, problem-solving and process skills. A considerable number of mediations end inconclusively for various reasons, including the inability to pay for further sessions.

It may be better for questions to remain unsettled, if they cannot be 'settled right'. Of course there may be different views as to what actually constitutes a 'right' settlement.[3] As discussed in what follows, a 'right' settlement requires informed and well-considered agreements between participants following legal and/or financial advice and which, most importantly, take account of the needs, feelings and contributory ideas of their children. There are rarely easy solutions and it may be very hard to find a balance that feels right to all concerned. Mediators help participants to look for a balanced outcome that both of them feel is 'right' for their children and themselves, or as nearly right as possible. Arrangements worked out in mediation may differ from the kind of order the court might make in the same circumstances, but they should fall within the parameters of a possible court order. A mediation summary is likely to include more child-focused details than a court order would do.

If mediation comes to an end with settlement proposals on all issues, this suggests that the mediator has used process, interpersonal and problem-solving skills to good effect. Nevertheless, even where full resolution appears to have been achieved, there is scope for problem-solving skills in anticipating and possibly pre-empting further difficulties that could cause co-operation to break down again. If participants seem satisfied that they have reached a settlement that will enable them to move on, this may be a good moment to ask them: 'Can you think of anything that is likely to happen that could cause things to go wrong again?' Humorous responses to this question indicate more relaxed communication and commitment to understandings that have been reached. But one or both participants may foresee a stumbling-block that needs to be addressed. One couple said they felt very satisfied with the outcome of their mediation and were confident they could agree on their own how to divide the contents of the family home. The mediator said encouragingly: 'Yes, I'm sure you can – but watch out for the ginger-jar!' They both looked bemused: 'What ginger-jar?' The mediator explained that, although most contents of the family home are shared out without problems, there can be one special possession that

---

[3]   See **10.2** above on 'just settlement'.

both partners want very much because of its emotional or symbolic value. This is the 'ginger-jar'. Later on, the couple reported back that everything was going smoothly in deciding about the contents of the family home until, all of a sudden, they found themselves arguing fiercely over one particular object. They stopped, looked at each other, said 'Ginger-jar!' and laughed. They were then able to get over this sticking-point as well.

All the mediator's skills are needed when concluding a mediation, with or without any basis for agreement. There may be opportunities for further ideas or strategies to overcome barriers to agreement, or an agreed truce to allow time for further reflection and advice before recourse to the court (unless delay would benefit one party and disadvantage the other). Where there is continuing deadlock on financial matters, mediators should ensure they have made full use of BATNA, WATNA and MLATNA questions,[4] possibly including them in a confidential summary that records each party's position on outstanding issues. The principal focus of this chapter is on process skills, because written summaries of mediation require considerable mastery of process skills. Opportunities for mediation practice need to follow swiftly after completion of foundation training. Otherwise, there may be risks that inexperienced mediators forget training that is particularly important with regard to the preparation of mediation summaries. For this reason, FMA mediators who have not yet passed the Assessment of Professional Competence[5] are required to send the draft of a final summary to their professional practice consultant (PPC) to be checked, before the summary is sent to the clients. Mediators should be encouraged, in any case, to request a fellow mediator to read and comment on a final summary in draft form from the perspectives of each participant and legal advisers. The final summary builds on interim summaries or 'Note of Mediation Session' that are generally sent to clients in the course of their mediation. Notes of Sessions are often written informally in letters addressed to both participants in the same terms and using a more personal style that continues the mediation 'conversation'. The final mediation summary is a formal document that should be produced to high professional standards in an approved format and which must contain certain required paragraphs. Its style and phrasing can however convey the mediator's empathy and interpersonal skills and, as suggested above, can incorporate problem-solving skills as well. The final summary would normally be sent to clients with a closing letter from the mediator/s. Some mediators enclose a client feedback form as well.

12.2 WHY IS A STANDARD FORMAT NEEDED FOR WRITTEN SUMMARIES OF MEDIATION?

The final stages of mediation in which participants reach terms or proposals for agreement are likely to require a confidential written summary setting out their arrangements for their children and/or proposals for financial settlement. Where needed, a separate, 'open' summary of financial information is also

---

4   See **11.10** above on BATNA, WATNA and MLATNA questions.
5   See **14.11** below.

provided by the mediator, listing the supporting documents supplied by participants and available to them both. Participants are encouraged to take these summaries to their legal advisers for (further) advice and possibly some 'fine-tuning'. One lawyer, having ascertained the other party's agreement, may then draft a consent order based on the confidential mediation summary or alternatively, an agreement may be confirmed in an exchange of 'open' letters between solicitors (see **12.6** and **12.10** below). Legal costs can be greatly reduced by a clear and comprehensive mediation summary of a proposed settlement on financial and property matters, accompanied by an Open Financial Summary providing full financial disclosure, with the necessary supporting documents.

However, in the post-LASPO world, the reality is that many couples cannot afford to take legal advice on their mediation summaries, while the Help with Mediation scheme available to publicly funded mediation clients does not allow time for lawyers to give detailed consideration and advice. Lawyers may be unwilling to draft a consent order setting out terms for a full and final settlement for which they may be held responsible, when they have not had the opportunity to examine the financial disclosure on which it is based, nor ascertain how options for settlement were explored.

In consequence, some couples may 'take the law into their own hands' and use the confidential mediation summary to apply for a consent order themselves, to obtain a full and final settlement in divorce proceedings without using lawyers. As explained in Chapter 1,[6] it is possible for both parties jointly to waive the 'without prejudice' privilege attaching to their confidential mediation summary, in order to facilitate the court making a consent order by explaining the rationale for the proposed settlement and the options considered in mediation. Joint consent to waive confidentiality should be given in writing. Particularly in court-referred mediations, it may be helpful for confidentiality to be waived in order to facilitate orders being made with consent.

As previously suggested,[7] mediation is paradoxical in a number of respects. On the one hand, the aim is to facilitate agreements being reached by the parties themselves, without advice or guidance from the mediator. On the other hand, mediators need to restrain participants from entering into a premature or unsafe 'agreement' that could disadvantage either or both of them. With many clients unable to access the legal advice they need, mediators need to exercise the greatest care and caution in preparing a confidential summary that could be used as the basis for seeking a consent order. There are risks for the parties and also for the mediator, if a consent order is sought without both parties having received sufficient professional advice on its terms. The parties themselves may not recognise significant omissions or lack of clarity and may not be able to grasp the long-term consequences of their proposals. An inexperienced mediator without sufficient legal knowledge may also fail to recognise these shortcomings. It is very worrying, therefore, that some mediators appear to be

---

[6]   See **1.10** above on the confidentiality of mediation in relation to the court.
[7]   See **3.11** above on the basic paradox of mediation.

drafting consent orders themselves, in the absence of lawyers. The mediator's professional indemnity insurance may not protect the mediator in the event of a professional negligence claim brought by a mediation client who claims to have suffered substantial financial loss as a result of formalising a settlement based on incomplete or erroneous financial facts.

Yet, the counterpoint to these arguments is that the 'empowerment' of the mediation process derives from its flexibility and from the creativity of all participants, including the mediator. Participants work out personal and family arrangements that are written up by the mediator in their chosen terms, whereas court-imposed settlements with their constraints and legal language may be more like a straitjacket than a tailor-made garment. Written summaries of mediation need to lay the foundations for lasting agreement and co-operation in the longer term. They need to be comprehensive, intellectually rigorous and accurate. For this reason, most Member Organisations of the FMC have a standard template for the summaries that are prepared at the end of the mediation process. What follows is one way of preparing summaries, modelled on the precedents of the Family Mediators Association. It is not intended to be prescriptive or to limit invention. For the mediator, developing a personal (but not too personal) style is important, but it is also essential for participants to feel that the written summary provides an accurate record of their concerns, objectives and proposals. For example, many mediators end the summary with a note of encouragement, but this might seem patronising to some participants or might strike a jarring note. Feedback from lawyers and participants assists the continuing evolution of a mediator's style in writing up mediation outcomes, as well as in face-to-face meetings.

12.3 THE CONFIDENTIAL SUMMARY OF MEDIATION (MEMORANDUM OF UNDERSTANDING)

The Agreement to Mediate that participants sign before beginning mediation explains that at the end of the process (and if needed also during the process) the mediator offers to prepare a confidential summary of the mediation (often referred to as the Memorandum of Understanding – MOU – or 'Summary of Proposals') summarising the outcome and proposals for settlement. Depending on the issues brought to mediation, the summary sets out parents' arrangements for their children and proposals for settlement of financial and property matters, thus providing the basis for a Consent Order in divorce-related financial relief proceedings or, if needed, for a consent order on child arrangements. Proposed agreements on family matters other than separation and divorce should be similarly summarised. Copies of correspondence and records should have been kept in the case file throughout the mediation, recording dates of sessions, issues considered and a brief summary of each session. An interim summary or Note of Meeting is often provided to help participants obtain professional advice, consider options and prepare for the next session.

The objectives of the mediation summary are:

- To explain proposals and identify questions on which legal advice is needed, so that participants can be fully informed and clear about the likely consequences before they seek to formalise an agreement in legally binding terms.

- To provide a clear summary of proposed terms of agreement that participants accept as an accurate summary. Otherwise, if each of them gives their own version to their legal advisers, further work will be needed by their lawyers to clarify the outcome of the mediation.

- To explain the rationale for proposed terms of agreement, to help legal advisers understand the reasons for their clients deciding on one particular option over other possible options that they have also considered in mediation.

- To reinforce co-operation between participants, especially where children are involved, by emphasising their mutual concerns and shared objectives as parents.

- To explain not only the issues and aspects that have been covered in the mediation, but also issues or aspects that have not been considered – possibly because of lack of time.

- Where there are outstanding issues, to explain each participant's position in neutral terms, clarifying the issues, narrowing areas of dispute and reducing misunderstandings.

- To maintain a written record on file. This is needed in any event and especially if further mediation takes place after an interval.

- To protect the mediator in the case of complaint. The use of correct standard wording is essential for the mediator's professional indemnity insurance.

- To fulfil the mediator's contractual obligations to participants (see Chapter 5 and Appendix E).

- In legally aided mediation, to meet LAA requirements and enable a claim to be submitted for the work done.

Separating and divorcing couples need a solid structure on which to build their post-separation lives. The summary lays foundations and provides scaffolding. If the scaffolding needs adjustment with the help of legal advisers, adjustments can be made without dismantling the whole framework. In an early study of pilot projects on all-issues mediation, the researchers found that 'most clients felt that the mediation summary represented a fairly accurate record of what had been agreed.'[8]

---

[8]   Walker, McCarthy and Timms *Mediation: the Making and Remaking of Co-operative Relationships* (Relate Centre for Family Studies, University of Newcastle, 1994), p 136.

12.4 INTERIM ARRANGEMENTS

Every mediation session has some form of outcome, even if there is continuing disagreement. It is usually desirable to provide a written note of the session for participants, even where it simply confirms arrangements to meet again and provide certain information (a 'task list'). This is another area of evolving practice, with some mediators providing a 'session record', whereas others provide an interim summary or Outcome Note (this may be particularly important where there are court proceedings). Other services may summarise the outcome of a meeting in a personalised letter. Clarity and rigour are as essential in recording interim arrangements as in the final summary – clarity of purpose, clarity as to what is proposed or actually agreed and, perhaps most of all, clarity as to whether any understanding is confidential or 'open'.

If parents tend to argue or do not communicate easily, they may need a written note after each mediation session to avoid confusion or arguments over dates or times of visits. If details are recollected differently, each parent may complain that the other parent broke their agreement or got it wrong. When parents need clarity on interim child arrangements, it is possible for these arrangements to be confirmed between lawyers. Sometimes parents want a letter or note of arrangements that they can show to new partners or other third parties. Depending on the ages of their children, parents may show it to their children too. If understandings are verbal only, there can be muddle and misunderstanding. Mediators help participants to work out proposals for settlement and agreement,[9] but they should avoid recording an 'agreement' which parents mistakenly understand to be binding on them both and possibly enforceable. A written summary recording an 'agreement' should be considered with great care and provided only in very limited circumstances, such as:

12.4.1 Interim child arrangements

Where there is urgency to confirm short-term arrangements, such as times of picking up and returning a child the following weekend, the mediator may draw up an Interim Summary recording the arrangements on an 'open' basis, making it clear that the document is 'open' and not legally privileged. Parents do not need legal advice as to whether their child is to be picked up from a swimming lesson or from Aunty Sue's home. They can agree such limited practical details on a short-term basis that does not establish a 'status quo'. If they both sign a short summary, it may reduce scope for confusion or further argument.

12.4.2 Proposed use or disposal of a minor asset, in relation to total assets

Participants sometimes wish to record an agreement on the sale or disposal of a minor asset in circumstances where they do not require legal advice. In one

---

[9]   See **1.10.2** above and **12.7.6** below

case, a couple wanted to clear a debt by selling a valuable china vase. Their total assets were such that neither partner's position would be prejudiced by the sale of the china vase for their joint benefit. In another mediation, the couple owned three cars and they decided to sell one of them and split the proceeds 50:50. They also owned two properties in joint names. Their interim agreement on the sale of the third car recorded that the division of sale proceeds on a 50:50 basis was to be taken into account in any future division of matrimonial assets. Mediators need to have enough legal knowledge and expertise to deal safely with an agreement involving the use or disposal of a financial asset, even if it appears to be a minor one. They need to be able to recognise when independent legal advice should be sought.

In all cases, mediators should take care to conclude mediation with positively worded closing letters and, where appropriate, written summaries. When mediation ends without any basis for agreement, closing letters should conclude the mediation clearly, with encouragement to return to mediation at any stage. Research shows that personal commitment is a key factor in lasting agreements. Many parents trust each other's commitment where their children are concerned. Others do not have this trust and in any case, as children get older, circumstances are liable to change. If parents' previous experience in mediation was positive, they are more likely to return to mediation to renegotiate their arrangements.

12.5   WHAT DO PARTICIPANTS NEED IN THEIR MEDIATION SUMMARY?

- A document that explains proposals and priorities accurately and clearly.
- Clear and comprehensible language, with a minimum of legal terminology.
- Impartial wording, no opinions or value judgements on the part of the mediator.
- Accurately recorded facts, figures and details of actual or proposed arrangements.
- Precise drafting that does not give scope for different interpretations.
- Sufficient focus on the children, usually with more details about parenting plans and arrangements than would be found in a court order.
- Proposals that participants feel they own.
- A document that will facilitate the legal process, reducing legal costs and avoiding delay.
- Sufficient explanation of reasons for selecting a particular course of action.
- In some cases, reference to concerns that have emotional rather than legal significance.
- Positive and sensitive phrasing that strikes a balance between formality and informality.

- Reference to points on which legal or other expert advice is needed, in terms the participants understand.

- A summary that will assist them to achieve a lasting and, where needed, legally binding, settlement.

12.6 WHAT DO LEGAL ADVISERS LOOK FOR IN THE MEDIATION SUMMARY?

- A heading and standard wording explaining the function and legal status of the document.

- The name/s of the mediator and the mediator's practice or agency, information about the duration of the mediation and approach used (eg single or co-mediation).

- Background information about the participants: names, addresses, date of marriage or cohabitation, names of children and dates of birth, whether the parents are separated, with whom the children are living, date of separation and so on. The background information should be provided in a short preamble to the main body of the summary.

- The issues brought to mediation, with a concise summary of proposals or positions on each issue, set out in a clear structure with sub-headings.

- The legal framework for settlement explaining whether the couple have separated and (in the case of married couples) whether a divorce petition has been filed and whether the content of the petition is accepted by the respondent.

- Financial disclosure: lawyers need to know whether a separate OFS has been produced and signed by both parties confirming that full financial disclosure has been made and information agreed, with supporting documents.

- Clarity: a professionally presented document, well organised and easy to follow.

- Precise drafting: proposals should state for example the amount of monthly child maintenance payments, the date on which payment will be made and how it will be made, provision for review and so on.

- Explanation: lawyers need sufficient explanation of the rationale for the proposals so that they can understand the reasons for preferring a particular option among a range of possible options.

- Comprehensiveness: lawyers need to see whether the issues brought to mediation have been covered fully and that all relevant questions arising from these issues have been addressed. If some matters have not been addressed in mediation, the reason for not addressing them, such as lack of time, should be explained.

- Concise drafting: lawyers do not want lengthy explanations of each party's feelings or concerns and details of their discussions. They may however like to have an indication that there are still high levels of stress, anxiety, uncertainty or conflict. Mediators can give such indications in wording agreed with both parties.

- Specific points on which legal advice is needed.
- Proposals, not agreements – unless an interim agreement on child arrangements is appropriate and does not need legal advice.
- An action plan setting out the next steps: are solicitors being asked to liaise in order to finalise the proposed settlement?
- Whether mediation has ended.

12.7 STRUCTURE OF THE CONFIDENTIAL MEDIATION SUMMARY

12.7.1 Cover page

As the summary is intended as a permanent document for the participants and as a good advertisement for the mediator or their service, it needs to look professional. A standard cover page setting out the status of the document (eg Interim/Final), the participants' names and the name of the service is advisable. The document should be marked 'Confidential and Legally Privileged'.

12.7.2 Required introductory paragraphs

The required introductory wording should be used,[10] so that there is no ambiguity as to the purpose and legal status of the summary. The participants' full names should be given at the beginning. Most mediators then proceed to refer to them by their first names, if first names have been used in the mediation.

12.7.3 Background information

A paragraph of background information is intended to assist legal advisers by providing brief details – names and dates of birth, date of marriage/or length of cohabitation and where applicable, date of separation or divorce. Names, ages and dates of birth of the children of the family should be given, also the address and living arrangements for each parent and the children. Each party's occupation and approximate net monthly or annual earnings should be given.

12.7.4 Issues brought to mediation

The number of mediation sessions should be stated with their dates, to show the time-scale of the mediation. The main issues brought to mediation should be listed, so that the range of the mediation can be grasped quickly.

---

[10] See Sample Mediation Summary at **12.11** below.

12.7.5 Separation/divorce

Usually this major issue needs to be addressed first, so that it is clear whether there is mutual acceptance of the need for separation or divorce and if so, in what time-scale. The summary should record whether some general information has been given about divorce and divorce procedure. It is important that couples understand and consider their options in relation to separation and divorce. When there is continuing dispute about separation or divorce, each partner's position needs to be explained sensitively, without reopening wounds. It may be important to acknowledge strong feelings on separation, divorce or other issues, without any implication of blame or causing further hurt. Information concerning actual or intended co-habitation or remarriage should also be given.

12.7.6 Proposals for settlement

Proposals need to stand out clearly, preferably in bold type. Otherwise, a key proposal may get buried in explanations. There is no need to record the whole content of discussions. As explained in **12.4** above, the words 'agreement' or 'agree' should be avoided, because proposals for settlement worked out in mediation are subject to legal advice to each party. If the words 'agree' and 'agreement' are used, they cause confusion and may increase conflict, especially if there is amendment or further negotiation following legal advice from solicitors. Many mediators set out the specific proposals as a separate section at the end of the document.

12.7.7 Arrangements for (names of children)

Where parents have emphasised in mediation that their children are their first priority, this section should underline their commitment to their children and mutual wish to give their children as much support as possible and/or concern to help their children adjust to the separation (provided these statements emphasise the parents' expressed wishes and objectives, not the mediator's personal views). When parents have already decided arrangements for their children before coming to mediation on financial issues only, the arrangements should be explained briefly. Rather than referring to participants by their first names throughout, it is helpful to emphasise parent–child relationships: 'will live mainly with their' referring to 'both parents' or to 'their mother' or 'their father' and using the names of the children, eg 'both parents accept that Jessica and Richard will continue to live with their mother and spend substantial periods of time with their father on a regular basis, as explained below.' It is helpful to put the children's names in the sub-heading of the section on child arrangements, as well as in detailed arrangements, to show that personal attention has been given to them as individuals, rather than treating them collectively.

Details should be given as far as necessary of the times or periods that the children will spend with their father/mother, including weekdays and weekends, school holidays, Christmas and other festivals, birthdays. Both parents' involvement in other areas of the children's upbringing and development, such as education and school events, should also be mentioned. It is helpful to record whether the parents will communicate directly with each other on day-to-day matters and review arrangements for the children periodically. If the parents have talked with their children and explained new arrangements to them, this should be mentioned, as well as any arrangement for a child or young person to be consulted directly. A parenting plan may be appended but as noted above, if the Cafcass Parenting Plan document is used, it is essential to clarify its status.

12.7.8   Property and future accommodation/housing

Brief information should be given: the address of one or more properties, date of purchase, how it was financed, in whose name and loans outstanding. The summary should explain to what extent possible options have been considered and the main reason/s for the preferred option, if there is one. Proposals for the continuing occupation of the home (eg by one parent and the children) and/or purchase of a new property by one or both parties should be explained clearly, with sufficient detail. Is one party seeking to maintain an interest either in the home or in a new property to be purchased by the other? What would be the triggers for repayment of a charge? What level of borrowing would be needed? Have enquiries been made?

Schedules of projected future monthly income and outgoings for each parent (as opposed to actual monthly income and outgoings summarised in the Open Financial Statement) may be attached to the summary, so that participants and their legal advisers can check that their housing proposals are financially viable.

12.7.9   Proposals for division of capital and other assets

A schedule should be provided, so that the proposed 'package' can be read easily at a glance. It is not necessary to replicate all the detailed information contained in the Open Financial Statement. It may be more useful to record in succinct terms the considerations and discussions that led to a particular plan being preferred. Mediators may set out the 'net effects' of a series of options, to remind participants and explain to legal advisers how a set of proposals was arrived at.

12.7.10   Child maintenance

The summary should state the level of proposed child maintenance and method of payment, the day of the month on which the payment will be made and over what period of time. Even where there is no intention to make an application to the Child Maintenance Service (CMS), the summary should state that relevant information has been given. Participants making an application to the CMS need to be aware that costs are involved and that it encourages private ordering of disputes.

12.7.11   Spousal maintenance

Is either party seeking spousal maintenance from the other, or are claims to be mutually dismissed? If there is a proposal for spousal maintenance, is it intended to be time limited and should there be index linking? It may be helpful to note that the borderline between clean break and nominal spousal maintenance where there are children is controversial and may require (further) legal advice.

12.7.12   Tax, tax credits and welfare benefits

The summary should record whether the tax implications of proposals have been considered and that the parties have been encouraged to take tax advice.

The summary should state whether information has been given about possible entitlement to welfare benefits, especially those that would automatically trigger the CMS becoming involved. If an estimate of the Child Maintenance calculation has been obtained by either parent, this should be stated. It is often necessary to inform people in receipt of Tax Credits that they need to notify the Tax Credit Office of their changed circumstances within one month of separation, or the Benefits Agency if they are in receipt of welfare benefits.

12.7.13   Pensions

Full details and supporting documents should be given in the Open Financial Statement. The confidential summary should state whether the mediator has provided basic information regarding pension options and whether options have been considered. The summary should also record that both parties have been encouraged to seek legal and financial advice regarding pension provisions and potential claims.

12.7.14   Inheritance

The summary should record whether either party has recently received an inheritance or has immediate prospects of receiving an inheritance that would have a bearing on the division of matrimonial assets. The summary should also record that both parties have been encouraged to seek legal advice on inheritance matters.

12.7.15   Wills

The summary should record that information has been given about the effect of divorce on Wills and the need to take legal advice on drawing up new Wills. They will need their lawyers' advice as to any interim arrangements that should be put in place.

12.7.16   House contents/personal possessions

Brief details should be given of proposals and/or intentions to agree the division of house contents and possessions without the need for detailed discussion in mediation.

12.7.17   Outstanding issues

The summary should list issues that were not dealt with in the mediation, either because of lack of time or because participants did not wish to discuss them. Questions raised by the mediator should be summarised: eg 'Questions were raised as to whether ... and ... were encouraged to consider these questions and take further legal advice on them.' Where some or all issues remain unresolved, the summary should give a concise and impartially worded statement of each participant's position, to facilitate movement towards settlement, with advice from solicitors.

12.7.18   Questions on which legal or financial advice is needed

The main points on which legal and/or financial advice is needed should be summarised. Even where there appears to be a basis for full agreement between participants, it is useful to anticipate legal advisers' responses to the proposals ('Well, you could do better than that') by framing neutrally worded questions for participants to put to their legal advisers in order to formalise a settlement.[11]

12.7.19   Next steps and time-scale for action

The summary should set out the next steps that participants intend to take, such as seeking legal advice and clarifying whether one partner's solicitor is to be asked to draw up a Consent Order. Time-scales should be given if possible and, if needed, the date for a further mediation meeting.

12.7.20   Ending

The summary often ends on a positive note that underlines participants' stated intentions to maintain their co-operation, especially with regard to their children. A review or further meeting may be offered, after legal advice has been taken or at some future stage, for example if parents need to discuss changes in their arrangements for their children, because the children are older and/or because of changes in family circumstances. The summary should be signed and dated by the mediator but not by the participants, as it could then be construed as a formal agreement or contract. The mediator's address and contact details should be given at the end of the document.

A sample mediation summary is included at the end of this chapter.

---

[11]   See **11.10** above on BATNA, WATNA and MLATNA questions.

12.8   OPEN STATEMENT OF FINANCIAL INFORMATION (OFS)

In concluding mediation on all issues or solely on financial and property matters, there should be an Open Statement of Financial Information (OFS) setting out the financial information provided by participants, including a schedule of accompanying supporting documents. The legal status of the Open Financial Statement differs from that of the confidential summary. Whereas the confidential summary is not reportable to the court, except with the joint written consent of both parties or where the court requires disclosure, the Financial Statement and supporting documents are 'open', meaning that they may be referred to in financial relief proceedings or to support a consent order. This saves unnecessary duplication in gathering financial information both with lawyers and mediators. As the legal status of the two documents is different, the Open Financial Statement should not be stapled or otherwise attached to the confidential summary.

A common error is to mix the contents of the two different summaries. It follows from its 'open' status that it is vital that the Open Financial Statement contains no information that forms part of proposals for settlement reached between the participants. Similarly, but with less risk, it is also unhelpful to slavishly repeat all the financial information in the mediation summary. FMC Member Organisations have their own precedents. Usually, it is helpful to have short explanatory notes and an overview of the finances in tabular form (which can be transcribed from the flip-chart). The opening paragraphs of the Open Financial Statement should use approved standard wording, stating that both parties agreed in writing at the outset to provide full financial information. It should state that while certain supporting documents have been obtained (copies listed and attached), the mediator did not undertake to verify the information supplied. The Statement should also record whether both parties have confirmed that full disclosure has been made and the date on which they signed the Statement to this effect, in case there is delay between the signing of the Statement and seeking legal advice on it. They need to be aware that, having signed to confirm that full disclosure has been made, any subsequent agreement based on information provided in mediation could be set aside, if it emerged later that the information had been inaccurate or incomplete. In cases where mediation has ended inconclusively, the OFS should state that it records *the information disclosed so far*. Clients and their solicitors can then take matters forward to amplify the information gathered in mediation, without needing to go back to square one.

12.9   DRAFTING OF SUMMARIES AND CHARGES

Confidential mediation summaries should provide a clear summary of arrangements and proposed terms of settlement, reinforcing co-operation by emphasising mutual concerns and objectives. Relevant considerations should be explained concisely, impartially and positively, without conveying any opinion or value judgement on the part of the mediator. Summaries should be well drafted and presented to a high standard as they are the main product on which mediators' professional standards are judged by legal advisers, as well as by participants themselves. As in so many other areas of mediation, a balance has to be struck. The document should be neither too short (there should be at least some explanation as to how options were rejected or acceptable) nor too long (it is not necessary to provide a 'blow by blow account'.) Its style should be neither legalistic nor overly informal, but should convey the mediator's personal style while being clear and easily comprehensible to the participants. It is good practice to read the draft document through a number of times through different 'eyes' – for example, through the eyes of each participant (particularly the one who may feel they have the 'worse deal' in some respects), their children, the lawyers and the judge, and, of course, as the proof reader! It is better to avoid using the first person as this could give the mediator an intrusive presence. The passive tense is preferable ('Various options have been considered'). Headings should be used, to make the summary easier to follow.

The preparation of these documents takes time. When one or both participants are publicly funded, a claim for preparing the summary may be made to the LAA and paid at a standard rate. Charges to private clients need to be discussed and agreed with them in advance. Sometimes clients do not see a need for a summary and do not wish to pay for one. If the mediation file does not contain adequate case notes, a mediator could have difficulty constructing summaries at a later stage.

12.10   FORMALISING AGREEMENTS

The Ministry of Justice, the Mediation Task Force and mediators themselves have been giving more attention to encouraging people into mediation than to what happens at the end of the process. The Mapping Paths study[12] found that a large number of participants were frustrated by the fact that an agreement reached in mediation, unless approved by the court in a consent order, did not provide a legally binding and enforceable settlement:

> 'The lack of enforceability of a mediated agreement other than through court order was a source of dissatisfaction to the majority ... as well as a reason to choose court or other FDR (family dispute resolution process).'[13]

A separated husband complained that he and his wife had agreed a settlement in mediation nine years previously, but when they divorced, she refused to be bound by it. Another father said he and his ex-partner had agreed interim contact with a review in mediation six weeks later, at which point she denied him further contact and refused to return to mediation. He wished he had gone to court in the first place. The researchers found that while some parents welcomed the flexibility of their arrangements, most participants were anxious to know whether understandings and terms of agreement would be legally

---

[12]   Barlow, Hunter, Smithson and Ewing *Mapping Paths to Family Justice – Briefing Paper and Report on Key Findings* (Universities of Exeter and Kent, June 2014).
[13]   Ibid, p 18.

binding and, if necessary, enforceable. When there is little trust between them, separated couples may have little confidence that arrangements worked out in mediation will survive, once they leave the mediation room. Especially where there is a history of intractable conflict, co-operation may be fragile. Parents who do not trust each other look for an agreement that is more than a verbal understanding. Although some parents see the benefit of having flexible arrangements for their children and resist being tied down to a fixed schedule, others want contractual arrangements they can rely on.

Mediators encourage participants to take professional advice on their confidential mediation summary and consider whether, subject to this advice, it should be formalised in some way. The ambiguous term, 'mediated agreement', is cropping up more often and the legal status of mediation outcomes is becoming increasingly complex and controversial. Although there are major differences between civil and family law and procedure, family mediators need to heed significant judgements in civil cases such as *Brown v Rice*,[14] where the judge considered very carefully whether or not an agreement had been reached in mediation. At the risk of greatly oversimplifying an area of law that is evolving in the re-formed family justice system, four possible ways of formalising mediation outcomes are touched on as follows:

12.10.1 Financial consent orders in divorce proceedings

Proposals for a full and final settlement on financial and property matters in divorce proceedings may be taken to legal advisers – either privately or under the Help with Mediation scheme for those with public funding for mediation – for advice and assistance in seeking a consent order based on the settlement proposals worked out in mediation. The terms of settlement are sometimes fine-tuned by solicitors but do not often seem to be rejected or recast completely. Decisions about where children will live or have their main home may be implicit in the terms of a consent order covering property matters.

12.10.2 Open agreement by exchange of letters

The confidential mediation summary may be taken to legal advisers with a request to confirm arrangements in an 'open' exchange of letters. 'Open' correspondence between solicitors confirming arrangements can be made available to the court and may be taken into account by the judge. However, many parents do not have solicitors and a separation agreement prior to divorce, even where it is stated to be the intended basis for a full and final divorce settlement, does not provide any guarantee that its terms will be adhered to in the final divorce settlement, if it can be shown that one party's circumstances have changed significantly in the meantime.

---

[14] *Brown v Rice* [2007] EWHC 625 (Ch), see **1.12.3** above.

12.10.3   Consent orders on child arrangements

Since judges and magistrates follow the 'no order' principle of the Children Act, parents may feel frustrated if they reach agreements on child arrangements that they want to be legally binding on them both. They are encouraged to use the new parenting plan available from Cafcass,[15] which can be filled in online by one or both of them. This is an 'open' document that can be produced to the court: it is not legally privileged and 'without prejudice', like the confidential mediation summary. The Government has considered the role of the parenting plan in court proceedings and takes the view that: 'The welfare of the child must be the court's paramount consideration; it would therefore not be appropriate for the parenting plan to carry evidential weight in the court's final decision, as it cannot be assumed that such a plan would necessarily reflect the child's best interests. However, the new Child Arrangements Programme makes it clear that the parenting plan is a useful tool for the court to understand which issues have been agreed between parents and which remain in dispute.'[16] Parents may therefore produce their parenting plan to the court, but if the court follows the 'no order' principle, it would be difficult for parents to obtain a child arrangements order by consent: the only way to obtain an order would be through contested proceedings and at the discretion of the judge.

The position is not at all clear cut. Diligent readers who reach the final page (page 24) of the C100 Form will discover the following: 'If both parties agree, you can ask the court to endorse what you have agreed by issuing a consent order. The mediator can help you to decide whether your case is complicated and does in fact need the court to consider the situation and make an order.'[17] Also: 'If you are applying for an order by consent you should tick the box on page 1 and attach the draft order to this form'.[18] The C100 Form gives the impression that it is now possible to seek a consent order on child arrangements.[19] However, judges may be unwilling to make a consent order approving arrangements they have not considered and parents may be deterred by the court charge – currently £215, the same as for contested proceedings. It remains to be seen, therefore, whether a child consent order may be facilitated by attaching a parenting plan or by both parents waiving the privilege attaching to their confidential mediation summary and attaching this summary to their application for a child consent order.

12.10.4   Registering a parental agreement on child arrangements

It would be much simpler if at the end of mediation, parents who wish to record agreements concerning their children could take their parenting plan or confidential mediation summary counter-signed and dated by them both and,

---

[15]   See www.cafcass.gov.uk and 7.12 above.
[16]   Department for Education and Ministry of Justice *A Brighter Future for Family Justice* (August 2014), p 33.
[17]   C100 Form, p 24, para 29.
[18]   Ibid, p 22, para 6.
[19]   Saunders 'Mediation and Child Consent Orders' [2014] Fam Law 1187.

with joint consent, register it at the court in a simple administrative procedure. Mediated agreements over children have legal force in other countries, such as Sweden. The ability to register a mediated agreement on child arrangements would increase confidence and commitment to mediation even though, if the agreement broke down and court proceedings ensued, the court would review the situation and would not necessarily enforce the previous agreement. Registering a parental agreement would not imply the court's endorsement of arrangements any more than registering a birth implies that the parents have been approved as 'fit parents'. In the 1970s, under the so-called special procedure in divorce, petitioners with dependent children were required to attend a children's appointment with the judge, also known as the 'section 41 appointment'. For a divorce to be granted, the judge had to declare that the parents' arrangements for their children were satisfactory, or the best that could be devised in the circumstances. A study carried out at Bristol University found that the average time spent by the judge at the children's appointment was four and a half minutes.[20] In more recent years, judicial review of the 'statement of arrangements' for children within divorce proceedings became a paper exercise and was abandoned by the Children and Families Act 2014. Parents who reach agreed arrangements for their children in mediation spend much longer than four and a half minutes with a professionally qualified mediator (or possibly two mediators) who must at all times 'have special regard to the welfare of any children of the family'.[21]

Many parents work very hard in mediation and they need something tangible and reliable at the end. 'Fine words butter no parsnips', as the proverb says. If parents could go together to the court to register an agreement on child arrangements, as they do in registering the birth of a child together, this joint act of commitment to agreement and co-operation as parents would have concrete and symbolic value, despite not having evidential weight.

---

[20] Parkinson *Conciliation in Separation and Divorce* (Croom Helm, 1986), p 22.
[21] FMC Code of Practice 2010, 5.7.1.

12.11 SAMPLE MEDIATION SUMMARY

MEDIATORS UNITED LTD [LOGO]

FINAL CONFIDENTIAL SUMMARY OF PROPOSALS

(MEMORANDUM OF UNDERSTANDING)

HELEN JANE SIMPSON and IAN ROBERT SIMPSON

prepared by

Anna Makepeace

Family Mediator

This document is confidential and legally privileged

CONFIDENTIAL SUMMARY OF PROPOSALS FOR SETTLEMENT

(MEMORANDUM OF UNDERSTANDING)

Helen Jane Simpson (Helen) and Ian Robert Simpson (Ian) have been taking part in mediation with Anna Makepeace, accredited family mediator, United Mediators Ltd. Helen and Ian wish to agree their arrangements for their children and to reach a settlement on financial and property matters to be finalised in a consent order in their divorce proceedings.

This summary of the proposals which Helen and Ian have arrived at in mediation is 'without prejudice' and legally privileged. It does not record or create a binding agreement between them. It is intended to assist them in obtaining independent legal advice on their proposals for settlement, as the mediator has recommended them to do before they take steps to enter into an agreement, whether through solicitors or informally between themselves. Unless and until they decide to enter into a binding agreement, no such agreement exists between them.

Ian and Helen have also signed an Open Statement of their current financial circumstances. This Open Statement, dated ... sets out in more detail the information below and contains a schedule of supporting documents. Helen and Ian have confirmed their understanding that the financial information they have provided may be produced to the Court (unlike this confidential summary).

The necessity for full and complete disclosure has been explained to them and recorded in writing. This confidential summary may of course, be produced to legal advisers upon the basis that it is, and remains, a legally privileged document.

The mediation was carried out in accordance with the professional requirements and Code of Practice of the Family Mediation Council.

Background information

Helen Simpson, aged ... (born ...) and Ian Simpson, aged ... (born ...) married on ...

They lived together from ... to ... and separated on .... Helen continues to live at 38 Clashfield Road ... with the children. Ian is staying temporarily with his parents, Colin and Mary Simpson at ....

Ian and Helen have two children, Alice, aged 6, born ... and Thomas aged 4, born .... The children live with their mother and spend time with their father on a regular basis.

Helen is a qualified teacher. She is currently earning ... per month as a supply teacher. She intends returning to full-time teaching when Thomas starts school. Helen receives Child Benefit and Child Tax Credit.

Ian is an accountant employed by .... His current salary is ... per annum (gross/net).

All the family are in good health.

Helen and Ian attended separate assessment meetings, followed by three mediation meetings on [...], [...] and [...].

Helen qualified for publicly funded mediation. Ian is paying privately. They have taken preliminary legal advice. Helen's parents are contributing to the cost of Helen consulting a solicitor privately.

The issues that Helen and Ian wished to resolve through coming to mediation were:

- The ending of the marriage in divorce proceedings initiated by Helen.
- Arrangements for Alice and Thomas.
- The family home.
- Proposals for a full and final settlement on financial and property matters.
- Child maintenance.
- Any other matters arising.

1. The ending of the marriage in divorce

Ian and Helen accept that their marriage has broken down irretrievably. They have come to this decision over a period of time and after taking part in counselling for several months. Ian has stated that he is willing to accept a divorce petition to be filed by Helen. There has been some discussion in the mediation of divorce procedure and of the 'facts' to be relied on by Helen in the divorce petition. Helen will request her solicitor to send the draft petition to Ian's solicitor to be forwarded to Ian so that he has the opportunity to consider it and request an amendment if necessary of any particular clause. Ian is willing to share the costs of filing the divorce petition.

2. Arrangements for Alice and Thomas

Both parents understand that they have continuing joint parental responsibility for their children, Alice and Thomas. They recognise the importance of the children's continuing relationship with them both.

Alice and Thomas live with their mother and spend time with their father on a regular basis. Interim arrangements for the children were summarised in the Interim Mediation Summary dated …. These arrangements are working well. When Ian is settled in his new home, there are plans for the children to spend alternate weekends with him, staying on Saturday night and possibly Friday and/or Sunday nights as well, depending on Ian's work commitments. The children will also spend part of each school holiday with their father. Both parents think it is better for Ian to come into the family home briefly when he collects the children and when he brings them back, as this makes the hand-overs easier for them.

Both parents have also considered in mediation how they will share major decisions concerning the children's health, education and upbringing. They are very concerned to co-operate as much as possible so that the children do not experience conflicts of loyalty. They have assured each other that they will not criticise each other or each other's family in front of the children. They will explain new arrangements to the children together and will continue to give them reassurance. If circumstances change so that different arrangements are needed, they expect to be able to work them out together. If, however, they are unable to agree matters on their own, Helen and Ian have said that they would seek further mediation. Both parents feel that the children are very close to them both and that both children are able to express their feelings, even though they are very young. In view of their ages and good communication in the family, it was felt that there was no need for the children to see a child counsellor or be involved directly in the mediation. Neither do they see the need to apply to the Court for a Child Arrangements Order.

Birthdays, Christmas and special events: Ian and Helen feel that the children will benefit from celebrating the children's birthdays together as a family, without however giving the children any misleading impression that their parents are getting back together. Helen and Ian have not yet worked out arrangements for Christmas and the New Year, but they expect to be able to do so between themselves.

3. Property and housing

Helen and Ian bought their home at 38 Clashfield Road in joint names in [...] for £[...] with a repayment mortgage of £[...]. It is a four-bedroom property and based on three recent valuations ranging from £[...] to [...], they decided to take the value as £[...] for their negotiations. There is a repayment mortgage with a balance of around £[...], leaving equity of £[...]. Ian has provided Helen with a copy of the latest mortgage statement.

Financial and property issues have been discussed in considerable detail. Ian and Helen have sought independent legal advice on various aspects during mediation. Various options have been considered, including the possibility of Helen remaining in the family home with the children. Having considered the financial cost of maintaining the family home and Ian's need for a home where the children can come to stay with him, they are in favour of selling the family home so that they can each buy a smaller property.

Ian and Helen wish to buy properties in the same area so that the children can move easily between them and so that there will be no need for Alice to change schools. Helen has looked at properties and expects to be able to buy a property in the region of £.... She has enquired about her borrowing capacity and has ascertained that she can raise a mortgage of ... and manage monthly payments of ... Ian has also looked at properties and says that he can buy a property in a similar price range. He has made enquiries about borrowing and has established that he can raise a mortgage of £....

The net proceeds of sale of 38 Clashfield Road are estimated at £ . . ., after deduction of costs of sale. Subject to their proposals on all issues, it is proposed that Helen should receive 65% of the net proceeds and that the balance of 35% should go to Ian.

At the third mediation meeting on ... Ian and Helen reported that a friend has made them an offer of £... for the family home, subject to survey. If this offer is confirmed, they would like to accept it. There will then be some urgency to reach a settlement so that Helen and Ian can proceed with the sale and the purchase of their new homes. Conveyancing arrangements will need to be synchronised.

4. Other assets

Building Society accounts

Helen and Ian propose that the balance of £... in the Halifax Building Society account and the balance of £... in the Leeds Permanent Building Society account should be split equally between them. They have said that they will not make further withdrawals from these accounts pending a settlement being reached.

Natwest and Barclays Bank accounts

These are current accounts which are not regarded as relevant assets for division as the balances fluctuate. Ian and Helen consider that Ian should keep his current account with NatWest and that Helen should keep her current account with Barclays.

British Telecom shares

Ian is willing for Helen to keep the BT shares registered in her name. The shares are currently valued at £....

Life assurances

There are two life assurance policies which are merely term assurances with no current value. They are in Ian's name and Ian intends to continue paying into both of them.

5. Pensions

Ian has a pension with Scottish Equitable with a CTV of £[...]. Since [...] Helen has contributed £[...] to a pension with [...] with a CTV of .... They have provided each other with copies of both pension statements to take to their solicitors, together with any other pension details.

Helen and Ian propose that they should each maintain their own pension arrangements (see details attached to Financial Summary). Although Ian has the larger pension fund, these are relatively small amounts, and since it is proposed that Helen should receive 65% of the net proceeds of sale of the family home, she has stated that she is not inclined to make an application in respect of Ian's pension. Ian and Helen are therefore proposing that all pension rights and claims between them should be waived in the divorce proceedings. The mediator has encouraged them however to seek professional advice from a pensions expert or Joint Financial Adviser.

6. Cars

Ian and Helen envisage Ian retaining the Ford Fiesta and Helen retaining the Renault. They have a joint loan of £[...] for their two cars and joint debts on two credit cards (£[...] on Helen's card and £[...] on Ian's card) making a total of £[...]. Helen and Ian wish to share these debts equally and to clear them by agreement as part of their settlement.

7. Child maintenance

Ian is currently paying Helen £... on the 26th day of each month by standing order, in addition to paying the main outgoings on the family home (see Interim Summary dated ...). Ian is willing to pay £... per month to Helen for the children from the 26th day of the month in which Helen moves into her new home.

Helen does not intend to apply to the Child Maintenance Service but she has checked online how much Ian might be required to pay. She is satisfied that Ian is, and will be, paying a higher level of child maintenance than the CMS would be likely to require. Ian and Helen acknowledge that maintenance for the children must be reviewed on a regular basis.

8. Spousal maintenance

Helen does not wish to seek maintenance from Ian for herself. She intends returning to full-time work as a teacher in ... months' time, when Thomas starts school. Meanwhile, Ian is willing to contribute to the cost of additional and special items for the children.

9. Jewellery

Ian wishes Helen to keep the jewellery which she inherited from her grandmother. It is valued at £... for insurance purposes.

10. Contents of the home

Helen and Ian expect to agree the division of house contents informally between themselves. When Helen has bought her new property, she will arrange with Ian for him to collect some furniture and possessions from the family home including the following:

- The smaller leather sofa.
- Stereo and a TV.
- Garden furniture.

- A bookcase and some books.
- Some other items from the attic.

11. Inheritance

Neither Helen nor Ian has a prospect of receiving an inheritance in the foreseeable future.

12. Wills

When they divorce, Ian and Helen will need to draw up fresh Wills to be effective after their divorce. They will need their lawyers' advice as to any interim arrangements that should be put in place.

13. Tax, tax credits and benefits

There do not appear to be any significant tax or welfare benefits implications in these proposals, but Helen and Ian are encouraged to check this with their advisers. Helen has informed the Tax Credit Office of the date of their separation and her Child Tax Credit has been adjusted accordingly.

14. Summary of proposed division of capital (see s 5 on pensions)

	Helen	Ian
Net proceeds of sale of 38 Clashfield Rd.		
Halifax account		
Leeds account		
BT shares		
Cars		
Jewellery		
Totals		

15. Next steps and time-scale

Helen and Ian intend to consult their solicitors as soon as possible regarding their divorce and the intended sale of the family home, so that the sale can proceed without delay.

Ian and Helen will also take advice with regard to finalising their settlement in a Consent Order in divorce proceedings, based on the arrangements they have worked out together in mediation. Subject to the legal advice she receives, Helen will ask her solicitor to draw up a Consent Order incorporating their proposals, before the Decree Absolute is applied for, to be sent to Ian's solicitor for Ian's approval and signature.

Both parents have shown great commitment to working out arrangements for their children, Alice and Thomas. They have emphasised throughout their strong wish to maintain their co-operation and to take as full account as possible of their children's needs and feelings.

No further mediation meetings have been arranged, but Ian and Helen are very welcome to return to mediation if they should encounter any further difficulty.

Dated: _____

Signed: _____

Anna Makepeace

Family Mediator

Mediators United Ltd

CHAPTER 13

RESEARCH ON FAMILY MEDIATION

'Can you know what is emerging, yet keep your peace while others discover it
for themselves?
You can do this if you remain unbiased, clear and down to earth.'[1]

'And the end of all our exploring
Will be to arrive where we started
And know the place for the first time.'[2]

CONTENTS

13.1 EVALUATING MEDIATION

Mediation is seen as a positive means of resolving conflict and improving communication, to the benefit of participants and their children. People are therefore expected to take a good dose of mediation before following the signpost marked 'To the Court'. When Alice fell down the rabbit-hole (Lewis Carroll, *Alice's Adventures in Wonderland*), she came upon a table with a small bottle on it:

---

[1]   Lao Tzu *Tao Te Ching*.
[2]   T S Eliot *Four Quartets – Little Gidding* (Faber, 1959), p 59.

'and tied round the neck of the bottle was a paper label with the words 'DRINK ME' beautifully printed on it in large letters. It was all very well to say 'Drink Me', but wise little Alice was not going to do **that** in a hurry. 'No, I'll look first', she said, 'and see whether it's marked 'poison' or not'... However, the bottle was not marked 'poison', so Alice ventured to taste it.'[3]

Information about mediation explains the main principles, but it does not list all the ingredients. Like Alice, once people feel satisfied that mediation is not a dangerous remedy, many of them decide to accept it without knowing its exact ingredients. As outlined in Chapter 2, family mediation offers various mixtures of ingredients, all carrying the same label. Mediators bring different professional backgrounds and styles of working. Claims about mediation's benefits need to be examined and substantiated to justify its continuing role in the family justice system. There may be unrealistic expectations of what mediation can achieve, and for whom. Social scientists cut through the rhetoric of mediation in examining practice and outcomes. But this is no simple task. Lines of enquiry do not always produce reliable results. Investigators do not always get the answers they were hoping for, as the schools inspector found when he asked a small boy in a primary school how many sheep he could see in the field and got the answer 'All o' them'.

Research literature on family mediation has accumulated over several decades, growing in volume and sophistication. The results need to be interpreted with caution, however. Comparability across studies is low, because research has been undertaken with disparate client groups using different types of mediation process over varying periods of time. Irving and Benjamin[4] reviewed fifty research studies on family mediation and found that:

> 'although two services might look the same on paper, they may provide very different services to different client groups using very different service models and differently trained mediators ....'

A recent study commissioned by the Ministry of Justice of mediators' practice at information and assessment meetings found similar variations in their approach.[5] As reported in Chapter 3,[6] the researchers found that assessments of the suitability of mediation varied according to mediators' views as to what mediation is able to achieve, the type of help needed and commercial pressures resulting from the reduction in solicitor referrals. Three different 'types' of mediator were described as 'purists', 'realists' and 'optimists'.

Interpretations of findings are complicated further if experience and outcomes from small samples in different settings are generalised to mediation as a whole.

---

3   Carroll *Alice's Adventures in Wonderland* (First published 1865, Folio 1961), p 7.
4   Irving and Benjamin 'Research in Family Mediation – an Integrative Review' in Irving and Benjamin (eds) *Family Mediation – Contemporary Issues* (Sage, 1995), p 408.
5   Bloch, McLeod and Tooms *Mediation Information and Assessment Meetings (MIAMs) and mediation in private law disputes – Qualitative research findings* (Ministry of Justice Analytical Series, 2014).
6   See **3.2** above.

In all forms of dispute resolution, there are variations in the timing of interventions, the types and level of dispute referred to dispute resolution processes and the approaches used by practitioners. A criticism levelled at some studies is that they lacked objectivity because the researchers were mediators themselves. The methodology and findings were therefore liable be skewed by eagerness to demonstrate the benefits of mediation. Maintaining impartiality presents challenges for mediators. Researchers, too, need to demonstrate that they do not have a bias either towards or against mediation. Sometimes there seems be a wish to deflate confidence in mediation, rather than present the evidence objectively. For example, Dingwall's[7] assertion that 'mediation fared little better in the Davis evaluation' overlooked findings in the Davis study[8] reported below. Dingwall noted low conversion rates from assessment meetings to mediation, but mediation is not always suitable and 'non-conversions' include couples who decide to work things out between themselves, without needing further help from mediators or lawyers. Mediators tend to be accused of over-egging the mediation cake, but a researcher might cut into one slice of a fruitcake and analyse it as though it were the whole cake.

13.2   THE AIM OF MEDIATION – SETTLING DISPUTES OR RESOLVING CONFLICT?

As Deutsch[9] pointed out, conflict is not always open and direct. Whereas a dispute is overt, conflict may be suppressed or channelled into other areas. The words 'conflict' and 'dispute' tend to be used interchangeably, but they are not synonymous. Felstiner and colleagues[10] identified three stages in the evolution of a dispute: (1) the 'naming' stage when a grievance is perceived and identified; (2) the 'blaming' stage when responsibility for the grievance is attributed to another person or group; and (3) the 'claiming' stage in which a remedy is sought to rectify or compensate for the grievance. In settling a dispute, the disputants may accept terms that involve a compromise or concessions. A settlement may be reached because both sides recognise it to be necessary, but their attitudes to each other may remain antagonistic and they may have no need for further communication with each other.

Mediation aims to help participants to reach consensual decisions and settle disputes. It may also help them to resolve conflict. But it is unrealistic to expect a brief process to resolve the deep anger and pain of a broken relationship. It can take years for a partner who feels abandoned and betrayed to come to terms emotionally with separation and divorce. Some never do so. Mediation does not offer counselling or psychotherapy. Yet the process of working towards a settlement on certain issues enables some couples to hear each other,

---

7   Dingwall 'Divorce mediation: should we change our mind?' (2010) 32 *Journal of Social Welfare & Family Law* 109.

8   Davis et al *Monitoring Publicly Funded Family Mediation – Report to the Legal Services Commission* (Legal Services Commission, 2000).

9   Deutsch *The Resolution of Conflict* (Yale University Press, 1973).

10 Felstiner, Abel and Sarat 'The Emergence and Transformation of Disputes' (1980–81) 15 *Law and Society Review* no 3.

perhaps for the first time. Some couples, in hearing and understanding each other, find that their perceptions and attitudes alter a great deal. At one end of the spectrum, a settlement can be reached without changing attitudes and without resolving anger. At the other end, some couples seem to experience a kind of catharsis in which they move from angry recriminations to a different relationship built on co-operation and renewed trust. One of the differences, therefore, between family mediators and the theories they follow is whether they aim only to settle disputes by reaching a concrete agreement or whether they also seek to help participants to resolve the psychological and emotional conflicts that underlie their disputes. At each end of the scale, practice diverges widely, yet these different aims are not necessarily incompatible. Many mediators blend them in some way. If agreement is seen as the opposite of dispute, this fails to recognise that there is a continuum between conflict and co-operation. Disputants are not only at different points on the continuum but may move along it in either direction at different points in time. In cases where mediation does not lead to agreement, mediation has not necessarily 'failed': it may have opened a door to communication that is more important than getting an agreement. A study by the Centre for Research on the Child and Family[11] found that:

> 'existing legal interventions have limited capacity to facilitate contact or reverse a downward spiral in contact relationships. ... Resources should be directed towards more creative work to improve parental and parent-child relationships rather than repeated attempts at imposing a solution.'

One of many problems in evaluating mediation is deciding the criteria to be used and applying 'technically robust' indicators. Researchers face methodological difficulties in obtaining representative samples of clients and establishing a control group with whom valid comparisons can be made. Research studies based on client groups of varying sizes, with or without control groups, have been conducted on different aspects including:

- the take-up of mediation and settlement rates;
- follow-up studies of consumer experience and satisfaction;
- follow-up to see whether mediated agreements last over time;
- analysis of mediators' methods and techniques;
- comparison of mediation costs with legal costs;
- comparisons between mediators and lawyers;
- consideration of what makes one mediator more effective than another.

In the 1980s, researchers evaluated mediation mainly in terms of settlement rates and client satisfaction. More attention is now given to outcomes over longer periods of time and to different elements of the mediator's role – the input as well as the outcome. Researchers recommend that mediation should 'consider a longer-term horizon for adults rather than concentrating on

---

[11] Trinder, Beek Connolly *Making contact: How parents and children negotiate and experience contact after divorce* (2002) Joseph Rowntree Foundation Findings 092, p 4.

short-term dispute resolution'.[12] Mediators face many challenges if they are expected not only to settle disputes but also to improve relationships between separated parents and between children and their parents.

13.3 EXPERIENCE OF IN-COURT CONCILIATION

Before considering studies of the mediation process and participants' experiences of mediation, it may be useful to look at experience and outcomes of in-court conciliation. The Private Law Programme introduced in 2004 encouraged early dispute resolution for parents involved in proceedings relating to children. This Programme was found to be very successful in enabling the majority of disputes to be settled by consent at the First Dispute Resolution Hearing (FDRH). The amount of time spent by Cafcass on in-court conciliation increased, while the number of reports reduced.[13] The Revised Private Law Programme implemented by the Practice Direction of 1 April 2010 built on the earlier programme and took account of recent developments in law and practice. Hunt[14] found evidence from a number of studies that it is now relatively unusual for a family case to end in a fully contested hearing. In-court conciliation has been found very effective in avoiding further litigation. 72% of parents in Trinder's study[15] reached full (45%) or partial agreement (27%) and 62% of these parents said they were satisfied with their agreements. Although many of these agreements did not last, a quarter of them were renegotiated by the parents concerned, without further professional intervention. Only a minority of parents re-litigated to arrive at a new arrangement. Overall, only 21% of agreements were judged to have failed. The main benefit reported by parents was:

> 'having a structured, managed, and fair opportunity to establish communication and reach agreement. Other themes were the value of having an unbiased person dedicated to achieving a workable set of agreed arrangements and the role of conciliation in encouraging the parties to focus on the child's interests.'[16]

58% of parents had felt anxious, however, before the conciliation meeting and 61% said the meeting had been tense and unpleasant. Resident parents were significantly more likely than non-resident to report feeling under pressure, both from the conciliator and from their ex-partner. There were twice as many 'father win, mother lose' cases as vice versa (35% compared to 16%). Resident parents reported less choice about entering the process, more anxiety beforehand and more tension in the meeting. They felt more dissatisfied with the amount of time available, less able to say all they wanted to and less likely to see the Cafcass officer and District Judge as helpful. They were more likely to

---

12 Walker and Hornick *Communication in Marriage and Divorce* (The BT Forum, 1996), p 65.
13 Cafcass Annual Report 2006–2007.
14 Hunt *Parental Perspectives on the Family Justice System in England and Wales: a review of research* (Report for the Family Justice Council, December 2009).
15 Trinder, Connolly, Kellett, Notley and Swift 'Making contact happen or making contact work? The process and outcomes of in-court conciliation' (2006) *DCA Research Series* 3/06.
16 Ibid, p 83.

feel their concerns were not understood, dismissed or marginalised and to feel pressurised into agreement by their ex-partner. 40% of women expressed feelings of anxiety and worries about intimidation, increasing their sense of confrontation and being at risk. Parents who had sat next to their ex-partner had felt uncomfortable. Mantle[17] suggests a triangular arrangement might be more acceptable. This arrangement is normally used in out-of-court mediation.[18] Perry and Rainey[19] reported that some parents felt obliged to accept arrangements that they did not feel were appropriate or which fell far short of what they wanted. Some of them were disconcerted that the judge seemed more focused on getting them to find a solution themselves than on adjudicating for them and they were not happy with this approach. Fathers, in particular:

'became angry when the courts seemed to imply that parents themselves should be able to find a solution. It was as if they did not go to court to be told to try harder themselves; rather they went to court to have the right solution imposed upon the recalcitrant spouse.'[20]

Where children themselves were concerned, 61% of parents in Trinder's study[21] said that the session had focused on children's needs, but of those who reached agreement, less than half (48%) thought the agreement was in their child's best interests. At the time the studies were undertaken, 'it was rare for children to take part in conciliation directly. Hence the child's views would typically be presented through one or both parents'.[22]

Conciliation is a brief intervention. It may consist of a single meeting lasting not more than an hour and often less. While most parents seem to accept the limited time, a substantial minority would have preferred to have more time with the conciliator.[23] A two-year follow-up study found that:[24]

'hammering out a deal and getting contact going does not in itself repair relationships or address the underlying or embedded conflict that probably gave rise to the contact dispute in the first place.'

---

[17] Mantle *A consumer survey of agreements reached in county court dispute resolution (mediation)* (Essex Probation Occasional Paper 2, 2001).
[18] See Chapter 4, s 3.
[19] Perry and Rainey *Supervised, supported and indirect contact: orders and their implications* (Report to the Nuffield Foundation, University of Wales, Swansea, 2006).
[20] Smart, May, Wade and Furness *Residence and Contact Disputes in Court* (Dept of Constitutional Affairs, London, 2005), Vol 2; quoted in Hunt *Parental Perspectives on the Family Justice System in England and Wales: a review of research* (Report for the Family Justice Council, December 2009), p 27.
[21] Trinder, Connolly, Kellett, Notley and Swift 'Making Contact happen or making contact work? The process and outcomes of in-court conciliation' (2006) *DCA Research Series 3/06*.
[22] Ibid, p 89.
[23] Ibid.
[24] Trinder 'Conciliation, the Private Law Programme and Children's Well-being' [2008] Fam Law 338 at 341.

Hunt[25] reported that 'parents find the whole experience of going to court traumatic and alienating' and that:

> 'court proceedings may be effective in restoring contact and increasing the extent of contact [but] do not appear ... to improve parental relationships and therefore their capacity to manage post-separation parenting.'[26]

A study of parents' experience of relocation disputes found that, whether they won or lost their case, parents described the court process as 'horrible ... emotionally distressing ... probably one of the worst days of my life'.[27]

13.4 RESEARCH ON THE FAMILY MEDIATION PILOT PROJECT 1996–2000

Before Part III of the Family Law Act 1996 was implemented nationally, the Legal Services Commission funded a four-year research study on publicly funded family mediation.[28] Although it was undertaken during the Family Mediation Pilot Project when many mediators were only just beginning to mediate on all issues, this research is the only significant, large-scale study of mediation prior to 2014. The researchers analysed 4,593 case monitoring forms supplied by 33 mediation providers. These included mediation 'intakes meetings' attended by one party only. The main study focused on data from five services providing all-issues mediation (102 cases) and child-focused mediation (298 cases). 70% of the referrals to mediation came from lawyers, 18% were self-referred and 12% were court-referred. 148 mediations sessions were recorded with clients' permission and follow-up interviews were conducted with 47 clients. Of the parents who took part in mediation in child-related issues, 82% considered the mediator had been impartial, 70% had found mediation either very or fairly helpful and 78% thought the mediator had understood their situation either very well (51%) or fairly well (27%). 71% said they would recommend mediation to others in a similar situation. Experience of mediation on financial matters was also positive. Most participants thought it had been helpful and said they would recommend it to others experiencing similar problems. The researchers concluded that mediation had its own distinctive and positive features and should be supported as a separate system running in parallel to the court system. Their findings supported their earlier recommendations that 'prior to legal aid being granted, the possibility of reaching agreement ... should be fully explored'.[29]

---

[25] Hunt *Parental Perspectives on the Family Justice System in England and Wales: a review of research* (Report for the Family Justice Council, December 2009), p 121.

[26] Ibid, p 118.

[27] George and Bader 'Parents' experience of relocation disputes' [2014] Fam Law 836.

[28] Davis et al *Monitoring Publicly Funded Family Mediation – Report to the Legal Services Commission* (Legal Services Commission, 2000).

[29] Davis and Lees *A Study of Conciliation – its Impact on Legal Aid Costs and Place in the Resolution of Disputes arising out of Divorce* (Dept of Social Administration, University of Bristol, 1981), p 164.

This study also compared clients' satisfaction with mediators with their satisfaction with lawyers. Lawyers are partisan, even if they aim to settle cases wherever possible. Individuals going through separation and divorce need legal advice and may look for partisan support. Mediators do not provide advice or partisan support. They mediate with both partners, generally face-to-face, whereas lawyers normally have separate meetings with their own client and, unless they are collaborative lawyers, may negotiate at arm's length with 'the other side'. The research on the Family Mediation Pilot Project[30] found that solicitors scored more highly than mediators on most measures of approval, but acknowledged that they might not have been studying 'directly comparable populations'. Listening to and advising one's client, one-to-one, is very different from mediating between two parties who are in dispute with each other. The roles of lawyers and mediators are complementary: neither is a substitute for the other. Well-organised combinations of mediation and legal advice are likely to enhance settlements and reduce costs. Research studies both in England and Australia[31] recognise that it is unrealistic to expect mediators to replace lawyers and courts. A nexus of paths is needed, with frequent intersections between them leading to different settlement processes that can be used in different ways at different points in time.

A report by the National Audit Office in 2007 stated that 42% of those who had not been referred to mediation said that they would have accepted it, had they known about it. The report concluded that: 'Confrontation in court cannot always be avoided, but the alternative of mediation should be pursued wherever possible – to the benefit of disputing individuals and the taxpayer'.[32] Three years later, the Evaluation Report of the In-Court Mediation Trial[33] found that 73% of parties who were referred to an information and assessment meeting by the court accepted the offer of mediation. In 43% of cases, they had not previously considered mediation. Assessment by a mediator who listens, asks questions and observes reactions is likely to be more thorough than a purely legal triage. When each party is seen separately prior to any mediation, the composite picture that emerges from separate assessments with each of them is likely to have more depth and detail than information given by one of them to a legal advisor, or a routine check by Cafcass.

13.5   DO MEDIATORS SETTLE JUST THE EASY CASES?

It may be assumed that couples who accept mediation at the pre-court stage are intrinsically more co-operative than those who go to court. It has therefore been argued that mediators settle easy cases that are likely to settle anyway. Davis and Roberts[34] pointed out, however, that:

---

[30]   Davis, Finch, Fitzgerald 'Mediation and Legal Services – The Client Speaks [2001] Fam Law 110–114, p 113.

[31]   Rhoades 'Revising Australia's parenting laws' (2010) *Child and Family Law Quarterly* 172.

[32]   National Audit Office Review of Legal Aid and Mediation for people involved in family breakdown (March 2007).

[33]   Legal Services Commission (August 2010), 5.

[34]   Davis and Roberts *Access to Agreement* (Open University Press, 1988).

'it might be thought that the parents' decision to take their quarrel to a mediation agency is itself indicative of a willingness to negotiate. But this is not always the case.'

To find out whether parental and child-parent relationships are improved by mediation, it is necessary to compare levels of conflict and co-operation pre-mediation with post-mediation levels. Pearson and Thoennes undertook a large-scale study[35] of court-referred mediation in contested child custody cases to test the hypothesis that parents who reach agreement through mediation are intrinsically more co-operative than those who seek a court decision. Parents were randomly assigned to two groups. The first group was referred to mediation, while the second group was not referred. A third group was formed of couples who went to court having refused the offer of mediation. A conflict scale was used to control for pre-existing characteristics, including the level and duration of dispute. In all three groups there were couples who described their ability to co-operate with each other as 'just about impossible'. Outcomes were then studied in all three categories. Even at the top end of the conflict scale, those who took part in mediation were found to have become more co-operative, compared with those who did not go to mediation. In the third follow-up interview, over 60% of those who reached agreement reported some co-operation with their former partner, twice the rate of co-operation (30%) among those who had not tried mediation. A number of research studies have found that high initial levels of anger and conflict do not present insuperable barriers to reaching agreement through mediation.[36] Kelly et al[37] compared the experience of divorcing couples who used mediation with those who litigated. Co-operation increased significantly in the mediation group, but there was a high drop out rate, explained primarily as due to cost and in some cases to feeling overwhelmed. Withdrawal from mediation did not necessarily mean that participants were unhappy with the process. Half of those who withdrew were found to be either neutral or satisfied. Many had reached some basis for agreement, while some had withdrawn for reasons that had little or nothing to do with mediation. Citing drop out from mediation as evidence of 'failed mediation' would therefore be an over-simplification.

13.6 SATISFACTION WITH MEDIATION AND DISPUTE RESOLUTION

Irving and Benjamin's survey[38] of research on family mediation in different jurisdictions found in the studies they looked at that 60–80% of mediation

---

35 Pearson and Thoennes 'Divorce Mediation Research Results' in Folberg and Milne (eds) *Divorce Mediation – Theory and Practice* (Guilford Press, 1988), pp 429–452.

36 Depner, Cannata and Ricci Client evaluations of mediation services (1994) 32(3) *Family and Conciliation Courts Review* 306–325; Kelly and Duryee 'Women's and men's views of mediation in voluntary and mandatory settings' (1992) 30(1) *Family and Conciliation Courts Review* 43–49.

37 Kelly 'A Decade of Divorce Mediation Research' (1996) 34 *Family and Conciliation Courts Review* 373–385.

38 Irving and Benjamin 'Research in Family Mediation – an Integrative Review' in Irving and Benjamin (eds) *Family Mediation – Contemporary Issues* (Sage, 1995).

participants reported high levels of satisfaction with the mediation process and its outcome. More recently (as mentioned in Chapter 1), the Mapping Paths to Family Justice study[39] reported on the usage, experience and outcomes of three out-of-court dispute resolution processes: lawyer negotiation, collaborative law and mediation. These three client groups are not strictly comparable and there are significant differences in process. People on low incomes and welfare benefits may see mediation as their only option, since legal aid is available for mediation but not for collaborative law and only to a very limited extent for lawyer negotiation. Around two thirds of those who had used solicitor negotiation (44 respondents) were satisfied with the process and welcomed the support it offered them at a very stressful time in their lives. There were common criticisms, however, of delay and higher than expected costs, with some clients complaining that correspondence between solicitors had exacerbated conflict and was sometimes used tactically to cause delay. Satisfaction among users of collaborative law, both with the process and with the outcome, was predominantly high, but it should be borne in mind that there were only eight respondents in this group. Almost three quarters of the sample of mediation users (56 respondents) said they were satisfied with the process of mediation. They appreciated the structure that mediation provided for:

> 'a managed discussion both in terms of an agenda outlined at the start, and in terms of the mediator keeping the parties on track in working towards solutions. They also appreciated the fact that agreements made in the session were written down so could not be forgotten. Mediation was viewed as quicker and cheaper compared to the alternatives. Some participants welcomed it as an amicable way of resolving a dispute, though this was not universal. Helpful features that were mentioned included opening up communication, the suggestion of new angles, overcoming emotional stalemates and taking even small steps forward, (for instance in getting contact re-started).'[40]

There were also areas where the researchers made recommendations to improve mediation practice, including:

- Avoid the impression of alignment with one party before the first joint session.

  The second party who comes to an assessment meeting knowing the mediator has already met with the other party may suspect that the mediator is already biased towards the first one. As the researchers point out, it is extremely important for mediators to demonstrate their impartiality, emphasising that as a mediator they are used to hearing different sides of the story and do not form judgements or opinions as to who may be right or wrong, but rather seek to understand each participant's concerns and help them both equally. Some services use a different mediator to carry out the assessment meeting from the one who will undertake the mediation. Client feedback in one study (reported verbally) was strongly in favour of keeping the same mediator throughout.

---

[39] Barlow, Hunter, Smithson and Ewing *Mapping Paths to Family Justice – Briefing Paper and Report on Key Findings* (Universities of Exeter and Kent, June 2014).
[40] Ibid, p 11.

Otherwise, the mediator has to rely on information and impressions from the 'intake' gained second-hand, while clients have to start afresh with another stranger.

• Anticipate and respond to parties' need for legal advice in encouraging them to obtain legal advice before commencing mediation. However, Help with Mediation is not available before commencing mediation and many separated parents, especially women, cannot afford to pay for legal advice. Mediation clients expressed dissatisfaction over the lack of legal advice and non-enforceability of mediation outcomes:

> 'Some found the lack of legal context difficult, either in having a counsellor mediator who was not aware of all the legal implications, or simply in the fact that the mediator could not give legal advice when the party felt the need for it. A number of people commented that the main problem for them had been the non-enforceability of agreements reached during the sessions. Some felt that mediation was never going to work, but they had to attempt it for legal aid reasons, or to show willingness with the aim of convincing their ex-partner, solicitors or judges in future about their seriousness in terms of child issues.'[41]

Possible ways of converting mediation outcomes into legally binding agreements and strengthening both parties' commitment to maintaining their arrangements were considered briefly in the previous chapter (**12.10**). The researchers also recommended that there should be greater opportunities for children's voices to be heard in mediation (see Chapter 8 above on child-inclusive mediation).

13.7 RECOMMENDATIONS FOR IMPROVEMENTS IN MEDIATION PRACTICE IN RELATION TO DOMESTIC ABUSE AND POWER IMBALANCES

A frequently expressed source of dissatisfaction with mediation in the Mapping Paths study related to inadequate screening for domestic abuse and failure to address power imbalances. There were complaints about lack of impartiality when power imbalances or high conflict were not managed adequately by the mediator. The researchers recommended more frequent use of gender-balanced co-mediation to address concerns about impartiality. Some participants said they had found mediation very stressful and felt they had been pressured into accepting it. There were a number of reports that domestic abuse had been overlooked in some cases by the mediator or not considered sufficiently carefully:

> 'Whilst practitioners in our sample were all aware of and took seriously the requirement to screen, we found a number of cases (13) in our party sample where on the party's account, effective screening was sidestepped, and a further number

---

[41] Ibid, p 11.

of cases where mediation was recommended by solicitors, parties were referred to mediation by a judge or accepted by mediators where there had been violence.'[42]

The researchers recommended more careful screening for domestic abuse and high levels of conflict.

Research both in the UK and the United States has found that even in the court system abused women did not feel adequately protected.[43] Girdner[44] and Neumann[45] have argued for 'feminist informed' models of mediation that address the needs and rights of those experiencing and/or fearing violence and abuse. An Australian study[46] found that women who had suffered domestic violence and abuse generally experienced less pre-mediation anxiety, more positive experience of the mediation process and a higher level of satisfaction with agreements where the woman:

- had been subject to emotional abuse, one-off physical threats, or threats only;

- had been separated from their ex-partner for a considerable time;

- had received personal counselling (as opposed to relationship counselling);

- reported that she no longer felt intimidated by her ex-partner; and

- felt confident in her legal advice and knew what she could reasonably expect from the settlement;

and where mediators:

- asked specific questions about violence and abuse, including non-physical abuse;

- offered specific guidance in considering the possible impact of violence and abuse on the mediation process;

- offered separate time with the mediator before, during and after sessions;

- worked as a gender-balanced co-mediation team;

- demonstrated that they understood fears and concerns both within and outside the mediation session by implementing specific strategies to deal with these concerns;

- demonstrated that they could control abusive behaviour within the session; and

---

[42]   Ibid, p 8.

[43]   Corcoran and Melamed 'From coercion to empowerment: spousal abuse and mediation' (1990) 7(4) *Mediation Quarterly* 303–316; Erickson and McKnight 'Mediating spousal abuse divorces' (1990) 7(4) *Mediation Quarterly* 377–388; Hunt *Parental Perspectives on the Family Justice System in England and Wales: a review of research* (Report for the Family Justice Council, December 2009).

[44]   Girdner 'Mediation triage: screening for spouse abuse in divorce mediation' (1990) 7(4) *Mediation Quarterly* 365.

[45]   Neumann 'How mediation can effectively address the male and female power imbalance in divorce' (1992) 9 *Mediation Quarterly* 227–239.

[46]   Keys Young Social Research Consultants *Research Evaluation of Family Mediation Practice and the Issue of Violence* (Legal Aid and Family Services, Commonwealth of Australia 1996).

- assisted a vulnerable individual to deal with any harassment and intimidation which occurred outside the actual mediation session itself.

13.8 SATISFACTION WITH OUTCOMES

A Government Green Paper[47] reported in 2010 that:

> 'the full and partial success rate of publicly funded mediations now stands at 70% (with the full resolution of cases accounting for 66% of this).'

A recent press release from the Ministry of Justice reported that almost seven in every ten couples using mediation reached agreement.[48] Are these settlements satisfactory, compared with the outcomes that participants might have obtained in court? North American studies, using control groups, found that settlements reached through mediation did not differ significantly from lawyer-negotiated settlements or from litigated settlements. In these studies, couples who used mediation were likely to consider that they had reached an outcome fair to them both.[49] Researchers have been concerned to establish whether mediation provides fair and balanced outcomes for men and women equally. Attempts have been made to compare men's and women's experiences of going to court with their experiences of going to mediation. One study found that mediation seemed to produce greater benefits for men than for women,[50] but this was later explained as reflecting men's greater dissatisfaction with their experience in court, rather than women's dissatisfaction with mediation.[51] Despite concerns that women would inevitably be disadvantaged in mediation by gender inequalities and lack of bargaining power, Davis et al found that 'women's responses were, on the whole, slightly more positive than those of men'.[52] Irving and Benjamin reviewed feminist objections to mediation and concluded from their survey of research findings in several countries that mediation does not systematically disadvantage women.[53] Women in these studies generally reported that they found the process balanced and helpful, although where there were complex financial issues and/or high levels of conflict, a single, inexperienced mediator was unable to manage the process adequately.

---

47 Green Paper *Legal Aid Reform 2010*, para 4.71.
48 Ministry of Justice press release, 20 August 2014.
49 Kelly 'Mediated and Adversarial Divorce: Respondents' Perceptions of their Processes and Outcomes' (1989) 24 *Mediation Quarterly* 71–88; Pearson 'The equity of mediated divorce settlements' (1991) 9 *Mediation Quarterly* 179–197.
50 Emery and Wyer Child Custody Mediation (1987) 55 *Journal of Consulting and Clinical Psychology* 179–186.
51 Emery and Jackson *The Charlottesville Mediation Project: mediated and litigated child custody disputes* (1989) 24 Mediation Quarterly 3–18.
52 Services Commission (2000), para 17.2.
53 Irving and Benjamin 'Research in Family Mediation – an Integrative Review' in Irving and Benjamin (eds) *Family Mediation – Contemporary Issues* (Sage, 1995).

Concerns have been raised by the finding in the Mapping Paths to Family Justice Study[54] of 'a strong and regularly stated perception of gender bias in mediation'. Many men felt that the process was biased against them, while some women felt that male mediators were biased against them, or that the whole family justice system was biased towards fathers' interests. A third said they were dissatisfied. Some said they had compromised or capitulated to protect their children or to avoid court proceedings and get things over and done with. The researchers found that men and women do not bring the same norms and values to dispute resolution processes. The predominant norms held by fathers both in children and financial matters were formal equality and rights, whereas the predominant norms of mothers were child welfare and concern to meet their needs as the children's primary carer. With such a fundamental polarity between the norms and priorities of mothers and fathers, does the relatively high settlement rate reflect genuine agreement or capitulation under pressure? There are doubts about the quality of some settlements reached through dispute resolution. In one collaborative law case in which sessions were recorded by the researchers, one primary carer mother settled for less than half of the liquid capital and no pension, because she knew that her husband would not agree to anything more and 'she just wanted to get out'.[55] However, the majority of participants in collaborative law settled because they reached a settlement they viewed as fair. In solicitor negotiations, the primary reason for settlement was a perceived 'good' outcome or acceptance of a lower offer on the advice of the lawyer. A high proportion of clients who used solicitor negotiation said they were satisfied with the process, although (as mentioned in 13.6 above) there were also complaints of increased hostility, high costs and delay being used as a deliberate tactic. Under half were satisfied with the outcome of solicitor negotiations, while 29% considered they were dissatisfied, with almost a quarter very equivocal.[56]

Despite stressful and sometimes negative experiences in mediation, almost three quarters of participants in mediation said they liked the process and just over half were satisfied with the outcome. In relation to financial settlements, legal advice during and following mediation is important, to enable participants to check and consider whether their proposed settlement is equitable and sound.

Clients' experience and satisfaction have also been the subject of some small-scale studies. Day Sclater[57] obtained a sample of thirty participants with the help of local mediators and solicitors and gathered full case-study material from eleven of them. For the remaining nineteen participants, the data gathered were incomplete, 'owing to the difficulties ... of maintaining contact with participants and sustaining their commitment to research which is dealing with sensitive and emotionally painful material.'[58] In the eleven case studies, four

---

[54]   Barlow, Hunter, Smithson and Ewing *Mapping Paths to Family Justice – Briefing Paper and Report on Key Findings* (Universities of Exeter and Kent, June 2014), p 12.

[55]   Ibid, p 20.

[56]   Ibid, p 18.

[57]   Sclater *Divorce: A Psychosocial Study* (Ashgate, 1999).

[58]   Ibid, p 121.

participants who had taken part in mediation went on to instruct solicitors to negotiate on their behalf about property, finances and children. Day Sclater readily acknowledged that her sample was not a random one and she made no claims for the generalisability of her findings. The four participants who had abandoned mediation were perhaps more motivated to maintain contact with the researchers because they had a greater need to recount their grievances than those who had resolved them. Nevertheless, mediators need to listen to the voices of dissatisfied clients just as attentively as to those of satisfied ones. Dissatisfied clients may be more inclined to respond to requests for feedback than those who are moderately satisfied or equivocal. Feedback is important in providing snapshots of how the process worked for particular individuals, but should not be generalised too readily. Mediators need to address areas of practice that need improvement and also hear from satisfied clients that they valued 'knowledge combined with empathy, total fairness, instinctive recognition of and respect for boundaries.'[59]

Since there is strong evidence that prolonged conflict between parents has harmful consequences for children, it is important to consider whether agreements reached through mediation benefit children, even if one or both parents are not fully satisfied with arrangements they consider less than fair from their own perspectives. In 2013–14, 5,434 couples took part in mediation to resolve a dispute concerning their children. 72% (3,888 couples) reached full agreement on child arrangements and the majority (63% – 2,720 couples) reached agreement in only one mediation session.[60] When parents are encouraged in mediation to focus on their children's needs and feelings, a great many agree that their children are their primary concern and thus they are able to regain or rebuild their joint commitment to their children, as the statistics indicate. However, where there is entrenched conflict between parents, a single session is unlikely to produce a lasting agreement. When conflict is intense or entrenched, step-by-step agreements reached over a series of mediation sessions allow more time to explore the needs of all concerned and work gradually towards sustainable arrangements. Direct consultation with the child or young person may be needed.[61] Mediation's effectiveness may be reported by the government in terms of the number of agreements reached, but the quality and sustainability of mediated agreements need evaluation in follow-up studies to establish whether they are associated with reduced conflict between parents in the longer term and with increased contact and communication between children and their non-resident parent.

13.9   DURABILITY OF AGREEMENTS

When settlements are reached in mediation, do they actually last? A three-year follow up study[62] found that users of mediation on all issues were more likely

---

[59]   Feedback from a recent client of Family Mediation Centre Staffordshire.

[60]   https://www.gov.uk/government/news/more-free-mediation-sessions-for-separating-couples.

[61]   See **8.4** and **8.10** above on children's positive experiences of child-inclusive mediation.

[62]   McCarthy and Walker 'The longer-term impact of family mediation' (1996) *Joseph Rowntree Findings* 103.

than users of 'child-only' mediation to reach agreements that survived and that they were also less likely to experience fresh disputes affecting their children. Both types of mediation helped couples to come to terms with the ending of their relationship and/or have a better relationship with their children. The researchers concluded that reaching agreements in mediation is a vital component in making and maintaining co-operative relationships between separated parents.[63]

An American study[64] used a control group to measure the effects of mediation in the longer term. Parents in dispute over child custody who had been randomly assigned to mediation or court proceedings were followed up over a twelve-year period. This study found that, compared with litigating parents, non-resident parents in the mediated group had much more contact with their children and were much more involved in their children's lives. 19% of the non-resident parents who took part in mediation saw their children one–three times per month, compared with 14% of parents who litigated. A further 30% of non-resident parents who mediated said they saw their children weekly or more often, compared with 8% of parents who litigated. 54% of non-resident parents said they talked to their children once a week or more, compared with 13% who litigated.[65] The increased involvement of the non-residential parent was not found to be associated with increased conflict. The parents who mediated made more changes in their children's living arrangements over the twelve-year period and generally showed increased flexibility and co-operation. The researchers emphasised, however, that their findings may not generalise to mediation and litigation in other courts or jurisdictions.

Experience suggests that there are some divorcing couples who work out arrangements for their children and proposals for financial settlement in mediation and confirm a year later that they have maintained their co-operation, yet neither parent has taken action to apply for the decree absolute and consent order. In one such case, the couple acknowledged ambivalent feelings about ending their marriage, but did not wish to get back together. In contrast, there are some highly antagonistic couples who reach a financial settlement in mediation culminating in a consent order, but their hostility towards each other does not diminish. Positive outcomes can be demonstrated more easily where a consent order results from mediation, but are harder to prove with semi-divorced couples whose progress in mediation is more ambiguous. While warning of the low comparability between studies, Irving and Benjamin[66] found that mediation generally led to an improvement in co-parental relationships in 60–70% of cases, measured in terms of decreased conflict, improved communication and fewer serious problems. Researchers in Australia, Canada, the United States and the UK have all found increased

[63] Ibid, p 1.
[64] Emery et al 'Child Custody Mediation and Litigation: Custody, Contact and Co-parenting 12 years After Initial Dispute Resolution' (2001) 69(2) *Journal of Consulting and Clinical Psychology* 323–332.
[65] Ibid, p 326.
[66] Irving and Benjamin 'Research in Family Mediation – an Integrative Review' in Irving and Benjamin (eds) *Family Mediation – Contemporary Issues* (Sage, 1995).

parental co-operation following mediation.[67] One of the main benefits reported by parents is that the mediator helped them focus on their children and consider their children's needs and feelings.[68] Mediation offers opportunities to restore or build parental co-operation and move forward from embedded conflict.

13.10   MEDIATOR INFLUENCE ON PROCESS AND OUTCOME

In general, the perceived quality of the mediator seems to be to be a key factor in the experience and outcome of mediation.[69] Early research focused on take-up and settlement rates, whereas later studies analysed mediators' techniques and interventions and use of authority.[70] The main aim of mediation is to 'empower' participants to reach their own decisions. A number of studies have shown, however, that it is naïve to believe that 'the mediator controls the process but not the outcome'. Gulliver[71] pointed out that mediators are bound to have their own views, values and interests, while Abel[72] warned that informal processes of dispute resolution are liable to oppress, as well as empower. Greatbatch and Dingwall[73] found in their analysis of audio-taped mediation sessions that mediators influenced the mediation process and outcome by encouraging some proposals and discouraging others. This study was criticised for not seeking participants' perspectives and using evidence selectively, but the findings nonetheless caused concern. Could mediators be wolves in sheep's clothing, driving frightened participants into a settlement corner? Piper[74] conducted an empirical study based on observation and tape recordings of child-focused mediation with 24 couples in a mediation service run by the local divorce court welfare service (pre Cafcass). The ethos of the divorce court welfare service was not found to result in 'differences of message or outcome'.[75]

[67] Bordow and Gibson *Evaluation of the family court mediation service* (Family Court of Australia Research and Evaluation Unit, 1994); Davis et al *Monitoring Publicly Funded Family Mediation – Report to the Legal Services Commission* (Legal Services Commission, 2000); Emery *The Truth about Children and Divorce* (Viking, 2004); Kelly 'A Decade of Divorce Mediation Research' (1996) 34 *Family and Conciliation Courts Review* 373–385; Pearson and Thoennes 'Divorce Mediation Research Results' in Folberg and Milne (eds) *Divorce Mediation – Theory and Practice* (Guilford Press, 1988), 429–452.

[68] Walker, McCarthy and Timms *Mediation: the Making and Remaking of Co-operative Relationships* (Relate Centre for Family Studies, University of Newcastle, 1994).

[69] Barlow, Hunter, Smithson and Ewing *Mapping Paths to Family Justice – Briefing Paper and Report on Key Findings* (Universities of Exeter and Kent, June 2014), p 10.

[70] Donahue, Allen and Burrell 'Mediator communicative competence' (1988) 55 *Communication Monographs* 104–119; Greatbatch and Dingwall 'Selective facilitation: some preliminary observations on a strategy used by divorce mediators' (1989) 23 *Law and Society Review* 613–641; Slaikeu, Pearson and Thoennes 'Divorce Mediation Behaviors: A Descriptive System and Analysis' (1988) in Folberg and Milne (eds) *Divorce Mediation – Theory and Practice* (Guilford Press, 1988), pp 475–495.

[71] Gulliver *Disputes and Negotiations* (Academic Press, 1979).

[72] Abel *The Politics of Informal Justice* (Academic Press, 1982) vol 1.

[73] Greatbatch and Dingwall Selective facilitation : some preliminary observations on a strategy used by divorce mediators' (1989) 23 *Law and Society Review* 613–641.

[74] Piper *The Responsible Parent – A Study in Divorce Mediation* (Harvester Wheatsheaf, 1991).

[75] Ibid, p 17.

The mediator's level of experience is an important factor. Pearson and Thoennes[76] found major improvements among mediators who had mediated six or more cases. Those who had mediated six to ten cases helped couples reach settlement in 64% of cases, compared with 30% of cases involving inexperienced mediators. In England and Wales, Davis et al[77] found that:

> 'mediators have become more skilled in negotiating settlements than appeared from earlier data collected in the 1980s.'

Effective mediators help participants generate options that benefit from the mediator's accumulated knowledge and experience, without assuming that what worked in one situation will necessarily work in another.

13.10.1   A dynamic, pro-active approach

Pro-active mediators achieve a higher rate of agreement than passive facilitators. It is important to recognise that being proactive is not synonymous with being directive. Pearson[78] and Pearson and Thoennes[79] found in analysing audiotapes of mediation sessions that effective mediators intervened actively, structured the process well and spent time exploring options. In cases where little progress was made, the mediator had focused more on gathering facts and made less headway, especially when participants communicated poorly. Audiotapes of mediation sessions transcribed and analysed by Donohue, Allen and Burrell[80] also found that mediators who intervened actively during mediation sessions were more likely to get good results than those who merely facilitated exchanges between the parties. Positive outcomes were associated with three particular interventions by mediators:

- laying down and enforcing procedural rules;

- structuring the process to obtain relevant information;

- reframing the parties' statements to identify important issues and proposals.

Examination of sessions that ended in deadlock found a tendency among the more passive mediators 'to let the couples go for a while to see how they interact'. The researchers found that a non-interventionist approach by

---

[76] Pearson and Thoennes 'Divorce Mediation Research Results' in Folberg and Milne (eds.) *Divorce Mediation – Theory and Practice* (1988) Guilford Press 429–452.

[77] Davis et al *Monitoring Publicly Funded Family Mediation – Report to the Legal Services Commission* (Legal Services Commission 2000) para 18.7.

[78] Pearson, 'An evaluation of alternatives to court adjudication' (1982) 7 *Justice System Journal* 420–444.

[79] Pearson, and Thoennes 'Divorce Mediation Research Results' in Folberg and Milne (eds.) *Divorce Mediation – Theory and Practice* (1988) Guilford Press 429–452.

[80] Donohue, Allen and Burrell 'Mediator communicative competence' (1988) 55 *Communication Monographs* 104–119.

mediators 'may create a runaway freight train that mediators are unable to stop with tools designed for slower-moving traffic'.[81]

13.10.2 Clear structure and focused questions

Kressel and colleagues[82] found that the techniques mediators used to gather information were an important component of effectiveness. The choice of question form was important and the use of structure to gather information systematically.[83] Kressel et al's[84] analysis of audiotapes and videotapes of mediation sessions found that mediators tended to be either settlement-seekers or problem-solvers. Problem-solvers were more flexible in the way they moved between participants to maintain a balance between them. They actively encouraged productive exchanges and discouraged destructive ones. The problem-solving approach was associated with durable agreements and with greater satisfaction on the part of participants, compared with a more inflexible, settlement-seeking approach.

The American Bar Association[85] considered factors defining good quality mediation practice in the context of civil/commercial mediation, based on interviews with lawyers, mediation users and mediators. The ABA identified 'good quality' in four categories:

- Good preparation by the mediator, representatives and parties.
- Adapting the mediation process to meet the needs of the individual case/parties.
- 'Analytical' techniques used by the mediator.
- 'Persistence' by the mediator.

Creativity and flexibility, showing an ability to adapt the mediation process to manage different levels of conflict and power imbalance without losing the integrity of the process, are surely among the characteristics of a good mediator.

13.11 ARE TWO MEDIATORS BETTER THAN ONE?

The use of shuttle mediation and gender balanced co-mediation teams may enable some issues to be mediated that would not be possible for a sole mediator with both participants together in the same room.[86] Hunt's[87] survey

---

[81] Donahue, Lyles, and Rogan 'Issue Development in Divorce Mediation' (1989) 24 Mediation Quarterly 19–28.

[82] Kressel, Butler-DeFreitas, Forlenza, and Wilcox, *Research in Contested Custody Mediations* (1989) 24 *Mediation Quarterly* 55–70.

[83] See Chapter 6 above.

[84] Kressel, Frontera, Forlenza, Butler and Fish 'The settlement-oriented versus the problem-solving style in custody mediation' (1994) 50(1) *Journal of Social Issues* 67–83.

[85] American Bar Association *Final Report – Task Force on Improving Mediation Quality* 2008.

[86] See **4.10** above.

[87] Hunt *Parental Perspectives on the Family Justice System in England and Wales: a review of research* (Report for the Family Justice Council, December 2009).

found only two studies, both pre-Cafcass, that looked at parental views on the gender or ethnicity of the conciliator and whether having two workers was, or might have been, helpful. Most of the parents in one study did not think it mattered whether there were one or two conciliators. 91% thought that the conciliators' gender or race was immaterial. Another study reported more mixed results: 65% of those with a single conciliator thought a gender balance was not important, whereas 50% of those who had experienced male/female co-working believed that it was: 'I think there should be one of each gender in all meetings so that both parties' views can be looked at in different ways plus giving the impression that both are equally represented.'[88]

Irving and Benjamin[89] concluded that there are significant benefits in using male-female co-mediators, suggesting that a gender-balanced team helps to give equal attention to male and female perspectives. A gender-balanced team has opportunities to facilitate and model negotiating and positive communication. Irving and Benjamin also consider that interdisciplinary co-mediation, combining a mediator with family law expertise with a mediator experienced in a psychosocial discipline, offers an 'interweaving of divergent sources of expertise' that enhance creativity.[90]

13.12   DOES MEDIATION REDUCE LEGAL COSTS?

One of the main advantages claimed for mediation is that it reduces legal costs. In an early study in Bristol,[91] researchers explored the impact of child-focused mediation on legal aid costs and found that where mediation led to agreement, there was a considerable reduction in legal aid applications. Solicitors considered that mediation had reduced legal costs in 54% of cases. Kelly[92] compared the costs of mediated divorces in California with those of divorces conducted through lawyers. She found that all-issues mediation cost considerably less than the use of two lawyers to negotiate or litigate a final settlement. The two groups of mediated and non-mediated divorces were comparable in the complexity of their issues, levels of income, extent of reported marital conflict, initial levels of hostility or co-operation and expected degree of difficulty in reaching settlement. Kelly warned, however, that her results should be viewed with caution, since the respondents were self-selected and not representative of the divorcing population as a whole.

Another American study conducted by Pearson[93] compared mediated and non-mediated cases. Legal costs were found to be 28–48% higher for those

---

[88]   Ibid, p 82.

[89]   Irving and Benjamin 'Research in Family Mediation – an Integrative Review' in Irving and Benjamin (eds) *Family Mediation – Contemporary Issues* (Sage, 1995).

[90]   Ibid, p 448.

[91]   Davis and Lees *A Study of Conciliation – its Impact on Legal Aid Costs and Place in the Resolution of Disputes arising out of Divorce* (Dept of Social Administration, University of Bristol, 1981).

[92]   Kelly 'Is mediation less expensive? Comparison of mediated and adversarial divorce costs' (1990) 8(1) *Mediation Quarterly* 15–26.

[93]   Pearson *The equity of mediated divorce settlements* (1991) 9 Mediation Quarterly 179–197.

who settled their divorce proceedings through lawyers, compared with those who used mediation. Proving that mediation reduces expenditure on legal proceedings is no easy task, since estimates of savings based on avoidance of litigation assumes that litigation would have taken place without mediation. Variables in client circumstances and negotiating strengths, in the model of mediation and in the experience, knowledge and skills of mediators make it very difficult to draw firm conclusions. Mediation could appear to increase costs in cases where no settlement is reached and court proceedings ensue, but it may still have been of use in obtaining financial disclosure and narrowing the issues in dispute.

Australia, New Zealand and Canada have all reported positive experience from their well-developed and well-resourced provisions for out of court dispute resolution, indicating a potential for around 30% of separating and divorcing couples to reach settlements through these services.[94] Norway introduced mandatory mediation in the 1990s for divorcing couples with children and has found that around a third can benefit from mediation, while the remainder either settled matters on their own or were in such high conflict that they needed to go to court.[95]

In the year 2004/2005, the British government spent £14.2 million on publicly funded family mediation, representing 4.2% of public expenditure on private family law.[96] The National Audit Office subsequently examined the cost-effectiveness of public expenditure on family mediation and reported to Parliament that:

> 'mediation is generally cheaper, quicker and less acrimonious than court proceedings and research shows it secures better outcomes, particularly for children …. On average a mediated case takes 100 days and costs £752, compared with 435 days and £1,682 in cases where mediation is not used.'[97]

As referred to in Chapter 2 (at **2.1** above) in the year from July 2013 to June 2014, Legal Aid Agency expenditure on MIAMs and mediation fell from £13,150,000 to £6,738,000 – a reduction of virtually 50%, despite the evidence that in addition to its other benefits, the use of mediation reduces public expenditure on disputes in private family law proceedings.[98]

---

[94] Mediation Task Force Report 2014, para 20.
[95] Ibid.
[96] Legal Services Commission, 2005.
[97] National Audit Office *Review of Legal Aid and Mediation for people involved in family breakdown* (March 2007).
[98] https://www.gov.uk/government/uploads/system/uploads/attachment_data/file/358092/legal-aid-statistics-apr-jun-2014.pdf.

13.13   PREDICTORS OF POSITIVE MEDIATION OUTCOMES

There do not seem to be any reliable predictors of positive mediation outcomes. Some researchers[99] have focused exclusively on client attributes in considering who is most likely to be helped by mediation. Waldron and colleagues[100] concluded that two main factors determine whether couples are likely to benefit from mediation:[101]

> 'The first determinant is a level of personality development that allows the subject to view the world not as black and white but as a gamut of greys ... The capacity for empathy, the ability to see two sides of an issue and the capacity to separate the parenting relationship from the marital relationship are essential.'

The second important determinant is that both partners can let go of their marital/couple relationship sufficiently to be able to work on decisions and issues. There needs to be a capacity to face forwards, to listen and to want to solve problems.

Some studies have found that positive outcomes are best predicted by the 'fit' and interaction between the couple's characteristics and dynamics and the mediator's attributes and skills. Pearson and Thoennes[102] found that relevant inter-related factors were client characteristics, the nature of the couple's disputes and the mediator's attributes. Donahue and colleagues[103] also found that agreements reached through mediation were related to the interaction between the parties' attributes and the mediator's communication skills. The interplay of factors in the mediation process illustrates the relevance of chaos theory and ways in which minor variations can help to transform discord into some degree of harmony. Variations in mediation models and small interventions, such as relevant questions, acknowledgements, reframing at appropriate moments, may make significant differences during the process and to its outcome.

13.14   IS THERE SUFFICIENT EVIDENCE TO FORM CONCLUSIONS?

It is clear that mediation is not a universal panacea. Much depends on the experience and skills of the mediator, as well as on the motivation and commitment of participants. A consistent gold standard of justice obtainable through the courts cannot be guaranteed any more than holding a perfect balance in mediation. Where child welfare is concerned, judges do not apply a

---

[99]   Emery and Wyer Child Custody Mediation (1987) 55 *Journal of Consulting and Clinical Psychology* 179–186.

[100] Waldron, Roth, Fair, Mann and McDermott *Therapeutic Mediation Model for Child Custody Dispute Resolution* (1984) 3 *Mediation Quarterly* 5–20.

[101] Ibid, at p 18.

[102] Pearson and Thoennes 'A preliminary portrait of client reactions to three court mediation programs' (1985) 23(1) *Conciliation Courts Review* 1–14.

[103] Donahue, Allen and Burrell *Mediator communicative competence* (1988) 55 Communication Monographs 104–119.

set formula in deciding the best interests of a child in particular circumstances. Parents know their children better than the judge can do. If parents take careful account of their child's best interests, wishes and feelings, the arrangements they make jointly for their children with the help of a skilled mediator are attuned to their child's needs and more likely to last than a court order. Mediation is a brief process aimed at improving communication and helping participants to work out agreed decisions. Circumstances and interpersonal dynamics are so variable that it cannot be expected to produce standard outcomes. It offers a pathway towards settlement that may be helpful for many people, but not for all. As two of the most experienced researchers in the United States have pointed out:

> 'the forum in which disputes are resolved is, after all, only a piece in the complex puzzle of couples' divorce experiences. In evaluating the utility of mediation we must consider not only the nature of the mediation intervention and the degree and nature of parents' exposure to adversarial systems, but must also weigh a myriad of factors related to the parties and their marital and separation history.'[104]

The findings from research on family mediation cannot be considered conclusive, but the weight of evidence from many countries supports the view that mediation assists a significant proportion of separated and divorcing couples and other family members to settle their disputes, communicate better and achieve more positive longer term outcomes for their children. The quality and experience of the mediator are critical factors. Mediators' training and continuing professional development are the subject of the following chapter.

'So hope for a great sea-change
On the far side of revenge
Believe that a further shore
Is reachable from here'

Seamus Heaney, The Cure at Troy

---

[104] Thoennes and Pearson 'Response to Bruch and McIsaac' (1992) 30(1) *Family and Conciliation Courts Review* 142–143; Barlow A, Hunter R, Smithson J and Ewing J *Mapping Paths to Family Justice – Briefing Paper and Report on Key Findings* (Universities of Exeter and Kent, June 2014).

CHAPTER 14

BECOMING A FAMILY MEDIATOR

'Be the change that you wish to see in the world.'[1]

'One must make the skills one's own. Light your own torch from other's candles, but make the skills fit your person ... Try to be whole'[2]

CONTENTS

14.1   MEDIATION – SCIENCE OR ART?

Mediation is increasingly accepted as a discipline in its own right, with its own body of theoretical and practical knowledge, principles and ground-rules. Like other branches of science, mediation has accumulated a body of knowledge based on case studies, classification of cases and analysis of outcomes. Mediators and researchers have tended to approach mediation in a linear way, dividing mediation into a series of steps or stages with outcomes classified as successful, partially successful or unsuccessful, according to whether participants are able to reach agreement, partial agreement or no agreement.

---

[1]   Mahatma Gandhi quoted by B'Hahn *Reclaiming Children and Youth* (Bloomington 2001, vol 10, No 1), p 6.

[2]   Patrick Davis 'Special Education Mediation' in Kolb and Associates *When Talk Works – Profiles of Mediators* (Jossey-Bass 1994), p 60.

This approach to mediation uses 'left-brain thinking' which may be characterised as logical, analytical and task-oriented.

When family mediation is seen as a science, emphasis is put on the need for:

- an intellectual grasp of mediation as a rational process consisting of a sequence of steps in which facts are gathered, differences are clarified, available options identified and proposals for settlement worked out;
- knowledge, including knowledge of the law and financial knowledge including tax, pensions and welfare benefits; knowledge of the experience and impact of divorce for adults and for children; knowledge of child and adult development and family dynamics, availability of support services;
- numeracy and the ability to analyse financial data;
- knowledge and experience of negotiated and litigated divorce settlements: structuring of settlements, trends, current issues;
- negotiation and bargaining techniques involving logic and reasoned thinking;
- adherence to the discipline of mediation, with knowledge of research studies on mediation.

When family mediation is recognised as an art, emphasis is put on the need for:

- empathy, intuitive understanding and ability to engage with people;
- maturity and life experience, not just textbook knowledge;
- skills in responding to the emotional as well as practical needs of separating couples, including skills in crisis management where irrational reactions from participants may heighten and prolong disputes;
- a personal and flexible style of working which enables the structure and pace of the process to be varied according to the dynamics of the couple or family;
- concern for the family as a whole, in which good relationships and co-operation between family members are valued more highly than agreements per se;
- communication skills – use of clear and appropriate language, questions, reframing.

Mediators rely mainly on spoken and written language, but spoken and written language constitutes only a small part of the way people communicate.[3] Mediators need to use all five senses – observing, listening, feeling (touching emotions), tasting (testing) and 'scenting'. Training needs to develop observation skills and awareness of body language, including our own. It should also develop the ways we feel – towards everyone we meet and the way we feel about ourselves. Knowledge is important, but knowledge needs the warmth of human understanding to infuse it with intuition and inspiration. Family mediation is therefore best understood both as a science and as an art, a crucible in which emotion and reason are merged. A weekend in the biennial

---

[3]   See **6.3** above.

series on Mediation, Science and the Arts, held in October 2014 in a beautiful location in Derbyshire, was entitled 'The Mediation Crucible – the Reworking of Family Relationships through Mediation'.[4] Medieval alchemists regarded fire not as the destroying element, but as the transforming element. 'Fire is a process of transformation and change, by which material elements are rejoined into new combinations.'[5] When alchemists tried to transmute base metals into gold, they heated them in a crucible. Family mediation is a crucible in which different, often very hot, elements and emotions are blended and fused in new combinations. Mediators hold the crucible and seek to blend emotion and reason by controlling the emotional temperature and calibrating the proportion of elements – emotion and reason – that seethe or simmer in the crucible at any one time. 'Alchemy is small in scale ... and contains a substantial body of speculative theory.'[6] Although the 'base elements' may not transmute into the pure gold of harmony, degrees of transformation may take place in mediation, for family members and for mediators themselves. A blend of knowledge, empathy and skills are needed, to help family members engage in dialogue during stressful periods in their lives, so that they are able to shift from battling and blaming to co-operating with each other through renewed trust and understanding. Foundation training in mediation cannot be more than the first stage of a continuing journey in becoming a mediator.

Human behaviour is highly variable and unpredictable, especially in the turmoil of separation and divorce. Family mediation is a complex process that needs to be attuned to the emotional state of each participant in helping them to manage major changes and transitions in their family: it is not 'just about settlement'.[7] The reactions and patterns of interaction between separating and divorcing couples vary over time, although some patterns are highly resistant to change. In family mediation, the volatile dynamics of separating couples can be managed in varying ways and degrees by the active involvement of the mediator. The process of mediation consists of a series of interactions: it is neither a re-enactment of familiar conflict nor a conveyor belt to agreement. Mediators need to combine the logical, systematic approach of 'left-brain thinking' with 'right-brain thinking' which encourages creativity and intuition. 'Right-brain thinking' seeks to make connections holistically. It works on different levels and can make connections or intuitive leaps between them. It looks at patterns and at relationships in circular, rather than linear, ways.

14.2 MAKING THE TRANSITION TO THE ROLE OF MEDIATOR

Most family mediators in the UK have professional qualifications and experience in family law, social work or therapy. Family mediation is a relatively new discipline and the mediation 'child' needs to draw from the

---

4   Organised by Lisa Parkinson and Neil Robinson with the Family Mediation Centre Staffordshire.
5   Bronowski *The Ascent of Man* (BBC, 1973), p 142.
6   Ibid, p 134.
7   See Chapter 13 on mediation objectives and outcomes.

knowledge and experience of parent disciplines, including psychology, sociology, family therapy and family law. Co-mediators from complementary professional backgrounds resemble co-parents with joint parental responsibility. Those coming from a family law background bring a fund of professional knowledge and experience in relation to separation, divorce and family matters and they are likely to have well-honed negotiation skills. However, family lawyers, including those trained in collaborative law, may be challenged by the powerful emotions that separated couples bring to mediation and by the complexity of issues concerning children. Counsellors, social workers and therapists are more likely to have experience and skills in conjoint work with couples and families, but they too need to make a conscious transition to the role of mediator and acquire further knowledge and skills. Unless already cross-trained as a lawyer and therapist, trainee family mediators need courage to move into unfamiliar professional territory and face fresh challenges. Courage and capacity for change are put to the test.

> 'Being a mediator demands a new approach from virtually all occupations of origin. Mediators need to draw on experience in a new way, and may have to discard some old habits. Many mediators find this a challenging process.'[8]

Training as a mediator involves acquiring new abilities and skills and putting aside practice and habits that are not part of the mediator's role. The longer one has worked in a particular professional role, the harder it may be to change one's practice and habits. Some people move naturally into the role of family mediator, whereas others experience considerable difficulty. There needs to be a conscious transition from an existing role as lawyer, therapist, social worker or counsellor (or other background) to the different and distinct role of family mediator. One of the first steps is to recognise the differences between mediating, advising and counselling. Mediators need legal knowledge to explain the law, legal terminology and court process in general terms, but the knowledge is applied differently in the impartial role of mediator. Mediators do not advise participants on their legal rights nor on how legal principles would apply in their particular circumstances. Anne Hall Dick,[9] founder and first Convenor of the Family Law Association in Scotland, remarked on the differences between acting as a lawyer and acting as a mediator: 'Lawyers undertaking mediation training are usually quite stunned by how challenging the transition is.' Lawyers need to understand the differences and maintain the boundaries between the roles of legal adviser and mediator. Some trainees reveal an unexpected capacity to 'change their spots' in the course of training. There have been some striking instances of adversarial leopards or lions not turning into lambs, exactly, but changing their approach through increased self-awareness and mindfulness.

---

[8]   Brown and Marriott *ADR: Principles and Practice* (Sweet & Maxwell, 2nd edn, 2011), p 375.
[9]   Anne Hall Dick, paper given at Sweet & Maxwell's Family Law Conference, London, 17 May 1996.

Legal advisers	Family mediators
Work within the discipline of the law	Multi-disciplinary
Advise individual clients	Impartial, balanced help to both or all participants
Often start with a history of the dispute	Participants invited to explain their issues and needs
Advise within a framework of legal rights	Focus on interests and mutual concerns
Financial information collected and exchanged between lawyers	Financial information gathered and shared within the mediation process
Use legal terminology	Use ordinary language as far as possible
Address clients' rights and claims	Focus on parental responsibilities and children's needs
Not trained in psychological processes	Trained in conflict management and mediation
Rely on their individual client's account of events and positions	Discuss with both parents together. Children and young people may be included directly
Advise clients on best course of action	Explore options in a non-directive way
Negotiate with 'the other side' by correspondence and/or round table meetings	Participants negotiate in face-to-face meetings
Draft applications to the court	Do not draft legal documents

The reduced opportunities for legal advice and representation following LASPO[10] pose fresh challenges for mediators who find themselves obliged to cover more legal aspects than formerly, when lawyers were far more available to complement the mediator's role. Nevertheless, the boundaries between the roles of mediator and legal adviser need to be maintained.

The boundaries between mediation, counselling and therapy are harder to delineate and more susceptible to being blurred. The following tables suggest some key differences.

---

[10] Legal Aid, Sentencing and Punishment of Offenders Act 2012 (LASPO).

Counsellors, therapists	Family mediators
May counsel one partner alone	Must engage with both partners from the outset
Clients may be seeking reconciliation	Mediate mainly between separating/divorcing couples
Not linked to legal process	Has links with legal process
Unlikely to start with written contract	Agreement to Mediate signed by both parties
May be long-term	Usually short-term
May explore personal/family history and experience to help adjust to the present	Focus on present and future, rather than the past
Focus on feelings, perceptions and relationships	Focus on agreed decisions and parenting arrangements
Focus on adult perspectives and needs	Focus on child-parent relationships and children's needs
Provide adult-related information	Provide child and family-related information
Aim to increase personal insight	Aim to help participants communicate better
May use psycho-analytic theory	Use mediation theory, systems theory etc.
Facilitate reflection	Structure discussions, explore options actively
Client-counsellor relationship may involve some dependency for a time	Seek to empower participants and increase autonomy, avoiding court proceedings
May not end with a written agreement	Draw up a Memorandum of Understanding

Family therapists	Family mediators
Help families to manage their problems	Help participants to resolve disagreements

Family therapists	Family mediators
Often work with 'intact families'	Work mainly with separating/divorcing couples
Children may be involved at the outset	Children may be involved at a later stage
Usually work without a written contract	Start with a signed Agreement to Mediate
No links with the family justice system	Links with the family justice system
Communication not structured, may observe how family members communicate	Facilitate communication in a structured way, to ensure balanced participation
Focus on family processes	Focus on options and family arrangements
Consider underlying problems	Focus on overt issues and identified tasks
May give messages, rather than information	Give impartial, neutral information
May develop hypotheses to explain family functioning that are not shared with the family	Seek to assist participants through open communication
If a one-way screen is used, communication with consultants is not heard by the family	Co-mediators work together and communications are shared openly with participants
May give paradoxical instructions without explaining reasons	Discuss and agree tasks with participants
Work strategically in ways that involve family members	Help parents to consider how to talk with and listen to their children, children sometimes included
May end without a written outcome	Draw up written summaries of mediation

Mediation with changing families, in a social and legal environment that is itself going through profound change, requires fresh thinking and adjustments at many levels. Training and developing as a mediator involves changing ourselves from the inside. These changes may seem exciting and inspirational, but they can also be scary. In *Alice in Wonderland*, the caterpillar asks Alice: 'Who are *you*?' and Alice replies: 'I hardly know, sir, just at present – at least I know who I *was* when I got up this morning, but I think I must have been changed several times since then.'[11] Mediation training involves putting aside one's identity as a lawyer, social worker, counsellor or Cafcass officer. A barrister training as a mediator experienced momentary distress: 'If I'm not a barrister, I don't know who I am.' Training as a mediator is not simply learning a set of techniques. Changes need to be made from the inside, to the extent that we may wonder if we are still the same person. Another lawyer recounted that during his mediation training, he walked into his partner's office when something had made his partner angry. When he didn't react in the way his partner expected, his partner looked at him and said: 'What's happened to you?'

14.3   THE EUROPEAN FORUM ON FAMILY MEDIATION TRAINING AND RESEARCH

One of the first opportunities for family mediators from European countries to come together to share their ideas and experience was provided by the first European conference held in Caen, France in November 1990. Following this conference, the *Association pour la Promotion de la Médiation Familiale (APMF)* in Paris invited a group of mediation trainers to work together to define standards of training for family mediation based on common principles and objectives. This group, initially comprising trainers from Belgium, France, Germany, Italy, Switzerland and the UK, set up a voluntary association, the European Forum on Family Mediation Training and Research. Convivial multi-lingual meetings in Paris, Geneva, Brussels and Hamburg led to the publication in French and English of the European Charter on Standards for family mediation.[12] The Standards define the main elements of family mediation training (knowledge and skills), the qualifications of trainers, criteria for those seeking training, the length of foundation training and requirements for accreditation.

The European Forum established a Steering Committee and a Training Standards Committee composed of qualified and experienced family mediation trainers.

The Training Standards Committee met in Hamburg in January 2000 to discuss and revise the Training Standards. There was consensus on fundamental points:

- Family mediation training should be interdisciplinary. Trainers and trainees should have a background in family law and/or psychosocial disciplines. Trainees from different disciplines and backgrounds learn as much from each other as from the trainers.

---

[11]   Lewis Carroll *Alice's Adventures in Wonderland* (Macmillan, 1874), p 60.
[12]   European Standards for Family Mediation Training, APMF, Paris 1992, published in English and French.

- The training programme should be developed and co-ordinated by training director/s who must be practising family mediators. The training must include practical exercises and role-plays. It should not consist of a series of academic lectures from visiting experts who lack first-hand experience of family mediation practice.

- It is important to make a clear distinction between mediation awareness training and a full course of training lasting at least 180 hours leading to a recognised qualification to practise as a family mediator. Mediation awareness training provides an introduction to mediation but does not equip participants to undertake the role of mediator.

Countries that have introduced legislation and national standards for family mediation training and practice now have less need for the Forum, but its standards merit attention and provide guidelines for countries where family mediation is at an earlier stage. The European Forum demonstrated the value of mediation trainers working together internationally to share ideas and experience. There was unanimous agreement among the original members of the Forum's Committee on Standards that family mediation requires the integration of savoir, savoir-faire and savoir-être – professional knowledge, practical skills, self-awareness and ethical conduct.[13]

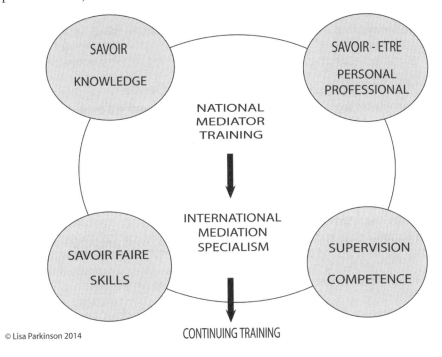

St Augustine emphasised the difference between *scientia*, meaning 'knowing about, or being skilled in' and *sapientia*, meaning insight and wisdom. At the fulcrum between the two, Augustine placed 'the eye of the heart', which he defined as seeing with compassion.

---

[13] European Forum Standards 2001, s 5.

14.4   APTITUDE FOR FAMILY MEDIATION

Many mediators seem to be 'born mediators' who possess a natural aptitude for peace-making, negotiating and resolving conflict. There are certain personal qualities that family mediators need to have and effective mediators are likely to demonstrate many, even most, of the following qualities (not listed in order of importance):

- Warmth – ability to engage with people and show empathy.
- Compassion – St Augustine's 'eye of the heart'.
- Respect for individuals – open-minded, non-judgmental.
- Non-directive – facilitating, not prescribing solutions.
- Optimism – a positive approach to conflict, tempered by realism.
- Balance – ability to relate to conflicting views and manage power imbalances.
- Self-knowledge – awareness of one's own values, weaknesses and prejudices.
- Ability to communicate.
- Firmness – ability to manage conflict without stifling it, challenging when necessary, keeping rules and time boundaries.
- Understanding – of emotions and needs, capacity to allow safe expression of feelings.
- Patience – ability to cope with setbacks.
- Sense of humour, used sensitively.
- Intelligence and analytic skills in drawing from and applying a wide range of knowledge.
- Common sense – practical and down-to-earth.
- Maturity – life experience.
- Personal integrity.
- Professionalism and objectivity.
- Ability as a team player – ability to co-mediate.
- Humility – readiness to acknowledge mistakes, willingness to learn.
- Stamina and energy.
- Imagination in generating ideas, brainstorming, creativity.

It is really rather difficult for one person to embody all these qualities.

Although maturity and life experience are valuable, it is not necessarily the case that older and more experienced practitioners bring more 'mediator qualities' than younger colleagues. Observation of young people who have trained as mediators shows that many of them have innate qualities, as well as formal skills. Should there be a minimum age for training as a family mediator, or could even undergraduate courses in mediation be a first step towards qualifying as a mediator?

14.5 ENTRY REQUIREMENTS AND LENGTH OF TRAINING

The FMC Standards[14] state that applicants for FMC-approved training in family mediation should demonstrate ability to work at graduate level, either through possession of a degree or equivalent-level professional qualification, or experience of work in a role that requires an equivalent level of thinking and application. They should also demonstrate ability to understand and use an adequate level of written and spoken English (or Welsh for courses in the Welsh language). Thirdly, they should demonstrate ability to work with conflicts and manage interpersonal relationships at a professional level, gained either through typically two or three years' experience as a professional dealing with families, or a similar amount of time as a mediator or non-adversarial dispute resolution practitioner in another field.

Initial training in the UK typically consists of a total of eight days, organised in three modules. It is designed as post-professional training for experienced practitioners. These intensive short courses, combined with background reading and course assignments, are just the first stage in a mediator's journey towards accreditation and continuing professional development. However, it can certainly be argued that eight days of initial training are insufficient, especially now that these courses have to incorporate MIAMs training as well. In some European countries, much longer training is required for certification as a family mediator. In France, a decree of 2 December 2003 created the Diplôme d'Etat de Médiateur Familial, the state diploma in family mediation. Satisfactory completion of this diploma is required for state recognition as a family mediator. Following review and evaluation of the diploma, modifications were made in a law passed on 19 March 2012. The French state diploma in family mediation requires 315 hours of training in the process of mediation and techniques, together with 161 hours of theoretical training in law, psychology and sociology, followed by 105 hours of supervised practice in a mediation service and 14 hours' supervision on the preparation of a dissertation. The total length of French training is 595 hours. Credits for certain modules may be granted on the basis of previous professional qualifications and the diploma may be extended beyond 600 hours to obtain a master's degree. Draft law in Germany on mediator certification requires a minimum of 120 hours' certified training, to include practical training, role-play and supervision.

Many universities offer courses in mediation and dispute resolution leading to a master's degree, but even when combined with experiential exercises, academic study directed by tutors who are not themselves accredited mediation trainers with substantial mediation experience does not provide adequate preparation for practice. Knowledge alone is insufficient. The skill of the mediator lies not only in the way knowledge is applied, but also in the ability to recognise what is **not** known and which needs to be found out – by participants and/or by mediators. An academic degree in mediation does not certify professional competence to practise (see **4.6** and **4.11** below). To obtain a driving licence,

---

14   FMC Manual on Professional Standards and Self-Regulatory Framework, September 2014, p 25.

knowledge of the law and the rules of the road are not sufficient. Learner drivers have to take a driving test with a qualified instructor to demonstrate competence in driving a car, controlling it in traffic and applying the brakes when necessary. Learning to ride a motorbike is probably a better analogy than driving a car, because a motorcyclist needs flexibility and balance. To negotiate a bend, a motorcyclist needs to lean into the bend. With good balance and flexibility, mediators can lean in different directions without losing their centred position.

14.6 FOUR PILLARS OF FAMILY MEDIATION TRAINING

Family mediators need a solid knowledge base and a wide range of skills which they use sensitively and competently. To change metaphors again, the family mediation 'building' needs to be supported by more than a single pillar. Taylor[15] proposed four pillars constructed from:

- mediation, conflict resolution and negotiation skills;
- legal and financial knowledge and skills;
- knowledge of adult, child and family development;
- helping professional skills.

These pillars are not free-standing. If any one of them is missing or shorter than the others, the structure of family mediation will be unsteady and liable to collapse. Trainee mediators who are qualified and experienced in a relevant professional discipline come with a high level of contextual knowledge in their own discipline, but, unless they are cross-trained both as a lawyer and as a therapist, they are likely to have gaps in other areas. Training needs therefore to be interdisciplinary and designed to build on and extend existing knowledge, without duplicating what is known already. Training manuals list the knowledge base needed for family mediation, covering mediation principles, policies and procedures, standard documents and precedents, requirements for accreditation and so on.

In his essay for Stephen Cretney's *Festschrift*, Neil Robinson[16] suggested that the family law syllabus (or indeed the whole of the jurisprudence/law school syllabus) could be transformed by in-depth study of private ordering through mediation and other forms of dispute resolution. An extended version of Neil Robinson's proposed content could provide the knowledge base for intensive, practice-oriented mediation training, which focuses on the acquisition and development of specialist skills:

- The theory, philosophy and history of conflict resolution by peaceful means.

---

[15] Taylor 'The Four Foundations of Family Mediation: Implications for Training and Certification' (1994) 12(4) *Mediation Quarterly* 77–87.

[16] Neil Robinson 'Shapeshifters or Polymaths – a Reflection on the Discipline of the Family Mediator' in *Fifty Years in Family Law – Essays for Stephen Cretney* (Intersentia, 2012).

- Systems of family dispute resolution in English and comparative law – adversarial, inquisitorial and private ordering; emerging trends in dispute resolution, particularly of disputes relating to children.

- Case-law, practice and sanctions relating to the development of mediation jurisprudence.[17]

- Specific areas of law relating to mediation privilege and confidentiality.

- Specific areas of family law such as the limits of judicial discretion, the no order and welfare principles, concepts of and challenges to shared parental responsibility and shared parenting.

- Mediation models and practices – structured, transformative, narrative, ecosystemic.

- Cultural diversity; cross-cultural families, social migration.

- Child and adolescent development; family systems theory and the theory of attachment and loss; the family life-cycle and family dynamics; experiences of separation and divorce for adults, children and young people; family transitions and family crisis, re-ordered families and extended families; resources and support services for adults and children.

- Gender and power issues, domestic abuse, safeguarding and child protection.

- Depictions of family relationships and conflicts in the arts and sciences: poetry, literature and the fine arts, insights from anthropology and neuroscience.

The list could go on! A master's course consisting of modules in these different areas (with certain modules optional for those demonstrating relevant professional qualifications and experience) could provide a solid foundation for skills training and accreditation as a family mediator.

FMC-accredited initial training is only the first step in becoming a professionally qualified, FMC-accredited family mediator and maintaining this status. There are staging-posts along the way:[18]

1. Completion of FMC-accredited training, with satisfactory assessments, leading to membership of a Member Organisation (MO) of the FMC.

2. Completion of post-training requirements with an FMC-recognised Professional Practice Consultant (PPC), subject to certain restrictions.

3. Accreditation (see **4.11** below).

---

[17] See *Halsey v Milton Keynes General NHS Trust* [2004] EWCA (Civ) 576: 'the value and importance of ADR have been established within a remarkably short time. All members of the legal profession who conduct litigation should now routinely consider with their clients whether their disputes are suitable for ADR.'

[18] For further details, see the FMC Manual on Professional Standards and Self-Regulatory Framework, September 2014.

4.   Renewal of FMCA status every three years, based on sufficient evidence of
      mediation practice under the FMC Code of Practice, together with
      evidence of professional practice consultancy and professional develop-
      ment.

It is considerably easier to list areas of contextual knowledge for mediation
than it is to design and deliver training that facilitates the transition to the role
of mediator. This essentially interactive, as opposed to didactic, training process
needs to extend the trainee's self-awareness and mindfulness, as well as
developing practical mediation skills. Mediation training should not be geared
solely to meeting standards and passing tests of competence. It should be
informative, mind-stretching, enjoyable and inspirational. It should also
provide opportunities to co-mediate and discover how to co-mediate effectively
in partnership.[19] One of the great benefits of co-mediating is that co-mediators
draw from each other's strengths, contribute different abilities and provide
support to each other.[20] A period of co-mediation practice with case discussion
and professional practice consultancy should be a compulsory stage of practical
training. It broadens perspectives and develops skills.

Additional specialist training is required for some areas of mediation, such as
direct consultation with children, child-inclusive mediation and international
family mediation. With the Government's renewed emphasis on the importance
of hearing the voice of the child, the FMC needs to set unified standards and
requirements for considering and, when appropriate, undertaking direct
consultation with children and young people, since careful direct consultation
can be highly beneficial both for children themselves and for their parents (see
Chapter 8).

14.7   TRAINING – THE MEANS AND THE MEDIA

Academic courses leading to a master's degree or diploma provide theoretical
knowledge, but may not develop the practical skills that family mediators need
to use. Experience as a co-trainer on training modules in a number of countries
suggests that some courses are heavy on knowledge but light on skills. The
framework of knowledge may be seen as the architecture of training. The art of
training lies in its design and delivery. Some trainers who are also accomplished
musicians, like Neil Robinson, can move easily from speaking to singing and
can use music to illustrate themes and make imaginative connections. Not all
trainers are similarly gifted. Some use visual aids including pictures, diagrams
and film. Most trainers use experiential techniques. In Spain, Daniel Bustelo
and Ana Sanchez Duran used an initially bewildering exercise called 'Picking up
sticks', which involved putting trainees in pairs, blindfolding them and placing
a stick between the forefingers of their right hands! This exercise needs to be
demonstrated, with musical accompaniment, to explain how it works and
demonstrate the learning it brings.

---

[19]   See **4.8** above on pre-requisites for effective co-mediation.
[20]   Ibid, at **4.4.1.2** above for an example of cross-cultural co-mediation.

Training family mediators is rather like teaching people to swim. The trainer starts by talking about swimming in a general way and may demonstrate basic strokes, but the best way of teaching a new skill is not to talk about it or show how it is done. We learn best by doing it ourselves. Learning to swim needs practice and a positive frame of mind to develop the necessary autonomy, confidence and buoyancy – the ability to keep one's head above water and feel at ease in the water, even when the breakers are coming in fast. Role-playing helps to:

- understand the feelings of other people in the room and different ways in which they may express or withhold their feelings;

- practise being a mediator, in a safe and supportive setting;

- identify mediator behaviour which is productive or counter-productive;

- explore new ways of working with difficult problems;

- become more aware of our own values and habitual ways of responding;

- share our reactions and difficulties and get fresh ideas;

- experience being a mediation client and the powerful emotions that are often aroused – and discover what is helpful or unhelpful in the mediator's response.

Role-plays can be designed to practise different stages of the mediation process and/or to practise a particular skill or skills, or devised to explore a situation that raises an ethical dilemma for mediators. There should be a carefully constructed scenario for each role-play with individual, confidential briefings for each role – mediators, participants and observers. If the briefing for the participants is both realistic and imaginative, they may slip into their role as easily as donning a costume and identify with their characters with remarkable intensity. The flames of conflict ignite and there may be fierce anger and real tears. The role-play groups create their own intimacy and containment and it would be inhibiting to have a trainer listening in. However, trainers should be 'at the side of the pool', so that they can spot when a trainee is suddenly in trouble. Role-plays resonate with personal experience and may stir up acute feelings of personal loss. Trainers have a responsibility to take care of those they train, noting signs of anxiety and providing support in a thoughtful and sensitive way. Role-playing with written briefing for each role generates spontaneous interactions and gives scope to develop interventions. If the drama is acted out, the strong emotions of mediation can be experienced in role and not merely observed. Trainers must be alert, however, for a trainee in personal crisis. During one training course, a participant disclosed for the first time her own experience as a victim of child sexual abuse. There should always be one or more co-trainers, one to take care of an individual while the other maintains responsibilities towards the group as a whole. Trainers can observe body language without being able to hear what is said in a small group. If a trainee is suddenly in distress and other members of the group are unaware, a trainer needs to jump in and throw a life-raft. Recall of a personal crisis triggered by a role-play is like getting cramp during swimming. Trainers need to be strong enough swimmers (holding someone during emotional crisis) to rescue and give support. After recovery, ways of continuing can be considered, with ongoing support. If there is focused planning in pairs or small groups before starting a role-play, using the written briefings provided by the trainers, 'performance anxiety' is reduced and there is less flamboyant splashing by a trainee swimmer which threatens to drown others around them!

Some trainees find role-play more useful than others, but provided it is planned and managed well by the trainers, they generally find they learn from it and enjoy it. At the end of a role-play, participants need to 'de-role' (or 'unroll' as a Scottish trainer puts it), ie come out of role. Role-playing arouses intense feelings and those who played the separated couple may continue to argue after the role-play ends. Some may feel demoralised because they found the role-play was difficult to manage. Everyone needs to be able to express their feelings safely, receive constructive feedback and support, and resume their own identity. Practising to co-mediate in role-play is essential preparation for co-mediating in practice.

14.8   CONVERSATIONAL ANALYSIS

Stokoe[21] takes the view that traditional role-play is an artificial training method that departs from real life and encourages 'playing to the gallery', to impress trainers or fellow trainees. These shortcomings may be minimised, however, as suggested above. Stokoe has developed a method called 'Conversation Analytic Role-Play Method' (CARM) that works 'by transcribing and anonymising extracts from recordings that demonstrate different ways that mediators and their support staff formulate and organise particular actions (eg offering mediation)'.[22] Stokoe's research, based on recording and analysing approximately two hundred intake calls to community mediation services in the UK, identified 'barriers to mediation' that discourage disputants from engaging in mediation. Training in CARM assisted community mediators to manage intake calls differently, describing mediation more effectively and expressing empathy towards callers. This analytic approach may be already familiar to family mediators and it is useful, since mediators need to use their heads as well as their hearts. Nevertheless, analysis of explanations cannot be a substitute for the *free conversations* that take place between trainers and trainees in which spontaneous interactions in role-plays generate conditions for active learning. This learning continues in constructive debriefing following role-play, in which co-mediators and 'clients' share observations and reflections in helpful ways that build confidence, rather than undermining it.

14.9   SELF-AWARENESS AND MINDFULNESS

References to mediators' self-awareness and self-presentation are rather scarce in mediation literature, but first impressions are important. Children and young

---

[21]   Stokoe 'Overcoming Barriers to Mediation in Intake Calls to Services: Research-based Strategies for Mediators' (July 2013) *Negotiation Journal* 289–314.

[22]   Ibid, p 312.

people have views on how mediators should 'come across' and be dressed: 'The mediator should be smiley and nice, a friendly mediator definitely not dressed in a suit but not in jeans as that would look as if they weren't taking it seriously.'[23] A tall and imposing barrister came to the first day of training dressed in a dark three-piece suit. He was surprised by the suggestion that parents – let alone a child – might find him intimidating. The next day he came in a red polar-neck sweater and fawn trousers: 'Look! Colour!' Obviously it is not just outward appearance that matters. Mediation training helps to develop self-awareness of personal qualities and style, strengths, weaknesses and mannerisms. Watching oneself on video is uncomfortable, but an important learning experience. Personal qualities are as important in mediation as professional knowledge and technical skills.

The mediator's personality, manner and values are a significant part of the 'mediation system' in an ecosystemic approach. Mediators bring their own family history and experience, cultural conditioning, views, values and beliefs. It is important to be aware of influences that may have a conscious or unconscious influence. Mediators also bring their own norms, values and biases to the mediation process, consciously or unconsciously. A mediator may feel more drawn to one participant than the other, or feel the need to defend one participant against the other. When they continue to argue, it may be tempting to act as arbitrator and tell them what they ought to do. Training needs to develop mediators' self-awareness and ability to manage their own reactions, to avoid becoming triangulated in the conflicts that are brought to mediation and maintain 'equidistance'. Role-plays and other experiential exercises give trainee mediators opportunities to experience challenging situations at first-hand, to recognise their own reactions and develop skills in managing conflict without taking sides or responsibility for resolving the dispute. Self-awareness and skills go on growing in the continuing journey from foundation training through practice, reflective thought and further reading, with the support and encouragement of the mediator's professional practice consultant.

Mindfulness may be defined as 'the intentional, accepting and non-judgmental focusing of one's attention on the emotions, thoughts and sensations occurring in the present moment.'[24] The concept of mindfulness is derived from 'sati', an essential element in Buddhist practice. Its use in processes of non-violent communication and conflict resolution was developed from the 1960s by Marshall Rosenberg and others in a communication process also known as Collaborative Communication.[25] This process focuses on three aspects of communication: self-empathy (defined as a deep and compassionate understanding of one's own inner experience), empathy (listening to another with deep compassion) and honest self-expression (defined as expressing oneself authentically in a way that is likely to inspire compassion in others).

---

23 Quotation provided by Nicola Tiernan, mediator.
24 Wikipedia.
25 Gates, Wray and Gear *Behavioural Distress: Concepts and Strategies* (Bailliere Tindall, 2000).

Some mediation trainers use mindfulness techniques in their training to develop this intense and compassionate self-awareness as a component of empathy in responding to others. Mindfulness focuses attention on the personal qualities that mediators need to possess and demonstrate, rather than on mechanistic adherence to structure and techniques. As Gilbert[26] points out in a book that should be required reading for all mediators, 'helping people develop compassion for others and, especially, themselves, is not always easy'. Gilbert defines the essence of compassion as 'a basic kindness, with a deep awareness of the suffering of oneself and other living things, coupled with the wish and effort to relieve it'.[27] Although mediation focuses on the settlement of specific issues under a number of practical constraints, notably cost, there are broader aims to improve communication and 'buttress' families through stressful periods of family change. Mediators' personal qualities and capacity for compassion and mindfulness are very important factors in the way participants experience the mediation process and also in the outcomes they reach. Cloke,[28] writing on 'Mediation and meditation: the deeper middle way', suggests that there are actually two middle ways with entirely different outcomes. The first consists of adding two things together and finding their average. The deeper, 'transformational' middle way involves authentic and committed listening, open-hearted communication, empathetic dialogue, collaborative negotiation and creative problem-solving.

14.10   TRAINING FOR INFORMATION AND ASSESSMENT MEETINGS (MIAMS)

The extensive knowledge and skills needed for information and assessment meetings are similar, but not identical, to those needed for mediation itself. Because of fears of an insufficient number of mediators qualified to undertake assessment meetings, during a limited period from April 2011 to December 2014 newly trained mediators could acquire a separate 'MIAM qualification' if they met certain criteria, including attendance at a one day MIAMs course. This fast-track route to MIAM qualification is being discontinued. As from 1 January 2015, authorisation to undertake publicly funded MIAMs and mediations will be based on a single qualified status (APC, see **14.11** below).

Information and assessment meetings are by no means a routine exercise. Mediators need to engage with angry or apprehensive people, put them at ease and gauge their ability to take information on board, while making careful and sensitive assessments of the suitability of mediation or other non-court dispute resolution process. The amount and pace of information-giving needs to be tailored to the individual's situation and emotional state. Mediation skills for assessment meetings need to include:

- Interpersonal skills to engage and build rapport with angry and distressed individuals who may come in a bewildered state, at varying stages of

---

[26] Gilbert *The Compassionate Mind* (Constable, 2009), p xxi.
[27] Ibid, at p xiii.
[28] Cloke *Mediation and meditation: the deeper middle way* (2009) mediate.com Weekly, No 266.

separation and with different levels of conflict. Each partner is generally at a different stage from the other. A partner who does not accept the ending of the marriage or relationship may be in a state of shock and have difficulty processing information. Mediators need to be aware of gender imbalances and able to assess emotional and psychological capacity for mediation.

- Communication skills to acknowledge concerns and explain mediation and other dispute resolution processes clearly and helpfully. Information needs to be tailored to the needs of each person receiving it, not a standardised discourse from a disengaged assessor. Mediators need to be aware of body language and responsive to non-verbal communication. Mediation conversations begin in initial assessment meetings and continue in mediation itself.

- Screening for domestic abuse, child protection concerns and any contra-indications for mediation. Mediation provides a forum where participants should be able to negotiate with each other in safety, without risk or fear of abuse or of being bullied into submission. Any indication of harm or risk of harm to a child requires immediate referral to the local safeguarding agency. Assessing safety and suitability for mediation is a highly skilled task that needs to be undertaken *with* the individual, rather than *of* the individual.[29] Responsibility for the assessment rests with the mediator.

- Competence in assessing eligibility for legally aided mediation. These financial assessments have become much more complicated and time-consuming now that capital has to be assessed as well as income. Bank statements must be produced, together with evidence of savings and other assets, supported by valuations as necessary. Evidence of income from all sources must be provided and/or recent written evidence of welfare benefits that 'passport' the recipient for legal aid. Income from self-employment is particularly difficult to assess, as some income may be 'cash in hand' and hard to determine. If the client is living with a new partner, the value of their income and jointly owned property must be assessed as well. The mediator may need to work out the average of variable weekly earnings. Lawyers may be accustomed to making financial assessments, whereas mediators from social work and counselling backgrounds need additional training and sufficient numeracy to assess eligibility. Assessment is not compulsory for those who choose to pay privately for mediation. However, if there are financial and property issues, the mediator needs to explain that full financial disclosure will be needed, with supporting documents, for mediation on financial and property matters.

- A combination of personal, process and problem-solving skills in proposing a 'tailor-made' mediation model with imagination tempered by

---

[29] See Screening Conversation, Appendix C and Pre-Mediation Screening and Suitability Assessment Record Form, Appendix D.

realistic appraisal: screening out of mediation in some circumstances, while in others, offering co-mediation and/or some combinations of caucusing and shuttle mediation.[30]

14.11   ASSESSMENT OF PROFESSIONAL COMPETENCE

The Final Report of the Family Justice Review called for 'a clear plan ... to maintain and reinforce standards of competence and to ensure the effective regulation of mediation ... Without that there are clear risks to children and their parents, and of discredit to the whole approach.'[31] Following the Government Response to the Family Justice Review, the FMC commissioned a report by Professor John McEldowney on standards and regulation of family mediation training and practice. In his report, Professor McEldowney observed that:

> 'Family mediation draws on a wide range of skills and techniques that range across a broad spectrum of disciplines and it needs to be distinguished from mediation in general. It uniquely addresses complex financial and related issues as well as children and their welfare ... [It] requires a modern and up-to-date system of regulation that sets standards, regulates the profession and provides an up to date licensing and accreditation scheme.'[32]

The McEldowney report warned of the 'risks around poor regulation exposing people to poor quality services'.[33] Rather than Member Organisations of the FMC applying variable standards to accredit their own training courses and mediators, there should be a single, independent accrediting body. The FMC commissioned Dr Stan Lester, an expert on professional standards, to undertake a Scoping Study in which working groups were set up under Dr Lester's guidance to consider revised standards for mediator training, accreditation, professional development, professional practice consultancy and other aspects. Following Dr Lester's report on the Scoping Study, the FMC approved a raft of new standards and requirements.[34]

From 1 January 2015, all family mediation initial training and other mediation courses must be approved by the FMC and there will be a single accreditation standard to which all mediators must work in order to pass the Assessment of Professional Competence (APC) and obtain FMCA status (FMC Accredited Family Mediator). Mediators will be required take the APC within three years of completing their initial training. The FMC Professional Standards and Self-regulatory Framework sets out the requirements for competence assessment and requirements for the role and responsibilities of professional practice consultants (PPCs, see **14.12** below). To apply for the APC, the mediator must

---

[30]   See Chapter 4 above.

[31]   Family Justice Review *Final Report* (November 2011) para 4.102.

[32]   McEldowney, *Family Mediation in a Time of Change*, FMC Final Review 2012,. para 15 and para 75.

[33]   Ibid, para 4.

[34]   FMC Manual on Professional Standards and Self-Regulatory Framework, September 2014.

submit a portfolio including documentation from three completed mediations (with identifying details removed), reflective case commentaries, answers to dilemmas that mediators may face and a testimony from their PPC, based in part on direct observation of the mediator's practice. Mediators who pass the APC successfully acquire FMCA status and the Legal Aid Agency's authorisation to undertake publicly funded information and assessment meetings (MIAMs) and publicly funded mediation. They can then be entered on the Government database of professionally qualified mediators. Mediators providing publicly funded MIAMs and mediations must also have a contract with the Legal Aid Agency to undertake this work.[35]

Mediators who are already accredited through the FMA or Resolution and/or who are authorised by the Legal Aid Agency to undertake publicly funded MIAMs and mediation will be automatically 'passported' to FMC Accreditation (FMCA), **provided that they have current membership of their Member Organisation that satisfies CPD and PPC requirements.** Subject to agreement by the FMC Professional Standards and Accreditation Board (PSAB), Law Society accredited family mediators will also automatic qualify for FMCA status.

14.12 PROFESSIONAL PRACTICE CONSULTANCY

The FMC Manual on Professional Standards states that professional practice consultancy is a relationship of support and oversight between a Professional Practice Consultant (PPC) (who must be an experienced, FMC-accredited and currently practising family mediator) and a family mediator who may be either FMC accredited, or registered as working towards accreditation ('registered'), or neither accredited nor registered. Family mediators are required to have a specified minimum level of initial and ongoing PPC support as a condition of registration and accreditation. The PPC's role includes acting as a mentor and sounding-board for the mediator, and providing a second professional opinion when requested by the mediator, the FMC or the mediator's Member Organisation (MO), for instance in response to a complaint or difference of opinion. It also involves maintaining oversight of the mediator's work insofar as is possible within the stipulated minimum requirement for PPC contact. While it is not a policing role, the PPC must draw the mediator's attention to any matters that may lead to contravention of the FMC Code of Practice, and, should the mediator continue to contravene the Code in spite of the PPC's advice and warnings, must report such contraventions to the mediator's MO for consideration under its complaints and disciplinary procedures. PPCs are also encouraged to discuss with their mediators (and, if necessary, in order to arrive at a decision on acceptability, consult with the MO concerned) any issues, which, while they do not directly contravene the Code, could be considered borderline in terms of good practice. PPCs must act confidentially and in line with data protection requirements in relation to their mediators and to any information they are privy to about mediation clients, while making clear that

---

[35] See Mediation Quality Mark at www.justice.gov.uk/legal-aid.

there are limits to confidentiality where there is risk of harm, money laundering, serious breach of the Code of Practice, or where directed to reveal information by a court. The PPC cannot be held responsible for any failings in the mediator's work unless they result from a clearly substantiated neglect of these duties. MOs should note that PPCs cannot be considered sufficiently independent to carry out a formal investigation of a complaint against a mediator whom they support and supervise, though, as stated above, they may be asked to provide a second opinion to aid informal resolution.'[36] A draft code of practice for PPCs has been prepared by the FMC. The PPC's role includes:

- supporting the consultee's professional practice;
- stimulating fresh insights and understanding, offering new ideas and approaches;
- reviewing case files and providing consultancy on case notes and summaries;
- helping to deal with problems encountered and to reflect on possible strategies;
- giving personal support – mediation is stressful and can be debilitating;
- helping to consider how the consultee's values and attitudes may impact on their practice;
- making suggestions to help develop new models and forms of partnership;
- helping to plan continuing professional development;
- providing information on current developments, research etc;
- encouraging further reading and ways to extend areas of knowledge;
- providing consultancy on the portfolio for competence assessment;
- providing a testimonial in support of an application for competence assessment;
- assisting the consultee and where necessary, their MO, to deal with a complaint in accordance with FMC and MO requirements and complaints procedures;
- in general, being a friend, as well as mentor.

The PPC's joint responsibilities towards their consultees and also towards their MO and the FMC to maintain standards of practice can cause tensions between the PPC and a consultee. The investigation of a client complaint against the mediator must be undertaken by an independent panel and not by the PPC. PPCs need support themselves. The PPC's own PPC is a source of support as well as the occasional, thought-provoking challenge. A PPC network or 'buddy group' such as the FMA's Regional PPC Network is valuable in providing support to individual PPCs and in disseminating information and updates on mediation developments and current issues. A PPC e-group offers a useful vehicle for ongoing debate and sharing information at a time of rapid change and development. The role and responsibilities of PPCs will assume greater

---

[36] FMC Manual on Professional Standards and Self-Regulatory Framework, September 2014, p 32.

importance from 1 January 2015 onwards under the new FMC Standards. Members of the FMC Scoping Study working groups worked hard to achieve higher quality standards and greater consistency in the role and duties of PPCs. Continued co-working will be needed between PPCs who are members of different MOs in order to iron out differences and develop creative approaches in their own form of inter-mediator mediation!

Regardless of their experience, all mediators need regular opportunities for reflective discussions and consultancy. At times, practitioners experience anxieties and dilemmas, feel stressed or over-involved and encounter difficulties on which consultancy is needed. It is important to be able to share problems and learn from shared experience. Members of helping professions are often so preoccupied with helping their clients that they fail to respond to each other's needs and may neglect their own. They may mediate effectively, but fail to acknowledge their colleagues' efforts and concerns. Mediation skills are needed between mediators and within the mediation profession, sometimes acutely so.

Family mediation is stressful work. Mediators are vulnerable to the pain and distress they encounter in mediation, especially when they are under stress themselves. The emotional intensity of mediation sessions and pressures on the mediator can lead to exhaustion and burn-out, or reactions which may impair the mediator's judgment and ability to practise effectively.[37] At such times, the ready availability and support of a consultant are very important. Mediators need to maintain a balance between empathy and objectivity. When participants feel better understood, their need to present their side of the argument may lessen and they become more capable of listening. But as their emotional receptivity increases, the mediator's empathetic listening can create internal pressures and ambivalence within the mediator. The PPC can help consultees to recognise and deal with their own feelings and avoid identifying with a particular person or problem. Inevitably, mediators feel more rapport towards some participants than others. Certain personalities and types of behaviour may trigger a subjective reaction, or even antipathy. If a mediator becomes aware of feeling sympathetic towards one partner and critical of the other, this indicates the need to step back, examine what is happening and consider ways of regaining balance, such as involving a co-mediator. Discussion with the PPC may be needed. In this, as in other areas, a PPC-led case discussion is a powerful learning tool.

Mediators are sometimes tempted to bend the rules and may have strong reasons for doing so, but they should pause and reflect on possible consequences and preferably consult with their PPC. In a thought-provoking disquisition, Wilson[38] observed that 'naughty departures'[39] in mediation have been noted for some years as 'disparities between received mediation orthodoxy

---

[37] De Mayo 'Practical and ethical concerns in divorce mediation' (1996) 13(3) *Mediation Quarterly* 217–228.

[38] Wilson '"Naughty Departures": Expertise, Orthodoxy and the Role of Theory in the Practice of Mediation' in Deleuran ed. *Conflict Management in the Family Field and in other close relationships* (DJØF 2011), p 18.

and actual behaviours'. An inclination to bend the rules could be a danger signal that in responding to pressure from one or both participants, a mediator risks losing control or becoming over-involved. There is need for consultancy as to whether bending the rules would meet the needs of both participants equally and, importantly, whether it would entail a breach of national standards and code of practice. It is important to avoid mixing mediation with other processes or allowing it to lapse into no process at all. An inclination to depart from accepted mediation practice could be a sign of being drawn into the couple's conflict and becoming triangulated in it.[40] Wilson[41] points out that naughty departures may not be 'wilful, unethical violations: they occur because skilled practitioners are endeavouring to perform optimally in complex situations'. Mason,[42] a therapist, refers to the need for genuine curiosity and the avoidance of premature certainty when shifting from first to second order thinking.[43] Mediation requires creativity, rather than standardised responses, and creativity, like mediation itself, involves risks as well as opportunities. Provided that the risks are recognised and evaluated carefully, opportunities for creative practice are essential if mediation is to continue to evolve, instead of stagnating.

14.13   COMBINING INTUITIVE RESPONSES WITH REASONED ANALYSIS

Clarkson, a psychotherapist, has written that:

> 'one of the primary skills required today is the fast processing of minimal cues in uncertain conditions. Intuition can be the fastest and most accurate way of doing this ... intuition skills are like those demanded in white-water rafting, where you have to know how to react, as information surfaces from the rush of data coming towards you.'[44]

In his book, *Thinking, Fast and Slow*,[45] Kahneman gives examples of the intuitive understanding we rely on in everyday life. We detect anger when an angry person begins to speak, we recognise when we enter a room that we were the subject of the conversation and we react quickly to signs that the motorist in the next lane is driving dangerously. When confronted with a problem, we often recognise the situation and our intuitive response is likely to be what is needed. But it is not infallible. When we feel stuck, we may switch to a slower, more analytical kind of thinking. Kahneman calls intuitive thinking 'System 1' and analytical thinking 'System 2'. System 1 is generally effective, because our reactions to familiar situations (the word 'familiar' has a double meaning for

---

[39]   Hoffman and Lintern 'Eliciting and Representing the Knowledge of Experts' in Ericsson et al (eds) *Cambridge Handbook of Expertise and Expert Performance* (Cambridge University Press, New York, 2006), p 215.

[40]   See Chapter 4 above.

[41]   Wilson, op cit, p 18.

[42]   Mason 'Relational risk-taking and the therapeutic relationship' in Flakas et al (eds) *The Space Between: Experience, Context and Process* (Karnak Books 2005), pp 157–170.

[43]   See also Chapter 2 above.

[44]   Clarkson *Learning to unlearn*, University of Surrey paper, 1998.

[45]   Kahneman *Thinking, Fast and Slow* (Penguin Books, 2012).

family mediators) and short-term predictions are usually accurate. However, System 1 has biases that make it prone to error, because it relies on learnt impressions that may be misleading. System 2 is needed to work out solutions to difficult problems. System 2 is used for searching one's memory, making complex calculations and comparisons, careful planning and conscious choice. However, System 2 is also prone to error and is 'not a paragon of rationality. Its abilities are limited and so is the knowledge to which it has access. We do not always think straight when we reason'.[46] Kahneman argues that a combination of Systems 1 and 2 is highly efficient, because it minimises effort and optimises performance. Mediation training fosters skills that combine System 1 intuitive thinking with System 2 analytic thinking. Mediators need both. As Kahneman says, 'developing expertise takes longer, because expertise is not a single skill: it is a collection of skills'.[47]

14.14 ACHIEVING POSITIVE CHANGES WITHIN OURSELVES

It may be arrogant to imagine that we can assist other people to change their situation and resolve their problems. We need to start by changing ourselves. Change is hard. Mediators need to walk the talk and we don't always succeed. Changing familiar ways of thinking and working needs motivation within ourselves and inspiration from other people. It is easy to become encased in a hard shell of set ideas and familiar ways of thinking. It may be difficult to develop a new approach, like a fragile creature that needs to emerge from its shell and stretch its wings. We need to believe in our capacity to go on learning and exploring new ways of working. According to Einstein 'the world cannot be changed without changing our thinking'.

To transform conflict into co-operation, we need continuing reflective practice to increase the neuroplasticity of our brains. Recent studies on the brain suggest that continuing reflective practice enhances the development of cognitive abilities:

> 'a commitment to working at a skill over and over and meticulously zeroing in on faults ... At mid life, the brain is on the cusp – what we do matters and even what we think matters ... Our brains build up patterns of connections, interwoven layers of knowledge.'[48]

Although with increasing age we may forget people's names or what we went to fetch in a particular room, neural networks can go on building and strengthening in middle age and even later.

> 'Neuroplasticity exists across the life span – you're never too old to improve your brain function.'[49]

---

[46] Ibid, p 415.

[47] Ibid, p 241.

[48] Strauch *The Secret Life of the Grown-Up Brain* (Penguin Books, 2011) Introduction, p xvii.

[49] Ibid, p 121.

Co-mediating with a mediator from a different discipline builds new neural networks and the synapses fire faster! Kahneman suggests[50] that human beings have an inbuilt optimism bias that leads us to view the world as more benign than it actually is. Mediators need an optimism bias. In May 2000 thirty family mediation trainers from eleven countries took part in a two-day Family Mediation Trainers Exchange Forum, held near London. It was an enriching and inspiring experience, leading to the conclusion that family mediators seek:

- to listen in a certain spirit which comes from the heart and not only from the head;
- to respect the individuality of each person;
- to show humility, compassion and tolerance;
- to maintain an appropriate distance;
- to facilitate communication in ways that convey human warmth and understanding;

'Change will not come if we wait for some other person or some other time. We are the ones we've been waiting for. We are the change that we seek.'[51]

Mediation/Meditation

> *An easy mistake, I often*
> *Type meditation for mediation*
> *And vice versa,*
> *Slightly amused at the difference*
> *The letter T makes to the meaning.*
>
> *But perhaps it's not so great;*
> *In meditation we become*
> *More aware of reality,*
> *Escaping from automatism*
> *Of habitual responses*
> *And from enslavement to*
> *Our negative emotions.*
> *Thus freed we live and love with*
> *Greater strength and greater understanding*
> *And so, among other things,*
> *Can mediate with more effect.'*
>
> *Adam Curle[52]*

---

[50] Kahnemann *Thinking, Fast and Slow* (Penguin Books, 2012).
[51] Barack Obama, Speech to the Democratic National Convention, Washington DC, 28 August 2008.
[52] Curle *Recognition of Reality – Reflections and Prose Poems* (Hawthorn Press, 1987), p 29.

CHAPTER 15

INTERNATIONAL FAMILY MEDIATION AND FUTURE DIRECTIONS

'The oneness of human beings is the basic ethical thread that holds us together.'

Muhammed Yunus 2006

CONTENTS

15.1 FAMILY MEDIATION IN EUROPE

The ethos of mediation and peace-making has travelled across the world from east to west and west to east over many centuries, rather like the acanthus leaf in architecture. In Europe, family mediation spread rapidly in the last quarter of the 20th century and continues to develop. Many countries have introduced legislation on mediation, while international exchanges have multiplied through mediation literature, conferences and the Internet. However, much remains to be done to increase public awareness and use of mediation. A picture of family mediation in Europe resembles a patchwork quilt or mosaic. The pieces making up the patchwork have similar designs and colours, but the patterns vary and there are missing pieces. A variegated patchwork that recognises cultural differences is preferable to uniformity. Northerners may need a different kind of family mediation from southerners. On the other hand, the expansion of the European Union and the mobility of individuals and families across state boundaries increase the need for universally accepted principles and consistency. Legislation on mediation is increasing, with a considerable degree of consensus on its objectives and principles of voluntary participation, confidentiality, mediator impartiality and 'empowerment' of parties to reach agreement through mediation, in place of litigation. Before taking a brief look at the 'mediation mosaic' showing varying stages of growth and development in Europe, it may be useful to look at the framework provided by the Council of Europe's Recommendation of 1998 and the European Parliament's Directive on Mediation of 2008.

15.2　COUNCIL OF EUROPE RECOMMENDATION 21 JANUARY 1998

A study undertaken during the 1990s by the Council of Europe's Committee of experts on family law found that:

> 'research in Europe, North America, Australia and New Zealand suggests that family mediation is better suited than more formal legal mechanisms to the settlement of sensitive, emotional issues surrounding family matters. Reaching agreements in mediation has been shown to be a vital component in making and maintaining co-operative relationships between divorcing parents: it reduces conflict and encourages continuing contact between children and both their parents.'[1]

The Committee's recommendations were formally adopted by the Council of Europe in Recommendation No. (98) 1 of 21 January 1998:

> 'Realising that a number of States are considering the introduction of family mediation (and) convinced of the need to make greater use of family mediation, [the Council of Europe] recommends the governments of Member States:
> i.　to introduce or promote family mediation, or, where necessary, strengthen existing family mediation:
> ii.　to take or reinforce all measures they consider necessary with a view to the implementation of the following principles for the promotion and use of family mediation as an appropriate means of resolving family disputes.'

The Recommendation defines the aims of mediation as follows:[2]

> '(a)　to promote consensual approaches, thereby reducing conflict in the interest of all family members;
> (b)　to protect the best interests and welfare of children in particular, by reaching appropriate arrangements concerning custody and access;
> (c)　to minimise the detrimental consequences of family disruption and marital dissolution;
> (d)　to support continuing relationships between family members, especially those between parents and their children;

---

[1]　*Report of the Working Party on Mediation and Other Processes to Resolve Family Disputes* (CJ-FA-GT2).
[2]　At para 5.

(e)   to reduce the economic and social costs of separation and divorce, both to families and to States.'

The Recommendation points out that family disputes have special characteristics that need to be taken into account in mediation:[3]

'There are usually continuing and interdependent relationships. The dispute settlement process should facilitate constructive relationships for the future, in addition to enabling the resolution of current disputes. Family disputes usually involve emotional and personal relationships in which feelings can exacerbate the difficulties, or disguise the true nature of the conflicts and disagreements. It is usually considered appropriate for these feelings to be acknowledged and understood by parties and by the mediator. Disputes that arise in the process of separation and divorce have an impact on other family members, notably children, who may not be included directly in the mediation process, but whose interests may be considered paramount and therefore relevant to the process.'

15.3   EUROPEAN DIRECTIVE ON MEDIATION 2008

Ten years after the Council of Europe's Recommendation, the European Parliament and the Council of the European Union issued a Directive on Certain Aspects of Mediation in Civil and Commercial Matters:[4]

'to promote the amicable settlement of disputes by encouraging the use of mediation and by ensuring a balanced relationship between mediation and judicial proceedings.'

The Directive recognises that:

'agreements resulting from mediation are more likely to be complied with voluntarily and are more likely to preserve an amicable and sustainable relationship between the parties. These benefits become even more pronounced in situations displaying cross-border elements.'[5]

Mediation is defined as:

'a structured process ... whereby two or more parties to a dispute attempt by themselves, on a voluntary basis, to reach an agreement on the settlement of their dispute with the assistance of a mediator. This process may be initiated by the parties or suggested or ordered by a court or prescribed by the law of a Member State.'[6]

A mediator is defined as:

---

[3]   At para 15 of the Explanatory Memorandum.
[4]   European Parliament *Directive on Certain Aspects of Mediation in Civil and Commercial Matters* 2008/52/EC 21 May 2008.
[5]   See Preamble, para 6.
[6]   Ibid, Art 3.

'any third person who is asked to conduct a mediation in an effective, impartial and competent way, regardless of the denomination or profession of that third person in the Member State concerned and of the way in which the third person has been appointed or requested to conduct the mediation.'[7]

The Directive applies specifically: 'to mediation in cross-border disputes, but nothing should prevent Member States from applying such provisions also to internal mediation processes.'[8] The Directive has been implemented by all EU Member States apart from Denmark, where it does not apply.

The following brief overview of mediation developments in some European countries is limited in scope and needs constant updating. It gives some indications of legislation and developing practice.

15.3.1   Austria

Austria is a pioneer in this field. A pilot project on family mediation paved the way for the Federal Act on Mediation in Civil Matters that came into force on 1 May 2004. This established the legal framework for mediation in all private law areas, including family law. An earlier Directive on Mediation issued on 1 January 2000 had set out the principles and requirements for family mediation. 'Mediation shall take place only if the participation of the clients is completely voluntary' (Article 5(4)). 'As far as possible, co-mediation shall take place in a setting with one female and one male co-mediator' (Article 8(2)). A co-mediation model, teaming a mediator qualified in law with a mediator from a psychosocial discipline, was found to encourage 'interdisciplinary cooperation … in order to ensure optimal coverage of the areas of law and psycho-dynamics during divorce and separation' (Preamble, p 2). A structured model of mediation is used, starting with a pre-mediation phase and proceeding through five stages of mediation, with follow-up if needed.

15.3.2   Denmark

In Denmark, separated parents normally continue to hold joint custody of their children and are encouraged to make their own arrangements. If they are unable to agree on residence and/or visiting arrangements, the State Administration offers mediation and child welfare counselling to help them reach agreement. Only lawyers and judges may be appointed as court mediators and their training is likely to be generic, rather than specialised training in family mediation. There are no requirements to screen for domestic abuse or child protection issues. Private mediation on all issues, including finance and property, is provided on a fee-charging basis by two associations of lawyer mediators www.familiemediatorer.dk/english.html and www.mediatoradvokat-er.dk. Mediatoradvokater, with around two hundred members including family law mediators, is linked to the Association of Danish law firms. The State

---

[7]   Ibid, Art 3b.
[8]   Ibid, Art 8.

Administration (Statsforvaltningen) offers in-house mediation to its employees, free of charge, using either sole or co-mediators.

15.3.3 Finland

Municipalities in Finland are required under the Marriage Act 1987 to provide mediation as a voluntary service for parents in dispute over their children. For many years, however, mediation was not recognised as a discrete process and there was no specific training for family mediation. In consequence, local authority social workers continued to use counselling, therapy and social work techniques under a generic label of 'mediation'. This situation is changing through the work of a multi-disciplinary research and development project called FASPER. Launched in 2009, FASPER has been working with six municipalities to create a unified, collaborative approach to family mediation as a short-term, structured intervention for parents in conflict and secondly, to develop a specialised training programme in family mediation that can eventually be rolled out nationally. The overall aim is to change the culture of family conflict in Finland, so that parents are encouraged to use mediation to resolve disputes and co-operate with each other in the best interests of their children.

Finland is also developing a system of in-court conciliation in child custody disputes. The parents meet with a judge and a child expert – a psychologist, therapist or social worker with expertise in child development – who help them reach agreement over custody arrangements for their children. Legal aid is available to cover the cost of the court and lawyers' fees and a time-limit is applied, so that a custody dispute is set down for conciliation within six weeks. In 26% of cases in a pilot project, the parents requested conciliation in their application to the court. In other cases where custody proceedings were already in train, the parents were referred to conciliation by the court. If no agreement was reached, the case was referred back to the original judge. A new law on 'expert-assisted court conciliation' came into force on 1 May 2014 and is being implemented across the country.

The same term in Finnish, 'sovittel', covers in-court conciliation and out-of court mediation. These dispute settlement processes share the same philosophy and aims, but, as pointed out in Chapter 1 (**1.9**), there are risks of confusion if the same term is used for an in-court process imbued with the court's authority and an out-of-court process in which parents are encouraged to reach their own agreements without involving professionals holding statutory responsibilities. It is not only a question of the stage at which the dispute resolution process is used. Court-directed conciliation and out-of-court mediation are complementary, with features suited to different levels of conflict and different kinds of family functioning. Some parents battling over 'possession' of their children need a judge and child expert to make them more aware of and responsive to their children's needs. Other parents need support and time to regain their ability to talk to each other and reach joint decisions. Mutual trust and good communication are vital if parents' arrangements for their children are to work well in the longer term. Parents who take part in in-court conciliation, consisting of one, or if needed, two meetings usually lasting three to six hours, are guided towards agreements that are endorsed by the judge. In community-based mediation, parents are encouraged to focus on their children's needs and reach agreement with the help of qualified but 'power-less' mediators. In Finnish society, authority may generally be exercised in a humane and low-key way and thus these distinctions may have less significance than in countries with more authoritarian régimes. Children and young people are not generally involved directly and it will be interesting to see whether more attention will be given in future to hearing the voice of the child in mediation, subject to the necessary pre-conditions and consents (see Chapter 8). The Finnish mediation system is still emerging and the relationship between different ways of resolving family conflicts is being explored as steps are taken towards further development.

15.3.4   France

The first steps to develop family mediation in France were taken in the early 1990s by social workers, psychologists and lawyers who recognised the need for mediation and took voluntary initiatives to develop this new field of professional practice. A group travelled to Quebec for training in family mediation and some of the first French training programmes involved experienced family mediators from North America and England.[9] These voluntary initiatives paved the way, as they did in England and other countries, for legislation on mediation. The law on joint parental authority of 4 March 2002 and the reform of divorce law implemented on 1 January 2005 empowered family court judges (the Juge aux Affaires Familiales, known as the JAF) to refer parties to mediation with a requirement to receive information on mediation and to take part in mediation if they both consent.

The European Directive on Mediation of 21 May 2008 was implemented in France under Ordonnance No 2011-1540 of 16 November 2011 and Décret no 2012-66 of 20 January 2012. There are further developments promoting the use of mediation in family proceedings. A draft law on parental authority and the best interests of the child was passed on its first reading on 27 June 2014 in the Assemblée Nationale. This draft law provides a definition of family mediation:

> 'La médiation familiale, qui a pour finalité d'apaiser le conflit et de préserver les relations au sein de la famille, est un processus structuré et confidentiel de résolution amiable des différends familiaux. Avec l'aide du médiateur familial, tiers qualifié, impartial et indépendant, les personnes tentent de parvenir à une solution mutuellement acceptable, qui tient compte de l'intérêt de l'une et de l'autre et de celui de leurs enfants éventuels et qui peut prendre la forme d'accords susceptibles d'être homologués par le juge.'

This definition may be loosely rendered in English as follows:

---

[9]   Babu and Bonnoure-Aufière 2003.

'Family mediation is a structured and confidential process of family conflict resolution aimed at the amicable settlement of differences between family members and the preservation of family relationships. With the assistance of a family mediator – a qualified, impartial and independent third party – the parties seek to reach mutually acceptable solutions that take account of each other's needs and those of their children and which may be formalised in agreements capable of being ratified by the judge.'

Article 17 of the draft law would maintain the 2002 regulation on referral to mediation. Further to this regulation and in order to promote agreement between parents on the joint exercise of their parental authority, parents may be required under new legislation to undertake up to two mediation sessions with a mediator appointed by the judge.

15.3.5 Germany

After training provided by mediators from the United States, Canada and Israel, the national association of family mediators, BAFM (Bundes-Arbeitsgemeinschaft für Familien-Mediation) was founded in Germany in 1992 with the aim of establishing and maintaining voluntary standards for family mediation training. Members of BAFM must have two years' practice experience in their profession of origin, mediation training of at least 200 hours and practical training under supervision, with documentation of four completed mediations. 50% of BAFM members come from psychosocial professions and 50% from the legal profession. Mediation training must be interdisciplinary, both in the structure of the group (50% psychosocial professionals, 50% lawyers) and in the composition of the training team. Family mediation is offered on all issues in separation and divorce (children and financial matters) and mainly takes the form of interdisciplinary co-mediation.

Under national law (Mediationsgesetz of 26.07.2012) on the promotion of mediation and other forms of out of court dispute resolution, mediation must be considered by the parties and their lawyers before application is made to the court on family matters. Parties to court proceedings are required to inform the court whether they have attempted mediation and if not, whether reasons were given as to why mediation should not take place. There is a possibility of cost sanctions applying if a party has not attended a mediation information session without providing a satisfactory reason. Family court judges have power to order attendance at an information meeting with a mediator and proceedings can be adjourned to allow mediation to take place. If the parties accept mediation, the usual provisions apply with regard to adjournment of proceedings and suspension of limitation periods. Mediation information meetings are free of charge but there is no public funding for mediation itself, either at national or regional level, and mediators generally charge privately.

The EU Mediation Directive and the national mediation law of 26 July 2012 highlighted the need for regulation. A draft law addressing the training and certification of mediators (Verordnung über die Aus- und Fortbildung von zertifizierten Mediatoren of 31.01.2014[10]) is due to be passed in late 2014. As Walsh has explained,[11] in order to meet the joint aims of quality assurance of mediation services and market transparency, the legislation sets certain pre-requisites – a professional qualification or a degree plus two years' professional experience – together with the certified mediator training that is required for practice as a certified mediator. Certified mediator training is set at a minimum hour level of 120 hours training including practical training, role-play and supervision. After qualification, mediators are required to undertake a minimum of 20 hours' professional development over a two year cycle and, to maintain their practical skills, must mediate or co-mediate a minimum of four cases over a two year period. These cases must be documented and supervision must also be undertaken.[12]

15.3.6   Ireland

The Mediators' Institute of Ireland (MII),[13] the professional association for mediators in Ireland, is a not-for-profit organisation providing mediation in single-issue and multi-issue disputes between two parties or in multi-party conflicts. MII defines mediation as 'a voluntary process of conflict prevention and resolution that allows the parties an opportunity to address their issues in a confidential, private, and safe environment'. The divorce rate in Ireland has risen from 8.7% in 2006 to 9.7% in 2011/2012 but use of mediation has remained low, despite statistics from MII showing a settlement rate for mediation averaging 80%. In a recent press statement, Helen Collins, a family law solicitor in West Cork, commented that changes are urgently needed: 'We need a sea-change in terms of separation and divorce. We need to move away from the adversarial model and support our families in a different way when they set about separation or divorce'.

There are a number of pilot schemes in existence in Ireland, both in the Circuit and District Courts. A scheme run jointly by the Courts Service, the Legal Aid Board and the Family Mediation Service is based in Dolphin House, Dublin. The aim is to make mediation available in all cases relating to children, that is, guardianship, custody and access cases (approximately 40% of all cases in the past 10 years). Applicants are offered a mediation information session and with their consent the service contacts the other party. If both are willing, they attend a joint mediation information session and then, if they wish, proceed to mediation. There is no charge. Preliminary figures for the first year of the project show that there were 1,623 applications to the District Court in relation to children. Between March 2011 and March 2012, more than 400 couples attended mediation information sessions and around 50% went on to mediate. By the end of March 2012, 293 of these had reached mediated agreements and many more were still in progress. As more than 90% of these applicants would

---

[10]   For the text in German see www.dgm-web.de/download/RVO_MedG.pdf.
[11]   Walsh *Proposed regulations on Mediator Certification in Germany* retrieved from www.kluwermediationblog.com, 6 March 2014.
[12]   For further information see http://kluwermediationblog.com/author/sabinewalsh.
[13]   www.themii.ie.

have been eligible for legal aid, it was estimated that net savings to the State resulting from issues being resolved through mediation was over €102,000 (Irish Times, June 2012). The project continues and further progress reports are planned, with expansion to other District Court areas in due course. 98% of family law applications are made in the Circuit Court and a number of court rules have been introduced. Order 19A of the Circuit Court Rules (inserted in 2009) permits a Judge or County Registrar to invite the parties to 'use an ADR process' and adjourn proceedings to facilitate dispute resolution.

The recently published Draft General Scheme of Mediation Bill 2012[14] proposes legislation to encourage greater awareness and use of mediation. Under the new legislation, judges would be empowered to refer cases to mediation and a statutory obligation would be placed on solicitors and barristers to inform their clients concerning mediation. Lawyers providing information on mediation to their clients would be expected to estimate, as far as possible, the likely costs and duration of court proceedings to help potential litigants recognise the benefits of mediation in time and cost terms, encouraging them to seek to resolve matters at an early stage. There are some concerns as to whether mediation might be made compulsory under new legislation. MII argues that the essentially voluntary nature of mediation and confidentiality of discussions in mediation must be preserved. MII also favours more robust regulation of mediation, but the nature of this regulation remains to be decided.

15.3.7 Italy

There is a growing number of Italian associations and agencies committed to developing family mediation and building a network to increase public awareness and greater use of mediation. The Università Cattolica S. Cuore in Milan provides a Masters programme in family and community mediation and hosts international conferences on families in transition and mediation. The Centro Studi e Richerche sulla Famiglia at this university has made important contributions to the conceptual understanding of family relationships.[15] In Florence, the highly committed team at *Mediamente* runs training courses and organises seminars and conferences. A new law came into force in Italy on 10 February 2013 requiring mediation organisations to adopt a common code of practice setting standards for training and practice, and to publish registers of mediators who have obtained a 'certificazione di qualità'. National mediation associations are expected to work together to develop unified norms and standards. The challenges of this new law and related developments were presented at the national conference of the Società di Mediazione Familiare (SIMeF) held in Florence in October 2013. In many regions, such as Lombardy, regional law provides for free mediation meetings (up to eight). There is debate in Italy about requiring an information meeting with an authorised family mediator before application is made to the Court.

---

14   For further comments see http://kluwermediationblog.com/author/sabinewalsh.
15   See for example Rigenerare i Legami: la mediazione nelle relazione familiare e comunitarie (Vita e Pensiero, Milano 2003).

15.3.8   The Netherlands

Since 1 April 2005, family courts in the Netherlands have been able to refer parties to mediation during court proceedings. The statutory framework for divorce mediation is contained in the Post-Divorce Continued Parenthood Act, in force since 1 March 2009. This Act defines parental responsibility and requires parents to submit their parenting plan to the divorce court. Parents may divorce only after they have submitted a parenting plan explaining how they intend to carry out their parenting responsibilities after divorce. Divorce mediation in the Netherlands is mainly concerned with the consequences of divorce for children and maintaining family ties between parents and their children, but may also deal with financial and property matters. Judges in the Netherlands are not permitted to be mediators themselves but all judges receive training in assessing and referring cases to mediation. Legal proceedings are suspended during mediation and can be resumed if the parents are unable to reach agreement. Half the mediation cases are completed within a month and one-third within 14 days. If agreement is reached, the court proceedings are terminated. Judicial checks on agreements take place only at the request of the parties. Follow-up studies have shown that large majority of mediation participants were satisfied with the mediation process and with the mediator. Over 80% of participants and their lawyers said that in a similar situation they would choose mediation again and would also recommend it to other people. This was equally the case among parents who did not reach agreement. The mediation referral procedure has been implemented at all district courts and courts of appeal and in the period from 2005 to 2009 there were approximately 10,000 referrals, with a settlement rate of 61%.[16]

Under new statutory rules introduced on 1 January 2009, parenting plans must show in what way the parents have involved their children in drawing up the plan. Depending on the age of the child and other circumstances, the mediator may talk with children on their own. Child-inclusive mediation is used in many cases and is likely to become more common. Mediators who undertake to see children without their parents being present agree with the parents and explain to the child that what the child says to the mediator will remain confidential (apart from child protection issues). As in child-inclusive mediation in Britain (see Chapter 8), the mediator checks carefully with the child at the end of their meeting whether the child wants anything fed back to the parents by the mediator and if so, exactly what the mediator should tell the parents. The mediator should also consider whether anything the child has said might get the child into trouble if a parent were to find out about it. Divorce mediation in the Netherlands takes place before and during court proceedings. In view of the requirement to submit a parenting plan prior to divorce being granted, there is a view that mediation should logically precede divorce proceedings. No comparable statutory framework exists in the Netherlands for other forms of mediation in family matters, such as children's contact with grandparents and disputes over family business or inheritance.

---

[16]   Pel et al 'Family Mediation in the Netherlands' *International Family Law* (2009) 4, 255–259.

15.3.9 Norway

The law both in Norway and Sweden makes it clear that arrangements agreed by parents themselves are generally preferable to decisions by the court. Therefore, the courts should always encourage parents to try to reach jointly agreed solutions. In Norway, unlike other European countries, mediation is mandatory and free of charge in legal disputes concerning children. Under a change to the Marriage Act effective from 1993, married couples with children under 16 must attend a mediation meeting before they can obtain a separation or divorce. Mediation is also mandatory before parents can bring a dispute over their children before the County Governor or the Court. Only one hour of mediation is compulsory, but this requirement can be extended for a further three hours if a continuation of mediation is considered likely to produce agreement. Mediation in Norway embodies certain key values:

- Families continue, despite separation and divorce.

- Children need to main their relationships with both parents, in the great majority of cases.

- Decisions agreed by parents themselves are more likely to work in practice.

- Mutually acceptable solutions can be reached more quickly through mediation and can be tailored to the needs of individual families.

- The individual claims and interests of each parent need to be understood and addressed in the context of the continuing needs and well being of the family as a whole (Tjersland 1995).

The County Governor in each region is responsible for the provision of family mediation by qualified social workers employed by the local authority. Couples meet with one mediator, the mediation is free of charge and normally limited to four sessions of one hour each. The first session is used to clarify any issues, exchange information and plan further sessions, if needed. The second session focuses on the children and the third on finances (regulated more simply in Norway than in many other countries). The fourth session may focus on relationships to family and friends and a fifth session may be used to draw up written agreements and to issue the parents with a certificate showing that they have attended mediation. Agreements reached in mediation are legally binding but not enforceable. Norwegian mediators educate parents about children's needs in separation and divorce and seek to make parents aware of the consequences of their behaviour and decisions for their children. The mediator also has an obligation to inform parents that according to the Norwegian Children Act, children over 12 should be listened to (but not asked to make decisions) before important decisions are taken concerning the child. Children are not usually involved directly, but they may meet with the mediator in some circumstances.

More recently, Norway has developed a procedure called 'Conflict and Conciliation'. Following an application to the court on child custody, residence or contact, the parents are invited to meet with the judge and a mediator who work together. At the first court meeting, the discussion focuses on immediate objectives that the parents agree to work on together with the mediator for the next three months. These plans are recorded and a date set for the second meeting in court about three months later. During these three months, the mediator and the parents (and usually also the children) meet regularly to try to resolve all the issues. If they reach a long-term agreement before the three months have elapsed, the mediator helps the parents to write it down, sign it, and send it to the court. The court ratifies the parents' agreement to make it enforceable and the case is closed.

If, however, matters are not resolved at the end of the three months, the parents are offered a further period of three months to try to reach a solution, but no more. If the issues are not settled after six months, the case is handled in the traditional way with a social work enquiry and assessment on custody or other matters. The court then takes its decision. The 'Conflict and Conciliation' procedure is not offered to parents in cases involving violence, abuse, drugs, mental illness, etc.

15.3.10   Poland

Although victim-offender mediation was introduced in Polish law in 1997, mediation in the family justice system started only in 2005, when an amendment to the Civil Procedure Code made it possible for courts to refer cases to mediation. The court keeps a list of mediators recommended by professional and social organisations to whom the court can refer. Mediation is voluntary in Poland and although parties are not compelled to accept it, many do so. The court can also be requested by the parties to make an adjournment to enable them to go to mediation. Family mediation is also available prior to court proceedings. Family mediators on court lists are members of associations or agencies in different parts of Poland. There are professional standards for training and practice and most mediator associations are represented on a national council advising the Ministry of Justice on ADR. The ADR Council, jointly with the Ministry of Justice, has recently launched a public awareness campaign to make mediation better known (including TV and radio publicity).

Recent developments in district courts include the appointment of mediation co-ordinators (judges) with responsibility for encouraging the use of in-court and court-referred mediation. In 2009, a further important legislative change increased the number of family mediation cases. The amended Family Code introduced obligatory 'parenting plans' in cases where parents seek joint custody of children after divorce. However, public awareness about children's needs in divorce and other family disputes is still low. Many parents, especially mothers whose chances of getting a sole custody order are over 80%, may not be interested in mediating, if they expect to do better in court. Another major deterrent is the cost, as mediation costs must be paid fully by the parties themselves: legal aid is not available for mediation.

15.3.11 Portugal

At the end of the 1990s, the first officially recognised family mediation service in Portugal was set up in a joint initiative taken by the Ministry of Justice and the Order of Lawyers. This court-referred mediation service was restricted to matters concerning parental responsibility and catered only for parents resident in certain districts of Lisbon. Following the establishment of the 'Dirección General de Administración Extrajudicial' in the year 2000, family mediation became more widely available in Portugal. Mediators now accept self-referrals from separated parents, instead of solely from the courts. Known as the 'Sistema de Mediación Familiar', family mediation in Portugal continues to be supported and regulated by the Ministry of Justice, providing mediation independently of court proceedings, as well as court referrals. Over the last decade, family mediation has developed in Portugal more rapidly than in other fields, to comply with European standards and directives in relation to international cross-border mediation in cases of parental child abduction.

15.3.12 Russia

There has been considerable progress in the development of family mediation in Russia following adoption of the Russian Law on Mediation in 2011. Although public awareness of mediation and the opportunities it offers remain very low, there is a clear upward trend in the number of family disputes being resolved amicably through mediation. This slow but steady increase is an encouraging sign. The Centre for Mediation and Law was established in Moscow in 2005 and the promotion of family mediation forms an important part of its activities. The Centre has undertaken many projects to increase awareness and understanding of mediation, including translation into Russian of books and articles on family mediation, training courses in mediation and meetings for mediators to share their experiences. The now standard foundation training in mediation taught at the Centre includes role plays to provide future mediators with some preparation for family mediation practice. More advanced courses on family mediation are also offered by trainers at the Centre.

Following Russia's accession to the 1980 and 1996 Hague Conventions, international family mediation began to be used in cases of alleged parental child abduction. The first international cross-border cases were referred to the Centre by the French-Russian Commission. The Centre for Mediation and Law supports the work of the Federal Institute for Mediation (FIM), the only statutory body in the Russian Federation dealing with policy and implementation in the field of mediation and ADR. To encourage the use of mediation in cross-border family cases, FIM has developed a project in co-operation with the Ministry of Education (which acts as the Central Authority for 1980 and 1996 Hague Convention cases) and with the Centre for Mediation and Law to establish a group of qualified international family mediators in Russia. The professional standards recently developed by expert organisations under the Centre's leadership includes specialisation in family mediation. Active co-operation has also been established between the Centre and child protection services and with the Department of Social Support and Protection. The Centre's pioneering work is increasing awareness of mediation among social workers and the general public, thus helping to develop family mediation at the domestic level as well as in international cases. Sharp debates about the introduction of mandatory court-annexed mediation for some types of disputes (including divorce) led to an understanding that such measures would be premature and would undermine the concept of mediation as a voluntary process. There are concerns that if the government were to impose mediation as a mandatory requirement, people would see it as an obstacle to obtaining justice at court, rather than as the natural way to resolve family disputes themselves. A regulation on referral to mediation would also depend on mediation being provided free of charge or at least on a subsidised basis. Professor Shamlikashvili, President of the Moscow Centre, considers that the priorities are to maintain high quality standards and avoid mediation being mandated by the courts in ways that would jeopardise the extensive efforts to promote mediation in Russia as a service for families.

15.3.13 Scotland

Scotland has a separate legal system from England and Wales. Family mediation in Scotland is provided by CALM (Comprehensive Accredited Lawyer Mediators recognised by the Law Society of Scotland) and by Relationships Scotland, who provide support to local services across Scotland. The confidentiality of mediation (non-disclosure to the court) provided by mediators in these two organisations has the formal approval of the Lord President of the Court of Session. The Scottish Civil Courts Review, known as the Gill Review (September 2009) recommended a free mediation service for lower value claims in civil cases to encourage out-of-court settlements, but did not propose measures to encourage greater use of family mediation. The Courts Reform Bill and its Programme for Government 2013–2014 sets out a major restructuring and modernisation of the civil justice system with increased use of mediation, initially in small claims and personal injury matters. The proposed new tier of court will take family cases and the Bill has implications for referral to mediation in family matters. The Scottish Mediation Network is exploring ways to integrate the use of mediation in the civil justice system.

15.3.14 Spain

Spain's first state law on mediation (Law 5/2012 on Civil and Commercial Mediation and RD 980/2013) incorporated the European Directive 2008/52/EC into Spanish law. This law did not refer specifically to family mediation, but its principles and criteria are equally applicable to family mediation, since family law in Spain forms part of Spanish civil law. Most autonomous regions of Spain had already enacted laws on family mediation in the decade 2001–2011. Although these regional laws lacked a common definition of mediation and had varying provisions for its use, they were compatible with State law on requirements and standards for the practice of civil and commercial mediation

The new draft federal law[17] on joint parental responsibility following separation is on its way through Parliament. This law introduces many changes to the legal procedure for divorce and separation, its principal aim being to promote the welfare of the child through facilitating agreement and reducing parental conflict. The draft law states that family mediation is a fundamental means of encouraging parental agreement, avoiding litigation and promoting shared parental responsibility following separation. Judges would be empowered under the new law to suspend proceedings and require parents to attend an information meeting with a family mediator. Parenting plans and mediated agreements should be presented to the court for ratification in a consent order.

State law, unlike regional laws, does not restrict the practice of family mediation to certain professions. Qualified mediators are required to have a university degree or equivalent before undertaking a course of at least 100 hours including 35 or more hours on mediation. Registration on a central register is voluntary under civil law, but there are requirements for continuing training. State law upholds the key principles of voluntary participation by the parties, neutrality and impartiality of the mediator and confidentiality of the process. The content and outcome of mediation are not reportable to the court, unless the parties agree to waive confidentiality or, in exceptional cases, if the judge requires evidence to be provided. Public authorities have a duty to inform the public of the availability of mediation as an alternative to litigation and publicly funded mediation may be available to parties who demonstrate financial hardship. In some regions, family mediation may be free of charge, regardless of income. Just over 50% of services providing publicly funded and private family mediation use a follow-up procedure about six months after a mediation comes to an end. Adherence to mediated agreements was found in 75% of cases.[18]

15.3.15 Sweden

In Sweden as in Norway, qualified social workers in the Family Law Office help separated parents to reach agreement on child-related issues. Parents may refer themselves at any time during or following separation for what are known in Sweden as 'co-operation talks'. Sessions are generally co-mediated, preferably by male-female co-mediators. On average there are three to five sessions. Municipalities in Sweden provide this help free of charge to parents who request it. Each parent is first seen separately and there is screening for domestic violence, child protection issues or circumstances that would make joint meetings unsuitable. The courts refer disputes over custody or access to

---

[17] Anteproyecto de Ley sobre el Ejercicio de la Corresponsabilidad Parental y Otras Medidas a adopter tras la Ruptura de la Convivencia, Ministry of Justice, Madrid, 10.04.14.

[18] García, L.V. *Paper given at ESFR Conference* (Milan, October 2010).

the Family Law Office but parents' participation is voluntary. A government report on Child Custody and Access published in 1997 stated that family mediation is the most cost-effective form of preventive social work. In 1998 the Swedish Parliament amended the law so that parental agreements on custody and access reached through 'co-operation talks' have the same juridical status as a court decision, provided the agreement has been approved by the social worker as being in the best interests of the child. The aim formerly was to assist parents to reach agreements over their children on the basis that parental agreement benefits children. With greater awareness of the impact of domestic abuse on women and children and the continuing risks they may experience, mediators in Norway and Sweden now focus more strongly on ensuring children's safety and well being. Over the last ten years, child-inclusive mediation has become more common. New partners and other family members may also be included.

The Norwegian Conflict and Conciliation procedure is now being used in several Swedish courts. It has had good results in both countries. The use of conciliation and mediation reduces the role of lawyers in both countries where family matters are concerned. Legal aid is very limited in Sweden, but lawyers' fees may be reduced or subsidised through paying into a home insurance scheme.

15.3.16   Switzerland

Conciliation as a method of conflict resolution has a long history and recognized role in civil and criminal procedures in Switzerland, but mediation has only recently become part of the legal system. The first unified Federal Code of Civil Procedure introduced on 1 January 2011 abolished the 26 different cantonal codes of civil procedure and gave an important place to mediation (Arts 213–218 and 297 – see: http://www.admin.ch/ch/e/rs/272/index.html) The Federal Code supports ADR and makes conciliation compulsory in most civil matters, whereas family mediation is voluntary, except in international cases. The court or child protection authority now has the possibility to strongly recommend parents to attempt mediation (Art.297 CP and Art 314 of the Civil Code (CC – see: http://www.admin.ch/ch/f/rs/210/a314.html). The costs of mediation for child-related issues may be publicly funded in some circumstances, especially if mediation was proposed by the court. The Code recognises the benefits of family mediation, both in reducing litigation and in the quality of outcomes. The regulation of mediation training and practice remains in the hands of private family mediation associations, without active government involvement.

Under the Swiss Federal Act on International Child Abduction of 1 July 2009[19]), mediation is compulsory when application is made for the return of a child abducted into Switzerland from a Hague Convention Member State (Arts 4 and 8). The International Social Service network (ISS) has responded to

---

[19]   http://www.admin.ch/ch/e/rs/211_222_32/index.html.

the recommendation from the Hague Conference to EU Member States to establish a central point of contact for international family conflicts in each country. In a joint project, the German and Swiss branches of ISS have opened a service for private individuals and government bodies to provide a central point of contact and centre of expertise for cross-border family conflicts. 'Parents often feel abandoned, finding that their concerns are not fully understood or that they are not adequately advised. Professionals also face additional challenges in situations of cross border family conflict: language problems, different cultural values, varying procedures for conflict resolution and in the application of international or foreign law. Geographical distance may prevent the implementation of previously agreed solutions.'[20]

The Swiss government proposed that the Swiss provisions for international family mediation should be incorporated in amendments to the Hague Convention and adopted at multilateral level, serving as a model for other States wishing to improve their practice in parental child abduction cases. However, Switzerland has not so far managed to convince a majority of Hague Convention Member States to follow the Swiss example. The use of mediation is encouraged in the constitution of the canton and republic of Geneva which came into force on 1 June 2013. Three articles on mediation in the constitution (Arts 36, 115 and 120) refer to the promotion of mediation in general, mediation in the work place and mediation between public administration and individuals. Mediation is progressively becoming part of the legal system in Switzerland.

15.4 HARMONISATION OF LEGAL SYSTEMS IN EUROPE

The harmonisation of legal systems in Europe is very important, because disputes with a cross-border element may be complicated by the simultaneous involvement of two or more jurisdictions following different sets of legal principles and presumptions. To reduce confusion or competition between different jurisdictions, significant moves have been made to harmonise civil and family law in Europe. The Regulation known as Brussels I (1968) regulated the Jurisdiction and Enforcement of Judgements in Civil and Commercial Matters. This regulation may be used to enforce orders or judgements in matrimonial maintenance claims, but not matrimonial property rights.

The European Convention on the Exercise of Children's Rights, which came into force on 1 July 2000 has the aim of protecting the best interests of children. The Regulation known as 'Brussels II' (the Regulation on Jurisdiction in Matrimonial Matters and Matters of Parental Responsibility), which came into force on 1 March 2001, introduced uniform jurisdictional rules throughout the EU (with the exception of Denmark). Brussels II provides for almost automatic recognition of all matrimonial judgments granted by the courts of Member States. With effect from 1 March 2005, Brussels II Revised (also

---

[20] For further information see www.family-conflicts.ch (Swiss website in English) and www.zank.de (German website).

known as Brussels II bis) extended this recognition further, to cover legal proceedings over children, irrespective of whether divorce proceedings are issued. Brussels II Revised seeks to ensure a common judicial area within the European Union, with stronger consideration of the interests of the child. It provides for uniform recognition of decisions by family courts in EU Member States on parental responsibility for children of married or unmarried parents, including stepchildren. The Court in the originating State is entitled to make the final ruling. This Regulation is also of relevance for the recognition and enforcement of mediated agreements.

In the field of civil and commercial mediation, the European Code of Conduct for Mediators of July 2004 was developed by a group of stakeholders from different countries who worked together with the assistance of the European Commission. Other Instruments contributing to the international harmonisation of legal systems include the Hague Convention of 23 November 2007 on the International Recovery of Child Support and Other Forms of Family Maintenance and the Protocol of 23 November 2007 on the Law Applicable to Maintenance Obligations.

15.5   THE HAGUE CONFERENCE ON PRIVATE INTERNATIONAL LAW

The European Convention on Children's Rights and EU legislation provide an overarching framework covering European law. Global law has even wider significance, particularly where child protection and child welfare are concerned. Child protection and child welfare lie at the heart of the 1989 United Nations Convention on the Rights of the Child and the Hague Conventions dealing with child welfare and child protection: the 1980 Hague Child Abduction Convention, the 1996 Child Protection Convention and the Inter-country Adoption Convention 2002. To date, 193 countries have ratified the United Nations Convention on the Rights of the Child, including every member of the United Nations apart from the United States of America, now that Somalia has announced its intention to ratify the Convention. 91 States, including Russia and Japan, have ratified the 1980 Hague Child Abduction Convention. The 1996 Child Protection Convention has 39 Contacting States and is in force in all EU Member States apart from (to date) Italy. The 1996 Convention enables contact orders to be automatically enforceable internationally, although the process of ratification has proved more complex than envisaged. Recent Hague Conventions encourage the use of mediation and dispute resolution as a means of achieving agreed solutions in cross-border disputes over children. In the UK, legal aid is available for Hague child abduction cases and for mediation. There must be provision for recognition and enforcement of a mediated agreement in all relevant States, not only the State in which the mediated agreement is recognised but also in the State/s where the agreement has effect.

15.6 JUDICIAL CO-OPERATION IN INTERNATIONAL CROSS-BORDER CASES

The Council of Europe's Recommendation on Family Mediation (1998) recognised the increasing number of disputes involving children in which there is a cross-border element. 65% of children born in London in 2010 had at least one foreign parent. The breakdown of cross-cultural relationships and work-related relocations are leading to more cases in which a parent removes, or threatens to remove, a child to another country without the other parent's agreement. Religious law and cultural factors bring additional complications to these relocation cases. In Jewish communities, family disputes have historically been referred to the rabbinical courts and are still referred to them, even where there are secular courts with parallel jurisdiction. In cases involving cross-border conflict, if either or both jurisdictions refer the case to the local religious court, problems of jurisdiction and enforcement become even more complex. Apart from South Africa and Morocco, no African countries are contracting members of the Hague Conventions and in the Middle East, only Israel. Nigeria has three different legal systems that operate concurrently: customary law, Sharia law and the common law. Customary law is further complicated by the fact that 350 different ethnic groups in Nigeria all have their own, slightly different versions of customary law. This multiplicity of legal systems makes accession to the Hague Conventions even more difficult. There is need for an International Family Court to provide global jurisdiction and to encourage international co-operation between lawyers and judges dealing with cross-border cases.

15.6.1 'The Malta Process'

A particularly important form of international co-operation over children is known as the 'Malta Process', initiated at the 1st Malta Conference of 2004. Three Malta Conferences laid the groundwork for a gradually increasing dialogue and engagement between Western and Islamic jurisdictions over issues of child abduction and child contact. The aim is to seek solutions to difficult disputes in situations where the relevant international legal framework is *not* applicable. To this end, the process encourages co-operation between judges, senior government officials and experts from countries that are parties to both the 1980 Child Abduction Convention and the 1996 Child Protection Convention, and those from countries that are not parties to the Conventions and whose legal systems are based on or influenced by *Sharia*. The focus of the Malta Process is the protection of children and in particular to support the child's right to maintain contact with both parents, even when they live in different countries, and to combat international child abduction. Experts from 12 states were invited to join the 'Malta Process' Working Party. Six are contracting states to the 1980 and 1996 Conventions, namely Australia, Canada, France, Germany, the United Kingdom and the United States of America. The other six are non-contracting states – Egypt, India, Jordan, Malaysia, Morocco and Pakistan, although Morocco has since ratified the 1980

Convention. South Africa has joined the Working Party and Jordan has established a mediation centre for international family disputes.

In August 2009, judges from 23 jurisdictions (Hague and non-Hague members) took part in the second International Family Justice Judicial Conference for Common Law and Commonwealth Jurisdictions. Lord Justice Thorpe, who was then Head of International Family Justice in England and Wales, opened the conference by describing the work of the Office of International Family Law in London and the steep increase in demand for its services since its creation in 2005. In 2007 the Office reported a 333% increase in the number of cases handled. The majority of these cases are at European level but the Office also facilitates judicial co-operation in international cross-border cases involving countries outside Europe. The Pakistan Protocol signed in January 2003 between Pakistan and the UK was negotiated at the highest judicial level. Judges are working together internationally to improve family justice systems. The Family Court of Trinidad and Tobago has introduced procedural reforms drawn from New Zealand that encourage referral to mediation and counselling services. The Conclusions and Recommendations of the 2009 International Family Justice Judicial Conference include the recommendation that mediation in cross-border child abduction cases should be recognised and supported, using mediators trained in this specialist field. A register of trained and competent mediators should be compiled and made readily available to the judiciary in each participating state.[21]

In 2012 the Hague Conference was mandated to set up a Group of Experts to address the problems of recognition and enforcement of mediated agreements. The agreement needs to be drafted by the parties' lawyers in a consent order that is capable of enforcement in both or all relevant States. 'Enforceability is a key concern with regard to any decisions made under the Hague Convention and problems have developed in Convention cases where orders made in one State have not been enforced in the other State. For mediation to have a positive effect on Hague Convention applications it is vital that agreements reached are capable of being enforced in both States' (Vigers 2007, Annex 1, 3.5).

15.7 INTERNATIONAL FAMILY MEDIATION IN CROSS-BORDER DISPUTES

In April 2006 the Permanent Bureau of the Hague Conference on Private International Law was asked by its Members to 'prepare a feasibility study on cross-border mediation in family matters, including the possible development of an instrument on the subject'. The Feasibility Study, published in 2007, defined cross-border family mediation as 'mediation in family disputes (concerning maintenance, family assets or matters of parent responsibility) where the parties have, or are about to have, their normal residences in different countries. This working definition includes cross-border mediation in the literal sense of being

---

[21] Baker 'The International Family Law Judicial Conference for Common Law and Commonwealth Jurisdictions' *International Family Law* (2009) 250–254.

conducted across borders (for example bi-national mediation involving parties and mediators located in two countries), as well as mediation occurring in one country, but involving parties and/or mediators from two countries. The definition also covers the situation in which two parties resident in the same country enter mediation in order to resolve the problems surrounding the intended relocation by one party with a child to another country'.[22] Acting on the recommendations of this study, the Permanent Bureau convened an international working party to assist in the preparation of a Guide to Good Practice on Mediation in the context of the 1980 Child Abduction Convention. This Guide was published in July 2012 in English and French.

Parallel developments included the conference organised by the European Academy of Law in Trier, Germany in April 2007 to consider practice and experience of mediation in international cross-border disputes over children. There was consensus that specialised training for international family mediation should be developed and that a central register should be set up of family mediators qualified to mediate in international cross-border disputes over children. The Council of Europe's 7th Conference on Family Law in Strasbourg in 2009 focused on family mediation throughout the world. Speakers reported on experience of family mediation in Europe and also in Caribbean, Latin America and Ismaili Muslim communities. Judge Winter from Austria[23] welcomed this worldwide, rather than Eurocentric focus. Child welfare is fundamental in countries following *Sharia* as in other jurisdictions. In line with 1400 years of Islamic tradition, the 49th Imam, His Royal Highness Aga Khan IV, established National and International Conciliation and Arbitration Boards to encourage amicable resolution of conflicts through impartial conciliation, mediation and arbitration. Some 800 Ismaili mediators in over 15 countries of Asia, Africa, Europe, North America and the Middle East have been trained in modern techniques of mediation both in the family and commercial fields.[24] In Portugal, Ismaili trainers provide training on mediation for the Ministry of Justice, designed for professionals in the family justice field. In Syria in 2006, seven High Court judges from outside the Ismaili community participated in a mediation training programme conducted in Salamieh. In India in the same year, three High Court judges attended the training programme, and one, a female judge, participated as a trainer. These training programmes found unanimous agreement on the need to harmonise systems for international family mediation, to specify qualifications and agree equivalences, and to create a central register to assist individuals and authorities to identify and contact qualified family mediators with specialist training for international cross-border mediation.

However, opportunities for referral to mediation are often missed for a number of reasons:

- lack of awareness of mediation;

---

[22] Vigers *Feasibility Study on Cross-Border Mediation in Family Matters* Permanent Bureau, Hague Conference on Private International Law (March 2007) 5.1.

[23] Council of Europe's 7th Conference on Family Law, Strasbourg 2009, Conference Conclusions.

[24] Keshavjee *Islam, Sharia and Alternative Dispute Resolution* (IB Tauris, 2013).

- lack of a central register to facilitate access to suitably qualified mediators in different countries;

- costs of mediation – fees, travel, interpreters if needed;

- disparities in laws regulating mediation practice, such as limits of confidentiality;

- fears that mediation will cause delay (although *reunite*, the leading British agency in this field, found that mediation does not generally delay the final hearing under the Hague Convention (reunite Pilot Project Report, October 2006);

- the shortage of mediation models adaptable to non-European as well as European family disputes.

In France, a court dealing with a Hague Convention case may refer parents to mediation, generally to the French agency MAMIF (Mission d'aide à la médiation internationale pour les familles). MAMIF, created in 2001 within the French Ministry of Justice, can intervene in international child abduction and contact disputes, either pursuant to the Hague Convention or outside its scope. MAMIF has been involved in single State mediations in Convention cases where MAMIF mediators work together to mediate and also in bi-national mediations involving a MAMIF mediator and a mediator from the other State. In 1998 the Ministers of Justice in France and Germany set up a Franco-German Parliamentary Mediation Commission. This led to a Franco-German bi-national professional mediation scheme which ran from February 2003 until 1 March 2006. In this pilot scheme, a French mediator co-mediated with a German mediator in cross-border disputes over children (Carl et al 2004). There are now several non-governmental, national and bi-national agencies providing cross-border mediation. These agencies include *reunite* in the UK, MiKK[25] in Berlin and French, Italian and Swiss agencies. Paul and Walker[26] report that conflict is high in cross-border cases and many parents feel helpless and despairing. The left-behind parent fears losing contact with the child even if a contact order is made, while abducting parents fear they will not receive fair treatment in the country of abduction, because they are often not citizens of that country. Young children are likely to forget the language of the left-behind parent or never to have learned it: communication as well as contact then becomes hard or impossible to sustain. *reunite* conducted a research study over a year using a sample of 34 cases.[27] This study found that where a court agreed to the relocation of a child, the child's relationship with the non-resident parent was unlikely to be maintained in the longer term because of the prohibitive costs of travel and other difficulties. The study also found that although relocation cases focused on the issue of contact, the impact on children of being removed to a different country was not only in

---

[25] Mediation bei internationalen Kindschaftskonflikten.
[26] Paul and Walker 'Family Mediation in International Child Custody Conflicts' *American Journal of Family Law* (2008) 22(1) 42–45.
[27] reunite Pilot Project *Mediation in International Parental Child Abduction* (October 2006).

losing their contact and relationship with the left-behind parent. Wider family relationships were often lost as well. Many children experienced profound dislocation at every level.

International mediation needs to be readily available, quickly accessible and used more widely. It offers a quickly organised and child-centred process, whereas legal processes can take months or years, escalating the conflict and risking prolonged trauma and harm for the child. In cases where an abducting parent is unable to return with the child and the left-behind parent is unable to care for the child, a child returned by court order to the country of habitual residence may be removed from *both* parents and placed in a succession of foster-homes until a final court order is made.[28] It was suggested in the previous edition of this book that the psychological harm to a small child, and indeed to older children, of being separated from both parents for months, even years, is so serious that 'child abuse' may not be too strong a term. In a judgment that recognises that any child abduction case is likely to arise from a missed opportunity for a relocation application, which is itself a missed opportunity for mediation, Mostyn J said recently: 'Child abduction seldom, if ever, has a happy ending. It has rightly been described as a form of child abuse.'[29] The rights and needs of the child should be prioritised over parental rights, with children of sufficient age and maturity having the opportunity to express their views and wishes in a safe and well supported way, without being subjected to pressure or fear of repercussions.

15.8 QUESTIONS TO CONSIDER IN RELATION TO MEDIATION IN CHILD ABDUCTION CASES

- Are any or all of the countries concerned partners under the Hague Conventions 1980 or 1996?
- Are both or all countries EU member states (apart from Denmark)? If so, Regulation Brussels II Revised applies and takes precedence over the Hague Conventions.
- What is the stage of legal proceedings, if any (see below, Stages for Referral to Mediation)?
- Are qualified cross-border family mediators available in, or able to travel to, the country or region concerned? Who would appoint the mediators?
- If mediation is appropriate, which model/s would be appropriate or possible?
- Is there a time limit for mediation under international conventions and/or set by the court?
- Who would contact the parents to offer mediation and assess suitability?
- Would the mediation be child-focused or child-inclusive?

---

[28] Bucher 'The New Swiss Federal Act on International Child Abduction' *Journal of Private International Law* (2008) 139–165.
[29] *TC and JC (Children: Relocation)* [2013] EWCA 292 (Fam) para 56.

To increase the use of mediation in international cross-border cases, referral should be encouraged as early as possible, as well as being considered at later stages.

Stage 1: before a parent removes a child to another country, to help parents reach agreements that avoid parental child abduction and court proceedings.

Example

A separated couple asked for mediation urgently, six weeks before the wife was due to return to Australia with the couple's two young children. Both parents were Australian and had been living in England for several years. The mother was acutely aware of the children's attachment to their father, but felt her own psychological survival was also critical and that she needed her family's support. Her husband had left a few months previously to live with a new partner. Three mediation meetings took place during the six weeks before the wife left for Australia. Financial information was gathered and in conjunction with each parent taking legal advice, agreements were reached on child support payments and on the ownership and occupation of two jointly owned properties, one in England and one in Australia. A great deal of discussion took place in mediation about how to help the children stay in contact with their father. The father bought a computer for his wife to take back to Australia. He and the older child keep in touch by e-mail and the father speaks regularly with both children on the phone, to keep his relationship with them and help bridge the periods between holiday visits.

Stage 2: where application has been made for leave to remove a child from the jurisdiction, or pending a court hearing of an application for return of an abducted child.

Stage 3: where a defence is raised against an order to return a child, on the grounds that return would be harmful to the child, mediation can facilitate communication over the best interests of the child, explore options and look for an agreed outcome.

Stage 4: following the return of an abducted child under a court order, to facilitate agreements over the child's residence and contact arrangements and also, after the return of the child has been ordered, to help make arrangements for the child's return and arrangements for contact following the return.

15.9 DIFFERENT MODELS OF INTERNATIONAL FAMILY MEDIATION

Various models have been developed for international family mediation, including bi-national mediation, interdisciplinary co-mediation, direct and indirect mediation. The model needs to be adapted for different cultures and circumstances and may consist of:

- A single mediator who mediates with both parents in person (direct, face-to-face mediation).

- Co-mediators (interdisciplinary, gender-balanced, bi-national) who mediate with both parents together in the same venue, or who use video/teleconferencing facilities for simultaneous meetings with parents in two different States (direct/distance mediation).

- Shuttle mediation in which mediators meet with each parent separately and the mediators liaise with each other. This can take place across two separate States with one mediator and one parent in each State, or in the same State with mediation taking place at different times or at the same time, in different rooms. Mediation may also take place online, using Skype and video conferencing.

- Co-mediation including members of the extended family and religious/community leaders.

MiKK's bi-national cross-border mediation projects are based on the following model:[30]

- A gender-balanced team of co-mediators, so that gender issues are understood and both parents feel heard.

- Cross-cultural, so that each parent feels able to relate to and be understood by a mediator from the same nationality or culture.

- Bilingual mediators, so that each parent can speak freely in their first language.

- Interdisciplinary backgrounds, one mediator trained and experienced in a psychosocial discipline while the other mediator must be a lawyer, both with specialist knowledge of international family law and international conventions.

- The parents' lawyers need to be readily accessible and involved, although not taking part directly, to advise their clients and to enable agreements to be ratified in legally binding terms in the country with jurisdiction.

15.10   TRAINING AND CERTIFICATION FOR INTERNATIONAL FAMILY MEDIATION

International family mediators need to know 'the rules of the road', that is, which jurisdiction takes precedence under what circumstances. Admission to a register of international family mediators should be based on the mediator's professional qualifications and substantial experience in domestic family mediation followed by additional specialist training for international family mediation.

The American Bar Association ran its first training in international family mediation in November 2013. In Europe, MiKK in Berlin runs bi-national mediation projects (currently Germany/France, Germany/England, Germany/

---

[30]   Breslauer Erklärung zur bi-nationalen Kindschaftsmediation (2008).

Poland, Germany/United States and Germany/Spain). A French/Italian training programme leading to the Certificat d'Accréditation Européen en Médiation Familiale Internationale (CAEMFI) is a 180 hour programme. It was organised during 2011–2012 in different locations in France, Italy and Switzerland and including some distance learning. Child Focus, a Belgian NGO dealing with international child abduction, led an EU-funded European project on Training in International Mediation (TIM) in partnership with the Katholieke Universiteit Leuven, MiKK in Berlin and the International Child Abduction Centre (Centrum IKO) in the Netherlands. Mediators from 27 EU Member States, including Turkey, took this training. The aim is to create a EU network, but many child abduction cases involve a child being taken from an EU country to a country outside the EU. The training team included a Muslim trainer linked to a network of Muslim mediators in India, Pakistan and Middle East countries, and a Spanish trainer linked to networks in the Iberian peninsular and South America.

The structures and histories of families caught up in international, cross-border and cross-cultural disputes over children are extraordinarily complex. The ecogram below was designed by International Social Service (ISS) Berlin for their three-day training programme for ISS lawyers and psychologists in a 'mediation-oriented approach' in cross-border cases.

It shows a Norwegian couple, Marika and Sven, who separated in 2010. They have two children, Bjorn aged 9 and Anja aged 7. The family formerly lived together in Paris and the children's country of habitual residence is France. After Marika and Sven separated, the children remained with their mother in the former family home. Marika still lives in Paris with Bjorn and her new partner, Pierre, has moved in with them. Sven returned to Norway where he is living with a new partner called Inger. Sven and Inger have a baby daughter called Christa. Sven came to Paris a few weeks ago to see the children and he arranged to take Anja back to Norway with him to meet her little half-sister and to visit his elderly parents. Bjorn did not want to go to Norway with his father and Anja, because he had sporting activities he was unwilling to miss. A dispute has arisen because Sven has not returned Anja as agreed. He claims that she wants to remain with him and Inger and their baby. Marika is making an application for Anja's immediate return under the Hague 1980 Convention on International Child Abduction.

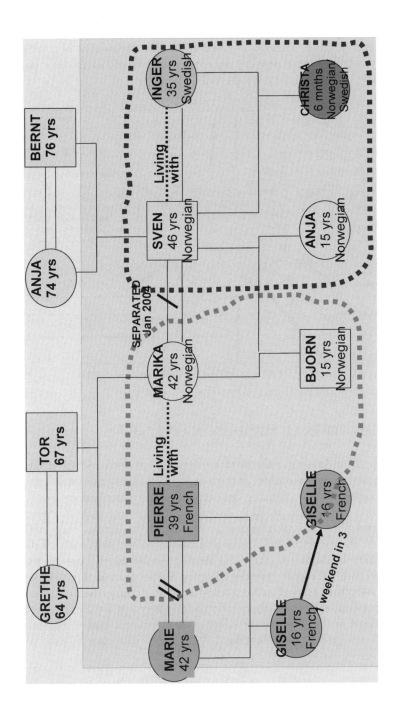

After constructing an ecogram showing the composition of the family, the names and ages of the children, with whom each child is currently living and other key pieces of information, the next step would be to focus on the child or children who are at the centre of an international, cross-border family dispute. The diagram below is an example of a 'focus on the child' that places the child in the centre, as the child should be, with details of the child's nationality or culture, language/s spoken, health, any special needs and so on. The child's parents, siblings, other key family members and the child's 'support system' are displayed around the child, to help parents consider the child's attachments and needs and ways of reaching a possible agreement that would meet these needs and maintain the child's attachments as well as possible.

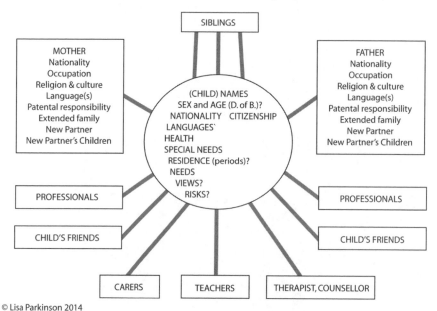

© Lisa Parkinson 2014

15.11   INTERNATIONAL MEDIATION ONLINE

Traditional mediation involves face-to-face meetings, but geographical distance and travel costs may prohibit face-to-face mediation in international cross-border cases. It is difficult to facilitate communication between participants who are unable to talk directly with one another. If they are unwilling or unable to take part in a conference call or share contact details with each other, the mediator may need to email or Skype with each of them separately. Online communications[31] can be augmented by the use of VOIP (voice over internet protocol) services such as Skype that enable telephone conversations over the internet at no additional cost, irrespective of distance. Negotiations between family members living a long way apart (or even nearby) can be 'buttressed and enhanced by electronic communication'.[32] Mediators with facilities for video conferencing, Skype and a webcam can offer

---

[31]   See also **4.10**.
[32]   Melamed *The Internet and Mediation* mediate.com Weekly (2009) 298.

telemediation – long-distance mediation. These facilities enable parents who live a long way apart to communicate without the time and cost of travel. Parents can see each other on screen, hear each other's voice and explore options directly with each other. This facility is of obvious value in cross-border cases, enabling parents and mediators in different countries to mediate on screen, if meeting face-to-face is impracticable. Important relationships can be sustained through electronic communications such as emails, Facebook, Twitter and so on.

15.12   INTERNATIONAL SOCIAL SERVICE (ISS)

Parents, lawyers and courts all over the world frequently contact International Social Service (ISS)[33] for help regarding one parent's unlawful removal of a child from one State to another. The ISS head office in Geneva has produced an informative and user-friendly Guide to international family mediation for parents and professionals. It includes commonly asked questions about the availability, organisation and benefits of mediation in relocation and child abduction cases and provides clear answers illustrated by colourful graphics and quotations from parents. The Guide can be downloaded from the ISS website free of charge in French or English[34] and has been translated into other languages, including Russian.

The Guide is drafted in general terms so that it can be distributed via many different networks and translated into more languages. The next step is to include country-specific information on the website and to facilitate access to information for families, professionals and administrative authorities. Discussions are also underway on the development of an international charter and international standards of practice, as well as on an accreditation system for family mediators specialised in cross-border cases. This charter and code of professional conduct, undersigned by professional associations, is part of ISS's ongoing work to create a reliable global network of IFM mediators. Parents with disagreements over relocation and those involved in cross-border disputes over children need to be encouraged to use mediation as early as possible and assisted to find suitably qualified mediators, especially where there are international implications, because litigation in these cases can take a very long time in the life of the child.

15.13   THE CONTINUING EVOLUTION OF FAMILY MEDIATION

Nationally and internationally, mediators mediate between the private world of families and the public world of institutions. Private decisions and arrangements worked out in mediation need to be congruent with the law. To gain juridical effect, mediated settlements need to be drawn up in unambiguous

---

[33]   www.iss-ssi.org.
[34]   Caratsch *Resolving Family Conflicts – a Guide to International Family Mediation* (International Social Service, Geneva, 2014).

legal terms and formalised in legally binding orders approved by a judge. Mediators seek to empower family members to reach their own decisions in their own way. Public funding constrains the time they can offer and mediators' independence is compromised if the state imposes mediation without assessment of its suitability and/or makes use of mediators as a resource for the court. The mediator's primary responsibility is towards the individuals and families who come to mediation. Mediators should not be used as agents of social, moral or political control, particularly as the personal and cultural values of mediation participants may diverge from those of the dominant social group or government.

The whole process of mediation is a balancing-act. Mediators walk a tightrope stretched between individual needs and public constraints. They need good balance to stay on this tightrope, managing the power imbalances and tensions that threaten mediation both internally and externally. A bearable 'lightness of being' helps to resist the downward drag of unremitting disputes. Maintaining buoyancy needs good support and mediators need to nurture each other, as well as other people. Dynamic energy, balance and 'lightness of being' are precious qualities. When they are combined, fragile threads of dialogue can carry a weight of feeling without breaking down. Mediators need to work within a supportive structure that encourages flexible movement, co-operation and trust. We need practical common sense infused with imagination, holding a balance between the craft of mediation and its creativity. We need to find ways of working together across frontiers – personal, professional and global – to encourage peaceful ways of resolving conflicts.

The task of the next generation is 'to push towards the widening of the circle of recognition'[35] so that the divisions that cause conflicts – in families, ethnic groups, gender, cultures, religions, nations and between West and East – can be transcended by the common needs and values of our shared humanity. Utopia is a long way off, but if we want to change the world, as well as ourselves, conflict management skills should be part of the core curriculum in schools for children of all ages, using the experiential methods that children and young people enjoy. In helping children to acquire second order learning so that they can disagree and listen to each other without declaring all-out war, maybe we adults could learn more of it ourselves as well. Mediation is evolving through the continuing exploration of the 'oneness' of our common humanity.

---

[35] Ramsbotham et al *Contemporary Conflict Resolution* (Polity Press, 2nd edn, 2005) at p 331.

APPENDICES

APPENDIX A

FAMILY MEDIATION IN ENGLAND AND WALES: A GUIDE FOR JUDGES, MAGISTRATES AND LEGAL ADVISORS (FMC/FJC 2014)

This document, circulated to all in judicial office in April 2014, informs the judiciary and the legal profession of the key principles of mediation and provides the basis for local models that facilitate good relationships between mediators and the court.

***

'I commend this helpful and brief guide to family mediation. Mediation is an established and valued part of the dispute resolution process of which the Family Court also forms a part. It is important for judges to be aware of the advantages that mediation can bring to resolving disputes between separated parents and to bear these in mind when cases come before them which may benefit from mediation. I would also encourage judges to become familiar with the mediation services which are available in their areas.'

Sir James Munby
President of the Family Division

HISTORY AND LEGISLATIVE FRAMEWORK

Family Mediation has been available in England and Wales for over 30 years. Initially used by Courts as an alternative to conflicted litigation in children's applications, the practice of mediation has grown to cover all areas of divorce and separation including finance and property.

Called 'All Issues' mediation, it was agreed that when making decisions about children's futures post separation, decisions about where families would live and how to share the marital/relationship assets went hand-in-hand with making future arrangements for the children.

A number of successive Acts of Parliament have sought to increase the use of family mediation as the benefits have become increasingly recognised and more widely understood:

- Family Law Act 1996.

- Access to Justice Act 1999.
- Children and Adoption Act 2006.
- Legal Aid Sentencing and Punishment of Offenders Act 2013.
- Children & Families Act 2014.

REGULATION AND GOVERNANCE

Family mediators are regulated and governed by six member organisations, all of which are members of The Family Mediation Council (FMC).

The FMC provides the Code of Practice for family mediators and sets minimum standards for the practice requirements of family mediation.

The FMC is responsible for the accreditation of family mediators.

Overarching all legislation for family mediators is the Children Act 1989, the Welfare Checklist and the principles of paramountcy for child welfare.

THE PROCESS AND PRACTICE OF FAMILY MEDIATION

Pre-proceedings: The Mediation Information and Assessment Meeting (MIAM)

Attendance at a Mediation Information and Assessment Meeting (MIAM) is required for any Applicant in relevant family proceedings (see *section 10 Children and Families Act 2014)* and should be expected and encouraged for all respondents.

Additionally, a MIAM can be ordered as an activity under s.11A and 11C Children Act 1989. This is to ensure that parties have an opportunity to find out about mediation and other forms of family dispute resolution.

The MIAM provides an opportunity for parties to meet with a mediator. At this meeting the mediator will:

- provide information about the process of mediation and other forms of family dispute resolution.
- start to clarify the areas where there are disputes, and provide options for resolving them.
- identify other sources of support including financial, emotional & legal.
- provide parties with more detailed information about additional services that encourage reaching settlement.

At the MIAM the mediator will talk to the parties about their concerns and their immediate priorities, with the aim of setting an agenda for areas to be negotiated. This typically includes children, finance and property issues. Discussions will take place separately until/unless it is recognised to be safe for any meeting to take place together.

As well as providing information about what mediation can provide, the mediator is making an assessment about the parties' ability to mediate. In some cases mediation might not be suitable.

There may be other over-riding factors which mean the court does not consider attendance at a MIAM is suitable in any particular case. FPR Rule 3.8(1) sets out the circumstances in which a requirement to attend a MIAM does not apply.

In summary, the main exemptions are:
- domestic violence/child protection;
- bankruptcy;
- the availability of an authorised mediator within a specified timescale;
- a MIAM has already been attended in the four months prior to making the application.

The full definition of these exemptions can be found at paragraphs 18-25 of the Practice Direction.

In the absence of evidence which satisfies the domestic violence exemption criteria, judges should be aware that the MIAM incorporates risk and safety screening. Mediators have no statutory authority and are not able to undertake risk assessment in the same way as Cafcass.

Court obligations to review opportunities for non-court dispute resolution

1. The Child Arrangements Programme makes clear that mediation and other forms of non-court dispute resolution should be considered at every stage of a court process.

2. The Practice Direction places an expectation on judges to inquire at first hearing if the MIAM requirement has been met. Paragraphs 33, 34 and 35 of the PD provide guidance on the specific nature of the inquiries to be made.

3. The Judge can assist parties (especially litigants in person) to understand the choices available to them and the likely outcome of: continuing court involvement (with or without Cafcass); mediation &/or other non-court dispute resolution interventions.

What can mediation achieve?

Mediation works, and is right for the majority of people provided it is safe and the parties are willing and able to negotiate. Part of the outcome of the MIAM is to ensure parties know if it is right for their situation.

Mediation can help sort out the options available on:

- arrangements for children;
- child maintenance payments;
- how to divide property and money, including savings, joint debts, pensions and mortgages.

It will also help parties develop skills for working together in the future as separated parents.

Mediation is confidential and privileged.

The mediation process

Family mediation is governed by four principles:

- It is **voluntary**, both parties and the mediator have to agree mediation is suitable.
- It is **confidential**, except where there are concerns of risk of harm to a child or vulnerable adult.
- The mediator is **impartial**, he/she facilitates negotiation and has no vested interest in the outcome.
- **Decision making** rests with the participants to the mediation.

These four principles are central to the practice of family mediators in England & Wales. They are embedded in the FMC Code of Practice, and applied by all mediation representative and governing bodies. They are reproduced in documentation provided by mediators to clients.

Working within these principles ensures that mediation provides a highly effective non-court dispute resolution process.

A *voluntary process*

At the MIAM, clients are fully informed of the principles, process, benefits and any cost of mediation. The clients <u>and</u> the mediator have to agree that mediation is suitable. Mediation will not take place until the 'agreement to mediate' is in place and signed by all parties.

Mediation differs from Cafcass dispute resolution services. Cafcass offers a court based service, which does not require the consent of the participants; it is Court directed and the outcomes of Cafcass dispute resolution can be shared with the Court.

Confidentiality and legal privilege

A MIAM is a confidential meeting. Mediation is a confidential process. The only exception to this arises in the rare case where a statement made in mediation indicates a safeguarding risk.

Any client entering a mediation process is asked to sign an 'Agreement to Mediate' which sets out both the scope of and limitations to confidentiality.

By signing the agreement to mediate, the parties understand that all communications, (except the disclosure of financial information) to which the mediator are party, are made solely for the purpose of attempting to reach a settlement and are made on the basis that the communications are:

(a)   confidential;

(b)   will not be referred to in evidence in any court proceedings about the same issues;

(c)   will not be used in affidavits or statements. However, this promise of confidentiality does not prevent the mediator disclosing information where there is significant risk to the life, health or safety of children, the parties, or anyone else, or in relation to money laundering/other unlawful act/s.

Similarly the court is not able to require mediators to disclose information about any mediation that has taken place.

Confidentiality can be waived with the consent of both parties.

If agreement is reached, the mediator will draft a memorandum of understanding. This can be used to form the basis of a consent order or a binding agreement. Participants in mediation are advised to take legal advice on the proposals they have made.

Impartial mediators

Mediators act as an impartial third person, and facilitate negotiation to assist people to reach their own, informed decisions. It is therefore important that mediators are understood to be independent of the court.

Decision-making rests with the participants

Mediators help to achieve an outcome which suits the whole family. Typically more than one session is required to reach an enduring outcome which is likely to stand the test of time and deal with underlying issues of conflict. The court may need to adjourn the proceedings to allow this process to be completed. Mediation appointments take place within a time-frame that is practical for clients, and can involve testing agreed arrangements. Despite the adjournment period, the time taken in mediation to reach full agreement is usually considerably shorter than the full court process.

Costs of family mediation

Legal Aid is available for mediation for those who are eligible. Parties can check whether they are eligible at www.gov.uk/check-legal-aid.

A mediator with a Legal Aid Agency (LAA) contract is able to undertake the eligibility assessment.

The LAA will cover the costs of **both** parties to attend a MIAM if one party is eligible. This encourages anyone who is not eligible for Legal Aid to find out about family mediation.

Legal Aid is also available for legal advice provided under the LAA's 'Help with Mediation' scheme. This can provide advice on proposals made in mediation and assistance with drafting consent orders.

The LAA allows court premises to be used as designated outreach facilities for the purpose of assessing suitability and eligibility for legally-aided mediation. This only covers the cost of delivering the MIAM.

Before mediation proper can take place the client has to produce means evidence to confirm their entitlement to public funding. It is unlikely that parties at court have with them proof of income evidence, and therefore parties should understand if mediation is to take place in the precincts of the court and before income evidence is produced, there will be costs associated with the mediation delivery.

Mediation providers working in courts will have available a schedule of their charges.

Authorised mediators

Family mediators are specialists who work with all aspects of divorce and separation. They are skilled at negotiating agreements and accustomed to working with conflict.

Only authorised mediators who are qualified and approved by the Family Mediation Council, the governing body for family mediators, should be used.

A list of authorised mediators can be found at

www.fmc.org.uk
Family Mediation Council, P.O. Box 593, Exeter, EX1 9HG
Family Justice Council

APPENDIX B

FAMILY MEDIATION COUNCIL
CODE OF PRACTICE

The Family Mediation Council Code of Practice governs family mediation practice in England and Wales. This Code of Practice may be subject to revision in accordance with current developments.

THE FAMILY MEDIATION COUNCIL
Code of Practice for Family Mediators
Agreed by the Member Organisations

1. DEFINITIONS

1.1   This Code of Practice applies to all family mediation conducted or offered by mediators who are members of the Member Organisations of the Family Mediation Council.

1.2   Family mediation is a process in which those involved in family breakdown, whether or not they are a couple or other family members, appoint an impartial third person to assist them to communicate better with one another and reach their own agreed and informed decisions concerning some, or all, of the issues relating to separation, divorce, children, finance or property by negotiation.

1.3   This Code applies whether or not there are or have been legal proceedings between the participants and whether or not any, or all of them, are legally represented.

1.4   In this Code, 'mediation' means the family mediation to which this Code applies. 'Mediator' means any person offering such mediation. 'Participant' means any family member taking part in mediation.

2. AIMS AND OBJECTIVES

2.1   Mediation aims to assist participants to reach the decisions they consider appropriate to their own particular circumstances.

2.2   Mediation also aims to assist participants to communicate with one another now and in the future and to reduce the scope or intensity of dispute and conflict within the family.

2.3   Where a marriage or relationship has irretrievably broken down, mediation has regard to the principles that the marriage or relationship should be brought to an end in a way that:

- minimises distress to the participants and to any children;

- promotes as good a relationship between the participants and any children as is possible;

- removes or diminishes any risk of abuse to any of the participants or children from the other participants; and

- avoids any unnecessary cost to participants.

3. QUALIFICATIONS AND TRAINING

3.1 Mediators must have successfully completed such training as is approved by a Member Organisation and accredited by the Council to qualify them to mediate upon those matters upon which they offer mediation.

3.2 Mediators must be a member of a Member Organisation and must therefore have successfully demonstrated personal aptitude for mediation and competence to mediate.

3.3 Mediators must satisfy their Member Organisation that they have made satisfactory arrangements for regular professional practice consultancy with a professional practice consultant who is a member of and approved for the purpose by a Member Organisation.

3.4 Mediators must agree to maintain and improve their skills through continuing professional development courses approved by a Member Organisation and/or the Council.

3.5 Mediators may only undertake direct consultation with children when they have successfully completed specific training approved by their Member Organisation and/or the Council and have received specific clearance from the Criminal Records Bureau.

3.6 Mediators undertaking publicly funded mediation must have been assessed as competent to do so by a recognised assessment scheme.

3.7 Mediators must not mediate upon any case unless they are covered by adequate professional indemnity insurance.

3.8 Mediators must abide by the complaints and disciplinary procedures laid down by the Member Organisation of which they are a member.

4. SCOPE OF MEDIATION

4.1 Mediation may cover any or all of the following matters:

4.1.1 options for maintaining or ending the marital or other relationship between the adult participants and the consequences of doing so;

4.1.2 arrangements for dependant children: with whom they are to live; what contact they are to have with each parent and other family members; any other aspect of parental responsibility such as, but not exhaustively, schooling, holidays, religious education;

4.1.3 the future of the family home and any other property or assets, including pensions, belonging to the adult participants; issues of child maintenance and spousal maintenance; issues relating to debts;

4.1.4   how adjustments to these arrangements are to be decided upon in the future.

4.2   Participants and mediators may agree that mediation will cover any other matters which it would be helpful to resolve in connection with relationship breakdown between the participants and which the mediators consider suitable for mediation.

5. GENERAL PRINCIPLES

5.1   **Impartiality and Conflicts of Interest**

5.1.1   It is the duty of the mediator at all times to ensure that he or she acts with impartiality and that that impartiality is not compromised at any time by any conflict of interest, actual or capable of being perceived as such.

5.1.2   Mediators must not have any personal interest in the outcome of the mediation.

5.1.3   Mediators must not mediate in any case in which they have acquired or may acquire relevant information in any private or other professional capacity.

5.1.4   Mediators must not act or continue to act if they or a member of their firm has acted for any of the parties in issues not relating to the mediation.

5.1.5.   Mediators must not accept referrals from any professional practice with whom they are employed, in partnership or contracted, on a full or part-time basis and which is involved in advising one of the participants on matters which relate or are capable of relating to the mediation, even though the practices are separate legal entities.

5.1.6   Mediators must not refer a participant for advice or for any other professional service to a professional practice with whom they are employed, in partnership or contracted, on a full or part-time basis on matters which relate or are capable of relating to the mediation even though the practices are separate legal entities.

5.1.7   Mediation must be conducted as an independent professional activity and must be distinguished from any other professional role in which the mediator may practice.

5.2   **Voluntary Participation**

Participation in mediation is voluntary at all times and participants and the mediator are always free to withdraw. Where mediators consider that a participant is unable or unwilling to take part in the process freely and fully, they must raise the issue and possibly suspend or terminate the mediation.

5.3   **Neutrality**

Mediators must remain neutral as to the outcome of a mediation at all times. Mediators must not seek to impose their preferred outcome on the participants or to influence them to adopt it, whether by attempting to predict the outcome of court proceedings or otherwise. However, if the participants consent, they may inform them that they consider that the resolutions they are considering might fall outside the parameters which a court might approve or order. They may inform participants of possible courses of action, their legal or other implications, and assist them to explore these, but must make it clear that they are not giving advice.

5.4   **Impartiality**

5.4.1   Mediators must at all times remain impartial as between the participants and conduct the mediation process in a fair and even-handed way.

5.4.2   Mediators must seek to prevent manipulative, threatening or intimidating behaviour by any participant. They must conduct the process in such a way as to redress, as far as possible, any imbalance of power between the participants. If such behaviour or any other imbalance seems likely to render the mediation unfair or ineffective, mediators must take appropriate steps to seek to prevent this including terminating the mediation if necessary.

5.5   **Confidentiality**

5.5.1   Subject to paragraphs 5.5.3, 5.5.4 and 5.5.5 below mediators must not disclose any information about, or obtained in the course of, a mediation to anyone, including a court welfare officer or a court, without the express consent of each participant, an order of the court or where the law imposes an overriding obligation of disclosure on mediators.

5.5.2   Mediators must not discuss the mediation or correspond with any participant's legal advisor without the express consent of each participant. Nothing must be said or written to the legal advisor of one party regarding the content of the discussions in mediation which is not also said or written to the legal advisor(s) of the other.

5.5.3.   Where it appears necessary so that a specific allegation that a child has suffered significant harm may be properly investigated or where mediators suspect that a child is suffering or is likely to suffer significant harm, mediators must ensure that the relevant Social Services department is notified.

5.5.4   Mediators may notify the appropriate agency if they consider that other public policy considerations prevail, such as an adult suffering or likely to suffer significant harm.

5.5.5   Where mediators suspect that they may be required to make disclosure to the appropriate government authority under the Proceeds of Crime Act 2002 and/or relevant money laundering regulations, they must stop the mediation immediately without informing the clients of the reason.

5.6   Privilege and Legal Proceedings

5.6.1   Subject to paragraph 5.6.2 below, all discussions and negotiations in mediation must be conducted on a legally privileged basis. Before the mediation commences the participants must agree in writing that discussions and negotiations in mediation are not to be referred to in any legal proceedings, and that mediators cannot be required to give evidence or produce any notes or records made in the course of the mediation, unless all participants agree to waive the privilege or the law imposes upon mediators an overriding obligation of disclosure upon the mediator.

5.6.2   Participants must agree that all factual information material to financial issues must be provided on an open basis, so that it can be referred to in legal proceedings.

5.6.3   All information or correspondence provided by either participant should be shared openly and not withheld, except any address or telephone number or as the participants may agree otherwise.

5.6.4   Privilege will not apply in relation to communications indicating that a child or other person is suffering or likely to suffer significant harm, or where other public policy considerations prevail.

5.7   Welfare of children

5.7.1   At all times mediators must have special regard to the welfare of any children of the family. They should encourage participants to focus on the needs and interests of the children as well as on their own.

5.7.2   Mediators must encourage participants to consider the children's wishes and feelings. If appropriate they may discuss with them whether and to what extent it is proper to consult the children directly in order to ascertain their wishes and feelings.

5.7.3 Where mediators and both participants agree that it is appropriate to consult any children directly, the consent of the children must first be obtained. Mediators consulting directly with any children must have been specifically trained to do so and have received specific enhanced clearance from the Criminal Records Bureau. Such mediators must provide appropriate facilities for direct consultation.

5.7.4 Where qualified mediators undertake direct consultation with any child, they must offer that child confidentiality as to any disclosure that that child may make to them. This must be explained to the participants before they agree to the direct consultation. Confidentiality in direct consultation with children must always be exercised subject to paragraphs 5.5.3, 5.5.4, 5.5.5, and 5.6.4 above.

5.7.5 Where mediators suspect that any child is suffering or likely to suffer significant harm, they must advise the participants to seek help from the appropriate agency. Mediators must also advise the participants that, in any event, they are obliged to report the matter to the appropriate agency in accordance with paragraph 5.5.3.

5.7.6 Where mediators consider that the participants are or are proposing to act in a manner likely to be seriously detrimental to the welfare of any child of the family or family member, they may withdraw from the mediation. The reason for doing this must be outlined in any further communication.

5.8 **Abuse and power imbalances within the family**

5.8.1 Mediators must be alert to the likelihood of power imbalances existing between the participants.

5.8.2 In all cases, mediators must seek to ensure that participants take part in the mediation willingly and without fear of violence or harm. They must seek to discover through a screening procedure whether or not there is fear of abuse or any other harm and whether or not it is alleged that any participant has been or is likely to be abusive towards another. Where abuse is alleged or suspected mediators must discuss whether a participant wishes to take part in mediation, and information about available support services should be provided.

5.8.3 Where mediation does take place, mediators must uphold throughout the principles of voluntary participation, fairness and safety and must conduct the process in accordance with this section. In addition, steps must be taken to ensure the safety of all participants on arrival and departure.

5.8.4 Mediators must seek to prevent manipulative, threatening or intimidating behaviour by either participant during the mediation.

6. CONDUCT OF THE MEDIATION

6.1   All assessments for suitability for mediation must be conducted at meetings on a face-to-face basis. Assessment meetings can be conducted jointly or separately depending on client preference, but must include an individual element with each participant to allow mediators to undertake domestic abuse screening.

6.2   Mediators must manage the mediation process. They should consult the participants on management decisions such as the ordering of issues and the agenda for each mediation session but must not relinquish control of the process to the participants.

6.3   Throughout the mediation mediators must keep the possibility of reconciliation of the participants under review.

6.4   Participants must be clearly advised at the outset of the nature and purpose of mediation and how it differs from other services such as marriage or relationship counselling, therapy or legal representation.

6.5   Participants must be informed of all the general principles set out in Section 5 above, including the nature and limits of the principles of confidentiality and privilege and mediators' special concern for the welfare of any children of the family.

6.6   Participants must be informed of the extent of any disclosure which will be required in cases relating to their property and finances.

6.7   Each participant must be supplied with written information covering the main points in this Code and given the opportunity to ask questions about it.

6.8   Mediators must ensure that the participants agree the terms and conditions regulating the mediation before dealing with the substantive issues. This must be in the form of a written agreement which reflects the main principles of this Code. The agreement must also set out the client fees.

6.9   Participants must be requested to notify any legal advisors acting for them of the appointment of a mediator.

6.10   Where during a privately funded mediation, mediators become aware that one or more of the participants may qualify for public funding, they must inform the client of this and, if they do not undertake publicly funded work, of the potential services of a mediation practice with an LSC contract.

6.11   Mediators must assist participants to define the issues, identify areas of agreement, explore the options and seek to reach agreement upon them.

6.12   Mediators must seek to ensure that participants reach their decision upon sufficient information and knowledge. They must inform participants of the need to give full and frank disclosure of all material relevant to the issues being mediated and assist them where necessary in identifying the relevant information and supporting documentation.

6.13   Mediators must ensure each participant is given the opportunity to make enquiries about information disclosed by any other participant and to seek further information and documentation when required. They must promote the participants' equal understanding of such information before any final agreement is reached.

6.14   Mediators must make it clear that they do not themselves make further enquiries to verify the information provided by any participant, that each participant may seek independent legal advice as to the adequacy of the information disclosed before reaching a decision; that in any court proceedings a sworn affidavit, written statement or oral evidence may be required and that authoritative calculations of liability under the Child Support Act 1991 can only be made by the Child Support Agency or may replacement organisation established under the Child Maintenance and Other Payments Act 2008.

6.15   Mediators must inform participants of the advantages of seeking independent legal or other appropriate advice whenever this appears desirable during the course of the mediation. They must advise participants that it is in their own interests to seek independent legal advice before reaching any final agreement and warn them of the risks and disadvantages if they do not do so.

6.16   Mediation meetings are commonly conducted without lawyers present. However, solicitors or counsel acting for the participants may be invited to participate in the mediation process and in any communications if the participants agree and the mediator considers that it would be appropriate.

6.17   When appropriate and with the consent of both participants, arrangements may be made for the attendance of professional third parties other than lawyers, such as interpreters, accountants, actuaries, independent financial advisors, and other advisors.

6.18   When appropriate and with the consent of both parties, arrangements may be made for the attendance of third parties with an interest in the proceedings, such as new partners, parties with a legal or beneficial interest in property that is the subject of dispute, or other family members.

6.19   Mediators must seek to ensure that agreements reached by participants are fully informed and freely made. Participants must have as good an understanding as is practicable of the consequences of their decisions for themselves, their children and other relevant family members.

APPENDIX C

SCREENING QUESTIONS

This list of screening questions prepared by Paul Kemp of The Worcester Family Mediation Practice is included with his kind permission. They are an example of the preliminary questions that mediators need to ask at initial assessment and information meetings (MIAMs, or AIMs) in conversation with each person, not as a bureaucratic check-list. Where there are indications of abuse or risk, these preliminary questions must be followed by specific risk assessment questions, as in the Cafcass Mediation Risk Assessment Tool referred to at **3.4**.

The Worcester
Family Mediation
Practice

Pre Mediation Screening Conversation

Mediation Party _____ Date of Conversation ___/___/201___ Mediator: _____

Before seeing [partner] and you together, I need to be sure that mediation is safe and appropriate for you. I want to ask some questions to help me to make that assessment. Is that OK with you?

So that you know what to expect, my questions will address issues of abusive and controlling behaviours as well as other things that might affect your ability to freely put your concerns and issues on the table in the course of mediation.

I'd like to ask you some general questions about your relationship, and especially the time when you lived together.

☐ When [partner] and you were together, how did you make decisions about general issues affecting your family?

☐ What happened if the two of you argued – what course would an argument take?

☐ How does [partner] react when s/he is angry?

☐ How do you?

☐ How would I know if you were feeling angry or anxious during a mediation meeting?

☐ How would I know if [other party] was feeling angry or anxious during a mediation meeting?

☐ Has anger between you ever risen to the level where you have been afraid? If so, what where the circumstances

I'd like to ask some questions about what people sometimes do when they are angry. Have any of these occurred in your relationship? **Notes** (include dates – esp noting dates of most recent incidents):

Name-calling?	☐ By you	☐ By the other party
Shouting?	☐ By you	☐ By the other party
Pushing/jostling?	☐ By you	☐ By the other party
Hitting?	☐ By you	☐ By the other party
Other violence	☐ By you	☐ By the other party
(Description required)		

☐ Have weapons been used/threatened to be used against you or someone in your household?

☐ Have you ever used/threatened to use weapons against [partner] or soemone in your household?

Other controlling patterns:

☐ When you were together, did you feel that you were being controlled by [partner] to the extent that you did not feel free to make choices about your daily life? If so, how, do you feel the control was being exercised? What was the effect on you?

☐ Did [partner] discourage you from having contact with your family? What about other friends?

☐ Did you feel that you could disagree with [partner] without fear?

Pre Mediation Screening Conversation

Mediation Party _____ Date of Conversation ___/___/201___ Mediator: _____

Before seeing [partner] and you together, I need to be sure that mediation is safe and appropriate for you. I want to ask some questions to help me to make that assessment. Is that OK with you?

So that you know what to expect, my questions will address issues of abusive and controlling behaviours as well as other things that might affect your ability to freely put your concerns and issues on the table in the course of mediation.

I'd like to ask you some general questions about your relationship, and especially the time when you lived together.

☐ When [partner] and you were together, how did you make decisions about general issues affecting your family?

☐ What happened if the two of you argued – what course would an argument take?

☐ How does [partner] react when s/he is angry?

☐ How do you?

☐ How would I know if you were feeling angry or anxious during a mediation meeting?

☐ How would I know if [other party] was feeling angry or anxious during a mediation meeting?

☐ Has anger between you ever risen to the level where you have been afraid? If so, what where the circumstances

I'd like to ask some questions about what people sometimes do when they are angry. Have any of these occurred in your relationship?   **Notes** (include dates – esp noting dates of most recent incidents):

Name-calling?	☐ By you	☐ By the other party
Shouting?	☐ By you	☐ By the other party
Pushing/jostling?	☐ By you	☐ By the other party
Hitting?	☐ By you	☐ By the other party
Other violence	☐ By you	☐ By the other party
(Description required)		

☐ Have weapons been used/threatened to be used against you or someone in your household?

☐ Have you ever used/threatened to use weapons against [partner] or soemone in your household?

Other controlling patterns:

☐ When you were together, did you feel that you were being controlled by [partner] to the extent that you did not feel free to make choices about your daily life? If so, how, do you feel the control was being exercised? What was the effect on you?

☐ Did [partner] discourage you from having contact with your family? What about other friends?

☐ Did you feel that you could disagree with [partner] without fear?

APPENDIX D

PRE-MEDIATION SCREENING & SUITABILITY ASSESSMENT RECORD

This Pre-Mediation Screening and Suitability Assessment Record Form was prepared by Paul Kemp of The Worcester Family Mediation Practice and is included with his kind permission. This form indicates the areas that the mediator needs to explore in assessing the suitability of mediation in particular circumstances and in considering whether, if both parties are willing, mediation may be arranged under certain conditions, with safeguards as necessary. It shows the wide range of considerations and assessments that are needed and may usefully be compared with the Cafcass Mediator Risk Assessment Tool which is being piloted in certain areas.

Permission to make use of this form and/or the Screening Questions listed at Appendix C should be sought from Paul Kemp at the Worcester Family Mediation Practice at the address given.

The Worcester
Family Mediation
Practice

**Pre Mediation Screening &
Suitability Assessment Record**

Parties: *(MP = Mediation Party)*

MP1   MP2   Case Ref:

Screened on: MP1 ____/_____/2014 MP2: ____/_____/2014 Assessment completed:
____/_____/2014

Mediator's decision as to suitability of case/issues: ☐ Yes issues susceptible to mediation
☐ No + Reason: ☐ Requires adjudication ☐ MP2 has not engaged ☐ Other [state reason]

MP1:   MP2:
☐ Agrees to mediate? ☐ Feels safe to mediate?   ☐ Agrees to mediate? ☐ Feels safe to
mediate?

Mediator's decision as to suitability to parties: ☐ Yes ☐ No ☐ Requires further consideration

Reasons for 'No' decision:

MP1:   MP2:
☐ Ineligible LA and cannot afford?   ☐ Ineligible LA and cannot afford?
☐ Reports Domestic Abuse (complete overleaf) ☐ Reports Domestic Abuse (complete overleaf)
☐ Fear of Partner/Lack of Trust   ☐ Fear of Partner/Lack of Trust
☐ Mental Acuity Issues   ☐ Mental Acuity Issues
☐ Other Reason: ☐ Other Reason:

POWER IMBALANCE

Is there any issue of power imbalance in the relationship?   ☐ Yes ☐ No ☐ Not mediating

If yes, what are the issues?

SAFETY ISSUES (refer also to abuse screening notes overleaf)

Is there any safety issue?   ☐ Yes ☐ No ☐ Not mediating

What protective measures taken?
☐ staggered arrivals/departures ☐ staff member to observe and assist: ☐ Vulnerable MP to seat
closest to door
☐ Co-mediation ☐ Shuttle mediation ☐ Other – give details

CO-MEDIATION INDICATORS
☐ High conflict between couple   ☐ History of Domestic Violence
☐ Previous involvement counselling/therapy ☐ Current involvement counselling/therapy
☐ Emotional neediness   ☐ High Net Worth
☐ Foreign Element   ☐ Other Indicator:

Mediator's signature _____ Date

☑ = Yes ☒ = No - where only one check box available

The Worcester
Family Mediation
Practice

Domestic Abuse Screening

IDENTIFICATION OF ISSUE

Is domestic violence an issue?

MP1 ☐ MP2 ☐ Now

MP1 ☐ MP2 ☐ In the past: date of most recent incident ___/_____/ 20__

Has a court order been made or undertaking given? ☐   Date of Order ___/_____/ 20__

Is child protection an issue?   MP1 ☐ MP2 ☐ Have Children's Services been involved? ☐

If so, give details

CATEGORISATION OF ABUSE

☐ Male controlling battering   ☐ Habituated interpersonal   ☐ Female initiated

☐ Neurotic/Psychotic   ☐ N/P with mental health overlay   ☐ Separation engendered

Comments:

DESCRIPTION OF ABUSE

☐ Physical   ☐ Single incident   ☐ Repetitive/Serial

☐ Serious physical (treatment needed)   ☐ Single incident   ☐ Repetitive/Serial

☐ Psychological   ☐ Single incident   ☐ Repetitive/Serial

☐ Shouting/Rows   ☐ Single incident   ☐ Repetitive/Serial

☐ Abuse from extended family   ☐ Abuse witnessed by children

☐ Other (give description)

CONCLUSIONS

☐ Not suitable for mediation   ☐ Suitable with safeguards   ☐ Suitable without safeguards

If abuse is an issue and is other than 'Separation engendered' but you consider that mediation is suitable, set out reasons why mediation can nonetheless proceed and give details of precautions overleaf.

☑ = Yes ☒ = No - where only one check box available

APPENDIX E

AGREEMENT TO MEDIATE

It is essential that mediators use an Agreement to Mediate that contains all the mandatory areas approved by their member organisation, including mediation principles, the nature and limits of confidentiality, and a complaints section. Otherwise, the mediator's insurance may be invalid. As at October 2014, both the FMA and Resolution are revising this document and mediators should check for revised versions. Mediation services may also develop their own document which may incorporate further terms and conditions. Additional clauses should be added for signature by legal advisors, interpreters or other third parties attending the mediation. This model document is designed by Lisa Parkinson and Neil Robinson.

AGREEMENT TO MEDIATE (EXAMPLE)

The following terms set out the basis for the mediations we undertake as members of the Family Mediators Association (FMA) recognised by the Family Mediation Council (FMC).

Please would you read each point carefully, noting any questions you may have and bring them to your first mediation meeting. At this meeting you will be invited to sign this Agreement to confirm your understanding and commitment to the process and the terms explained below. We will also sign, to demonstrate our commitment and responsibilities under the FMC Code of Practice for mediators, which explains the following principles:

Mediation is Voluntary

1. Mediation is voluntary. You choose to take part because you wish to resolve issues in need of settlement, without taking these issues to Court if possible. You have the right to end the mediation at any time, if you wish, although before doing so we hope you would be willing to explain your concerns in the hope that they could be addressed and resolved. Mediators also retain the right to end mediation if we consider that it would be more appropriate or helpful to do so. In some circumstances, we may involve a co-mediator (with /without additional cost to you – detail as necessary).

2. When there are financial issues needing settlement, we ask you both to provide complete and accurate disclosure of your financial circumstances, with supporting documents. We do not verify the completeness and accuracy of the information provided and you will be asked to sign and date a statement confirming that you have made full disclosure. If it later emerges that full disclosure has not been made, any agreement based on incomplete information can be set aside and the issues re-opened.

Mediators are Impartial

3. As mediators, we are impartial and we seek to help all participants equally. We do not make judgements or express opinions about who may be right or wrong, and we do not take sides. We assist you to reach your own decisions and to work out arrangements by mutual agreement as far as possible.

4. Mediators provide legal and financial information in a neutral way to help you understand the options available to you. We do not provide advice on your 'best interests' and the choices and decisions remain yours.

5. Where children are concerned, we also have a special duty towards children to consider with their parents (or those with parental responsibility) the arrangements that are most likely to support the children's relationships and well-being, now and in the future.

Mediation is Confidential – with exceptions

6.   Mediators have a professional duty of confidentiality. Discussions in mediation about possible terms of agreement and settlement are 'without prejudice' and legally privileged (i.e. they cannot normally be disclosed to the Court, except as explained below).

7.   You each agree not to call the mediator/s to give evidence in Court.

8.   At your request, either during mediation or at the end, we can prepare an interim or final Summary of arrangements for your children and/or your proposals for settlement of financial and property matters. Mediation summaries are prepared on a 'without prejudice' basis and can be made available to the Court with your joint written consent if, having taken legal advice as far as necessary, you both consider that providing a copy of the mediation summary would facilitate the Court making a consent order in the terms you are seeking.

9.   The 'without prejudice' confidentiality protects the content of mediation and its outcome from disclosure to the court (except where you have both given your joint written consent). However, this 'without prejudice' confidentiality could be overridden by the court, if, in exceptional circumstances, the judge requires some information concerning the process or outcome of your mediation to be disclosed in subsequent court proceedings.

10.   If you are taking legal advice, a copy of your mediation summary can be sent to your solicitors to assist them in advising you.

Exceptions to confidentiality

11.   Where any person (particularly a child) is alleged to be at risk of harm we have a duty to contact the appropriate authorities (with or without your permission).

12.   Where required to make disclosure to the appropriate government authority under the Proceeds of Crime Act 2002 and/or relevant money laundering regulations and/or any other law.

13.   Exceptionally, we may disclose personal data in connection with the alleged or established commission of an unlawful act.

14.   We are 'processors' of personal data for the purposes of the Data Protection Act 1998. You consent to our processing your personal data for the purposes of this Agreement to Mediate. You understand that this includes our retaining and storing your personal data for as long as is necessary in connection with this Agreement. We may retain data for research and statistical purposes but on the understanding that if used for this purpose all identifying details would have been removed.

15.   Our quality assurance standards require that we monitor our mediation files. Periodically, our practice supervisors and/or the Legal Aid Agency (in relation to any publicly funded mediation) may have sight of files, but access is strictly controlled and on a similarly confidential basis.

16. All the information you provide in mediation, including correspondence and communications from either of you, will be shared openly with you both, apart from an address or telephone number which either of you wishes to keep confidential, or where information refers to a child or adult who is, or may be, at risk of harm (see 11 above), or otherwise as may be agreed with you both.

17. Your financial information is provided on an 'open' basis, which means that it is available to your legal advisers and can be referred to in court, either in support of an application made with your joint consent or in contested proceedings. This avoids a need for the information to be provided twice.

Charges

18. If your mediation is provided under the Legal Aid Agency Scheme, there will be no charge to you for mediation sessions or for a mediation summary. If you are not eligible, our charges are £[   ] per session, per person, plus VAT, payable at the end of each session. Sessions are usually scheduled for 90 minutes.

19. There is an additional charge of £[   ] plus VAT per person, for the written summary at the conclusion of your mediation.

20. If mediation does not proceed, or if it breaks down and a copy of Form C100 or Form A is required by the court, with relevant sections completed and signed by the mediator, a charge of £87.00 plus VAT is payable by those not in receipt of publicly funded mediation.

Concerns and complaints

21. Our practice is governed by the Family Mediators Association (FMA) and our mediations are conducted in accordance with the Family Mediation Council Code of Practice (copy available on request). We follow the FMA's complaints procedure, a copy of which may be obtained from us. Any concern you may have as to our practice should be raised with us in the first instance and thereafter, if unresolved, in writing to the FMA. In this event, in signing this Agreement to Mediate, you also give your advance consent to the release of the file to the Complaints Adjudicator.

Your decisions and responsibility

22. We shall do our best to help you both. We seek to help you to reach agreed decisions and arrangements in a way that meets the needs of all concerned, especially children. You are in charge of your own decisions and we ask you to show respect to each other and commitment to the mediation process and to co-operate as fully as possible in looking for workable solutions.

I understand and agree to the above:

Signed: Signed:

Date: Date:

Signed: Signed:

Mediator   Mediator

Date: Date:

APPENDIX F

ADDITIONAL GROUND RULES FOR COURT–REFERRED MEDIATION[1]

Where mediation is commenced alongside court proceedings, it is especially important to re-assert the principles on which it operates. The transformation of the adversarial arena into a place for co-operative resolution is hard for many clients to understand. It may help to underline the differences by reference to ground rules or additional principles, as suggested by Neil Robinson in Appendix F.

Note for clients: Mediation has four main principles, which are in block capitals below. When you are involved in court proceedings alongside mediation, it is especially important to remember these principles, to consider how they may be refined, and what other ground rules you also consider important.

1.   MEDIATION IS VOLUNTARY. THIS MEANS:

- Even if you have been referred to mediation by the Court or directed to attend a mediation information and assessment appointment, mediation itself is voluntary and requires the continuing agreement of all participants, including the mediator(s).
- We all have a responsibility to be non-abusive, protect safety and provide a safe environment.
- We will remain respectful and open-minded, civil, polite and child-centred, so we all have an opportunity to say what we need to say.
- We will not interrupt, and will let everyone have their turn.

2.   MEDIATORS ARE IMPARTIAL. THIS MEANS:

- Unlike the Court case in which you are involved, mediators do not judge or find facts or fault, but explore the scope for common ground. We encourage you to do the same.
- Mediation is not adversarial; it is aimed at bringing an end to litigation wherever possible.
- In mediation, we all look for what can be agreed, not what remains in dispute; we solve the problem *together*, not continue fighting the battle on separate sides.
- Mediators have a special care for children, but we have no investigatory or welfare role; we may work alongside Cafcass if both are needed.
- We will gain information about your children's needs and wishes not through independent investigation but through your own consultation with them, and often by their direct participation in the mediation.

3.   MEDIATION IS CONFIDENTIAL. THIS MEANS:

- What is discussed in mediation remains inside the mediation room, unless:
- We **all** agree that a summary of the outcomes of the discussions can be shared with the Court, or
- There is a risk of harm to a child or an adult which needs to be reported.

4.   YOU ARE RESPONSIBLE FOR THE OUTCOMES; YOUR MEDIATOR IS RESPONSIBLE FOR THE PROCESS. THIS MEANS THAT MEDIATION IS:

- An opportunity for a fresh start.

- Facing the future, not examining the past.
- Positive and optimistic.
- Focused on you as parents, on your mutual interest in co-operative parenting, and making arrangements run more smoothly.
- Unlike the Courtroom, a place where *you* remain in control.
- Task-centred and time-limited.
- Your best chance to sort things out.

YOUR ADDITIONAL GROUND RULES:

-
-
-
-

YOUR GROUND RULES FOR COMMUNICATION OUTSIDE MEDIATION, BETWEEN EACH OTHER AND WITH YOUR CHILDREN

-
-
-
-

I understand and am committed to the ground rules above.

(Signed) ....(Dated) ....

(Signed) ....(Dated) ....

APPENDIX G

CO-MEDIATION FILE SHEET[1]

Mediators who provide publicly funded mediation face an increasingly uphill struggle to obtain additional funding for co-mediation from the Legal Aid Agency (LAA). This is the latest version of a form devised by Neil Robinson and adopted by the FMA. A detailed file note is also necessary, as the LAA can recoup payment for co-mediation on audit, if there is not sufficient justification in the case file.

Client Names ....and ....File number ....

Complete as applicable:

1. I have considered that <u>**co-mediation**</u> is **necessary** in this matter, after discussion with my PPC/manager,[2] and that mediation would be likely to be unsuitable if it were not co-mediated.

2. Co-mediation is appropriate by reference to one or more of the following factors:[3]

(please complete specific reasons and amplify in file note; the following guidance footnotes may help – refer also to any co-mediation protocol of Service or FMA/ lead body Protocols)

•   Vulnerability of a participant or relevant child

....

•   Vulnerability of a mediator

....

•   Significant management issue – including shuttled or caucused mediation

....

•   Requirement of specialist skills, or specialist area of work

....

•   Complexity

....

---

[2]   **The LAA Guidance** requires any decision to use co-mediation to be recorded on the file including, where appropriate: reasons as to the complexity, legal, psychological or otherwise of the case; a risk assessment for the participants and/or mediator; any reasons as to the requirement of specialist and/or expert skills; any management issues for the mediation.

[3]   **Vulnerability of a participant or relevant child** – current or past domestic violence, drugs or alcohol influence, limited ability of participant, safety issue, allegations of abuse; other 'high risk' issues; **Vulnerability of a mediator** – Complaint about supplier or previous supplier; borderline conflict issue; safety issue; inexperience of mediator; referral of complex case from another service; **Significant management issue** – significant imbalance of perception, understanding, pace, power, experience of participants; significant impasse; shuttle mediation; high conflict; communication management; gender issues; pressure to complete quickly; **Requirement of specialist skills** – Any situation where the complementary skills, competence or experience of a second mediator are appropriate – e.g. specialist financial/ legal knowledge, drugs/alcohol/abuse; therapeutic background/ conflict management skills; recognised specialist skills in direct consultation with children, child care mediation (nb these last two areas are likely to require co-mediation in any event because of their multi-party nature and issues of power); **Complexity** – Legal or psychological complexity; multiplicity of issues; multiplicity of parties to the mediation; **Other exceptional circumstance which might prejudice the successful outcome of the mediation if not co-mediated** – policy of individual service; opportunity to empower the 'victim'.

- Other exceptional circumstance which might prejudice the successful outcome of the mediation if not co-mediated

....

3. Co-mediation is appropriate in this case for other reasons, on the understanding that this is a privately funded case[4] or that, if publicly funded, the LAA will not cover the additional costs of the co-mediation,[5] namely ....

---

[4] Mediators undertaking privately funded work only do not need to use this form and indeed their reasons for co-mediating may be much wider. Nevertheless it may provide a useful checklist of considerations.

[5] **Other reasons** may include both the particular circumstances of the case or those of the service or any mediator, such as inexperience, but these may not of themselves justify a **claim** as co-mediation to the LAA.

APPENDIX H

MIDLAND REGION FAMILY JUDGES AND MAGISTRATES: WHAT THE FAMILY COURT EXPECTS FROM PARENTS

This statement from Family Judges and Magistrates in the Midland Region (Judiciary of England and Wales, 2009) gives authoritative encouragement to the sharing of parental responsibility and parental co-operation.

The courts consider that these guidelines apply to all children and all parents. Please don't think that your case is an exception.

ARE YOU A PARENT THINKING OF ASKING FOR A COURT ORDER?

The court wants you to think about these things first:

- As parents, you share responsibility for your children and have a duty to talk to each other and make every effort to agree about how you will bring them up.
- Even when you separate this duty continues.
- Try to agree the arrangements for your child. If talking to each other is difficult, ask for help. Trained mediators can help you talk to each other and find solutions, even if things are hard. The court staff can give you details.
- If you cannot agree you can ask the court to decide for you. The law says that the court must always put the welfare of your child first. What you want may not be the best thing for your child. The court has to put your child first, however hard that is for the adults.
- Experience suggests that court-imposed orders work less well than agreements made between you as parents.

The court therefore expects you to do what is best for your child:

- Encourage your child to have a good relationship with both of you.
- Try to have a good enough relationship with each other as parents, even though you are no longer together as a couple.
- Arrange for your child to spend time with each of you.

Remember, the court expects you to do what is best for your child even when you find that difficult:

- It is the law that a child has a right to regular personal contact with both parents unless there is a very good reason to the contrary. Denial of contact is very unusual and in most case contact will be frequent and substantial.
- The court may deny contact if it is satisfied that your or your child's safety is at risk.
- Sometimes a parent stops contact because she/he feels that she/he is not getting enough money from the other parents to look after the child. This is not a reason to stop contact.

Your child needs to:

- Understand what is happening to their family. It is your job to explain.

- Have a loving, open relationship with both parents. It is your job to encourage this. You may be separating from each other, but your child needs to know that he/she is not being separated from either of you.
- Show love, affection and respect for both parents.

Your child should not be made to:
- Blame him/herself for the break up.
- Hear you running down the other parent (or anyone else involved).
- Turn against the other parent because they think that is what you want.

You can help your child:
- Think about how he or she feels about the break up.
- Listen to what your child has to say.
- About how he/she is feeling.
- About what he/she thinks of any arrangements that have to be made.
- Try to agree arrangements for your child (including contact) with the other parent.
- Talk to the other parent openly, honestly and respectfully.
- Explain your point of view to the other parent so that you don't misunderstand each other.
- Draw up a plan as to how you will share responsibility for your child.
- When you have different ideas from the other parent, do not talk about it when the children are with you.

If you want to change agreed arrangements (such as where the child lives or goes to school):
- Make sure the other parent agrees.
- If you cannot agree, go to mediation.
- If you still cannot agree, apply to the court.

If there is a court order in place:
- You must do what the court order says, even if you don't agree with it. If you want to do something different you have to apply to the court to have the court order varied or discharged.

APPENDIX I

RESOURCE LIST FOR MEDIATORS, PARENTS AND CHILDREN

SUGGESTED FURTHER READING FOR FAMILY MEDIATORS

Barlow A, Hunter R, Smithson J and Ewing J *Mapping Paths to Family Justice – Briefing Paper and Report on Key Findings* (Universities of Exeter and Kent, ESRC, June 2014)

Brown, Henry and Marriott, Arthur *ADR Principles and Practice* Sweet & Maxwell (3rd edn, 2011)

Brown, Rebecca and Ward, Harriet *Decision-Making within a Child's Time-frame – an overview of current research evidence for family justice professionals* (Childhood Wellbeing Research Centre, Working Paper No 16, October 2012)

Butler I, Robinson M and Scanlan L *Children's Involvement in Family Decision-Making* (Joseph Rowntree Foundation findings 0365, July 2005)

Caring for Children after Parental Separation (Department of Social Policy and Intervention, University of Oxford, Family Policy Briefing 7, May 2011)

Fehily, Rachel *Split – True Stories of Relationship Breakdown in Ireland*

Fortin J, Scanlan L, Hunt J 'Taking a longer view of contact: perspectives of young adults who experienced parental separation in their youth' [2013] Fam Law 104

Gerhardt, Sue *Why love matters – how affection shapes a baby's brain* (Routledge, 2004)

Gilbert, Paul *The Compassionate Mind* (Constable, 2009)

International Social Service *Resolving Family Conflicts – a Guide to International Family Mediation* (ISS, 2014) www.iss-ssi.org, info@iss-ssi.org

McGee, Christina *Parenting Apart* (Resolution)

Midland Region Family Judges and Magistrates *What the Family Courts expect from Parents* (Judiciary of England and Wales, 2011)

Mnookin, Robert *Bargaining with the Devil – When to Negotiate, When to Fight* (Simon & Schuster, 2010)

Moore, Christopher *The Mediation Process – Practical Strategies for Resolving Conflicts* (Jossey–Bass, 1986)

Office of the Children's Commissioner *Don't Just Listen... Act* (Consultation Response to the Family Justice Review July 2011)

Ramsbotham O, Woodhouse, T, Miall, H *Contemporary Conflict Resolution* (2nd edn, Polity Press, 2005)

Schaffer, HR *Making Decisions about Children – Psychological Questions and Answers* (Blackwell 1990)

Timms JE, Bailey S and Thorburn J *Your Shout Too!: a survey of the views of children and young people involved in court proceedings when their parents divorce or separate* (NSPCC, Policy and Practice Series, 2007)

RESOURCES FOR PARENTS

Information Video (Courts Service and Ombudsman for Children's Office, Ireland) http://youtu.be/LkAlPrfaT2E

Basciano, Christina *Relationship Breakdown – a Survival Guide* (Ward Lock, 1997)

Charlish, Anne *Caught in the Middle – Helping Children to Cope with Separation and Divorce* (Ward Lock, 1997): positive and helpful

Calman, Claire *Lessons for a Sunday Father* (novel)

Curtis, Jill and Ellis, Virginia *Where's Daddy?* (Bloomsbury, 1996)

Faber, Adele *How to Talk so that Kids Will Listen and Listen so Kids will Talk*

International Social Service *Resolving Family Conflicts – a Guide to International Family Mediation* (ISS, 2014) www.iss-ssi.org, info@iss-ssi.org

Quinn, Mickey and Terri *What Can a Parent Do? A Handbook for Parents* (The Veritas Parenting Programme, Dublin 1986): very useful, practical advice for parents, with comments from other parents – do get this if you can)

Wells, Rosemary *Helping Children Cope with Change and Loss*

Woodall, Karen *The Guide for Separated Parents: Putting Children First*

WEBSITES

www.cafcass.gov.uk/grown-ups/parenting-plan.aspx – Cafcass Parenting Plan

www.findamediator.org.uk

www.oneparentfamilies.org.uk

www.oneplusone.org.uk

www.thefma.co.uk – website of the Family Mediators Association

www.theparentconnection.org.uk

www.fatherhoodinstitute.org – Dad info – being a dad

www.resolution.org.uk

www.separatedfamilies.org.uk

www.sortingoutseparation.org.uk

RESOURCES FOR CHILDREN AND YOUNG PEOPLE

Information Video (Courts Service and Ombudsman for Children's Office, Ireland) on YouTube for young people whose parents are separating http://youtu.be/LkYXqggg9Xc

Brown, Laurene Krasny and Marc Brown *Dinosaurs Divorce – a Guide for Changing Families.* This is the book that parents and younger children seem to like best

Cole, Julia *How do I feel about my Parents' Divorce*, Suitable for 5–11 year olds.

De Smet, Maria and Talsma, Nynke *I have Two Homes*

Family Mediators Association *An Introduction to Mediation for Young People* www.thefma.co.uk

Grinsell, A. *Let's Talk about Stepfamilies* (Gloucester Press, 1995)

Lamb, Kathryn *Is Anyone's Family as Mad as Mine? – A Survival Guide for Teenagers* (Piccadilly Press, 1997). Although not about separation/divorce, good on teenager-parent communication, for parents also

Masurel, Claire and MacDonald Dention, Kady *Two Homes*

Powell, Jillian *What do we think about Family Break-Up?* (Hodder Wayland, 2004). Very clear and helpful text with a lot of photographs of children of different ages and ethnicity and a useful glossary. Highly recommended

Stones, Rosemary *It's Not Your Fault – What to Do When Your Parents Divorce* (Piccadilly Press, 1994). Good for children over 10 who are good readers

Swan-Jackson, Alys *Caught in the Middle – Teenagers Talk about their Parents' Divorce* (Piccadilly Press, 1997)

Thomas, Pat and Harker, Lesley *My Family's Changing – First Look at Family Break-Up (What About Me?)* (Macdonald Young Books). Reassuring and helpful explanations for four year olds and upwards

Winchester, Kent and Beyer, Roberta *What in the World do you do when your parents divorce – A survival Guide for Kids*

A brighter future: a young person's guide to what's happened since the Family Justice Review (Ministry of Justice and Department for Education, August 2014). The guide explains family mediation, the Family Court and child arrangement orders

WEBSITES FOR CHILDREN AND YOUNG PEOPLE

www.kidsinthemiddle.co.uk

www.teenagehealthfreak.org. Health information and advice for teenagers, includes a page on divorce

FICTION FOR CHILDREN

Baum, Louis *Are we nearly there?*

Blume, Judy *It's Not the End of the World*

Cole, Babette *Two of Everything*

Curtis, Jill and Ellis, Virginia *Where's Daddy?*
Fine, Anne *Madame Doubtfire*. For older children
Goggle-Eyes (about accepting mother's new partner)
Step by Wicked Step (about living with a step-parent)
Gray, Kes *Mum and Dad Glue*
Ironside, Virginia *The Huge Bag of Worries*
McAfee, Annalena and Browne, Anthony *The Visitors Who Came to Stay*
Palacio, R J *Wonder* ('You can't blend in when you were born to stand out')
     powerful and life-affirming
Striker, Susan and Kimmel, Edward *The Anti-Colouring Book*
Thomas, Pat *My Family's Changing* (for young readers)
Walsh, Melanie *Living with Mum and Living with Dad*
Wilson, Jacqueline *Clean Break*
—*The Suitcase Kid*
—*Sleep-overs*
—*Love Lessons*
—*Secrets*

APPENDIX J

BIBLIOGRAPHY

Abel, R *The Politics of Informal Justice* (Academic Press, 1982), vol 1

Adam-Cairns 'Why Instruct a Single Joint Expert Valuer?' [2010] Fam Law 656–7

Adler P and Barnes B 'Mediation and Lawyers – the Pacific Way' (1983) 18 Hawaii Bar Journal 37–52

Ahrons C *The Good Divorce* (Bloomsbury, 1994)

Ainsworth M 'Attachment: Retrospect and Prospect', Chapter 1 in Murray Parkes and Stevenson-Hinde (eds) *The Place of Attachment in Human Behaviour* (Tavistock, 1982)

American Bar Association *Final Report – Task Force on Improving Mediation Quality* (2008)

Angyal 'A Logic of Systems' in FE Emery (ed), *Systems Thinking* (Penguin Books, 1969), vol 1

Bagshaw, D *Disclosure of Domestic Violence in Family Law Disputes: Issues for Family and Child Mediators* (Conflict Management Research Group, University of South Australia, 2001)

Baker, H 'The International Family Law Judicial Conference for Common Law and Commonwealth Jurisdictions' (2009) International Family Law 250–4

Banham-Hall M 'Children Act First Appointment Scheme' [2008] Fam Law 1054–5

Barenboim, D *Everything is Connected – The Power of Music* (Weidenfeld and Nicolson, 2008)

Barlow A, Hunter R, Smithson J and Ewing J *Mapping Paths to Family Justice – Briefing Paper and Report on Key Findings* (June 2014)

Barsky, AE *Conflict Resolution for the Helping Professions* (Wadsworth, 2000)

Bateson G *Steps to an Ecology of Mind* (Chandler, San Francisco, 1972)

Bellamy C, Platt J and Crichton N 'Talking to Children: the Judicial Perspective' [2010] Fam Law 647

Benjamin R 'The Constructive Use of Deception: Skills, Strategies and Techniques of the Folkloric Trickster Figure and their Application by Mediators' (1995) 13(1) Mediation Quarterly

Bentovim A 'Jazz and family therapy – my journey' (June 2011) *Context, the magazine for family therapy and systemic practice* 33

Bérubé, L *Workshop at International Family Mediation Trainers Conference* (Edinburgh, April 2002)

Bloch A, McLeod R and Tooms B *Mediation Information and Assessment Meetings (MIAMs) and mediation in private law disputes – Qualitative research findings* (Ministry of Justice Analytical Series 2014).

Boal, A *Games for Actors and Non-Actors* (Routledge, 1992)

Bodtker A and Jameson J 'Mediation as mutual influence: re-examining the use of framing and reframing' (1997) 14(3) Mediation Quarterly

Bohannan, P *Divorce and After* (Doubleday, New York, 1970)

Bordow, S and Gibson, J *Evaluation of the family court mediation service* (Family Court of Australia Research and Evaluation Unit, 1994)

Borkowski, M, Murch, M and Walker, V *Marital Violence* (Tavistock, 1983)

Bowlby, J 'Loss: Sadness and Depression', Vol 3 in *Attachment and Loss* (Hogarth Press, London, 1980)

Bronowski, J *The Ascent of Man* (BBC, 1973)

Brown, G 'Early Loss and Depression', Chapter 12 in Murray Parkes and Stevenson-Hinde (eds) *The Place of Attachment in Human Behaviour* (Tavistock, London, 1982)

Brown, H and Marriott, A *ADR Principles and Practice* (Sweet & Maxwell, 3rd edn, 2011)

Bryant, D *An Australian perspective on the Family Justice Review,* paper delivered by the Chief Justice of the Family Court of Australia at the International Family Law Lecture (London 2012)

Bucher, A 'The New Swiss Federal Act on International Child Abduction' (2008) Journal of Private International Law 139–65

Bunting, M 'Our history told in just 100 objects' *Guardian Weekly* 07 January 2011

Burrell, N, Donahue, W and Allen, M 'The impact of disputants' expectations on mediation' (1990) 17 Human Communication Research 104–39

Burton and Kitzinger with Kelly and Regan (1988) *Young People's Attitudes Towards Violence, Sex and Relationships: A Survey and Focus Group Study*, Edinburgh: Zero Tolerance Trust

Bush, RAB and Folger, JP *The Promise of Mediation* (Jossey-Bass, 1994)

Cafcass Parenting Plan www.cafcass.gov.uk/grown-ups/parenting-plan.aspx

Camara, K and Resnick, G 'Marital and parental sub-systems in mother-custody, father-custody and two-parent households: effects on children's social development' in J Vincent (ed) (1987) 4 Advances in family assessment, intervention and research Greenwich 165–96

Cantwell, B 'CAFCASS: In-court conciliation and Out-of-court Mediation' [2006] Fam Law 389–92

Cantwell, B 'Battling Parents: are they getting the right treatment?' [2007] Fam Law 743–8

Cantwell, B 'The Emotional Safeguarding of Children in Private Law' [2010] Fam Law 84–90

Caratsch, C *Resolving Family Conflicts – a Guide to International Family Mediation* (International Social Service, Geneva, 2014)

Carroll, L *Alice's Adventures in Wonderland* (1865) and *Through The Looking-Glass* (1872)

Carter, J *Keeping Faith – Memoirs of a President* (Bantam Books, 1982)

Casals, M Martin *Divorce Mediation* (European Academy of Law Conference, Trier, March 2005)

Cassidy, D and Davey, S 'Family Justice Children's Proceedings' (2011) Ministry of Justice Research Summary 5/11

Childline *Unhappy Parents, Unhappy Children* (1998)

Children's Society *Here to Listen?* (London, 2013)

Cigoli, V and Gennari, M (eds) *Close Relationships and community psychology: an international perspective* (FrancoAngeli, 2010)

Clarkson *Learning to unlearn* (University of Surrey paper, 1998)

Cloke, K 'Politics and values in mediation: the Chinese experience' (1987) 17(3) Mediation Quarterly 69–82

Cloke, K 'Mediation and Meditation – the Deeper Middle Way' mediate.com weekly 266 (March 2009)

Cobb, S and Rifkin, J 'Neutrality as a discursive practice' in Sarat and Silbey (eds) *Studies in law, politics and society* (JAI Press, USA, 1991)

Cobb, S 'A Narrative Perspective on Mediation' in Folger, J and Jones, T (eds) *New Directions in Mediation – Communication Research and Perspectives* (Sage Publications, 1994)

Cockett, M and Tripp, J *The Exeter Family Study: Family Breakdown and its impact on children* (University of Exeter Press, 1994)

Cohen, LJ and Campos, JJ 'Father, mother and stranger as elicitors of attachment behaviour in infants' (1974) 10 Developmental Psychology 146–54

Coogler, J *Structured Mediation in Divorce Settlement* (Lexington Books, 1978)

Corcoran, K and Melamed, J 'From coercion to empowerment: spousal abuse and mediation' (1990) 7(4) Mediation Quarterly 303–16

Council of Europe *Recommendation No R (98) 1* (21 January 1998)

Crum, T *The Magic of Conflict* (Touchstone, 1987)

Curle, A *Recognition of Reality – Reflections and Prose Poems* (Hawthorn Press, 1987)

Dancey, M *Contact* 'Activities: Parenting Information Programmes' [2010] Fam Law 1101–5

Davis, G.and Lees, P *A Study of Conciliation – its Impact on Legal Aid Costs and Place in the Resolution of Disputes arising out of Divorce* (Dept of Social Administration, University of Bristol, 1981)

Davis, G and Roberts, M *Access to Agreement* (Open University Press, 1988)

Davis, G et al *Monitoring Publicly Funded Family Mediation – Report to the Legal Services Commission* (Legal Services Commission, 2000)

Davis, G, Finch, S and Fitzgerald, R 'Mediation and Legal Services – The Client Speaks' [2001] Fam Law 110–14

De Bono, E *Conflicts – A Better Way to Resolve Them* (Penguin, 1991)

De Mayo, R 'Practical and ethical concerns in divorce mediation' (1996) 13(3) Mediation Quarterly 217–228

Department for Education and Ministry of Justice *A Brighter Future for Family Justice* (August 2014)

Department of Social Policy and Intervention *Caring for Children after Parental Separation*, Family Policy Briefing 7, May 2011

De Shazer, S *Keys to solution in brief therapy* (Norton, 1985)

Depner, C, Cannata, K and Ricci, I 'Client evaluations of mediation services' (1994) 32(3) Family and Conciliation Courts Review 306–25

Deutsch, M *The Resolution of Conflict* (Yale University Press, 1973)

Diduck, 'A Justice by ADR in private family matters: is it fair and is it possible?' [2014] Fam Law 616–19

Dingwall, R 'Divorce mediation: should we change our mind?' (2010) 32(2) Journal of Social Welfare & Family Law

Donahue, W, Allen, M and Burrell, N 'Mediator communicative competence' (1988) 55 Communication Monographs 104–19

Donahue, W, Lyles, J and Rogan, R 'Issue Development in Divorce Mediation' (1989) 24 Mediation Quarterly

Doughty, J and Murch, M 'Judicial independence and the restructuring of family courts and their support services' (2012) 24(3) Child and Family Law Quarterly

Dunn, J and Deater-Deckard, K *Children's Views of their Changing Families* (Joseph Rowntree Research Findings, 2001) 931

Emery, F *Systems Thinking: Selected Readings* (Vol 1, Penguin Education, 1969)

Emery, R *The Truth about Children and Divorce* (Viking, 2004)

Emery, R et al 'Child Custody Mediation and Litigation: Custody, Contact and Coparenting 12 years After Initial Dispute Resolution' (2001) 69(2) Journal of Consulting and Clinical Psychology 323–32

Emery, R, Margola, D, Gennari, M and Cigoli, V 'Emotionally Informed Mediation: processing grief and setting boundaries in divorce' in Cigoli and Gennari (eds) *Close relationships and community psychology: an international perspective* (FrancoAngeli, 2010)

Emery R, and Jackson, J 'The Charlottesville Mediation Project: mediated and litigated child custody disputes' (1989) 24 Mediation Quarterly 3–18

Emery, R and Wyer, M 'Child Custody Mediation' (1987) 55 Journal of Consulting and Clinical Psychology 179–86

Erickson, S and McKnight, M 'Mediating spousal abuse divorces' (1990) 7(4) Mediation Quarterly 377–88

European Forum on Family Mediation Training and Research, Training Standards (1992, revised 2003) www.europeanforum-familymediation.com

European Parliament Directive on Mediation 2008/52/EC (21 May 2008)

Family Justice Review *Interim Report* (Ministry of Justice, London, March 2011)

Family Justice Review *Final Report* (Ministry of Justice, London, November 2011)

Family Justice Review *Government Response* (Ministry of Justice, London, February 2012)

Family Mediation in England and Wales – A Guide for Judges, Magistrates and Legal Advisors (Family Justice Council and Family Mediation Council, 2014)

Family Mediation Council, England and Wales *Code of Practice* (2010)

Family Mediation Council, England and Wales *Professional Standards and Self-Regulatory Framework* (2014)

Fehily, R *Split – True Stories of Relationship Breakdown in Ireland* (Y Books, Dublin, 2011)

Felstiner W, Abel R and Sarat, A 'The Emergence and Transformation of Disputes' (1980–81) 15(3) Law and Society Review

Ferri, E and Smith, K *Parenting in the 1990s* (Family Policy Studies Centre, 1996)

Fiadjoe, A 'Family mediation in the Caribbean' *Paper given at the Council of Europe's 7th European Conference on Family Law – International Family Mediation*, Strasbourg, March 2009

Finer Report *Report of the Committee on One-Parent Families* Cm. 5629 (1974)

Fisher, R and Ury, W *Getting to Yes – Negotiating Agreement Without Giving In* (Arrow Publications, 1997, Penguin Books, 1983)

Fisher, T (ed) *Family Conciliation within the UK* (Family Law, 1990)

Folberg, J and Taylor, A *Mediation* (Jossey-Bass, 1984)

Folberg, J and Milne, A (eds) *Divorce Mediation – Theory and Practice* (Guilford Press, 1988)

Folger, J and Bush, B 'Transformative Mediation and Third-Party Intervention' (1996) 13(4) Mediation Quarterly

Follett, MP *Dynamic Administration: The Collected Papers of Mary Parker Follett* ed Metcalf, H and Urwick, L (Harper, 1942)

Fortin, J, Scanlan, L and Hunt, J, 'Taking a longer view of contact: the perspectives of young adults who experienced parental separation in their youth' [2013] Fam Law 104

Garcìa, LV *Paper given at ESFR Conference* (Milan, October 2010)

Garwood, F *Children in Conciliation* (Scottish Association of Family Conciliation Services, 1989)

Gates, Wray and Gear *Behavioural Distress: Concepts and Strategies* (Bailliere Tindall, 2000)

Gaus, JM *The Frontiers of Public Administration* (University of Chicago Press, 1936)

Genn, H *Judging Civil Justice* (Cambridge University Press, 2009)

Genn, H 'What is civil justice for? Reform, ADR and Access to Justice' (2012) 24(1) Yale Journal of Law and the Humanities

George, R and Bader, K 'Parents' experience of relocation disputes' [2014] Fam Law 836

Gerhardt, S *Why love matters – how affection shapes a baby's brain* (Routledge, 2004)

Gibran, K *The Prophet* (Pan Books, 1991)

Gilbert, P *The Compassionate Mind* (Constable, 2009)

Gilligan, C *In a Different Voice: psychological theory and women's development* (Harvard University Press, 1982)

Girdner, L 'Mediation triage: screening for spouse abuse in divorce mediation' (1990) 7(4) Mediation Quarterly 365–86

Gleick, J *Chaos* (Heinemann, 1988)

Government Response to the Family Justice Review (February 2012)

Greatbatch, D and Dingwall, R 'The Interactive Construction of Interventions by Divorce Mediators' in Folger, J and Jones, T (eds) *New Directions in Mediation – Communication Research and Perspectives* (Sage, 1994)

Grillo, T 'The mediation alternative: process dangers for women' (1991) 100(6) Yale Law Journal 1545–610

Gulliver, P *Disputes and Negotiations* Academic Press (1979)

Hague Conference *Guide to Good Practice on Mediation in the context of the 1980 Child Abduction Convention* (July 2012)

Hancock, E 'The dimensions of meaning and belonging in the process of divorce'(1980) 50(1) American Journal of Orthopsychiatry 18–27

Hart, B 'Gentle jeopardy: the further endangerment of battered women and children in custody mediation' (1990) 7(4) Mediation Quarterly 317–30

Harte, E and Howard, H 'Encouraging positive parental relationships' [2004] Fam Law 456

Hawthorne, J, Jessop, J, Pryor, J and Richards, M 'Supporting children through family change' (2003) 323 *Joseph Rowntree Foundation Findings*

Hayes, S 'Family Mediators in the UK – A Survey of Practice' [2002] Fam Law 760

Haynes, J *Divorce Mediation – A Practical Guide* (Springer Publishing, 1981)

Haynes, J *Alternative Dispute Resolution – the Fundamentals of Divorce Mediation* (Old Bailey Press, 1993)

Herrnstein, BH 'Women and mediation: a chance to speak and to be heard' (1996) 13(3) Mediation Quarterly 229–41

Hester, M and Radford, L *Domestic Violence and Child Contact in England and Denmark* (Polity Press, 1996)

Hetherington, EM, Clingempel, WG, et al 'Coping with Marital Transitions – A Family Systems Perspective' (1992) 227 Society for Research in Child Development 57

Hoffman, R and Lintern, G 'Eliciting and Representing the Knowledge of Experts' in Ericsson et al (eds) *Cambridge Handbook of Expertise and Expert Performance* (Cambridge University Press, New York, 2006), 203–22

Holmes, T and Rahe, H 'The social readjustment rating scale' (1967) 11 Journal of Psychosomatic Research 213

Humphreys, Judge C *Zen Buddhism* (Unwin Paperbacks, 1984)

Hunt, J *Parental Perspectives on the Family Justice System in England and Wales: a review of research Family* (Justice Council, London, 2009)

International Social Service *Resolving Family Conflicts – a Guide to International Family Mediation* (ISS, 2014) www.iss-ssi.org, info@iss-ssi.org

Irving, H and Benjamin, R *Family Mediation – Contemporary Issues* (Sage Publications, 1995)

Johnston, J and Campbell, L *Impasses of Divorce – the Dynamics and Resolution of Family Conflict* (Free Press, 1988)

Johnston, J and Campbell, L 'A clinical typology of interparental violence in disputed custody divorces' (1993) 63(2) American Journal of Orthopsychiatry 190–9

Johnston, J and Roseby, V *In the Name of the Child: a developmental approach to understanding and helping children of conflicted and violent divorce* (Free Press, 1997)

Kahneman, D *Thinking, Fast and Slow* (Penguin Books, 2012)

Kaspiew, R et al *Evaluation of the 2006 family law reforms* (Australian Institute of Family Studies, 2009)

Kelly, J 'Mediated and Adversarial Divorce: Respondents' Perceptions of their Processes and Outcomes' (1989) 24 Mediation Quarterly 71–88

Kelly, J 'Is mediation less expensive? Comparison of mediated and adversarial divorce costs' (1990) 8(1) Mediation Quarterly 15–26

Kelly, J 'Power Imbalance in Divorce and Interpersonal Mediation: assessment and intervention' (1995) 13(2) Mediation Quarterly 85–8

Kelly, J 'A Decade of Divorce Mediation Research' (1996) 34 Family and Conciliation Courts Review 373–85

Kelly, J and Duryee, M *Women's and men's views of mediation in voluntary and mandatory settings* (1992) 30(1) *Family and Conciliation Courts Review* 43–9

Keshavjee, M *Islam, Sharia and Alternative Dispute Resolution* (IB Tauris, 2013)

Keys Young Social Research Consultants *Research Evaluation of Family Mediation Practice and the Issue of Violence* (Legal Aid and Family Services, Commonwealth of Australia, 1996)

Kitson, Lopata, Holmes and Meyering 'Divorcees and widows: similarities and differences' (1980) 50 American Journal of Orthopsychiatry

Krementz, J *How It Feels When Parents Divorce* (Gollancz, 1985)

Kressel, K, Jaffee, N, Tuchman, B, Watson C and Deutsch, MA 'Typology of Divorcing Couples' (1980) 19(2) Family Process 101–16

Kressel, K, Butler-De Freitas, F, Forlenza, S and Wilcox, C 'Research in Contested Custody Mediations' (1989) 24 Mediation Quarterly 55–70

Kressel, K, Frontera, E, Forlenza, S, Butler F and Fish, L 'The settlement-oriented versus the problem-solving style in custody mediation' (1994) 50(1) Journal of Social Issues 67–83

Kübler-Ross, E *On Death and Dying* (Macmillan, 1969)

Lamb, ME 'Father-infant and mother-infant interaction in the first year of life' (1977) 48 Child Development 167–81

Law Society of England and Wales *Family Mediation Code of Practice* (1999)

Leach, P *Your Baby and Child* (first published 1977, reissued Penguin Health Books, 2010)

Leach, P *Family Breakdown* (2014)

Legal Services Commission *Quality Mark Standard for Mediation* (December 2002)

Lewis, Papacosta and Warin 'Cohabitation, separation and fatherhood' (Joseph Rowntree Foundation Findings, 2002) 552

Lodge, D *Therapy* (Penguin Books, 1996)

Lorenz, K *On Aggression* (University Paperbacks, 1968)

Lyon, Surrey and Timms *Effective Support Services for children and young people when parental relationships breakdown – a child-centred approach* (University of Liverpool, 1998)

Lund, M' Research on divorce and children' (1984) 14 Family Law 198–201

Maida, P 'Mediating disputes involving people with disabilities' Chapter 12 in Kruk, E (ed) *Mediation and Conflict Resolution in Social Work and the Human Services* (Nelson-Hall, 1997)

Mantle, G *A Consumer Survey of Agreements reached in county court dispute resolution (mediation)* (Essex Probation Occasional Paper 2, 2001)

Markman, H, Stanley, S and Blumbers, S *Fighting For Your Marriage* (Prentice Hall, 1996)

Marzotto, C (ed) *Gruppi di parola per figli di genitori separati* (Vita e Pensiero, 2010)

Mason, B 'Relational risk-taking and the therapeutic relationship' in Flakas et al (eds) *The Space Between: Experience, Context and Process* (Karnak Books, 2005), 157–70

Mathis, R 'Couples from Hell: Undifferentiated Spouses in Divorce Mediation' 16(1) Mediation Quarterly 37–49

McCarthy, P and Walker, J 'The longer-term impact of family mediation' (Joseph Rowntree Findings, 1996) 103

McEldowney, J *Family Mediation in a Time of Change* (Family Mediation Council, 2012)

McIntosh, J 'Child-Inclusive Mediation' (2000) 18(1) Mediation Quarterly

McIntosh, J, Wells, Y, Smyth, B and Long, C 'Child-Focused and Child-Inclusive Divorce Mediation: Comparative Outcomes' (2008) 46(1) Family Court Review

McIntosh, J, Smyth, B, Kelaher, M, Wells, Y and Long, C *Post-separation parenting arrangements and developmental outcomes for infants and children* (Family Court of Australia, Attorney-General's Department, 2010)

McIntosh J *Beyond the Baby Wars – toward an integrated approach to the post-separation care of very young children*, keynote address to the inaugural conference of the AFCC Australian Chapter, August 2014

McIsaac, H 'Towards a Classification of Child Custody Disputes: an Application of Family Systems Theory' (1986/7) 14/15 Mediation Quarterly 39–50

Mediation Task Force Report, Ministry of Justice, June 2014

Mehrabian, A and Ferris, S 'Inference of Attitudes from Nonverbal Communication in Two Channels' (1967) 31 Journal of Counselling Psychology 248–52

Melamed, J 'The Internet and Mediation' (2009) mediate.com Weekly 298

Midland Region Family Judges and Magistrates *What the Family Courts expect from Parents* (Judiciary of England and Wales, 2009)

Mills, O 'Effects of Domestic Violence on Children' [2008] Fam Law 165–71

Ministry of Justice *Family Justice Review, Terms of Reference* (London, 2010)

Ministry of Justice *A brighter future: What's Happened since the Family Justice Review?* (Ministry of Justice and Department for Education, August 2014)

Mitchell, A *Children in the Middle* (Tavistock, 1986)

Mitchell, J 'Inquisitorial family justice' [2014] Fam Law 1180

Mnookin, R and Kornhauser, L 'Bargaining in the shadow of the law: the case of divorce' (1979) 88 Yale Law Journal 950–97

Mnookin, R *Bargaining with the Devil – When to Negotiate, When to Fight* (Simon & Schuster, 2010)

Moore, C *The Mediation Process – Practical Strategies for Resolving Conflicts* (Jossey–Bass, 1987)

Morris, D *Bodytalk: the Meaning of Human Gestures* (Crown Trade Paperbacks, 1995)

Morrow, V *Children's Perspectives on Families* (Rowntree Research Findings, 798, July 1998).

Munro, E *The Munro Review of Child Protection – a child-centred system* (DfE, 2011)

Murch, M *Justice and Welfare in Divorce* (Sweet and Maxwell, 1980)

Murch, M 'The Voice of the Child in Private Law Proceedings in England and Wales' [2005] IFL 8

Murray Parkes, C *Bereavement* (Tavistock Publication, 1972)

National Alternative Dispute Resolution Advisory Council *Report on Standards* (Australia, 2001)

National Audit Office *Review of Legal Aid and Mediation for people involved in family breakdown* (March 2007)

National Family Mediation *Policy on Domestic Violence* (London, 1996)

Neale, B and Wade, A *Parent Problems – children's views on life when parents split up* (Young Voice, 2000)

Neumann, B 'How mediation can effectively address the male and female power imbalance in divorce' (1992) 9 Mediation Quarterly 227–39

O'Connor, J and Seymour, J *Introducing NLP – Neuro-Linguistic Programming* (Thorsons, 1995)

O'Quigley, A *Listening to children's views: the findings and recommendations of recent research* (Joseph Rowntree Foundation, 2000)

Office for National Statistics *Non-resident parental contact* (Omnibus Survey Report 2008, No 38)

Office of the Children's Commissioner *Don't Just Listen, Act* (Consultation Response to the Family Justice Review, July 2011)

Paolucci, B et al *Family Decision-Making – an Ecosystem Approach* (John Wiley, New York, 1977)

Parkinson, L *Bristol Family Conciliation Service* (unpublished paper, 1978)

Parkinson, L and Westcott, J 'Bristol Family Conciliation Service' Law Society's Gazette (21 May 1980)

Parkinson, L 'Conciliation – a new approach to family conflict resolution' (1983) 13 British Journal of Social Work 19–38

Parkinson, L *Conciliation in Separation and Divorce – Finding Common Ground* (Croom Helm, 1986)

Parkinson, L 'Co-mediation with a lawyer mediator' [1989] 48 Family Law

Parkinson, L *Family Mediation* (Sweet and Maxwell, London, 1997)

Parkinson, L 'A family systems approach to mediation with families in transition' *Context, the magazine for family therapy and systemic practice* (October 2002)

Parkinson 'A Happy Concatenation?' in Westcott (ed) *Family Mediation – Past, Present and Future* (Family Law 2004) 33–46

Parkinson, L 'Child-Inclusive Family Mediation' [2006] Fam Law 483–8

Parkinson, L *Developing International Cross-border Family Mediation and Harmonising Standards,* paper given at the Council of Europe's 7th European Conference on Family Law, Strasbourg, March 2009

Parkinson, L *Family Mediation – Appropriate Dispute Resolution in a new family justice system* (2nd edn, Fam Law, 2011)

Parkinson, L 'Adults should talk to kids more' [2012] Fam Law 346–51

Parkinson, L 'Child Care Mediation in Public Law Proceedings' (presented at Stafford, 27–28 November 2012)

Parkinson, L 'Taking a Longer View of Contact: messages that adults need to hear' [2013] Fam Law 294–9

Parkinson, L 'The Place of Mediation in the Family Justice System' [2013] (2) Child and Family Law Quarterly 200–14

Parkinson, P and Cashmore, J 'Judicial Conversations with children in parenting disputes: the views of Australian judges' (2007) 21 International Journal of Law, Policy and the Family 160

Paul, C and Walker, J 'Family Mediation in International Child Custody Conflicts' (2008) 22(1) American Journal of Family Law 42–5

Pearson, J 'An evaluation of alternatives to court adjudication' (1982) 7 Justice System Journal 420–44

Pearson, J 'The equity of mediated divorce settlements' (1991) 9 Mediation Quarterly 179–97

Pearson. J and Thoennes, N 'A preliminary portrait of client reactions to three court mediation programs' (1985) 23(1) Conciliation Courts Review 1–14

Pearson, J and Thoennes, N 'Divorce Mediation Research Results' in Folberg and Milne (eds) *Divorce Mediation – Theory and Practice* Guilford Press (1988) 429–52

Pel, M et al 'Family Mediation in the Netherlands' (2009) 4 International Family Law 255–9

Pendlebury, M 'Divorce and separation: listening to children and young people in mediation' [2008] Fam Law 1255

Perry, A and Rainey, B *Supervised, supported and indirect contact: orders and their implications* (Report to the Nuffield Foundation, University of Wales, Swansea, 2006)

Piper, C *The Responsible Parent – A Study in Divorce Mediation* (Harvester Wheatsheaf, 1991)

Pruitt, D and Carnevale, P *Negotiation in Social Conflict* (Open University Press, 1993)

Quartermain, S *Sustainability of mediation and legal representation in private family law cases: analysis of legal aid administrative datasets* (Ministry of Justice Series 8/11, TSO, 2011)

Ramsbotham, O, Woodhouse, T and Miall, H *Contemporary Conflict Resolution* (2nd edn, Polity Press, 2005)

Rapoport, A *The Origins of Violence* (Paragon House, 1989)

Rapoport, R 'Normal crises, family structure and mental health' (1965) 2 Family Process 68–80

reunite Pilot Project *Mediation in International Parental Child Abduction* (October 2006)

Rhoades, H 'Revising Australia's parenting laws' (2010) Child and Family Law Quarterly 172

Roberts, M *Mediation in Family Disputes* (2nd edn, Ashgate Publishing, 1997)

Roberts, M *An A-Z of Mediation* (Palgrave Macmillan, 2014)

Roberts, S *Order and Dispute – an Introduction to Legal Anthropology* (Penguin Books, 1979)

Robey, J 'Mediation and the Revised Private Law Programme' [2009] Fam Law 67–70

Robinson, L *Cross-cultural child development for social workers* (Palgrave Macmillan, 2007)

Robinson, N 'Developing Family Mediation' [2008] Fam Law 926–8

Robinson, N 'Developing Family Mediation: Innovative Approaches to ADR' [2008] Fam Law 1048–53

Robinson, N 'Developing Family Mediation' [2009] Fam Law 734–44

Robinson, N 'A Mediator's Guide to Pre and Post Marriage Agreements' [2011] Fam Law 529

Robinson, N 'Shape-shifters or Polymaths – a Reflection on the Discipline of the Family Mediator' in *Fifty Years in Family Law – Essays for Stephen Cretney* (Intersentia, 2012)

Robinson, N and Brisby, T 'ADR Professional' [2001] Fam Law 59–64

Rodgers, B and Prior, J *Divorce and separation: the outcomes for children* (Joseph Rowntree Foundation, 1998)

Rothman, J *Resolving Identity-based Conflict in Nations, Organisations and Communities* (Jossey-Bass, 1997)

Rutter, M 'Resilience in the Face of Adversity' (1985) 147 British Journal of Psychiatry 598–611

Ryder LJ *Judicial Proposals for the Modernisation of Family Justice* (Ministry of Justice, July 2012)

Salter, D 'A Decade of Pension Sharing' [2010] Fam Law 1294–8

Saposnek, D *Mediating Child Custody Disputes* (Jossey-Bass, 1983)

Saunders, L 'Mediation and Child Consent Orders' [2014] Fam Law 1187–8

Schaefer, C et al 'The health-related functions of social support' (1981) 4(4) Journal of Behavioral Medicine 381–406

Schaffer, HR *Making Decisions about Children – Psychological Questions and Answers* (Blackwell, 1990)

Schore, A and McIntosh, J 'Family Law and the neuroscience of attachment', Part 1 (2011) Family Court Review 49

Sclater, SD and Richards, M 'How Adults Cope with Divorce – Strategies for Survival' [1995] Fam Law 143

Sclater, SD *Divorce: A Psychosocial Study* (Ashgate, 1999)

Shattuck, MT *Mandatory Mediation* in *Divorce Mediation – Theory and Practice* eds Folberg, J and Milne, A (Guilford Press, New York, 1988)

Slaikeu, K, Pearson, J and Thoennes, N 'Divorce Mediation Behaviors: A Descriptive System and Analysis' in Folberg and Milne (eds) *Divorce Mediation – Theory and Practice* (Guilford Press, 1988) 475–95

Smart, C *Equal shares: rights for fathers or recognition for children?* (Critical Social Policy, 2004) 484

Smart, C and Neale, B 'It's My Life Too – Children's Perspectives on Post-Divorce Parenting' [2000] Fam Law 163–9

Steinberg, JL 'Towards an Interdisciplinary Commitment' (July 1980) Journal of Marital and Family Therapy 259–67

Steinman, S 'The Experience of Children in a Joint Custody Arrangement' (1981) 51 American Journal of Orthopsychiatry 403–14

Stokoe 'Overcoming Barriers to Mediation in Intake Calls to Services: Research-based Strategies for Mediators' (July 2013) Negotiation Journal 289–314

Strauch, B *The Secret Life of the Grown-Up Brain* (Penguin Books, 2011)

Tannen, D *That's Not What I Meant* (Virago, 1992)

Thoennes, N and Pearson, J 'Response to Bruch and McIsaac' (1992) 30(1) Family and Conciliation Courts Review 142–3

Timms JE, Bailey S and Thorburn J *Your Shout Too!: a survey of the views of children and young people involved in court proceedings when their parents divorce or separate* (2007) NSPCC, Policy and Practice Series

Tjersland, O 'Mediation in Norway' 1995 12(4) Mediation Quarterly 339–51

Trinder, L et al *Making contact: How parents and children negotiate and experience contact after divorce* (Joseph Rowntree Foundation Research Findings 092, October 2002)

Trinder, L et al *Making contact happen or making contact work? The process and outcomes of in-court conciliation* (DCA Research Series 3/06, 2006)

Trinder and Kellett, J *The Longer Term Outcomes of In-Court Conciliation* (Ministry of Justice, 2007)

Trinder, L 'Conciliation, the Private Law Programme and Children's Wellbeing' [2008] Fam Law 338–42

Trinder, L 'Shared Residence: A Review of Recent Research Evidence' [2010] Fam Law 1192–7

UK College of Family Mediators *Code of Practice and Standards for Mediators and Approved Bodies* (1995, reissued 2000) and *Children, Young People and Family Mediation – Policy and Practice Guide-lines* (2002) www.ukcfm.co.uk

Ury, W *Getting Past No* (Century Business Books, 1991)

Vigers, S *Note on the development of mediation, conciliation and similar means to facilitate agreed solutions* (Permanent Bureau, Hague Conference on Private International Law, October 2006)

Vigers, S *Feasibility Study on Cross-Border Mediation in Family Matters* Permanent Bureau (Hague Conference on Private International Law, March 2007)

Waldron, J, Roth, C, Fair, P, Mann, E and McDermott, J 'A Therapeutic Mediation Model for Child Custody Dispute Resolution' (1984) 3 Mediation Quarterly 5–20

Walker J 'How can we ensure children's voices are heard in mediation?' [2013] Fam Law 191

Walker J, McCarthy, P and Timms, N *Mediation: the Making and Remaking of Co-operative Relationships* (Relate Centre for Family Studies, University of Newcastle, 1994)

Walker, J and Hornick, J *Communication in Marriage and Divorce* (BT Forum, 1996)

Walker, J and Robinson, M 'Conciliation and Family Therapy', chapter 9 in Fisher, T (ed) *Family Conciliation within the UK* Family Law (1990)

Wallerstein, J and Kelly, J *Surviving the Break-up – how children and parents cope with divorce* (Grant McIntyre, 1980)

Wallerstein, J 'Children of Divorce – the psychological tasks of the child' (1983) 53(2) American Journal of Orthopsychiatry

Wallerstein, J and Blakeslee, S *Second Chances – Men, Women and Children a Decade After Divorce* (Bantam Press, 1989)

Walsh, S Mediation Pilot Projects in Ireland (www.kluwermediationblog.com, September 2012)

Westcott, J (ed) *Family Mediation – Past, Present and Future* (Family Law, 2004)

Whitaker, C 'Process Techniques of Family Therapy' (1977) 1 *Family Process* 4

Wilson, B '"Naughty Departures": Expertise, Orthodoxy and the Role of Theory in the Practice of Mediation' in Deleuran ed *Conflict Management in the Family Field and in other close relationships* (DJØF, 2011)

Wilson, J *Domestic Abuse: Practice and Precedents* (Law Society Publishing, 2010)

INDEX

References are to paragraph numbers.